TRAVELER

ITALY

NATIONAL GEOGRAPHIC
TRAVELER

ITALY

by Tim Jepson
photography by Matt Propert

National Geographic
Washington, D.C.

CONTENTS

■ **Pages 2–3: The alluring town of Atrani on the Amalfi Coast**
Opposite: The campanile of Florence's Duomo towers above the surrounding neighborhood.

TRAVELING WITH EYES OPEN

Alert travelers go with a purpose and leave with a benefit. If you travel responsibly, you can help support wildlife conservation, historic preservation, and cultural enrichment in the places you visit. You can enrich your own travel experience as well.

To be a geo-savvy traveler:

- Recognize that your presence has an impact on the places you visit.

- Spend your time and money in ways that sustain local character. (Besides, it's more interesting that way.)

- Value the destination's natural and cultural heritage.

- Respect the local customs and traditions.

- Express appreciation to local people about things you find interesting and unique to the place: its nature and scenery, music and food, historic villages and buildings.

- Vote with your wallet: Support the people who support the place, patronizing businesses that make an effort to celebrate and protect what's special there. Seek out local shops, restaurants, and inns. Use tour operators who love their home—who love taking care of it and showing it off. Avoid businesses that detract from the character of the place.

- Enrich yourself, taking home memories and stories to tell, knowing that you have contributed to the preservation and enhancement of the destination.

That is the type of travel now called geotourism, defined as "tourism that sustains or enhances the geographical character of a place—its environment, culture, aesthetics, heritage, and the well-being of its residents." To learn more, visit National Geographic's Center for Sustainable Destinations at *nationalgeographic.com/maps/geotourism.*

TRAVELER

ITALY

ABOUT THE AUTHOR & THE PHOTOGRAPHER

Tim Jepson has been a passionate and lifelong devotee of Italy. Since graduating from Oxford, he has spent long periods of time living and traveling in the country, including a year in a remote Umbrian village—where he learned fluent Italian—and five years as a writer and journalist in Rome. Over the years he has written some 15 books on the country, as well as numerous articles for the *Daily Telegraph, Vogue, Condé Nast Traveller,* and other publications. For National Geographic he wrote the following guides in the National Geographic Traveler series: *Florence & Tuscany, Naples & Southern Italy, Piedmont & Northwest Italy,* and *Sicily.*

Now based in London, Jepson continues to visit Italy regularly, and, as a keen hiker and outdoor enthusiast, he takes a particular interest in the country's mountain and wilderness areas. He also revels in Italy's more sedentary pleasures—the food, wine, art, and culture—and hopes one day to indulge them all from a small Venetian apartment of his own.

Jepson has also worked on Italian programs for the BBC and commercial British television, and his career has included spells in a slaughterhouse, on building sites, and as a musician playing piano and guitar in streets and bars across Europe.

Matt Propert is a freelance photographer and photo editor based in Santa Cruz, California. His photography has been shown in one-person exhibitions and published nationally and internationally. His work has been featured in many National Geographic books and special edition magazines. He has photo-edited more than 30 books for the National Geographic Society on topics ranging from Mount Everest to the history of Christianity. In addition to this guidebook, Propert has photographed two other travel guides for National Geographic: *Miami and the Keys* and *The Caribbean.* He is a member of Visura and is represented by Nat Geo Creative.

CHARTING YOUR TRIP

No other country has Italy's perfect combination of art, culture, food, fashion, wine, opera, people, and landscape, or the same vivid blend of the old and new, the beguiling and the beautiful. Few countries, as a result, offer quite the same variety or bewildering choice of vacation, all of which makes planning, more than usual, an essential part of your trip.

How to Visit & Get Around

Italy has five superb, pivotal cities—Rome, Florence, Venice, Naples, and Milan—and notable smaller centers of great intrinsic interest—Turin, Verona, Bologna, Genoa, Bari, and Palermo—in which you could spend a few days before exploring smaller towns and rural enclaves nearby. Fly into one and out of another to maximize your time.

Base yourself in the historic city centers, where you should be able to see virtually everything of note on foot. Take the train to move between cities; only fly for the longest journeys—Venice to Palermo, for example. Italy has an excellent, extensive, and inexpensive rail network, Trenitalia (see Travelwise p. 345). Connections between the major cities and points in between are superlative, while the trains also serve smaller towns and cities, often on charming and scenic routes. You'll only need to rent a car (an expensive option; see Travelwise p. 344) to make the most of rural regions, especially in the south and Sicily, where a car is invaluable. Italian roads are generally good and well signed and maintained.

If You Have Only a Week

A trip that takes in Florence and Tuscany—Europe's quintessential city of art and the pastoral region of cypress-topped hills, olive groves, and vineyards most often associated with Italy—as well as Rome will deliver in a week the great Italian pleasures of art, ice cream, culture, food, wine, and landscape. Start by flying to Florence, where you'll spend **Days 1 and 2** marveling at Brunelleschi's famed dome atop Santa Maria del Fiore (aka the Duomo), Michelangelo's "David" in the Galleria dell'Accademia, and the magnificent Uffizi, Bargello, and Palazzo Pitti art galleries (reserve tickets for the Uffizi and "David"). You will also have time for the major churches, Santa Croce and Santa Maria

Dome of St. Peter's Basilica, Vatican City

Novella; the Ponte Vecchio; and smaller artistic jewels such as the Cappella Brancacci and Palazzo Medici-Riccardi, as well as an hour or two for shopping.

On the morning of **Day 3,** board a regional train for the 90-minute trip to Siena, 31 miles (50 km) south as the crow flies, and spend the rest of the day in this fine and easily explored medieval city in the heart of Tuscany—and your base for the next few days. Be sure to see the Campo, the main square and setting for the famous Palio horse race; the Duomo; the Museo Civico; the Museo dell'Opera del Duomo; and Santa Maria della Scala.

Devote **Days 4 and 5** to the Tuscan countryside. On one day, rent a car and make a 115-mile (185 km) loop that takes in Pienza, the abbeys of Sant'Antimo and Monte Oliveto Maggiore, and the wine towns of Montalcino and Montepulciano in southern Tuscany. On the other day, take one of the regular buses from central Siena to the picturesque but popular hilltop village of San Gimignano, about an hour northwest.

On the morning of **Day 6,** board a train for Rome, allowing two to three hours for the 150-mile (241 km) journey south, depending on connections. Stretch your legs in the afternoon with a walk via the Campidoglio to the Foro Romano and Colosseo, perhaps dropping into the nearby churches of San Clemente and San Pietro in Vincoli. In the evening see the Spanish Steps and Fontana di Trevi. Start **Day 7** in Piazza Navona and Campo de' Fiori, then see the Pantheon and Santa Maria sopra Minerva, followed by a walking tour and one or both of two central and manageable galleries, the Palazzo Altemps and Palazzo Doria Pamphilj. In the afternoon, allow an hour for St. Peter's Basilica and shopping, a major museum, or the pretty Trastevere quarter.

NOT TO BE MISSED:

Walking around Rome's Foro Romano and Colosseo 50–56

A boat trip to Bellagio 117

A nighttime water-bus ride on Venice's Canal Grande 133

Hiking in the Dolomiti 181

Ravenna's Byzantine and early Christian mosaics 196–198

The paintings in the Galleria degli Uffizi, Florence 216–219

Siena's Duomo, Campo, and Palazzo Pubblico 244–247

The art-filled Basilica di San Francesco, Assisi 274

Herculaneum's ruins 295–296

Online Information

The best source of general information before you travel is the Italian Tourist Board, **ENIT** (enit.it or italiantourism.com). For information on Rome, visit 060608.it; Florence, firenzeturismo .it; and Venice, veneziaunica.it. Use key words such as turismo, comune, or ufficio informazioni or pro loco (visitor centers) plus a town name to find official websites for smaller centers. For museums, museionline.info is a good resource, and for national, regional, and other parks and reserves, go to the excellent parks.it. Trains can be researched and booked at trenitalia.com.

If You Have More Time

On longer visits, still choose convenient hubs to start and finish your trip, but work in more regional and rural variety.

Northern Itinerary: Fly into Milan and spend the morning of **Day 1** seeing the Duomo and Leonardo's "Last Supper" (in Santa Maria delle Grazie; reserve your ticket ahead of time)

Essential Facts

Most stores, banks, post offices, churches, visitor centers, and museums close for lunch (typically 1 p.m.–3 p.m.), especially in summer, before opening again until 7:30 p.m. or 8 p.m. All-day opening *(orario continuato)* in stores is more common in big cities or tourist areas. Bars are more like cafés than their U.S. or U.K. equivalents—pay for what you want first at the cash desk and then take your chit to the bar and place your order. Tipping is less prevalent than in the United States—leave around 10–12 percent in restaurants, unless service *(servizio)* is included.

before taking a 2.5-hour train ride south to La Spezia, where you pick up a cab to take you to lovely Portovenere on the Ligurian coast; base yourself here for the next couple of days. Devote **Days 2 and 3** to the Cinque Terre, just north of Portovenere, especially Vernazza and Manarola, best seen by boat, with a train excursion to Portofino and/or Genoa. On **Day 4** take a 2.5-hour train ride from La Spezia southeast to Florence, stopping on the way for the best part of the day in the wonderful medieval town of Lucca.

For **Days 5 through 9** follow the itinerary given for Days 2 through 5 in the week-long itinerary, adding an extra day to your exploration of southern Tuscany (base yourself in Pienza or Montalcino).

On **Day 10,** drive northeast into Umbria, known for its coronet of hill towns, by way of Cortona, a lofty Tuscan town on the Umbrian border. In the afternoon, make your way southeast 43 miles (70 km) to stay overnight in Assisi and visit the art-filled Basilica di San Francesco. On **Day 11,** drive over Monte Subasio to Spoleto, 53 miles (86 km) south, visiting Spello, sleepy Bevagna, Trevi, and Montefalco (known for its wine and a fine art gallery) along the way. In Spoleto, see the Rocca and Ponte delle Torri. That evening, press on about 50 minutes westward to overnight in Todi, a delightful, increasingly chic hill town.

After wandering around Todi the morning of **Day 12,** drive west some 22 miles (35 km) and visit Orvieto, famed for its Duomo, before heading south via the A1 to Rome, 80 miles (130 km) away. Spend **Days 13 and 14** in Rome (see the days for Rome in the itinerary on p. 9).

Southern Itinerary: Travel in southern Italy is less straightforward than in the north, with poorer visitor infrastructure, and it offers less in terms of art and culture. At the same time, the south often conforms to some of the traditional stereotypes of old Italy, notably in Naples, its rambunctious main city, and has

Best Times to Visit

Italy's range of climate and terrain means that optimal seasonal visiting times vary by region. Spring (April–May) is definitely the best time to visit the countryside (Tuscany, Umbria, Sicily, the Italian Lakes), though rain and low temperatures are still possible; wait until May or June to visit the mountains (Dolomiti, Alps, Abruzzo region, high Apennines). The weather is usually more reliable everywhere from mid-September to October, but the countryside will have been burned brown by the summer sun. July and August are too hot and oppressive to visit the cities, and only suitable for a sedentary villa vacation; beach resorts will be crowded. The low season (Nov.–Feb.) can be an excellent time to visit usually crowded cities such as Rome, Florence, and Venice.

some great set pieces, most famously Pompeii, the Greek temples of Sicily, the island of Capri, and the spectacular (if often costly and crowded) Amalfi Coast.

Fly to Naples and spend **Days 1 and 2** in this city overlooking its bay; be sure to visit the Museo Archeologico Nazionale and the Capodimonte and San Martino art galleries. On **Day 3,** make a day trip by train to Pompeii and Herculaneum, towns destroyed by the eruption of Vesuvius in A.D. 79, and perhaps ascend Vesuvius itself.

On **Day 4,** travel by boat from Naples's harbor to one of the towns on the Amalfi Coast, basing yourself in Sorrento or the more attractive, but more expensive, Positano or Ravello. Spend the rest of the day and **Day 5** exploring the Amalfi Coast by boat or bus, or rent a car for the day. On **Day 6** take a ferry from Amalfi, Positano, or Sorrento to spend two nights on the island of Capri, visiting Anacapri and making the ascent of Monte Solaro, and perhaps exploring the Blue Grotto sea cave.

On the morning of **Day 8,** return to Naples by ferry and board a train for the 6.5-hour journey south down the Italian peninsula and across the Strait of Messina to Taormina in Sicily. Explore the town in the evening, especially the Teatro Greco, and on **Day 9** rent a car or join a tour for a full day exploring the slopes of nearby Etna, Europe's highest active volcano.

On **Day 10,** drive south 75 miles (120 km) to Syracuse early, devoting the morning to exploring the historic center of Ortigia, with an hour or so in the Parco Archeologico, before making the 2.5-hour-plus-long drive (135 miles/217 km) west to Agrigento by way of the superb Roman mosaics near Piazza Armerina. Visit the Greek temples in Agrigento's Valle dei Templi on the morning of **Day 11** before driving two hours north to Monreale to see the town's celebrated Norman cathedral. Afterward, drive the few minutes into Palermo and spend the next two nights in the Sicilian capital before flying home, visiting the cathedral, Palazzo dei Normanni, Catacombe dei Cappuccini, and the many sumptuous churches and oratories of the old center. ■

HISTORY & CULTURE

■ Bust of Emperor Claudius, Musei Vaticani
■ Opposite: Interior of Parma's Duomo, a 12th-century Romanesque cathedral

ITALY TODAY

Italy has created many of the world's most sublime works of art, literature, and architecture and spawned some of the greatest empires of the ancient and medieval world. It also has evolved one of the world's finest cuisines and possesses landscapes as beautiful and varied as any in Europe. Few cultures are as beguiling, and few countries are as rich and endlessly fascinating.

People

In 1861, the year of Italian unification, patriot Massimo D'Azeglio made a comment that has haunted politicians ever since. "We have made Italy," he remarked, "now we must make Italians." More than 150 years later—when "Italians" number over 60 million—it is a moot point whether he and his like-minded followers succeeded. For there has never been, and probably never will be, a typical Italian despite the clichéd archetypes with which we're all familiar—possessive *mamma,* Latin Lothario, olive-skinned beauty (think Sophia Loren), Mafia godfather . . .

Italy's history has been too long and divisive for uniformity. Southern Italy includes Arabs, Greeks, Phoenicians, Normans, Spanish, and others among its ethnic mix. In the northwest, the

Most Italians have a sensual appreciation of the finer things in life—and no wonder in a country where the finer things in life are so prevalent.

Valle d'Aosta and Piedmont have strong French ties; German is the first language of many in Alto Adige to the north; and, in the northeast, the linguistic and ethnic cocktail even embraces Slovenian. Dotted across the country there are pockets of Arbëresh (Albanian), Occitan (Provençal), and Ladin (Old Swiss) cultures. Sardinia, with its unique language and people—blends of Italian, Spanish, and several other elements—is a law unto itself.

Modern mass media is now producing a degree of cultural homogenization, but for the most part Italians retain regional loyalties that reflect their history. A Tuscan is a Tuscan, first and foremost, not an Italian; and then not just a Tuscan, but a Pisan, Florentine, or Sienese. The Italian word for it is *campanilismo*—the idea that your loyalties and worldly concerns extend no farther than the reach of your church bell tower, or *campanile.*

Taken to their logical conclusion, these tightly focused loyalties end with that most close-knit of all social groupings—the family. This is also evident in the world of business: Although the percentage of family-run companies is in line with Europe, the management of almost 70% of them in Italy is made up of family members as opposed to 10% in the U.K. and 25% in France. At the same time, Italy's birthrate, averaging 1.32 children per couple, is among the lowest in Western Europe, giving the lie to the notion of Italy as a country of large families, or of one in thrall to the Catholic Church. Some 90 percent of Italians are baptized, but only 10 percent now regularly attend Mass. Divorce and abortion have all been freely available since the 1970s.

In emphasizing Italians' diversity, however, we should not underestimate their common traits. Most are pragmatic and spontaneous. Most are realists; many are self-reliant. They are also rather formal and conservative—the notion of *bella figura,* of cutting a "beautiful figure," by dressing well and not making a fool of yourself, is an important one. Many have flair, and it is not surprising that Italian fashion and design are big business. Most Italians have a sensual appreciation of the finer things in life—and no wonder in a country where the finer things in life are so prevalent.

Politics

Italians are naturally wary and weary of authority—the country was long fragmented and ruled, often badly, by foreigners down the centuries. The experience of the last

■ **Pedestrians and scooters throng the crowded, narrow streets of Naples at night.**

50 years has hardly helped. Despite the Constitution of the Republic framed in 1948 with good intentions—to prevent a return to fascism—a succession of weak and sometimes corrupt governments ensued over the years. The political upheavals of the early 1990s, which appeared to mark the system's death throes, have so far proved a false dawn.

Closer ties with Europe through the European Union, and the financial and institutional disciplines these demand, are now forcing change on recalcitrant politicians. No one would be surprised, however, if the Italians merely pay lip service to this entity as one more authoritarian body far removed from the realities of daily life.

Why blame them when self-reliance has served Italians well, allowing them to transform their country in less than a century? And make no mistake: Italy has been transformed. Sixty years ago, it was an agricultural backwater: Poverty was rife and emigration a fact of life. Today, it is one of the world's most powerful economies—region for region, experts say. The north keeps up with Germany (Europe's driving force) while the reality of the south resembles that of Greece. The general economic growth has led to a pronounced decline in emigration but there are still a great number of people, particularly among the young, that pursue their fortune abroad.

Vital Statistics

- **Population: 60,391,000**
- **Foreigners resident in Italy: 5,234,000 (62,780 in 1961)**
- **Birth rate: 7.4 births per 1,000**
- **Death rate: 10.5 deaths per 1,000**
- **Median age: 45.2 years**
- **Life expectancy at birth: male 80.8 years, female 85.2 years**
- **Average number of children per woman of child-bearing age: 1.32**

The Land

Italy is a small country. From north to south, the distinctive "boot" measures barely 750 miles (1,200 km) and covers 116,000 square miles (300,000 sq km). Of this, 35 percent is mountainous, rising to above 2,300 feet (700 m), 40 percent hilly, and just 21 percent plain.

The main relief features are the high, rugged mountains of the Alps, which form a broad arc across the north of the country—Mont Blanc (Monte Bianco), the highest point, on the border between Italy and Switzerland, reaches 15,781 feet (4,810 m); the Apennines are the lower central mountains, hunched in a narrow spine along the length of the peninsula. The broadest plain is Pianura Padana, the plain of the Po, Italy's longest river, which stretches 405 miles (650 km) and drains a densely populated area between the Alps and the Apennines.

Italy's oft-ignored coastline extends for 4,660 miles (7,500 km) and is washed by two major seas—the Tyrrhenian to the west and the Adriatic to the east (with the Ionian to the southeast). Scattered off its shores are numerous islands, including Sicily and Sardinia, the first and second largest islands in the Mediterranean.

Italy's basic landscape, however, is riddled with anomalies. Of these, the most famous are the active volcanoes of Vesuvius, Etna, and Stromboli, all linked to the residual movement of the tectonic plates that formed the Apennines. The same movement accounts for seismic activity in parts of central and southern Italy, which produces earthquakes such as the powerful tremors that shook Naples in 1980, Umbria in 1997, Abruzzo in 2009, and several provinces of the central regions in 2016.

▪ **A very active volcano, Stromboli in full flow becomes a fountain of fiery lava.**

Climate divides into three broad bands: Alpine in the north, characterized by cold winters and warm summers; temperate across the Po plains, with cold, damp winters and hot, humid summers; and Mediterranean across most of the peninsula and islands, with mild winters and long, hot, dry summers. This said, all manner of variations pertain: Icy blasts from Central Asia can produce freezing conditions, while the sirocco (a warm dust-laden wind) and heat of North Africa can bring blast furnace conditions to the south. Vegetation mirrors the variety of climate and relief, ranging from the pine forests of the Alps to the familiar vines, olive and fruit trees of the Mediterranean south. ▪

FOOD & DRINK

Imagine you are on a desert island, a special sort of desert island. Here you are allowed to enjoy the cuisine of any country in the world. The only catch—you have to eat it for the rest of your life. What would it be? French? Chinese? Japanese? Mexican? None seem quite right . . . but Italian? Well, most of us could probably live with Italian food for the rest of our days, and live quite happily.

Neapolitan *pizzaioli* (pizzamakers) load pizzas into a wood-burning oven.

Italian Cuisine

The food is healthy; the ingredients—meat, fish, fruit, and vegetables—are fresh; the quality is first-rate; there is huge regional and local variety; and the cooking methods are quick and simple. The principal staple—pasta—is endlessly versatile, coming in all shapes and sizes to form the base of countless recipes. The fast food—pizza—has no peers; and as for dessert—well, where would we be without ice cream?

Italian cuisine is actually many regional cuisines rolled into one. In Milan, rice rather than pasta dominates; in the far north, where Austrian influences are strong, you'll be offered dumplings and apple strudel; and, in Sicily, where the influence of the sea and North Africa prevail, you might dine on tuna, couscous, and spicy Arabian-style peppers. The variety is endless. The only rough rule of thumb is that the farther you go from the cities and into the countryside, the simpler the cuisine becomes.

But few rules are hard and fast. Even in the poorest areas, where tomato, olive oil, and pasta reign, you'll find endless regional specialties. Umbria and Piedmont offer one of the world's rarest foodstuffs—the truffle (see pp. 90–91); Parma has two great Italian staples—Parma ham and Parmesan cheese; Campania and Puglia have mozzarella cheese; and Liguria has created *pesto alla Genovese* (a blend of oil, basil, garlic, cheese, and pine nuts), one of many sauces to have reached beyond Italian shores.

Certain items are universal—olive oil is invariably excellent, as is the coffee. So, too, is the Italian passion for the social and sensual side of eating. Italians, like the French, live to eat, but without their northern neighbors' fuss and fanfare. It follows that food should be one of the great pleasures of an Italian sojourn—anything from an oven-fresh roll (brioche) with your morning cappuccino to the final mouthful of gelato or zabaione last thing at night. Try experimenting from region to region and seek out the more obscure restaurants—a far cry from the obvious tourist traps that will leave you thinking you could have done better at home.

Wine

While you might happily live on Italian food forever, no one is going to obligate you to prefer Italian wine to the many others in existence. Italy is the largest wine producer in the world and is among the first in terms of exportation. Both of these records are attributable to Italy's optimal climate, which makes it possible for each region to develop particular types of vines (there are over 500 in the country) and to produce an assortment of wines that differ greatly both in variety and quantity.

The country's wine has long had to live with the image of the straw-covered flask, for years the mainstay of old-time Italian restaurants at home and abroad. Fortunately, the enamel-stripping tannins of the rough, watery reds are largely a distant memory. A new breed of producers has sprung up, casting off the old-fashioned techniques and prejudices of centuries in favor of innovative methods. Super Tuscan have opened up new avenues in viticulture but today, the old indigenous grape varieties are regaining a stronghold (the inquisitive will find a wide array to choose from) as are natural wines, often full of character.

Some older wines have always been highly prized. Barolo and Barbaresco, from Piedmont, are two of Europe's foremost reds; Prosecco is a light, sparkling white from the Veneto; and, in Tuscany, Brunello and Vino Nobile are reds of the highest distinction.

As with food, the regional variety of wine is enormous. Indeed, one of the great pleasures of traveling in Italy is the chance to taste the many local wines. In Sicily, for example, there is Marsala, a dark and powerful dessert wine, as well as the lighter Malvasia wines of Etna and Lipari; in Umbria, try Sagrantino, a voluptuous red made from a grape found nowhere else;

Origins of Pasta

Just one thing unites Italians, said Giuseppe Garibaldi, one of the 19th-century fathers of Italian unification—pasta. There are more than 350 varieties, but all are variations of the same ingredients: water and flour from hard durum wheat, or egg (uova) instead of water in pasta all'uovo. Yet pasta's origins are a mystery. Numerous cultures have similar dishes, and noodles were probably being eaten in China at least 4,000 years ago. The Arabs may have introduced durum wheat to Sicily in the seventh century—though others say it came back from the New World with Christopher Columbus. The word has Greek roots, may be alluded to in Italian in 1279, and has a first recorded usage as an English word as late as 1874.

and, in Campania, one of the favorite tipples is Lacryma Christi (Christ's Tear), a white wine teased from vines grown on rich volcanic soils.

This said, Italian table wine will rarely match its French or New World cousins, but it is nearly always a perfect accompaniment to the food. And, if the wine doesn't please, ask for one of Italy's famed liqueurs—grappa and limoncello are just some worth sampling.

HISTORY OF ITALY

Italy is formed on a patchwork of people. Clearly defined tribes emerged circa 1800 B.C., notably in the south. Later came the Piceni and Messapians, peoples from the Balkans who settled on the Adriatic coast. Then came the Italic peoples—Umbrians, Samnites, Latins, and others—who colonized the north and center of the peninsula. The Phoenicians founded colonies in Sicily and Sardinia about 800 B.C., French-born Celts arrived about 600 B.C.

The Greeks

Settlement patterns achieved greater coherence in the south with the arrival of the Greeks around 735 B.C. Greece had long traded with parts of Italy, and it was inevitable that Greek migrants would become permanent residents. Independent Greek cities such as Acragas and Katane (known today as Agrigento and Catania) grew up across southern Italy and Sicily, creating a region known as Magna Graecia (Greater Greece). In the process they enriched the artistic, cultural, and agricultural prowess of Italy's indigenous populations.

Many of the new colonies eventually eclipsed the cities of Greece itself, leading to friction between Magna Graecia and the mother country. In 413 B.C., a naval attack by Athens on Syracuse, the most powerful of Sicily's Greek cities, was repulsed in one of the greatest sea battles of the ancient world. Further challenges to Magna Graecia came from the Etruscans to the north (see below) and from Carthage in North Africa.

Italy's Iceman

A graphic monument to Italy's earliest inhabitants came to light in 1991, when a leathery, partially preserved male corpse was discovered protruding from the ice of a glacier high in the Italian Alps. Named Ötzi, after the Ötztal region in which he was discovered, the body was 5,300 years old, from the Chalcolithic (Copper) Age, and belonged to a 45-year-old man who had died in mysterious, quite probably violent circumstances. He was 5 feet 5 inches (1.65 m) tall and weighed 110 pounds (50 kg). Ötzi and the artifacts found with him are now on display in the archaeology museum in Bolzano.

Carthage

The city began life as a Phoenician colony on the North African coast. By Magna Graecia's heyday, it had become a power in its own right and soon established colonies alongside those of the Greeks in Sicily and elsewhere. Conflict followed. Only in the third century B.C. did the two enemies set aside their differences, and only then in the face of a new superpower that threatened both rivals—Rome. Syracuse fell to the new power in 211 B.C. Carthage put up more of a fight—and survived a little longer.

The Etruscans

While the Greeks and Carthaginians fought over southern Italy, another major civilization, the Etruscans, imposed a degree of hegemony on the fractured domains to the north. Who these people were and where they came from are two of history's great

Rome's Arco di Costantino (left) and Colosseo (right), legacies of the Roman Empire

mysteries. First recorded around 900–800 B.C., they were probably a mix of indigenous and foreign peoples who assimilated other tribes—notably the Umbrians—and eventually developed a common language and shared social and cultural outlooks.

Society was structured around a loosely affiliated 12-city federation and ruled by priestly kings. Evidence of their art and culture is scant, however, as many of their cities were built of wood and quickly succumbed to the passage of time. Virtually the only archaeological evidence of their existence comes from their tombs. Their technical and cultural sophistication kept them unchallenged in central Italy for some 400 years, only to fall eventual prey to the Romans, who by 350 B.C. had defeated or absorbed most of their cities.

The Roman Empire

Legend claims Rome was founded in 753 B.C., but evidence found on the city's Campidoglio (Capitoline Hill) suggests the date was nearer to 1200 or 1400 B.C. By the ninth century B.C., the low hills on the banks of the Tiber were probably covered with scattered villages. The site then assumed a position of strategic importance between the territories of the Etruscans to the north and the Latins—another central Italian race—to the south. Over the next three centuries, the region prospered through trade and came under the control of the Etruscan kings.

■ **Julius Caesar enjoyed absolute power for just four years before being assassinated.**

In 509 B.C., Rome's citizens overthrew their Etruscan overlords, installing a system they called a *res publica,* or republic, a state where the "people were kings." The city then continued to prosper, its only weakness a growing gulf between the "common people," who became known as plebeians, and the burgeoning political and military elite—the patricians. This and other failings were addressed in 494 B.C., when a tribune, or magistracy, was created to protect plebeian interests.

A more robust political base allowed Rome to embark on a program of conquest. Etruscan-, Samnite-, and Greek-dominated areas of southern Italy soon fell, leading to confrontation with Carthage, a standoff that resulted in three protracted campaigns known as the Punic Wars. The first of these (264–241 B.C.) saw Rome capture islands of Sicily, Sardinia, and Corsica. The second (218–202 B.C.) pitched Rome against Hannibal, a Carthaginian general who inflicted stunning defeats on Rome before his campaigns collapsed in 202 B.C. Carthage finally succumbed during the Third Punic War (149–146 B.C.), an encounter that left Rome dominant across much of the Mediterranean.

While Rome prospered abroad, at home it was increasingly ravaged by civil strife. Disputes between patricians and plebeians found their most violent expression in the Social Wars of 92 to 89 B.C. Unrest resulted in a military clampdown under the leadership of Sulla, a general whose brutal regime marked the emergence of the army as a political force. His period in power is best remembered for helping spark the Slaves' Revolt (73–71 B.C.), an ultimately doomed rebellion led by a former gladiator, Spartacus.

Another general, Pompey, came to the fore after Sulla's death. He ruled in conjunction with Crassus, an ultimately peripheral patrician figure. When military matters plucked

Pompey from Rome, a third leader, Julius Caesar, appeared. Caesar had joined the army in 81 B.C. to pay off debts, but by 63 B.C. had achieved the office of Pontifex Maximus, Rome's ceremonial high priest. In 60–59 B.C., he joined Crassus and Pompey in a power-sharing triangle known as the First Triumvirate.

Originally distinguished by his oratory and financial acumen, Caesar quickly proved his ability in the military sphere, embarking on a ten-year campaign that saw him win notable victories in present-day Britain, Germany, and France. These triumphs rankled Pompey, who tried to turn Rome against his partner. Returning to Italy in 49 B.C., Caesar marched his armies across the Rubicon, a river close to modern-day Bologna, thus flaunting a decree that forbade armies from crossing the river without senatorial permission. Pompey fled, forewarned of Caesar's advance, causing political resistance in Rome to crumble.

In 48 B.C., Caesar was appointed Rome's ruler for life. He then embarked on a policy of reform and renewal, encouraging a sustained construction program and rejuvenating legal and other institutions. However, the new dictator's powers provoked jealousy and on March 15 (the Ides of March), 44 B.C., a clique of conspirators, which included his adopted son Brutus, murdered Caesar as he walked to the Senate.

Bedlam followed Caesar's assassination. The Second Triumvirate took initial charge, a coalition of prominent men—Mark Antony, Lepidus, and Octavius. This was followed by 12 years of turbulence during which Mark Antony and Octavius vied for control. Antony's liaison with the Egyptian queen, Cleopatra, undermined his ambitions, his final defeat coming with Octavius' victory at the Battle of Actium in 31 B.C. Octavius changed his name to Augustus and in 27 B.C. adopted the title of emperor, ushering in the Augustan Age, the heyday of Imperial Rome.

Augustus' rule was inspired. Expansion was reined in, military successes were consolidated, and massive building projects were instigated across the empire. Augustus' boast would be that he "found Rome brick and left it marble." Cultural life blossomed, particularly in literature, where writers such as Ovid, Virgil, and Horace produced some of the masterpieces of the classical canon.

> **The empire reached its greatest territorial extent under Trajan in A.D. 117, while in Hadrian, Rome found the most cultured and astute of its leaders.**

Augustus' successors proved less adept. Tiberius (A.D. 14–37), Claudius (A.D. 41–54), and Nero (A.D. 54–68) were mostly venal and decadent, successful only in squandering their considerable inheritance. Only the great riches of the empire masked the economic and bureaucratic shortcomings. Nero's tenure proved particularly traumatic and saw the start of widespread persecution of Christians.

The Flavian dynasty (A.D. 69–96)—emperors Vespasian, Titus, and Domitian—was generally more accomplished, as was the Antonine (A.D. 96–192) and its incumbents Nerva, Trajan, Hadrian, Antoninus Pius, and Marcus Aurelius. The empire reached its greatest territorial extent under Trajan in A.D. 117, while in Hadrian, Rome found the most cultured and astute of its leaders.

Decline & Fall: The death of Marcus Aurelius in A.D. 180 proved a watershed and saw the first genuine threats to the Roman Empire from external foes. Rome's deficiencies, long masked by imperial bluster, now came home to roost. Inflation raged and the economy faltered. Imperial assets were mortgaged to pay debts. Cultural life withered and emperors began to come and go with increasing regularity. Agriculture and trade at home collapsed as the spoils of empire dried up. Social, military, and other institutions became weak and moribund.

Attempts were made to arrest the process, notably the division of the empire in A.D. 286 into eastern and western dominions, each with emperors in Rome and Constantinople. Such measures brought temporary respite, as did the appearance of an unusually robust emperor. Rome prospered under Constantine (A.D. 306–337), the first to extend freedom of worship to Christians. Such respites proved temporary. In A.D. 402, the western empire's capital was moved from Rome to the more easily defended Ravenna in the northeast. A few years later, Rome was sacked by Alaric the Goth, the leader of a tribe of Baltic origin and one of the first Barbarians. The end was approaching. In A.D. 475 or 476, another Goth, Odoacer, displaced Romulus Augustulus, the western empire's last emperor. In A.D. 493, Odoacer was followed by Theodoric, who ruled most of Italy from the last capital, Ravenna.

Sicily Falls to the Arabs

In its day, the Roman Empire had fought off a challenge from North Africa, defeating the Carthaginians during the Punic Wars. During the ninth century, the African challenge was resurrected, this time in the shape of the Arabs, or Saracens, who invaded Sicily from North Africa in 827. They remained on the island for almost two centuries, introducing countless cultural, architectural, gastronomic, and other innovations, many of which (such as ice cream!) enrich our lives to this day.

Franks & Byzantines

Across the Mediterranean, however, the old eastern empire, or Byzantium, escaped the fate of its western neighbor. Between 536 and 552, its emperor, Justinian, reconquered large areas of Italy, imposing a Byzantine hold that would linger across much of the country for centuries. Complete hegemony was prevented by the arrival of the Lombards (567–774), a mostly pagan Germanic people who established powerful duchies across non-Byzantine areas of northern and central Italy.

The peninsula's territorial jigsaw was further complicated by the involvement of the Franks, a Christian people from Gaul (modern-day France). The Franks' position in Gaul was weakened by the existence of two rival royal dynasties, the Carolingian and Merovingian. This conflict was addressed by Pepin the Short, the Carolingian leader, who appealed to the papacy, an institution with increasing temporal authority, to arbitrate in the affair. Pope Stephen III sanctioned Pepin's rule in 754, but demanded in return that the Franks drive the Lombards from Italy.

This they did, partly under Pepin, and partly under Pepin's son, Charlemagne, who was crowned Holy Roman Emperor by Pope Leo III on Christmas Day, 800, an act of immense symbolic importance. Charlemagne then awarded the papacy the central Italian territories captured from the Lombards, thus creating the germ of the Papal States, territories that provided the papacy with the financial resources to wield genuine political power.

The transfer of territory also forged enduring links between the papacy and empire. These ties remained largely friendly while Charlemagne and his more powerful successors controlled the empire (while the Frankish empire eventually disintegrated, the Holy Roman Empire remained a coherent entity). As time passed, however, and the fortunes of the popes and emperors wavered, so relations between the two became strained. When issues of legitimacy arose, both parties harked back to Charlemagne's fateful coronation:

■ **A 19th-century painting from the French school shows Charlemagne's coronation as Holy Roman Emperor at St. Peter's Basilica in Rome on Christmas Day, A.D. 800.**

Popes claimed the right to sanction emperors, emperors the right to appoint popes. The consequences of the standoff, as well as the names of the respective camps and their supporters—Guelphs (the papal party) and Ghibellines (the imperial party)—would resonate through Italian history for centuries.

Arabs & Normans

Events in southern Italy followed a different course. The Arabs (see sidebar opposite) and the Byzantines, the latter still dominant elsewhere in southern Italy, eventually fell prey to the Normans, a race of Scandinavian descent who had settled in Normandy in northern France. Far-ranging in their search for plunder, they arrived in southern Italy as mercenaries, but by 1030 they had established a self-contained kingdom in Puglia as a springboard for conquest. From here, they invaded Sicily in 1061, establishing a royal dynasty—kings Roger I and II were the most notable incumbents—that had kinship with England's 11th-century nemesis, William the Conqueror.

Events during this period colored southern Italy's development for centuries. When Roger II was crowned king of Sicily, for example, he united a kingdom—the Kingdom of Naples and Sicily—that survived in one form or another until 1860. In the short term, however, Norman hegemony was soon undermined. The main culprits here, as in the north, were the papacy and the Holy Roman Empire.

The Norman decline was sparked by the marriage in 1186 of Henry VI, the Holy Roman Emperor, and Constance of Hautville, a Norman princess. When the Norman royal line died out in 1194, Henry's fortuitous union made him heir to the Norman throne. The papacy had sanctioned Norman rule in the south, much as it had done with Charlemagne, and deeply resented the appearance of the empire. Henry's son, Frederick Hohenstaufen (1197–1250), one of the great figures of the Middle Ages, proved impervious to papal resentment—he simply ignored his excommunication in 1228, for example—and ruled the

south adroitly, acquiring the title Stupor Mundi (Wonder of the World) in recognition of his many artistic, scientific, and military achievements.

Frederick's son, Manfred, proved less adept and was defeated in 1266 by Charles of Anjou, son of King Louis VIII of France, to whom the popes had appealed in 1260 to rid them of the Hohenstaufens. Charles then moved his capital to Naples, where he and his Anjou (or Angevin) successors established a dynasty that ruled for two centuries. Only Sicily, always something of a law unto itself, slipped from their control, a lapse precipitated by the Sicilian Vespers, an anti-Anjou uprising in 1282 (the revolt was sparked at the hour of vespers on March 30). During the revolt, Sicily's nobles looked to outside powers for help, this time to Spain's Peter III of Aragon. Not only did the Aragonese seize Sicily, but in 1442, in one of history's ironic twists, the Aragonese ruler, Alfonso V, was later named as heir to the last of Naples's Angevins, thus uniting the south under Spanish control until the 18th century.

City-states

Northern Italy, meanwhile, had seen the emergence of the *comuni,* or city-states, during the 11th and 12th centuries. In the first instance, these independent enclaves were nurtured by the weakness of the papacy and the Holy Roman Empire, the two bodies that could have exercised power in the region. Most emperors proved unable to combine their imperial obligations in northern Europe—their main power base—with the task of imposing authority in Italy. The papacy, for its part, was weakened by its bickering with the empire, and it eventually fell prey to French domination, being forced to move to Avignon in 1309, where it remained under French "protection" until 1377.

Cities took advantage of the power vacuum to forge increasingly independent identities. The Maritime Republics—Genoa, Pisa, Amalfi, and above all Venice—grew rich through overseas trade. Cities such as Florence and Siena prospered through textiles and banking. Others—Milan, Bologna, and Verona—flourished astride important trade routes. Eventually, some 400 city-states stretched across the north of the country. Only in the south, where the Spanish and the old feudal system held sway, was progress stifled, a situation that prevailed until the 20th century.

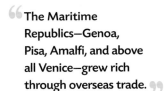

" **The Maritime Republics—Genoa, Pisa, Amalfi, and above all Venice—grew rich through overseas trade.** "

Initially, most of the cities enjoyed a degree of democratic rule, electing merchants and minor nobles to their ruling bodies. As time went by, however, cities were increasingly riven by internal dissent and disputes with rival cities. Against this background, there often emerged a single powerful figure or wealthy family, the only people able to exert authority in troubled times—the Medici in Florence, Visconti in Milan, Montefeltro in Urbino, Este in Ferrara, Gonzaga in Mantua, Scaligeri in Verona, among the many.

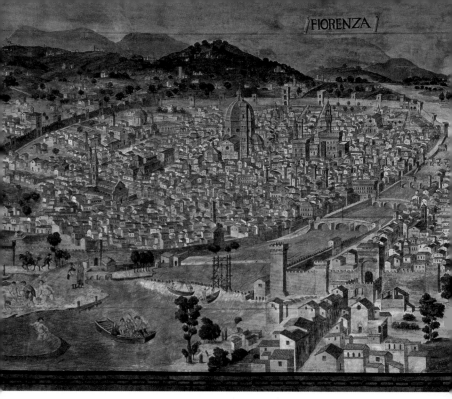

A panorama of 1490 shows Florence in its Renaissance heyday. The city was then one of about 400 independent Italian city-states.

Although often despotic, these wealthy clans provided the stability required for economic prosperity. They were also often enlightened artistic patrons, and the cities they controlled became sophisticated centers of learning. The result was an unparalleled explosion of artistic and cultural endeavor. In the literary field, the period saw the emergence of Dante Alighieri (1265–1321), Petrarch (1304–1374), and Giovanni Boccaccio (1313–1375). In painting, it produced innovators such as Giotto (1266–1337), Cimabue (ca 1240–1302), and Duccio (1255–1318). In architecture, it spawned Arnolfo di Cambio (ca 1240–1302), responsible for Florence's great cathedral, and, in sculpture, the figures of Giovanni Pisano, Nicola Pisano, and many others. The age's dynamism was also reflected in spiritual matters, where figures such as St. Francis (1182–1226) revitalized and challenged the prevailing religious orthodoxies. It was also manifest in the area of scholarship, which saw a revival of classical learning and the creation of some of Europe's oldest universities (notably Padua and Bologna).

Lay patronage freed artists from their earlier obligations to religious art, obligations that had resulted in conservative modes of expression. Similar freedoms appeared in scholarship, where writers and thinkers were able to turn from theology to the study of classical and humanist texts. From here it was a short step to a revival of the classical ideal in art and to the vast upsurge in artistic and other cultural activity known as the Renaissance (from the Italian *rinascimento,* or rebirth; see pp. 34–35).

But even as Italy was enjoying what in retrospect would be seen as a golden age, the first powerful hints of its eventual demise were already evident. Spain and Portugal's discovery of the New World and of improved trade routes to the East undermined the Mediterranean and mainland trade on which the considerable prosperity of Venice and other maritime powers was based. The rise of the Ottoman (Turkish) Empire also threatened the power of Venice, and by implication Italy, while the greater prominence of the Italian states on the European stage inevitably brought them into greater contact with the continent's other major powers.

History on the Streets

Dates from 19th- and 20th-century Italian history feature time and again—always in Roman numerals—in street names in every town, city, and village in Italy. Here's what some of them mean:

XXV Aprile: The day Italy was liberated from the Nazis in World War II.

XXIV Maggio: The day in 1915 when Italy entered World War I.

XX Settembre: The day in 1870 that Italian troops entered Rome to complete Italian reunification.

IV Novembre: The day in 1918 that Italy's armistice with Austria took effect, marking the end of World War I in Italy.

France & Spain

The turning point came with the death in 1492 of Lorenzo de' Medici, whose control of Florence had helped ensure a period of relative peace. Henceforth, foreign powers began to turn on Italy with an ever greater vengeance.

The first was Charles VIII (1470–1498) in 1494. The French king entered Italy at the "request" of the Duke of Milan, who had become embroiled in an argument with the Kingdom of Naples. Charles justified his interference on the basis that his French Anjou ancestors had once ruled Naples and much of southern Italy (see p. 26). Within three months he had seized, looted, and then abandoned the city of Naples.

In 1526, it was the turn of Charles V (1500–1558), the Holy Roman Emperor and heir to the Austrian and Spanish thrones. Within a short time he had defeated the French, captured Rome, and established puppet regimes in Milan, Tuscany, and Genoa. In 1559, the power of his Spanish successors in Italy was formalized by the Treaty (or Peace) of Cateau-Cambrésis, an agreement that left virtually only Venice and the Papal States free of foreign control.

In the late 17th century, Spain's grip on its foreign dominions was weakened by internal conflict, precipitating a further fragmenting of Italy's political jigsaw. The Treaty of Utrecht (1713) saw Sardinia pass to Austria; Piedmont and Sicily were handed to the French House of Savoy in 1713 and 1718; and, in 1735, Naples and southern Italy were given to the Bourbons. Later in the century, Napoleon's campaigns (1796–1800) made him master of the Italian peninsula, a short-lived interruption to the Italian status quo, which was restored by the Congress of Vienna in 1815.

Unification

The move toward Italian unification—known as the Risorgimento (Resurgence)—was hampered by the variety of forces ranged against it. In the north, much of Lombardy and the Veneto were controlled by the Austrians; in central Italy, power was held by the papacy; and in Naples and the south, authority was wielded by the Bourbons. Unification had been an issue for centuries, but it only became a serious possibility when Napoleon's integration of the peninsula underlined the potential for a unified state.

The first hints of change were contained in the Carbonari, secret societies active against the Austrians and Papal States in the 1820s. These were followed in 1831 by the foundation of a political movement known as Giovane Italia (Young Italy), whose aim was the creation of an Italian republic. Its leader was Giuseppe Mazzini (1805–1872), one of unification's three founding fathers.

Unification's second major proponent was Count Camillo Cavour (1810–1861), prime minister of Piedmont, an independent kingdom whose Savoy rulers Cavour hoped to install as kings of a united Italy. Its third leader was Giuseppe Garibaldi (1807–1882), a charismatic military leader who would help unite the opposing republican and royalist ambitions of Mazzini and Cavour.

The first efforts at change came during the revolutionary turmoil that swept Europe in 1848. Cavour and Garibaldi declared a republic in Rome, while ill-fated uprisings against the Austrians were led in Venice by Daniele Manin (1804–1857) and Carlo Alberto, the Savoy king, in Lombardy. The Austrian army crushed the revolts in the north, while the French, under Napoleon III, restored the power of their papal allies in Rome.

Things would change, however, over the next ten years. First, Piedmont sided with Britain, France, and Turkey against Russia in the Crimean War, and won increased sympathy from its allies with regard to what had become known as the "Italian Question." Second, Cavour's political skill produced an alliance with the French against

■ **Giuseppe Garibaldi, pictured circa 1861, one of the founding fathers of Italian unification**

Austria, resulting in a combined French-Piedmontese force: In 1859, it defeated the Austrians in northern Italy at the battles of Magenta and Solferino. Lombardy then fell to the Savoys, followed soon afterward by Tuscany and Emilia, both scenes of spontaneous uprisings.

Within four months, Garibaldi had captured the south from the Bourbons, aided by the Mille (Thousand), his famous troop of red-shirted volunteers. The Papal States fell soon after, save for Rome, which was still protected by its French garrison. The Kingdom of Italy was proclaimed in Turin on March 17, 1861. Venice and the Veneto region joined in 1866, when Austria was defeated by Bismarck and the Prussians at the Battle of Sadowa. Rome, the final link, was occupied in 1870, when the French withdrew following their defeat in the Franco-Prussian War. Rome was declared capital of the new country a year later.

Italy United

Politicians made concerted efforts to modernize Italy in the decades after unification. Highways and railroads were built, education improved, and industry encouraged. Colonies were acquired—parts of Eritrea (1882) and Libya (1911–1912) were
conquered in North Africa—and, in 1912, the first elections were held with universal
male suffrage (women had to wait until 1946 for the vote).

Italy remained neutral at the outbreak of World War I in August 1914, but within nine
months (on May 24, 1915) rallied to the Allied cause, seduced by the possibility of further
colonial gains in Africa and the acquisition of the *terre irredente* (Italian-speaking areas of
northeast Italy still held by the Austrians). Italy's nascent army initially proved no match
for the Austrians and lost several major battles before a remarkable rearguard victory at
Vittorio Veneto in 1918.

Italy received some of what it had hoped for from the peace treaty of 1919, but the
country suffered grievously in the economic and social upheavals that followed the war.
Political chaos ensued, providing a fertile breeding ground for extremism. A former social-
ist journalist, Benito Mussolini (1883–1945), adroitly exploited the situation, using his
black-shirted followers to foment unrest on the streets, and seduced Italy's nervous upper
and middle classes with the power of his rhetoric.

A threatened general strike in 1922 provided the catalyst for change. Mussolini made
his famous "March on Rome" from Milan, leading King Vittorio Emanuele III (1869–
1947)—fearful of civil war—to sanction Mussolini as prime minister, despite the still paltry
showing of his Fascist Party in parliament. Mussolini quickly consolidated power, eventually assuming the title of Duce, or Leader. By 1925, he had forged a dictatorial fascist state
that drifted inexorably toward alliance with Nazi Germany in the buildup to war.

▪ **A match of UEFA Nations League in 2018. Today, passion for soccer is probably what
unites Italians most.**

Italy made common cause with the Nazis in 1940, expecting easy gains on the back of sweeping German victories in Poland and France. But the Italian armies were ill-prepared, ill-motivated, and suffered losses in Greece, Ethiopia, and elsewhere that culminated in the Allied invasion of Sicily in July 1943. An armistice followed in September 1943, Mussolini was imprisoned, and—amid chaotic scenes—a new Italian government declared war on Germany. Hitler then freed Mussolini by force, installed him as head of a puppet state in northern Italy, and began a hard-fought war of attrition against the advancing Allies.

Rome was eventually taken on June 4, 1944, but the Allies would not cross the Po in northern Italy until April 24, 1945. Mussolini was captured by partisans while attempting to escape to Switzerland and executed on April 28.

To the Present

Italy's remarkable postwar transformation began in June 1946, when a national referendum narrowly voted to replace the country's monarchy with a republic. The Marshall Plan then provided the catalyst for an economic boom, fueled by the availability of cheap labor and the Italians' voracious appetite for material change. The country's emergence into the European mainstream was symbolized by the 1957 Treaty of Rome, a document that laid the foundations of the European Union, of which Italy was one of the six founding members. It was further cemented when Rome hosted the 1960 Olympic Games, in the same year as Federico Fellini's famous *La Dolce Vita*, a movie that captured the flavor of Italy during a decade of extraordinary change.

> **Italy's remarkable postwar transformation began in June 1946, when a national referendum narrowly voted to replace the country's monarchy with a republic.**

Italy's transformation was not without its problems. By the 1960s, the boom had largely run its course. Coalition governments became weaker, and the economy faltered, leading to violent social tensions. Unrest exploded in the *autunno caldo* (literally, "hot fall") of 1968, when worker and student demonstrations swept the country.

Worse was to come in the next few years, when Italy was ravaged by political terrorism of all shades. The low point came in 1978, when the feared group Brigate Rosse (Red Brigade) kidnapped and murdered the former prime minister, Aldo Moro. No sooner had the terrorist menace been nullified, however, than Italy's political system was wracked by the corruption scandals of the early 1990s. At the time it seemed the experience had demonstrated for the first time Italy's desire for institutional change. In the event, the Second Republic (1994) proved something of a false dawn, although the country's ties with the European Union have recently produced a degree of change by default.

Italy today continues to appear fractured, much as it has been for centuries. The economic developments of the north and the south proceed at very different paces and the Mafia continues to be an unwieldy presence. In recent years, Italians have seen a series of unstable governments, caretaker governments, and controversial or ineffective reforms; some parties are even questioning the country's relationship with Europe. Even though everyone seems to be talking about "national debt" and "immigration," the percentage of eligible voters who don't go to the polls is high, a sign of the waning trust in politics. And yet it seems hard to imagine that Italy will not prosper again, overcoming circumstance in the same inspired and triumphant manner it has for much of its checkered past. ■

THE ARTS

Italy's immense artistic and cultural heritage is its greatest legacy. Over almost 3,000 years, the paintings, sculptures, mosaics, operas, and works of literature of the country's countless artists, composers, and writers have helped shape and define Western civilization.

Painting & Sculpture

Greece & Rome: Greek art was introduced to Sicily and southern Italy in the eighth century B.C. with the arrival of Greek settlers to Magna Graecia (see p. 20). Its most obvious memorials are the temples at Paestum, Agrigento, and elsewhere and the semicircular theaters of Taormina and Syracuse. Little survives of Hellenistic painting of the time, although its influence can be seen in the tomb and vase paintings of the Etruscans in central Italy and in the fresco decoration of Roman villas, of which the most exhilarating examples survive at Pompeii and Naples's Museo Archeologico Nazionale.

Etruscan and Roman art also looked to Greece for the mosaic, a medium that found favor on the walls and floors of domestic and religious buildings across Italy. Naples and Pompeii again preserve fine Roman-era mosaics, although the best of all belong to the third-century A.D. hunting lodge at Piazza Armerina in Sicily. Of still greater influence was Hellenistic sculpture, whose impact was felt not only during the Roman period, but also during the Renaissance and the neoclassical revival of the 18th and 19th centuries. Museums across Italy contain numerous masterpieces of Roman sculpture, works whose debt to Greece is belied by exquisite execution. Much the same can be said of Etruscan sculpture, examples of which are rarer—the best are found in Rome's Villa Giulia and the smaller provincial museums of Tuscany, Umbria, and Lazio.

> **Etruscan and Roman art also looked to Greece for the mosaic, a medium that found favor on the walls and floors of domestic and religious buildings across Italy.**

Byzantine Empire: The art of the Byzantine Empire was an entity born of the decision to divide the old Roman empire in two: a western empire with its capital in Rome and an eastern empire centered on Constantinople (Istanbul). Given its eastern and Roman roots, Byzantine art developed along distinctive lines, emerging as a hybrid of classical and more ornate oriental styles. Its most predominant medium was the mosaic, a form that proved perfectly suited to the Byzantine penchant for ornamentation, abstraction, and the characteristic use of gold and other richly colored backgrounds.

Byzantium's first major incursion onto Italian soil came with Justinian, the Byzantine emperor who reconquered areas of Italy from the Goths, invaders from central Europe, in the sixth century. He established his capital at Ravenna, a town still graced with Europe's finest Byzantine mosaics, although other magnificent Byzantine-influenced mosaics exist in Aquileia, Milan, Rome, and elsewhere. One of Byzantium's most

■ **A late-13th-century depiction of the Virgin and Child, Gallerie dell'Accademia, Venice**

remarkable aspects was its longevity, the mosaic tradition having remained a component of buildings such as the Basilica di San Marco in Venice and Florence's Battistero
di San Giovanni until the 12th century and beyond.

Pre-Renaissance: Byzantium's influence was especially slow to fade in the sphere
of painting, where three stylized images dominated Italian art for more than 500
years: portraits of saints; the iconic Madonna and Child; and *Christus Triumphans,* a
painted figure of Christ on the cross. By the 14th century, as the increasing wealth
and cultural sophistication of the city-states took hold, these images had begun to
seem tired and anachronistic. However, the move toward new idioms—harbingers
of the Renaissance—was gradual.

One of the first artists to grapple with new forms of expression was the Roman
Pietro Cavallini (ca 1250–ca 1330), a Byzantine-trained mosaicist who began in mid-
career to explore the possibilities of fresco painting. For a while he worked in the Basilica
di San Francesco (1228) in Assisi, a seminal building in the development of Italian art.
Here he met Cimabue, famously described by the Renaissance art critic Giorgio Vasari
as the "father of Italian painting." Soon after, he worked with Cimabue's pupil, Giotto di
Bondone (ca 1266–1337), the single most influential figure in European pre-Renaissance
art. Building on the tentative advance of Cimabue and others, Giotto introduced realism, narrative, emotion, and spatial depth into paintings, breaking Byzantium's stilted
stranglehold on both the style and substance of Italian art. Similar advances were made
in sculpture, a long neglected art form, in particular by the Tuscan-based artists Nicola
Pisano (ca 1220–1284) and Arnolfo di Cambio.

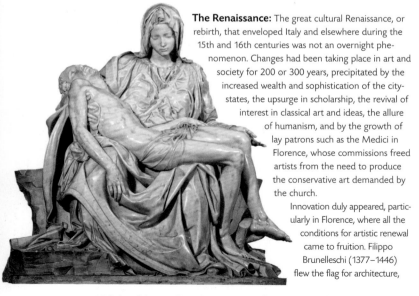

The Renaissance: The great cultural Renaissance, or
rebirth, that enveloped Italy and elsewhere during the
15th and 16th centuries was not an overnight phenomenon. Changes had been taking place in art and
society for 200 or 300 years, precipitated by the
increased wealth and sophistication of the city-
states, the upsurge in scholarship, the revival of
interest in classical art and ideas, the allure
of humanism, and by the growth of
lay patrons such as the Medici in
Florence, whose commissions freed
artists from the need to produce
the conservative art demanded by
the church.

Innovation duly appeared, particularly in Florence, where all the
conditions for artistic renewal
came to fruition. Filippo
Brunelleschi (1377–1446)
flew the flag for architecture,

■ Michelangelo's 1499 "Pietà," a masterpiece of Renaissance sculpture

Donatello (1386–1466) pioneered advances in sculpture, and Masaccio (1401–1428) set new standards in painting. Thereafter, the floodgates of genius and achievement opened in cities across Italy. The most notable center was Venice, whose immense wealth and cosmopolitan élan found artistic expression in the works of Vittore Carpaccio, Giovanni Bellini, Titian, Jacopo Tintoretto, and many others.

High Renaissance & Mannerism: The Renaissance can be said to have lasted the best part of the 15th century, at least as far as parameters can be defined. Its final years, more or less the first quarter of the 16th century, are referred to as the High Renaissance. Three hallowed names dominate this period, Leonardo da Vinci (1452–1519), Michelangelo (1475–1564), and Raphael (1483–1520), men of consummate individual genius whose work transcends category or classification.

The Art of Frescoing

Frescoes take their name from *fresco,* or fresh, because they were painted on wet, or "fresh," plaster—a technique popular in the Renaissance period. Add paint to dry plaster and any moisture or physical deterioration in the wall eventually lifts off the paint. But put paint pigments on wet plaster—a mixture of lime, water, and fine sand—then, as the plaster dries, the lime (calcium hydroxide) combines with carbon dioxide in the air to create calcium carbonate. This then crystallizes around the sand and pigment particles, fixing them and leaving them resistant to further action by water. However, the technique restricted the range of pigments, and thus colors, that could be used. Pigments were also difficult to mix, unlike oil paints, making it hard to achieve depth of tone or subtlety of shade, and artists could only work on areas small enough to complete before the plaster dried. Stripping off the plaster and starting again was the only way to rectify mistakes.

Renaissance self-confidence was eventually punctured by Italy's increasingly troubled political situation, whose perilous state found its most dramatic expression in 1527 with the attack on Rome and the papacy by Charles V's imperial army. The uncertainty of the times was reflected in mannerism, the artistic genre that bridged the Renaissance and baroque periods. As the name suggests, its approach was more mannered, putting style above substance and artifice above naturalism. Previously unquestioned conventions such as color, proportion, and composition were deliberately subverted. Michelangelo's and Raphael's late work displayed mannerist hints, many of which were taken up and developed by artists such as Pontormo (1494–1556), Rosso Fiorentino (1494–1540), and Parmigianino (1503–1540).

The Baroque: Baroque art was an expression of the new spirit of self-confidence engendered during the late 16th century by the Counter-Reformation, a movement promulgated by the Roman Catholic church to challenge the rise of Protestantism. The Italian writer Luigi Barzini produced a view shared by many of much of baroque art, describing it as "anything pointlessly complicated, otiose, capricious and eccentric" (*The Italians*, 1964). The style prospered hugely in Rome, where the papacy became Italy's greatest 17th-century patron, but it also found triumphant expression in Naples, Lecce, Turin, and Palermo. Its most obvious memorials are sculptural and architectural, its greatest exponents the exuberant Gianlorenzo Bernini (1598–1680) and his more troubled and introverted rival, Francesco Borromini (1599–1667).

Baroque painting, while less high profile, also had its masters, principally Caravaggio (1573–1610), who produced works of graphic and revolutionary realism, and the Carracci dynasty (Ludovico, Annibale, and Agostino), whose approach tended toward the cooler and more restrained precepts of classical art.

To the Present: The approach exemplified by the Carraccis was also pursued in the 18th century, when Europe was swept by a renewed passion for the classical ideal in art. Neoclassicism, as the movement was known, was most marked in sculpture, where the style's sober virtuosity was exemplified by artists such as Antonio Canova (1757–1822). Painting of the period tended more to the florid world of rococo, a sensual style born in France that found a natural home in the decadent world of 18th-century Venice with painters such as Giovanni Battista Tiepolo (1696–1770).

> **Used extensively across Italy, the Romanesque style's popularity was fostered by the spate of church building that followed the emergence of city-states.**

The middle of the 19th century was enlivened by the Macchiaoli, a Tuscan-based group of painters whose new approach to style and color mirrored that of the French Impressionists. Paris seduced Italy's most celebrated late 19th-century painter, Amedeo Modigliani (1884–1920), who spent much of his life in that city. Paris was also the birthplace of futurism, a movement founded in 1909 by a group of Italians there, which aimed to embody the drama and dynamism of the mechanical age.

During the 20th century, Italy's artistic influence was peripheral—surrealist Giorgio de Chirico (1888–1978) was the country's last painter of international renown. Today, its long artistic tradition finds more oblique, but no less glorious expression in other mediums—those of design and high fashion—where Michelangelo, Leonardo, and other past greats would doubtless be working were they alive.

Architecture

Among the oldest architectural creations found in Italy are the prehistoric *nuraghi* of Sardinia, circular stone dwellings of which extremely little is known. Next in age are the great temples and theaters of Magna Graecia, the area of southern Italy colonized by the Greeks from about 800 B.C. The classical elements of these and other buildings influenced Etruscan and Roman architecture, although little survives of the Etruscans save their central Italian necropoli, or burial grounds (most Etruscan buildings were made from wood and so perished over the years). All but a handful of Roman architectural forms were derivative—the triumphal arch and basilica were notable exceptions—although the innovative use of the arch and new materials such as concrete (in the Pantheon, for example) enabled the Romans to build on a grander scale than the Greeks.

Byzantine architecture borrowed both from Rome (and therefore Greece) and the Orient. Many buildings of the era were based on the basilica or the Greek cross, the

■ **Buildings of the size and complexity of Pisa's cathedral often took hundreds of years to complete.**

latter a design in which a dome was raised above a square or rectangular base. The Orient's heavily decorated traditions are seen to best effect in the basilicas of San Marco in Venice and San Vitale in Ravenna, and to a lesser extent in the cathedral of Monreale in Sicily, where Byzantine forms were mixed with exotic and northern European elements introduced by Arabs and Normans.

This intermingling of traditions influenced Italian architecture for centuries, particularly the Romanesque styles that developed around the tenth century. The style's simple, round-arched forms varied greatly by region, from the buildings of Sicily and Puglia, often tinged with ornate Arab-influenced decorative details, to the black and white marble-striped and sculpture-embellished appearance of Lombard- and Pisan-Romanesque buildings in the north. Used extensively across Italy, the Romanesque style's popularity was fostered by the spate of church building that followed the emergence of city-states.

From about the late-13th century, the Romanesque was enlivened and eventually replaced by Gothic architecture, a style that at its most basic is identified by a pointed arch, vaulting, and rose windows, and by its propensity for airy interiors and an emphasis on verticality. The form was largely introduced from France, finding its earliest expression in simple but influential buildings such as the Basilica di San Francesco in Assisi. Like the Romanesque, it proliferated and mutated quickly, its spread facilitated by the profusion of civic and church building in the wealthy and now well-established city-states. Romanesque-Gothic hybrids predominated, largely because of the length of time it took to complete buildings. This fusion is most notable in the great cathedrals and public palaces of Siena, Pisa, Florence, and Orvieto. Only rarely did the Gothic predominate, most gloriously in Milan's cathedral and the Doge's Palace in Venice.

Renaissance architecture saw the reemergence of classical forms and ideals. Even as the Gothic reached its apogee, architects such as the Florentine Filippo Brunelleschi were adapting ancient forms to new buildings. Brunelleschi's work was developed by Michelozzo, Leon Battista Alberti, and Bramante—who conceived the basic plan for

St. Peter's Basilica in Rome—although the most important architect of the period was Andrea Palladio (1508–1580), whose reworking of classical idioms in Venice, Vicenza, and elsewhere continues to influence architecture to the present day.

Renaissance purity of line and form gave way to the baroque, an exuberant style whose complex, theatrical, and highly decorated elements expressed the self-confident optimism of the Counter-Reformation. Religious and architectural ebullience found their greatest expression in Rome, where papal patronage fueled a 17th-century building boom led by the greatest architects, Gianlorenzo Bernini and Francesco Borromini.

Baroque's energy and invention eventually gave way to the bland creations of 18th-century neoclassicism, a further reworking of classical forms that lacked the earlier subtlety of Palladio and his contemporaries. Art nouveau also made a brief 19th-century appearance, most notably in the covered glass arcades of Milan and Naples. In the modern age, Italian architecture has mirrored the burgeoning fortunes of Italian design, as celebrated architects such as Renzo Piano, responsible for Paris's Centre Pompidou, Mario Botta, and Stefano Boeri, a leader in extensive urban planning, have given renewed impetus to a distinguished 3,000-year-old tradition.

■ **A lavish performance of Verdi's *Aida*, staged outdoors in Verona's Roman amphitheater**

Music

Italy's immense contribution to the world of classical music bore early fruit in the 11th century when a Tuscan monk, Guido Monaco (ca 992–ca 1050), devised the musical scale and forms of notation still used today.

The country also produced one of the world's first documented composers, Francesco Landini (ca 1325–1397). Religious and choral music predominated during much of the Middle Ages, culminating in the work of Giovanni da Palestrina (1525–1594). Secular music of the period often took the form of madrigals, a genre in which poems were set to music, or of wedding entertainments, both of which helped lay the foundations of Italy's greatest musical legacy—opera.

> **Opera's precise origins are disputed. Many trace the genre to the *intermedii* of Florentine and other wedding ceremonies.**

Opera's earliest manifestations, however, were largely overshadowed by the development of instrumental music. A triumvirate of composers perfected and advanced such music: Girolamo Frescobaldi (1583–1643) wrote largely for the organ, Arcangelo Corelli (1653–1713) for the violin,

and Domenico Scarlatti (1685–1757) for the harpsichord. Venice, then one of the great centers of Italian music, thanks in part to the choir and orchestra of the Basilica di San Marco, gave birth to Antonio Vivaldi (1678–1741), somewhat ignored in his own day—he died impoverished in Vienna—but he is now celebrated for works such as *The Four Seasons*. The composer wrote some 454 concertos, thus helping to establish the concerto's classic three-movement structure (fast-slow-fast). Tomaso Albinoni (1671–1750), a similar composer and close contemporary of Vivaldi, has also achieved modern fame—his stately *Canon* is perhaps his best known work.

Opera: Opera's precise origins are disputed. Many trace the genre to the *intermedii* of Florentine and other wedding ceremonies. These entertainments included a series of tableaus involving singing, dancing, and static performance. Members of a Florentine academy known as the Camerata, inspired by these entertainments, then began to combine elements of Greek drama with musical declamation. In 1597, two of the academy's members, Jacopo Peri and Ottavio Rinuccini, produced *Dafne,* what many consider to be the first opera, as well as *Euridice,* the first opera to have survived in its complete form.

The first well-known composer to grapple with the new form was Claudio Monteverdi (1567–1643), whose *Orfeo* (1607) first established opera in the musical mainstream. Various refinements to the form then took place during the 17th century, notably the division between *opera seria,* which dealt with weightier themes—usually drawn from mythology—and *opera buffa,* or comic opera, which frequently drew on the stock characters and situations of *commedia dell'arte.* Every major Italian city soon had its own opera house, and in Naples Alessandro Scarlatti (1660–1725) established the opera's classic opening overture and the division between the individually sung arias and the joint recitative essential for the development of plot.

Henceforth, many of the great names of opera were Italian. The notable exception was, of course, Mozart (although it was an Italian, Lorenzo da Ponte, who wrote the librettos for the maestro's greatest operas, *Don Giovanni, Così fan tutte,* and *Le Nozze di Figaro*). Gioacchino Rossini (1792–1868) was one of the earliest masters of comic or light opera *(William Tell, The Barber of Seville).* Contemporaries who worked in a similar vein included Vincenzo Bellini (1801–1835), whose melodic genius found expression in works such as *Norma,* and Gaetano Donizetti (1797–1848), who combined melodrama *(Lucia di Lammermoor)* with more lightweight fare *(L'Elisir d'Amore).*

Opera's golden age dawned at the end of the 19th century with the arrival of the genre's giants—Giuseppe Verdi (1813–1901) and Giacomo Puccini (1858–1924). Verdi's lush, romantic works, with those of Mozart, form the bedrock of the operatic canon *(Aida, Rigoletto, Nabucco,* and *La Traviata).* Puccini, no less performed, explored more modern themes, embracing the trend toward *verismo,* or realism, in operas such as *Tosca, Madame Butterfly,* and *La Bohème.*

> **When Mussolini opened Rome's famous Cinecittà studios in 1938 it was with the boast that movies would be 'our greatest weapon.'**

Modern Italian music stands in opera's long shadow. The most famous composer today is Ennio Morricone (1928–), who wrote scores for many award-winning movies. Italy's musical heritage, however, is celebrated in prestigious festivals across the country, most notably Verona's Festival Lirico, Florence's Maggio Musicale, and Spoleto's Festival dei Due Mondi.

Cinema

Italian cinema accounts for much of what we know, or think we know, of modern Italy. Neorealist moviemakers after World War II, Federico Fellini's *La Dolce Vita,* and stars such as Sophia Loren and Marcello Mastroianni have all contributed to our idea of how Italians look and behave.

The industry's roots are old. The first Italian movie studio was built in Turin in 1905. The first full-length movie, *Cabiria,* appeared in 1914. Within a few years the business had moved to Rome, lured by the capital's kinder weather and impressive range of locations. Fascism, when it came, proved a boon, but only in terms of quantity. Most movies of the thirties were lightweight baubles, escapist fare that pandered to the streak of sentimentality in the Italian character. Others were little more than propaganda: When Mussolini opened Rome's famous Cinecittà studios in 1938 it was with the boast that movies would be "our greatest weapon."

Italian moviemaking came of age after the war. A new generation of directors pioneered a genre known as neorealism, a gritty style grounded in hard-hitting social *vérité.* Roberto Rossellini's *Roma, Città Aperta* (1945) was its first masterpiece, an almost documentary-style movie of deliberately jerky camera work, real locations, and a narrative that rarely pulled its punches.

Rossellini's lead was followed by Luchino Visconti, Michelangelo Antonioni, and Vittorio de Sica, and later by Pier Paolo Pasolini and Federico Fellini, each of whom, in his own way, explored the changing face of postwar Italy. Neorealism quickly colored

Hollywood's approach to films noirs and the French New Wave, as well as drawing foreign mainstream moviemakers to the Italian studios (*Cleopatra* and *Ben Hur* were just two of the blockbuster movies partly made at Cinecittà).

The glory days were soon over, however. Neorealism's iconoclasm—although influential—proved short-lived, while rising costs pushed Italian studios into soft porn and spaghetti westerns to make ends meet. The old names—Fellini and Visconti—worked on, and still sprung the odd surprise, but by the late seventies the pioneering fervor of 20 years earlier had vanished.

Today, both the language and the inspirations of the Italian movie industry have changed. Often, they are focused on analyzing particular aspects of the country and its inhabitants. Franco Zeffirelli and Bernardo Bertolucci have been the big names in Italian cinema in recent decades but other directors have reached international fame and won important awards as well: Giuseppe Tornatore, Roberto Benigni, Matteo Garrone, Paolo Sorrentino.

A scene from Benigni's *Life Is Beautiful*, winner of the 1999 Oscar for best foreign language film

Literature

Early Italian literature is the literature of the classical canon, notably the Roman poets Virgil and Ovid, authors of *Aeneid* and *Metamorphoses,* respectively, and writers such as Pliny *(Historia Naturalis),* Julius Caesar *(The Gallic Wars),* and Suetonius *(The Twelve Caesars),* who chronicled the history of Rome and its empire. In drama, Seneca explored the tragic idiom, while Plautus and Terence were the masters of comedy. Juvenal stands out among the satirists—he coined the phrase *panem et circenses* (bread and circuses) to mock the decadence of a Roman populace that bartered its freedom for food and entertainment.

Latin's linguistic primacy continued until the 13th century, when poets from the Sicilian School and Franciscans, such as Jacopone da Todi and St. Francis of Assisi, borrowing from the troubadour traditions of Provence, began to write in the everyday Italian of the period. This trend was continued by three of Italy's greatest literary figures: Dante Alighieri, Petrarch, and Giovanni Boccaccio. Dante's *Divine Comedy* (ca 1321) is one of the finest epic poems of any age or language, an all encompassing work inspired by the poet's doomed love for Beatrice. Love also inspired Petrarch, whose passion for Laura produced the lyrical sonnets of the *Canzoniere,* or Songs. Boccaccio is remembered for the narrative finesse of *Il Decamerone* (1348–1353), a series of one hundred tales told by ten people over ten days as the Black Death raged in Florence.

Petrarch and Boccaccio were not entirely wedded to the vernacular but joined attempts to revive Latin and Greek as literary languages, forming part of the humanistic and classical vanguard that paved the way for the Renaissance. Classical ideals found expression in the works of humanists such as Leonardo Bruni and Poliziano, and in the verse of Michelangelo, who, as well as being a painter, sculptor, and architect, also wrote accomplished sonnets and other poetry.

Other hugely influential works of the period included Baldassare Castiglione's *Courtier* (1528), a handbook of courtly manners read across Europe, and Ariosto's *Orlando Furioso,* an epic poem based on the exploits of the knight Orlando and his paramour Angelica. *The Prince* (1513), a masterly political analysis that combined politics with an unerring study of human nature, was Niccolò Machiavelli's masterpiece.

Italian literature after the Renaissance continued to produce outstanding individual exponents of the various literary movements that swept Europe in the 18th and 19th centuries. Alessandro Manzoni's *I Promessi Sposi* reflected the development of the novel as a form—his epic tale of young love written in idiomatic Italian (a revolution in literary terms) remains required reading for Italian students to this day. In drama, the dominant figure was Carlo Goldoni (1707–1793), whose bright, incisive comedies bear similarities to the plays of the 17th-century French dramatist Molière. In poetry, the lyrical poems of Giacomo Leopardi (1798–1837) represented Italian Romanticism at its best, while the works of Giosuè Carducci (1835–1907) presaged the more troubled undercurrents of the modern age.

These undercurrents found expression in the novels of Italo Svevo (1861–1928), whose existential and psychoanalytical concerns mirrored those of contemporaries such as Czech-born Franz Kafka and France's Marcel Proust. Similar concerns were addressed in the plays of Luigi Pirandello (1867–1936), whose work explored human alienation and the contradictions of personality. The 20th century also marked the emergence of female writers, in particular Grazia Deledda (1875–1936), winner of the Nobel Prize for literature in 1926.

Fascist repression produced its own masterpieces, notably Primo Levi's powerful accounts of his experiences in the Nazi death camps and Carlo Levi's *Christ Stopped at Eboli* (1945), an account of the poverty encountered by a writer exiled to southern Italy. Both were starkly realistic, as were the works of Alberto Moravia (1907–1990), a writer whose portrayal of the rapidly changing Italy of the postwar era found an audience beyond his home country. The same can be said of Umberto Eco (1932–2016) and Italo Calvino (1923–1989), whose subtle and often magical novels and short stories have been widely translated. ■

Italian Love of Crime

Some of Italy's best-selling contemporary novelists are crime and thriller writers. Publishing house Mondadori helped start the phenomenon in 1929, when it began publishing thrillers, often translated from the English, in garish yellow *(giallo)* covers. Thrillers became known colloquially as *gialli,* and the name has stuck. The best known modern writer of gialli is Andrea Camilleri, famed for his Inspector Montalbano crime novels, the first of which, *La forma dell'acqua,* was published in 1994, when the writer was 69. The books are set in the fictional Sicilian town of Vigata, based on Camilleri's hometown of Porto Empedocle. The town, recognizing a good thing, adopted Vigata as a second name in 2003.

A romantic city filled with museums, galleries, churches, fountains, and glorious monuments to almost a thousand years of empire

ROME

■ The Colosseo, a first-century A.D. legacy of the Romans

ROME

Rome (Roma) is without equal. No other city can match its artistic, historical, or architectural riches, and no city presents quite such an intimidating sightseeing prospect—merely visiting the main highlights will take several days. It also has more than its share of modern problems—noise, traffic—and, especially in the sweltering summers, can seem too busy and bustling for comfort. This note only serves as a warning—it is easy to forget that Rome has a problematic present as well as a glorious past.

■ Views east from St. Peter's Basilica stretch across Bernini's Piazza San Pietro to the Alban Hills.

Your best approach to Rome is an oblique one. Avoid the big-name sights at the outset, and ease yourself gently into the city with a stroll around its more intimate squares—Piazza Navona and the market-filled Campo de' Fiori are two of the best. Remember that enjoying a city is not only about seeing the monuments, so leave time for aimless exploration of these districts as well as Trastevere and the Ghetto, two of the most rewarding old quarters.

Once you are ready for the sights, a clear map and basic sense of direction will stand you in good stead, as orienting yourself in the old city is not difficult.

Branch Out From Piazza Venezia

Head first for Piazza Venezia, a vast traffic-filled square that lies more or less at the city's heart. Overlooking it is the Monumento a Vittorio Emanuele II, a colossal shrine to

INSIDER TIP:

Most museums and churches close between 1 and 4 p.m. or so. Do as the locals do and enjoy a nice long lunch and a nap or saunter around town.

—CHRISTOPHER SOMERVILLE
National Geographic author

Italian unification, flanked on its right by the Campidoglio (Capitoline Hill), the core of the ancient city. Three principal roads lead from the square, each providing a useful focus for sightseeing expeditions.

First of these is the Via dei Fori Imperiali, which runs south past the Foro Romano (Roman Forum) and Colosseo (Colosseum), two of the city's big set pieces. It also provides easy access to the Fori Imperiali, San Pietro in Vincoli (known for its huge Michelangelo statue of Moses), and two of the city's most interesting churches, San Clemente and San Giovanni in Laterano. All of these sights could be comfortably seen in a day, although the last major church in this district, Santa Maria Maggiore, lies in a slightly isolated position in the unlovely area around Termini, Rome's main train station.

West of Piazza Venezia runs Corso Vittorio Emanuele II, the second of Rome's principal thoroughfares, which cuts through what is often called the city's medieval and Renaissance heart. In truth, as elsewhere in Rome, the district it divides—the city's most appealing—is a medley of monuments from every era. Its key sights are the Palazzo Doria Pamphilj, one of the city's top art galleries, and two major squares: Piazza Navona and Campo de' Fiori.

All manner of other churches, palaces, and little nooks and corners lie scattered around the area, and you could spend a couple of days exploring this quarter alone. If time is short, stick to the Pantheon, Rome's best preserved ancient monument, and the churches of San Luigi dei Francesi (paintings by Caravaggio) and Santa Maria sopra Minerva (a fine Michelangelo sculpture).

An almost equally appealing area lies astride the third of Piazza Venezia's thoroughfares, the Via del Corso running to the north, whose side streets conceal well-known attractions as the Fontana di Trevi (Trevi Fountain) and Spanish Steps, not to mention the Palazzo Barberini (a major gallery) and streets around Via Condotti that make up the city's main shopping district. At its northern end, the Corso opens out into Piazza del Popolo, beyond which stretches the Villa Borghese, Rome's main park and the setting for two leading museums: the Galleria Borghese (paintings and sculpture) and Villa Giulia (ancient art and artifacts).

Across the Tevere (Tiber), Rome's river, stands St. Peter's Basilica, which requires most of a morning to see, including about an hour in Castel Sant'Angelo. In the same area, the tiny independent state of Vatican City, are the Musei Vaticani (Vatican Museums), home to the Cappella Sistina (Sistine Chapel) and the world's single greatest museum complex. ∎

NOT TO BE MISSED:

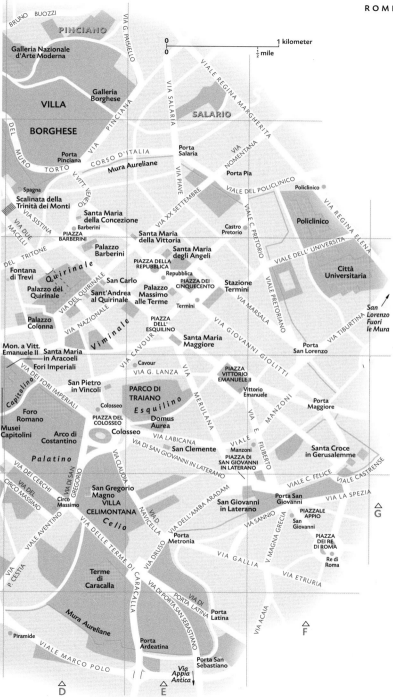

ANCIENT ROME

From the back of the Campidoglio, the Foro Romano stretches for almost half a mile. Alongside it lie excavated portions of the later Fori Imperiali, built to enlarge and beautify an increasingly cramped downtown area. Opposite you, toward the right, is the Palatino, and farther away, to the left, you can just make out the top of the Colosseo.

An equestrian statue of Emperor Marcus Aurelius sits at the center of the Piazza del Campidoglio.

Campidoglio

🅰 46 C3

Campidoglio

Piazza Venezia is dominated by the Monumento a Vittorio Emanuele II, a shrine to Italian unification known locally as the "typewriter" or "wedding cake" after the shape and dazzling whiteness of its marble bulwarks. Its construction resulted in the destruction of countless medieval buildings and altered forever the contours of the Campidoglio or Capitolino (Capitoline Hill), the heart of

ancient Rome and the most important of the city's original Seven Hills.

Inhabited since the Bronze Age, the Campidoglio's southern summit once contained the city's most venerated temple, a shrine to Jupiter, while its northern promontory housed the Arx, Rome's earliest defensive citadel. Today, its main focus is the **Piazza del Campidoglio,** completed to an original design by Michelangelo in the 17th century. Palaces on either side

INSIDER TIP:

The inscription SPQR (a Latin abbreviation of "the Senate and Roman People") on many road grates is a quick reminder of Rome's enduring past.

—ADAM THEILER
*National Geographic
International Channel*

contain the linked **Musei Capitolini** (Capitoline Museums), home to a picture gallery and some of the city's most remarkable pieces of Roman and Greek statuary. The most impressive of all is the second-century equestrian statue of Emperor Marcus Aurelius, installed on the first floor of the Palazzo dei Conservatori on the right (the statue in the square is a copy). Walk to the rear left of the piazza for some memorable views over the Foro Romano.

A flight of more than one hundred steps leads to the church

of **Santa Maria in Aracoeli,** an approach built in 1348 as a votive offering to celebrate the passing of the Black Death. A less demanding approach is possible from the rear of Piazza del Campidoglio. Inside, the building has a musty, magical charm, particularly at dusk, when delicate chandeliers illuminate the gold-tinged ceiling and shadowy ancient columns. Artistic highlights include Pinturicchio's frescoes on the "Life of San Bernardino" (1484-86), in the first chapel in the south aisle.

The **Fori Imperiali** (Imperial Forums) is the name given to the five forums created by Julius Caesar and his successors after the original Foro Romano became too crowded for further building. Many of their monuments now lie entombed beneath the Via dei Fori Imperiali, a road scythed through the area by Mussolini in 1931–33. Estimates suggest only one-fifth of the original area remains above ground. The work that is currently being done to connect the two sectors of emperor Trajan's Foro di Traiano

Musei Capitolini

⛰ 46 C3

✉ Piazza del Campidoglio 1

☎ 06 0608 for information and reservations or online at museiincomune roma.it

🕐 Closed Jan. 1, May 1, Dec. 25

💲 $$ (more during special exhibitions)

🚌 Bus: 60, 64, 81, 87, & all other buses to Piazza Venezia

museicapitolini.org

Passes & Combined Tickets

Reduce the cost of seeing Rome's top sights with one of these passes:

Colosseo and Foro Pass *(tel 06 3996 7700 or coopculture.it, $$)* A pass to the Foro Romano, Palatino, and Colosseo. The shortest lines are at the Foro Romano entrance off Via dei Fori Imperiali by Via Cavour. Tickets bought by phone or online must be picked up at the Colosseo.

Foro Romano-Palatino Super *(tel 06 3996 7700, coopculture.it, $$)* Can be bought alone or as an upgrade of the previous

pass. It is a one-day ticket including one entrance to the Foro Romano and to seven special sights (according to availabilities).

Roma Pass *(tel 06 0608, romapass.it, $$$–$$$$)* These two- or three-day passes provide free admission to the first one or two major museums or archaeological sites visited, and discounted admission to those visited afterward. It also offers free travel on buses, trams, and the subway. Available by phone, online, and at visitor centers and information points.

Foro Romano

🅰 47 D3

✉ Entrances at Largo Romolo e Remo (at the junction of Via dei Fori Imperiali & Via Cavour) & Via di San Gregorio 30

☎ 06 0608. Non-compulsory reservations 06 3996 7700 or online at coopculture.it

💲 $$ (includes entry to Colosseo & Palatino)

🚌 Bus: 75, 81, 175, 204, 673; tram 30, & all other buses to Piazza Venezia. Metro: Colosseo

parcocolosseo.it

will bring new wonders to light. In May 2019, a marble head of Diony-sus from the 1st–2nd century A.D. was recovered.

Julius Caesar was the first to build on any scale outside the original forum, but time has been unkind to his creation, the **Foro di Cesare** (54–46 B.C.). His imperial successor, Augustus, was equally undermined by posterity—the ruins of the Temple of Mars Ultor, flanked by columns on three sides, is more or less all that survives of his **Foro di Augusto** (inaugurated in 2 B.C.). Two large columns and a delightful frieze are the highlights of the **Foro di Nerva**, built by an emperor who reigned for just two years (A.D. 96–98). However, most people overlook this and the **Foro di Vespasiano** (A.D. 71–75)

(30 m) pillar was once the same height as the surrounding land, emphasizing the scale of the quar-rying required to excavate the forum. The superbly preserved monument—widely considered the masterpiece of all Roman carving—was raised in A.D. 113 to commemorate victories over the Dacians, a warrior tribe who occupied much of present-day Romania. An intricate spiral frieze 656 feet (200 m) in length winds around the column's 18 marble drums. Woven into its majestic marble narrative are scenes from Trajan's victorious campaigns—including some 2,600 figures.

Foro Romano

For almost a thousand years, the Foro Romano (Roman Forum) was the heart of ancient Rome and the nerve center of an empire that extended across most of the world known to Europeans. Today, all that remains is a jumble of romantic ruins, although its wistful beauty and myriad historical echoes still make it Europe's most impor-tant archaeological site. Altered and rebuilt over many centuries, its monuments—one superim-posed on another—are often confusing. But they hint at past splendors and the gentle charm of a once great site.

The forum began life as a marshy valley between the Pala-tino and Campidoglio. During the Iron Age it served as the cemetery on the fringes of a village, a loca-tion giving rise perhaps to the name (from Latin *foris,* "outside"). Later, it became a garbage dump

■ A slice of Roman life on the edge of the Foro Romano

in favor of the **Foro di Traiano** (A.D. 107–113), the most extravagant of the five forums.

Trajan's forum is dominated by **Trajan's Column,** centerpiece of the Fori Imperiali. The top of the 97-foot

Vestal Virgins

Vestal Virgins were required to tend Rome's sacred flame, a perpetually burning symbol of Rome's eternal character kept in the Tempio di Vesta. All were aged between six and ten at induction and were chosen only from the grandest patrician families. They served 30 years before being awarded a state pension and allowed to marry. Ten years were spent in learning, ten in performing ritual tasks, and ten in teaching.

Incumbents who lost their virginity—a vestal's blood could not be spilled—were buried alive, and the offending male was flogged to death. Those allowing the flame to die were whipped by the Pontifex Maximus, Rome's high priest, and forced to rekindle the fire using sacred pieces of wood. In return for their services, the virgins enjoyed high social esteem and had special rights, among them the power of mercy over condemned criminals, the right of way on all streets, permission to drive in carriages within the city limits (a right usually granted only to empresses), and the safekeeping of wills, including those of the emperor. Any injury inflicted on a virgin was punishable by death.

for nearby settlements, and later still a communal marketplace. Its first distinct monuments probably appeared in the seventh century B.C. during the reigns of the first Etruscan kings.

As the empire flourished, so the forum began to accumulate all the structures of civic, religious, and political life. Patrician houses, shops, temples, and markets jostled for space, and merchants, politicians, and emperors competed to fill the area with ever-more magnificent monuments.

By the second century A.D., the building frenzy had run its course, largely because all available room had been taken up. The site remained a vital symbolic focus, however, despite the shift of political power to the Palatine, trade to the Mercato di Traiano (Trajan's Market), and new building to the Fori Imperiali.

After Rome's fall, time began to take its toll. Fire had ravaged the site in the third century, followed by earthquakes and the assaults of barbarian invaders in the fifth century. During the Middle Ages, stone was pillaged for churches and palaces and precious marbles reduced to dust in the lime kilns of builders. Eventually, the forum was so reduced that it became known as *campo vaccino*, or cow pasture. Coherent excavations only began toward the end of the 18th century and continue to this day.

The Site: Be sure to grasp an overview of the forum before exploring the site, the best of which can be obtained from Via del Campidoglio and the steps behind the Palazzo Senatorio on Piazza del Campidoglio. You need a good site plan and a great deal of imagination to make full sense of the ruins. What follows is a guide only to the better-preserved and more evocative monuments.

From the main entrance on Via dei Fori Imperiali, bear right on the Via Sacra, the ancient forum's most important street, and follow a roughly counterclockwise route. This will leave you at the Arco di Tito exit, where you have the choice of walking up to the Palatino (see sidebar opposite) or proceeding directly to the Colosseo (see pp. 53–56).

The first temple on your right, the **Tempio di Antonino e Faustina** (A.D. 141), is one of the forum's best preserved, largely because it was converted in the 11th century to the church of San Lorenzo in Miranda. The original temple was raised by the emperor Antoninus Pius in honor of his wife, Faustina (Roman gossip at the time suggests the emperor was the only man in the city unaware of his wife's numerous infidelities). Beyond, on the right, lies the **Basilica Aemilia** (179 B.C.), once a business and banking complex and reputedly among the forum's most beautiful buildings

(it was all but destroyed during Alaric the Goth's attack on Rome in A.D. 410).

At the end of the Via Sacra stand two unmistakable monuments: the austere, brick-built **Curia** and the **Arco di Settimio Severo.** The space in front of them was known as the **Comitium,** probably the forum's first important meeting place and the hub of its early social, judicial, and civic life. Processions, funerals, and sacrifices took place here, local politicians met and voted in its halls, and judgments were handed down by the praetor in its law courts. The Curia was home to the Roman senate and its 300 senators (it became a church in the seventh century). The *arco* (A.D. 203), or arch, was raised to celebrate the military triumphs of the emperor Septimius Severus, its four principal reliefs decorated with battle scenes, the goddess of

■ **Dusk falls on the scattered ruins of the Foro Romano, the heart of ancient Rome.**

victory, and panels lauding Septimius' sons, Geta and Caracalla.

Below the arch stretches a ruined brick wall, all that remains of the **Imperial Rostra,** orators' platforms that took their name from the bronze ships' rostra, or prows, used to ram other boats in battle. Such prows were taken as spoils of war and once adorned the platforms. It was here that Mark Antony reputedly delivered his "Friends, Romans, and countrymen" speech after the murder of Julius Caesar. Behind the arch to the left stand the eight red-gray columns of the **Tempio di Saturno** (498 B.C., rebuilt in 42 B.C. and in A.D. 283), the oldest of the forum's early temples. It was dedicated to Saturn, god of agriculture, Rome's early power having been deemed to stem from its agricultural prowess. The temple also housed Rome's treasury.

With your back to the temple, the area in front of you to the right is the **Basilica Giulia** (54 B.C.), once a central courthouse. Beyond it are the three lonely columns of the **Tempio di Castore e Polluce.** Farther beyond lie two of the forum's most evocative sights, the **Tempio di Vesta** and **Atrium Vestae,** respectively the Temple of Vesta, goddess of the hearth, and the House of the Vestal Virgins (see sidebar p. 51). The former held Rome's eternal sacred flame, a symbol of the city's well-being. Citizens ritually extinguished their fires on the first day of the Roman New Year (March 1) before relighting them with tapers taken from the flame. The extinguishing of the flame,

tended by the Vestal Virgins, was considered the worst of all possible portents, foretelling the fall of Rome. Ashes from the fire were scattered on the Tiber on June 15 each year as part of a pagan ritual of continuity and regeneration.

Palatino

The Palatino (Palatine) was one of Rome's original Seven Hills. It was also the site of the city's earliest settlement—predating the forum—and the spot on which the legendary she-wolf is said to have suckled the twins Romulus and Remus.

One of Rome's earliest residential districts, it later became a favored location for the city's grandest imperial palaces (the word "palace" shares the same root as the Latin *palatium*). Its ruins are now more confusing than those of the forum, but its views, lovely gardens, shady orange groves, and peaceful corners make this a wonderful area in which to take a break from sightseeing.

On the left beyond the Atrium rises the **Basilica di Massenzio** (A.D. 306), whose vast trio of vaults make up one of the forum's most physically impressive sights. The **Arco di Tito** near the east entrance is an arch built in A.D. 81 to commemorate the capture of Jerusalem by the emperor Titus. Its reliefs show Titus's triumphal return to Rome and the removal of treasures from the Holy Temple.

Colosseo

The Colosseo (Colosseum, or Flavian Amphitheater) is the Roman world's largest surviving structure, its majestic impact undimmed either by the passage

Colosseo

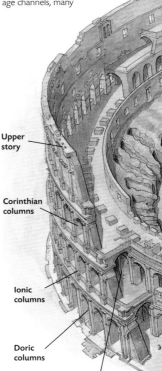

🅰 47 D3

✉ Piazza del Colosseo

☎ 06 0608. Reservations 06 3996 7700 or online at coopculture.it

💲 1st floor $$$$ (includes entry to Palatino & Foro Romano)

🚌 Bus: 60, 75, 81, 175; tram 30. Metro: Colosseo

parcocolosseo.it

INSIDER TIP:

To avoid waiting in line for tickets to the Colosseo, first visit the less crowded Foro Romano, where you can buy a ticket good for both sites.

—BRIDGET A. HAMILTON
National Geographic Books editor

of time or the blight of today's encircling traffic. Once its walls echoed to the sounds of gladiatorial combat and the roar of the Roman mob, and later to the chink of hammers as its stones were pillaged to build Rome's medieval churches and palaces. Today, its half-ravaged walls are still standing, defying the famous prophecy that "while the Colosseum stands, Rome shall stand; when the Colosseum falls, Rome shall fall; when Rome falls, the world shall fall."

Rise & Fall: The Colosseo was the brainchild of the emperor Vespasian in A.D. 69, who wanted a monument to celebrate his military triumphs in the Middle East. Unfinished at his death in A.D. 79, the building was continued by Vespasian's son, Titus, its inauguration taking place in A.D. 80. Finishing touches were added by Titus's successor, Domitian (A.D. 81–96), who like his predecessors was a member of the Flavian dynasty, hence the name by which the arena was originally known—the *Amphitheatrum*

Flavianum. Its present name may derive simply from its size, or, more probably, from the presence (it is now lost) of the nearby Colossus of Nero, once the world's largest bronze statue.

The Colosseo's vast scale presented huge engineering problems, not least those offered by the marshy site—chosen for its proximity to the forum and the Palatino—previously used as a ceremonial lake for the Domus Aurea, or Golden House, of the emperor Nero (its restoration worksite can be visited using virtual reality). Immense drainage channels, many

Upper story

Corinthian columns

Ionic columns

Doric columns

Internal corridor

still extant, honeycombed the foundations, while huge quantities of light volcanic tufa and brick-clad cement were used to form the walls. More than a million cubic feet (100,000 cubic meters) of travertine marble gilded its surfaces, a decorative veneer held in place by 300 tons (272 tonnes) of iron brackets (these brackets were wrenched out in A.D. 664, hence the puzzling holes that pockmark the exterior).

The completed amphitheater was a model of simplicity and function, providing a template not only for other Roman amphitheaters but also for numerous stadiums of the modern age. Some 70,000 spectators could enter and leave by any one of the 80 numbered *vomitoria,* or exits, while 240 wooden masts on the upper story supported a broad *velarium,* or sail-cloth awning, swung into place to protect crowds from the sun.

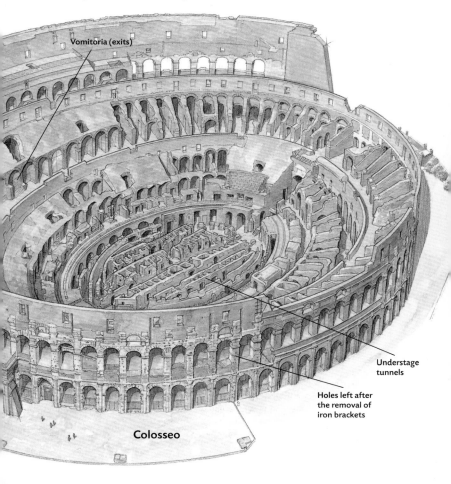

Vomitoria (exits)

Understage tunnels

Holes left after the removal of iron brackets

Colosseo

Sand covered the amphitheater's floor, its purpose to prevent combatants slipping and to soak up the blood of gladiatorial combat (the Latin *arena* [sand] would be used from this time on to describe places of spectacle). All manner of understage tunnels, pulleys, and lifts enabled animals and contestants to be brought to the arena. You can also join a guided tour to the underground areas.

Arco di Costantino

Immediately alongside the Colosseo stands the Arco di Costantino, a triumphal arch built in A.D. 315 to celebrate the emperor Constantine's victory three years earlier over his rival, Maxentius. One of Imperial Rome's last great monuments, it features many decorative reliefs pilfered from earlier classical buildings.

The building fell into decline early. Fires in the third century destroyed much of the stage area and upper seating, both of which were constructed largely of wood. Further conflagrations and earthquakes compounded the damage over the next two centuries. After Rome's fall, natural calamities, and the Romans themselves led to its deterioration. Stone was ruthlessly plundered from the site, finding its way in to new buildings, such as the Palazzo Farnese, Palazzo Venezia, Palazzo Barberini, and any number of smaller palaces, churches, and latter-day bridges. Two-thirds of the monument vanished over the years—more would have gone had it not been for Pope Benedict XIV, who consecrated the site in 1749 in honor

of the Christians supposedly martyred here. Subsequent popes and administrators then began a process of restoration, excavation, and consolidation that continues to the present day.

The Games: One of the Colosseo's most enduring myths—that it ran red with the blood of Christian martyrs—is just that: a myth. Evidence suggests few, if any, Christians died here. Many others, however, certainly did die here.

Gladiators had originally fought in ritual combat to prepare for battle, a practice inherited by the Romans from the Samnites and Etruscans. By Vespasian's time, the practice had been debased, the games, or *munera* (dutiful gifts), having become part of the decline of a population. Wealthy individuals initially sponsored the events, but by Domitian's time, the games were so important that they were the gift of emperors alone.

Daily performances usually followed a set order. First came the *venationes,* or animal hunts. Then came public killings, often preceded by bouts of torture and completed with the use of gruesomely complicated instruments of death. The playing out of macabre episodes from Greek and Roman mythology were added refinements. The main highlight, the gladiatorial games themselves, came last.

Gladiatorial contests survived until A.D. 438, while the last animal extravaganza was recorded in A.D. 523. ∎

THREE MONTI CHURCHES

The neighborhood of Monti is home to three churches of note. Santa Maria Maggiore is one of Rome's seven pilgrim churches. After St. Peter's Basilica, San Giovanni in Laterano is the most important Roman Catholic church in the world. And the intriguing San Clemente presents a fascinating study of architectural styles through the centuries.

Ferdinand and Isabella of Spain donated the gold used to gild the ceiling of Santa Maria Maggiore.

Santa Maria Maggiore

Santa Maria Maggiore was founded after A.D. 431. It was reputedly built to celebrate a summer snowfall in A.D. 356, during which the snow marked the outlines of the future church. Today, it is Rome's finest early Christian basilica, an important point of pilgrimage, and the largest of the city's churches devoted to the Virgin.

The first feature to catch the eye is the sumptuous ceiling, supported by 42 massive columns removed from ancient Roman buildings. Swathes of decoration cover nearly every surface: The most outstanding is the mosaic (1290–1295) in the apse by Jacopo Torriti, widely considered the apogee of Rome's medieval mosaic tradition. Equally important recently restored mosaics adorn the nave and triumphal arch, a more extensive sequence than Torriti's, dating from the fifth century with scenes from the Old Testament. Elsewhere, be sure to look at the **Cappella Sistina** (1585), off the right aisle, almost a church within a church. It was built

Santa Maria Maggiore

🗺 47 E4

✉ Entrances on Piazza dell'Esquilino & Piazza Santa Maria Maggiore

☎ 06 6988 6800

🕐 Loggia mosaics closed p.m. Nov.–Feb.

🚌 Bus: 16, 70, 71, 714, & all services to Piazza dei Cinquecento. Metro: Cavour

San Giovanni in Laterano

🗺️ 47 E2–F2

✉️ Piazza di San Giovanni in Laterano 4

☎️ 06 6988 6433 (sacristy)

🕐 Scala Santa closed 2 p.m.–3 p.m.; baptistery closed 12:30 p.m.–4 p.m.

🚌 Bus 16, 81, 85, 87, 186. Metro: San Giovanni

by Domenico Fontana for Pope Sixtus V. Across the nave lies the **Cappella Paolina** (1611), commissioned by two popes, Paul V and Clement VIII, showing outstanding decoration by Cavalier d'Arpino and Guido Reni.

Within the **high altar** are the relics that draw most of the church's pilgrims: five pieces of iron-bound wood said to be fragments of Christ's Bethlehem crib, a prize revealed to public scrutiny on the night of Christmas Eve. To the altar's right lies the church's loveliest sepulchral monument, the tomb of Cardinal Consalvo Rodriguez (died 1299), adorned with beautiful marble inlay by Giovanni di Cosma, one of a family of craftsmen that gave its name to this much-copied form of decoration.

San Giovanni in Laterano

San Giovanni is Rome's cathedral church, not St. Peter's as many visitors assume. It is also the "Mother and head of all the churches of the city and the world," according to the Latin inscription across its towering facade. Built around A.D. 314 by Constantine, the first Christian emperor, the church has witnessed all manner of historical events: Charlemagne was baptized here in 774, popes were crowned at its altar until the 19th century, and, with the signing of the Lateran Treaty in 1929, it saw Mussolini and the papacy formalize relations between church and state.

The interior, much altered by fire, earthquakes, and rebuilding

> **INSIDER TIP:**
>
> Spend some time to visit the San Giovanni metro station (C line), which is also a museum displaying Roman remains and a first-/second-century drainage system.
>
> —LORENZO SAGRIPANTI
> *Travel guide editor*

over the centuries, is largely the work of Borromini, a tortured baroque genius who remodeled much of the church between 1646 and 1650. Certain earlier parts of the building survive, notably the superb wooden ceiling and the Gothic tabernacle (1367) above the altar—said to contain the skulls of saints Peter and Paul. However, these pale beside the sublime **cloister** ($), located off the south aisle.

Linked to the church, but entered separately, is the **baptistery** ($), one of Italy's earliest, whose octagonal form was the model for similar buildings across the country. Although much restored, it is the only surviving fragment of the original fourth-century church: Its centerpiece is a scintillating fifth-century mosaic. On the northeast flank of the church square lies the **Scala Santa,** recently restored together with its 16th-century frescoes, reputedly the marble staircase from Pontius Pilate's Jerusalem palace that Christ ascended during his trial. Penitents mount on their knees the stairs, covered with hickory beams to protect them from wear.

San Clemente

At San Clemente three phases of Rome's long religious history lie layered one above another. The first is encapsulated by a peerless medieval church (ca 1108–1130), beneath which lies an older one, founded in A.D. 395, perhaps earlier. Below this again are the ruins of a temple dedicated to Rome's most important Oriental cult.

The most eye-catching highlights of the medieval church are the nave's *schola cantorum* with a **choir screen,** pulpits, and parts of the baldachino, or altar canopy. A 12th-century **mosaic** behind the altar depicts "The Triumph of the Cross," below which stands a marble tabernacle and frescoes of saints. Important paintings on the "Life of St. Catherine" (1428), the work of Florentine artist Masolino da Panicale, swathe a chapel next to the church's side entrance.

Steps lead down to the older church, built in honor of San Clemente, Rome's fourth bishop and pope. It was destroyed by the Normans in 1084 but preserves faded frescoes from the fifth or sixth century. The church was only discovered in 1857.

More steps go down to the oldest area of the complex (first century A.D.), a series of chambers and tunnels that include the remains of a **Mithraic temple** and the partially excavated remains of a Roman street, warehouse, and patrician palace. The sound of running water comes from an underground stream that runs to the Cloaca Maxima, ancient Rome's principal sewer. ■

San Clemente

🗺 47 E3

✉ Corner of Via di San Giovanni in Laterano & Via Labicana

☎ 06 774 0021

🕐 Closed 12:30 p.m. –3 p.m. & Sun. a.m.

💲 Second & third levels $$

🚌 Bus: 85 & 117 to Via di San Giovanni in Laterano, or 51, 85, 87 to Via Labicana

basilicasanclemente .com

■ A serene courtyard fronts San Clemente's west facade.

CAMPO MARZIO & AROUND

In Roman times, the Campo Marzio or Campus Martius (Field of Mars) was a broad expanse of land that stretched from the Quirinal Hill to the Tiber River. It eventually shrank in size and came to be identified primarily with the area tucked into the curve of the Tiber that faces Castel Sant'Angelo and St. Peter's Basilica. This is one of the oldest parts of modern Rome, home to Piazza Navona, the sculpture-filled Palazzo Altemps, and the bustling Campo de' Fiori.

Fontana dei Quattro Fiumi, centerpiece of Piazza Navona

Piazza Navona
- 46 C4
- Bus: 70, 81, 87, & 116 to Corso del Rinascimento

Sant'Agnese
- 46 C4
- 06 6819 2134
- Closed Mon. & 1 p.m.–3 p.m.

santagneseinagone
.org

Piazza Navona

Piazza Navona is Rome's loveliest square, ideal for people-watching, day or night, while ensconced at one of its many cafés. Broadly elliptical in shape, the piazza's outline matches that of the Circus Agonalis—from which the square's name derives—a vast 30,000-seat stadium inaugurated by the emperor Domitian in A.D. 86.

In 1644, Pope Innocent X embarked on a radical program of baroque rebuilding. Chief among the monuments were two outstanding fountains by Bernini, the **Fontana del Moro** (at the square's southern end) and the **Fontana dei Quattro Fiumi**, or Fountain of the Four Rivers. Statues on the latter symbolize Danube, Nile, Plate, and Ganges, at the four corners of the known world—Asia, Africa, Europe, and America.

On the square's western side is the church of **Sant'Agnese,** its concave façade (1653–1657) by Francesco Borromini. It stands on the site of the martyrdom of St. Agnes, a 13-year-old virgin killed for refusing to marry a pagan.

Palazzo Altemps

The Palazzo Altemps houses part of Italy's state collection of antiquities, the **Museo Nazionale Romano.** It boasts some of the greatest of all Roman sculpture, including the Ludovisi Collection, amassed by Ludovico Ludovisi, a nephew of Pope Gregory XV, and acquired by the state in 1901. The sublime Renaissance palace is worthy of a visit in its own right, too.

Beyond the palace's relatively plain façade, you walk into a lovely courtyard that sets the tone for the frescoed and decorated rooms. The palace was built for Girolamo Riario, lord of Imola and Forlì, in 1480 and passed through several hands before being bought by the state in 1982.

On the **ground floor,** around the courtyard and flanking salons, the highlights are the Room of the Herms (with two first-century figures depicting Apollo the Lyrist), closely followed by the "Ludovisi Athena," showing the goddess taming a serpent.

On the **upper floor,** the palace's pretty chapel (Sant'Aniceto) and northern loggia are outstanding. In the adjoining rooms, you'll find the first-century B.C. "Ludovisi Orestes and Electra" by Menelaus, along with the "Ludovisi Ares," a seated figure. The latter work, probably a Roman copy of a Greek original, was restored by Bernini in 1622. Also here is the "Ludovisi Throne," one of the city's most celebrated sculptures; though some claim it is a fake, it is generally considered a fifth-century B.C. Greek work brought to Rome from a Greek settlement in southern Italy when the Romans conquered the region in the third century B.C.

Campo de' Fiori

Campo de' Fiori ("field of the flowers") has a wonderful street market, where every day except Sunday the square overflows with fruit, fish, flower, and vegetable stands and stallholders. Campo de' Fiori does not have a church—a rare occurrence in Rome. Nothing symbolizes the piazza's secular nature better than the half-hidden statue at its heart, the somber, cowled figure of Giordano Bruno, a humanist philosopher burned for heresy here in 1600.

Piazza Farnese, a bright, open square to the south, provides a counterpoint to the Campo's more cramped charms. Here all is decorum and refinement, thanks mainly to the **Palazzo Farnese** (1515), now the French Embassy, considered one of the most beautiful Renaissance buildings in Rome. Be sure to explore **Via Giulia,** one of Rome's most elegant streets, to the rear of the palace. ■

Palazzo Altemps

🅰 46 C4

✉ Piazza Sant'Apollinare 46

☎ 06 684 851, 06 3996 7700/01 or online at coopculture.it

🕓 Closed Mon.

💲 $

🚍 Bus: 70, 81, 87, & 116 to Corso del Rinascimento

museonazionale romano.beniculturali .it

Campo de' Fiori

🅰 46 C3–C4

Palazzo Farnese

🅰 46 C3

✉ Piazza Farnese

🕓 See monthly calendar

💲 $$

inventerrome.com

EXPERIENCE: The Cult of the *Aperitivo*

One of the quintessential Roman experiences involves a warm, early summer's evening, dinner booked for an hour or two hence around the corner, and an animated group of locals sipping drinks at the bar. This is the cult of the *aperitivo*—an aperitif, or predinner drink—which has its origins in Turin, in northwest Italy, where the practice has always been popular. In the last decade, however, this equivalent of the "happy hour" has spread to most Italian cities. You'll find many larger Roman bars full of locals chatting and tucking into the spread of all-you-can-eat olives, nuts, sandwiches, finger food, and pasta salads that most establishments offer free with a drink to help tempt customers. Campari soda or a glass of Prosecco (sparkling white wine) are the classic *aperitivi*, but the nonalcoholic Crodino is also popular.

The places of the moment vary, but try **Salotto 42** (Piazza di Pietra 42, tel 06 678 5804, closed Aug.), just northeast of the Pantheon; **Freni e Frizioni** (Via del Politeama 4–6, tel 06 4549 7499, frenie frizioni.com) in Trastevere; or **VinAllegro** (Piazza Giuditta Tavani Arquati 114, tel 06 589 5802, vinallegro.com), also in Trastevere, close to the Ponte Sisto.

THE PANTHEON & AROUND

The downtown area around the Pantheon is an unusual mélange of ancient, medieval, and Renaissance history, notable for a pagan temple turned national monument, the 13th-century Santa Maria sopra Minerva, and the magnificent Palazzo Doria Pamphilj.

The Pantheon's large oculus lets in rain as well as light. There are drainage holes in the floor.

Pantheon

🗺 46 C4

✉ Piazza della Rotonda

☎ 06 6830 0230

🕐 Closed Jan. 1, May 1, Dec. 25, & p.m. on public holidays

🚌 Bus: 30, 40, 62, 64, 81, 87, 492

pantheonroma.com

Pantheon

After the ravaged but romantic beauty of the Foro Romano and the shattered majesty of the Colosseo, the pristine grandeur of the Pantheon provides Rome's most powerful illustration of how the ancient city might once have appeared. The emperor Hadrian completed the Pantheon in A.D. 125—probably to his own design—replacing much of an earlier temple on the site raised in 27 B.C. by Marcus Agrippa, son-in-law of the emperor Augustus. Hadrian retained the pediment's imposing inscription, which attributed

the building to Agrippa: The Latin text reads "Marcus Agrippa, son of Lucius, consul for the third time, built this."

The building's miraculous state of preservation stems from its conversion to a Christian church in A.D. 608, a transformation that ensured that the removal of even a single stone would constitute a mortal sin. On November 1 of the same year, the church was christened Santa Maria ad Martyres (the Virgin and all the Martyrs), a date commemorated ever since as All Saints' Day.

Today, the building is still a church, and both its interior and exterior look virtually as they did in the second century. Not all the interior marbles are original, but their patterning and arrangement are believed to conform to Hadrian's original scheme. Around the walls lie the **tombs** of Raphael and two Italian kings, Umberto I and Vittorio Emanuele II.

The **dome** is one of the masterpieces of Roman engineering. Bigger than St. Peter's, it was the largest concrete construction undertaken until the 20th century and the world's largest freestanding dome until as recently as 1960. The dome's oculus, the circular hole that opens to the sky, was a key feature of Hadrian's original plan, its purpose being both practical—it helped illuminate the interior—and spiritual, allowing those in the temple direct contemplation of the heavens.

Santa Maria sopra Minerva

Santa Maria's plain Gothic facade is unique in Rome, a city where most churches were reworked along baroque lines during the 16th and 17th centuries. As singular in its way is Bernini's **elephant statue** (1667) in front of the church, an idiosyncratic work in which the elephant is supposed to represent piety and wisdom, Christianity's founding virtues; the Egyptian obelisk on the elephant's back dates from the sixth century B.C. The present church (1280) was built over (sopra) an earlier Roman temple to Minerva—hence its name.

Pride of place among the interior's many paintings goes to

a series of frescoes (1488–1492) by the Florentine artist Filippino Lippi. They portray the "Annunciation" and "Episodes from the Life of St. Thomas Aquinas" (first chapel of the south transept). Another Florentine painter, Beato Angelico, is buried near the high altar, as is one of Italy's patron saints, Catherine of Siena (minus her head, which is in Siena). The church's sculptural masterpiece is Michelangelo's "Redeemer" (1519–1521), criticized on its unveiling for appearing too much like a pagan god.

Santa Maria sopra Minerva

- 46 C4
- Piazza della Minerva 42
- 06 6992 0384
- Closed Sat. & Sun. 12:30 p.m.–3:30 p.m.
- Bus: 119 to Piazza della Rotonda

santamariasopra minerva.it

Roman Coffee & Gelato

A fierce debate rages about which café serves Rome's best cup of coffee. Some say the **Tazza d'Oro** (Via degli Orfani 84, tel 06 678 9792, tazzadorocoffeeshop .com), moments from the Pantheon, just off Piazza della Rotonda. Others claim the honor goes to nearby **Caffè Sant'Eustachio** (Piazza Sant'Eustachio 82, tel 06 6880 2048, santeustachioilcaffe.it). More people agree on the city's best ice cream, which comes courtesy of **Il Gelato di San Crispino,** either at its original home (Via della Panetteria 42, tel 06 679 3924, ilgelatodisancrispino.com) near the Fontana di Trevi or the more recent outlet just north of the Pantheon (Piazza della Maddalena 3, tel 06 9760 1190, closed Tues. mid-Sept.–mid-March).

Palazzo Doria Pamphilj

Strands of Rome's long past are still woven into the city's present, few of them more marked than the Palazzo Doria Pamphilj, a rambling thousand-room palace that still belongs to the Pamphilj, one of Rome's preeminent medieval

EXPERIENCE: Study Italian in Italy

If you want to learn a language quickly and properly, there is no substitute for basing yourself somewhere the language is spoken and immersing yourself in the culture in question. Italy offers innumerable opportunities to learn or improve your Italian, from weekend courses in private homes to year-long programs of regular, formal lessons.

Students practice speaking Italian at a convivial gathering.

You need to consider many things when choosing where to study: How much you can achieve in a short time; how much work you are prepared to put in; whether preparatory study prior to a course is needed; and whether you want to combine learning with sightseeing.

Accommodations are also a consideration, as a home-stay with an Italian family has obvious benefits, as does access to a television, which can be a valuable aid to improving comprehension, especially if you already have a little Italian.

All the major cities have a variety of schools. In Rome, opt for schools where lessons are held in the historic center, rather than the suburbs, and where accommodation can be arranged. A good choice is the **Scuola Leonardo da Vinci** *(Piazza dell'Orologio 7, tel 06 6889 2513, scuolaleonardo.com)*, where author Elizabeth Gilbert was a student while researching *Eat, Pray, Love*. It offers a wide range of courses, from a week to a year, across several ability bands. Among the options are courses designed specifically for more mature students over age 50.

In Florence, one of the longest established and most reliable schools is the **British Institute of Florence** *(Piazza Strozzi 2, tel 055 267 781, britishinstitute.it)*. Its range of courses includes one-, two-, and three-month semesters, at beginner, intermediate, and advanced levels. It can also arrange shorter courses, including a week-long Christmas special, with three hours of lessons given daily, Monday to Friday, and time off for sightseeing and shopping. Art courses are also available.

Venice is also a popular option, and the **Istituto Venezia** *(Campo Santa Margherita 3116a, Dorsoduro, tel 041 522 4331, istituto venezia.com)* is typical of the smaller organizations offering lessons. Among its options are weekend courses, low-budget intensive courses, and home-stays of between one and four weeks, in single or double rooms with private bathrooms, or a room in a delightful historic cloister on the Giudecca island.

If you're more adventurous, consider studying in one of Italy's less visited cities. In Naples, the **Centro Italiano di Napoli** *(Vico Santa Maria dell'Aiuto 17, tel 081 552 4331, centroitaliano.it)* offers courses at its school in the city's historic heart. Choose between intensive courses (ten individual one-hour sessions over a week) or one-, two-, three-, and four-week programs. Courses can be combined with lessons in Neapolitan cooking, pizza-making, and Italian culture and design. The company can also organize courses for visitors staying in Sorrento or on the islands of Capri or Ischia.

INSIDER TIP:

In early September Rome celebrates Notte Bianca, or White Night. Piazzas fill with live entertainment, and museums are open and free throughout the night.

—MAURA PALELLA
National Geographic researcher

patrician families. Part of the palace is given over to the family's private art collection, a collection that ranks with those of the Musei Vaticani (see pp. 78–81) and Galleria Borghese (see p. 71) as one of the finest in the city.

The collection was founded by Pope Innocent X, a member of the Pamphilj dynasty, and augmented when subsequent family members married into the equally elevated Doria and Borghese clans. Today, the paintings are ranged around part of the palace's first floor, their beautifully appointed setting almost as splendid as the works of art themselves. Guided tours around other areas of the palace are available most mornings for a small additional fee.

The pictorial highlights are many. Make a special point of seeking out Velázquez's celebrated portrait of "Innocent X" (1650), a picture that captures all too clearly the man's suspicious and feebleminded nature. Pope Innocent himself is said to have complained that the portrait was "too true, too true." Also look for works by Titian, Tintoretto, Filippo Lippi, and Caravaggio, as well as Raphael's magnificent "Portrait of Two Venetians." ■

Palazzo Doria Pamphilj

🗺 46 C4

✉ Via del Corso 305

☎ Reservations 06 679 7323, 331 164 1490 (apartments)

🕐 Gallery closed Jan. 1, Easter, Dec. 25., & 3rd Wed. of month

💲 Gallery $$, additonal $ for apartments

🚌 Bus: 40, 46, 62, 64, 70, 81, & all other buses to Piazza Venezia

doriapamphilj.it

trustfdp.it

■ Piazza della Minerva's marble elephant statue, designed by Bernini and sculpted by Ercole Ferrata

A WALK THROUGH MEDIEVAL ROME

From Piazza Colonna, this walk explores some of Rome's more enchanting back streets, wending through artisans' quarters and the old Ghetto before crossing the Tiber River to finish in the atmospheric district of Trastevere.

Start at **Piazza Colonna ❶**, named after the Colonna di Marco Aurelio, a second-century relief-covered column celebrating the military triumphs of Emperor Marcus Aurelius. Beyond it stands Bernini's Palazzo di Montecitorio (1650), now the lower house of the Italian parliament. Then walk west on Via degli Uffici del Vicario, aiming for **Sant'Agostino,** a church off Via della Scrofa known for paintings by Caravaggio and Raphael. More canvases by the former hang in **San Luigi dei Francesi ❷** (see p. 82) to the south. From here, walk east on Via Giustiniani to visit the **Pantheon ❸** (see pp. 62–63) and **Santa Maria sopra Minerva ❹** (see p. 63).

From the Piazza della Rotonda next to the Pantheon, walk west to Corso del Rinascimento by way of Piazza Sant'Eustachio. On the way, note the Palazzo della Sapienza, whose courtyard contains the entrance to **Sant'Ivo alla Sapienza** (1642–1660), a church with a twisting tower designed by Francesco Borromini. Cross the Corso and enter **Piazza Navona ❺** (see p. 60), leaving the square midway down its western side on Via di Tor Millina.

Bear right (north) toward Via dei Coronari, a street known for its antique shops. Follow it west until Via del Panico, where you should turn left and twist through the back streets to the **Chiesa Nuova ❻**, a church celebrated for paintings by Rubens and a baroque fresco cycle by Pietro da Cortona. Cross Corso Vittorio Emanuele II in front of the church, and continue straight before turning left on Via del Pellegrino and then almost immediately right onto Via dei Cappellari. Lined with dusty furniture workshops, the latter presents a picturesque view of old Rome.

Follow the street to **Campo de' Fiori ❼** (see p. 61), and then turn right into Piazza Farnese. Take Vicolo dei Venti from this

---

NOT TO BE MISSED:

San Luigi dei Francesi • Pantheon • Santa Maria sopra Minerva • Campo de' Fiori • Trastevere

---

square's southern corner past the **Palazzo Spada,** known for its decorated facade and Borromini's trompe l'oeil colonnade.

Turn left on Via Arco del Monte and then right on Via Giubbonari. Cross Via Arenula, and follow Via dei Falegnami into the pretty web of streets that once made up Rome's Jewish Ghetto. In Piazza Mattei, a short distance farther down the street, is one of the city's most charming fountains, the **Fontana delle Tartarughe** (1581), named after Bernini's quaint bronze *tartarughe* (tortoises).

Turn right out of the piazza heading south and then left on Via del Portico d'Ottavia, a street named after the Roman ruins at its eastern end, once the *portico* (entrance) to a vast library and temple complex. Follow the street as it bends right, passing Rome's main synagogue and the circular bulwarks of the **Teatro di Marcello ❽**, a first-century B.C. amphitheater later covered by medieval houses.

Across the Tiber to Trastevere

Cross the riverside street, the Lungotevere, and take the Ponte Fabricio ahead to the **Isola Tiberina ❾**, an island largely given over to a hospital dating from 1538. Drop into the church of **San Bartolomeo all'Isola** (*Piazza di San Bartolomeo all'Isola 22, tel 06 687 7973, sanbartolomeo.org*), built in the 11th century over a pagan temple to Aesculapius, god of the healing arts.

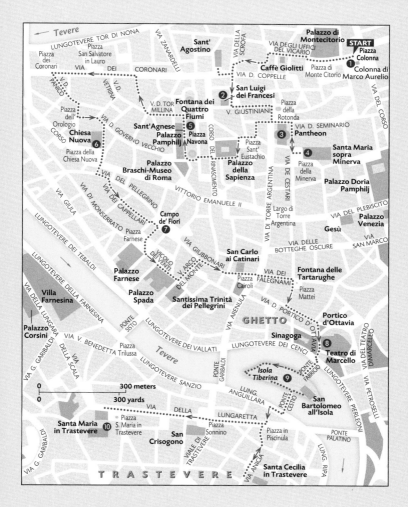

Cross the Ponte Cestio to the district known as **Trastevere** (literally "over the Tiber"). Traditionally a blue-collar enclave, this is a colorful area known for its restaurants and nightlife, though the trendier bars and clubs are increasingly shifting farther south to an area around Testaccio. Beyond the Lungotevere, walk south on Via Anicia from Piazza in Piscinula to look at the church of **Santa Cecilia in Trastevere** (see p. 82), known for its ninth-century mosaic,

- Also see area map, p. 46 C3 & C4
- Piazza Colonna
- 5 hours
- 3.25 miles (5.25 km)
- Piazza Santa Maria in Trastevere

and then double back to pick up Via della Lungaretta. Follow this to **Santa Maria in Trastevere** ⑩ (see p. 82), another fine mosaic-laden church set at the heart of Trastevere.

FONTANA DI TREVI & PALAZZO BARBERINI

Instantly recognizable, the giant **Fontana di Trevi** (Trevi Fountain) lies tucked away among narrow side streets, cunningly built into the side of a patrician palace. No less impressive is the nearby **Palazzo Barberini**, a huge baroque palace now housing the Galleria Nazionale d'Arte Antica, part of the national art collection.

Baroque in style, the Fontana di Trevi is the most beautiful of the city's many fountains.

Fontana di Trevi

 47 D4

 Piazza di Trevi

Bus: 62, 80, 117, & 119 to Via del Corso

Fontana di Trevi

It has to be one of the most memorable images from postwar movies: Anita Ekberg, black-clad and bosom heaving, trails through the placid waters of the Fontana di Trevi (Trevi Fountain) in *La Dolce Vita,* Fellini's paean to the indolent, easy-living days of Rome in the late 1950s.

The first fountain on this site was built in 1453 for Pope Nicholas V, taking its waters from the Acqua Vergine, an aqueduct constructed by Agrippa in 19 B.C. The present fountain, modeled

on the Arco di Costantino (see sidebar p. 56), was built between 1732 and 1762 for Clement XII, probably to a design by Nicola Salvi (1697–1751). Few sights in Rome are as lovely at first glimpse, narrow cobbled lanes suddenly opening up to reveal the fontana ranged across an entire wall of the Palazzo Poli. The fountain's name derives from these lanes—the *tre vie* (three streets) that meet here.

At the fountain's center stands a statue of the Greek Titan god Oceanus, god of all waters, flanked by horse-riding Tritons that symbolize a stormy sea (left) and the sea in repose (right). The niche statues behind Oceanus represent Health and Abundance, and the pediment statues represent the four seasons with their gifts.

Palazzo Barberini

The Palazzo Barberini has a distinguished pedigree: Its architects were three of the biggest names of their day—Bernini, Carlo Maderno, and Borromini—while its founding family, the Barberini, was one of Rome's greatest medieval dynasties.

Today, its magnificent baroque interior houses the Galleria Nazionale d'Arte Antica, part of Italy's national art collection and one of Rome's premier galleries.

The palace is an attraction in itself, all sweeping staircases, grandiose suites, and labyrinthine apartments. Few rooms, even in Rome, can match the almost overblown splendor of its great set piece, the **Gran Salone,** crowned with a dazzling ceiling fresco by Pietro da Cortona depicting an "Allegory of Divine Providence" (1632–1639).

Only paintings of the first rank can compete with such surroundings, paintings such as Raphael's famous "La Fornarina," possibly a portrait of the artist's mistress, a baker's daughter (*fornaio* means "baker"). The work was completed in the year the painter died. Other exceptional works from the early Renaissance period include pictures by Fra Angelico, Filippo Lippi, and Perugino, while the late Renaissance is represented by, among others, Titian, Tintoretto, Lorenzo Lotto, Caravaggio, and Andrea del Sarto. ∎

Palazzo Barberini

🅰 47 D4

✉ Via delle Quattro Fontane 13

☎ Information 06 481 4591; reservations 06 32810 or tosc.it

🕐 Closed Mon. & Jan. 1, May 1, & Dec. 25

💲 $$

🚌 Bus: 61, 62, & 85 to Via Barberini. Metro: Barberini

barberinicorsini.org

EXPERIENCE: See Rome by Vespa

Few experiences are more Roman than riding a Vespa around the streets—half the city's population, young and old, seems to own and use these iconic motor scooters. **Happy Rent** (*Via delle Sette Chiese 276e, tel 06 488 4215, happyrent.com, $$$$$*) offers five guided and themed city tours on vintage Vespas and Lambrettas, another classic scooter. Most tours range around four hours long. On the "Roman Holiday Tour," you'll ride as a passenger with a guide and emulate Gregory Peck and Audrey Hepburn in *Roman Holiday* (1953), visiting the locations that featured in the movie, many of them instantly recognizable even today, such as the Trevi Fountain. Another popular ride is the "Secret Rome Tour," which visits off-the-beaten-path locales to give visitors a sense of the Rome most tourists don't see.

PIAZZA DI SPAGNA
TO VILLA BORGHESE

Rome's central Trident neighborhood has many attractions. It includes the Piazza di Spagna, home to the famous Spanish Steps; the Villa Borghese, a large park that contains the Galleria Borghese and Villa Giulia; and innumerable churches, including Santa Maria del Popolo. It is also a prime shopping district.

■ Romans and visitors find respite in the Villa Borghese park.

Piazza di Spagna
🅰 46 C5

Keats-Shelley Memorial House
✉ Piazza di Spagna 26
☎ 06 678 4235
🕐 Closed Sun., 1 p.m.–2 p.m. Mon.–Sat.
💲 $
🚍 Bus: 119. Metro: Spagna
keats-shelley-house .org

Piazza di Spagna

The Piazza di Spagna and the Spanish Steps (Scalinata) are one of Rome's great set pieces. Both the square and its famous flight of steps take their name from the Palazzo di Spagna, built in 1622 as the residence of the Spanish ambassador to the Holy See.

During the heyday of the Grand Tour (see pp. 72–73), the area around the square was a magnet for artists and foreign visitors. Hotels, studios, and cafés attracted many famous names, among them Byron, Liszt, Stendhal, and Wagner—you can sample something of the flavor of the times at a survivor of the period, the **Antico Caffè Greco** (Via Condotti 86).

The English Romantic poet John Keats, who came to Rome in 1820 seeking a cure from tuberculosis, died in a house alongside the Spanish Steps. Today, the building is known as the **Keats-Shelley Memorial House,** a museum given over to Keats, Shelley (who also died in Italy), and other 19th-century literary figures.

Other sights on the square include the eccentric little **Fontana della Barcaccia** at the foot of the steps, designed—possibly by Bernini—to resemble a half-submerged boat, in memory of the floods of 1598. Many visitors will also be seduced by the fine stores and galleries on surrounding streets—the area is Rome's premier shopping district.

Santa Maria del Popolo

Santa Maria del Popolo fronts Piazza del Popolo, a broad square close to the city's old northern gateway. Church and square both take their name from the *populus,* or hamlet, which stood here during the Middle Ages. Santa Maria was founded in 1099 over the tomb of Emperor Nero, its purpose to reclaim for Christianity ground sullied by contact with the pagan demagogue. Much of the present building is by Bramante and Bernini and dates from the 16th and 17th centuries.

The interior's most prized sight is the **Cappella Chigi** (1513), commissioned from Raphael by the Sienese banker Agostino Chigi, who instructed the artist that his chapel should "convert earthly things into heavenly." All the decoration here is by Raphael, except for a few Bernini medallions on the Chigi tombs and Sebastiano del Piombo's altarpiece painting of the "Birth of the Virgin." Other treasures include two paintings by Caravaggio (north transept), a set of **frescoes** (1485–1489) by Pinturicchio behind the high altar, and a pair of tombs (1505–1507) in the choir by Andrea da Sansovino.

INSIDER TIP:

Visit the top of the Spanish Steps at the end of the day to catch a spectacular sunset over the city.

—RUTH GRUBER
National Geographic author

Villa Borghese

The open spaces and shady walks of Rome's central park are home to two of the city's most important galleries: the Galleria Borghese and the Villa Giulia. The park, the first of its kind in Rome, was originally laid out between 1613 and 1616 for the Borghese family to provide them with a shady country retreat from the heat of Roman summers. Today, the lakes, fountains, woods, and grassy spaces make it perfect for a stroll or siesta, even on Sundays, when the park is at its busiest.

The **Galleria Borghese** at its heart was once the Villa Borghese's *casino* (little house), the name given to the principal building of an Italian country estate. The word's later association with gambling stems from the fact this was often the major pursuit of such houses' inhabitants. Although smaller than many galleries in Rome, the Borghese's collection is widely considered the city's most ravishing.

Many of the works were commissioned by Cardinal Scipione Borghese, a nephew of Pope Paul V, and bought by the state in 1902. Scipione was a great patron of Bernini, one of the baroque's leading lights, whose works dominate the gallery's sculpture sections. The most notorious sculpture, however, is by Antonio Canova: an erotic statue (1805–1808) of Paolina Borghese, sister of Napoleon and wife of Camillo Borghese. Among the many valuable paintings are exquisite works by Raphael, Titian, Botticelli, and Caravaggio.

The **Villa Giulia** nearby was built as a pleasure palace for Pope Julius III. Today, the villa houses what is widely considered the world's greatest museum of Etruscan art. Highlights include the terra-cotta statues of Apollo and Herakles, the contents of the Bernardini Tomb, and the sixth-century B.C. Sarcofago degli Sposi, a statue of a reclining and enigmatically smiling married couple. ∎

Santa Maria del Popolo
- 46 C5
- Piazza del Popolo 12
- 06 361 0836
- Closed 12:30 p.m.–4 p.m. Mon.–Fri., 1:30 p.m.–4:30 p.m. Sun., & during services
- Bus: 119. Metro: Flaminio

www.santamariadel popolo.it

Galleria Borghese
- 47 D6
- Piazzale Scipione Borghese 5
- 06 841 3979 Required reservations 06 32810
- Closed Mon. & Jan. 1 & Dec. 25
- $$$
- Bus: 52, 53, & 910. Metro: Flaminio

galleriaborghese beniculturali.it

gebart.it

tosc.it

Villa Giulia
- Piazzale di Villa Giulia 9
- 06 322 6571 Reservations 06 328 101
- Closed Mon. & Jan. 1, May 1, & Dec. 25
- $$

villagiulia. beniculturali.it

museoetru.it

tosc.it

THE GRAND TOUR

Italy has long seduced the curious and world weary of colder climes, bewitching with its art and culture, befuddling with its charm, inexpensive wine, and siren call to the senses. However, modern tourism is a far cry from the decorous days of the Grand Tour, a ritualized progression through the cities of Europe without which the education of 18th-century gentlemen—rarely ladies—was deemed incomplete.

The ruins of ancient Rome, including the Colosseo, were popular with Grand Tourists.

For most Grand Tourists, the attraction was the lure of imperial Rome and the city's great monuments of antiquity—the Colosseo, Pantheon, Palatino, and Foro Romano. Close behind came the astounding collections of classical statuary, notably found in the Musei Capitolini and the Vatican's Bramante Court-yard, whose peerless statues—the "Laocoön" and "Apollo Belvedere"—made it the Tour's Holy of Holies.

Not all visitors came for culture. In 1765, the British diarist James Boswell caught venereal disease and crab lice during an orgy of noctur-nal sightseeing. The Duchess of Devonshire and Lady Elizabeth Foster (two among many) came to conceal the birth of illegitimate children. In 1594, the English dramatist Thomas Nashe—no sightseer he—boasted, "I was at *Pontius Pilate's* house and pissed against it." Other visitors formed part of the tribe of foreign eccentrics

Artists on a Grand Tour found inspiration in Rome's sights, including the Vatican's Royal Staircase.

who have found refuge in travel. The aristocratic Thomas Hackman walked to Rome from London studiously "taking no notice of anything," while George Hutchinson, a Presbyterian firebrand, came to Rome in 1750 "by God's command," his mission to "preach mightily against statues, pictures, umbrellas, bag-wigs, and hoop petticoats."

Many had equally pressing but more poignant reasons for a visit, none more so than the English poet John Keats, who arrived in 1820 desperately seeking deliverance from tuberculosis. It proved a wretched affair, the poet describing his stay in the city—where he was to die after three months—as a "posthumous life" in which he "already seemed to feel the flowers growing over" him.

"At Florence, you think," runs an old Italian proverb, "at Rome, you pray; at Venice you love; at Naples, you look." Only a handful of visitors to the capital, however, spent any time on their knees. Far more hedonistic pleasures filled their days. Breakfast, often after a night of whoring, might be taken in the infamous Caffè degli Inglesi near the Spanish Steps, a "filthy vaulted room" and favored den of gossip and drink. Mornings would be spent seeing the sights, often in the company of the so-called bear leaders, the much put-upon tutors detailed to chaperone the wayward *milordi*, as the English (noble or otherwise) were known. Afternoons meant tea at Babingtons in Piazza

di Spagna (still serving today) or a nap in the English Club on Via Condotti.

For those not engaged in Boswellian pursuits, evenings were a fashionable time to visit the catacombs or sculpture galleries, where guttering candles added to the erotic charm of the latter and the eerie romanticism of the former. At some point, virtually every visitor of means found time to sit for a portrait, a pastime that by the mid-18th century had become an integral part of the Tour. The main reason was cost: In 1760, Sir Joshua Reynolds' fee for a half-length painting in London was more than £150. Rome's leading practitioner, Pompeo Batoni, would produce one for £25.

And not for the milordi the present-day keepsakes of T-shirts, cheap art, and religious kitsch. A Grand Tour souvenir meant the real thing—statues, furniture, prints, and paintings. Such was the obsession with artifacts that many echoed the sentiments of the Earl of Chesterfield, who despaired, as he put it, of those who "run through Italy *knick-knackically*." British writer Horace Walpole admitted in 1740 that "I am far gone in medals, lamps, idols, prints," adding that he "would buy the Coliseum [*sic*] if I could . . . ." One of the keenest collectors, Charles Townley, whose collection was sold to the British Museum, sacked Rome of its treasures on no fewer than three Grand Tours.

VATICAN CITY

St. Peter's—the church built over the tomb of the Apostle Peter—is the center of Roman Catholicism and the largest basilica of Christianity. It is also the external face of Vatican City, the world's smallest independent city-state. Despite its minuscule geographical dimensions, however, the Vatican wields immense power and influence. Much of Vatican City today is occupied by the immense Musei Vaticani, galleries offering incomparable works of art.

Bernini's bronze altar canopy at the heart of St. Peter's stands above the supposed tomb of St. Peter the Apostle.

St. Peter's Basilica

The Basilica di San Pietro can hardly fail to impress: It is the largest church in Christendom (capable of accommodating an estimated 60,000 people), represents the heart of Roman Catholicism, serves as a seminal point of pilgrimage, and is crowned by a stupendous Michelangelo-designed dome that offers sweeping views across much of the Eternal City. The church owes its site and spiritual legitimacy to Peter the Apostle, the first pope, who is believed to have been buried here after his crucifixion close by in the Imperial Gardens in either A.D. 64 or 67.

A shrine was probably built on the site around A.D. 155, or earlier, but the first church for which records survive was begun around A.D. 320 by Pope Sylvester I during the reign of Constantine, the first Christian emperor. This church was to survive until 1452, when its perilous state prompted Pope Nicholas V to consider the creation of a new basilica. Almost 200 years elapsed before this church was completed, during which time the leading architects of their day produced a succession of different plans, false starts, and half-finished schemes.

EXPERIENCE: A Papal Audience

Pilgrims and visitors have enjoyed papal audiences for almost two millennia. Today, the public audiences are usually held on Wednesday mornings in the modern **Paolo VI Hall** or in the Basilica.

Arrive early to allow time for the stringent security checks—you take a seat among hundreds of other devotees from all over the world, including numerous nuns and monks from a vast range of religious orders. Depending on the order of the day, the precise course of the 1- to 1.5-hour-long audience may vary, but generally the pope repeats the same address in several languages, occasionally identifying large groups in the crowd. The pope also says prayers and offers a blessing at the end.

Each attendee needs a ticket. Travel agents can make arrangements for you to take part, but they will charge a fee. You can apply for the free ticket by sending a fax at least ten days in advance to the **Prefecture of the Papal Household** *(06 6988 5863);* include the full names of those attending, your mailing address, and your preferred date and language. Some same-day tickets may be available—enquire at the Prefettura, reached via the Porta di Bronzo.

Applications can also be made online through **St. Patrick's American Community** *(stpatricksamericanrome.org)* two to three weeks before. Tickets must usually be collected at the church in person on the Tuesday before the audience.

In 1506, Bramante put forth the first significant proposal, a design built around a church arranged in the form of a Greek cross. The next came from Antonio da Sangallo in 1539, a plan that required the alteration of work in progress to accommodate a church based on a Latin cross. Raphael, Baldassare Peruzzi, and Giuliano da Sangallo also made contributions. In 1547, Michelangelo, then 72, was appointed to make sense of the increasingly muddled project. He promptly obliterated Sangallo's work and started building the dome—both the drum and cupola's distinctive twin columns are his.

By 1603, Carlo Maderno had reinstated the Latin cross and widened the facade to more or less its present width. Bernini then created the magnificent square outside—**Piazza San Pietro**—and

made a few alterations to the interior. The new church was finally consecrated in 1626, about 1,300 years after the original basilica.

The Basilica: Bramante spared little of the original St. Peter's, for which he earned the damning nickname Bramante Ruinante—Bramante the Destroyer. Among the handful of works to escape his modernizing zeal were the church's **central doors** and a **mosaic fragment** above them on their inner arch. The latter, called the Naricella, is the work of Giotto and it portrays the Apostles' ship and the figure of Christ walking on water. (The Porta Santa—the farthest right of St. Peter's five doors—is usually opened only once every 25 years during Holy Years.) The equestrian statues flanking the doors depict Charlemagne (on

St. Peter's Basilica

🗺 46 A4

✉ Piazza San Pietro

☎ 06 6988 3229 to reserve audio guides

🕐 Church & dome closed during religious services

🚌 Bus: 64. Metro: Ottaviano–San Pietro

vaticanstate.va

NOTE: A dress code applies—no shorts, short skirts, or bare shoulders. Allow plenty of time to stand in security lines before entry.

the left) and Constantine (by Bernini) on the right.

Once inside the church, the first breathtaking impressions are of its staggering size, although after wandering endlessly amid the cascades of marble, somber tombs, and mountains of baroque decor, you realize that the interior is surprisingly bereft of major works of art. One notable exception is Michelangelo's **"Pietà"** (1499), located in the first chapel off the south aisle.

Moving down the church, note the measurements set into the nave, markers indicating the size of other churches in relation to St. Peter's. The crossing is dominated by the unmistakable bulk of

the baldacchino (1633), or **altar canopy,** a work created by Bernini. Behind it, at the rear of the church, lies the **Cathedra Petri** (1665), also by Bernini, an ornate throne crafted to enclose a wood and ivory chair reputedly used by St. Peter to address his first sermon to the Romans (scholars believe the chair actually dates from the fourth century).

On either side of the Cathedra are two of the more outstanding of the church's plethora of tombs and statues: On the left stands Guglielmo della Porta's **Tomb of Pope Paul III,** while on the right lies Bernini's **Tomb of Urban VIII** (1647), a model for countless funerary monuments that

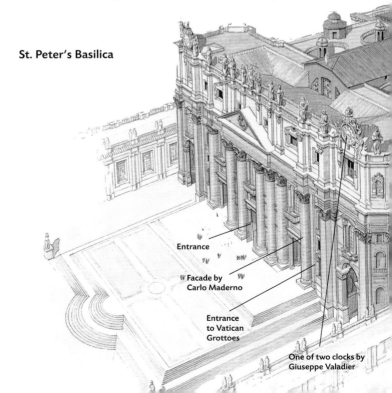

St. Peter's Basilica

Entrance

Facade by
Carlo Maderno

Entrance
to Vatican
Grottoes

One of two clocks by
Giuseppe Valadier

followed. Also hunt out Antonio del Pollaiuolo's **Tomb of Innocent VIII** (1498), a lovely Renaissance work located between the second and third bays of the left aisle. Don't miss the bronze **statue of St. Peter,** attributed to Arnolfo di Cambio and located by the front right of the crossing's four pillars. It is an unmistakable work, thanks to its worn

right foot, caressed by millions since Pius IX granted a 50-day indulgence to anyone kissing it following confession.

Finally, on no account fail to explore the so-called **Vatican Grottoes,** tomb-filled underground chambers

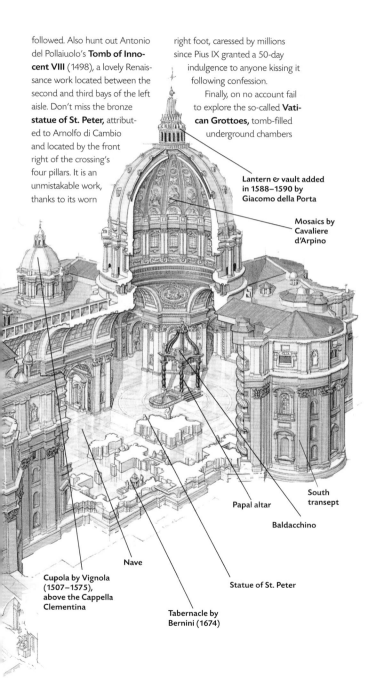

Lantern & vault added in 1588–1590 by Giacomo della Porta

Mosaics by Cavaliere d'Arpino

South transept

Papal altar

Baldacchino

Nave

Cupola by Vignola (1507–1575), above the Cappella Clementina

Statue of St. Peter

Tabernacle by Bernini (1674)

■ The Hellenistic "Belvedere Torso" highly influenced Renaissance, mannerist, and baroque artists.

Musei Vaticani

- 🅰 46 A5
- ✉ Main entrance on Viale Vaticano
- ☎ 06 6988 4676 or 06 6988 3145
- 🕐 Closed Sun. (except 9 a.m.– 2 p.m. last Sun. of month) & religious & public holidays
- 💲 $$$. Free last Sun. of month. Tickets available online at biglietteriamusei .vatican.va
- 🚌 Bus: 19, 32, & 81 to Piazza del Risorgimento. Metro: Cipro– Musei Vaticani

museivaticani.va

below the church, nor to climb the **dome** ($) for unforgettable views of Piazza San Pietro and the city beyond. The dome's entrance lies off the south aisle; access is by stairs or elevator.

Musei Vaticani

It is hard to think of any greater museums than those of the Vatican. Other galleries may match the broad span and myriad origins of the artifacts in the Vatican Museums, but none can also offer works of art that include entire rooms painted by Raphael and the ceiling frescoes of the Cappella Sistina. Exhibits are scattered around many separate museums and several hundred rooms; to see them all involves a walk of some 5 miles (8 km).

See the obvious highlights— the Museo Pio-Clementino, Cappella Sistina (Sistine Chapel), Raphael Rooms, and Pinacoteca

(art gallery)—and then make for museums that reflect your own interests. This might mean choosing between the Egyptian and the Etruscan exhibits. Or it might involve deciding between rooms devoted to modern or pagan art, admiring tapestries and precious manuscripts, wandering corridors lined with ancient maps, or enjoying rooms crammed with medieval furniture and classical sculpture. Whatever your choice, allow plenty of time and arrive early—the high-season crowds can be overwhelming.

The Musei Vaticani contain enough classical sculpture to last a lifetime. If you want to see the best statuary, make straight for the **Museo Pio-Clementino,** laid out in the 18th century by popes Pius VI and Clement XIV. The museum's finest pieces are arranged in the Cortile Ottagono, or **Octagonal Courtyard.** Here you'll find the famous "Laocoön," carved on the island of Rhodes in 40 B.C. but only rediscovered close to the Colosseo in 1506. The sculpture exerted much influence on the art of the High Renaissance, as did another of the courtyard's works, the celebrated **"Apollo del Belvedere,"** a Roman work of A.D. 130 copied from a Greek original (330 B.C.).

The museum's many other highlights include the first-century **"Apoxyomenos"** (literally the "Scraper"), which shows an athlete scraping the sweat and dust from his body after a wrestling match; the first-century B.C. **"Belvedere Torso,"** a work that greatly impressed Michelangelo; a figure of Hermes shown throwing a cloak over his shoulders; the statue of **"Apollo Sauroktonos,"** which portrays the god about to kill a lizard; Canova's neoclassical **"Perseus"** (1800); and the **Candelabri Barberini,** a pair of second-century lamps from Hadrian's Villa at Tivoli.

Stanze di Raffaello: In 1503, Pope Julius II commissioned Raphael, then just 26, to decorate a suite of four modestly sized rooms in the Vatican. The result was the Stanze di Raffaello, or Raphael Rooms, one of the great masterpieces of Western European art.

He first painted the **Stanza della Segnatura** (1508–1511), from the *Signatura,* the highest department of justice of the Holy See. The principal paintings here explore themes such as Theology, Poetry, Philosophy, and Justice,

each of them a complex interweaving of classical, religious, and contemporary characters and allusions. Raphael then moved to the **Stanza di Eliodoro** (1512–1514), a private antechamber, where the main quartet of paintings explore the theme of Divine Providence intervening to defend Faith.

A new pope, Leo X, ascended the papal throne during work on the room, which is why one of

Other Vatican Attractions

Other areas worth seeing in the Musei Vaticani include the **Galleria delle Carte Geografiche,** whose walls are decorated with a 40-panel sequence of pictorial maps (1580). The **Cappella Niccolina** contains frescoes by Beato Angelico on the "Life of St. Stephen and St. Lawrence" (1447–1451), while the nearby **Appartamento Borgia** features equally celebrated frescoes by the Umbrian artist Pinturicchio. The **Museo Gregoriano Etrusco** boasts the world's finest collection of Etruscan art after the Villa Giulia, while the **Museo Gregoriano Egizio** is a treasure chest of Egyptian artifacts.

the walls depicts a scene of "Leo I Repulsing Attila." Leo's insistence on the inclusion of his illustrious namesake, Leo I, was intended to secure glory for himself by proxy. This less than subtle form of self-promotion was carried over into the third room, the **Stanza dell'Incendio di Borgo** (1514–1517). Most of the paintings here involve previous Leonine popes; their content is less eye-catching than their manner, which reveals Raphael painting in a grander style than in earlier rooms, his color more virulent, his emphasis on the human figure more marked. It is thought the change owed much to the influence of Michelangelo, then working close by in the Cappella Sistina. Further development of Raphael's style was cut short by his premature death in 1520, and only one painting in the final room, the **Sala di Costantino,** is based on his drawings.

Cappella Sistina: The Sistine Chapel, Western art's most famous masterpiece, started life as a chapel built for Pope Sixtus IV in 1477. Its earliest decoration dates to 1481, when the lower walls were painted by a group of leading artists who included Botticelli, Perugino, and Luca Signorelli. The ceiling remained relatively unadorned until 1508, the year Pope Julius II approached Michelangelo to begin one of the world's most celebrated paintings.

The work took four years to complete, four years in which Michelangelo endured extremes of heat and cold and weeks of cramped misery spent painting on his back. More than 300 figures populate the scenes, which divide into nine basic sections. Each is read chronologically in the order you walk through the chapel. First come the five seminal events from the Book of Genesis: the "Separation of Light and Darkness," the "Creation of the Heavenly Bodies," the "Separation of Land and Sea," the "Creation of Adam," and the "Creation of Eve." These are followed by the "Fall and

The Musei Vaticani's monumental spiral staircase, designed by Giuseppe Momo in 1932

Expulsion from Paradise," the "Sacrifice of Noah," the "Flood," and the "Drunkenness of Noah."

Rome was a different city and Michelangelo a different man when he came to paint the Cappella Sistina's other masterpiece, the vast fresco of the **"Last Judgment"** (1536–1541), which covers the chapel's rear wall. More than 20 years had elapsed since his work on the ceiling, during which time Rome had been traumatized by the 1527 sack by Charles V. For his part, Michelangelo had become embittered by, among other things, his work on the tomb of Julius II, his former employer. As a result, the painter's vision of the Day of Judgment is dark and uncompromising, its content a departure from earlier interpretations of the theme in which forgiveness and redemption had laced vengeance and Divine ire. The doomed are shown sinking to their fate on the painting's right, faces and bodies contorted, while the saved—merely relieved rather than overjoyed—rise powerfully on the painting's left.

Pinacoteca: The minor Vatican museum with the most general appeal is the art gallery, whose 18 rooms contain the cream of the Vatican's collection of medieval and Renaissance paintings. The most celebrated pictures here are Raphael's last work, the **"Transfiguration"** (1520), which hung above the artist as he lay in state; the same artist's "Madonna of Foligno"; Giotto's "Stefaneschi Triptych"; a "Deposition" by Caravaggio; and Melozzo da Forlì's portrait of Sixtus IV and his librarian. The gallery also has Rome's only painting by Leonardo da Vinci, an unfinished monochrome of St. Jerome, as well as works by nearly every other Italian and European artist of note. ■

Outside the Walls

Visiting the scenarios that open up beyond the sections of the ancient city walls that have survived is well worth a detour. The city gates gave access to the consular roads, including the Via Appia to the south, that runs along the **Appia Antica Regional Park** (tel 06 512 6314, parcoappia antica.it) where you can bike amid ancient cobblestones and spectacular catacombs (see p. 82). Farther west is the **Basilica di San Paolo Fuori le Mura** (Piazzale San Paolo 1, tel 06 6988 0800, basilicasanpaolo .org). Mosaics and ornaments of inestimable value are conserved there. South, visitors can find the **EUR** zone, built in the 1930s for the 1948 Rome World's Fair and famous for its rationalist architecture. Today it has become a great place to visit museums as well as the new convention center and Massimiliano Fuksas's la Nuvola, inaugurated in 2016.

North of the city is the **MAXXI** (Museum of the Arts of the 21st Century, Via Guido Reni 4a, tel 06 32810, fondazione maxxi.it). Dedicated to modern art and architecture, it was designed by Zaha Hadid and inaugurated in 2010. Together with the nearby **Parco della Musica,** Europe's biggest performance venue designed by Renzo Piano, it constitutes an area that differs greatly from the ancient Rome that tourists are more used to.

More Places to Visit in Rome

Churches

Between Piazza Navona and the Pantheon is **San Luigi dei Francesi** (*map 46 C4, Piazza di S. Luigi de' Francesi, tel 06 688 271, closed 12:45 p.m.–2:30 p.m. Mon.–Fri. & Sun., 12:15 p.m.–2:30 p.m. Sat.*), which features three dramatic paintings of the apostle Matthew by Caravaggio. In Trastevere, try to visit **Santa Maria in Trastevere** (*map 46 B3, Piazza Santa Maria in Trastevere, tel 06 581 9443*), renowned for the 12th-century mosaics that adorn both its facade and interior. Nearby **Santa Cecilia in Trastevere** (*map 46 C3, Piazza Santa Cecilia 22, tel 06 4549 2739, closed 12:30 p.m.–4 p.m. & Sun.*) contains more mosaics (ninth century) and an altar canopy (1293) by Arnolfo di Cambio. Across the river, the portico of **Santa Maria in Cosmedin** (*map 46 C3, Piazza Bocca della Verità*) houses the famous Bocca della Verità, the Mouth of Truth, whose stone jaws are supposed to clamp shut on the hands of dissemblers. Santa Maria's medieval interior provides a contrast to the prevailing baroque tone of most of the city's churches. Foremost among these are the **Gesù** (*map 46 C4, Piazza del Gesù, tel 06 697 001, chiesa delgesu.org, closed 12:30 p.m.–4 p.m.*), mother church of the Jesuits, and the modest yet distinguished churches—**San Carlo** (*map 47 D4, Via del Quirinale 23*) and **Sant'Andrea al Quirinale** (*map 47 D4, Via del Quirinale 29*), by Borromini and Bernini, respectively, the baroque's leading lights. One of Bernini's most famous sculptures, the erotically charged "Ecstasy of St. Theresa," graces **Santa Maria della Vittoria** (*map 47 E4–E5, Via XX Settembre 17*). Equally memorable is the macabre decoration of **Santa Maria della Concezione** (*map 47 D5, Via Vittorio Veneto 27*), which features skulls and lovingly arranged human bones.

Palazzo Massimo alle Terme

Italy's state collection of antiquities is scattered among several museums in Rome, with the lion's share housed in the Palazzo Massimo alle Terme. The Palazzo Massimo also holds the best of the state collection, its array of Roman and Greek sculpture, mosaics, and other artifacts spread over three floors. Don't miss the frescoed rooms on the top floor, notably the House of Livia, part of a first-century B.C. villa that belonged to the wife of Emperor Augustus, as well as murals of the same period found in a palace near the Villa Farnesina.
coopculture.it 🅐 47 E4 ✉ Largo di Villa Peretti 1, off Piazza dei Cinquecento ☎ 06 3996 7701 🕒 Closed Mon. 💲 $$

Other Museums & Monuments

Few ancient Roman reliefs are as well preserved as those adorning the **Ara Pacis** (*map 46 C5, Via di Ripetta Lungotevere in Augusta, corner of Via Tomacelli, tel 06 0608, arapacis.it, $$*), a masterpiece of the Augustan era, and few as imposing as the **Teatro di Marcello** (*map 46 C3, Via del Teatro di Marcello, closed to the public*), in its day one of Rome's largest theaters. Roman remains on the old city's fringes include the **Terme di Caracalla** (*map 47 D1–D2, Viale delle Terme di Caracalla 52, closed Mon. p.m.*), a colossal bath complex, and the well-preserved, tomb-lined portion of Roman road Via Appia Antica. It is close to sets of early Christian catacombs; the best are **San Sebastiano** (*Via Appia Antica 136, tel 06 785 0350, catacombe.org, closed Sun. & Dec., $*), **San Callisto** (*Via Appia Antica 110, tel 06 513 0151, catacombe.roma.it, closed 12 p.m.–2 p.m., Wed., & Feb., $*), and, along the Roman Via Ardeatina, **Santa Domitilla** (*Via delle Sette Chiese 282, tel 06 511 0342, domitilla.info, closed 12 p.m.–2 p.m., Tues., & mid-Dec.–mid-Jan., $$$*).

Among Rome's many minor museums, the most notable is the **Castel Sant'Angelo** (*map 46 B4–B5, Lungotevere Castello 50, tel 06 681 9111, castelsantangelo.com, $$*) near St. Peter's Basilica, a fortress cum mausoleum built in A.D. 135 and now a museum of medieval and other artifacts.

The allure of two major cities—Turin and Genoa—sublime food
and wine, and beautiful mountain and coastal landscapes

NORTHWEST ITALY

■ Decorative stonework,
Palazzo Madama, Turin

NORTHWEST ITALY

Northwest Italy introduces three regions—Piedmont (Piemonte), Liguria, and the Valle d'Aosta—and three very different types of landscape—the peaks, forests, and deep-cut valleys of the Alps; the flatlands and meandering rivers of the Po plain; and the cliffs, coves, and beaches of the Mediterranean coast.

Piedmont takes its name from *pedemontis* or *piede dei monti*—the foot of the mountains—after the Alpine wall that guards its plains, tidy towns, and pastoral, vine-covered hills. At its heart lies Turin (Torino), a beautiful baroque city full of cobbled streets, shady arcades, and elegant sidewalk cafés. It was the cradle of Italy's unification movement, home to the Savoys, dukes of Piedmont and first kings of a united Italy. Their mansions outside Turin, especially the Venaria Reale, have become important tourist destinations.

Agriculture thrives in the region, and the hills of Monferrato yield truffles, Asti Spumante, and two of the country's premier red wines—Barolo and Barbaresco. Vermouth and *grissini* (bread sticks), mainstays of bars and Italian restaurants across the world, also have their origins here.

Wedged hard up against the Alps is the Valle d'Aosta, home to some of Italy's grandest scenery, including its greatest national park—the Parco Nazionale del Gran Paradiso—and three of Europe's highest mountains: Mont Blanc, Monte Rosa, and Monte Cervino (Matterhorn). Aosta is the main town,

while along the valley floor looms a succession of gaunt castles, monuments to a time when mountain passes such as the Great St. Bernard made the region a strategic corridor between Italy, France, and Switzerland. Today, tunnels such as the St. Bernard maintain the area's role as a vital European route.

Liguria is Italy's maritime region par excellence. Genoa (Genova), its briny capital, is one of the country's largest ports, while the nooks and crannies of its fractured coastline contain beguiling scenery. A narrow sliver of territory, the region runs from the French border as far as Tuscany, forming a long coastal strip—the Italian Riviera—sheltered by the Ligurian Alps. West of Genoa, the palm-fringed coast is known as the Riviera di Ponente; to the east is the Riviera di Levante. Both are strung with resorts and towns. The best are the Cinque Terre, five delightful little cliff-hung villages, and Portofino, a romantic jewel set on a beautiful coastal promontory. ■

⏐ TURIN

"Turin is not a city . . . to make a fuss about," complained Henry James in *Italy Revisited* (1877), a still common belief among those unfamiliar with this unsung and unvisited city—prior to the 2006 Winter Olympic Games, anyway. Dour and un-Italian, at least by reputation, its center at first glance is a grid of mostly 19th-century streets, its outskirts a tangle of industrial suburbs.

■ The Palazzo Madama dominates Piazza Castello, one of Turin's two main squares.

Turin

🗺 84 C3

Visitor Information

✉ Two locations in Piazza Carlo Felice and at Via Garibaldi 45a (corner of Piazza Castello)

☎ Call center 011 535 181

**comune.torino.it
turismotorino.org
fondazione
torinomusei.it**
(museum information
& online tickets)

On closer inspection, Turin (Torino) emerges as an elegant city, full of parks, palaces, arcades, venerable cafés, and fine baroque architecture. It is also home to the much-disputed Turin Shroud and to the giant Fiat corporation, former bulwark of the city's industrial might.

Turin began life as the capital of the Taurini, a tribe of Celtic origin. Later it became a modest Roman military outpost. Its rise to real prominence came when the princes of Savoy, an ancient Italo-French dynasty, made the city the seat of their court in 1574. Savoy patronage and two outstanding baroque architects, Guarino

Guarini (1624–1683) and Filippo Juvarra (1676–1736), then turned the city into a social and architectural showcase. In the 19th century, the family became prime movers in the unification movement and the first kings of Italy. In the 20th century, large companies such as Fiat, founded in 1899, attracted vast pools of migrant labor, particularly from southern Italy, leading to the growth of major new suburbs during the 1950s and '60s.

Central Turin is a close-knit area that is easy and pleasant to explore on foot. On its western side lies the fashionable Piazza San Carlo, the most architecturally distinguished of the city's squares.

Turin's attractive main street, Via Roma, all cobbled squares and tempting stores, leads east to the Piazza Castello, the city's other main square. Around both squares range an interesting collection of museums, palaces, and churches.

Piazza San Carlo

Only London and Cairo have comparable ancient Egyptian collections to that of Turin's **Museo Egizio,** housed in the Palazzo dell'Accademia delle Scienze. The city owes its windfall to the Savoys, who in 1824 brought the artifacts accumulated by Bernardo Drovetti, a Piedmont-born French consul general posted to Egypt during the Napoleonic Wars. To these were added finds from excavations made by Italian archaeologists in 1911, as well as outstanding treasures such as the rock temple of Thutmose III (1450 B.C.) from Ellessya, gifted by the United Arab Republic to the museum in 1967 for its help during the excavations that preceded the building of the Aswan Dam. The museum recently reopened after a dazzling contemporary makeover. Its highlights include the Colossus of Seti II and a black diorite statue of Ramses II (1299–1233 B.C.). Upstairs, the exhibits run the gamut of Egyptian civilization, embracing everything from objects linked to weaving, farming, and fishing to complete tombs such as the sepulchres of Kha and Merit (14th century B.C.) and a collection of papyri that includes the reputedly world's oldest topographical map.

Superga

Superga *(Strada di Superga 73, tel 011 899 7456),* **a grand baroque basilica, is the masterpiece of the architect Filippo Juvarra. Built between 1717 and 1731 atop a 2,198-foot (670 m) hill, 6 miles (9.6 km) east of Turin, it was raised in thanksgiving for Turin's deliverance from the French army in 1706. The exterior terraces offer superb views of the city and its surroundings, while the interior contains the royal tombs of the Savoy family.**

A few steps from the Museo Egizio lies the **Palazzo Carignano,** built between 1679 and 1684 for the Carignano, a branch of the Savoy family, and distinguished by Guarini's unusual curved brick facade. Unified Italy's first king, Vittorio Emanuele II, was born here in 1820, and between 1861 and 1864, the palace served as the seat of Italy's first parliament. Today, it houses the 27-room **Museo Nazionale del Risorgimento,** a museum devoted to the 19th-century unification of Italy.

Piazza Castello & Around

At the center of Piazza Castello, the huge square north of the palace, stands the **Palazzo Madama.** It owes its present appearance to Filippo Juvarra (see p. 86) but has its origins in the Roman fortifications and medieval fortress that once stood on the site. The palace is named for its 17th-century occupant, "Madama" Marie-Christine of France, mother of Carlo Emanuele of Savoy. Inside it houses the **Museo Civico d'Arte Antica,** a museum whose wide-ranging collection includes

Museo Egizio
- Via Accademia delle Scienze 6
- ☎ 011 440 6903
- ⏱ Closed Mon. p.m.
- $ $$

museoegizio.it

Palazzo Carignano
- Via Accademia delle Scienze 5
- ☎ 011 564 1791 or 011 564 1733
- ⏱ Closed Mon.
- $ $

polomusealepiemonte
.beniculturali.it

Museo Nazionale del Risorgimento
- Via Accademia delle Scienze 5
- ☎ 011 562 1147
- ⏱ Closed Mon.
- $ $$$$

museorisorgimento
torino.it

Palazzo Madama & Museo Civico d'Arte Antica
- Piazza Castello
- ☎ 011 443 350
- ⏱ Closed Tues.
- $ Museum $$

palazzomadama
torino.it

NOTE: The **Torino+ Piemonte Card** *(turismo torino.org)* offers free or discounted entry to 180 museums and other sights in Turin and the Piedmont region, plus free above-ground public transport and discounts on guided tours, concerts, parking, car rental, and the circular hop-on-hop-off City Sightseeing bus tour *(torino.city-sight-seeing.it)*. Valid for one, two, three, or five days, the cards *($$$–$$$$$)* can be bought from the visitor center.

paintings and objets d'art spanning three millennia. Its highlights are the famous "Portrait of a Man" (1476) by Sicilian painter Antonello da Messina and the Duc de Berry's sumptuously illustrated 15th-century *Book of Hours.*

Turin's cathedral, the **Duomo di San Giovanni** *(Piazza S. Giovanni, tel 011 436 1540, closed 12:30 p.m.– 3 p.m.),* begun by Tuscan architects in 1491, is the city's only major Renaissance monument, but the city's baroque geniuses could not hold their hand—Juvarra designed the crown (1720) of the restrained brick campanile (1468–1470).

controversial relic, better known as the **Shroud of Turin,** is the winding sheet used to wrap Christ after his crucifixion. To doubters, it is a 13th-century fake. Carbon dating in 1988 seemed to vindicate the skeptics, but many have since questioned the validity of the dating techniques. The shroud is supposed to have been taken from Jerusalem to Cyprus, and from there to France, where it came into the possession of the Savoys in 1453 then was first displayed in the cathedral in 1694.

The **Palazzo Reale,** or Royal Palace was the Savoys' principal seat from 1646 to 1865. Today, it is visited for its gardens *(free)* and lavish state apartments. The **Armeria Reale** is one of the world's largest and most important collections of arms and military memorabilia. The collection was amassed by the Savoys and comprises weapons from Greek and Roman times, medieval and Renaissance items, and military hardware from as far afield as China and Japan.

The **Galleria Sabauda** moved to a wing of this impressive palace in 2014. It contains paintings accumulated by the Savoys from the 15th century onward, a collection donated to the state following unification in 1860. Among the many Dutch and Flemish works, look for Rembrandt's "Old Man Asleep"; Hans Memling's "Passion of Christ"; and Antony Van Dyck's "Children of Charles I of England." Italian painters include Mantegna, whose wistful "Madonna" is one of the gallery's loveliest works; members of the Venetian school such as Giovanni

■ Equine armory displays, Armeria Reale

Musei Reali (Cappella della Sacra Sindone, Palazzo Reale, Armeria Reale, Galleria Sabauda)

✉ Piazzetta Reale

☎ 011 521 1106

🕐 Closed Mon.

💲 $$

museireali .beniculturali.it

Immediately east of the Duomo is the huge complex of the **Musei Reali,** which include many sights. The **Cappella della Sacra Sindone** (1668–1694) is a magnificent chapel that had been damaged by fire in 1997. Reopened in 2018, Guarini's masterpiece once again houses a relic, the *Sindone,* or Holy Shroud, that escaped the conflagration unscathed. To believers, this

EXPERIENCE: Sip a Drink in a Historic Café

Turin's many historic cafés are proudly prized and fondly frequented by its citizens. The cafés feature lots of old wood; plush velvet seats; plenty of cozy nooks; elegant marble tables; mirrors and glittering chandeliers; frescoed ceilings; and the intoxicating perfumes of coffee, cakes, chocolate, and classic cocktails. One of the most alluring is **Al Bicerin** *(Piazza Consolata 5, bicerin.it)*, a tiny delight founded in 1763. The essential drink here is the eponymous *bicerin*, a decadent mixture of coffee, chocolate, and cream.

Some of Turin's most famous cafés are in Piazza San Carlo and Piazza Castello, the city's main squares. **Baratti & Milano** *(Piazza Castello 27–29, barattiemilano .it)*, founded in 1873, was for decades

supplier to the Savoy royal family. Nearby **Mulassano** *(Piazza Castello 15)* is much smaller, with a classic wood-paneled interior from 1907 and a wonderful marble bar.

Equally seductive are **Abrate** *(Via Po 10)*, just around the corner, founded in 1866, and **Caffè Fiorio** *(Via Po 8)*, a center of the city's social life since 1780.

Other smarter and more ornate cafés also suit the dressed-up, early evening demands of the aperitif, notably two rivals on Piazza San Carlo: **Caffè San Carlo** *(Piazza San Carlo 156)* and **Caffè Torino** *(Piazza San Carlo 204, caffe-torino .it)*, both temples of baroque splendor with more than a century of history behind them.

Bellini, Tiepolo ("The Triumph of Aurelius"), Veronese ("The Meal at the House of Simon"), and Tintoretto; and an impressive roster of Tuscan artists—Fra Angelico ("Madonna"), Filippino Lippi ("Three Archangels"), and Sodoma ("Madonna and Saints"). Also keep an eye open for Orazio Gentileschi's "Annunciation" and Bernardo Bellotto's views of 18th-century Turin.

Walk east from Piazza Castello on Via Giuseppe Verdi and you come to the **Mole Antonelliana,** Turin's most prominent sight. For a while during the 19th century, this was one of the world's tallest buildings, standing at 548 feet (167 m). Begun as a synagogue by architect Alessandro Antonelli in 1862, it was finished by the Turin city council in 1897. Today, the Mole serves as an exhibition center and home to the excellent

Museo Nazionale del Cinema, a museum that traces the Italian movie industry from its earliest days in Turin. A viewing platform midway up offers airy views to the Alps and Po Valley.

The Lingotto Area

The Fiat industrial complex was built between 1916 and 1930. It quickly became a symbol of the city and has remained so ever since. In the 1980s, when car manufacture halted, the architect Renzo Piano was commissioned to convert the **Lingotto,** a difficult task. Today, the building houses an exposition center, hotels, offices, and retail space.

Moving towards the River Po, visitors will find the **MAUTO,** one of the best automotive museums in the world with an information center and more than 200 automobiles. ∎

Mole Antonelliana /Museo Nazionale del Cinema

⊠ Via Montebello 20

☎ 011 813 8564–565

⊡ Closed Tues.

⑤ $$ (museum), $$ (panoramic elevator)

museocinema.it

MAUTO-Museo dell'Automobile di Torino

⊠ Corso Unità d'Italia 40

☎ 011 677 666

⊡ Closed Mon. p.m.

⑤ $$

🚇 Metro: Lingotto from Porta Nuova station

museoauto.it

TRUFFLES

Piedmont is a truffle capital, home to the fabled white truffle—*Tuber magnatum*— one of the world's rarest foodstuffs. Truffles have been known, if not understood, since ancient times. The first written record dates from the fifth century B.C. They were enjoyed by the Babylonians, the Greeks, and the Romans, who consumed them as much for their reputed aphrodisiacal qualities as their gastronomic allure.

In Italy, truffle hunters use highly trained—and valuable—dogs to sniff out the prized foodstuff.

Classical writers were mystified by truffles. Plutarch believed they were mud cooked by lightning; Juvenal that they were the product of thunder and rain. Pliny, bewildered by their origins, considered them nature's greatest miracle. During the Middle Ages, they were considered a manifestation of the devil. And no wonder, for here was a "plant" apparently without root, branch, or stem; without leaf, fruit, or flower.

Truffles are actually a form of fungus that has sunk underground, probably as part of an evolutionary defense against the elements. Their spores are spread not by the wind, but by various truffle-eating animals such as rodents, deer, slugs, and wild boars. Their underground home precludes photosynthesis, meaning they rely for nutrients on a symbiotic relationship with the roots of certain trees, most commonly oak, hazel, beech, and lime.

Truffles usually attain their final dimensions—anything from the size of a pea to the size of a soccer ball—over a few days during the spring. Protected from the weather, they are then able to mature slowly, often over the course of several months. Only when ripe— from about November onward—do they give off the distinctive perfume, and only then for about ten days, thus ensuring they are snaffled up only when laden with viable spores. Thereafter, they become poisonous and rot. But to ensure they're rooted out, they need to advertise their presence.

This is where the truffle's famous perfume comes in, not to mention dogs and pigs, foremost among the ragbag of sleuths used to nose out the prized tuber (goats, foxes, and ferrets are also used, and even bear cubs, in Russia). Pigs love truffles, at least female ones,

INSIDER TIP:

In Piedmont, truffle festivals
and auctions take place in late
autumn, while in the Marche
they are held in winter.

—JANE SUNDERLAND
National Geographic contributor

for among the countless volatile compounds
exuded by the truffle is one that closely
resembles the musky sexual pheromones of the
wild boar. In fact, a truffle gives off almost twice
the amount of this scent as the male boar, the
idea being to attract the sow and so disperse
its spores. Sows are huge and unmanageable,
however, and they're also prone to attacks of
sexual frenzy when close to the truffle, the
main reasons they've been replaced by dogs.

The Truffle Mystique

But why the fuss and mystique surrounding
truffles? They are nothing to look at and
the perfume, best described as "essence
of undergrowth," has been compared to
leaf mold, overripe cheese, garlic, herbs,

methane, and sweaty armpits. For cooks,
the appeal is the truffle's unique and subtle
flavor. Elizabeth David, in her classic cook-
book *Italian Food* (1954), called the truffle
the "most delicious of all foods anywhere."
Brillat-Savarin, the distinguished 19th-
century French gastronome, went further,
stating that "without truffles there can be
no truly gastronomic meal."

The truffle's mystery, its seemingly spontaneous appearance and ethereal existence, is also
significant. Equally important is the rarity and
thrill of the hunt—it is one of the only foods of
any description that cannot be grown to order.
It is also gloriously unpredictable, something that
has made cultivation something of an agricultural holy grail. One tree will yield truffles while
its apparently identical neighbor will not—and no
one knows why. Money also plays a part. Weight
for weight, truffles are among the world's costli-
est foodstuffs: Only saffron costs more.

Only a relatively modest amount, however,
needs to be spent to enjoy the truffle's exalted
qualities. Nowhere, save central France, can you
relish their sublime flavor better than in the restaurants of Piedmont, Umbria, and—to a lesser
extent—Tuscany and the Marche.

EXPERIENCE: Go Truffle Hunting

On a misty fall morning you are walking
through the woods with a guide and a
man with a small dog. Suddenly the dog
stops, nose in the air, and starts scrabbling
at the undergrowth. The man pulls the
dog gently back, produces a small trowel,
and then lifts a small, dark nugget from
the ground. You are several feet away, but
the sudden, otherworldly scent of the
truffle is powerful and unmistakable.

Truffle hunting is fun, wherever you
do it, and combines a gentle hike, a good
morning in the outdoors, lovely scenery,
and numerous fascinating insights into
this most unusual and prized of foodstuffs
(plus you can eat what you find).

A good place to truffle hunt is in
Umbria—one of Italy's main truffle regions
(see pp. 269–286). For a memorable
experience, partake of the three-day,
two-night truffle-hunting special offered
by the **Palazzo Seneca** *(Via Cesare Battisti
12, Norcia, tel 0743 817 434, palazzoseneca
.com)*, in Norcia, Umbria. A gastronomic
and cultural delight, the package includes
two nights, breakfast included, two din-
ners, a two-hour experience in the woods
with a truffle hunter, admission to the
wellness center and other hotel services.
The price of the entire package varies
€355–€830 ($404–$946) per person
in a "Romantica" double room.

PARCO NAZIONALE DEL GRAN PARADISO

Italy's first national park began life as a royal hunting reserve maintained exclusively for Vittorio Emanuele II of Savoy and his family in 1856. In 1920, Vittorio Emanuele III presented the reserve to the state, and three years later the area was declared a national park. Today, the Parco Nazionale del Gran Paradiso extends across 270 square miles (70,000 ha), spanning the regions of Piedmont and the Valle d'Aosta, and protecting the majestic mountain scenery on and around the 13,323-foot (4,061 m) Gran Paradiso massif.

■ The Valnontey Valley typifies the spectacular scenery throughout the Parco Nazionale del Gran Paradiso.

Parco Nazionale del Gran Paradiso
🗺 84 B4–C4
Visitor Information
parks.it
pngp.it

NOTE: The park has several visitor centers and information points, many only open seasonally; they are listed online at *pngp.it*.

Landscapes in the park's Alpine region are a patchwork of high mountain wilderness, meadows, and dulcet valley bottoms. Year-round snow and glaciers shroud its inner fastness, from which crashing streams plunge into flower-strewn pastures and forests of larch, fir, and pine. Waterfalls, deep-cut valleys, and pastoral corners also abound, all within easy reach, thanks to the park's good roads and well-maintained trails.

The region can be reached from Piedmont in the south, but perhaps the most convenient and interesting approach is from the **Valle d'Aosta** and the north (see pp. 94–95). The best tactic is to take one of the trio of roads that follow the major valleys on the park's northern flanks—the Val di Rhêmes, Val Savarenche, and Val di Cogne. Any of these roads offers prodigious views, wonderful landscapes, and the opportunity to pick up trails for hikes of varying lengths and difficulty.

Val di Cogne

In an ideal world, you would explore all three roads, but if time is short the best route is the SS507 along the Val di Cogne, an approach that brings you to the park's major resort at Cogne, a busy little place some 30 minutes' drive from Aosta. En route you can stop off to admire the castle at **Aymavilles** and follow the short signposted road diversion to **Pondel**, a tiny hamlet famed for its superb third-century B.C. Roman bridge and aqueduct.

Cogne is a good place to stay and pick up trail details (trails are indicated by the Italian Alpine

Club's official trail numbers and markings), although for the best scenery you need to follow two smaller roads that push a couple of miles deeper into the park. One finishes at **Lillaz,** a peaceful little village where many of the houses still preserve their traditional slate roofs (you can also walk here along the river from Cogne). Some short hikes, from Cogne or from Lillaz, lead to the beautiful Urtier stream waterfalls.

Alternatively, follow the minor road south to **Valnontey,** a busier village, and the trailhead for one of the park's most deservedly popular hikes, the walk to the **Vittorio Sella** mountain refuge (trail 18) and back via the Lago di Lauson and Sella Herbetet refuge (trail 18b, for trained hikers). Allow a full day for the walk and try to avoid weekends, when the route is busy. Valnontey is also known for the **Giardino Botanico Alpino Paradisia** (tel 0165 753 011, closed mid-Sept.–early-June, $), founded in 1955, where you can admire some of the park's many wild Alpine plants and flowers growing in controlled conditions.

Wildlife

Scenery aside, one of the Gran Paradiso's major attractions is its wildlife and the ease with which much of it can be seen. Chief among its animals, and chosen as the park's symbol, is the *stambecco* (ibex), a member of the deer family. Virtually extinct elsewhere in Europe, this wild animal thrives in the region—the park has some 5,000—where it has been protected since 1821.

If anything, there are too many, the lack of predators allowing herds to proliferate beyond naturally sustainable limits. Plans to introduce wolves and lynx have so far proved unsuccessful. Numbers of antelopelike chamois are

---

EXPERIENCE:

Hiking in Gran Paradiso

Early morning starts on Parco Nazionale del Gran Paradiso's hiking trails are easy from the region's many valley-bottom villages. Walk across dew-covered and flower-filled pastures, and then start to climb through the cool pine forests that cover most of the steep lower slopes of the area's glaciated valleys. Or cut out the hardest climbing by taking a cable car. Either way, you'll soon find yourself above tree line, in meadows full of spring flowers well into June.

Hikes are easily organized—excellent maps are readily available, trails are well marked and well kept, and visitor centers can advise on hikes to suit your time and abilities. Gran Paradiso is also one of the "easiest" 4,000-meter (13,120 ft) peaks to scale in the Alps, but you will need a guide. To hire a guide, contact the Società delle Guide del Gran Paradiso (guidegranparadiso.com), **an umbrella site with links to the area's regionally based guides and officially sanctioned guide organizations.**

---

also considerable, as are those of marmots, a small furry mammal whose piercing warning whistle is a common sound on the park's trails. The Valnontey walk has almost guaranteed sightings of ibex and chamois. The bearded vulture, a rare bird extinct in many Alpine areas, recently returned to live here again thanks to a reintroduction program. ■

Cogne

🗺 84 B4

Visitor Information

✉ Via Bourgeois 33

☎ 0165 74040

🕐 Closed 1 p.m.–3 p.m.

cogneturismo.it

A DRIVE ALONG THE VALLE D'AOSTA

This stunning drive takes you through high Alpine scenery from Pont-St.-Martin to Courmayeur and the foot of Mont Blanc via the historic town of Aosta.

Pont-St.-Martin ❶ is known for its vineyards and the small first-century B.C. Roman bridge at its heart. Consider a diversion here on the SR44 along the **Val di Gressoney,** a perfect Alpine valley of meadows, traditional houses, and soaring mountains whose inhabitants, the Walser, descendants of 12th-century Swiss migrants, still speak an ancient German dialect.

A few minutes beyond Pont-St.-Martin on the SS26 lies the brooding **Forte di Bard** *(tel 0125 833 811, closed Mon., $–$$, fortedibard. it),* first of the 70 or more fortresses for which the Valle d'Aosta is renowned. Dismantled on Napoleon's orders, it was largely rebuilt in the 19th century. Today, it houses a variety of museums and exposition areas as well as a free panoramic pedestrian path. A little farther along the same road is the superb **Castello di Issogne** ❷ *(tel 0125 929 373,*

NOT TO BE MISSED:

Val d'Ayas • Castello di Fénis • Parco Nazionale del Gran Paradiso • Mont Blanc cable car (take your passport)

closed 1 p.m.–2 p.m. & Mon., $$), built in 1498 by Georges de Challant, a member of the family that controlled much of the Valle d'Aosta for centuries. Across the river lies the **Castello di Verrès** *(tel 0125 929 067, open daily Apr.–Sept.; closed 1 p.m.–2 p.m. & Mon. Oct.–March, $),* also built by the Challant, but gaunt in appearance, as its purpose was more defensive than residential.

A side road at Verrès, the SR45, leads north along the **Val d'Ayas** ❸, the prettiest of all the side valleys on the drive: Cable cars from the village of **Champoluc** at its head run to one of the Alps' grandest viewpoints, with vistas of Monte Rosa and Monte Cervino, the two highest mountains in Europe after Mont Blanc.

Hotel-filled **St.-Vincent** is known for its casino and for the road

FRANCE
Glacier du Géant
VAL FERRET
Punta Helbronner
❼
La Palud
Entrèves
SS26 dir
Courmayeur
Pré-St.-Didier
SS26
Morgex
La Salle
Dora Baltea
Colle del Piccolo San Bernardo
SS26
Avise
2976m
Arvier
Ville-neuve
St-Pierre
Sarre
VALLE
AOSTA ❺
A5
SS27
2625m
Aymavilles
Pondel
VAL DI COGNE
3090m
Vieyes
Val di Rhêmes
Val Savarenche
❻
PARCO NAZIONALE DEL GRAN PARADISO
3996m
Giardino Alpino Paradisia
Cogne
Lillaz
Valnontey

up the Valtournenche to **Breuil-Cervinia,** a winter resort. Press on to the intriguing **Castello di Fénis** ❹ *(tel 0125 764 263, open daily Apr.– Sept.; closed 1 p.m.–2 p.m. & Mon. Oct.–March, $),* an outstanding castle renowned for its 15th-century frescoes and exquisite furniture.

Aosta & Beyond

Don't despair at the industrial suburbs of **Aosta** ❺ *(visitor information, Piazza Porta Pretoria 3, tel 0165 236 627, lovevda.it),* for at its heart the region's capital is a pleasant historic town of Roman ruins, medieval churches, and tranquil old squares. Captured from the local Salassi tribe by the Romans, the town was christened Augusta Praetoria in honor of the emperor—"Aosta" is a corruption of "Augustus." Over the centuries, its strategic position brought considerable wealth, its current prosperity bolstered by tourism, trade, and the Mont Blanc and St. Bernard tunnels. Aosta's nickname, the "Rome of the Alps," overstates things just a touch, but the tally of Roman remains is still impressive. In the old center, see the Roman

forum (with a spectacular cryptoporticus), theater, and amphitheater; farther afield visit the Porta Pretoria, Arch of Augustus, and old Roman bridge. Roman and other early artifacts are the mainstay of the **Museo Archeologico Regionale** *(Piazza Roncas 12, tel 0165 275 902),* a modest museum next to the forum. Close by stands the town's 12th-century **cathedral,** filled with fine tombs, choir stalls, and mosaic pavements. It also has the little **Museo del Tesoro** *(Piazza Giovanni XXIII, tel 0165 40413, call for hours, cattedraleaosta.it).* The town's other main church is the lovely 11th-century **Collegiata di Sant'Orso** *(Via Sant'Orso),* a beguiling medieval complex comprising a priory, a Romanesque cloister, and an ancient crypt.

A side road beyond Aosta at Sarre leads to Cogne on the SR47 and the **Parco Nazionale del Gran Paradiso** ❻ *(see pp. 92–93).* After this essential detour, return to the main SS26, which climbs ever closer to the vast peaks at the head of the valley. Sarre has yet another castle, as do the picturesque villages of St.-Pierre and Avise.

At Pré-St.-Didier, the SS26 toward the Colle del Piccolo San Bernardo offers more scenic diversions. Allow time for the **cable car** ride *(montebianco. com, $$$$$)* up Mont Blanc. The well-signposted ride starts at **La Palud** ❼, a hamlet close to the resort town of Courmayeur. Most people ride as far as Punta Helbronner, but other stages *(July–Sept. only)* go across the mountain into France. Return to La Palud by cable car.

Monte Cervino

Monte Rosa

Champoluc

3316m ▲ Testa Grigia

▲ Breuil-Cervinia

VAL D'AYAS

8 kilometers
4 miles

Ayas

❸

2722m ▲

Valtournenche

SS406

Evançon

St.-Vincent

Brusson

Chambave   Châtillon

A O S T A

Nus

llefranche

❹ Castello di Fénis

SS26

Dora Baltea

2482m ▲

SR45

Castello di Verrès
Verrès

Castello di Issogne ❷

Arnad

SS26

A5

Forte di Bard ❶

Pont-St.-Martin

START

GENOA

Genoa's (Genova's) fame has been built on the seafaring exploits of its mariners and the trading potential of Italy's once premier port. La Superba (The Proud), as the city is known, lacks obvious sights, but by burrowing beneath the city's rumpled appearance and confining yourself to the historic core, you will uncover its eclectic wealth of churches, palaces, and galleries.

■ Piazza San Matteo claims the charming black-and-white-striped Gothic church of San Matteo.

Genoa
🗺 84 D2
Visitor Information
✉ Via Garibaldi 12/r
☎ 010 557 2903
visitgenoa.it
lamialiguria.it

Cattedrale di San Lorenzo
✉ Piazza San Lorenzo
☎ 010 209 1863
🕐 Closed 12 p.m.– 3 p.m. & Sun. a.m.

With its strategic position and fine natural harbor, Genoa's historical rise was almost inevitable. During its 14th-century heyday, the territories of this city-state extended as far as Syria, North Africa, and Crimea. Defeat by Venice in 1380 curtailed maritime expansion, but within two centuries, diversification into banking and other areas of trade had restored its primacy. Great families enriched the city with palaces, parks, and works of art, a second golden age undermined by the eventual loss of colonies to Venice and the Ottomans and the increasing share of trade taken by other Mediterranean ports.

Genoa's historic center is a jumble of streets and alleys with twists, turns, and ever changing levels. Begin in **Piazza Matteotti,** one of the larger squares, dominated by the gargantuan **Palazzo Ducale** *(tel 010 817 1600, palazzoducale.genova .it).* Built over several centuries as the erstwhile home of Genoa's ruling medieval doges, it now hosts exhibitions and other cultural events. From here, walk a few steps west to San Lorenzo.

San Lorenzo & Around

Cattedrale di San Lorenzo is Genoa's cathedral. Begun in the ninth century and completed in 1118, it received countless embellishments over the centuries, creating a medley of styles inside and out. The interior's broadly baroque appearance is tempered by the great **Cappella di San Giovanni,** a glorious Renaissance chapel (1451–1465) dedicated to St. John the Baptist, Genoa's patron saint. The cappella contains a 13th-century French sarcophagus once said to have concealed the remains of St. John the Baptist. In the church's **treasury** *($)*, entered from the sacristy, is the "Sacro Catino," a blue platter reputedly used to serve up the saint's head to Salome. Also here is a green glass bowl said to have been used during the Last Supper.

Just north of San Lorenzo stands **Piazza San Matteo,** one of Genoa's most quaint squares—its small church and old houses were rebuilt and restored in 1278. To the south lie the best of old Genoa's many churches. Charming **San Donato** has a lovely octagonal bell tower, doorway, and a painting of the "Adoration of the Magi" by Joos van Cleve, while Gothic **Sant'Agostino** nearby is worth a look for its museum of frescoes, sculptures, and archaeological fragments.

Romanesque **Santa Maria Castello** *(off Piazza Embriaci)* owes its name to an earlier Roman *castrum* (castle) on the site—a few ruins from that period still survive. The church also has several worthwhile frescoes and sculptures, but its most compelling treasures lie in the adjoining Dominican convent. Here the lower loggia of the second cloister features captivating 15th-century frescoes, while the upper loggia has a monochrome fresco of St. Dominic and a tabernacle of the Trinity, both late 15th-century Genoese works.

Via Garibaldi

Via Garibaldi is often called the most beautiful street in Italy. Laid out between 1551 and 1558, the Strada Nuova, or New Road, as it was then called, was created for newly rich merchants eager to escape the cramped confines of the medieval quarter. Today, many of its palaces have been converted into offices or dazzling stores, although the facades, fountains, frescoes, and half-hidden interior gardens remain as grand as ever.

Palace follows palace in a splendid parade: the Palazzo Cambiaso at No. 1, Palazzo Parodi (No. 3), Palazzo Carrega-Cataldi (No. 4), Palazzo Doria (No. 6), and Palazzo Podestà (No. 7). The **Palazzo**

Sant'Agostino

✉ Piazza Sarzano 35

☎ 010 251 1263

🕐 Closed Mon.

💲 $

The **Card Musei** *(museidigenova.it, $$$$–$$$$$)* offers unlimited admission to 21 of Genoa's major museums for 24 or 48 hours. It is available at the participating museums.

Christopher Columbus

Remarkably little is known of Christopher Columbus (1451–1506). The navigator's handwritten will of 1498 states he was born in Genoa, but old city registers only record the name of his father, a weaver. Some scholars claim he was born in Piacenza in Emilia-Romagna; others have him as Swiss, Corsican, French, or English. Some say he was a Spanish Jew forced into Italian exile by persecution, while a handful claim he was a Levantine corsair, Giorgio Bissipat. Genoa does not care: Cristoforo Colombo, as he is known in Italian, appears at every turn, from numerous statues and paintings to the streets, piazzas, fountains, bars, and city airport that bear his name.

Palazzo Doria-Tursi, Palazzo Bianco, & Palazzo Rosso

- ✉ Palazzo Doria-Tursi: Via Garibaldi 9
- ✉ Palazzo Bianco: Via Garibaldi 11
- ✉ Palazzo Rosso: Via Garibaldi 18
- ☎ 010 557 2193
- 🕐 Closed Mon.
- 💲 $$ single combined ticket for all three palaces

Palazzo Spinola

- ✉ Piazza Pellicceria 1
- ☎ 010 270 5300
- 🕐 Closed Sun. & Mon.
- 💲 $ or $$ combined ticket with Palazzo Reale

Acquario

- ✉ Ponte Spinola, Strada Aldo Moro
- ☎ 010 23451
- 💲 $$$

acquariodigenova.it

Palazzo Reale

- ✉ Via Balbi 10
- ☎ 010 271 0236
- 🕐 Closed p.m. Mon., Tues. & Wed.; a.m. Sat. & Sun.
- 💲 $

palazzorealegenova
.beniculturali.it

Doria-Tursi (No. 9) is now the town hall and home to a municipal art museum that includes three letters by Christopher Columbus and a violin that belonged to the famous Genoa-born violinist Nicolò Paganini (1782–1840).

Another essential stop is the **Palazzo Bianco** at No. 11, home to one of the city's principal art collections. Some of the paintings are by worthy but otherwise little known Genoese artists, but there are also pieces by high-profile Italian masters—Caravaggio, Veronese, and Filippino Lippi among them—as well as exceptional Dutch and Flemish works by Memling ("Christ Blessing"), Joos van Cleve ("Madonna and Child"), and Jan Provost ("St. Peter").

Virtually opposite the Palazzo Bianco lies the **Palazzo Rosso** (No. 18), where you can admire similarly outstanding paintings. These include portraits by Antony Van Dyck and paintings by Dürer, Veronese, Palma il Vecchio, and lesser Genoese artists.

Palazzo Spinola

The third of Genoa's triumvirate of galleries, the Palazzo Spinola lies to the southwest of the Palazzo Rosso. The beautifully appointed salons from the 17th and 18th centuries in which the exhibits are hung are almost as beguiling as the artwork. Genoese artists naturally figure large—Lazzaro Tavarone's ceiling frescoes (1615) are particularly fine—but there are also paintings of wider renown, notably Joos van Cleve's sublime "Adoration of the Magi," Antonello

da Messina's "Ecce Homo," Rubens' equestrian portrait of Gio Carlo Doria, and Van Dyck's winsome "Portrait of Lady and Child."

Around Genoa's Port

Celebrations in 1992 to commemorate the 500th anniversary of Columbus's voyage to the New World saw much of Genoa spruced up, in particular the port, where Renzo Piano, one of Europe's leading architects, transformed previously derelict swaths of waterfront. By far the most popular sight is the **Acquario,** a state-of-the-art and very expensive aquarium—Europe's second largest—based around 50 vast basins and containing some 20,000 marine creatures. Here you can see dolphins, seals, sharks, and penguins, along with countless smaller fish and marine life.

With a combination ticket, visitors can enjoy other interesting attractions in the old port such as the **Galata Museo del Mare** *(Calata de Mari, tel 010 234 5655, closed Mon. Nov.–Feb., galatamuseo delmare.it, $$–$$$),* the largest maritime museum in the Mediterranean. Using captivating, interactive displays, visitors can explore the relationship between man and the sea: expeditions, migration, journeys, and even storms!

North of the Acquario, be sure to visit the sumptuous **Palazzo Reale,** begun by the patrician Balbi family in the 17th century, with its host of lavishly decorated salons and chambers and fine temporary exhibitions. ■

PORTOFINO

Portofino is the jewel of an already gloriously embellished coastline. Romantic and beautiful, this former fishing village is now one of Italy's most exclusive and expensive little resorts. When you tire of the yachts, the exclusive stores, the summer crowds, the tangle of cobbled streets, the chic cafés, and the candlelit restaurants, then you can stroll through pine-scented woodlands or follow one of the easy trails that crisscross the promontory above the village.

Explore the village and then walk to the church of **San Giorgio** *(Salita San Giorgio),* home to the reputed relics of San Giorgio (St. George), brought from the Holy Land in the 12th century by homeward-bound crusaders. Then go past the old castle and follow the path to the lighthouse, a walk of about 2.5 miles (4 km). This is the most popular of many local walks, and you can see why, for the views, particularly at dusk, are ones you will take to the grave. Almost equally magical vistas are possible from the corniche road linking the village with the resort town of Santa Margherita Ligure.

Parco Naturale Regionale di Portofino

Much of the promontory above Portofino is protected by the Parco Naturale Regionale di Portofino, where Aleppo and maritime pines flourish along with a fragrant undergrowth of herbs, juniper, heathers, cistus, and more than 700 species of wildflowers. All manner of tranquil paths fan out across the area from Portofino and from **Camogli,** a fishing village on the promontory's western edge. The best of the longer walks from Portofino is to **San Fruttuoso,** an 11th-century monastery idyllically set amid olives and pines at the head of a narrow bay. This 4-mile (6.5 km) walk takes some five hours round-trip, but you could make either outward or return legs (or both) by boat, an unbeatable way to enjoy the area's beautiful coastal scenery firsthand. ∎

Portofino

🗺 85 E2

Visitor Information

✉ Via Roma 35

☎ 0185 269 024

🕐 Closed 12:30 p.m.–2:30 p.m.

comune.portofino .genova.it

Parco Naturale Regionale di Portofino

Visitor Information

✉ Viale Rainusso 1, Santa Margherita Ligure

☎ 0185 289 479

parcoportofino.it

EXPERIENCE: Search for Cetaceans

In the water in front of you, a school of dolphins; in the distance, the cliffs and hazy mountains of the beautiful Ligurian coast. The sea off Liguria has one of the Mediterranean's highest populations of whales and dolphins, and from mid-May to mid-September it is possible to join week-long scientific research cruises as a paying volunteer. You'll help local experts of a nonprofit Italian organization gather and record data on the various cetacean populations, and also receive lectures on marine biology and conservation. Participants—6 to 12 per course—are also full members of the crew aboard the research vessel. Training is given, and no experience of the sea or research is required. Costs start at €795 ($895), excluding flights; visit *responsibletravel.com* or *whalesand dolphins.tethys.org* for more information.

CINQUE TERRE

Most secrets are eventually discovered, and this, sadly, is true of the Cinque Terre (Five Lands), a quintet of tiny seafront villages that until recently were all but inaccessible by road and all but unknown to visitors. So far the villages' charms remain unspoiled, as does the allure of their surrounding countryside, which is a jumble of plunging cliffs, vineyards, olive groves, and steeply terraced slopes.

Parco Nazionale delle Cinque Terre

Visitor Information

✉ Via di Scovolo, railway station, Manarola

☎ 0187 762600

parconazionale 5terre.it

prolocomonterosso .it

Cinque Terre

📍 85 E1–E2

Visitor Information

✉ Railway station, Riomaggiore

☎ 0187 920 633

✉ Railway station, Corniglia

☎ 0187 812 523

✉ Railway station, Vernazza

☎ 0187 812 533

✉ Railway station, Monterosso

☎ 0187 817 059

Levanto

📍 85 E2

Visitor Information

✉ Piazza Cavour

☎ 0187 808 125

🕐 Closed 1 p.m.– 3 p.m. & Sun. p.m.

visitlevanto.it

■ Tiny Manarola, picturesquely squeezed between the hills and the sea

You can take a car to most of the villages, but parking is all but impossible and the roads are a nightmare of twists, turns, and hellish grades. Instead, base yourself in one place or shuttle from village to village on foot, by rail, or—best of all—by boat. Accommodations are often in short supply, but try **Levanto,** a pleasant town to the north with plenty of hotels.

The attractions of all five villages are similar: intimate pebbly beaches, tiny coves, crisp white wines, romantic fish restaurants, and quaint huddles of pastel-colored houses. None should disappoint, and you'll soon find your own favorite. When you do want to move on, the trains and boats can whisk you to a neighboring village in minutes.

For many, **Manarola** is the favorite, closely followed by **Vernazza.** The most popular and, perhaps, least alluring village is **Monterosso,** but it has the largest beach and best choice of accommodations. **Riomaggiore,** too, has plenty of places to stay and is prettier. **Corniglia,** high above the sea, is the smallest village, a farming rather than fishing community, but privy to a long shingle beach. Try a little hiking—local visitor centers have details. The famous Via dell'Amore (Path of Love) is closed for maintenance until 2021 but there are many other paths to discover, possibly with an authorized, expert guide. ■

EXPERIENCE: Help Protect the Cinque Terre

The Cinque Terre is one of Europe's supreme landscapes, a unique combination of distinct communities with a remarkable social and historic heritage, and an environment that blends the sea, cliffs, and mountainous hinterland with the extraordinary terraces and 5,000 miles (8,000 km) of drystone walls of the man-made landscape.

But the Cinque Terre is also a landscape under threat. Only a tiny portion of the area remains under cultivation now, following the drift from agriculture and peasant subsistence farming in the 1950s—and terraces for vines and olives that were the work of centuries have crumbled in little under a generation. Once isolated villages are now prey to mass tourism, with the problems this brings: Tiny Vernazza's population of 800, for example, easily doubles on most summer days, and hikers on the celebrated trails between the Cinque Terre villages—Manarola, Vernazza, Monterosso, Riomaggiore, and Corniglia—can contribute to coastal erosion. This is why we suggest you also travel the "high" paths that run above the towns and that are less crowded. As you do, please follow the park's rules and signage.

Many organizations exist to help protect the area. You can find them by visiting sites such as *savevernazza.com,* or by searching online with keywords such as "volontario" or "volontari" with "Cinque Terre." You might join one of several volunteer programs that vary each year. These might include helping the local masons still skilled in the art of dry-stone walling repair terraces above

the villages, or "Vintage in Vernazza," where you help pick and transport grapes on the steep slopes, helping preserve a unique system of agriculture in decline due to the labor-intensive approach demanded by the terrain.

Longer volunteer opportunities to work in the area—two- to four-week stays—are offered by **Legambiente** *(legambiente.it),* one of Italy's leading and most respected nonprofit environmental organizations. Legambiente began working with the Cinque Terre National Park authorities in 2002. It now coordinates work camps centered on Riomaggiore, with volunteers involved in food production and the maintenance of paths and terraces.

From the villages you will climb quickly and steeply on trails used for millennia by workers in the olive groves and vineyards, carrying what you need for the day while enjoying superb views of the villages and the cliffs and other magnificent sceneries. You'll then help repair walls and terraces damaged by landslips, or replace guardrails and other parts of the trails, before a break for lunch in the shade of an olive grove.

For more information about volunteering with Legambiente and others, visit *vap.org.uk* (search for "Italy," "Cinque Terre," or "Riomaggiore"). Or, if your Italian is proficient, search for "Campi di Volontariato" on Legambiente's website.

■ The Cinque Terre's terraces have been cultivated for centuries.

More Places to Visit in Northwest Italy

Asti

The Piedmontese town of Asti sits at the heart of some of northern Italy's finest wine country and is best known for its eponymous sparkling white wine, Asti Spumante. The town's most dramatic festival, an annual horse race combined with much medieval pageantry, coincides with its wine fair and the first hints of the wine harvest, or *vendemmia*, in late September.

Many of the town's older monuments lie on or close to the main street, Corso Vittorio Alfieri, named after local poet and dramatist Vittorio Alfieri (1749–1803). Worth seeing are the crop of medieval towers at the street's western end, the 14th-century Gothic **Duomo,** and the 15th-century church of **San Pietro** *(Corso Vittorio Alfieri 2, tel 0141 399 489, closed Mon. & 1 p.m.–3/4 p.m., $),* celebrated for its 17th-century frescoes, cloister, and circular Romanesque baptistery. Just west of the central Piazza Alfieri lies the church of **Collegiata di San Secondo,** founded in the 13th century and distinguished by a series of 15th-century frescoes and a fine Renaissance altarpiece by Gandolfino d'Asti. *astiturismo.it* ⓜ 84 C3 **Visitor Information** ✉ Piazza Vittorio Alfieri 34 ☎ 0141 530 357 🕐 Closed Mon.–Sat. 1 p.m.–2 p.m. & 1 p.m.–1:30 p.m. Sun.

Lerici

At the easternmost end of the so-called Gulf of Poets lies a wealth of charming little villages with a quiet, picturesque atmosphere. It's not surprising that Lerici, Tellaro, and San Terenzo have all hosted a number of famous guests in the past: D. H. Lawrence, P. B. Shelley, and Byron. A former fishing village, Lerici sits on a bay under a glowering 13th-century Pisan fortress, from which there are superb views. Prettily painted houses line the waterfront, where you can watch boats, eat, and drink in the many bars and restaurants, or relax on the beaches. *comune.lerici.sp.it* ⓜ 85 F1 **Visitor Information** ✉ Via Biaggini 6 ☎ 0187 969 164

Portovenere

Western border of the Gulf of Poets, on the Riviera di Levante, the town seduces visitors with its harbor, colored houses, and knot of little streets. It is part of the national park of the same name, which includes the town and the group of islands that lie in front of it–a marvel of antique architecture and uncontaminated Mediterranean nature. Sights include the church of **San Pietro,** founded in the sixth century. From its location at the end of the waterfront, you can enjoy views of the island of Palmaria, the biggest of the archipelago. In the upper village, visit the 12th-century church of **San Lorenzo.** Note the relief above the door that shows the saint's martyrdom. Then clamber to the ramparts around the 16th-century **fortress** for a breathtaking panorama that takes in Lerici and the cliffs girding the Cinque Terre to the west. *portovenere.com, parconaturaleportovenere.it* ⓜ 85 E1 **Visitor Information** ✉ Piazza Bastreri 7 ☎ 0187 790 961 🕐 Closed 12 p.m.–3 p.m & Wed.

Sacra di San Michele

Those looking for the quintessential medieval monastery must visit Sacra di San Michele. Founded before A.D. 1000, eventually it became one of Europe's most powerful religious foundations, controlling more than 140 sister houses across Italy, France, and Spain. It appears a fortress, so dark and forbidding are its walls, so lofty and lonely its position—perched at an elevation of 3,156 feet (962 m). Some 154 rock-hewn steps, the **Scalone dei Morti** (Stairs of the Dead), lead to the main Portale dello Zodiaco, a Romanesque portal with fine early carvings. Inside, the monastery church features a variety of medieval paintings, less memorable, if truth be told, than the magnificent view from the church's esplanade. *www.sacradisanmichele.com* ⓜ 84 B4 ✉ Via alla Sacra, Sant'Ambrogio ☎ 011 939 130 🕐 Closed Mon. Oct.–Mar. & 12:30 p.m.–2:30 p.m. (Jul.–Aug. open daily) 💲 $$ 🚆 Train from Turin to Avigliana, then infrequent bus

A region known for bustling Milan—Italy's business capital—many beautiful, smaller historic towns, and idyllic lakes and mountains

LOMBARDY & THE LAKES

A luxuriant garden on Isola Bella, one of the Isole Borromee

LOMBARDY & THE LAKES

Lombardy rises from the Alpine heights ranged along its border with Switzerland, meanders through the lower and more lyrical landscapes of the Italian Lakes, and then expires gently on the great city-studded plains of the Po River. Named after the Lombards, sixth-century invaders from northern Europe, the region has a long and distinguished history.

The Plain of Lombardy offers little by way of scenic reward, save for the distant shadowy outline of the Alps. Cities are its raison d'être, commerce its driving force. The biggest city, Milan, is Italy's mercantile heart. Lombardy is also an agricultural region, its vast fields and floodplains perfectly suited to farming on an almost industrial scale: Fruit, cereals, and market gardening are all big business, and *risotto* (rice), not pasta, is the region's gastronomic mainstay.

Lombardy's prosperity is not a modern phenomenon, for powerful city-states held sway throughout much of the medieval period. And where there were powerful city-states in Italy, backed by powerful noble families with powers of patronage, there were usually jewel-like medieval city centers, majestic palaces, and sublime works of art. Thus in Milan, where the presiding dynastic families were the Sforzas and Viscontis, the city's modern appearance is belied by an extraordinary range of art-filled palaces

and galleries. In Mantua, one of Italy's most unexpected treasures, the Gonzaga family oversaw the creation of a flourishing court and two stupendous palaces. Smaller centers are no less alluring, not least Bergamo, a lofty hilltop citadel, and sleepy Cremona, birthplace of the violin maker Antonio Stradivari.

The Italian Lakes

Carved by glaciers, the lakes strung across northern Italy have been celebrated by poets and painters for centuries. Their shores, blessed with mild weather, are scattered with quaint villages, venerable resorts, soaring mountains, and an array of villas and luxuriant gardens. Few areas are as romantic or as scenic, at least where the beauty and tranquility have not been compromised by fast, modern roads, pollution, and modern building occasionally blocking once peerless vistas.

This is just a gentle word of warning, for the good far outweighs the bad. Como, Maggiore, and Garda are the most celebrated; Orta and Iseo are

smaller and less known, while Lugano and Maggiore are shared with Switzerland. Maggiore is the most visited, Como the most beautiful. Spring, when the gardens are in bloom, is sublime. Twisting lakeside roads offer excellent touring routes, and you can just as easily get around by train. Traveling by boat is a sightseeing must—all the lakes are crisscrossed by numerous car and passenger ferries.

There are endless opportunities for outdoor activities, all easily arranged on the spot. Visitor centers can provide details of golf courses, water-sport centers, and the many well-mapped hiking trails in the area. If the lake scenery seems too gentle, head north to the rugged beauty of the Alps, in particular the Parco Nazionale dello Stelvio, one of the country's premier parks. ■

MILAN

Italy's second city (population 1.4 million) is a brisk metropolis. Modern and northern European in manner and appearance, Milan (Milano) seems to have sacrificed art and beauty to the demands of style, fashion, and high finance. Amid the smart stores and sleek office blocks, however, shelter Europe's most extravagant Gothic cathedral, the world's most famous opera house, northern Italy's finest art gallery, and Leonardo da Vinci's celebrated "Last Supper."

■ A statue of Vittorio Emanuele II, the first king of a unified Italy, stands in the Piazza del Duomo.

Milan
🗺 105 B3
Visitor Information
✉ Piazza Duomo 14
☎ 02 8845 5555
turismo.milano.it
in-lombardia.it

Central Milan is not a difficult area to explore. Begin your tour in Piazza del Duomo, easily reached on foot, by cab, or by subway (*Metropolitana* or *Metro* in Italian). From here you can see the Duomo (Cathedral) before walking north to take in the nearby Teatro alla Scala opera house. Still on foot, you can then visit a trio of galleries to the north, among them the Brera, Milan's principal gallery. Nearby is the Quadrilatero, or rectangle, the name given to an area of fashion houses and luxury stores bounded by four streets: Via Monte Napoleone,

Via della Spiga, Via Borgospesso, and Via Sant'Andrea. Moving west, and still within walking distance, lies the Castello Sforzesco, a bristling medieval fortress. Leonardo's "Last Supper" is in the church of Santa Maria delle Grazie, several blocks southwest.

History

Location has long been Milan's strong suit—the city's power grew from its position astride vital trading routes. Home to the bulk of the Roman army in the third century B.C., Mediolanum, as the city was known, functioned as the empire's effective capital from

A.D. 286 to 402—it was here, for example, in A.D. 313, that the emperor Constantine issued his edict recognizing Christianity.

In the Middle Ages, the city became one of Italy's most powerful city-states, ruled by the Visconti and Sforza families, under whom it acquired the title of the "New Athens," due to the cultural sophistication of its courts. Capitulation to the French in 1499 prefaced several centuries of foreign interference, including periods of Spanish, Austrian, and Napoleonic domination. But nothing could stop its growth and today it represents the driving force of the nation in terms of economy and finance, with all of the resulting advantages and disadvantages.

Piazza del Duomo

The **Duomo,** Milan's cathedral, is not to all tastes. To fans of Gothic architecture, it is a masterpiece of decorative elaboration: "A poem in marble," remarked Mark Twain in *Innocents Abroad* (1869). It is adorned with over 3,400 statues, 135 spires, 96 gargoyles, and around half a mile (1 km) of tracery. To more demanding palates it is all too much: "an awful failure," according to Oscar Wilde.

Founded in 1386, the building was instigated by Gian Galeazzo Visconti, Milan's ruler of the time, hopeful that the commission would persuade Heaven to reward him with a male heir. Work continued for almost five centuries, the finishing touches being added on Napoleon's orders in 1807.

After the exterior's stonework pyrotechnics, the interior might disappoint. Size is the abiding impression—it comes as no surprise to discover that, at 522 feet (159 m) long by 305 feet (93 m) wide, the Duomo is Europe's third

Duomo

✉ Piazza del Duomo; Piazza del Duomo 14a (Info Point)

☎ 02 7202 3375

🕐 Cathedral, crypt, & treasury closed during services

💲 Duomo $; Terraces $$$ (on foot) or $$$$ (elevator); Archaeological area $. Tickets can be bought online

🚇 Metro: Duomo

duomomilano.it

A Changing Metropolis

Visitors to Milan can enjoy the sights of an extremely modern city, full of ancient and modern history, as well rich in charm and full of life.

The **Navigli** are canals that were once part of an extensive, complex system used for defense, water supplies and transportation of both people and cargo. There are few canals remaining but there is a project to re-open others. The two most popular are connected by a dock that was modernized for Expo 2015 and, as a favorite place to shop or have a drink, they pulsate with life. Nearby Via Tortona is full of exhibitions and design events during the Milan Furniture Fair. Here the **MUDEC** *(Museum of Cultures, Via Tortona 56, tel 02 54917, closed Mon. a.m., $–$$, mudec.it)* rose from the ashes of a former industrial complex in 2014. It houses an important permanent collection as well as temporary exhibits.

In recent years, international star architects have left their mark in some neighborhoods, including **Porta Nuova,** near the Garibaldi Station. At its heart is the futuristic Piazza Gae Aulenti. From the square, visitors can admire the nearby Bosco Verticale, or Vertical Forest, a world famous project with residential skyscrapers, which "house" trees that look at the metropolis from above and represent the birth of a new relationship between nature and the city.

largest church after St. Peter's Basilica in Vatican City and Spain's Seville Cathedral. The stained glass, dating back in places to the 15th century, is some of Europe's most extensive, while embedded in the nave near the entrance is the world's largest sundial (1786).

Other key works of art include a seven-branched, bronze candelabrum (14th century) of French or German origin in the north transept, and in the south transept, a macabre statue (1562) of St. Bartholomew, martyred by being flayed alive (the saint is carrying his folded skin). The same transept contains a lavish monument to Gian Giacomo Medici (1560–1563) and, outside, the entrance to the **roof** *($$)*, a spot you must visit to enjoy the exterior's decoration—some wonderful gables, pinnacles, and gargoyles—and views to the distant Alps that on a clear day extend to the Matterhorn.

Just south of the cathedral stands the **Palazzo Reale,** a royal palace built for the Austrian Grand Dukes in the 18th century. Today, one wing contains the cathedral museum, the **Museo del Duomo** *(Piazza del Duomo 12, tel 02 0202, admission included with Duomo entrance),* whose highlights are a variety of casts taken from the cathedral's statues, a lovely wooden model (1519) of the Duomo, and Tintoretto's "The Infant Christ Among the Doctors of the Church." The palace also hosts regular, major exhibitions *(closed Mon. a.m.).*

To the north of the cathedral lies the **Galleria Vittorio Emanuele II,** a beautiful glass-enclosed arcade (1865): A belle epoque masterpiece, it is best admired from one of the cafés nestled between its offices and luxury stores. Known to the Milanese as the city's *salotto,* or salon, it is a great place to escape sightseeing duties. Its unfortunate designer, Giuseppe Mengoni, tumbled through the roof and died just days before its inauguration in

Cathedral's spires and pinnacles were added in the 19th century.

17th-century central portal

1877. Watch to see if anyone pays attention to the zodiac mosaic on the pavement beneath the main cupola—standing on Taurus's testicles is supposed to bring good luck.

Piazza della Scala

Walk through the Galleria and you come to Piazza della Scala. On your left stands the world's most distinguished opera house, **Teatro alla Scala.** Inaugurated in 1778, the building took its name from an earlier church on the site, although much of the present plain-faced building

dates from 1946, when it was reopened after war damage. Renovations to the 2,800-seat auditorium and its vast stage were completed in 2004.

Tours take in the theater boxes for a peek at the sumptuous interior and famous gargantuan chandelier. You might also visit the **Museo Teatrale alla Scala,** which contains such operatic memorabilia as past sets, costumes, portraits, and Verdi's top hat.

Museo Teatrale alla Scala

Largo Ghiringhelli 1, Piazza della Scala

02 8879 7473 museum, 02 7200 3744 opera house

$$

Metro: Duomo

museoscala.org

teatroallascala.org

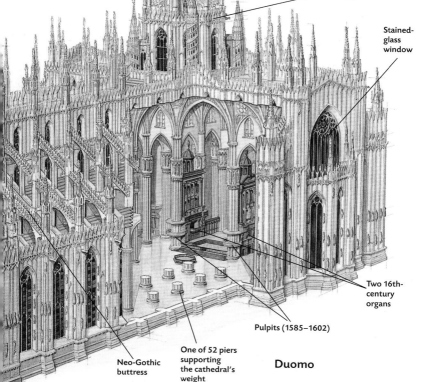

Octagonal drum by Giovanni Antonio Amadeo (1490–1500)

Stained-glass window

Two 16th-century organs

Pulpits (1585–1602)

One of 52 piers supporting the cathedral's weight

Neo-Gothic buttress

Duomo

Museo Poldi-Pezzoli

- ✉ Via Alessandro Manzoni 12
- ☎ 02 794 889
- 🕐 Closed Tues. & public holidays
- 💲 $$
- Ⓜ Metro: Montenapoleone

museopoldipezzoli.it

Museo Bagatti Valsecchi

- ✉ Via Gesù 5
- ☎ 02 7600 6132
- 🕐 Closed Tues.– Sun. a.m. & all day Mon.
- 💲 $$ (discounted on Wed.)
- Ⓜ Metro: Montenapoleone

museobagatti valsecchi.org

NOTE: Abbonamento Musei (*$$$$, lombardia. abbonamentomusei.it.*) offers unlimited free admission for 365 days to the more than 100 museums in the region (with the possibility to include the Piedmont region, *$$$$$*) as well as discounts on performances and events. The MilanoCard Pass (*milanocard.it*) offers free access to transportation and discounts on 200 tourist attractions (museums, shops and restaurants) for 24, 48, or 72 hours.

North of Piazza della Scala stretches Via Alessandro Manzoni, one of the city's busier and more fashionable streets. A short way up on the right stands the **Museo Poldi-Pezzoli,** home to an enchanting collection bequeathed to the city by wealthy aristocrat Giacomo Poldi-Pezzoli in 1879. Giacomo's eclectic taste ensured a wonderfully diverse collection of art and artifacts—you'll find everything from weapons, clocks, cutlery, and fabrics to bronzes, jewelry, paintings, porcelain, and furniture. The carpet and fabric collections, in particular, are outstanding.

Foremost among the museum's paintings are a "Madonna and Child" and "Portrait of a Man" by Mantegna; "St. Nicholas of Tolentino" by Piero della Francesca; a "Madonna" and a "Pietà" by Botticelli; a Tuscan picture of "Artemesia,"; the "Pietà" by Giovanni Bellini; and the gallery's most famous work, Antonio or Piero del Pollaiolo's "Portrait of a Young Woman." Many of these works generally hang in the Salone Dorato, or Golden Salon, the grandest of a series of rooms whose magnificent decoration is as alluring as the works of art themselves.

Museo Bagatti Valsecchi

After the Poldi-Pezzoli collection, you have a choice between another palace or more paintings. Turn left on Via Borgonuovo and you come to the Pinacoteca di Brera (see page opposite); turn right on Via Monte Napoleone, one of Milan's premier shopping

INSIDER TIP:

The wonderful neighborhood just east of Corso Venezia and Via Senato is a must-see. Both Via Serbelloni and Via Mozart are lined with incredible, architecturally interesting houses.

—ANTONY SHUGAAR
National Geographic contributor

streets, and you reach the **Palazzo Bagatti Valsecchi**. Begun in 1876, the palace is a Renaissance pastiche inside and out, the interior having been decorated after 1887 by its owners, Fausto and Giuseppe Bagatti Valsecchi, with original works of art or persuasive 19th-century copies. The house remained in the Valsecchi family until 1974 and opened as a museum in 1994. Like the Poldi-Pezzoli, the palace interior is as interesting for its decor as its art and artifacts, its decorative style reflecting the taste for Renaissance ornamentation that prevailed in much of late 19th-century Italy.

Pinacoteca di Brera

The Brera art gallery contains one of Italy's finest collections of paintings displayed through 38 renovated rooms. Although founded in 1776, it owes much to the efforts of Napoleon, who gathered works from churches and palaces across Italy to create a collection worthy of a city he had earmarked as capital of his "Cisalpine Republic."

Pinacoteca di Brera

- ✉ Via Brera 28
- ☎ 02 7226 3264
- 🕐 Closed Mon.
- 💲 $$ (free some Sat. & Sun.)
- 🚇 Metro: Montenapoleone, Lanza

**www.brera.beni
culturali.it**

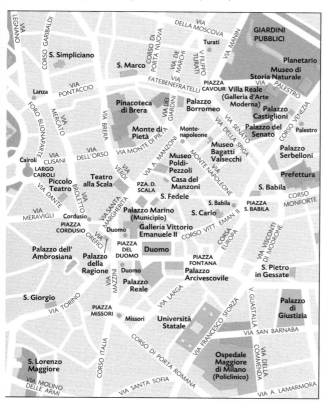

EXPERIENCE: A Night at La Scala

At La Scala, Italy's leading opera house, high-quality performances and sumptuous productions are virtually guaranteed. Here you experience the Italian opera-going public at its most stylish, a spectacle in itself—fine furs, diamonds, women in couture, men in the best cut evening wear—so be sure to dress the part.

This is also an opera crowd at its most critical and knowledgeable. If members of the audience disapprove of a production, expect them to make their feelings known. The expectant hush before the overture can be replaced by boos and catcalls as the performance wears on

and, in one or two celebrated cases, with opera stars flouncing off stage, never to return. There's sometimes a drama within a drama at the opera.

La Scala itself offers a glorious and extravagant backdrop for the music and the singing. The entire interior was renovated between 2002 and 2004, with everything replaced or refurbished.

The opera season runs from December 7, the feast day of Sant'Ambrogio (St. Ambrose), Milan's patron saint, to June. Book tickets online or in person (no phone sales) well in advance, as they sell out quickly (*teatroallascala.org*, $$$$$).

Castello Sforzesco

- ✉ Piazza Castello
- ☎ 02 8846 3700
- 🕐 Castle open daily, museums closed Mon.
- 💲 Castle free, museums $$
- Ⓜ Metro: Cadorna, Lanza, & Cairoli

milanocastello.it

Palazzo dell'Ambrosiana

- ✉ Piazza Pio XI 2
- ☎ 02 806 921
- 🕐 Closed Mon.
- 💲 $$
- Ⓜ Metro: Duomo

www.ambrosiana.it

In **Rooms 1–18,** medieval and renaissance painters, mostly of the Venetian school and from Lombardy, figure large, notably Giovanni Bellini, with a poignant "Pietà," and Mantegna, whose "Dead Christ" is among the gallery's most famous works. Veronese's "Supper at the House of Simon," "St. Mark Preaching in Alexandria," by Gentile and Giovanni Bellini, and Bernardino Luini's "Madonna del Roseto" also clamor for attention. This said, there are almost equally compelling works by Carpaccio, Tintoretto, Lorenzo Lotto, and Cima da Conegliano.

Rooms 20–30 are a journey into renaissance in Emilia-Romagna and central Italy, and into the works of great names. Visitors will admire Piero della Francesca's last documented work, the "Montefeltro Altarpiece," which portrays the Madonna surrounded by saints and members of Urbino's ruling Montefeltro family, Raphael's "Marriage of the Virgin", and the superb "Supper at Emmaus" by Caravaggio.

The last rooms show outstanding works by European artists and 18th- and 19th-century Italian paintings.

Castello Sforzesco

West of the Brera rises Milan's most imperious monument, the gaunt Castello Sforzesco, a huge redbrick fortress of high towers and bristling defensive walls. Begun by the Visconti in the 14th century, it was virtually destroyed in 1447 by mobs demonstrating against the family's monopoly of power, only to be rebuilt soon after by another dynastic clan, the Sforzas. It was never quite the same after Milan's defeat by the French in 1499, serving as little more than a glorified barracks until its conversion, in 1904, for use as a library, archive, and municipal museum.

Today, it contains several museums. The art gallery and fine arts museum are essential ports of call, but the others are minor affairs devoted to musical instruments, prints, photography, and archaeological exhibits. Highlights of the former, the **Pinacoteca** and **Museo d'Arte Antica,** are a polyptych by Mantegna, the "Pala Trivulzio" (1497), Bambaia's 1525 tomb and tomb reliefs of Gaston de Foix, and the unfinished "Rondanini Pietà," the last known work of Michelangelo. To the castle's north stretches the **Parco Sempione** (1893), Milan's largest, and most central, public park.

Palazzo dell'Ambrosiana

Milan's parade of art-filled palaces and galleries continues with the Palazzo dell'Ambrosiana (1609), home to a famous library founded in the 17th century by Cardinal Federico Borromeo (1564–1631), archbishop of the city, and to a first-floor gallery crammed with Lombard, Venetian, and Florentine masterpieces. Among the library's 750,000 volumes and 35,000 manuscripts are drawings by Leonardo da Vinci, a fifth-century copy of The Iliad, and early editions of works by Dante, Virgil, and Boccaccio.

Among the works of art, the prize exhibits are a cartoon by Raphael of his painting "The School of Athens" (now in the Vatican), a "Portrait of a Musician" (1485) by Leonardo da Vinci, and a fine "Portrait of a Young Woman" by one of Leonardo da Vinci's pupils, Ambrogio de Predis. Other paintings worthy of note are Caravaggio's "Basket of Fruit" (1596), one of the first still lifes in Italian art, and works by Botticelli, Ghirlandaio, Pinturicchio, Titian, and Tintoretto.

Sant'Ambrogio

About half a mile (1 km) west of the Palazzo dell'Ambrosiana, Sant'Ambrogio is Milan's most important church. Founded in 379 by Milan's patron saint

■ **Castello Sforzesco's imposing Filarete tower, rebuilt in 1905**

(the remains of German-born St. Ambrose, who died in 390, still rest in the crypt), the building's 11th–12th-century Romanesque form served as a model for countless Lombard Romanesque basilica churches across northern Italy.

Twin bell towers flank the austere facade and its stunning atrium (1088), one from the 9th century on the right, another from

Sant'Ambrogio

✉ Piazza Sant'
   Ambrogio 15

☎ 02 8645 0895

🕐 Closed for
   services, 12:30
   p.m.–2:30 p.m.
   Mon.–Sat., &
   Sun. a.m.

🚇 Metro:
   Sant'Ambrogio

**basilicasant
ambrogio.it**

Santa Maria delle Grazie

- ✉ Piazza Santa Maria delle Grazie 2
- ☎ 02 467 6111
- 🕐 Church closed 12:20 p.m.–3:30 p.m. Mon.–Sat. & Sun. a.m.; "Last Supper" closed Mon.
- 💲 "Last Supper" $$$
- 🚇 Metro: Cadorna

NOTE: Advance reservations (tel 02 8942 1146 or 02 9280 0360 or online at vivaticket.it) are required to see the "Last Supper," often at least a month ahead in summer and on weekends, for which there is an additional charge ($). Visits last 15 minutes, with 30 visitors per tour.

the 12th century on the left. The restored main portal features 9th-century bronze panels, probably made at about the same time as the interior's superb ciborium (in the sanctuary) and ravishing gold, silver, and jewel-studded high altar front. Also search out the 11th-century pulpit, among Italy's foremost Romanesque works, and the 4th-century sarcophagus beneath it. At the end of the south aisle, seek out the Sacello di San Vittore, a crepuscular chapel built in the 4th century over the site of an earlier Christian cemetery: Its mosaics and gold-domed ceiling date from the 5th century.

Milan Environs

An easy day trip 24 miles (38 km) to the south takes you to **Pavia,** a delightful historical town beside the Ticino River. Once the capital city of the Lombards, Pavia is rich in buildings from

the Romanesque and Renaissance periods, none more so than the nearby Certosa di Pavia. Be sure to visit the town's cathedral in Piazza Vittoria, the outstanding churches of **San Michele,** on Via Capsoni, and **San Pietro,** on Via Griziotti. The former Visconti castle is home to a rewarding little museum and art gallery (*Castello Visconteo,*

Leonardo's "Last Supper"

Few paintings are as familiar as Leonardo da Vinci's "Last Supper" (1494–1498), and few, it must be said, are quite as disappointing in the flesh. The "saddest painting in the world," wrote Aldous Huxley in *Along the Road* (1925). Painted on the refectory wall of Bramante's **Santa Maria delle Grazie**—a Renaissance church worth a look in its own right—the "Last Supper" owes its decay to Leonardo's predilection for oil over the traditional techniques of fresco. Painted onto wet plaster, pigments bind powerfully to a porous wall in a strong chemical reaction. Painted as oil, they simply rest on a surface and become prone to damp and weathering. Oil allows greater choice of color and tone, however,

and, in the short term, produces dazzling frescoes. In the long term, the result is often catastrophic deterioration.

Matters were made worse, in this case, by clumsy restoration and by sheer bad luck: At one point, the resident monks whitewashed part of the painting, at another Napoleonic troops billeted here used the wall for target practice, and in 1943 much of the building was destroyed by a World War II bomb. Today, the painting has been restored again to portray its former grandeur, sublime coloring, and dramatic composition—elements that, had the original survived intact, might have made it the world's single greatest painting.

■ **The fine facade of the Certosa di Pavia reflects the wealth and power of its medieval patrons.**

Piazza Castello, tel 0382 399 770, museicivici.pavia.it, closed Mon. & Tues.–Fri. a.m., open to groups with advance reservations, $$).

Certosa di Pavia: Certosa, Chartreuse, and Charterhouse are the Italian, French, and English names, respectively, for a Carthusian monastery, of which the most beautiful in Europe is the Certosa di Pavia. Intended as a mausoleum for the Visconti, Milan's ruling medieval dynasty, the building is the supreme expression of Lombard Gothic and Renaissance architecture, the decorative majesty of its exterior rivaled by few buildings in Italy.

Work on the Certosa began in the 1390s on the orders of Gian Galeazzo Visconti. No expense was spared. Marble was brought from as far away as Carrara on the Tuscan coast, while craftsmen were removed from their labors on Milan's cathedral to satisfy the Visconti whim. Work proceeded

for some 200 years, its defining moments provided mostly by Giovanni Antonio Amadeo, the architect responsible for, among other elements, much of the superb facade and its bewildering multicolored collection of statues and intricate marble ornament.

Decoration inside is equally excessive, some of it outstanding, some of it superficial froth. Highlights, located in the south and north transepts, respectively, include the fresco-framed tomb of Gian Galeazzo Visconti (1493–1497), the only Visconti buried here, and the monument (1497) dedicated to Lodovico Sforza and his child bride, Beatrice d'Este. Also look for the altarpiece of "St. Ambrose" (1492) by Bergognone in the Cappella di Sant'Ambrogio (sixth chapel of the north aisle), the inlaid wooden stalls of the choir (1498), and the dazzling ivory altarpiece of the old sacristy, a 15th-century Florentine work. ■

Pavia

🗺 105 B2

Visitor Information

✉ Palazzo del Broletto, Via del Comune 18

☎ 0382 079 943

🕐 Closed 1–2 p.m., Sat. & Sun. p.m. from Nov.–Feb.

visitpavia.com

vivipavia.it

Certosa di Pavia

✉ Viale Monumento, 6 miles (9 km) N of Pavia

☎ 0382 925 613

🕐 Guided tours except Mon. & 11:30 a.m.–2:30 p.m.

💲 Donation

🚌 Bus: (board Piazza Piave) from Pavia to Certosa

LAGO DI COMO

Lago di Como, or Lake Como, is the most varied and most dramatic of the Italian Lakes. Its banks are fringed with villas, lush gardens, and bucolic villages, while its hinterland is a patchwork of wood-swathed hills and rugged mountains. To sightsee, pick a base—Como is the largest town, Bellagio the prettiest village—and then explore by driving the scenic lakeshore roads or boarding one of the many ferries that link the lake's far-flung settlements.

■ Thanks to a mild climate, rich Mediterranean vegetation thrives along the shores of Lago di Como.

Como

⚠ 104 B3

Visitor Information

✉ Piazza Cavour 17; info points at the railroad station and Via Pretorio-Piazza Duomo

☎ 031 269 712; info points: 031 304 137

🕐 Closed 1 p.m.– 2:30 p.m. & Sun. p.m., & all Sun. Oct.–April; info points open daily

visitcomo.eu

Como

"Bosomed deep in chestnut groves," wrote poet William Wordsworth of the lake's capital in 1791, although these days a faint industrial fringe slightly tarnishes the town's allure. But Como is also enjoyable and full of culture. There are many remembrances of the scientist Alessandro Volta, one of the city's famous inhabitants, and in the old center, close to the water, you can happily wander the promenades and relax in pleasant cafés. Boats embark here for all points of the lake.

Principal sights in Como's historic town center include the **Duomo** *(Piazza Duomo),* the cathedral, founded in the 14th century: It has a fine facade and some interior treasures, of which several tapestries (1598) and the Renaissance altarpieces by Tommaso Rodari and Bernardino Luini are the most memorable. Next door stands the arched **Broletto,** the town's 13th-century town hall, while farther afield lie **San Fedele** *(Piazza San Fedele)* and **Sant'Abbondio** *(Via Regina Teodolinda),* two perfect Lombard Romanesque churches.

Cernobbio & Tremezzo

Just north of Como lies the village of Cernobbio, famed for the 16th-century Villa d'Este and its splendid garden, now part of a magnificent hotel and thus only open to lucky patrons. But all can visit two sets of gardens in Tremezzo, a village to the north: the **Parco Comunale,** and the more elaborate **Villa Carlotta**—the one garden on the lake you should visit if you see no other. The 18th-century villa contains a small sculpture gallery. Take excursions by boat to the wooded **Isola Comacina,** Lago di Como's principal island, and to the romantic gardens at **Villa del Balbianello** (tel 0344 56110, closed mid-Nov.–mid-March, Mon., & Wed., $$) near Lenno.

Bellagio

A dream of a place, nestled on a hilly promontory that overlooks both of Lago di Como's watery arms. Its name comes from the Latin bilacus, meaning two lakes. Views are matchless, the cobbled streets quaint, and the gardens of the **Villa Serbelloni** (tel 031 951 555, only guided tours mid-March–Oct. Tues.–Sun. at 11 a.m. & 3:30 p.m., $$) and **Villa Melzi d'Eril** (Lungolario Manzoni, tel 339 457 3838, giardinidivillamelzi. it, closed Nov.–March, $) as pretty and perfumed as any in Italy. The Serbelloni was reputedly built over a villa belonging to Pliny the Younger (A.D. 61–112), a noted Roman man of letters born nearby.

Bellagio's central position makes it an ideal base, but even if you are only visiting the village for the day, it is still worth taking a ferry from here to the lake's eastern shore to visit **Varenna.** The best of this village's many leafy retreats are the **Villa Cipressi Hotel** (closed Nov.–March, $) and **Villa Monastero,** the latter built over a former convent dissolved in the 16th century due to its nuns' wayward behavior. The village offers some lovely strolls, notably up to the ruined Castello Vezio for breathtaking views of the lake; along the shoreline to the Fiumelatte, reputedly Italy's shortest river; and from Fiumelatte to Baluardo, another lofty viewpoint.

INSIDER TIP:

Try to visit the lake in the fall, when shades of red and yellow tint the wooded hillsides.

—SUSAN BLAIR
National Geographic Books
illustrations editor

Menaggio

Back on the lake's western shore, you come eventually to Menaggio, probably the most fashionable resort and an ideal base for a sporting or hiking interlude. There is also an 18-hole golf course above the village, while **Monte Bregagno,** one of the region's more rewarding mountain peaks at 6,913 feet (2,107 m), lies close by. Consult local visitor centers for details of trails and water- or land-based sporting options in or near the lake's villages. ■

Villa Carlotta
- ⊠ Via Regina 2, Tremezzo
- ☎ 0344 40405
- 🕐 Closed Nov.–mid-March
- 💲 $$$

villacarlotta.it

Bellagio
- 🗺 105 B4

Visitor Information
- ⊠ Piazza Mazzini
- ☎ 031 950 204
- ⊠ Piazza della Chiesa 14
- ☎ 031 951 555

bellagiolakecomo .com

Villa Monastero
- ⊠ Corso Matteotti 3, Bellagio
- ☎ 0341 295 450
- 🕐 Garden closed Nov.–March, museum closed Nov.–March, Mon. Jun.–Jul., & Mon.–Wed. & Thurs. a.m. Sept.–Oct.
- 💲 Garden $$, villa & garden $$$

villamonastero.eu

Menaggio
- 🗺 105 B4

Visitor Information
- ⊠ Piazza Garibaldi 3
- ☎ 0344 32924
- 🕐 Closed 12:30 p.m.–2:30 p.m. Mon.–Sat., & Wed. & Sun. Nov.–March

menaggio.com

varennaturismo.com

proloco.menaggio .com

LAGO MAGGIORE DRIVE

This drive takes you along the attractive western shore of Lago Maggiore (Lake Maggiore), probably the best known of the Italian lakes, with the option of a diversion at Stresa to the celebrated Isole Borromee (Borromean Islands).

The best route to Lago Maggiore from the south is via Autostrada A8 or A26. Unfortunately, first impressions of a lake renowned across centuries for its romantic beauty involve a rather drab, factory-pocked shoreline and the no-nonsense market town of **Arona ❶** (visitor information, Largo Vidale 1, tel 0322 243 601, pro locoarona.it), best known for its colossal statue of Cardinal Charles Borromeo (1538–1584). Borromeo's family has long been the lake's leading light—even today it owns all of the lake's islands and its fishing rights. Charles became Archbishop of Milan at age 22, thanks to the influence of his uncle, Pope Pius IV. After exploring the older upper town and climbing the 120-foot (37 m) statue, or Colosso di San Carlo (tel 0322 249 669, closed 12:30–2 p.m. & Mon.–Fri. Oct.–March, & Mon.–Sat. Dec.–Feb., $), you have a choice of two routes north, both appealing. The SS33 follows the lakeshore, with worthwhile stops at **Lesa ❷** to see **San Sebastiano,** the lake's best Romanesque church, and the pleasing resort of **Belgirate,** where the scenery begins to improve. The other leads inland on the SS34 and runs through the pretty hills of the Vergante region and its string of attractive villages. Both routes meet just south of **Stresa ❸** (visitor information, Piazza Marconi 16, tel 0323 31 308, stresaturismo.it, closed Sat. p.m.–Sun. Nov.–mid-March & 12:30 p.m.–3 p.m.).

Stresa & Beyond

This mild-weather town is the lake's main resort, known for its fine setting, sedate waterfront promenades, luxuriant gardens—all palms and orange blossoms—and heart-melting views of the nearby Isole Borromee. Two local villas, blessed with lush lakeside gardens, merit a visit: **Villa Ducale** and **Villa Pallavicino.** Take time to stroll the town's placid cobbled streets,

NOT TO BE MISSED:

Lesa • Isole Borromee • Monte Mottarone • Pallanza

then to explore the **Isole Borromee ❹** (see p. 120) and **Monte Mottarone ❺,** the mountain rising 4,891 feet (1,491 m) above town. Make the ascent by the zigzagging toll road, signed off the SS33 west, just south of Stresa at Alpino, or by cable car from Stresa Lido (tel 0323 30 295, stresa-mottarone.it, $$ one way). On a clear day, the views from the summit are magnificent, embracing Lago Maggiore, the Lombard plain, a wide swath of the Alps, and many of the region's other lakes.

Proceed on the main lakeside SS33 as far as sleepy **Baveno.** Squeezed between crags and lakeshore, it has been a desirable resort since 1879, when Great Britain's Queen Victoria graced the village with her presence. German composer Richard Wagner also stayed here. Today, you can see the 11th-century church of Santi Gervaso e Protaso and an octagonal baptistery with 5th-century origins. Curving northward you come to **Pallanza ❻,** best known for the **Villa Taranto** (Via Vittorio Veneto 111, tel 0323 556 667, ticket office 0323 404 555, villataranto.it, closed Nov.–March, $$), built in 1831. It was rescued from semi-dereliction in 1931 by its Scottish owner, Neil McEacharn, who replanted the gardens with some 20,000 often rare and imported flowers, shrubs, and trees.

North of Pallanza

The lake and its villages become quieter as you follow the SS34 north of Pallanza. To continue northward eventually means either

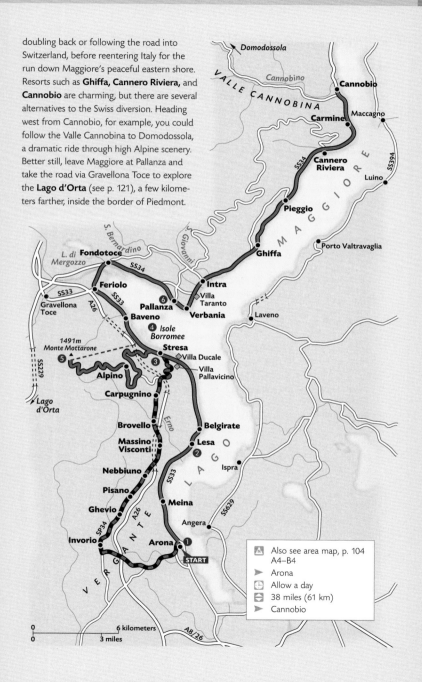

doubling back or following the road into
Switzerland, before reentering Italy for the
run down Maggiore's peaceful eastern shore.
Resorts such as **Ghiffa, Cannero Riviera,** and
Cannobio are charming, but there are several
alternatives to the Swiss diversion. Heading
west from Cannobio, for example, you could
follow the Valle Cannobina to Domodossola,
a dramatic ride through high Alpine scenery.
Better still, leave Maggiore at Pallanza and
take the road via Gravellona Toce to explore
the **Lago d'Orta** (see p. 121), a few kilometers farther, inside the border of Piedmont.

ISOLE BORROMEE

The Isole Borromee, or Borromean Islands, are a trio of almost impossibly idyllic islands lapped by the waters of Lago Maggiore. All three—Bella, Pescatori, and Madre—are usually jam-packed in high season, but it is worth putting up with people and high prices to enjoy the villas, gardens, and peerless views of the archipelago's loveliest retreats—the Isola Bella and Isola Madre.

Isole Borromee

🗺 104 A4

Visitor Information

☎ 0323 30556

🕐 Palaces &
gardens on both
islands closed
late Oct.–
late March

💲 Isola Bella
$$$$$, Isola
Madre $$$$, or
combined ticket
$$$$$

⛴ Boats to the
islands leave
regularly from
Arona, Stresa,
Baveno, & other
local towns.
Excursion tickets
give you the
freedom to
move between
the islands.

borromeoturismo.it

Isola Bella, the best known of the islands, was a rocky wasteland until 1632, when Count Carlo III Borromeo decided to transform it into a garden for his wife, Isabella. Huge quantities of soil and plants were brought from the mainland to create a theatrical garden arranged over ten terraces, each terrace a lush mix of laurel, cypresses, camellias, box hedges, and creamy magnolias. Work on the adjoining Palazzo Borromeo went on for generations, with the finishing touches made as late as 1959. The end result is less an architectural triumph than an amusing monument to decorative kitsch.

Sheer weight of numbers spoils the **Isola dei Pescatori,** writer Ernest Hemingway's favorite island, a place almost too quaint for its own good. It is probably only worth a passing visit en route to the **Isola Madre,** which is larger, less inundated, and in many ways scenically

INSIDER TIP:

While enjoying the café life before or after a visit to the islands, taste the delicious local Margheritine cookie, which originated in Stresa.

—MICHAEL BROUSE
National Geographic author

superior to the other islands. The Borromeos also toiled here for generations to produce a magnificent garden, perfect for languorous strolling. Pheasants, peacocks, and parrots add an exotic touch to the grounds, which are filled with early-blooming camellias, Europe's largest Kashmir cypress, and a wide variety of other rare plants and trees.

A fourth island in the group, San Giovanni, is private. ■

Boat Excursions on the Lakes

Boat trips are possible—and highly recommended—on all of Italy's major northern lakes, either as excursions offered by private operators or on board the public transit ferries and hydrofoils that operate between the lakes' major towns. Prices are reasonable, and day passes are usually available if you would like to spend more time on the water. Some larger ferries also carry cars.

Ferries are convenient, too, often leaving from jetties off a town's main lakefront piazza; they offer a good sight-seeing alternative to what, in summer, can be busy, traffic-filled roads.

To plan trips, contact **Navigazione Laghi** *(tel 030 914 9511 or toll-free in Italy 800 551 801, navlaghi.it),* which carries prices and schedules for services on lakes Como, Garda, and Maggiore.

LAGO D'ORTA

Lake Orta is a vision from a bygone age, its almost unsullied beauty a hint of how Como and Maggiore, its near neighbors, might once have appeared before crowds and commercialism took their toll. Both its tranquil capital, Orta San Giulio, and its island hideaway, the Isola San Giulio, are unspoiled gems, ideal for a few days' relaxation and gentle sightseeing.

The beguiling island of San Giulio sits at the heart of Lago d'Orta.

Orta San Giulio is a perfect base from which to explore the lake. Intimate and peaceful, the village and its leafy peninsula offer lovely views and a tangle of cobbled streets. Village life revolves around Piazza Motta, a lakeside square dominated by the arcaded Palazzotto (1582), Orta's former town hall. Walk up to the **Sacro Monte** above the village, a pretty group of tiny chapels (1590–1770) overlooking the lake. Still lovelier views can be enjoyed from the **Passeggiata del Movero,** a headland path near the village.

Boats from Orta run to the **Isola di San Giulio,** named after the fourth-century saint credited with clearing the island of snakes

and dragons. Having first sailed to its shores on his cloak, he then yoked wolves to a cart and proceeded to construct a church. For this reason, Giulio was annointed patron saint of builders.

Today, the successor to his church is the baroque **Basilica di San Giulio,** whose crypt reputedly contains the saint's relics. It also features some beautiful fourth-century sculptural fragments, probably from the saint's original tomb. The main body of the church boasts an 11th-century black marble pulpit adorned with reliefs of scenes from Giulio's life, also celebrated in the accomplished 15th-century frescoes off the church's north aisle. ■

Lago d'Orta

🗺 104 A3–A4

Visitor Information

✉ Via Panoramica, Orta San Giulio

☎ 0322 905 163

🕑 Closed Mon.– Tues. & 1 p.m.– 2 p.m.

🚢 Navigazione Lago d'Orta *(tel 345 517 0005, navigazionelago dorta.it)* runs frequent boat services from Orta to Isola San Giulio and eight other villages on the lake. It also offers lake tours *($$)* and scenic cruises.

distrettolaghi.it

orta.net

BERGAMO

Bergamo is a tale of two cities: the lower and mostly modern Bergamo Bassa, built across the Lombard plain at the confluence of the Brembo and Serio Rivers; and Bergamo Alta, an older and mainly medieval quarter perched on one of the foothills of the Orobian Alps.

■ **Medieval and baroque styles side by side in Bergamo Alta.**

Bergamo
🗺 105 C3

Visitor Information

✉ Via Gombito 13, Bergamo Alta

✉ Viale Papa Giovanni XXIII 57, Bergamo Bassa

☎ 035 242 226 or 035 210 204

🕐 Closed 12:30 p.m.–2 p.m. Mon.–Thurs.

visitbergamo.net

provincia.bergamo.it

Bergamo Bassa

Bergamo Bassa, the lower town, has its medieval moments, the best of them found on and around the palace-lined Via Pignolo, the steep street that climbs toward the upper town. Near it stands a trio of churches known for the altarpieces by Lorenzo Lotto (1480–1556), who was born in Bergamo: **Santo Spirito** *(corner of Via Torquato Tasso)*, **San Bernardino** *(Via San Giovanni)*, and **Sant'Alessandro** *(Piazzetta del Delfino)*. Lotto also left a wonderful "Madonna and Saints" in **San Bartolomeo,** a church overlooking Piazza Matteotti, Bergamo Bassa's broad main square.

The beauty of Lotto's paintings prepares you for the **Accademia Carrara,** an outstanding provincial art gallery full of leading names, in particular those of the great 15th-century Venetians. Gentile Bellini is represented by several ethereal portraits, his brother Giovanni by a delicate "Virgin with Child," and Carpaccio by a stately "Portrait of the Doge Leonardo Loredan." Other Venetian offerings include paintings by Antonio Vivarini, Titian, Tintoretto, Canaletto, Carlo Crivelli, Veronese, Tiepolo, and Guardi. The Florentines are not forgotten nor are non-Italians such as Holbein, Brueghel, Van Dyck, Velázquez, and Dürer.

Bergamo Alta

The imperious position of Bergamo Alta, the upper town, attracted Ligurian settlers from as early as 1200 B.C. Later the site was adopted by the Celts, who named it Bergheim or Berghem (hill town), then by the Romans, who renamed it Bergomum. Later a medieval city-state, it fell first to Milan's Visconti and then to Venice. The *condottiere,* or mercenary leader, Bartolomeo Colleoni (1400–1475), was born here as was the composer Gaetano Donizetti (1797–1848), who also died in the city. The medieval Bergamask dance originated here, as did the commedia dell'arte, comedy drama known for its stock

INSIDER TIP:

Ride the funicular *($)*
up to Bergamo Alta.
On Viale Antonio
Locatelli, it's easily
reached by bus from
the rail station.

—JANE SUNDERLAND
National Geographic contributor

characters, Harlequin, Pulcinella,
and Columbine.

Bergamo's old town huddles
within ancient walls built by the
Venetians, at its heart two closely
linked squares: **Piazza Vecchia** and
Piazza del Duomo. The former
fronts the **Palazzo della Ragione,**
one of Italy's oldest civic palaces
(1199). Take the elevator up the
square's 12th-century **Torre Civica**
for a bird's-eye view of the city.

The neighboring square's pride
is the exquisitely decorated **Cappella Colleoni,** commissioned in
1470–1476 as a mausoleum by
the eponymous condottiere from
Giovanni Antonio Amadeo, the
architect responsible for much of
the equally extravagant Certosa
di Pavia (see p. 115). Alongside it
stand a baptistery (1340) and the
Basilica di Santa Maria Maggiore (begun in 1137; *tel 035 223
327, closed 12:30 p.m.–2:30 p.m.
Mon.–Sat. & 1–3 p.m. Sun.*), the
latter an outstanding piece of
Lombard Romanesque architecture. Several outstanding Flemish
and Florentine tapestries redeem
the later baroque interior, as do
the lavish *intarsia* (inlaid wood)
panels of the chancel and choir.

North of the piazza, clamber
up to the ruined **Rocca,** or fortress, for views over the town.
Then follow Via Porta Dipinta
to the north, pausing to admire
the frescoes in **San Michele** and
the **Convento di Sant'Agostino.**
South of the piazza, take the
funicular up to the **Castello** for
more sweeping vistas. ∎

Accademia Carrara

- ✉ Piazza Giacomo Carrara 82
- ☎ 035 234 396
- 🕐 Closed Tues.
- 💲 $$

lacarrara.it

Torre Civica

- ✉ Piazza Vecchia
- ☎ 035 224 700
- 🕐 Closed Mon. March–Oct. & Mon.–Fri. Nov.–Feb.
- 💲 $

Cappella Colleoni

- ✉ Piazza Duomo
- ☎ 035 210 061
- 🕐 Closed 12:30– 2 p.m. daily & Mon. Nov.–Feb.

EXPERIENCE: Biking Brescia & Franciacorta

Brescia is located 31 miles (50 km) from
Bergamo and, with its Franciacorta region,
it's a destination full of culture, nature,
food, and wine that can't be missed. The
area is fairly level so its magnificent bike
tours are appropriate even for less experienced riders. Bicycles can be rented at
Iseo Bike *(Via per Rovato 26, tel 340/396-
2095, iseobike.com, also delivery service),*
located in Iseo, on the lake of the same
name, or at **Zecchini** *(zecchinibiciclette.com)*
with locations in Brescia *(Via Solferino 38,
030/375-5432)* and Desenzano del Garda
(Via Monte Grappa 28, 030/636-0740). The
website *franciacorta.net* offers maps that

propose five easy itineraries that can be
combined to make a longer ride.

Starting at the **Piazza della Loggia** in
Brescia, a spectacular Renaissance Square
dating back to the Venetian dominance of
the city, and riding into the countryside,
cyclists will find little villages and parish churches from long ago. No one can
resist a stop at one of the many wineries
(marked on the downloadable map) to
taste the area's pride and joy, **Franciacorta,** an exquisite sparkling wine made
from Pinot Grigio and Chardonnay grapes
using the classical method (the same used
for making champagne).

MANTUA

Inspired by its canals, lake-ringed surroundings, and almost faultless medieval center, Aldous Huxley described Mantua (Mantova) as the world's most romantic city. Locals know it as *la piccola Venezia*, or little Venice. The beautifully arcaded streets are among northern Italy's most evocative, and in the Palazzo Ducale and extraordinary Palazzo Te, the town boasts two of the country's most remarkable palaces.

An exceptional example of urban Renaissance planning, Mantua is a World Heritage site.

Mantua

📍 105 E2

Visitor Information

✉ Piazza Andrea Mantegna 6

☎ 0376 432 432

turismo.mantova.it

NOTE: Mantova Sabbioneta Card *($$$, mantovacard.it)* gives free access to Mantua's public transportation (included bus No. 17 and No. 17s to Sabbioneta), to the city's bike sharing service, and to the most important sights of the two towns for 72 hours.

Mantua lies among marshy lowlands—hence its lakes and canals—and was most likely founded as an island refuge by the Etruscans during the fifth or sixth century B.C. Starting from the late Middle Ages and during the Renaissance, the ruling Gonzaga family turned the town into a byword for courtly life and cultural endeavor, their patronage attracting the likes of Leon Battista Alberti (1404–1472), the great Renaissance architectural theorist, and painters such as Pisanello and Mantegna.

The historic center is an unmitigated delight. Here, three squares

create a focus—Piazza Sordello, Piazza Broletto (now a restoration site, after a 2012 earthquake), and Piazza delle Erbe—each bristling with medieval buildings and flanked with cobbled lanes and ancient arcaded streets. On Piazza delle Erbe you'll discover the **Basilica di Sant'Andrea** *(closed 12 p.m.–3 p.m. Mon.–Fri.),* an imposing 15th-century church designed by Alberti (the painter Mantegna is buried in one of its chapels), and the 11th-century **Rotonda di San Lorenzo,** a restrained Romanesque church with a lovely loggia and a colonnaded ambulatory.

Palazzo Ducale

Mantua's great sight, indeed one of northern Italy's greatest sights, is the Palazzo Ducale, or Ducal Palace, a vast edifice begun in the 14th century and expanded over the centuries, largely on behalf of the Gonzaga dukes. In its day, it was Europe's largest palace. When the Austrian Hapsburgs sacked it in 1630, they removed some 2,000 works of art from its hundreds of rooms.

Room follows room in a majestic parade, some immeasurably grand, others tiny, decorative fresco-filled jewels. Among their more notable works are a series of frescoes by the Veronese artist Pisanello (1395–1450), most of them inspired by episodes from the tales of King Arthur and the Knights of the Round Table. Also outstanding is the **Appartamento degli Arazzi,** or Room of the Tapestries, hung with Flemish tapestries crafted to designs and cartoons by Raphael. Best of all is the tiny **Camera degli Sposi** *(reservations required, tel 041 241 1897, $),* or Bridal Chamber, so called because, according to the Gonzaga family's archive, it is where a just married couple spent their first night. The room is almost entirely covered in one of the most breathtaking Renaissance fresco cycles (1465–1474), Mantegna's sublimely lyrical portraits of the Gonzaga family and the splendors of courtly life.

Palazzo Te

Situated in parkland on the edge of the old town, Palazzo Te was conceived as a country retreat for the Gonzaga family. Built between 1525 and 1535, it is a smaller and different creature to its more central rival. Both the design and many of the interior frescoes were the work of Giulio Romano (1492–1546), one of the age's most accomplished mannerist artists.

Stylized and deliberately shocking, the palace was conceived primarily as a pleasure dome, the preoccupation with hedonism most obvious in the **Sala di Psiche** (Room of Psyche), whose languorous frescoes—all satiated satyrs and frolicking nymphs—must be some of Italy's most erotic and sexually explicit paintings. The scenes, like many in the palace, borrow heavily from classical myth, although contemporary gossip suggested they celebrated Federico Gonzaga's passion for his mistress. More extraordinary paintings adorn the neighboring **Sala dei Giganti** (Room of the Giants), where the looming and grotesquely distorted figures of the Titans act out against Jupiter's rage. ■

Sabbioneta

On the Lombard plains southwest of Mantua, Sabbioneta is a planned town begun in 1558 by Vespasiano Gonzaga, a cultured mercenary leader. Hemmed in by a hexagon of walls, the Renaissance experiment is a delight, full of ordered streets and fine buildings that include the **Palazzo Ducale, Palazzo del Giardino** *(combined ticket $$ from visitor center),* and the **church of the Incoronata** (Vespasiano's burial place). The **Teatro Olimpico** was designed by Vincenzo Scamozzi, a pupil of Palladio.

Palazzo Ducale

- ✉ Piazza Sordello 40
- ☎ 0376 352 100 or for ticketing information tel 041 241 1897
- 🕐 Closed Mon.
- 💲 $$–$$$$

**mantovaducale
.beniculturali.it**

Palazzo Te

- ✉ Viale Te 13
- ☎ 0376 323 266
- 🕐 Closed Mon. a.m.
- 💲 $$$

museicivici.mn.it

Sabbioneta

- 🗺 105 D1

Visitor Information

- ✉ Piazza d'Armi 1
- ☎ 0375 221 044
- 🕐 Closed 1 p.m.– 2:30 p.m.

visitsabbioneta.it

More Places to Visit in Lombardy & the Lakes

Cremona

Cremona is worth a special visit if your interests include violins and violin maker Antonio Stradivari (1644–1737). Stradivari was part of Cremona's long instrument-making tradition, a tradition that continues to this day in the town's 150 or so workshops. Displays in the **Museo Civico** (*Via Ugolani Dati 4, tel 0372 407 269, closed Mon., $$*) explore the history of violinmaking. To see Cremona's very own Stradivarius and other precious instruments, visit the **Museo del Violino** (*Piazza Marconi, closed Mon., $$$$*). *turismocremona.it* ⚑ 105 D2 **Visitor Information** ✉ Piazza del Comune 5 ☎ 0372 406 391 🕐 Closed 1 p.m.–2 p.m.

Lago d'Iseo

The wild scenery, high mountains, and small villages of Lake Iseo, often overshadowed by the splendors of Como, Garda, and Maggiore, merit a look and can easily be incorporated on an itinerary that takes in the Dolomiti to the north.

The lake's major centers are **Iseo**, whose pleasant main square is graced with the pretty fresco-filled church of Sant'Andrea, and **Pisogne** to the north, whose church, Santa Maria della Neve, is also extensively frescoed. These and other villages on the eastern shore are popular with Italians on weekends. The western shore and the villages of Sarnico, Tavernola, and Riva di Solto are usually a bit quieter.

The single best sight on the lake is **Monte Isola** (*regular boat connections from several lake towns*), a verdant island crowned by the hilltop church of Madonna della Ceriola, from whence tremendous views of the lake and surrounding mountains abound. At **Cislano** you can admire one of the region's more unusual natural phenomena—the Fairies of the Forest—thin and strangely eroded rock spires and towers, many crowned with a precariously perched boulder. *visitbergamo.net* or *iseolake.info* ⚑ 105 D3 **Visitor Information** ✉ Lungolago Marconi 2c/d, Iseo ☎ 030 374 8733 🕐 Closed 12:30–3:30 p.m. (3 p.m. Oct.–March) & Sat. p.m.–Sun. Oct.–March

Parco Nazionale dello Stelvio

This national park, Italy's largest, protects a prime slice of Alpine scenery. It's a mountain playground with plenty of skiing opportunities and almost 1,000 miles (1,600 km) of marked hiking trails. The town of **Bormio** is the best base, the **Valle dello Zebrù,** a spectacular valley to its east, a good target for hikers. *stelviopark.it* or *parks.it* ⚑ 105 D4–D5

EXPERIENCE: All Aboard the Bernina Express

The **Bernina Express** (*rhb.ch*) travels 90 miles (145 km) between Tirano in Italy and St. Moritz in Switzerland, crossing the Alps' 7,392-foot (2,253 m) Bernina Pass in the process. So spectacular is the mountain scenery en route that the railway line features on UNESCO's World Heritage List.

Nicknamed the "Little Red Train" after its distinctive red carriages, the train dates from 1913, when the narrow-gauge line (Europe's highest transalpine railway) opened. Special long, curving panoramic windows allow you to admire the region's dense pine forests, ice blue lakes, lush Alpine pastures, and glaciers, as well as endless towering peaks.

You can reach Tirano easily by train from Milan or Bergamo, and the trip to St. Moritz takes almost three hours, so you can return to Italy the same day. The trip is popular, however: Reserve well in advance. The train runs year-round, even through the snowiest conditions in winter.

Canal-laced, history-laden, and art-filled Venice—a romantic
and intriguing city beyond description and compare

VENICE

■ A fancy, full-face mask for Carnevale,
adorned with feathers and gold leaf

VENICE

The world's most beautiful city rarely disappoints. Venice casts its magic spell year-round—whether you visit in the depths of winter, an icy mist spreading chill over the encircling lagoon, or in the shimmering, enervating heat of summer, when the canals, ancient churches, and endless palaces are dappled with the shifting light of the sun.

More than 400 bridges span the countless waterways that weave through Venice.

NOT TO BE MISSED:

Venice (Venezia) is a relatively young city, yet few places have remained as unsullied by the passing of time. Its lagoon was probably inhabited during the time of Christ, and small groups of refugees may have settled its islands following barbarian raids in the fifth century (myth dates the city's foundation to March 25, 421). Elected in 726, the first doge, or ruler, presided over a loose confederation of settlements rather than a single city. Later, the Frankish invasions of the eighth century forced some of the inhabitants to the Rivus Altus, or high bank, more easily defended islets that in time would become the cornerstone of present-day Venice.

By the tenth century, the nascent city had established trading links with the East and elsewhere. Prosperity increased during the Crusades and in the wake of the city's growing maritime prowess. Firm government provided political and social cohesion at home, and by the 13th century the city was mistress, in an oft-quoted phrase, of "one quarter and one half-quarter" of the old Roman empire. On the mainland, the city subdued its main maritime rivals, notably Genoa, and extended its reach across much of northeast Italy, an empire that remained intact until the arrival of Napoleon. Decline was due largely to the rise of the Turks, who gradually absorbed Venice's maritime empire, and to the long-standing enmity of other powers. The city-state's final dissolution came in 1797, courtesy of Napoleon, after which the city passed under Austrian control before joining a united Italy in 1866.

It's no surprise that Venice is one of the most visited cities in the world. Industry has moved to dry land and the city now lives on tourism. This creates some serious problems: The "hit-and-run" day-trippers don't enrich the city, the over 20 million visitors each year are literally consuming it, and the presence of huge cruise ships in the lagoon is becoming increasingly controversial. All of this will hopefully lead to the creation of a more sustainable model of tourism that could lead the way for other troubled "urban ecosystems."

What to See

Venice is divided into six *sestieri,* or districts, with three on either side of the Canal Grande, the city's watery main thoroughfare. Before embarking on the sights, take a ride along the Canal Grande, as an introduction to the city. Above all, don't plunge straight into Piazza San Marco, where the crowds could put you off the city before you even start. Instead, make for one of the city's smaller squares to sample areas of the city not entirely given over to tourism. Only then, acquainted with the more intimate side of Venice, should you surrender to the demands of sightseeing.

The city's two key churches are Santa Maria Gloriosa dei Frari and Santi Giovanni e Paolo (known as San Zanipolo), its principal art galleries the Accademia and Collezione Peggy Guggenheim. The major *scuole,* ancient art-filled buildings, are the Scuola Grande di San Rocco and the smaller Scuola di San Giorgio degli Schiavoni. Second-ranked galleries include the Museo Civico Correr, Ca' d'Oro, and Ca' Rezzonico, while lesser churches—a relative term, given that even the smallest Venetian churches have charm and treasures beyond compare—include Santa Maria della Salute and San Zaccaria. Finally, steel yourself for the "big two"—the Palazzo Ducale and Basilica di San Marco. ∎

Useful Museum, Church, & Transit Passes for Venice

Venice has a variety of museum, church, and transit passes that save money and also often save waiting in lines.

Chorus Pass *(tel 041 275 0462, chorus venezia.org, $$)* Allows one visit to each of the 16 churches that make up the Chorus Foundation. The pass is available online or at participating churches, which otherwise charge for individual entry *($)*.

MUVE Friend Card *(tel 041 240 5211, visitmuve.it, $$$$$)* Offers one entry to each of the city's 11 locations of the Musei Civici. Buy at participating museums, online at *vivaticket.it,* or via the Musei Civici website. Valid six months.

Actv Ticket *(actv.avmspa.it, $$$–$$$$$)* A ride on the city's *vaporetti* (water-buses) costs a steep €7,50 ($8.50). To save money, buy a pass for one, two, three, or seven days; valid also for land transport.

Venezia Unica City Pass *(veneziaunica .it)* This scheme allows you to buy and tailor-make museum and transit tickets and passes in advance (guaranteeing the lowest prices), and offers discounts on a range of other goods and services.

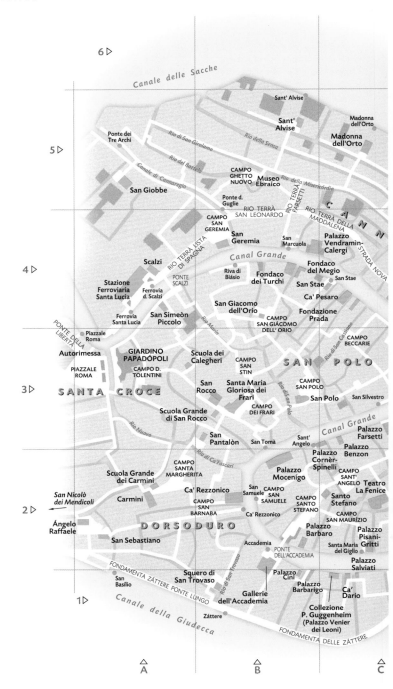

6 ▷

Canale delle Sacche

Sant' Alvise

Sant'
Alvise

Madonna
dell'Orto

5 ▷

Ponte dei
Tre Archi

Rio di San Girolamo

Rio della Sensa

Madonna
dell'Orto

CAMPO
GHETTO
NUOVO

Museo
Ebraico

Rio della Misericórdia

San Giobbe

Canale di Cannaregio

Rio del Battelo

Ponte d.
Guglie

RIO TERRÀ
SAN LEONARDO

RIO TERRÀ
FARSETTI

RIO TERRA DELLA
MADDALENA

C
A
N
N

CAMPO
SAN
GEREMIA

San
Geremia

San
Marcuola

Palazzo
Vendramin-
Calergi

STRADA NOVA

4 ▷

Scalzi

RIO TERRÀ LISTA
DI SPAGNA

Canal Grande

Riva di
Biásio

Fondaco
dei Turchi

Fondaco
del Mégio

San Stae

San Stae

PONTE
SCALZI

Stazione
Ferroviaria
Santa Lucia

Ferrovia
d. Scalzi

Ca' Pesaro

Ferrovia
Santa Lucia

San Simeòn
Piccolo

San Giacomo
dell'Orio

Rio Marin

Fondazione
Prada

PONTE DELLA
LIBERTÀ

Piazzale
Roma

CAMPO
SAN GIÁCOMO
DELL' ORIO

Rio di San Cassiano

CAMPO
BECCARIE

Autorimessa

GIARDINO
PAPADÓPOLI

Scuola dei
Caleghéri

SAN   POLO

PIAZZALE
ROMA

CAMPO D.
TOLENTINI

CAMPO
SAN
STIN

CAMPO
SAN POLO

Rio di San Polo

3 ▷

S A N T A   C R O C E

San
Rocco

Santa Maria
Gloriosa dei
Frari

San Polo

San Silvestro

Scuola Grande
di San Rocco

Rio Nuovo

CAMPO
DEI FRARI

San
Pantalòn

San Tomà

Sant'
Angelo

Canal Grande

Palazzo
Farsetti

CAMPO
SANTA
MARGHERITA

Rio di Ca'Foscari

Palazzo
Corner-
Spinelli

Palazzo
Benzon

Scuola Grande
dei Carmini

Ca' Rezzonico

Palazzo
Mocenígo

CAMPO
SANT'
ANGELO

Teatro
La Fenice

San Nicolò
dei Mendicoli

Carmini

CAMPO
SAN
BARNABA

San
Samuele

CAMPO
SAN
SAMUELE

CAMPO
SANTO
STEFANO

Santo
Stefano

2 ▷

Ángelo
Raffaele

Ca' Rezzonico

D O R S O D U R O

CAMPO
SAN MAURÍZIO

Palazzo
Barbaro

Palazzo
Pisani-
Gritti

San Sebastiano

Accademia

Santa Maria
del Giglio

Palazzo
Salviati

PONTE
DELL'ACCADEMIA

FONDAMENTA ZÁTTERE PONTE LUNGO

San
Basílio

Squero di
San Trovaso

Rio di San Trovaso

Palazzo
Cini

Palazzo
Barbarigo

Ca'
Dario

1 ▷

Canale della Giudecca

Záttere

Gallerie
dell'Accademia

Collezione
P. Guggenheim
(Palazzo Venier
dei Leoni)

FONDAMENTA DELLE ZÁTTERE

△
A

△
B

△
C

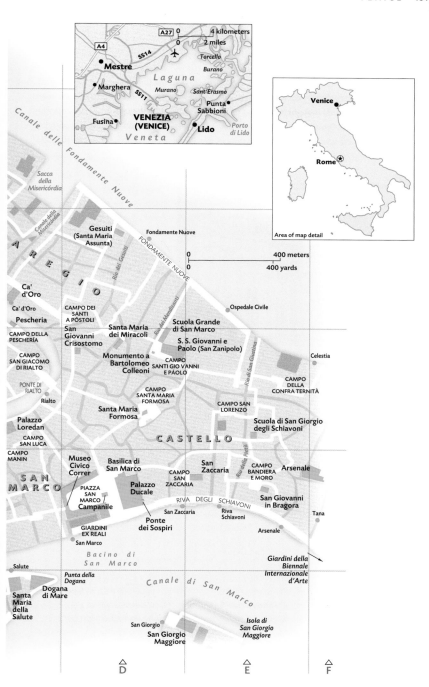

A27

A4

SS14

Mestre

Laguna

Torcello

Burano

Murano

Sant'Erasmo

Marghera

SS11

Punta
Sabbioni

**VENEZIA
(VENICE)**

Fusina

Lido

Porto
di Lido

V e n e t a

0   4 kilometers
0   2 miles

Venice

Rome

Area of map detail

Canale delle Fondamente Nuove

Sacca
della
Misericórdia

Canale della Misericórdia

Fondamente Nuove

FONDAMENTE NUOVE

0   400 meters
0   400 yards

**Gesuiti
(Santa Maria
Assunta)**

Rio dei Gesuiti

Rio dei Mendicanti

Ca'
d'Oro

Ca' d'Oro

Pescheria

CAMPO DELLA
PESCHERÍA

CAMPO DEI
SANTI
A PÓSTOLI

**San
Giovanni
Crisostomo**

**Santa Maria
dei Miracoli**

Ospedale Civile

**Scuola Grande
di San Marco**

**S. S. Giovanni e
Paolo (San Zanipolo)**

Celestia

CAMPO
SAN GIACOMO
DI RIALTO

**Monumento a
Bartolomeo
Colleoni**

CAMPO
SANTI GIO VANNI
E PÁOLO

PONTE DI
RIALTO

Rialto

CAMPO
SANTA MARIA
FORMOSA

CAMPO SAN
LORENZO

Rio di San Giustina

CAMPO
DELLA
CONFRA TERNITÀ

**Palazzo
Loredan**

**Santa Maria
Formosa**

CAMPO
SAN LUCA

C A S T E L L O

**Scuola di San Giorgio
degli Schiavoni**

CAMPO
MANIN

**Museo
Civico
Correr**

**Basilica di
San Marco**

CAMPO
SAN
ZACCARIA

**San
Zaccaria**

CAMPO
BANDIERA
E MORO

Arsenale

S A N
M A R C O

PIAZZA
SAN
MARCO

Campanile

**Palazzo
Ducale**

Rio della Pietà

RIVA   DEGLI   SCHIAVONI

**San Giovanni
in Bragora**

Tana

GIARDINI
EX REALI

San Marco

**Ponte
dei Sospiri**

San Zaccaria

Riva
Schiavoni

Arsenale

Salute

B a c i n o   d i
S a n   M a r c o

**Giardini della
Biennale
Internazionale
d'Arte**

**Santa
Maria
della
Salute**

**Dogana
di Mare**

Punta della
Dogana

C a n a l e   d i   S a n   M a r c o

San Giorgio

**San Giorgio
Maggiore**

Isola di
San Giorgio
Maggiore

D

E

F

CANAL GRANDE

There can be no more beautiful urban thoroughfare than the Canal Grande (Grand Canal), the broad artery that winds in a mesmerizing and serpentine loop through the ancient heart of Venice. Your first thought on arriving to the city should be to board one of the lumbering *vaporetti*, or water-buses, that ply its palace-lined length—an unforgettable odyssey of sights and sounds and an eye-opening first glimpse of the waterborne eccentricities of this daily life.

■ Venice's main corridor of transportation, the Canal Grande makes a large S-formation as it winds through the city.

Venice

🅰 130–131

Visitor Information

✉ Stazione Ferroviaria Santa Lucia (railroad station)

✉ Piazzale Roma

✉ Calle dell' Ascensione 71 /f

☎ 041 2424

turismovenezia.it

To the Rialto

Board a boat at Piazzale Roma or the railroad station for San Marco. The first church you see on your left beyond the bridge is the **Scalzi,** designed in 1656 by Baldassare Longhena (1598–1682), architect of Santa Maria della Salute and several of the canal's most prestigious palaces. Farther down on the left stands **San Geremia,** home to the prized relics of St. Lucy, a fourth-century martyr. On the opposite (south) bank, the arched **Fondaco dei Turchi,** now Venice's natural history museum, was the headquarters between 1621 and 1838 of Turchi (Ottoman) merchants, while the plain

15th-century **Fondaco del Megio** to its left served as an emergency grain store for use during famine or siege, while today it's home to a school (closed to the public).

Mauro Coducci's **Palazzo Vendramin-Calergi,** one of the canal's most famous palaces, is now home to the Casinò. One of its suites was occupied by the composer Richard Wagner between 1882 and 1883 during the last months of his life. Two other great palaces lie a short way beyond, the **Ca' Pesaro** and stunning **Ca' d'Oro** (see pp. 160–161), now museums of modern and medieval art, respectively. Almost opposite the Ca' d'Oro stands the neo-Gothic **Pescheria,** or fish market, heralding the arrival of the **Rialto,** the city's ancient heart, and the unmistakable outlines of the 16th-century **Ponte di Rialto,** or Rialto Bridge.

Beyond the Rialto, the 13th-century **Palazzo Loredan** and **Palazzo Farsetti** on the left form Venice's town hall, once home to the neoclassical sculptor Antonio Canova. Among the former inhabitants of the **Palazzo Benzon,** a few palaces down on the same side, was the Contessa Benzon, a leading 19th-century socialite. The poet Lord Byron lodged close by, in one of four palaces owned

EXPERIENCE: The Canal Grande by Night

If you don't mind sharing your romantic experience with others, then a nighttime journey down the Canal Grande in a *vaporetto*, or water-bus, is one of the most magical trips you can make in this most magical of cities.

Board in the middle of the gently rocking vessel, watch the deft moves of the *marinaio*, or boatman, as he unhitches the craft from the quay, then head forward or aft for the best views.

Lights ripple on the water, along with the reflections of palaces, while the sounds of the canal—the lap of water, the chug of boats, the singing of distant gondoliers—seem even more evocative and ethereal than by day. Ancient facades pass in a shadowy succession, some beautifully floodlit, others shuttered and with a faint air of foreboding. The dark, mysterious silhouettes of other boats drift by, and eerie alleys and narrow canals disappear into the gloom in the ferry's wake. Then, suddenly, come the lights of the Rialto, a blaze of color and life, before it is back to the black waters of the canal as it sweeps first past the Palazzo Mocenigo and then the Palazzo Dario.

The journey is easily made from the transit stops at Ferrovia Santa Lucia or Piazzale Roma to San Marco—both the 1 and 2 ply the length of the canal, with a restricted night service (N) into the small hours. Consider buying a multihour pass (see sidebar p. 129), as this is a journey you may well want to make more than once.

---

by the Mocenigo family on the Volta del Canal, the canal's great bend. With Byron during his two-year stay in the haunted **Palazzo Mocenigo,** opposite the San Tomà landing stage, were a dog, a wolf, and a monkey. Short-stay guests included Margherita Cogni, one of Byron's lovers, who reacted to his rejection of her by attacking him with a knife and then jumping into the canal. On the opposite bank, right on the bend, stands the **Ca' Rezzonico,** since 1936 dedicated to 18th century Venice (see pp. 148–149).

On the left beyond the Ponte dell'Accademia, last of the canal's bridges, stands the 15th-century **Palazzo Barbaro,** bought in 1885 by the Curtis family, a Boston dynasty whose guests included Claude Monet, John Singer Sargent, Cole Porter, and Henry James. The garish, modern mosaics on the palace almost opposite mark the **Palazzo Barbarigo,** now owned by a glass company. A short way down on the same bank stands the truncated **Palazzo Venier dei Leoni,** where the Collezione Peggy Guggenheim is housed (see pp. 152–153). Immediately beyond is the perilously leaning **Ca' Dario,** one of the canal's most charming-looking palaces but also one of the least desirable to own—Venetians have long considered it cursed. The mosaic-fronted **Palazzo Salviati,** two palaces farther down, like the Barbarigo, is owned by a glass company. Just beyond the Santa Maria del Giglio landing stage rises the Palazzo Pisani-Gritti, Venice's premier hotel, almost overshadowed by the church of **Santa Maria della Salute** (see p. 153). Soon afterward comes the first glimpse of the Palazzo Ducale and Piazza San Marco. ■

Canal Grande

🚤 Vaporetto 1, 2

💲 Single journey $$, valid for 75 minutes' travel

NOTE: Vaporetto 1 stops at every landing stage on the Canal Grande; the faster 2 makes fewer stops.

PIAZZA SAN MARCO

"The most beautiful drawing room in Europe," said Napoleon of the Piazza San Marco, or St. Mark's Square, Venice's famous central square, which provides not only the setting for two of the city's foremost buildings—the Basilica di San Marco and Palazzo Ducale—but also the home to historic cafés, the Campanile, and the Museo Civico Correr, whose displays provide a fascinating insight into Venice's long history.

The Piazza San Marco remains Venice's cultural heart.

Piazza San Marco

 131 D2

 1, 2, 4.2, 5.1, 5.2 to San Zaccaria; 1, 2 to Vallaresso

Piazza San Marco

The piazza's most distinctive smaller monuments are the two **columns** near the waterfront, brought from the eastern Mediterranean in 1170. One is topped with the lion of St. Mark (see sidebar p. 142), the other with St. Theodore, one of Venice's patron saints, flanked by a creature of unknown type or symbolic significance. The area between the pillars was once a place of execution, and

Venetians still consider it an unlucky spot to walk. To the west lies Jacopo Sansovino's **Zecca** (1545), the city's mint until 1870 and one of the few buildings in the city built entirely of stone as a precaution against fire. Alongside stands the **Libreria Sansoviniana** (1588), or state library, also by Sansovino, entered under the portico at No. 13a.

To the left (north) of the basilica, look up at the **Torre**

INSIDER TIP:

Entering Piazza San Marco via the Calle Larga XXII Marzo's darkened archway is a bit like finding the door in the back of C. S. Lewis's wardrobe.

—JOHNNA RIZZO
National Geographic author

dell'Orologio (*tel 041 520 9070 for compulsory reservations & guided tours, $$ includes other Piazza San Marco locations*), a clock tower built in 1499 whose Latin legend translates "I number only the happy hours." The two distinctive bronze figures are known as *I Mori,* or the Moors, after their dark patina.

The **Campanile,** Venice's tallest building at 323 feet (98.5 m), offers one of Europe's most entrancing viewpoints, but when it was first built around 912, it had three very different purposes: to act as bell tower for the basilica, to provide a lookout for the harbor below, and to serve as a lighthouse for ships at sea. Over the centuries it received all manner of minor alterations, none of them, unfortunately, directed at the foundations—which, unknown to anyone, were barely 65 feet (20 m) deep.

Lashed by wind and rain, corroded by saltwater, and struck repeatedly by lightning, the tower became ever weaker. When it finally collapsed on July 14, 1902, the only wonder was that it had not crumbled earlier. No one was killed in the disaster. Within

hours the city council vowed to rebuild the tower *"dov'era e com'era"* (where it was and how it was). The pledge was realized ten years later in 1912, when a new tower, identical but for the fact it was 600 tons (661 tonnes) lighter and better supported, was inaugurated on the Feast of St. Mark (April 25), a thousand years after the first campanile.

Flanking the piazza on three sides are the **Procuratie,** the arcaded buildings that once served as offices for the Procuratie, the

---

EXPERIENCE:
Drinks at Caffè Florian

Florian is expensive, certainly, and often busy, but it's worth treating yourself at least once to enjoy Venice's oldest and most opulent café—its beautiful old interior has barely altered since it opened for business in 1720. In that time it has served coffee, hot chocolate, and more to the likes of Casanova, Charles Dickens, and Marcel Proust. Visit in the evening or in winter, if possible, when it is less busy (*Piazza San Marco 56–59, tel 041 520 5641, caffeflorian .com, closed Wed. in winter*).

---

upper tier of Venice's administrative bureaucracy. Within part of these buildings is the **Museo Civico Correr,** whose exhibits offer a wonderful and often eccentric survey of Venice's long history. Ranged over three floors, the museum consists of a historical section, a picture gallery, and a more specialized section devoted to Italian unification. There is also a salon with early masterpieces by the sculptor Antonio Canova.

Campanile

✉ Piazza San Marco

☎ 041 270 8311

$ $$$

NOTE: Arrive early to avoid lines. Ascent is by elevator.

Museo Civico Correr

🅰 131 D2

✉ Procuratie Nuove-Ala Napoleonica, Piazza San Marco 52

☎ 041 240 5211

$ $$$$$ (includes Palazzo Ducale)

correr.visitmuve.it

Basilica di San Marco

🗺 131 D2

✉ Piazza San Marco

☎ 041 270 8311; online reservations venetoinside .com

🕐 Closed Sun. a.m.

💲 Loggia dei Cavalli $, museum $, sanctuary $, & treasury $

🚤 1, 2, & other boats to San Zaccaria

basilicasanmarco.it

Rooms in the first part are arranged by theme, beginning with a section devoted to topographical and other views of the city. Then come areas devoted to costumes, coins, flags, glassware, weapons, and maritime ephemera, although most people's favorite is the special footwear section and the extraordinary *zoccoli*, or platform clogs, once worn by Venetian women. Outstanding paintings in the surprisingly rich picture gallery include Carpaccio's famous "Two Women" (1507), also known as "The Courtesans," and a "Pietà" (1476) by the Sicilian artist Antonello da Messina.

Basilica di San Marco

It is hard to imagine another building in western Europe more beautifully or richly embellished with the architectural and artistic legacy of the centuries than the Basilica di San Marco (St. Mark's Basilica). A magnificent hybrid of a church, it served for almost a thousand years as the tomb of St. Mark, the private chapel of the doges (Venice's rulers), and the spiritual fulcrum and ultimate symbol of the power, authority, and continuity of the Venetian state.

St. Mark's first resting place was a modest chapel within the Palazzo Ducale, a sanctuary replaced first in 832, and again in 978, when rioting destroyed the earlier church and mausoleum. In 1063, Doge Contarini instigated a fourth building, demanding a church that would be "the most beautiful ever seen." Work on this nonpareil culminated in 1094, when the new basilica was consecrated and designated Venice's "official church of state." This is more or less the building you see today, although in 1094 it had yet to acquire its vast

■ The basilica's **Loggia dei Cavalli** offers a bird's-eye view of the Piazza San Marco.

EXPERIENCE: Join in the Revelry of Venice's Carnevale

The Venice Carnevale is not for everyone—though sometimes it can seem as if everyone is here during the event, held in the 12 or so days leading up to Shrove Tuesday. After being abandoned at the end of the 18th century, having taken place since at least the 13th century, Carnevale (from *carne levare*—the farewell to meat) has been a huge success since it was reborn in the 1970s, attracting upward of half a million people.

As a result, Carnevale time is not the occasion to visit Venice for sightseeing—if you're coming to Venice during Carnevale, then you must come ready to join in the celebrations.

For this you need costumes, masks, and resilience in the face of the huge crowds. Masks—simple eye masks or full-face masks outlined in silver and gold, many of the designs stemming from commedia dell'arte—can be bought year-round or at stalls that spring up during the festivities, while costumes can be rented, bought, or created beforehand. The theme? Think the waning decades of 18th-century Venice—a decadent and sinful period when Venetians indulged their every pleasure-seeking whim.

People spend the whole day in character, gathering in Piazza San Marco to compare outfits and to be photographed; preening in the windows of Caffè Florian; or, in the case of Venetians who stay in the city, going about their daily business in the classic costume of white mask, black cloak, and tricorn hat.

You can also attend some of the numerous street events, special concerts and theater shows, fashion and

Masks were banned under Mussolini, but they have been made and sold across the city since the revival of Carnevale in 1979.

design parades, processions, masquerades, and street performances that take place everywhere during Carnevale. Especially diverting are the pageants held on the water, featuring crews in costume and many of Venice's different types of traditional boats. Or you can join actors in costume as they take you to little-visited parts of the city and act out historical vignettes.

Museums and churches stay open late into the evening during Carnevale, the latter wonderfully evocative at night, especially those that host classical concerts, often with musicians also in costume and playing original 18th-century, or 18th-century-like, instruments.

To feel fully part of the proceedings, you should also try to attend one of Carnevale's lushly extravagant masked evening balls, with dancing and other entertainment, held in some of the city's most magnificent palaces such as Ca' Vendramin and Palazzo Dandolo. These masked balls can be expensive, with tickets for the more exclusive events hard to come by. **Venice Tours** (*venicecitytours.it*) can help source tickets.

For information on the balls, or on Carnevale in general, visit the website of **Consorzio Venezia Market & Eventi** (*carnevale.venezia .it*), which is the body responsible for co-coordinating Carnevale events.

array of artistic and architectural embellishment. Work on the mosaics began before 1100, but the bulk of the ornamentation appeared in 1204, much of it shamelessly looted by the Venetians from Constantinople during the Fourth Crusade.

Mosaics—some more than 900 years old—cover almost every surface of the basilica's interior.

Exterior: At first glance, the basilica appears an intimidating sightseeing prospect. In truth, the exterior, at least, is relatively straightforward. There are three facades: Start your visit beneath the right (south) facade, the side facing the water, where the outline of what was once the basilica's main entrance can still be seen.

The two freestanding **columns** against this facade, fifth-century Syrian works, came either from Constantinople or from Acre (in present-day Israel), where the Venetians defeated a Genoese force in 1256. The smaller column stump nearby, the **Pietra del bando,** almost certainly hails from Acre and was one of two such columns—the other is in the Rialto markets— once used to proclaim state decrees; it was also used to display the heads of executed criminals. High up on the facade is a small mosaic Madonna flanked by ever-burning oil lamps, originally lit to mark executions, when the condemned would turn to the Madonna with the cry of *"Salve Regina."* Others claim the mosaic was commissioned by the authorities to atone for a wrongful execution or in fulfilment of a promise made by an old sailor lost at sea and saved by the Virgin's intercession.

Many of the apparent treasures on the **main facade** are copies, most notably the famous bronze horses (the originals are inside) and the vast majority of the mosaics, only one of which is original: the **"Translation of the**

Venice's *Acqua Alta*

Venice's setting has always made it a watery hostage to the vagaries of wind and tide. It is no longer sinking—the lowering of the water table, and with it Venice, as the thick layer of silt and clay beneath the city dried and contracted, was arrested in 1973, when water extraction from more than 50 boreholes on the mainland was curtailed.

While the water table recovered, however, the subsidence, say experts, was "unrecoverable." So Venice is lower than it might be, and sea levels seem gradually to be rising, all of which means that the phenomenon known as *acqua*

alta, or high water, will continue, the sea invading Venice's streets and squares— most notably Piazza San Marco—on days when the tides are high or the wind blows in the wrong direction.

Sometimes the piazza is merely covered in a few large puddles; at others it is completely underwater. Venetians are unperturbed. They put on boots and know the authorities will swing into action, setting raised walkways across the square and along the city's main streets. Few, though, will choose to live at sea level—ground-floor real estate is the city's cheapest.

Body of St. Mark to the Basilica" (1260–1270), above the door on the extreme left. This same door, one of five, contains 14th-century sandstone bas-reliefs portraying the symbols of the Evangelists, together with an attractive architrave of panels and figures dating from either the 5th or 13th century. The facade's greatest works are the 13th-century **Romanesque carvings** above the central (third) portal, whose broad range of themes and figures includes (on the outer arch) the famous statue of a man biting his nails; Venetians claim he represents an 11th-century Greek architect chewing his nails in fury at criticism of his work.

Sights on the oft-ignored **north facade** include the Porta dei Fiori, or Door of Flowers, whose arches enclose a charming nativity scene. Alongside is the tomb of Daniele Manin (1804–1857), leader of a heroic but unsuccessful 19th-century uprising against

the Austrians. At the center of the first arch lies an eighth-century Byzantine relief of the Twelve Apostles, while between the arch and its neighbor is a quaint tenth-century relief portraying Alexander the Great's mythical quest to reach heaven on a chariot pulled by two griffons.

Interior: Crowds and services within the basilica are such that you cannot always wander at will or choose which of the many treasures you wish to see. (Nor can a short account do justice to the sights on show. In order to make the most of your visit and, in particular, to make sense of the quite bewildering array of mosaics, it pays to buy a specialist guidebook at the basilica's shop.) Aim to arrive early in the morning or late in the afternoon to avoid the worst of the crowds. And note that while admission is free to the main interior space, you need to follow the given path for groups or individual visitors.

Mosaics: Almost every available surface of the basilica—some 43,000 square feet (4,000 sq m) in all—is blanketed with golden-hued mosaics, an artistic medium, like the church's Greek cross plan, that was adopted from the Byzantine tradition. The earliest examples date from around 1100, but new additions were still being made 700 years later. Down the centuries, the leading artists of their day, notably Titian, Tintoretto, and

Veronese, often contributed the designs for new panels. Mosaics in the basilica's dusky interior largely portray episodes from the New Testament, while those in the **narthex,** or vestibule, the first area you come to just inside the basilica's main door, depict scenes from the Old Testament.

Loggia dei Cavalli: Stairs from the narthex lead to the Loggia dei Cavalli, or the Loggia of the Horses,

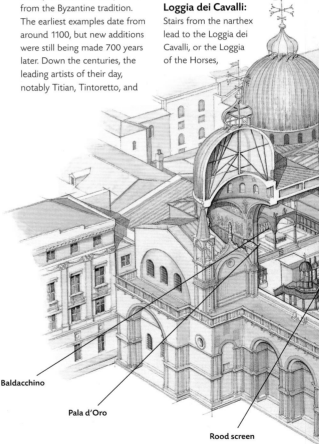

Baldacchino

Pala d'Oro

Rood screen

Basilica di San Marco

an external balcony that offers a lofty view across Piazza San Marco. It is also home to the basilica's famous **bronze horses,** brought from Constantinople in 1204—or rather copies of these horses, as the originals are now kept far from the corrosive assault of airborne pollution in the adjoining Museo di San Marco. Part of a *quadriga,* or four-horsed chariot team, the gilded creatures are the only such artifact to have survived from classical antiquity, although whether they are of Greek (fourth century B.C.) or Roman (third century A.D.) provenance is uncertain. All four found their way to Paris in 1797,

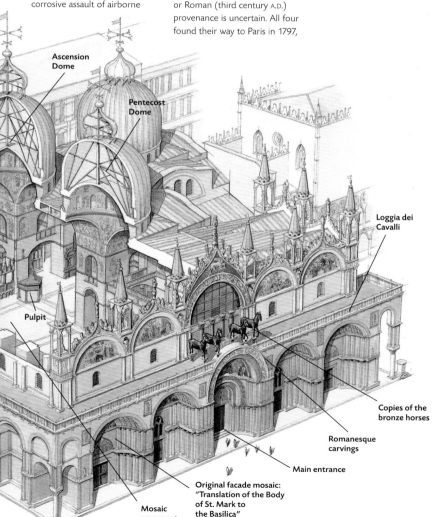

Ascension Dome

Pentecost Dome

Loggia dei Cavalli

Pulpit

Copies of the bronze horses

Romanesque carvings

Main entrance

Original facade mosaic: "Translation of the Body of St. Mark to the Basilica"

Mosaic pavement

St. Mark

Venice has long enjoyed a very special relationship with St. Mark, Apostle and Evangelist. Not that St. Mark enjoyed any relationship with Venice, a city still several centuries from existence during the saint's lifetime. The nearest he supposedly came to the city's site was on his return to Rome from Aquileia, a Roman colony on the Adriatic, when an angel appeared to the saint as he passed across the lagoon with the words, *"Pax tibi Marce, evangelist meus. Hic requiescet corpus tuum"* (Peace be with you Mark, my Evangelist. Here shall your body rest).

The story is probably a myth of Venetian invention, used to justify the theft of the saint's body and to lend valuable spiritual sanction to the foundation of a city that, in truth, had been disappointingly banal in its origins. The theft, a seminal moment in Venetian history, occurred in 828, although details of the event are encrusted in myth. The authorized version suggests the custodians of the saint's body, then in Alexandria in Egypt, became concerned at the Alexandrian king's plundering of the saint's tomb. Fearing further assault, they agreed to help the Venetians steal the body, hiding the relics beneath mounds of pork to distract the Muslim guards. After a tumultuous sea voyage, the remains were presented to the doge and Mark was duly declared Venice's patron saint.

courtesy of Napoleon, but were returned to Italy 18 years later—unlike many Italian works of art looted by the French emperor.

Sanctuary: The basilica's most compelling sight after the horses and the solemn beauty of the dimly lit interior is the area behind the high altar—the sanctuary—and its monumental altarpiece, the **Pala d'Oro** (Screen of Gold). This altarpiece lies to the rear of the altar, reputed final resting place of St. Mark, although many claim the saint's relics were destroyed in a fire in 976. The Pala is Europe's greatest piece of medieval gold and silverware, its dazzling frontage adorned with 15 rubies, 100 amethysts, 300 sapphires, 300 emeralds, 400 garnets, 1,300 pearls, and some 200 miscellaneous stones. Begun in 976, it was reworked in 1105 and again in 1209, when it was embellished with some of the flood tide of jewels looted from Constantinople during the Fourth Crusade.

Note the **pulpit** on exiting the sanctuary, traditionally the spot where a new doge was presented to the people, and the vast iconostasis, or **rood screen,** which is topped with 14th-century statues of the Virgin, St. Mark, and the Apostles.

Treasury: Booty from the Fourth Crusade makes up much of the collection in the basilica's *tesoro,* or treasury, located off the transept midway down the church's right (south) side. Made up largely of religious and other early Byzantine silverware, the collection is the finest of its kind in Europe, and, but for the antics of Napoleon, would have been finer still—some 55 gold and silver ingots were all that remained once he had melted down the cream of the collection. Note the large throne by the turnstile, the so-called **Throne of St. Mark,** carved in Alexandria and given to one of the lagoon's earliest religious rulers in 690. Note, too, the treasury's redoubtable **walls,** probably part of the original ninth-century Palazzo Ducale.

Palazzo Ducale

The Palazzo Ducale, or Doge's Palace, was home for almost a thousand years not only to Venice's doges, secret police, and principal law courts, but also to its prisons, torture chambers, and many of the city's myriad administrative institutions.

One of the world's finest Gothic buildings, the exterior is a beautiful mingling of columns, quatrefoils, and intricately patterned marbles. The interior is a labyrinth of gilt- and

INSIDER TIP:

Follow in the footsteps of the locals and grab a well-priced sandwich and beer at tiny Mio *(Frezzeria 1176).* It's a one-minute walk from Piazza San Marco's southwest corner.

—SHEILA F. BUCKMASTER
National Geographic Traveler
magazine editor at large

painting-smothered rooms, as well as a series of dark and intimidating dungeons that once confined the 18th-century adventurer Casanova, among others.

The first palace, a fortresslike structure, was built in 814, but it succumbed to fires in 976 and 1094. The present building began

Palazzo Ducale

- 131 D2
- Piazzetta-Piazza San Marco 1
- 041 271 5911
- $$$$$ combined ticket with Museo Civico Correr. Guided tours $$ extra
- 1, 2, & other boats to San Zaccaria

palazzoducale .visitmuve.it

The current Palazzo Ducale has withstood floods and other disasters for close to 700 years.

It is unknown who the sculpted Tetrarchs at the entrance to the Palazzo Ducale are meant to represent.

fires in 1574 and 1577 brought the building close to collapse, and for a while there were plans to demolish the palace and rebuild it along High Renaissance lines. As it turned out, a more modest restoration scheme saved the Gothic palace for posterity.

Exterior: Start your visit by walking to the bridge, the Ponte della Paglia, at the far end of the palace's waterfront facade. From the little bridge, you can admire the inexplicably famous Ponte dei Sospiri (1600), or **Bridge of Sighs,** reputedly named after the sighs of condemned men being led from the palace to the city's prisons. Then look up to the left to admire "The Drunkenness of Noah," one of three statues adorning three corners of the palace—the other two represent "Adam and Eve" and "The Judgment of Solomon." Walking back along the waterfront facade, note the statue of "Justice" (1579) above the central window. The capitals of the many pillars below are carved with allegories of the vices and virtues.

Around the corner, on the palace's other principal facade, look up to the loggia and its two anomalous red columns, reputedly stained by the blood of the tortured criminals who were hung here before execution. Left of the palace's flamboyant doorway, the **Porta della Carta** (1443), stand the famous **Tetrarchs,** a group of maroon-colored porphyry knights, probably fourth-century statues representing the emperor

to take shape in 1314, when work started on a great hall for the Maggior Consiglio, the Republic's parliamentary lower house. Three years after this was completed, in 1422, remaining parts of the older palazzo razed to make way for the palace's present main facade. Thereafter, the interior was constantly modified as the machinery of government grew, the palace attaining more or less its present shape in 1550. Major

Diocletian and three co-rulers of the Roman Empire.

Interior: In the palace court-yard is the Scala dei Giganti, or Giants' Staircase (1485), named after Jacopo Sanso-vino's statues of "Mars" and "Neptune" (1567), emblems of Venice's command of land and sea, respectively. Purchase an entrance ticket before climbing

---

INSIDER TIP:

While on a tour of the Palazzo Ducale, don't miss the vivid, artistic graffiti left behind by unfortunates on the walls of the prisons.

—PATRICIA DANIELS
National Geographic contributor

Sansovino's **Scala d'Oro,** or Golden Staircase (1557), to the start of a set itinerary through the palace's long succession of magnificently decorated rooms. The first of these, the **Sala dell'Anticollegio,** acted as an anteroom for visiting dignitaries, who, while awaiting an audience, could admire paintings by Tin-toretto and Veronese. The same painters decorated the **Sala del Collegio,** home to the Collegio, Venice's ruling council, and the Signoria, the Collegio's more powerful inner sanctum.

Highlights among the stream of rooms that follow include the gilt-laden **Sala del Senato** and the **Sala del Consiglio dei Dieci,**

Secret Itinerary Tours of the Palazzo Ducale

Book one of the popular Itinerari Segreti del Palazzo Ducale *($$$$; ticket includes admission to rest of palace)* **for a fascinating behind-the-scenes look at the doges' for-mer private apartments, the rooftop prison (or Piombi) and torture chambers, and the maze of corridors, passageways, and offices hidden from normal view in the Palazzo Ducale. Tickets must be booked in advance, online or at tel 848 082 000 (lines closed Sun., Sat. p.m., & 1–2 p.m.), though you can ask at the box office if any places remain on that day's tours. Tours in English generally take place three times a day, currently at 9:55 a.m., 10:45 a.m., and 11:35 a.m.**

the latter a meeting place for the Council of Ten, magistrates and overseers of Venice's feared secret police. The **Sala della Bussola** next door contains a Bocca di Leone (Lion's Mouth), a form of mailbox into which citizens could drop accusations. The Sala's rear door led to a small inner court-room, and from thence to the torture chamber and prisons.

A four-room armory follows until the itinerary, somewhat circuitous by this stage, arrives at the palace's star turn, the immense **Sala del Maggior Consiglio,** dominated by the world's largest painting, Tintoretto's gargantuan "Paradiso" (1592). The old prisons follow, reached via the Bridge of Sighs, strikingly dark and somber after the preceding splendor.

To see more than just the pub-lic rooms, take one of the Itinerari Segreti, excellent guided tours (see sidebar this page) that visit, among other places, the old dungeons. ∎

A SAN MARCO & DORSODURO STROLL

This walk runs west from Piazza San Marco through the heart of Venice, crossing the Accademia Bridge to explore the Dorsoduro district before reaching the Scuola Grande dei Carmini, headquarters of the Carmelite confraternity.

Leaving **Piazza San Marco** ❶ (see pp. 134–136), walk past the **Palazzo Ducale** (see pp. 143–145) to the waterfront and bear right. Go past the Giardini ex Reali and turn right up Calle del Ridotto to the church of **San Moisè**, noted for its exuberant baroque facade created by Alessandro Tremignon in 1668. Cross the bridge over the Rio di San Moisè to reach Calle Larga XXII Marzo, and take a short detour north on Calle del Sartor da Veste to **Teatro La Fenice**, the opera house. Follow the shop-lined Calle Larga XII Marzo west to Campo Santa Maria Zobenigo, where **Santa Maria del Giglio**

NOT TO BE MISSED:

Santo Stefano • Collezione Peggy Guggenheim • Santa Maria della Salute

stands, crammed with a bizarre medley of saintly relics. Continue west through Campo San Maurizio to Campo Santo Stefano.

Leave this square after visiting the church of **Santo Stefano** ❷ *(closed Sun., $)*, with its fine ceiling and calm interior. Campo San

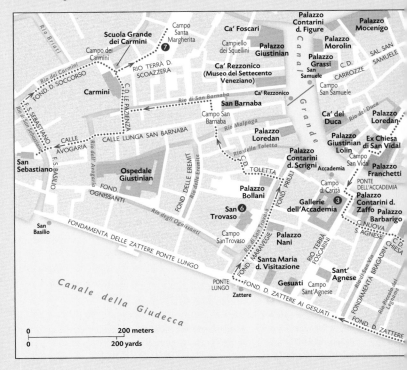

Vidal leads from the square's southern flank to the **Ponte dell'Accademia**, a bridge over the Canal Grande. Here you can absorb one of Venice's most mesmerizing views.

Follow the street Rio Terrà Foscarini to the left of the **Gallerie dell'Accademia ③** (see pp. 149–152), then bear left on Calle Nuova Sant'Agnese. Continue due east, past the **Collezione Peggy Guggenheim ④** (see pp. 152–153), to emerge at **Santa Maria della Salute ⑤** (see p. 153). Follow the waterfront promenade around the **Punta della Dogana** and the Zattere, a route with views to the island of the Giudecca and the church of San Giorgio Maggiore. Pass the church of the Gesuati and turn north on Fondamenta Nani along the Rio di San Trovaso canal. Note the *squero* (gondola boatyard) across the canal in front of the church of **San Trovaso ⑥** (closed Sun. & a.m.).

Cross the second bridge and follow Calle delle Toletta to emerge in Campo San Barnaba. Follow the canal left from the top of the square. Cross the bridge before the canal bends left and take Calle de le Pazienza north to the church of the **Carmini** (tel 041 296 0630, closed Sun. & a.m.), which has paintings by Lorenzo Lotto and Cima da Conegliano. Opposite stands the **Scuola Grande dei Carmini** (Campo Santa Margherita 2617, tel 041 528 9420, $$), noted for Tiepolo's 18th-century ceiling frescoes.

A loop west on Calle de le Pazienza, Calle Lunga San Barnaba, and Calle Avogaria takes you to **San Sebastiano** (closed Sun., $ or Chorus Pass), with paintings by Veronese. Continue north on Fondamenta San Sebastiano and east on Fondamenta del Soccorso, past the Carmini, to reach **Campo Santa Margherita ⑦**, one of Venice's prettiest piazzas.

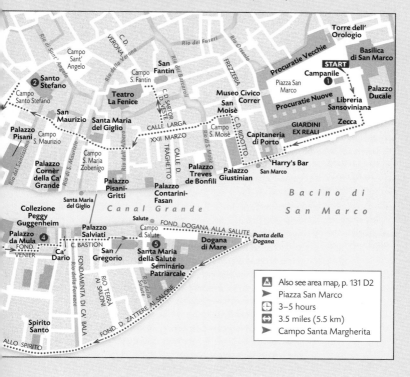

Also see area map, p. 131 D2
Piazza San Marco
3–5 hours
3.5 miles (5.5 km)
Campo Santa Margherita

DORSODURO

Wedged between the Canal Grande and the Canale della Giudecca, Dorsoduro—one of Venice's six *sestieri* (districts)—holds many attractions for visitors, most notably a slew of high-profile art museums. Art abounds in the 17th-century Santa Maria della Salute, too, which occupies pride of place at the mouth of the Canal Grande.

Look up to see the glittering chandeliers and beautifully decorated ceilings of the Ca' Rezzonico.

Ca' Rezzonico

- 130 B2
- Dorsoduro 3136
- 041 241 0100
- Closed Tues.
- $$ or combined Museum Pass
- 1 to Ca' Rezzonico

**carezzonico
.visitmuve.it**

Ca' Rezzonico

Venice has enjoyed many a colorful period, but few have been as striking as the decadent years of its 18th-century dotage, a period when, according to one popular adage, the "Venetians did not taste their pleasures but swallowed them whole." The Ca' Rezzonico, or Museo del Settecento Veneziano, is devoted to the period, its displays and palatial interior fashioned to reflect the artistic and social tastes of the city during its often frivolous decline.

The Ca' Rezzonico was begun circa 1649 by Baldassare Longhena, the leading baroque architect of

his day, and completed in fits and starts over the next hundred years. Among its long line of owners was Pen Browning, son of the English poet Robert Browning—Browning *père* died here in 1889. The building was bought by the state and opened as a museum in 1936.

The first eye-opener on a tour of the palace is the magnificent **ballroom,** spoiled only by the renowned but vulgar furniture of Andrea Brustolon (1662–1732), whose shackled wooden slaves make dispiriting viewing. Soon after comes the **Sala dell'Allegoria Nuziale,** with 18th-century ceiling frescoes by

Giovanni Battista Tiepolo (1696–1770), and then rooms adorned with portraits in pastel by Rosalba Carriera, Flemish tapestries, and beautiful lacquerwork furniture.

Part of the second floor is given over to an art gallery, where the highlights are works by Canaletto, Francesco Guardi's vignettes of Venetian high society, and Pietro Longhi's fascinating snapshots of Venetian daily life. Pride of place, however, goes to Giandomenico Tiepolo's satirical frescoes (1793–1797) in the last few rooms, a sequence moved here from the artist's country villa.

Gallerie dell'Accademia

It was no surprise that a city as singular as Venice should produce its own artists and its own artistic style. "All Venice was both model and painter," observed novelist Henry James, "and life was so pictorial that art could not help becoming so."

Venetian art was transcendent across several centuries, and not only those spanning the Renaissance and High Renaissance, Italy's obvious artistic zenith. It was also outstanding across earlier and later centuries, from the gold-backed Byzantine mosaics of Torcello and the Basilica di San Marco, to the photograph-sharp 18th-century cityscapes of Canaletto.

Some of the greatest of Venice's paintings, however, are gathered in a single gallery, the Gallerie dell'Accademia, founded in 1750 as an academy of the arts. Much of its collection was acquired in 1807, the year the academy moved to its present home. Most was collected from churches, convents, and monasteries suppressed and cleared by Napoleonic decree. Due to important restoration work started in 2017, some areas can be closed to visitors, but the artworks are being relocated in other rooms and their display guaranteed.

Gallerie dell'Accademia

🗺 130 B1–B2

✉ Ponte dell'Accademia, Campo della Carità, Dorsoduro, 1050

☎ 041 522 2247

🕐 Closed Mon. p.m. (lines closed Sat. p.m., Sun.)

🚤 1 & 2 to Accademia; 2, 5.1, 5.2, 6, 8, 10 to Zattere

💲 $$ Tickets available online or by phone. Additional charge during special exhibitions.

gallerieaccademia .it

Venetian Vocabulary

Understanding some of the words you'll encounter time and again on the streets of Venice will add to your understanding and enjoyment of the city. *Campo,* for example, is the name given to a square, from the Italian for field—note that Venice has only one "piazza," Piazza San Marco. A small square is a *campiello* or *campazzo,* and a courtyard or dead-end alley is a *corte. Rio* means canal, *rio terrà* a canal that has been filled in. A *calle* is a street, *ruga* an important street or one lined with stores, and a *fondamenta* or *riva* (bank) is a wide street running along a canal where a boat can dock. *Salizzada* refers to a paved street (which were once rare), and a *ramo*—from

the word for "branch"—is a short alley or the extension of another street. A *sotoportego* is an arcade or arched passage under a building.

Away from the streets, an *ombra* is a glass of wine, from the word for "shadow," perhaps after the idea of coming in from the sun for a refreshing drink—or perhaps from the days when wine was stored in barrels at the foot of the Campanile and had to be constantly moved into the shade to keep it cool. An *ombra* might be taken in a *bàcaro,* a traditional Venetian wine bar, and accompanied by *cicchetti,* a selection of small tapas-like snacks.

Byzantine Beginnings: The Accademia's opening room augurs well, its glorious gold-tinged ceiling providing a beautiful foil for the array of largely Byzantine-influenced paintings. The star turn is the glorious "Coronation of the Virgin" (1365) by Paolo Veneziano. One of the city's first great painters, he played a prominent role in transforming Venice's previous artistic preoccupation with

---

INSIDER TIP:

To find warmth on a cold sunny day after visiting the Accademia, weave through the narrow streets for about three minutes to the Zattere, the wide-open promenade on the Giudecca Canal.

—SHEILA F. BUCKMASTER
National Geographic Traveler
magazine editor at large

---

the mosaic into a preference for painting. Moving to **Room 2,** you skip a century to find yourself among early Renaissance masterpieces: Giovanni Bellini (1435–1516), perhaps the most sublime of all Venetian painters, is represented by the "Madonna and Saints" (1487), while another big name, Vittore Carpaccio (ca 1460–1526), makes an early appearance with the seductive "Presentation of Jesus in the Temple" and the graphic "Ten Thousand Martyrs of Mount Ararat." The latter alludes to the legend of

10,000 defeated Roman soldiers martyred by Armenian rebels.

Great Names: The tiny **Rooms 4 and 5** contain some of the Accademia's greatest paintings. Among them is Giorgione's remarkable "The Tempest" (1500), a work so enigmatic that no one has been able to explain its allegorical meaning (if one exists) with any success. Nearby is Giorgione's "Col Tempo," a more easily understood allegory of old age and passing time. Piero della Francesca (1416–1492), an almost equally enigmatic painter, is represented by a curious "St. Jerome," arranged alongside an almost indecent number of paintings by Giovanni Bellini—a painter heavily influenced by Piero—the most beguiling of which is the "Madonna and Child with Saints."

High Renaissance: Rooms 6–9 mark something of a hiatus in proceedings, a lull interrupted in spectacular fashion by Paolo Veronese's colossal "Supper in the House of Levi" (1573) in **Room 10.** It was originally intended as a depiction of the Last Supper, but Veronese (1528–1588) was forced to change the painting's title—but not its content—when the Inquisition objected to its inappropriate portrayal of what it termed "buffoons, drunkards, Germans, dwarfs, and similar indecencies." Two paintings by Jacopo Tintoretto (1519–1594), one of the giants of the Venetian High Renaissance, hang close by: the "Miracle of the Slave" (1548) and the "Translation of the Body of St. Mark" (1560, **Room 15**).

On the opposite wall hangs a "Pietà" (1576), a masterpiece by Titian (1485–1576), Tintoretto's foil and rival. Painted when the artist was more than 90, the red-cloaked figure to the right of Christ is probably a self-portrait.

"Miracles of the True Cross":

The gallery's main corridor and **Rooms 8** and **12–19** provide a handful of worthwhile distractions, most notably several works by Canaletto, pastels by Rosalba Carriera (1675–1757), one of Venice's best known women artists, and several fascinating little 18th-century vignettes of Venetian daily life by Pietro Longhi (1702–1785). Make sure you reserve energy for "Miracles of the True Cross" (1494–1510) in **Room 20,** an eight-painting sequence created by a variety of artists for the city's Scuola Grande di San Giovanni Evangelista. Each work ostensibly portrays a miracle associated with a fragment of the cross from the Crucifixion, presented to the *scuola,* although much of the paintings' charm derives from the cycle's wonderful accumulation of incidental narrative detail. Gentile Bellini's "Procession of the Holy Relic," for example, offers a marvelous portrait of Piazza San Marco as it appeared in 1496.

Carpaccio's St. Ursula:

Another painting cycle fills **Room 21,** but this time the nine-work sequence is by a single artist, Carpaccio, and the theme is the life and death of St. Ursula. Daughter of a Breton king, Ursula promises to marry an English prince on condition he let her and a train of 11,000 virgins go on a two-year pilgrimage. Carpaccio portrays a variety of scenes, often compressing several events into a single frame. Some of the best are the "Arrival of the English Ambassadors," the "Conditions of Marriage," the "Return of the Ambassadors," and Ursula's "Departure for Rome" (the last panel depicts no fewer than four distinct events). "London" is portrayed on the right, dark and barbaric (note the symbolic

Giovanni Bellini's "Virgin and Child," Gallerie dell'Accademia

sunken ship). The Breton capital, by contrast—founded on Humanist principles—is shown bright and marble decked. Each painting is crammed with the sort of incidental detail for which Carpaccio is famous (his little dog was a favored motif). Few scenes are as action-packed as the penultimate panel, which combines the martyrdom of the saint and her followers in Cologne—massacred by the

■ The Collezione Peggy Guggenheim boasts an impressive collection of contemporary art.

Collezione Peggy Guggenheim

🔺 130 C1

✉ Fondamenta Venier dei Leoni 701, Dorsoduro

☎ 041 240 5411

🕐 Closed Tues.

💲 $$$$$
Tickets can be purchased online.

🚊 1 & 2 to Accademia; 1 to Salute

www.guggenheim -venice.it

Huns then besieging the city—and her subsequent funeral.

Collezione Peggy Guggenheim

Peggy Guggenheim adored Venice and Venice adored her, making the American-born heiress an honorary citizen of the city she adopted as her own in 1949. Born in 1898, she moved to Europe in 1921, where she became a leading light in artistic circles—she enjoyed a brief marriage to painter Max Ernst—and a collector of the finest avant-garde art of her day. Much of her collection is now on display in the Palazzo Venier dei Leoni.

The palace gardens, on the banks of the Canal Grande, are a delight, thanks to their scattered works of sculpture, including pieces by Paolozzi, Giacometti, and Henry Moore. The 18th-century palace, while superbly adapted to the demands of the

collection, is less alluring, partly because it was never completed—hence its nickname, the "Non-finito," the Unfinished.

Guggenheim had a matchless eye for the exquisite, and virtually every exhibit is scintillating, even for those whose taste does not normally extend to the modern or avant-garde. Her enthusiasms were also wide-ranging, and most broad movements within modern 20th-century art are represented. Thus Picasso and Braque fly the flag for cubism, Francis Bacon for English modernism, and Mondrian, Malevich, and Pevsner for constructivism. Among the surrealists, one of Guggenheim's chief passions, the works of Dalí, Max Ernst, and Magritte stand out, as do those of Americans such as Jackson Pollock, Willem de Kooning, and Mark Rothko. Italian Marino Marini, however, produced the gallery's most provocative work, "Angel of the

Citadel," an equestrian statue complete with nude rider and erect phallus, overlooking the Canal Grande.

Santa Maria della Salute

Remove the towering Renaissance church of Santa Maria della Salute from Venice and you would lose one of the city's most distinctive landmarks. Perched at the mouth of the Canal Grande, the great white-domed edifice has occupied a pivotal point on the Venetian skyline for more than 350 years.

Santa Maria was built in 1631 to fulfill a pledge made a year earlier by the Venetian Senate. The vow promised the building of a church in honor of the Virgin should she deliver Venice from a plague that had claimed more than 40,000 lives, around a third of the city's population. When the pestilence lifted—a result of cold weather rather than divine intervention, per cynics—a competition was launched to choose the church's architect, a man who had to fulfill the senate's demand that the building should "make a good impression without costing too much." The winner was Baldassare Longhena, who later would design the Ca' Pesaro and Ca' Rezzonico. His winning entry was christened the Salute, meaning both health and salvation in Italian.

Santa Maria's main portal is opened only during the Festa della Salute, a festival held on November 21 to commemorate the passing of the 1630 epidemic. Entry via the small side door scarcely diminishes the impact of the interior—the beautiful marble pavement at your feet and the soaring dome above. The high altar features the "Virgin Casting Out the Plague" (1670), a sculpture designed by Longhena and executed by Josse de Corte. The figure on the Virgin's left symbolizes Venice, the figure to the right the banished plague.

Other major works of art include Titian's "Descent of the Holy Spirit" (1545), the third

Santa Maria della Salute

🗺 131 C1

✉ Fondamenta della Salute

☎ 041 241 1018 or 041 274 3928

🕐 Closed 12 p.m.– 3 p.m.

🚢 1 to Salute

basilicasalute venezia.it

Dogana di Mare

The Dogana di Mare, Venice's beautiful former customhouse, sits on the Punta della Dogana, the finger of land at the point where the Canal Grande and Canale della Giudecca meet. After a couple decades of sitting vacant, it reopened in 2009, having been beautifully restored by world-renowned Japanese architect Tadao Ando as an exhibition space—Palazzo Grassi–François Pinault Foundation (closed Tue., Punta della Dogana, Dorsoduro 2, tel 041 240 1308, palazzograssi.it, vaporetto 1 to Salute, $$$)—**for the collection of contemporary art belonging to François Pinault, the building's co-owner and benefactor. The works exhibited change from time to time, but around a hundred pieces are generally on view, including most of the big names of modern art, among them Cy Twombly, Jeff Koons, Cindy Sherman, Maurizio Cattelan, and Luc Tuymans.**

painting on the church's left side, and several paintings in the **sacristy** ($), of which the most notable are Tintoretto's "Feast at Cana" (1561) and Titian's trio of ceiling paintings and majestic "St. Mark and Saints Damian, Cosmas, Roch, and Sebastian" (1510). ∎

GONDOLAS

Dark, silent, and oddly sinister, the gondola, for all its romantic allure, is an equivocal vessel. Nothing summons Venice so swiftly to mind as the gondola's sleek shape and its easy gliding motion along mirror-smooth canals. Yet few objects so emblematic of a city are so mysterious in their origins, so rigid in their present-day appearance, or so convoluted in their evolution over the centuries.

■ A couple rides in the world's most romantic vessel through the world's most romantic city.

Gondolas today are remarkably uniform. All weigh around 1,500 pounds (700 kg), have 280 components, and employ eight different types of wood—lime, larch, oak, fir, cherry, walnut, elm, and mahogany. All have an oar—made from beech—and a *forcola,* or carved oarlock, each of which is custom-made to suit individual gondoliers and allows the oar to be manhandled in eight distinct maneuvers. All are 36 feet (exactly 11 m) long and 4.6 feet wide (exactly 1.4 m), and all have one side 10 inches (24 cm) longer than the other. This final feature, oddly enough, was one of the last in the boat's

evolutionary process. Added by a boatyard during the 19th century to compensate for the weight of the gondolier, the imbalance lends the gondola its distinctive lean and lopsided appearance.

Other refinements are much older. Some scholars claim the vessel dates back to 697. Most agree on a first documentary reference in 1094, when the word appears in part of a decree aimed at regulating boats using the lagoon. The name is a matter of debate—some claim Latin, Maltese, or Turkish origins, others that it derives from the Greek for "cup" or "mussel." The most macabre theory links the name to classical mythology and the ferry used by Charon to carry the dead to the underworld.

In reality, the gondola's evolution was gradual. The lagoon's shallows and mud flats required a shallow-drafted vessel from earliest times. In the 13th century, the requisite boat had 12 oars; by the 15th century, the "gondola" had shrunk in size but acquired a *felze,* or cabin. By 1562, it had accumulated such a wealth of decoration that a special law banning ostentation of almost any kind was introduced. Henceforth, gondolas became a uniform black, while their exteriors were restricted to just three decorative flourishes—a curly tail, a pair of sea horses, and the familiar multi-pronged *ferro,* or prow.

The origin and symbolism of the prow are even more contentious than the gondola's origins. Some *ferri* have five prongs, some six—emblematic perhaps of Venice's six districts. The single prong facing aft is described alternatively as a symbol for the Palazzo Ducale, the Giudecca, Cyprus (part of Venice's former empire), or Piazza San Marco. Meanwhile, the broad-edged "blade" above may represent the sea, a lily, a doge's hat, a Venetian halberd, or the Rialto Bridge. Depending on your source, the ferro was inspired by Roman galleys, the funerary barges of ancient Egypt, or a judicial axe.

Gondola Rides

Venice's cheapest gondola rides involve the *traghetti* (ferries) that ply the Grand Canal at regular intervals. (A Venetian stands up, but a *foresta,* or outsider, usually finds it safer to sit.) Tariffs are set for the "genuine" gondola excursions. You pay more between 8 p.m. and 8 a.m., and additional rates apply for every 25 minutes over the standard 50-minute ride. Musical entertainment also costs more. In practice, gondoliers are open to negotiation—you may want to follow a particular route, for example—but always confirm the price and duration of any trip *before* setting out. Remember prices are per boat (not per person), up to a five-passenger limit. To avoid rip-offs, consult visitor centers for current rates and location of official stands.

EXPERIENCE: Visit a Gondola Workshop

The canals of Venice teemed with more than 10,000 gondolas in the 16th century. Today, there remain but a few hundred. Only a handful of new boats are made every year, many of them bought by foreigners. Yet boats must be cleaned every three weeks, and if not treated properly, they can warp beyond repair in five years, whereupon they are pensioned off as *traghetti* (ferries) across the Canal Grande or burned in the glass furnaces of Murano.

Thus, there is still work for the small number of *squeri,* or gondola workshops, that survive—just—in the city. Visiting a *squero* is to witness a centuries-old craft. The yards are picturesque—old, often wooden, and scattered with boating ephemera. You can see the gondolas being made, the woods used to make them, and the special and often unusual tools used to shape them. You also will see gondolas under repair and, probably, some of Venice's other distinctive small wooden boats.

The yards are small and not generally geared up to accept visitors on a regular basis. However, ask at the visitor center (see p. 132) or consult your hotel concierge about arranging a visit. Note that squeri owners generally charge a fee. Also note that it is often best to go with an official guide for the weathered artisans of the squeri are more comfortable with an all but impenetrable Venetian dialect than they are with English.

SAN POLO

San Polo, Venice's smallest district, is well known for its churches—chief among them Santa Maria Gloriosa dei Frari, second only to the Basilica di San Marco in terms of importance—and its ornately decorated small palaces and other buildings. One of the latter, the Scuola Grande di San Rocco merits particular attention for its many paintings by Tintoretto.

Titian's "Assumption" altarpiece in Santa Maria Gloriosa dei Frari is 22.5 feet tall (6.9 m).

Santa Maria Gloriosa dei Frari

- 🅰 130 B3
- ✉ Campo dei Frari 3072, San Polo
- ☎ 041 272 8618 or 041 272 8611
- 🕐 Closed Sun. a.m.
- 💲 $
- 🚤 1 & 2 to San Tomà

www.basilicadei frari.it

Santa Maria Gloriosa dei Frari

Santa Maria Gloriosa dei Frari is Venice's second most important religious building. Begun around 1250, the colossal Gothic church was built for the Franciscans, from whom it takes its colloquial name, the Frari, a corruption of *frati,* meaning "friars." It boasts a surfeit of sculpture and paintings completely at odds with the Franciscan ideals of poverty and humility, and claims three of Italy's greatest Renaissance paintings.

The first of these paintings, Titian's gargantuan **"Assumption"** (1518), dominates the church from its position above the high altar. Everything in the Frari contrives to focus your attention on the work, most notably the 124-stall wooden choir (1468)—itself a masterpiece—whose arched entrance frames the painting from the church's rear.

The Frari's second great painting could hardly be more different. Giovanni Bellini's sublime **triptych** (1488) in the sacristy is the essence of meditative calm. It portrays the Madonna and Child between Saints Peter, Nicholas, Mark, and Benedict, its saints the namesakes of those who commissioned it—Pietro Pesaro and his sons Niccolò, Marco, and Benedetto.

The Frari's third major painting is Titian's **"Madonna di Ca' Pesaro"** (1526). Commissioned by Iacopo Pesaro, who lies buried in a tomb to the painting's right, the work contains several portraits of the Pesaro family. The most obvious is Iacopo's nephew and heir, Leonardo, the small boy who stares out at the onlooker in one of the painting's most familiar compositional flourishes. Iacopo himself is on the left in front of the knight (possibly a self-portrait of Titian). Pesaro was a bishop and admiral, and, in 1502, led a campaign against the Turks on the prompting of the Borgia pope, Alexander VI. This accounts for the Borgia and Pesaro coats of arms on the red banner and the turbaned Turk and slave on the left being led toward St. Peter, symbolizing their conversion and the Christian impulse behind Iacopo's campaign.

Tombs: There is no mistaking the Frari's most distinctive tomb: a huge white marble pyramid created in honor of Antonio Canova (1827). All that remains of the noted neoclassical sculptor within it, however, is his heart, the rest of his remains having been removed to his birthplace in the Veneto. Canova himself had originally designed the tomb as a new mausoleum for Titian (died 1576), who lies across the nave in a second-rate tomb designed by Canova's pupils. To the right of Canova's

pyramid stands the extraordinary monument to Doge Giovanni Pesaro (died 1659), a kitschy but oddly beguiling tomb.

Three tombs of greater intrinsic merit occupy the end wall of the south transept: These are monuments to Paolo Savelli (1407), Benedetto Pesaro (died 1503), and Beato Pacifico (1437). Savelli was a Roman *condottiere*, or mercenary, who died of the plague while leading Venice's army against Padua. Pesaro, by contrast, was a Venetian admiral who died in Corfu, hence the reliefs of ships and naval fortresses adorning his tomb. The tomb of Pacifico, a religious figure, is a rare Florentine work, its canopy and terra-cotta figures some of the prettiest objects in Santa Maria Gloriosa dei Frari.

INSIDER TIP:

Wandering around Venice at sunrise is wonderful. You get to see the city wake up, with municipal boat traffic—school "buses," trash barges—navigating the canals.

—AMY KOLCZAK
National Geographic
International Editions

Two tombs in the second chapel to the right of the high altar are almost equally pleasing, particularly the disarmingly modest effigy of Duccio degli Uberti (died 1336) on the left, with its protective and quaintly hovering statue of the

Venetian *Scuole*

The Venetian *scuola* was a combination of guild, charity, and religious confraternity. Some united merchants, craftspeople, or those with similar professions; others linked expatriates, religious orders, and individuals with humanitarian aims. Most were lay organizations with religious ties, their main purpose mutual assistance and charitable works. By the fall of the Republic in 1797, there were more than 300, of which the six largest and most prosperous had acquired the title of Scuola Grande.

As well as patron saints, each scuola often had its own church and specially commissioned meeting place, the latter usually a two-story building divided into an *albergo* (a committee room) and *sala del capitolo* (for services and ceremonies).

Scuole varied in size from the 600 members of the Scuola Grande di San Rocco to the 20-person sand merchants' scuola. Anyway, smaller scuole lacked nothing by way of status—the sand merchants, for example, were able to commission an artist of the stature of Bartolomeo Vivarini for the altarpiece of their chapel in the church of San Giovanni in Bragora.

Scuola Grande di San Rocco

🗺 130 B3

✉ Campo San Rocco 3052, San Polo

☎ 041 523 4864

💲 $$

🚤 1 & 2 to San Tomà

scuolagrande sanrocco.it

Madonna and Child. The chapel to the left features another Florentine work, a statue of "St. John the Baptist" (1438) by Donatello, the Tuscan sculptor's only work in Venice.

Scuola Grande di San Rocco

Of Venice's half dozen *scuole grandi* (see sidebar this page), the most important was the Scuola Grande di San Rocco, founded in 1478 in honor of San Rocco (St. Roch), a French-born saint widely invoked against infectious diseases. These credentials made him a prime candidate for veneration in plague-battered Venice and the obvious inspiration for an institution devoted to healing the sick, hence the large sum paid by the *scuola* to bring his relics from Germany to Venice in 1485.

The arrival of Roch's relics brought the scuola a flood of donations, allowing it to commission a magnificent new home

from architect Bartolomeo Bon in 1516. On completion, the interior remained relatively unadorned until 1564, when Tintoretto won a commission to decorate the *sala dell'albergo,* beginning an association with San Rocco that would last 24 years and produce 54 extraordinary paintings.

To follow Tintoretto's artistic progress through the scuola, make first for the small annex on the first floor known as the **Sala dell'Albergo.** Decorated between 1564 and 1567, it features the ceiling painting of "St. Roch in Glory" that first won Tintoretto his commission. Tintoretto trumped other painters competing for the commission by creating a finished painting—his rivals produced only sketches—and then had it secretly placed in situ on the ceiling before the judges' arrival. Like everything else in the room, however, the winning picture is overshadowed by the painter's vast "Crucifixion" (1565), widely considered one of the finest paintings in Italy. John

Ruskin, the eminent Victorian critic, thought it "beyond all analysis and above all praise."

The rest of the upper floor, the **Sala Capitolare,** features the main body of Tintoretto's work (1575–1581). The artist began his labors on the ceiling, where a multitude of paintings depict episodes from the Old and the New Testament. All were carefully selected to draw some parallel with the scuola's humanitarian aims—thus the obvious relevance of such scenes as "The Feeding of the Five Thousand" or "Christ's Healing of the Paralytic." The ten wall paintings deal with episodes from the New Testament, their volatile composition, unworldly coloring, and generally iconoclastic approach making them some of the city's most striking works of art. Don't, however, miss the wonderful collection of 17th-century **wooden carvings** around the walls. The two most famous are the "Painter," a caricature of Tintoretto, complete with brushes (near the altar), and "Curiosity," a macabre, spy-like figure in cocked hat, with one sinister eye peering over his cloak (left and below Tintoretto's "Resurrection").

Tintoretto was in his sixties when he moved to the scuola's **lower hall,** where eight huge canvases (1583–87) pick up from the New Testament scenes upstairs. The painter's invention here is equally breathtaking. Rarely can the subject of the Annunciation, for example, have been painted with such vigor or with quite such disregard for the conventions usually demanded of the subject.

The Virgin's tumbledown home is a chaos of splintered wood and shattered brick, her expression one of startled disbelief as the angel Gabriel descends from the darkened heavens with a cohort of dive-bombing cherubs.

Even more of Tintoretto's work can be seen in the church of **San Rocco** just outside the scuola.

Scuola dei Calegheri

🔺 130 A3
✉ Campo San Tomà 2857, San Polo

▪ **Detail of Tintoretto's celebrated "Crucifixion," Scuola Grande di San Rocco**

Scuola dei Calegheri

The headquarters of one of the smaller scuole, the Scuola dei Calegheri, or Shoemakers, can be seen a block from San Rocco, at the western end of Campo San Tomà. Look for the stone shoe by the door and the faded relief above the portal from 1478 by Pietro Lombardo, which depicts St. Mark healing the cobbler Anianus, later to become the Bishop of Alexandria and the patron saint of shoemakers. The building is now a library. ■

CANNAREGIO

The district of Cannaregio is mostly a quiet, peaceful residential neighborhood, worth a wander for a sense of everyday Venetian life. Notable sights are the Ca' d'Oro, a sumptuous palace now housing an art museum; and the churches of Santa Maria dei Miracoli and Madonna dell'Orto, the first blessed with a lovely facade and the second several paintings by Tintoretto.

■ The Ca' d'Oro was once intended to be the most magnificent building on the Canal Grande.

Ca' d'Oro

🅰 131 C4

✉ Canal Grande or Calle di Ca' d'Oro at Strada Nuova 3932

☎ 041 520 0345

🕐 Closed Mon. p.m.

💲 $

🚤 1 to Ca' d'Oro

cadoro.org

Ca' d'Oro

The Ca' d'Oro, or house of gold, takes its name from the veneer of gilt and other precious materials that once adorned its magnificent facade. Begun in its present guise in 1421, the palace endured a succession of lackadaisical owners and clumsy restorations before being bequeathed to the state and opened to the public in 1927. The facade has been returned to its ornate splendor and the interior now houses the Galleria Franchetti, an outstanding potpourri of medieval and renaissance paintings and sculpture.

The gallery is not large nor are the works of art numerous, although they are often exquisite, none more so than the first floor's pictorial masterpiece, Mantegna's **"St. Sebastian"** (1506). As a saint invoked against disease, Sebastian was a popular pictorial subject in plague-ridden Venice.

Other highlights include the late-15th-century "Bust of Young Couple" by Tullio Lombardo, six 15th-century bronze reliefs by Andrea Riccio, paintings by Carpaccio, Giovanni Bellini, and Antonio Vivarini, and works of art by Florentine masters such as Luca Signorelli and Antonio da Firenze.

A glorious age-worn staircase leads to the second floor and a room full of Flemish **tapestries,** in their day a far more valuable commodity than paintings. Secreted amid the hangings are a "Venus" by Titian and portraits by Tintoretto and Van Dyck, artistic preludes to several faded frescoes by Pordenone, Titian, and Giorgione in the nearby *portego,* an area that divided most Venetian palaces, its purpose to promote cooling breezes in summer.

INSIDER TIP:

If possible, approach Venice for the first time by boat: The vision of the golden city on the water is magical.

—PATRICIA DANIELS
National Geographic contributor

Madonna dell'Orto

Tranquil in its setting and blessed with a beautiful red-brick Gothic facade, Madonna dell'Orto was the parish church of Tintoretto. The first church here was founded in 1350 and dedicated to St. Christopher, whose statue still stands above the main portal. It was rededicated to the Madonna in 1377 following the discovery of a statue of the Virgin with miraculous powers in a nearby *orto* (garden).

For years the church's pride and joy was a Bellini altarpiece, but after its theft in 1993, the interior's artistic interest shifted to Cima da Conegliano's painting of **"St. John the Baptist"** (1493) on the first altar of the south wall. Almost every other work of note belongs to Tintoretto, who is buried, along with his children, in the chapel to the right of the choir. The choir itself contains two of the painter's masterpieces, the towering **"Last Judgment"** and **"The Making of the Golden Calf."** The artist completed all the paintings in the church free of charge, asking only for the cost of his materials.

Just south of the church, look for the three statues of Moors embedded in the wall of Campo dei Mori.

Santa Maria dei Miracoli

Santa Maria dei Miracoli, a half-hidden jewel of a church swathed in precious colored marbles, has one of Venice's most immediately beguiling exteriors. Pietro Lombardo (ca 1435–1515), one of the leading architects of his day, began Santa Maria in 1480, its purpose to house a miraculous image of the Virgin painted in 1409. Lombardo ignored structural complexity in favor of a church that relied for its exterior effect almost entirely on color. Inside, he was responsible, along with his sons Tullio and Antonio, for the fine carving on the pillars of the nuns' choir (near the entrance) and the pillars and balustrade of the raised choir by the altar. On the altar is the miracle-working image of the Virgin that gave the church its name (*miracoli* means "miracles"). ∎

Madonna dell'Orto

- 130 C5
- Campo Madonna dell'Orto
- 366 736 8390 or 041 79 59 91
- Closed Sun. a.m.
- $
- 4.1, 4.2, 5.1, & 5.2 to Madonna dell'Orto; 1 & 2 to San Marcuola

chorusvenezia.org

madonnadellorto.org

Santa Maria dei Miracoli

- 131 D3
- Campo dei Miracoli
- 041 275 0462
- Closed Sun.
- $
- 1 & 2 to Rialto; 4.1, 4.2, 5.1, & 5.2 to Fondamenta Nuove

chorusvenezia.org

CASTELLO

The largest of Venice's districts, Castello boasts the churches of Santi Giovanni e Paolo and San Zaccaria, as well as the Scuola di San Giorgio degli Schiavoni, a tiny *scuola* founded in 1451 to serve the city's large Slav population. All three contain spectacular works of art.

■ **Exquisite funerary monuments on the walls of San Zanipolo**

Santi Giovanni e Paolo

🅐 131 D3

✉ Campo Santi Giovanni e Paolo 6363, Castello

☎ 041 523 5913

🕐 Closed Sun. a.m.

💲 $

🚏 4.1, 4.2, 5.1, & 5.2 to Fondamenta Nuove or to Ospedale

basilicasantigiovanni epaolo.it

Santi Giovanni e Paolo

Santi Giovanni e Paolo, or San Zanipolo, is Venice's second most important church after Santa Maria Gloriosa dei Frari. San Zanipolo was the mother church of the city's Dominicans, who began the present building in 1246. Its fame rests on a profusion of superb funerary monuments—25 doges are buried here.

San Zanipolo's solemn interior is characteristic of Dominican churches, its unadorned **nave** designed primarily to preach to as large a congregation as possible. On the way in, you pass the tomb of one doge, Iacopo Tiepolo (died 1249), buried in the most ornate of the four tombs on the exterior facade. Three more tombs lie across the facade's interior wall,

all devoted to members of the Mocenigo family and all sculpted by Pietro, Tullio, and Antonio Lombardo, three of the most accomplished sculptors of their day. The finest belongs to Doge Pietro Mocenigo, remarkable for the fact that it contains barely a hint of the religious iconography often found in church tombs.

The second altar on the south wall features the church's greatest painting, Giovanni Bellini's "St. Vincent Ferrer with Sts. Christopher and Sebastian" (1465). To its right is an urn inside which lies the skin of Marcantonio Bragadin, a Venetian general captured by the Turks in 1571, tortured, and flayed alive. Across the nave, on the north wall, stands Pietro Lombardo's "Monumento al Doge Nicolò Marcello" (died 1474): a mature Renaissance work that contrasts with the same sculptor's canopied Gothic tomb—three altars to the right—of Doge Pasquale Malipiero (died 1462), carved some 15 years earlier.

The **south transept** features three eye-catching paintings: Alvise Vivarini's "Christ Carrying the Cross"; "The Coronation of the Virgin," attributed to Cima da Conegliano; and Lorenzo Lotto's marvelous "St. Antoninus Peruzzi Giving Alms to the Poor" (1542). Moving to the high altar, note the tomb of Doge Michele Morosini (died 1382) on the right-hand wall, a beautiful Byzantine-Gothic hybrid. High up on the opposite wall is an almost equally lovely Gothic tomb, the five-figured "Monumento al Doge Marco Corner" (died 1368), while to its right lies the "Monumento al Doge Andrea Vendramin" (died 1478), a vast white marble edifice by Pietro and Tullio Lombardo.

The **north transept** walls belong to the Venier, once among Venice's leading patrician families. The most eminent family member interred here is Doge Sebastiano Venier (died 1578), victorious commander of the fleet that confronted the Turks at the Battle of Lepanto (1571). A door leads to the **Cappella del Rosario,** where the best artworks are the ceiling panels by Veronese.

San Zaccaria

San Zaccaria is dedicated to Zacharias, the father of St. John the Baptist. The church's facade bears both Gothic and Renaissance elements. Inside, the second altar on the left contains Bellini's "Madonna and Saints" (1505), one of the city's greatest altarpieces. Across the nave, the second altar on the north wall contains the reputed relics of St. Zacharias, while alongside lies the entrance to a small museum.

The vaults in the Cappella di San Tarasio feature important early Renaissance **frescoes** (1442) by the Florentine artist Andrea de Castagno, while around the walls are three resplendent **altarpieces** (1443) by the Venetian painters Antonio Vivarini and Giovanni d'Alemagna.

Scuola di San Giorgio degli Schiavoni

Few works of art in Venice are as charming as the painting cycle of this tiny *scuola,* founded in 1451 to serve the city's large *Schiavoni* (Slav) population. The work of Carpaccio, the cycle deals mainly with events from the lives of Dalmatia's three patron saints: George, Tryphon, and Jerome. The nine-painting cycle (1507–1509) starts on the left wall with

"St. George Slaying the Dragon." Panels to the right portray "The Triumph of St. George," "St. George Baptizing the Gentiles," and the "Miracle of St. Tryphon," which captures the boy-saint exorcizing a demon. The central saintly theme, abandoned in the following paintings, "The Agony in the Garden" and "The Calling of St. Matthew," is picked up again in the last three pictures, each of which recalls an episode from the life of St. Jerome. ■

Bartolomeo Colleoni

To San Zanipolo's right stands Europe's finest equestrian monument, Andrea Verrocchio's 15th-century statue of Bartolomeo Colleoni, a mercenary soldier who served Venice for much of his life. Colleoni had hoped to be commemorated in Piazza San Marco. He left the bulk of his vast fortune to the city on condition that he be honored accordingly. Venice never encouraged the cult of the individual, however, and certainly not in its main square. But it wanted Colleoni's money and so cheated the mercenary by raising a statue in Campo San Marco.

San Zaccaria

- 131 E2
- Campo San Zaccaria 4693
- 041 522 1257
- Closed Sun. a.m. & 12 p.m.–4 p.m.
- Chapels $
- 1, 2, 4.1, 4.2, 5.1, & 5.2 to San Zaccaria

Scuola di San Giorgio degli Schiavoni

- 131 E3
- Calle dei Furlani 3259/a, Castello
- 041 522 8828
- Closed Sun. p.m., Mon. a.m., & 1 p.m.–2:45 p.m.
- $$
- 1, 2, 4.1, 4.2, 5.1, & 5.2 to San Zaccaria

THE LAGOON

The lagoon has been Venice's salvation, and its curse. Once its watery embrace provided a defensive barrier against the outside world and later helped foster a maritime tradition that secured a far-flung empire. But its high tides also flood the city, and its waters are a dumping ground for industrial waste from mainland factories. Few visitors will be aware of such problems, however, as they take a boat trip to one or more of its many outlying islands.

As the sun sets over Venice, a lone boatman makes his way across the lagoon.

The Lagoon

⛰ See map inset
p. 131

Museo del Vetro

✉ Palazzo
Giustinian,
Fondamenta
Giustinian 8,
Murano

☎ 041 739 586

💲 $$ or combined
ticket with
Museo del
Merletto ($$) or
Museum Pass
(see p. 129)

🚢 3, 41 to Museo
(ferry stop)

**museovetro
.visitmuve.it**

Murano

Murano—the closest, most famous, and least pretty of the islands—only prospered after 1291, when Venice's glass furnaces were moved here as a precaution against fire. It is worth a visit for its glass shops, glass museum, a pair of churches, and the chance to look at **San Michele,** Venice's main island cemetery, along the way. Fondamenta dei Vetrai has many of the largest glass shops and foundries. The church at its northern end, **San Pietro Martire,** is also home to some

grandiose wooden carvings, several Murano chandeliers, and one of the city's foremost altarpieces—Giovanni Bellini's "Madonna and Child with Doge Barbarigo and Saints Mark and Augustine" (1488). Close by is the **Museo del Vetro,** or Glass Museum, whose intriguing displays of glassware document the history and techniques of glassmaking. To the museum's right stands the seventh-century church of **Santi Maria e Donato,** notable for its unusual arcaded apse, a sixth-century pulpit, and a breathtaking 12th-century mosaic pavement.

Getting to the Islands

Most of the boats bound for the islands leave from the Fondamente Nove (or Fondamenta Nuove). You can purchase individual tickets to Murano ($$), although one- ($$$) or three-day ($$$$) passes are generally a better value if you plan to use boats elsewhere in the city more than three times a day or wish to visit Torcello. For general information, visit *actv.it* or telephone 041 24 241.

Burano

Burano is best known for its lace, which was made on the island since at least the 15th century. Today, much of the material on sale is imported, although a declining number of older women still make the fine *punta in aria* (points in air) lace. The **Museo del Merletto,** or Lace Museum, accurately displays ravishing works of old lace.

Burano is considerably prettier than Murano, thanks largely to its brightly colored houses, reputedly painted to help husbands identify their homes from their vantage points onboard boats far out at sea. The island also preserves the air of a genuine fishing community, with boats moored on its grassy banks and nets strung out to dry. This makes the island a joy to explore, the old fish market and peaceful shoreline being the best targets. It is also perfect for a

morning's excursion in combination with Torcello, just five minutes away by boat.

Torcello

Move heaven and earth to find the time to visit Torcello, one of the loveliest places in all of Venice. Now virtually uninhabited, the island was probably the first part of the lagoon to be settled in the fifth century—which would make it Venice's birthplace. Malaria and the silting of its canals sealed its fate in the 12th century. Today, the island has only a single huddle of buildings, easily reached by a pastoral canal-side walk from the landing stage.

On your right stands **Santa Fosca,** an 11th-century Byzantine church, and to the left the **Museo di Torcello** *(tel 041 270 2464, $),* a small museum devoted to the history of the lagoon. Straight ahead stands **Santa Maria Assunta** *(tel 041 730 084, $),* arguably the most glorious church in Venice. Founded in 639 by the exarch of Ravenna, everything in its interior is matchless, from the elegant 11th-century wooden ceiling and marble pavement to the rood screen, choir, and apse mosaic of the Virgin. The main body of the building dates from 1008, the facade and portico from about 864, and the crypt and high altar from the original seventh-century church. Don't miss the 11th-century mosaics in the chapel to the right of the altar or the ghoulish 12th-century mosaic of the Last Judgment on the rear wall. ■

Murano

🚤 4.1 or 4.2 from Fondamenta Nuove and other points in the city (boats every 20–25 minutes). Or take the 3 service from Piazzale Roma and Ferrovia (railroad station)

🕑 Journey time is 7 minutes from Fondamenta Nuove

Burano

🚤 9, 12, & 14 ferries from the Fondamenta Nuove (boats every 30 minutes, hourly early a.m. & p.m.)

🕑 Journey time is 40 minutes

Museo del Merletto

✉ Piazza Baldassare Galuppi 187, Burano

☎ 041 730 034

🕑 Closed Mon.

💲 $$ or combined ticket ($$) with Museo del Vetro or Museum Pass (see p. 129)

museomerletto .visitmuve.it

Torcello

🚤 12 service via Burano from the Fondamenta Nuove

🕑 Journey time is 45 minutes

More Places to Visit in Venice

Churches

Venice's most charming small church is **San Giovanni in Bragora** (map 131 E2, Campo Bandiera e Moro, tel 041 520 5906, closed 12 p.m.–3 p.m. & Sun.). Once the parish church of Antonio Vivaldi, it features nice Renaissance paintings and an altarpiece by Cima da Conegliano (1494). Another fascinating small church, ninth-century **San Giacomo dell'Orio** (map 130 B4, Campo San Giacomo dell'Orio, tel 041 275 0462, closed Sun., $) contains paintings by Veronese and a stunning altarpiece (1546) by Lorenzo Lotto. The interior of **San Sebastiano** (map 130 A2, Campo San Sebastiano, tel 041 275 0462, closed Sun., $) is filled with works by Veronese, who lived locally, buried in the church. **San Pantalòn** (map 130 B3, Campo San Pantalòn, tel 041 272 8611, sanpantalon.it, closed 12:30 p.m.–3:30 p.m.) is dominated by the work of the lesser known Antonio Fumiani, whose ceiling painting is reputedly the world's largest area of painted canvas. Close to the Rialto, **San Giovanni Crisostomo** (map 131 D3, Campo San Giovanni Crisostomo, tel 041 522 7155, irregular opening hours) has an altarpiece by Giovanni Bellini, while east of the Rialto, **Santa Maria Formosa** (map 131 D3, Campo Santa Maria Formosa, tel 041 277 0233, closed Sun., $) offers a painting by Palma il Vecchio of St. Barbara (1522–1524), patron saint of gunners, hence the cannon balls in the painting. Located in a lovely piazza, **Santo Stefano** (map 130 C2, Campo Santo Stefano, tel 041 275 0462, closed Sun., $) has a peaceful interior with captivating artworks. Don't miss Palladio's **San Giorgio Maggiore** (map 131 D1, Isola di San Giorgio Maggiore, tel 041 522 7827). The view from its campanile ($$) is the best in Venice.

Museums

You can immerse in the city's Jewish culture and its peculiar history with a stop at two synagogues and the beautiful **Museo Ebraico** (map 130 B5, Campo Ghetto Nuovo, Cannaregio 2902b, tel 041 715 359, closed Sat., $$, museo ebraico.it). The **Fondazione Prada** (map 130 C4, Calle de Ca' Corner, Santa Croce 2215, tel 041 810 9161, $$, fondazioneprada.org) offers modern art in a 1720 building with newly discovered frescoes. **Palazzo Cini** (map 130 B1, Dorsoduro 864, tel 041 241 1281, closed Tues., mid-Nov.–mid.-Apr., $, palazzocini.it), lesser known, is a pleasure to visit. It houses paintings by artists the likes of Piero della Francesca and Pontormo.

EXPERIENCE: Attend a Performance at La Fenice

While perhaps lacking the musical kudos of Milan's La Scala or Naples's San Carlo opera houses, La Fenice has much that its rivals must envy, not least its sublime setting. The tiered boxes drip with gold and a vast Murano glass chandelier hangs overhead. The interior, restored following arson in 1996, copies the opera house of 1836, itself a restoration after an earlier fire—hence the building's name, La Fenice, or The Phoenix, reborn from the flames.

As the lights dim and the orchestra strikes up the opening bars of the overture, you enjoy an experience shared by generations of earlier operagoers; those who attended the premieres of Verdi, Rossini, Stravinsky, or Britten. After the performance, as you emerge from the opera house with the animated Venetians, the sense of being outside time is heightened by the fact that you step into a tiny square surrounded by peaceful alleys and romantic canals almost unchanged in centuries.

The opera season runs from November to the end of June. You can buy tickets online, at the box office (Campo San Fantin 1965, tel 041 2424, teatrolafenice.it, $$$$$), or at some of the city's visitor centers.

A region notable for its sprinkling of historic cities, scenic Lago di Garda, and the Dolomiti, Italy's most spectacular mountain range

NORTHEAST ITALY

Basilica di Sant'Antonio, Padua

NORTHEAST ITALY

Northeast Italy is dominated by Venice, a city whose siren call to visitors often diverts attention from one of Italy's most scenically and ethnically diverse corners. Comprising three regions—the Veneto, Trentino–Alto Adige, and Friuli–Venezia Giulia—this is an area of lakes, city-scattered plains, and spectacular Alpine peaks.

If you can only spare a short time in the northeast, make for the Veneto, a prosperous region that corresponds roughly to the limits of Venetia, the mainland territory once ruled by the Venetian Republic. In earlier times, the region lay astride important Roman lines of communication, a position that led to the growth of colonies that evolved into the latter-day cities of Padua (Padova), Vicenza, and Verona. Padua boasts one of Italy's most celebrated fresco cycles, Vicenza is an urbane little city known for the architecture of Palladio, while Verona—the region's most alluring urban focus—is a treasure-house of art and architecture from a variety of historical eras. Verona is also a mere whisker away from the scenic Lago di Garda, Italy's largest lake.

North of Lago di Garda, the Veneto's densely populated plains and rippling hills give way to the Alps, and in particular to the

Dolomiti. If you are tempted by only one major Italian landscape, make it this one. Bolzano is the main center, but nearly every town and village in the region makes a suitable base.

The Veneto shares several of the 30 or more massifs in the Dolomiti with Trentino–Alto Adige, a curious region cobbled together from two historically and ethnically disparate areas. Trentino in the south, named after the regional capital, Trento, is distinctly Italian. The mainly German-speaking Alto Adige in the north extends across a region ceded to Italy from the former Austro-Hungarian empire after World War I (it is sometimes referred to as the Südtirol, or South Tyrol, its main city is Bolzano). German remains the predominant language, and there is a distinctly Teutonic flavor to everything from food to architecture, and an undeniably brisk and efficient air to all matters practical and bureaucratic.

All this makes the region a fascinating one for visitors. Architecture is enlivened by Austrian onion-domed churches, and the wooden

NOT TO BE MISSED:

balconies of the traditional Tyrolean houses are invariably adorned in summer with flowers. In the kitchen, Italian staples are complemented, or replaced, by *Knödel* (*canederli* in Italian, dumplings) and other specialties such as *blau Forelle* (mountain trout), *Speck* (cured smoked ham), goulash, and the ubiquitous apple strudel.

Other ethnic complexities shape the northeast's region Friuli–Venezia Giulia, whose position on the fringes of the Balkans and central Europe has made it a melting pot of Italian, Slavic, and Austro-German cultures. Its position may discourage visitors who have heard of Trieste, an intriguing city, but consider it is far from the rest of the country, if your stay is short. ■

VERONA

Refined, relaxed, and romantic, Verona is one of Italy's most prosperous cities thanks to its position astride trade routes. It was a thriving Roman colony for the same reasons and later became a prominent city-state under the rule of the Scaligeri, its medieval overlords. Subjection to Milan's Visconti and the Venetian Republic followed, with Venice holding control until the arrival of Napoleon. From then on, it remained under Austrian rule until Italian unification.

■ Piazza delle Erbe, built on the site of the Roman forum

Verona
🏛 168 B2

Visitor Information
✉ Palazzo Barbieri, Piazza Brà–Via degli Alpini 9
☎ 045 806 8680
turismoverona.eu
veronatouristoffice.it

Arena
✉ Piazza Bra
☎ 045 800 5151
🕐 Closed Mon. a.m.
💲 $$
turismoverona.eu
arena.it

Begin your tour in the vast **Piazza Bra** (from the German *breit,* meaning "spacious") and its cavernous **Arena,** the third largest amphitheater in the Roman world after Capua's, near Naples, and Rome's Colosseo. Completed in A.D. 30, the structure is in remarkably good shape: Only its original third tier has vanished, toppled by an earthquake in 1183. The 44 ranks of stone seats accommodate more than 20,000 people—roughly Verona's Roman-era population—and are now used for Verona's renowned summer opera festival (see sidebar p. 172). Be sure to clamber to the interior's upper reaches for some far-reaching views over the city.

On leaving the Arena, walk northeast on the pedestrians-only Via Mazzini, one of the city's premier shopping streets. This brings you to **Piazza Erbe,** site of the Roman forum and heart of the medieval city. Gathered around a bustling market, the cramped square is lined with tempting cafés and many varied period buildings, most notably the **Casa dei Mercanti** *(corner of Via Pellicai).* Built in 1301 as an exchange and merchants' storehouse, the building is all brick and bristling battlements.

The heart of the square contains several smaller monuments: the **Capitello,** a four-columned tribune from which medieval decrees were proclaimed; the **Berlina,** to which 16th-century convicts were tied and pelted with moldering fruit; the **Colonna di San Marco** (1523), topped by the Venetian lion of St. Mark; and a delightful **fountain** (1523) graced with a Roman statue known as the "Verona Madonna." Midway along the square's east side, hunt for the medieval **Arco della Costa** (Arch of the Rib), named after the whale's rib hung beneath it. Local legend claims the arch will tumble if a married virgin walks beneath it.

Walking through the Arco della Costa ushers you into **Piazza dei**

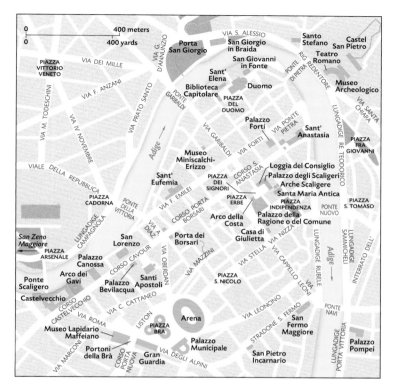

Signori, once Verona's principal public square, its array of buildings lovelier even than those of Piazza delle Erbe. To your right, as you enter the piazza, rises the striped **Palazzo del Comune** (begun in 1193). Once the town hall, it is also known as the Palazzo della Ragione, or Palace of Reason, after its later use as a law court. Turn sharply right and climb the palace's unmistakable **Torre dei Lamberti** for lofty city views. Straight ahead stands the brick-fronted **Palazzo degli Scaligeri,** or Prefettura, built as a palace for the Scaligeri, Verona's dynastic overlords, and later appropriated

by the city's Venetian governors. Left of the palazzo lies the Loggia del Consiglio (1492): An attractive Renaissance arcade with frescoed upper level, it served as a council chamber during Venetian rule.

The statue (1865) at the piazza's heart represents a stern-faced Dante, who, in 1301, was welcomed to the city by the Scaligeri, a family who for all their ruthless rise to power proved relatively just and cultured in office.

Leave Piazza dei Signori under its eastern arch and you come to the Romanesque church of **Santa Maria Antica,** former parish church of the Scaligeri, whose

Torre dei Lamberti

✉ Cortile Mercato Vecchio, Piazza dei Signori, Via della Costa 2

☎ 045 927 3027

$ $

EXPERIENCE: Opera Under the Stars

Attending an outdoor opera performance in Verona's Roman amphitheater offers a spectacle for the senses like no other. The productions are grand affairs, involving enormous choruses, extravagant sets, and—frequently, if the story calls for them—real horses, camels, and elephants.

People begin to fill the vast arena as the sun sinks and are traditionally invited to buy a candle as they enter. The less expensive seats are the simple stone seats of the original stadium. Exposed to the sun all day, they radiate heat, but they are also hard, so it pays to rent a cushion. Cushioned seats in the stalls below are more comfortable and expensive, but they often don't offer the same overall view of the stage.

Before the performance begins, food and beverage vendors pass through the crowd, often singing fragments of arias to draw attention to themselves. Some are rather good, and you'll hear smatterings of applause from distant corners of the arena in appreciation.

The performances start more or less as dusk falls, and as the musicians file in the crowd lights its candles, creating a magical effect. Thousands of tiny points of light illuminate the gathering darkness, while the first stars appear in the evening sky above. The air is still balmy, often with a gentle breeze, but on some nights, especially in August, thunderstorms occur, and then the musicians scurry for cover, and the performance ends until the storm passes. Spectators must manage the best they can, as the vendors reappear, this time selling rain jackets.

The **Fondazione Arena di Verona** (*arena.it*) can provide further information and details on tickets (*$$$$$*).

NOTE: The **Verona Card** (*turismoverona.eu*) offers one free entry to the Arena, Torre dei Lamberti, Castelvecchio, Casa di Giulietta, Tomba di Giulietta, Museo Archeologico al Teatro Romano, Museo Lapidario, and Museo di Storia Naturale, as well as the Duomo, San Zeno, San Fermo, and Sant'Anastasia. Valid for one (*$$$*) or two (*$$$$*) days, the card can be bought online, at the visitor center, participating sites, a number of hotels, and at bar-tobacconists (*tabacchi*).

remarkable tombs, the **Arche Scaligere** (*Via Santa Maria Antica 4*), lie ranged behind the adjacent iron grille. Notice the grille's repeated ladder motif, a pun on the Scaligeri's name (*scala* means "ladder"). Above the church's side door stands the tomb of the family's godfather, Cangrande I, who died in 1329. His smirking figure stares down from the reproduction equestrian monument (the original is in the Museo di Castelvecchio). The dynasty's founder, Mastino I, resides in a plain tomb against the church wall. He died in 1277, assassinated in Piazza dei Signori.

Visitors to Verona invariably get caught up in the *Romeo and Juliet* myth—Shakespeare's romantic tragedy is set in the city. Sooner or later you will have to visit the **Casa di Giulietta,** or Juliet's House. Located near the Scaligeri tombs, the building certainly looks the part, complete with balcony and much-groped statue of the eponymous heroine. However, although the Bard's fictional Capulets and Montagues were based on actual families, the Cappelletti and Montecchi, there is no evidence of a real Juliet, still less of any star-crossed lovers and blood-soaked vendettas. The house itself is a 13th-century inn, notable today mostly for the crowds cramming its courtyard and the extraordinary variety of lovers' graffiti scrawled across its entrance.

Walk northeast from Piazza dei Signori to reach the riverside **Sant'Anastasia,** Verona's largest church, built for the Dominicans between 1290 and 1471. Beyond the main portal, note the two holy water stoups, each supported by bizarre crouching figures known locally as *i gobbi* (the hunchbacks). The **sacristy** conceals the church's main sight, Pisanello's damaged fresco, "St. George Freeing the Princess of Trebizond" (1436). Elsewhere, the chapel to the right of the high altar, the **Cappella dei Pellegrini,** is adorned with terra-cotta bas-reliefs by 15th-century Tuscan sculptor Michele da Firenze. The first chapel in the south transept has a much prized fresco, "The Presentation of the Cavalli Family to the Virgin" (1380) by local artist Altichero.

Duomo

Verona's cathedral lies north of Sant'Anastasia in Piazza del Duomo. Begun about 1120, its facade is striped with local pinky-hued marble that lends many of Verona's buildings their warm, rose-colored appearance. The **west portal** (1139) is the work of Nicolò, one of two master craftsmen also responsible for the facade of San Zeno Maggiore (see p. 174), the city's other sculptural masterpiece. Try to identify the statues of Roland and Oliver among the carvings, two of Charlemagne's generals and favorite characters in medieval art and literature—Roland's name appears on his stone sword. The south portal, with old Roman pillars, is almost equally impressive—here the reliefs deal largely with the story of Jonah and the whale.

Chief attractions inside are a painting of the **"Assumption"**

(1535) by Titian (first chapel of the north aisle), Michele Sanmicheli's pink and gray marble choir screen (1534), Francesco Torbido's choir frescoes (1534), and the anonymous sculptural work of the Cappella Mazzanti (end of the south aisle).

The cathedral complex also includes the entrance to San **Giovanni in Fonte,** part of a tenth-century baptistery built over a fourth-century church, remains of which are nearby. Parts of another church, the 12th-century **Sant'Elena,** can also be seen, while a passageway to the cathedral's left leads to a Romanesque cloister, built over the remains of a fifth-century basilica.

Castelvecchio

Verona's main art collection resides in the Castelvecchio, a wonderfully evocative riverside palace cum fortress begun by Cangrande II in 1354. Alongside stands the most beautiful of Verona's many bridges, the **Ponte Scaligero,** painstakingly rebuilt after its destruction by retreating

Casa di Giulietta
✉ Via Cappello 23
☎ 045 803 4303
🕐 Closed Mon. a.m.
💲 Interior $
**casadigiulietta
.comune.verona.it**

Sant'Anastasia
✉ Piazza Sant'Anastasia
☎ 045 592 813
🕐 Closed Sun. a.m.
💲 $
chieseverona.it

Duomo
✉ Piazza del Duomo
🕐 Closed Sun. a.m., & 1 p.m.–1:30 p.m. Nov.–Feb.
💲 $
chieseverona.it

Castelvecchio
✉ Corso Castelvecchio 2
☎ 045 806 2611
🕐 Closed Mon. a.m.
💲 $
**museodicastelvecchio
.comune.verona.it**

■ Love notes, left on the exterior of the Casa di Giulietta

San Zeno Maggiore

✉ Piazza San Zeno

☎ 045 592 813

🕐 Closed Sun. a.m.
March–Oct.,
Sun. a.m. &
1 p.m.–1:30 p.m.
Nov.–Feb.

$ $

chieseverona.it

basilicasanzeno.it

Nazis in 1945. The 27-room **gallery,** opened in 1924, is one of northern Italy's most important, its collection running the gamut from Roman remains to Renaissance paintings.

The artistic highlights include Pisanello's "Madonna della Quaglia" (stolen in 2015, then recovered in 2016), Carlo Crivelli's "Madonna della Passione," the "Holy Family" by Mantegna, Veronese's "Descent from the Cross," and two Madonnas by Giovanni Bellini. Local and other Venetian and northern Italian artists are also well represented, illustrating the broad development

INSIDER TIP:

Juliet's balcony has nothing on the romance of a dusk *passeggiata*— Italian for "slow stroll." I suggest circling Piazza Brà or walking a stretch of the Adige River.

—JOHNNA RIZZO
National Geographic author

and interchange of ideas among the region's various schools of painting. Other exhibits include glassware, weapons, jewelry, and sculpture, the most noteworthy of which is the equestrian statue removed from the tomb of Cangrande I (see p. 172).

San Zeno Maggiore

Be sure to follow the river west or wander through the Parco dell'Arsenale, Verona's main park, to see San Zeno Maggiore, northern Italy's finest Romanesque church. Built in its present guise at the beginning of the 12th century, the church began life much earlier, probably as a small chapel over the tomb of St. Zeno, Verona's fourth-century patron saint.

Its treasures begin immediately, with the wonderful canopied **porch** (1138) flanked by carvings and polychrome reliefs (1140). These frame the church's mighty main doors, gilded with 48 12th-century bronze reliefs, among the first such works attempted since antiquity. Byzantine in inspiration, the reliefs depict biblical scenes and episodes from the life of St. Zeno and are probably the work of three sculptors: Those on the left date from around 1030, those on the right from 1137.

Inside, your eye is drawn to the magnificent **ship's keel ceiling** (1398), so-called because it resembles the wooden interior of an upturned boat. The nave's design copies that of an old Roman basilica, many of the capitals on the supporting columns having been salvaged from earlier classical buildings. Faded but lovely patches of fresco adorn the otherwise bare walls, a prelude to the interior's masterpiece, Mantegna's high altarpiece of the **"Madonna and Child with Saints"** (1457–1459). Notice how Mantegna has painted the Virgin's halo as a deliberate echo of the church's 12th-century rose window. Be sure to explore the adjoining cloister (1123) and the church's ancient and atmospheric crypt. ∎

VICENZA

Possessed of "all the advantages of a great city," wrote Johann Goethe in 1786 of Vicenza, an observation as true as ever of this sophisticated little town. Renowned above all for the buildings of Palladio (see sidebar p. 176), one of the most influential of all Renaissance architects, its streets are some of the most urbane and architecturally distinguished in Italy.

The Basilica and other buildings by Palladio in Vicenza have been designated World Heritage sites.

Vicenza's modern suburbs quickly give way to a glorious old center hinged around a single main street—**Corso Palladio**—and a single spectacular square, the **Piazza dei Signori.** The latter is dominated by Palladio's **Basilica,** a gargantuan medieval building once close to collapse until the architect enclosed it in a cradle of columns and arcades. The square also contains the **Loggia del Capitaniato** (1571), another Palladian building, and the Venetian lion of St. Mark atop a column: Vicenza enjoyed centuries of glory as a Roman *municipium* and independent city-state before falling to Venice in 1404. Wander into the adjoining Piazza delle Erbe, site of a colorful market, and then to the **Casa Pigafetta** *(Contrà Pigafetta, visible only from the outside),* an ornate house begun in 1440 and once owned by a crew member of Magellan's around-the-world voyage (1519–1522).

Architectural buffs could have a field day or two exploring

Vicenza

🗺 169 C2

Visitor Information

✉ Piazza Matteotti 12

☎ 0444 320 854

vicenzae.org

Teatro Olimpico

✉ Piazza Matteotti 11

☎ 0444 222 800
   or 0444 964380
   (booking)

🕐 Closed Mon.

💲 $$ or Museum
   Card $$–$$$

teatrolimpicovicenza.it

Museo Civico

- ✉ Palazzo Chiericati, Piazza Matteotti 37–39
- ☎ 0444 222 811
- 🕐 Closed Mon.
- 💲 $ or Museum Card $$–$$$

museicivicivicenza.it

Villa Valmarana ai Nani

- ✉ Via dei Nani 8
- ☎ 0444 321 803
- 🕐 Open daily
- 💲 $$

villavalmarana.com

La Rotonda

- ✉ Via Rotonda 29
- ☎ 0444 321 793
- 🕐 Villa open only mid-March–Nov. Wed. & Sat.; grounds closed Mon. & 12 p.m.–2:30/3 p.m.
- 💲 Villa & grounds $$, grounds $

villalarotonda.it

the Palladio's many buildings. Nonspecialists should stick to the fantastic **Teatro Olimpico** (1580), the architect's last work and Europe's oldest surviving indoor theater—Goethe called its interior "indescribably beautiful." Just off the Corso stands the city's most important church, **Santa Corona** (closed Mon., $), best known for Giovanni Bellini's "Baptism of Christ." Opposite the theater, housed in Palladio's Palazzo Chiericati (1551–1557), is the **Museo Civico,** recently expanded, rich in stuccoworks and frescoes, whose collection includes medieval and Renaissance works by Vicentine, Venetian, and other northern painters.

The Vicentine countryside is scattered with villas by Palladio and others, although only two are readily seen from the city itself. Before visiting either, take a cab to Monte Berico, the hill that cradles Vicenza, and to the **Santuario di Monte Berico** (open daily) at its summit, built to commemorate a double apparition of the Virgin during a 15th-century plague epidemic. Take in city views, then visit the basilica's refectory to admire Veronese's "Supper of St. Gregory the Great."

INSIDER TIP:

After looking at the statue-studded stage of the magnificent Teatro Olimpico, spend some time in the pretty courtyard.

—SHEILA F. BUCKMASTER
National Geographic Traveler
magazine editor at large

The **Villa Valmarana ai Nani,** a ten-minute walk from the basilica, has gardens that look out over vineyards, green hills, and feathery lines of poplars. The real reason for a visit, however, are the principal buildings that preserve much of their original furniture, rippling old stone floors, and some majestic wooden ceilings. The highlight: a series of often salacious 18th-century **frescoes** by Giovanni Tiepolo and his son, Giandomenico.

Palladio's Villa Capra Valmarana, better known as **La Rotonda,** is also easily reached from the basilica. Begun around 1551, it was frequently copied by other architects, not least Inigo Jones in England and Thomas Jefferson in America. ∎

Palladio

Palladio was born in Padua in 1508. He moved to Vicenza at the age of 16, working first as a stone mason, then as the protégé of Giangiorgio Trissino, a nobleman who introduced him to wealthy patrons. Until Palladio's death in 1580, he built palaces and villas in Vicenza and elsewhere that reinvented and redefined the idioms of classical architecture in a way that influenced architects for generations to come.

The **Palladio Museum,** inside Palazzo Barbarano (Contrà Porti, tel 0444 323 014, closed Mon., $$ or $$–$$$ Museum Card, palladiomuseum.org) is dedicated to his genius and offers an exhibit about his life, his times, and his works.

PADUA

Centuries of artistic and cultural splendor in Padua (Padova) were destroyed by just a few days' bombing during World War II. The miraculous survival of one of Italy's major fresco cycles, however, and the shrine of one of the country's best loved saints, means that the city still deserves a visit.

A statue-lined canal rings Padua's largest open space, Prato delle Valle.

Padua

▲ 169 C2

Visitor Information

✉ Piazzetta Pedrocchi

☎ 049 201 0080

🕐 Closed Sun.

✉ Stazione Ferroviaria (railroad station)

☎ 049 201 0080

🕐 Closed Sun. late p.m.

turismopadova.it

padovanet.it

Cappella degli Scrovegni & Musei Civici

✉ Piazza Eremitani

☎ 049 820 4550; advance reservations required at least 24 hours ahead, tel 049 201 0020 or reserve online

🕐 Museum closed Mon.

💲 Chapel $$

cappelladegli scrovegni.it

NOTE: The **Padova Card** (*padovacard.it, $$$$–$$$$$*), valid for two or three days, offers free or reduced admission to more than 20 major museums and monuments, including the Cappella degli Scrovegni.

Padua's most important sight is the **Cappella degli Scrovegni.** Commissioned in 1303 by local nobleman Enrico Scrovegni, this chapel owes its fame to Giotto's exquisite sequence of paintings (1303–1305), bathed in the ethereal blue light of the chapel's interior. The best painting is the scene on the rear (entrance) wall, the "Last Judgment," in which a small vignette just above the door shows Scrovegni presenting his chapel. Be sure to explore the adjoining museum complex, the **Musei Civici,** a superb ensemble filled with coins, paintings, sculpture, and archaeological exhibits.

Padua's other famous treasure is the 14th-century **Basilica di Sant'Antonio** (*Piazza del Santo,* *tel 049 878 9722),* burial place of St. Antony of Padua, one of Italy's most venerated saints. Pilgrims stream into the church past Donatello's statue (1453) of the mercenary leader Gattamelata. Highlights of the basilica's interior include Donatello's high altar reliefs and bronze statues, the intriguing collection of relics at the church's rear, and the nine bas-reliefs (1505–1507) around the saint's tomb, the work mostly of Tullio and Antonio Lombardo, and Jacopo Sansovino.

Also worth visiting are two squares, **Piazza della Frutta** and **Piazza dei Signori,** the beautifully frescoed **Baptistery** (1376), and the **Palazzo della Ragione** *(Piazza della Ragione, tel 049 820 5006, closed Mon., $),* one of Italy's largest medieval halls, built in 1218. ∎

A DRIVE AROUND LAGO DI GARDA

This drive takes you around Italy's largest and most scenically diverse lake, Lago di Garda (Lake Garda), beginning on its verdant southern coast and hugging the hillier slopes and cliffs of its northern reaches, before returning along its mountain-backed eastern flanks.

Lago di Garda's Western Shores

Start at **Peschiera del Garda,** a village dominated by a redoubtable Venetian fortress. Follow the lakeside road west toward **Sirmione** ❶ *(visitor information, Viale Marconi 6, tel 030 374 8721, sirmionebs.it),* the lake's most popular resort. Another fortress, **Rocca Scaligera** *(closed Mon., $),* built by Verona's Scaligeri family, broods over the village's tidy harbor and attractive huddle of houses. Boats embark here for most of the lakeside villages, which are worth taking for views of the lake, villas, and gardens invisible from the road. Local visitor centers have details of outdoor activities.

Head west on the lakeside road to **Desenzano del Garda,** Garda's largest town, known for its wines, Roman villa, and the proximity of Solferino, site of the bloody battle in 1859 that led to the foundation of the Red Cross. Beyond Desenzano, on the SP572, lies **Salò** ❷, remembered as the capital of the short-lived republic created by Mussolini after the Italian armistice of 1943. The western coast's most attractive base, it has a traditional air and a ravishing 15th-century cathedral.

Gardone Riviera *(visitor information, Corso Repubblica 8, tel 0365 20 636)* lies 3 miles (5 km) northeast of Salò on the SS45 bis. Once the lake's finest resort, it marks the start of Garda's more spectacular upland scenery. It is just half a mile (1 km) from the region's most extraordinary sight, the **Villa il Vittoriale** ❸ *(Via Vittoriale 12, tel 0365 296 511, vittoriale.it, museum closed Mon. Nov.–March, $$),* a villa transformed into a treasure-house of kitsch—everything from an embalmed tortoise to a World War I biplane—by Gabriele d'Annunzio (1863–1938), a noted poet, soldier, socialite, womanizer, and fascist sympathizer.

> **NOT TO BE MISSED:**
>
> Sirmione • **Tremosine road & views**
> • **Villa Il Vittoriale** • **Malcesine**
> • **Monte Baldo** • **Punta San Vigilio**

Moving north, you pass through several pretty villages—**Gargnano** ❹ is especially charming—and get the chance to make several scenic diversions away from the lake. The best run to stunning viewpoints at the sanctuary of **Madonna di Monte Castello** ❺ and the **Pieve di Tremosine** near Campione del Garda. (Take the signed road off the SS45 bis north of the road tunnel beyond Gargnano.) Inland and lakeside roads meet at **Limone sul Garda,** one of the lake's more developed resorts. Take the SS45 bis from Limone to **Riva del Garda** ❻ *(visitor information, Largo Medaglie d'Oro al Valor Militare 5, tel 0464 554 444, gardatrentino.it),* at the lake's northern tip. This is Garda's best known resort, popular with windsurfers. Its waterfront and medieval quarters, as in most of Garda's villages, retain much of their Old World charm.

Lago di Garda's Eastern Shoreline

Heading south along the lakeshore on the SS240 and SS249, you come to **Malcesine** ❼ *(visitor information, Via Gardesana 238, tel 045 740 0044, visitmalcesine.com),* the east coast's prettiest resort, known for its well-preserved fortress and the highly recommended cable car ride *(tel 045 740 0206, funiviedelbaldo.it, $$)* to **Monte Baldo.** Views from the upper ridges of this 7,277-foot (2,218 m) mountain are sensational, and there are numerous marked hiking trails. The area is also renowned for its flora and was once known as the *hortus europae,* or garden of Europe, after the huge variety of floral species that grow here. The lake's waters and the sheltering arc of the Dolomiti to the north create mild and varied microclimates that favor floral variety and anomalous vegetation—olives, figs, citrus, vines, and cypress. The balmy climate also encourages swimming and sunbathing at Malcesine and elsewhere.

Moving south on the SS249 along the olive tree-swathed shore, you pass **Torri del Benaco,** home to another Scaligeri castle, and the headland at **Punta San Vigilio,** one of the lake's most romantic spots—more than can be said for nearby **Garda,** a popular but unprepossessing resort developed after World War II.

Map labels:

Cascata del Varone
1991m
Val di Ledro
Riva del Garda
Sarca
Torbole
Piano di Tempesta
1621m Monte Orone
SS45 bis
Limone sul Garda
Navene
SS249
Monte Baldo
Campione
Pieve de Tremosine
1790m
Malcesine
Campione del Garda
2128m
Madonna di Monte Castello
Cassone
2218m Cima Valdritta
Porto di Brenzone
Gargnano
SS45 bis
Lago di Garda
Castelletto di Brenzone
Bogliaco
SS249
Pia
1582m
Toscolano--Maderno
Villa il Vittoriale
Torri del Benaco
SS45 bis
Gardone Riviera
Salò
SP572
San Felice del Benaco
Punta San Vigilio
Garda
Manerba del Garda
Bardolino
Moniga del Garda
Cisano
SS249
Lido di Lonato
Lazise
SP572
Sirmione
SS11
Desenzano del Garda
Colombare
Pacengo
Rivoltella
Peschiera del Garda
SS567
Solferino   A4
START   A4   SS11
884m

Legend box:

🏔 Also see area map, p. 168 A2–A3
▶ Peschiera del Garda
🕐 1–3 days
↔ 90 miles (145 km)
▶ Peschiera del Garda

Scale bars:
0   6 kilometers
0   3 miles

DOLOMITI

Of all the majestic ranges contained in the Alps' broad sweep, none quite compare with the Dolomiti, or Dolomites, a tightly packed collection of massifs in Italy's northeast corner whose peaks and pinnacles make this the most beguiling mountain region in the country. Wildlife and high Alpine flora are superb, while in the pastoral depths of the valleys you can enjoy flower-strewn meadows and the rural tranquility of age-old villages.

■ Jagged limestone pinnacles are the hallmark of the Dolomiti. Opportunities for hiking abound.

Madonna di Campiglio

🄼 168 A4

Visitor Information

✉ Via Pradalago 4

☎ 0465 447 501

parks.it

campigliodolomiti.it

None of the 30 or more massifs in the Dolomiti will disappoint. From a hiking point of view, the best approach is to pick one or two massifs and explore them in depth—the Dolomiti di Brenta are perfect for the first-time visitor. If you prefer to tour or admire the scenery from a car, then follow the Grande Strada delle Dolomiti, or Great Dolomites Road, which runs from the region's German-speaking capital at Bolzano (Bozen) to Cortina d'Ampezzo, the most prestigious of the area's many ski resorts.

Italians, on the whole, are not great walkers, but, in terms of culture and tradition, the Dolomiti are not Italy, or at least not the Italy of popular imagination. Much of the region still has strong Austro-German leanings, among which the Teutonic propensity for healthy exercise and the great outdoors looms large. Perhaps it is this more northern European attitude to landscape, together with the superb natural beauty of the Dolomiti, that gives the region its immensely hiker-friendly infrastructure.

Arrive in any town or village, and a comfortable and reasonably priced hotel is assured. Visitor centers will ply you with maps and recommendations for walks to suit all abilities. Strike into the mountains and you will find well-marked and well-worn trails, not to mention plentiful mountain huts *(rifugi)*, where you can stay overnight in simple dormitories or simply pause for refreshments (details from visitor information centers). Towns and villages are often on upper slopes, so trails quickly reach high elevations (in summer you can ascend via cable car, enabling you to follow high-line paths with minimal effort). All the massifs are mapped. Paths are well signed. Every town has outdoor stores selling boots and special equipment.

The **Dolomiti di Brenta** are a good place to start hiking, using the resort town of **Madonna di Campiglio** as a base. Many loop walks begin close to the town, located at 4,921 feet (1,500 m). A good option is to take the Grosté cable car to the Graffer refuge at 5,355 feet (1,632 m) and then follow the official trail 316 to the Rifugio Tuckett before dropping back to Madonna on trail 317 or 328/318. Other options include low-altitude lake strolls near the village of **Molveno.**

Touring by Car

Not everyone, however, wants to hike amid the high peaks or indulge in low-level lakeside and forest strolls. The roads are so good here and the mountains

Origins

The Dolomiti are set apart from the Alps' main thrust both geographically and geologically. Most of the massifs began life as ancient coral reefs, which were lifted from the seabed, hence the distinctive orange-pink hue of their stone—a rare *dolomia* limestone—and the still more distinctive eroded appearance of their soaring rock towers, pillars, and cliffs.

so dramatic, that touring by car still offers you excellent views of the scenery. The options are many. In the north, you could take the Autostrada A22 from Bolzano (Bozen) to Bressanone (Brixen), and then follow the glorious SS49 road along the Val Pusteria. From here you could head south on the SS244, either at San Lorenzo di Sebato (St. Lorenzen) down the Val Badia or take the SS51 at Dobbiaco (Toblach) through the Dolomiti di Sesto, one of the range's more noted massifs, to Cortina d'Ampezzo. From Cortina d'Ampezzo you can return to Bolzano on the 68-mile (110 km) Great Dolomites Road (SS48/SS241), built in 1909, which threads through the Catinaccio, Latemar, Marmolada, and other massifs. Alternatively, leave the designated route and detour along the Val Gardena (SS242), or follow higher mountain roads via Siusi (Seis) or Tires (Tiers). ■

More Places to Visit in Northeast Italy

Aquileia

Sleepy Aquileia boasts extensive Roman excavations—it was the Roman Empire's fourth-ranking Italian colony—the finds from which are displayed in local museums. More impressive, however, is the **basilica** on Piazza del Capitolo. It preserves areas of its breathtaking fourth-century mosaic floor. Visit the **Cripta degli Scavi,** with parts of the original church; the **Cripta degli Affreschi,** with 12th-century frescoes; and the **tombs** of the region's early Christian rulers.
turismofvg.it ⚌ 169 E3 **Visitor Information**
✉ Terminal Via Iulia Augusta ☎ 0431 91 491

Asolo

Asolo is a medieval gem set amid rolling hill country that offers a taste of quiet, small-town life. Excursions can be made to the Palladian villa at Maser, to the east, and to the interesting town of Bassano del Grappa, famous for its grappa, a fiery after-dinner drink.
asolo.it ⚌ 169 C3 **Visitor Information**
✉ Piazza Garibaldi 73 ☎ 0423 529 046

Trento

This tidy medieval town hosted the Council of Trent, convened to combat Lutheranism. Several council's sessions were held in the Duomo, which has fine exterior stonework. The nearby **Museo Diocesano** (*Piazza del Duomo 18, closed Tues. & 1–2 p.m., $*) contains treasures removed from the cathedral. The **Castello del Buonconsiglio** (*Via Bernardo Clesio 5, tel 0461 233 770, closed Mon., $$*), a 13th-century fortress, houses also a museum full of interesting objets d'art.
discovertrento.it ⚌ 168 B3 **Visitor Information**
✉ Via Manci 2 ☎ 0461 216 000

Treviso

The old walled town has a pleasant mix of canals, old balconied buildings, frescoed facades, and shady arcades. The north Italian master Tommaso da Modena (1325–1379) worked in the Romanesque-Gothic Dominican church of **San Nicolò** (*Via San Nicolò, closed Sat. p.m.–Mon. & 1–2 p.m.*).
visittreviso.it ⚌ 169 D2 **Visitor Information**
✉ Via Sant'Andrea 3 ☎ 0422 547 632

Trieste

On the extreme border of Italy, this city has been a melting pot for centuries, and its atmosphere leaves an impression. At the highest point of the city stands the **cathedral** (*Piazza della Cattedrale 2, tel 393 954 3131, sangiustomartire.it*), while at the lower is Piazza Unità d'Italia: You'll feel like you're in an Austro-Hungarian city, except for the sea.
turismofvg.it ⚌ 169 F2 **Visitor Information**
✉ Piazza Unità d'Italia ☎ 040 3478312

EXPERIENCE: Exploring the Northeast's Lagoons

South of Aquileia, a necklace of sandy islands along 20 miles (32 km) of coast creates the Laguna di Marano and Laguna di Grado. Their fringes are laced with canals, channels, marshes, and reed beds, creating habitats for a broad range of flora and fauna and refuge for migrating birds.

The nature reserves **Valle Canal Novo** and **Foci dello Stella** can be visited by boat (*$$$$$*) with rangers based at the reserves' wetlands center in Marano Lagunare (*Piazza Olivotto 1, tel 0431 67 551, visitmaranolagunare.it*). October and February are the best months to visit.

As you thread through the reeds, willows, and bulrushes, you pass isolated *casoni*, thatched wooden huts, fishermen's shelters. Mallard, teal, and black terns abound; rarities such as velvet scoters and goldeneyes are known. With luck, you may glimpse an elusive otter, one of the creatures the reserves were set up to protect.

A region boasting gastronomic centers (Parma and Bologna), lovely
countryside, and the charming towns of Ravenna, Ferrara, and Urbino

EMILIA-ROMAGNA
& THE MARCHE

Rounds of Parmesan cheese

EMILIA-ROMAGNA & THE MARCHE

Rich in industry and agriculture, Emilia-Romagna is one of the country's wealthiest region. The Marche is a more rural redoubt, and its attractions are mostly scenic where Emilia-Romagna's are cultural and culinary.

NOT TO BE MISSED:

Emilia-Romagna's location has long made it one of Italy's pivotal regions. Towns developed under the Romans along the Via Aemilia, a road that linked the Adriatic coast with the vital garrison town of Piacenza. Attention during the empire's dying days moved to Ravenna.

City-states emerged in the aftermath of the Dark Ages, states that in time fell prey to great noble families. Court life flourished as patronage on a grand scale attracted writers, poets, and painters, yielding a cultural heritage that illuminates the region's historic cities to this day. Under different rules, Emilia and Romagna then developed as separate states until 1860.

The Marche knew no such divisions, having existed for centuries as a largely forgotten backwater of the Papal States. A long, narrow, and mostly agricultural region, it is separated from Rome, Tuscany, and the rest of central

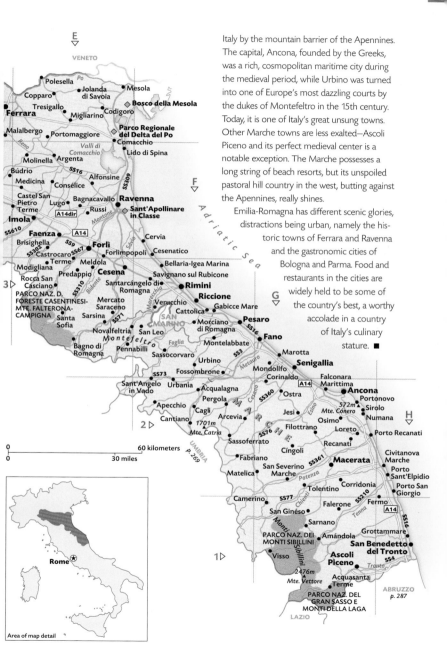

Italy by the mountain barrier of the Apennines. The capital, Ancona, founded by the Greeks, was a rich, cosmopolitan maritime city during the medieval period, while Urbino was turned into one of Europe's most dazzling courts by the dukes of Montefeltro in the 15th century. Today, it is one of Italy's great unsung towns. Other Marche towns are less exalted—Ascoli Piceno and its perfect medieval center is a notable exception. The Marche possesses a long string of beach resorts, but its unspoiled pastoral hill country in the west, butting against the Apennines, really shines.

Emilia-Romagna has different scenic glories, distractions being urban, namely the historic towns of Ferrara and Ravenna and the gastronomic cities of Bologna and Parma. Food and restaurants in the cities are widely held to be some of the country's best, a worthy accolade in a country of Italy's culinary stature. ∎

BOLOGNA

Bologna's food is reputedly Italy's best, hence the nickname *La Grassa,* or The Fat, while its university, one of Europe's oldest, has earned the city another plaudit, *La Dotta,* or The Learned. Better still, its tightly knit old center is a pleasing medieval patchwork of brick arcades, towers, churches, palaces, and fascinating museums. Yet for all of this, Bologna is surprisingly ignored by visitors to Italy, its culinary and cultural allure better known to Italians than foreigners.

■ Take time out to enjoy a cappuccino in Piazza Nettuno, one of Bologna's main squares.

Bologna

⬛ 184 D4

Visitor Information

✉ Palazzo del Podestà, Piazza Maggiore 1/e

☎ 051 658 3111

bolognawelcome.com

Collezioni Comunali d'Arte

✉ Palazzo D'Accursio, Piazza Maggiore 6

☎ 051 219 3998

🕑 Closed Mon.

💲 $

For so large a city, Bologna's medieval heart is surprisingly small. Most places of interest lie within easy walking distance of the main squares.

Piazza Maggiore & Piazza Nettuno

Pride of place in Piazza Nettuno goes to Giambologna's central **Fontana del Nettuno** (1566), or Neptune Fountain, a vast bronze affair that spouts water from every orifice—the locals call it *Il Gigante,* or The Giant. Also worth a look is the **Palazzo Comunale,** or D'Accursio, with its medieval Torre

dell'Orologio (soon to be open to the public), a huge building whose civic museum, the **Collezioni Comunali d'Arte,** contains a number of paintings by Bolognese painters spanning several centuries. Finer buildings still line Piazza Maggiore, including the 13th-century **Palazzo del Podestà,** the former governors' palace, and the magnificent **San Petronio.** This, Bologna's largest and most important church, is dedicated to St. Petronius, a fifth-century bishop and the city's patron saint. Founded in 1390, the church was originally intended to be twice its present size, but funds ran short during the 300 years it took to build. This left the brick-built facade shorn of its planned patterning and marble veneer; the main portal, however, was completed, adorned with a "Madonna and Child" (1425–1438) and other carvings by the great Sienese sculptor Jacopo della Quercia.

Inside, your attention is drawn to the nave's soaring Gothic vaulting. Such was the money lavished here, financial shortfalls notwithstanding, that the extravagance is said to have heavily influenced Martin Luther's revolt against Catholicism. The Cappella Bolognini, the fourth chapel off the north aisle, contains the best—a series of 15th-century frescoes by Giovanni da Modena and an altarpiece (1410) by Jacopo di Paolo.

The baroque Duomo is a composite of architectural styles. It certainly isn't one of the best you can see in Emilia, but its bell tower (opened to the public) will give you a magnificent view that extends from the city to the hills. The civic museum, the **Museo Civico Medievale,** that lies opposite, contains a first-rate collection of medieval and Renaissance paintings, sculpture, and applied arts. Sculptural highlights include Alessandro Algardi's "St. Michael and the Devil," works by Bernini, a magical "Madonna and Child with Saints" by Jacopo della Quercia, and a "Mercury" and working model for the Neptune fountain by Giambologna. Among the applied arts, watch for several fine 13th-century bronzes and a sumptuous 14th-century cope, a peerless example of *opus anglicanum,* or

English medieval embroidery work. The museum also contains collections of armor, glassware, ivories, ceramics, and musical instruments.

East of San Petronio is the city's archaeological museum. The **Museo Civico Archeologico** will appeal to devotees of Egyptian and Etruscan art. Etruscan influence reached as far north as Bologna, as did that of the Umbrians, a central Italian tribe absorbed by the Etruscans. Tomb remains from both cultures make up many of the displays, the best of which were removed from the necropoli of Felsina, the sixth-century B.C. Umbro-Etruscan settlement on Bologna's present-day site. Highlights among the Egyptian exhibits are stone reliefs from the 14th-century B.C. tomb of Horemheb. The museum also preserves prehistoric, Roman, and Greek artifacts.

South of the museum lies the **Palazzo dell'Archiginnasio** (1562–1563), built by the papal legate

San Petronio

- ✉ Piazza Maggiore
- ☎ 051 231 415
- 🕐 Closed 1:30 p.m.–2:30 p.m. Mon.–Fri.

Museo Civico Medievale

- ✉ Palazzo Ghisilardi-Fava, Via Manzoni 4–Via dell' Indipendenza
- ☎ 051 219 3916 or 051 219 3930
- 🕐 Closed Mon.
- 💲 $ (free first Sunday of the month)

Museo Civico Archeologico

- ✉ Via dell' Archiginnasio 2
- ☎ 051 275 7211
- 🕐 Closed Tues.
- 💲 $$

museibologna.it

Bologna's Past

Bologna's central location has long been its strength—roads and railroads still converge on the city from the rest of northern Italy. Of Etruscan or earlier foundation, its early history has a familiar ring—overrun by the Gauls in the fourth century B.C., conquered by the Romans, and then ravaged by the Barbarians. From about 1300 to 1500, it prospered as an independent city-state, a period of well-being cut short by violent aristocratic feuding. Here, as ever, one clan emerged triumphant, in this case the Bentivoglio. After some 50 years of autocratic rule, power passed to the papacy, which after 1506 ruled unchallenged until the appearance of Napoleon and Austria.

MASTER THE ART OF BOLOGNESE COOKING

Many towns, cities, and rural regions across Italy are celebrated for their gastronomy, but none enjoys quite the status of Bologna, which makes it an excellent place to learn the finer arts of north Italian cuisine. Classes can be spread over a week, making them a vacation in themselves, or you can opt for self-contained three-hour, four-hour, or full-day sessions.

Pasta forms the basis of many a Bolognese dish.

Founded in 1993 by Alessandra Spisni, **La Vecchia Scuola Bolognese** *(Via Stalingrado 81, tel 051 649 1576, vsb-bologna .it)* offers many options. The three-hour class (€100/$113) is firmly focused on pasta making. You learn how to turn flour and eggs into pasta, and then the tricks required to make the three most typical Bolognese pastas: tagliatelle, tortellini, and tortelloni, plus the spinach and ricotta mixture (secret ingredient: nutmeg) that can

be used in filled pastas. Lunch is included in the price of the course.

Longer courses are also available with **Cook Italy** *(tel 349 007 8298, cookitaly.com)*, founded in 1999. Here the emphasis is on conviviality and informality, small groups, and a typical and pretty Italian setting for lessons. One-, two-, and three-day courses are available; tailor-made courses, with accommodation and some meals, can be arranged. You will gain

a broad culinary education by walking with an expert around the city's markets, learning about the wealth of fruit, vegetables, and other ingredients. Customized half- and full-day cooking courses, combined with a market and city tour, are also available from €200 ($226) per person for groups of two or more.

The **Tavola della Signoria** association *(tavoladellasignoria .it)* has a different approach, offering four or five generally more intensive classes a month in the lovely period rooms of the 17th-century Palazzo Albergati *(albergati .com)*, 6 miles (10 km) west of the city. Courses generally run a full day, with the option of different modules, from pasta and breadmaking to desserts and fruit-and-vegetable courses. Lessons cost from €195 ($221) per person per day, and from €500 ($566) per person for the association's occasional three-day courses.

EXPERIENCE: A Day at the FICO

FICO (or "fig" in Italian) is an acronym for Fabbrica Italiana Contadina *(Via Paolo Canali, shuttle bus from the center, tel 051 002 9001, eatalyworld.it)*. It is the largest agribusiness park in the world, opened in 2017. Its almost 25 acres (10 ha) include barns, cultivated fields, laboratories for the transformation of raw materials, shops, and

eateries where visitors can buy and taste the products of this village. The thematic tours through the park allow you to experience first-hand farm life, its animals and its produce, farm work activities, and all of the secrets behind the culinary specialties that we usually find ready on our plates. All of this in the name of biodiversity.

in place of what would have been San Petronio's north transept. For centuries the palace formed part of Bologna's prestigious university; visit it to see the beautiful wood-paneled **Teatro Anatomico** (1637), the old medical faculty's dissection theater *(tel 051 276 811, closed Sun. p.m.)*. Students once sat in the tiered seats to watch the dissection of human corpses, a form of instruction first introduced in this university school.

Torre Garisenda & Torre degli Asinelli

The *Due Torri,* or two towers, are located just to the east of Piazza Nettuno. Begun around 1109, the Torre Garisenda and Torre degli Asinelli are two of only a handful of survivors of the 100 or more medieval towers that distinguished Bologna's skyline.

Both belonged to leading noble families, both were towers of the first rank, and both merited a mention in Dante's *Inferno.* Left unfinished, the 164-foot (50 m) Garisenda was shortened in the 14th century to prevent its collapse—even today the lean still looks alarming. Its 320-foot (97.5 m) rival is the fourth tallest in Italy. A lung-bursting haul up its 498 steps, accessible from Via di Porta Ravegnana, is rewarded with a glorious panorama.

Before leaving the area, take a look at the **Palazzo della Mercanzia** (1382–1384) in the adjacent Piazza Mercanzia. A former guild and merchants' meeting place, it is among the city's finest pieces of Gothic architecture. Be sure to explore the nearby **Strada Maggiore,** the most captivating of Bologna's old streets. In Via

Torre degli Asinelli

✉ Piazza di Porta Ravegnana

☎ 051 658 3111

🕑 Advance reservations through Bologna Welcome

💲 $ or Bologna Welcome Card

duetorribologna.com

bolognawelcome.com

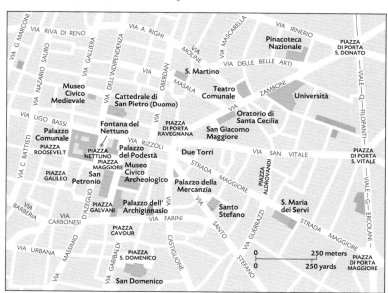

La Macchina del Tempo

- ✉ Via Zamboni 7
- ☎ 051 008 7519
- 🕐 Open by appt.
- 💲 $$

**lamacchinadel
tempo.eu**

San Giacomo Maggiore

- ✉ Piazza Rossini
- ☎ 051 225 970
- 🕐 Closed 12:30 p.m.
  –3:30 p.m.

Oratorio di Santa Cecilia

- ✉ Via Zamboni 15
- ☎ 051 225 970
- 🕐 Closed 1 p.m.–
  2 p.m. Oct.–
  May; 1 p.m.–3
  p.m. Jun.–Sept.

Pinacoteca Nazionale

- ✉ Accademia di
  Belle Arti, Via
  delle Belle Arti
  56
- ☎ 051 420 9411
- 🕐 Closed Mon.
- 💲 $

**pinacotecabologna
.beniculturali.it**

Santo Stefano

- ✉ Via Santo
  Stefano 24
- ☎ 349 150 1899
- 🕐 Closed during
  services

Zamboni there is a new museum, **La Macchina del Tempo** (The Time Machine), where visitors can surround themselves with the medieval city (and other attractions) using virtual reality, before heading to San Giacomo.

San Giacomo Maggiore

A few minutes' walk from the towers on Via Zamboni lies San Giacomo Maggiore, a pleasing Romanesque-Gothic church founded by the Augustinians

---

INSIDER TIP:

Try the crostini—tiny pieces of toast topped with mushrooms, meat, or other delectable morsels—offered in cafés all over Bologna.

—JOHNNA RIZZO
National Geographic author

---

in 1267. It has a fine exterior and a passable assortment of interior paintings and frescoes. The main reason for a visit, however, is the **Cappella Bentivoglio** (1486) at the end of the north aisle, created in 1445 as a mausoleum for the Bentivoglio family, Bologna's erstwhile rulers. Its altarpiece (1488) is the work of the painter Francesco Francia, while Lorenzo Costa was responsible for the frescoes of the "Apocalypse," the "Triumph of Death," and portraits of the Bentivoglio family in the company of the Madonna and various saints. In the ambulatory opposite the chapel stands the "Tomb of Anton Galeazzo

Bentivoglio" (1435), one of the last works of the Sienese sculptor Jacopo della Quercia.

Spare a minute on exiting the church for the **Oratorio di Santa Cecilia,** entered via the church's side portico, which contains more frescoes and paintings (1506) by Francia and Lorenzo Costa.

Pinacoteca Nazionale

Paintings by medieval Bolognese artists dominate the Pinacoteca Nazionale, the city's premier art gallery, beginning with early painters such as Simone de' Crocefissi and Vitale da Bologna, men heavily influenced by Byzantine art. Later works by local Renaissance artists occupy the **long gallery,** although the artists here are often outshone by competing works by Giotto, prominent Venetians such as Cima da Conegliano, and members of the Ferrara school such as Francesco del Cossa.

The most astounding painting is Raphael's celebrated "Ecstasy of St. Cecilia" (1515). It shows the patron saint of musicians with instruments at her feet, clutching an organ, which she is said to have invented. Other notable paintings include Parmigianino's "Madonna and Saints" and Guido Reni's "Pietà dei Mendicanti," plus works by masters such as Perugino, Giotto, Titian, El Greco, and Caracci.

Santo Stefano

Santo Stefano is not one church but several, part of a pretty monastic complex first mentioned in 887 that originally comprised at least seven separate churches. The lackluster **Crocefisso,** restored in 1924, is followed by the more interesting **San Sepolcro,** home to the shrine of Bologna's patron saint, St. Petronius. Beyond these lie the **Cortile di Pilato** and a lovely Romanesque **cloister,** the latter providing access to a small museum *(tel 051 223 256)* of paintings and religious ephemera. The *cortile* (courtyard) contains a large eighth-century basin with Lombard inscriptions, reputedly the bowl used by Pontius Pilate to wash his hands and absolve himself of responsibility for Christ's death. At the top of the courtyard lies the 13th-century **Chiesa della Trinità,** while alongside San Sepolcro stands the **Santi Vitale e Agricola,** Bologna's oldest church. Dating from the fifth century, it has been much altered since then.

San Domenico

Churches belonging to the Dominicans, a severe medieval order, are generally intimidating. Bologna's San Domenico, however, is an exception, chiefly because it is the burial place of St. Dominic himself, who died in the city in 1221. The tomb is a showcase of medieval art, featuring funerary carvings (1267) by Nicola Pisano and Arnolfo di Cambio, sculpted reliefs (1468–1473) by Niccolò da Bari, and a kneeling angel and two saints (1494) by a young Michelangelo. Other must-sees include Filippino Lippi's painting of the "Mystic Marriage of St. Catherine" (1501), some beautiful inlaid choir stalls (1451), and—in the sacristy museum *(closed Sun.)*— a bust of St. Dominic (1474) in polychrome terra-cotta by Niccolò da Bari. ■

San Domenico

- ✉ Piazza San Domenico 13
- ☎ 051 640 0411
- 🕐 Closed Sun. until 3:30 p.m., & Mon.– Sat. 12 p.m.– 3:30 p.m.

■ **Santo Stefano comprises seven religious buildings, including the lovely Chiesa della Trinità.**

PARMA

Northern Italy has many a well-heeled city, but none perhaps quite so prosperous or quietly devoted to the finer things in life as Parma. A byword for fine food—Parma ham and Parmesan cheese both come from here—this is a refined and genteel city that is crammed with elegant cafés, superb restaurants, and tempting luxury stores. If you want to treat yourself to an expensive meal or make some special purchases—and in between times visit a memorable museum and marvelous medieval square—then Parma is for you.

■ Parma's famous meats and cheeses are sold in shops across Italy and worldwide.

Parma

▲ 184 C5

Visitor Information

✉ Piazza Garibaldi 1

☎ 0521 218 889

turismo.comune .parma.it

Camera di San Paolo

✉ Via Melloni

☎ 0521 233 309

🕐 Closed Mon. & p.m.

$ $

Pride of place in Parma's historical core goes to the buildings around **Piazza del Duomo,** a faultless ensemble dominated by the 11th-century **Duomo** (*piazzaduomoparma.com*) and its graceful Gothic campanile (1284–1294). A Romanesque masterpiece, the cathedral is best known for the frescoes of the "Assumption" (1524–1530) in its main cupola, the work of Correggio (1489–1534), the leading light, with Parmigianino (1503–1540), of the Parma school of painting. Its other major work of art is a relief of the "Deposition" (1178) in the south transept, the

earliest known work of the sculptor Benedetto Antelami.

Antelami was also responsible for much of the exquisite octagonal **baptistery** (*$*). Begun in 1196, it's a distinctive and harmonious building built largely in Verona's orange-red marble. The sculptor designed the structure and created the sumptuous carving flanking the three main portals, as well as the interior's holy water stoup, altar, and many of the capitals and reliefs above the doors. The interior's most stunning feature, however, is its many frescoes (1260–1270), anonymous Byzantine-influenced works portraying biblical episodes.

More frescoes, this time by Correggio, can be seen in **San Giovanni Evangelista** *(closed Sun., Thurs., & 11:45 a.m.–3 p.m.)*, immediately behind the Duomo, and in the **Camera di San Paolo.**

There is no mistaking the **Palazzo della Pilotta**, a colossal brick edifice built for the Farnese, a powerful Roman papal family who ruled Parma between 1545 and 1731. Today, it holds some archaeological exhibits and two principal sites: the Teatro Farnese and the Galleria Nazionale. The **Museo Archeologico Nazionale** occupies two floors, its rooms embracing a wide range of prehistoric, Greek, Etruscan, Egyptian, and Roman exhibits. Of more general appeal is the **Teatro Farnese** (1617–1618), an extraordinary wood and stucco stage and auditorium based on Palladio's Teatro Olimpico in Vicenza (see p. 176). The superb **Galleria Nazionale** presents its myriad paintings in huge, airy salons, many of them graced with clever modern walkways and displays. The works of Emilian painters take center stage, with an obvious bias toward local artists such as Parmigianino and Correggio. The latter's "Madonna della Scodella" (1525–1530) is one of the gallery's star turns, although it is run close by Leonardo da Vinci's "La Scapigliata" and Cima da Conegliano's "Madonna and Child with Saints." Other paintings of note are by Beato Angelico, Van Dyck, Holbein, Canaletto, and Giulio Romano.

Overcome museum fatigue by walking in the **Parco Ducale** (1560), laid out as a retreat for the Farnese, just across the river from the Palazzo della Pilotta. Near its southeast corner lies the **Casa Toscanini,** birthplace of conductor Arturo Toscanini (1867–1957). The house contains a small but lovely museum.

Just outside the city, along the road to Sabbioneta (see p. 125), is an impressive Cistercian abbey that rises up alone on the plain. Its suggestive spaces include the **Centro Studi e Arhivio della Comunicazione,** opened in 2015, where a huge collection (owned by the university) of 12 million works of photography, design, art, and graphics, is displayed in rotation. ■

Palazzo e Musei della Pilotta

✉ Piazzale della Pilotta 15

☎ 0521 233 309 or 0521 233 617

🕐 Closed Mon. & Sun. a.m.

💲 $$

pilotta.beniculturali.it

Casa Toscanini

✉ Borgo Rodolfo Tanzi 13

☎ 0521 031 769

🕐 Closed Mon., Tues. p.m., Sun. a.m., & 1 p.m.– 2 p.m.

💲 $

museotoscanini.it

CSAC-Centro Studi e Arhivio della Comunicazione

✉ Strada Viazza di Paradigna 1

☎ 0521 033 652

🕐 Closed Mon.– Tues. & Thurs.– Fri. a.m.

💲 $$

csacparma.it

EXPERIENCE: See How Parmesan Is Made

Parmigiano-Reggiano cheese, or Parmesan, can only be made in a strictly delineated area around Parma and Reggio Emilia, a town half an hour's drive to the east. It's possible to visit many of the area's cheesemakers on free two-hour guided tours *(Mon.–Fri.)* that reveal the various processes that go into making Italy's most celebrated cheese—how milk is warmed in copper cauldrons, for example, and how the curds are broken up and the soft, white cheese is placed in the distinctive wheel-shaped molds before being aged.

Ask at Parma's visitor center for details of tours, or arrange visits through the **Consorzio del Formaggio Parmigiano-Reggiano** *(tel 0522 307 741, parmigiano-reggiano.it),* the consortium that controls all aspects of Parmesan production. Search its website under "Dove si fa" and "Visite guidate ai caseifici" for details on producers open to visitors. Tours are usually in Italian, but translators can be arranged.

FERRARA

Ferrara is a sleepy town stranded on the Emilian plains. Its historical heritage owes much to the efforts of a single family, the Este, whose often despotic behavior did little to temper the growth of a civilized court during the long years—1208 to 1598—when they controlled the town's destiny. Palaces, castles, and a magnificent set of walls are their most enduring legacy.

One of Ferrara's many flag-throwing teams practices its moves in the Piazza della Repubblica.

Ferrara

🗺 185 D5

Visitor Information

✉ Castello Estense

☎ 0532 209 370 or 0532 299 303

🕐 Closed 1 p.m.– 2 p.m. Jun.–Aug.

ferrarainfo.com

ferraraterraeacqua.it

Castello Estense

✉ Largo Castello– Piazza della Repubblica

☎ 0532 299 233

🕐 Closed Mon. Oct.–Feb.

💲 $$

castelloestense.it

Head first for Piazza della Repubblica, at the town's heart, the stage for the **Castello Estense** (begun in 1385), a grandiose fortress complete with towers, moat, drawbridges, and soaring buttressed ramparts. The Este's principal seat, its wonderful medieval interior once played host to writers and artists. Painters included members of the Ferrara school, led by Cosmè Tura, Francesco del Cossa, Lorenzo Costa, and Ercole de' Roberti. Writers included Tasso, Petrarch, and the author of the epic *Orlando Furioso*, Ludovico Ariosto (1474–1533), whose house can be seen at Via Ariosto 67.

The **Museo Nazionale dell'Ebraismo Italiano e la Shoah** is located to the southeast. Opened in 2017 in what was once the city's prison, it narrates the history that has inextricably tied the Jewish population and Italy for more than 2,000 years. Going back toward the castle will take you to the **cathedral** *(Piazza della Cattedrale, tel 0532 207 449, temporarily closed)*, fronted by a superb facade. The effect inside is less spectacular, the result of interior remodeling in the 18th century. The best of the surviving works of art reside in the **Museo della Cattedrale** *(Piazza della Cattedrale, tel 0532 249 949, closed Mon. & 1 p.m.–3 p.m., $)*, and include tapestries, manuscripts, Romanesque reliefs, painted organ panels by Cosmè Tura, and a "St. George," an "Annunciation" (1469), and a "Madonna" (1408) by the Sienese sculptor Jacopo della Quercia.

Beyond the Castello Estense, Ferrara's spacious northern margins are different in look and feel, largely because they form part of the so-called Addizione Erculea, or Herculean Addition, an urban development program commissioned by Duke Ercole I d'Este in 1492. His aim—consummately realized—was to transform the area into a model Renaissance quarter. The district is arranged around Corso Ercole I d'Este, the main street, while its chief focus is the **Palazzo dei Diamanti** (begun in 1492). Today, it houses the Pinacoteca Nazionale, an art gallery given over largely—but not entirely—to paintings by artists of the Ferrara school.

The fourth of Ferrara's great set piece buildings, the Palazzo Schifanoia, lies in the town's southwest corner. Walking there from the cathedral, follow Via Savonarola to see the **Casa Romei** (tel 0532 234 130, closed p.m. Sun.–Wed., a.m. Thurs.–Sat., $), a 15th-century town house with many original fittings and frescoed decoration. Detour a little to the north to admire the furniture, gardens, and ceilings of the **Palazzina di Marfisa d'Este** (1559).

The **Palazzo Schifanoia** was begun in 1385 as the Este's summer residence—its name means carefree. Today, it is getting an anti-seismic upgrade and is closed to the public for what may be a long period. We suggest you check with the information office for updated information about this jewel of stuccowork and frescoes.

A little to the south stands the **Palazzo Ludovico il Moro** (Via XX Settembre 124, tel 0532 66 299, closed Mon., $$), an outstanding but unfinished 15th-century palace now used to house the Museo Archeologico Nazionale di Spina, given over largely to finds from Spina, a former Greco-Etruscan port on the Po Delta. The wonderful church of the nearby convent of **Sant'Antonio in Polesine** (Vicolo del Gambone, tel 0532 64 068, closed Sun. & 11:30 p.m.– 3:15 p.m., donation) features several chapels smothered in early medieval frescoes. ∎

MEIS-Museo Nazionale dell'Ebraismo Italiano e la Shoah

- ✉ Via Piangipane 81
- ☎ 0532 769 137
- 🕐 Closed Mon.
- 💲 $$

meisweb.it

Palazzo dei Diamanti (Pinacoteca Nazionale)

- ✉ Corso Ercole d'Este I 21
- ☎ 0532 244 949
- 💲 $$$$

palazzodiamanti.it

Palazzina di Marfisa d'Este

- ✉ Corso della Giovecca 170
- ☎ 0532 207 450
- 🕐 Closed Mon. & 1 p.m.–3 p.m.
- 💲 $

Palazzo Schifanoia

- ✉ Via Scandiana 23
- ☎ 0532 244 949
- 🕐 Closed Mon.
- 💲 $

Ferrara's Este Family

Many medieval cities in central and northern Italy had dominant dynasties. Florence had the Medici; Milan, the Visconti and Sforza. In Ferrara it was the Este, an ancient family with roots in northern Europe, one branch of which yielded the Hapsburg emperors and the Hanoverian kings of Britain in the 18th and 19th centuries. Members of the line that dominated Ferrara from the time of Niccolò d'Este III (1384–1441), whose court was one of the most dazzling in Europe, were often great patrons of the arts and married into the royal houses of Europe. They also, as in the case of Isabella d'Este (1474–1539), who was painted by Titian and Leonardo da Vinci, became great personalities of their day.

RAVENNA & AROUND

Ravenna acquired Western Europe's finest Byzantine and early Christian mosaics almost by accident. In A.D. 402, as the power of Rome declined, it was made capital of the Roman Empire. After the empire's collapse, the town continued to prosper. The Ostrogothic king, Theodoric, ruled much of Italy from the city after A.D. 493, as did the Byzantine emperor Justinian after A.D. 540, both men greatly embellishing its churches and other religious monuments.

The Basilica di San Vitale has some of the best preserved Byzantine mosaics outside Istanbul.

Ravenna

185 E4

Visitor Information

Piazza S. Francesco 7

0544 35404

turismo.ra.it

ravennamosaici.it

ravennantica.it

Ravenna

Ravenna's star attraction is the **Basilica di San Vitale,** begun by Theodoric in A.D. 525 and completed in A.D. 547 by Justinian. On its own, the vast octagonal building would be judged an architectural masterpiece. What makes it still more remarkable are the number and quality of its sixth-century mosaics. The most fascinating of these adorn the side walls of the apse and portray the courtly retinues of Justinian (on the left) and his wife Theodora (on the right).

On the basilica's grounds stands a still more magical monument, the fifth-century **Mausoleo di Galla Placidia** *(for ticket information, see sidebar opposite),* or tomb of Galla Placidia, sister of Emperor Honorious I who sanctioned Ravenna's elevation to capital city in A.D. 402. The tiny chapel is studded with Italy's most beautiful mosaics, a glittering decorative spectacle presented in a quite breathtaking array of colors.

Elsewhere, part of San Vitale's tenth-century convent building is given over to the **Museo**

INSIDER TIP:

Ravenna's mosaics are the finest of the Byzantine civilization. If you are in a hurry, hire a local guide to take you on a tour of the most important mosaic sites.

—MARZIA BORTOLIN
Italian Government Tourist Board

Nazionale *(tel 0544 213 902, closed Mon., $)*, a museum noted in particular for its collection of ivories and old coins, but also for its archaeological exhibits, bronzes, fabrics, weapons, ceramics, and Roman, Byzantine, and early Christian mosaics.

Mosaics aside, Ravenna is a surprisingly pleasant and prosperous town in its own right. Wandering its alleys, visitors may run into studios and shops where artists interpret the tradition of mosaics in a modern key. Its medieval quarter centers on **Piazza del Popolo,** a square lined with fine old buildings and plenty of appealing cafés. You come here not for the Duomo, a disappointing 18th-century remodeling of a 5th-century original, but for the scattering of interesting buildings around it.

Chief among these is the **Battistero Neoniano** *(Via Battistero, tel 800 303 999, for ticket information, see sidebar this page)*, converted from a Roman bathhouse by Bishop Neon in the fifth century. Inside, the walls are almost entirely covered in mosaic, stucco, and other decoration (the lower mosaics are poorly preserved Roman originals, the higher ones better-conserved fifth-century examples). Compare the building with the equally important **Battistero degli Ariani** *(Vicolo degli Ariani, tel 0544 543 724)*, whose slightly later mosaics depict similar subjects.

Behind the cathedral, the first floor of the Archbishops' Palace contains the **Museo Arcivescovile** *(Piazza Arcivescovado 1, tel 0544 541 688, for ticket information, see sidebar this page)*, a museum dominated by four outstanding exhibits: the ivory "Throne of Maximian," a sixth-century work carved with biblical scenes; the silver "Cross of St. Agnellus" (A.D. 556–569); and two entire chapels adorned with fifth- and sixth-century mosaics.

South of Piazza del Duomo is the **Tomba di Dante** *(Via Dante Alighieri)*, burial place of the poet, who died here in 1321 while in exile from Florence. The adjacent tenth-century church of **San Francesco**, largely rebuilt in 1793, preserves several early Christian sarcophagi, a high altar fashioned

Basilica di San Vitale

✉ Via Argentario 22

☎ 800 303 999

$ See sidebar this page

Combination Ticket

A single combination ticket *($$)*—and the same opening hours—applies to Ravenna's San Vitale, Mausoleo di Galla Placidia, Battistero Neoniano, Museo Arcivescovile, and Sant'Apollinare Nuovo. Tickets for each of these individual sites are not available, and there is a €2 supplement for the Mausoleo di Galla Placidia from March 1 to June 15. The ticket can be bought at each participating site. For further information, visit *ravennamosaici.it* or call 0544 541 688.

EXPERIENCE:
Po Delta Bird Fair

Birders should aim to visit the Delta del Po in spring *(late March–early June)*, during the region's excellent annual **Po Delta Birdwatching Fair** *(primaveraslow.it)*—a three-month-long celebration of the delta and its birds. Among the many activities are weekend guided natural history hikes or dedicated birding walks, usually arranged by Ravenna's **Museum of Natural Sciences** *(tel 0544 528 710, opening hours vary, $, natura.ra.it)*. You can also join daily boat trips *($$$$$)* into the Comacchio lagoon *(tel 340 253 4267, vallidicomacchio.info)* and elsewhere across the delta *(tel 0533 81302 or 346 592 6555, podeltatourism.it)*.

Delta del Po

🗺 185 E5

Visitor Information

✉ Via San Basilio 12, San Basilio

☎ 0426 71200

from the fourth-century tomb of St. Liberius, and the original tenth-century crypt.

Mosaics also dominate the peripheral but outstanding **Sant'Apollinare Nuovo** *(Via Roma, tel 800 303 999, for ticket information, see sidebar p. 197)*, begun in A.D. 493 by Theodoric. The golden-hued, sixth-century mosaics run in bands along each side of the upper nave: The right side portrays 26 martyrs approaching Christ, the left 22 virgin martyrs behind the Magi. Above the bands on both sides are prophets, Church fathers, and episodes from Christ's life. Don't confuse the church with **Sant'Apollinare in Classe** *(Via Romea Sud 224, closed Sun. a.m., tel 0544 527 308, $)*, a sixth-century building some 3 miles (5 km) south of Ravenna. This building is almost all that remains of the old Roman port of Classis, and though in rather unlovely surroundings, its mosaics are as important as any in the town.

Delta del Po

Italy is not a bird-watching destination—too many birds have been shot by overenthusiastic hunters. But one area where you may still see birds in considerable numbers, particularly during the spring and fall migration periods, is the delta of the Po River, north of Ravenna. Much of the area stands protected as a regional park, **Parco Regionale del Delta del Po** *(parcodeltapo.it)*, with key smaller reserves found near Comacchio, the region's main center, and the ancient woodlands of the Bosco della Mesola. Watch for avocets, herons, egrets, terns, and other waterfowl. The delta's ethereal landscapes can be enjoyed by driving along the SS309 road or by taking boat trips from villages such as Taglio di Po. ∎

■ Italy's most breathtaking mosaics cover the walls of Ravenna's Mausoleo di Galla Placidia.

URBINO

Urbino was once one of Europe's great Renaissance courts. Its artistic and cultural life was promoted by the ruling Montefeltro dukes and reached its zenith during the reign of Duke Federico da Montefeltro between 1444 and 1482. Today, it is one of Italy's best kept secrets, its urbane streets and magnificent ducal palace little known to most foreign visitors. In truth, Urbino is the superior of many more famous towns in neighboring Tuscany and Umbria.

■ The Palazzo Ducale, begun by Federico da Montefeltro, who grew wealthy as a mercenary soldier

Palazzo Ducale

The Palazzo Ducale, or Ducal Palace, dominates hilltop Urbino, its towers and honey-colored stone bulwarks soaring above the pretty, rolling countryside that reaches up to the town's medieval walls. Its main architect was Dalmatian-born Luciano Laurana (1420–1479), who produced an almost perfect Renaissance palace, with a serene inner courtyard, a harmonious interplay of brick and stone, and a faultless purity of line and ornamentation. Against this setting, it is hardly surprising that cultural life flourished: Raphael and the architect Bramante were born in the town, and Baldassare Castiglione drew from his experience at the Montefeltro court for *Courtier,* a 16th-century handbook of Renaissance manners that was disseminated across Europe.

Wandering the palace's stately rooms is a pleasure in itself. As you explore, look for the eagle symbol emblazoned throughout, part of the Montefeltro crest, and for the words Fe Dux, from Federicus Dux —Duke Federico. Make a point, too, of seeking out the *studiolo,* the duke's private study, whose *intarsia* (inlaid wood) was crafted in places to designs by Botticelli.

Urbino
🗺 185 F3

Visitor Information
✉ Piazza Rinascimento 1
☎ 0722 2613

**turismo
.pesarourbino.it**

Palazzo Ducale & Galleria Nazionale delle Marche
✉ Piazza Duca Federico 107
☎ 0722 322 625
🕐 Closed Mon. p.m.
💲 $

**gallerianazionale
marche.it**

Colorful and detail-rich 14th-century frescoes adorn the Oratorio di San Giovanni Battista.

Casa Natale
di Raffaello
- Via di Raffaello 57
- 0722 320 105
- Opening hours vary March–Oct.; closed p.m. Nov.–Feb.
- $

Museo Diocesano
- Piazza Pascoli 1
- 0722 4818
- Closed Mon. & 1:30 p.m.–2 p.m., open daily Jun.–Jul.
- $

museodiocesano urbino.it

The palace lacks much of its original fittings, but the first-floor **Galleria Nazionale delle Marche** holds a wealth of Italian paintings, including three of Italy's greatest masterpieces: "La Muta", by Raphael, and "Madonna di Senigallia" and "Flagellation of Christ" by Piero della Francesca. Also noteworthy is Luciano Laurana's painting of the "Ideal City."

The Town

Small and contained within its walls, Urbino is a pleasure to explore. The first stop is a place of artistic pilgrimage, the **Casa Natale di Raffaello,** birthplace of Raphael, who lived here until he was 14 before moving to Umbria and Rome. Inside, the house preserves much of its period charm. On Via Barocci, make a point of seeing two small oratories: the **Oratorio di San Giuseppe** (closed Sun. p.m. & 1

p.m.–3 p.m., $), known for its 16th-century stucco *presepio,* or Christmas crib, and the **Oratorio di San Giovanni Battista** (closed Sun. p.m. & 1 p.m.–3 p.m., $), whose interior is adorned with 14th-century frescoes portraying the Crucifixion and the life of St. John the Baptist.

The **Duomo,** home to a celebrated 16th-century painting of the "Last Supper" by Federico Barocci, will reopen in 2020, as it is currently being rebuilt following the violent earthquake that hit the Marche in 2016. The nearby **Museo Diocesano** is also worth a look for its collection of ceramics, glassware, and ecclesiastical ephemera. Finally, be sure to walk part of the **Strada Panora-mica,** a scenic street leading from Piazza Roma, and to climb to the park above the town. Both offer rewarding views of Urbino and the appealing countryside. ∎

ASCOLI PICENO

Few squares, even in Italy, are quite as alluring as Ascoli Piceno's Piazza del Popolo, the centerpiece of the most beautiful town in the Marche after Urbino. Nestled in the pastoral upper reaches of the Tronto Valley, the town lies far from the commercial taint of the region's coastal resorts, its walled old quarter still laid out in the gridiron pattern of the old Roman colony, Asculum Picenum.

Restrained Renaissance buildings in the **Piazza del Popolo** stand cheek by jowl with more forceful Gothic palaces. Among them is the **Palazzo dei Capitani del Popolo,** whose facade is adorned with a Renaissance portal and statue (1549) of Pope

---

INSIDER TIP:

Be sure to have a drink, preferably an *anisetta,* a celebrated aniseed-based specialty, at the historic Caffè Meletti in Piazza del Popolo.

—TIM JEPSON
National Geographic author

Paul III by the local painter Cola dell'Amatrice (1480–1559). Almost equally prominent is the church of **San Francesco,** begun in 1262, its austere appearance softened by the adjacent Loggia dei Mercanti, or Merchants' Loggia, a Tuscan-influenced edifice dating from 1513.

Next, make first for Piazza Arringo, just east of Piazza del Popolo, where you'll find the Palazzo Comunale, once the town hall and currently home to the **Pinacoteca Civica,** or civic art gallery. The nearby 12th-century

Duomo has another facade by Cola dell'Amatrice, while inside the focal point is a stunning polyptych (1473) by Carlo Crivelli, a Venetian artist who based himself in town. There are more paintings by the same artist in the Pinacoteca, along with works by Titian, Van Dyck, Guido Reni, and others.

Wander down Corso Mazzini to view **Sant'Agostino,** a church noted for a fresco of "Christ Carrying the Cross" by Cola dell'Amatrice. Then head north on Via dei Torri to see the adjacent churches of 13th-century **San Pietro Martire** and the Romanesque **Santi Vincenzo e Anastasia.** ■

Ascoli Piceno
- 185 G1

Visitor Information
- ✉ Piazza Arringo 7
- ☏ 0736 253 045
- **visitascoli.it**

Pinacoteca Civica
- ✉ Palazzo Comunale, Piazza Arringo 1
- ☏ 0736 298 213
- 🕐 Closed Mon. &, mid Sept.–Mar. only, 1 p.m.–3 p.m. Tue.–Fri.
- 💲 $
- **ascolimusei.it**

Olive Ascolane

The delicious gastronomic delight *olive ascolane* originates from Ascoli Piceno. It is made using a large, sweet olive grown in an area limited to the provinces of Teramo and Ascoli Piceno. The olive is carefully hollowed out; stuffed with a seasoned mixture of minced beef, pork, and chicken; dredged in flour, eggs, and breadcrumbs; and then fried in extra-virgin olive oil. The treat can be eaten hot or cold. Excellent places to sample the specialty in Ascoli Piceno itself include **Gastronomia Migliori** *(Piazza Arringo 2, tel 0736 250 042),* **Il Desco** *(Via Vidacilio 10, tel 0736 250 757),* and **Kursaal** *(Via Luigi Mercantini 66, tel 0736 253 140).*

More Places to Visit in Emilia-Romagna & the Marche

Adriatic Coast

The coast of the Marche regions is so much more than beaches. Driving along the SS16, visitors will find cities that deserve a cultural visit, such as **Fano** *(visitor information Piazza XX Settembre, tel 0721 803 534)* with its harmony of Roman and Renaissance monuments. **Ancona** *(visitor information Banchina N. Sauro, tel 071 207 6431)* is a fascinating layered maritime city that reflects its long history. It offers a Romanesque Duomo "with a view" and a requalified heritage. *turismo.marche.it* 🔼 185 G3–H3

Fidenza

Fidenza's modern suburbs crowd in on a compact medieval center, visited principally for its 13th-century **cathedral,** an accomplished piece of composite Lombard-Romanesque and Gothic architecture in Piazza del Duomo. *comune.fidenza.pr.it* 🔼 184 B5
Visitor Information ✉ Piazza del Duomo 16 ☎ 0524 83377

Modena

Modena has several cultural sights—its **cathedral** is one of northern Italy's greatest, and the **Palazzo dei Musei** *(closed Mon., $)* contains a complex of museums bursting with paintings, sculptures, and manuscripts. The best is the **Galleria Estense** *(closed a.m. Sun. & Mon.)*. The city's attractions are also mechanical, after the firms of Ferrari and Maserati, based in the area. The **Museo Ferrari** is in Maranello *(Via Dino Ferrari 43, tel 0536 949 713, $$$)*, 12 miles (20 km) south, with memorabilia and vintage cars. *visitmodena.it* 🔼 184 D4 **Visitor Information** ✉ Piazza Grande 14 ☎ 059 203 2660

Piacenza

Due to its pivotal position, Piacenza served as an important Roman garrison (and still shows the original street plan). The principal attractions are the three **Musei Civici** *(Piazza Cittadella 29, tel 0523 496 661, closed Mon. & Tue.–Thurs. p.m., $, palazzofarnese.piacenza.it),* housed in the colossal Palazzo Farnese, begun in 1558. Its star turns are a painting of the "Madonna and Child with St. John the Baptist" by Sandro Botticelli and the rare "Fegato di Piacenza," or Liver of Piacenza, an Etruscan bronze depicting a sheep's liver marked with the names of Etruscan deities.

Other sights include the **Piazza dei Cavalli,** the main square, named after the two bronze statues of horses *(cavalli)* and riders. From the square walk to the Lombard-Romanesque **cathedral** (1122–1233) at the end of Via XX Settembre. The cathedral's interior warrants a few minutes' attention, as does the nearby church of **Sant'Antonino** *(Via Chiapponi)*, celebrated for the 12th-century bas-reliefs on its main door. *turismo.provincia.piacenza.it* 🔼 184 B5
Visitor Information ✉ Piazza Cavalli 10 ☎ 0523 492 001 🕒 Closed Mon. & 1 p.m.–3 p.m. (opening hours vary)

San Leo

Many people have heard of San Marino, a tiny independent republic between Romagna and the Marche. From a distance, its impressive hilltop location holds out great promise, but only the views are worth the journey. Fewer people have heard of nearby San Leo, a smaller and far more alluring hill town with an equally commanding position. Machiavelli, the medieval political philosopher, called its **fortress** Italy's finest military redoubt, while Dante drew inspiration from the castle for parts of his *Purgatorio*. The castle *($$)* survives, looking down from its craggy ramparts on to a quaint cobbled square flanked by a ninth-century parish church and Romanesque cathedral. *san-leo.it* 🔼 185 F3 **Visitor Information** ✉ Piazza Dante Alighieri 14 ☎ 0541 916 306

A city-size shrine to the Renaissance whose streets and galleries
showcase Europe's greatest artistic flowering

FLORENCE

■ Detail of a bronze relief on the east
doors of the Battistero di San Giovanni

FLORENCE

In Florence (Firenze), Europe's premier artistic capital, Renaissance treasures fill a host of museums, churches, and galleries, while the roll call of famous names from the city's past—Dante, Machiavelli, Michelangelo, and Galileo among them—are some of the most resonant of the medieval age. Lively markets, pretty piazzas, and Italy's most visited garden provide ample outdoor respite from the surfeit of art.

Florence was founded in 59 B.C., superseding an earlier Etruscan settlement (present-day Fiesole) in the hills. The colony owed much of its prosperity to the Arno River, navigable to this point and crossed by the Via Cassia, one of the Romans' strategic roads to the north. The city emerged from the Dark Ages as an independent city-state and quickly prospered as a result of its banking and textile industries. During the 13th century, it enjoyed a sophisticated form of republican government but in the 14th century fell prey to a powerful banking family—the Medici.

The last Medici ruler died in 1737, after a series of increasingly inept rulers. The city then passed by treaty to Francesco of Lorraine, the future Emperor Francis I of Austria. The city remained under Austrian rule—bar 15 years

of Napoleonic rule—until Italian unification in 1860 (with Florence as the capital from 1865 to 1871). Since then, its most publicized event was the 1966 flood that killed several people and damaged thousands of works of art. Today, the city is as wealthy as ever, grown fat from tourism and its still thriving textile industry.

Start your artistic odyssey with the two main squares: Piazza della Signoria and Piazza del Duomo, the latter home to Santa Maria del Fiore (the Duomo), Battistero di San Giovanni, and the campanile; climb the Duomo or the bell tower dome for fabulous views across Florence. From the squares, you can tackle three of the city's main galleries: the Uffizi (paintings), Bargello (sculpture), and Museo dell'Opera del Duomo (sculpture). Next come two major churches, Santa Croce and Santa Maria Novella, and then the sights with one-off attractions: the Galleria dell'Accademia (Michelangelo's "David"), the Palazzo Medici-Riccardi (frescoes by Benozzo Gozzoli), the Museo di San Marco (paintings by Fra Angelico), and the Cappelle Medicee (sculptures by Michelangelo).

At some point, cross the river, preferably via the celebrated Ponte Vecchio, and explore the district known as the Oltrarno. Here stand the Palazzo Pitti, whose art gallery is second only to the Uffizi, and the Cappella Brancacci, home to the city's most important fresco cycle. You will also find the Giardino di Boboli, the city's loveliest garden, as well as numerous artisans' workshops, antique stores, and quieter, more traditional streets and squares. Finally, don't miss the only sight beyond easy walking distance of the center—the superb church of San Miniato al Monte. ∎

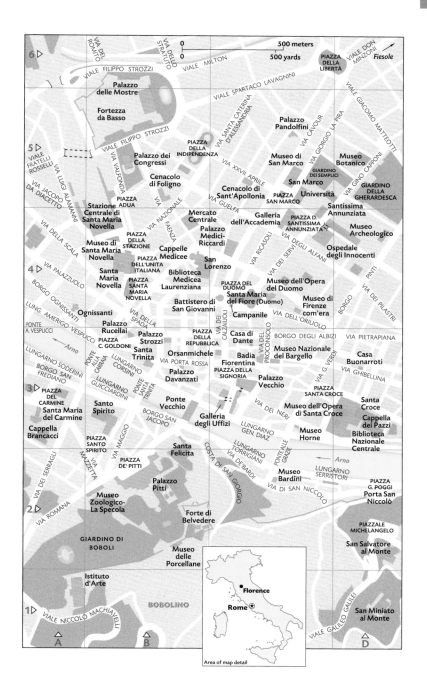

FLORENCE

0 _____ 500 meters
0 _____ 500 yards

VIA DEL ROMITO
VIA DELLO STRATUTO
VIALE MILTON
PIAZZA DELLA LIBERTÀ
VIALE DON MINZONI
Fiesole

VIALE FILIPPO STROZZI
VIALE SPARTACO LAVAGNINI
VIALE GIACOMO MATTEOTTI

Palazzo delle Mostre

Fortezza da Basso

VIALE FILIPPO STROZZI

VIA SANTA CATERINA D'ALESSANDRIA

Palazzo Pandolfini

VIA CAVOUR

VIA GIORGIO LA PIRA

VIALE FRATELLI ROSSELLI

VIA VALFONDA

PIAZZA DELLA INDIPENDENZA

Palazzo dei Congressi

Museo di San Marco

Museo Botanico

VIA GINO CAPPONI

VIA LUIGI ALAMANNI

Cenacolo di Foligno

VIA XXVII APRILE

GIARDINO DEI SEMPLICI

San Marco

GIARDINO DELLA GHERARDESCA

VIA JACOPO DA DIACETO

PIAZZA ADUA

VIA GUELFA

Cenacolo di Sant'Apollonia

PIAZZA SAN MARCO

Università

Stazione Centrale di Santa Maria Novella

VIA NAZIONALE

VIA FAENZA

Mercato Centrale

Galleria dell'Accademia

Santissima Annunziata

VIA DELLA SCALA

PIAZZA DELLA STAZIONE

Cappelle Medicee

Palazzo Medici-Riccardi

PIAZZA D. SANTISSIMA ANNUNZIATA

Museo Archeologico

Museo di Santa Maria Novella

PIAZZA DELL'UNITA ITALIANA

San Lorenzo

VIA RICASOLI

VIA DEGLI ALFANI

Ospedale degli Innocenti

VIA PALAZZUOLO

Santa Maria Novella

PIAZZA SANTA MARIA NOVELLA

Biblioteca Medicea Laurenziana

VIA DEI SERVI

PINTI

BORGO OGNISSANTI

Battistero di San Giovanni

PIAZZA DEL DUOMO

Museo dell'Opera del Duomo

VIA DEI PILASTRI

LUNG. AMERIGO VESPUCCI

Ognissanti

VIA DELLA SPADA

Santa Maria del Fiore (Duomo)

Museo di Firenze com'era

BORGO PINTI

PONTE A. VESPUCCI

Palazzo Rucellai

Campanile

VIA DELL'ORIUOLO

LUNGARNO AMERIGO VESPUCCI

PIAZZA C. GOLDONI

Palazzo Strozzi

PIAZZA DELLA REPUBBLICA

Casa di Dante

BORGO DEGLI ALBIZI

VIA PIETRAPIANA

Arno

Santa Trinita

VIA PORTA ROSSA

Orsanmichele

VIA DEL PROCONSOLO

Museo Nazionale del Bargello

Casa Buonarroti

LUNGARNO SODERINI

PONTE ALLA CARRAIA

LUNGARNO CORSINI

Badia Fiorentina

VIA G. VERDI

VIA GHIBELLINA

BORGO SAN FREDIANO

LUNGARNO GUICCIARDINI

Palazzo Davanzati

PIAZZA DELLA SIGNORIA

Palazzo Vecchio

PIAZZA DEL CARMINE

PONTE SANTA TRINITA

Ponte Vecchio

PIAZZA SANTA CROCE

Santa Croce

Santa Maria del Carmine

Santo Spirito

BORGO SAN JACOPO

Galleria degli Uffizi

VIA DEI NERI

Museo dell'Opera di Santa Croce

Cappella dei Pazzi

Cappella Brancacci

PIAZZA SANTO SPIRITO

LUNGARNO GEN. DIAZ

Museo Horne

Biblioteca Nazionale Centrale

VIA MAGGIO

Santa Felicita

LUNGARNO TORRIGIANI

VIA DE' BARDI

PONTE ALLE GRAZIE

Arno

VIA DEI SERRAGLI

VIA MAZZETTA

PIAZZA DE' PITTI

COSTA DI SAN GIORGIO

LUNGARNO SERRISTORI

PIAZZA G. POGGI

Palazzo Pitti

Museo Bardini

Porta San Niccolò

VIA ROMANA

Museo Zoologico-La Specola

VIA DI SAN NICCOLO

PIAZZALE MICHELANGELO

Forte di Belvedere

GIARDINO DI BOBOLI

Museo delle Porcellane

San Salvatore al Monte

Istituto d'Arte

Florence

VIALE GALILEO

BOBOLINO

Rome

San Miniato al Monte

VIALE NICCOLÒ MACHIAVELLI

VIALE GALILEO GALILEI

Area of map detail

A   B   C   D

PIAZZA DEL DUOMO TO PIAZZA DELLA SIGNORIA

The Piazza del Duomo and Piazza della Signoria are Florence's two main squares, around which lie some of the city's principal attractions. Most visitors make the Duomo (cathedral) and its attendant baptistery and campanile their first stop, then wend their way past the Orsanmichele, a 14th-century church, to the charms of Piazza della Signoria, where the Palazzo Vecchio and Loggia della Signoria await.

■ Piazza del Duomo, with the Battistero di San Giovanni in the foreground

Santa Maria del Fiore (Duomo)

🗺 205 C4

✉ Piazza del Duomo

☎ 055 230 2855

🕐 Closed Sun. a.m. & 1st Tue. of the month

💲 Free; combined ticket (see p. 209)

ilgrandemuseodel duomo.it

Piazza del Duomo

The Piazza del Duomo is the city's religious heart. Here stands the Duomo, Santa Maria del Fiore, and its imperious dome, one of the city's great symbols, flanked by its freestanding campanile, or bell tower. In the Duomo's shadow stands the Battistero di San Giovanni, Florence's oldest building, a place of spiritual and artistic importance

for well over a thousand years. Some of the art produced for these buildings has been removed for safekeeping to the square's fourth major component, the Museo dell'Opera del Duomo, a museum tucked behind the cathedral.

Santa Maria del Fiore: The Duomo, Europe's fourth largest cathedral, was begun in 1296 by

INSIDER TIP:

A great and little-known viewpoint is the tiny terrace of the Rinascente department store in Piazza della Repubblica. Go to the top floor for wonderful vistas of the Duomo, Campanile, Bargello, and Palazzo Vecchio.

—BEATRICE LAGHI
Hotel Brunelleschi

the architect Arnolfo di Cambio (1245–1302). Its vast scope was designed to reflect Florence's burgeoning importance as a city and to outshine the cathedrals of rivals Siena and Pisa. Consecrated in 1436, it was crowned with the largest dome since antiquity, a masterpiece of medieval engineering designed by Filippo Brunelleschi (1377–1466). The multicolored facade, a Gothic pastiche, dates from as recently as 1887, Arnolfo di Cambio's quarter-finished frontage having been pulled down in 1587.

The contrast between the cathedral's ornate exterior and apparently plain interior could hardly be greater. Size for its own sake seems to be the latter's overriding preoccupation. Closer investigation, however, reveals a surprising number of artistic treasures, as well as two worthwhile side attractions: the crypt, where you can see the remains of **Santa Reparata** (*closed Sun., $*), an earlier church on the site,

and the cathedral's **dome** (*closed Sun., advance reservations*), which offers an insight into Brunelleschi's engineering genius and a glorious panorama of Florence and its surrounding countryside.

Before you explore either of these, however, see the interior's other highlights. Start with three paintings on the left (north) wall: "Dante Explaining the Divine Comedy" (1465) is by Domenico di Michelino, and the other two are equestrian portraits of the mercenary soldiers Sir John Hawkwood (1436) and Niccolò da Tolentino (1456) by Paolo Uccello and Andrea del Castagno, respectively.

Florence's Ice-Cream Wars

For years, there was no contest in the title for Florence's best ice cream: **Vivoli** (*Via Isola delle Stinche 7r, tel 055 292 334, vivoli .it, closed Mon.*), founded near the church of Santa Croce in 1929, outshone all others. Now, however, there is a slick new challenger, **Grom** (*int. of Via del Campanile & Via delle Oche, tel 055 216 158, grom.it*), tucked away in a side alley off Piazza del Duomo. The **Gelateria della Passera** (*via della Toscanella 15r, 055 291 882, gelateria lapassera.wordpress.com*), in the heart of the Oltrarno, is also one of the best.

Colorful but trite frescoes (1572–1579) by Giorgio Vasari of the "Last Judgment" adorn the interior of the dome, distracting from the genuine treasures of the twin sacristies below. On the left, as you face the high altar, is the **Sagrestia Nuova,** or New Sacristy, decorated with exquisite 15th-century inlaid wood

Florence

🗺 205 & 243 D4

Visitor Information

✉ Via Cavour 1r

☎ 055 290 832

🕐 Closed p.m. & Sat.–Sun.

✉ Piazza San Giovanni

☎ 055 288 496

🕐 Closed Sun. p.m.

✉ Piazza della Stazione 4

☎ 055 212 245

🕐 Closed Sun. p.m.

firenzeturismo.it

NOTE: In Florence, business addresses are suffixed with "r," which stands for *rosso* (red). These numbers are displayed in red on the street.

paneling and protected by bronze doors (1446–1467) designed by Michelozzo and Luca della Robbia. Above the doors is a bluish white terra-cotta lunette (1442), also by Luca della Robbia. An almost identical lunette (ca 1440) by the same artist graces the **Sagrestia Vecchia,** or Old Sacristy, on the other side of the church. Between the two sacristies, in the central apse, is a magnificent **bronze reliquary** (1432–1442) by Lorenzo Ghiberti that holds the remains of St. Zenobius, Florence's first bishop.

Battistero di San Giovanni:

The baptistery is the city's oldest building. Constructed on the site of a first-century Roman building, it probably dates from around the fourth or fifth century, although the earliest documentary reference comes in 897, when it was explicitly mentioned as Florence's first cathedral. Much of its classically inspired decoration dates from 1059 to 1128–or later–a period of important remodeling that saw the addition of the exterior's geometric medley of pillars, cornices, and colored marble friezes.

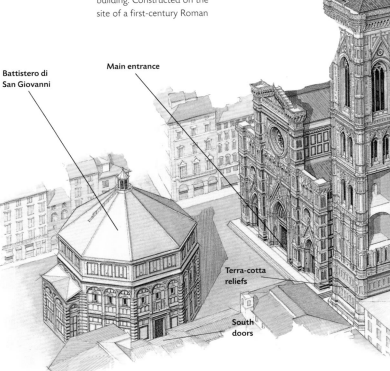

Campanile

Main entrance

Battistero di
San Giovanni

Terra-cotta
reliefs

South
doors

By far the baptistery's most eminent features are its **doors.** Those on the south face were the first to be made (1328–1336), designed by Andrea Pisano, a Pisan sculptor. They are decorated with 28 panels depicting, for the most part, scenes from the life of Florence's patron saint, St. John the Baptist, to whom the building is dedicated. The north doors (1403–1424) were commissioned from Lorenzo Ghiberti after a competition in 1401, a date often seen as marking the beginning of the Italian Renaissance. While following Pisano's earlier 28-panel scheme, Ghiberti's panels

Battistero di San Giovanni

🅰 205 C4

✉ Piazza San Giovanni-Piazza del Duomo

☎ 055 230 2885

🕐 Closed 10:15 a.m.–11:15 a.m. Mon.–Fri. & Sun. p.m.

💲 $$$ combined ticket to Duomo (free), Battistero, cathedral dome & crypt, Campanile, and Museo dell'Opera

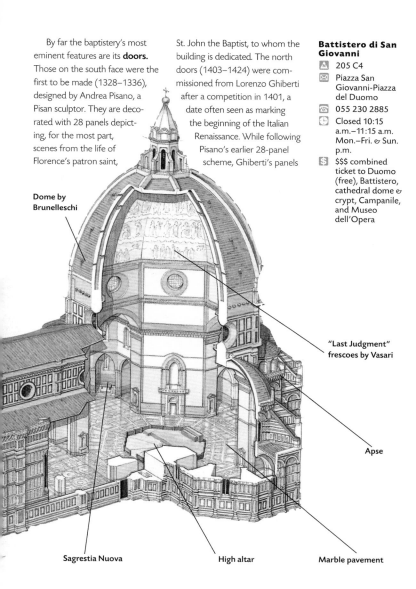

Dome by Brunelleschi

"Last Judgment" frescoes by Vasari

Apse

Sagrestia Nuova

High altar

Marble pavement

Santa Maria del Fiore (Duomo)

Campanile

 205 C4

 Piazza del Duomo

 055 230 2885

$ $$$ combined ticket (see p. 209)

display far greater artistic ambition than their predecessors—their subjects are episodes from the life of Christ, the Evangelists, and Doctors of the Church.

Still greater refinements appear in the most famous of the three portals, Ghiberti's east doors (1425–1452), the **Gates of Paradise,** whose ten panels depict Old Testament scenes with a previously unseen measure of narrative and technical sophistication. The panels are copies—the originals are in the Museo dell'Opera del Duomo (see page opposite).

The first impression of the baptistery's interior is of a bland shell. A glance upward, however, reveals a majestic mosaic-covered **ceiling,** a largely 13th-century work begun by Venetian craftsmen. Its immensely complex narrative embraces episodes from the lives of Christ, Joseph, the Virgin, and John the Baptist. To the right of the *scarsella,* or apse, lies Donatello and Michelozzo's **tomb of John XXIII,** antipope, an adviser and friend of the Medici who died in the city in 1419. Also worthy of note are the interior's band of granite columns, probably removed from the old Roman Capitol, and the intricately tessellated marble pavement, where the outline of the original octagonal font can still be seen.

Campanile: The campanile is the cathedral's bell tower. It was begun in 1334 under the guidance of the painter Giotto, then the city's *capo maestro,* or master of works. He completed only the first of the tower's five stories before his death in 1337. Work then proceeded in two phases, the first (1337–1342) under Andrea Pisano, designer

---

EXPERIENCE: Sampling Florence's Street Food

Florence's favorite, and traditional, street food is *trippa*—tripe—eaten in a crusty roll, usually topped with either a *salsa verde (*green sauce) or a spicy red sauce (ask for *trippa alla fiorentina*). Often rolls are offered *bagnato,* or dipped in the tripe's cooking juices.

Trippa is available from *trippai*—traditional street corner kiosks and stands—and from venerable outlets such as **Nerbone** *(tel 055 219 949, closed Sun.)* inside the Mercato Centrale, the city's covered central market. The trippai also sell other fillings, mostly variations on offal—such as *lampredotto,* made of the cow's fourth stomach—as well as robust red wine by the glass, often served from a flask.

Join the many Florentines standing in line at any number of trippai around town. One of the most convenient for Piazza del Duomo is in **Piazza dei Cimatori,** at the corner of Via de' Cerchi and Via dei Tavolini (off Via dei Calzaiuoli). Other central outlets can be found at **Lupen e Margo** *(Banco No. 75, corner of Via dell'Ariento & Via Sant'Antonio, closed Sun. April–Sept. & 2 weeks in Aug., lupen emargo.it),* by the San Lorenzo market; **Orazio Nencioni** *(Loggia del Porcellino, closed Sun., plus Sat. June–July),* at the Mercato Nuovo, a short distance from the Piazza della Signoria; and the venerable **Sergio Pollini** *(corner of Via de' Macci & Piazza Sant'Ambrogio, closed Sun. & Aug.),* near the Sant'Ambrogio market.

The mosaics on the ceiling of the Battistero di San Giovanni were completed in the 13th century.

of the baptistery's north doors, the second (1348–1359) under Francesco Talenti. Giotto probably left blueprints for the tower's decoration, although most of the first-story reliefs—the tower's decorative highlights—were executed by Pisano, Luca della Robbia, and assistants. The present reliefs are copies (the age-darkened originals reside in the Museo dell'Opera). A strenuous 414-step climb (no elevator) to the top of the 278-foot (84,7 m) tower is rewarded by sensational views of the city.

Museo dell'Opera
del Duomo: The Opera del Duomo was a body created in 1296 to care for the fabric of the cathedral. Since 1891, its former headquarters has been used to safeguard works of art removed over the centuries

from the Duomo, baptistery, and campanile. Occupying an impressive, modern space that reopened in October 2015 after a long period of restoration, its sculpture collection is second only to that of the nearby Bargello (see pp. 220–221).

The principal space is the museum's enclosed courtyard, where the young Michelangelo carved much of his famed "David." Today, though, the highlights are the restored panels from Lorenzo Ghiberti's Gates of Paradise doors on the Battistero di San Giovanni and a host of statues, most rescued from Arnolfo di Cambio's demolished cathedral facade. The most eye-catching are a figure of "St. John" by Donatello and two works by di Cambio: the "Madonna of the Glass Eyes," with its otherworldly gaze, and an almost comical statue of "Boniface VIII,"

Museo dell'Opera del Duomo

🅰 205 C4

✉ Piazza del Duomo 9

☎ 055 230 2885

🕐 Closed 1st Tue. of the month

💲 $$$ combined ticket (see p. 209)

ilgrandemuseodel duomo.it

Orsanmichele

205 C3

Via dei Calzaiuoli 42

055 210 305

a controversial medieval pope seen here with his distinctive hat.

Other standout statues include Michelangelo's **"Pietà"** (ca 1550), a late work probably intended for his own tomb (the New Testament figure of Nicodemus may be a self-portrait). Michelangelo became disillusioned by the piece and, in his frustration, smashed its left arm and leg. The damage was

Magdalene" (1455) and the bald-headed Old Testament prophet "Abacuc," or Habakkuk (1423–1425), one of 16 figures removed here from the campanile. You will also find many more refugees from the bell tower, including first-story allegorical reliefs by Andrea Pisano, Luca della Robbia, and their pupils. Other museum sections contain Renaissance paintings, reliquaries, and a fascinating

■ Full of charm and character, the streets off Via dei Calzaiuoli beckon visitors to explore.

later repaired by a pupil, but signs of the damage and the discrepancy in styles are evident.

Other rooms contain two stunning and contrasting *cantorie*, or **choir lofts,** one by Donatello (1433–1439), the other by Luca della Robbia (1431–1438). Both were removed from the entrances to the cathedral's sacristies. Close by are Donatello's celebrated wooden statue of "Mary

section devoted to Brunelleschi, notably a series of tools, as well as period and modern wooden models of this extraordinary work of architecture. Conclude your visit on the museum terrace with a dazzling view of the dome itself.

Orsanmichele

Walk south from Piazza del Duomo along Via dei Calzaiuoli, a pedestrians-only street; down on the right you pass the church of Orsanmichele, known chiefly for the extraordinary range of sculptures that adorns its otherwise plain exterior. The church takes its name from San Michele ad Hortum, the name of a seventh-century oratory that once occupied the *hortum* or *orto* (garden) of a Benedictine monastery on the site.

This oratory was replaced around 1284 by a grain market, although the site retained its religious associations thanks to an image of the Virgin accredited with miraculous powers painted on one of its pillars. Over the next century, the building was rebuilt on several occasions, and by 1380, its lower half had once again become a church—more or less the building you see today—while its upper levels were used as a granary during times of siege and famine.

As early as 1339, the city's guilds had been entrusted with the building's decoration, each of the exterior niches to be filled with a statue of a particular guild's patron saint. Some of the great names of early Renaissance sculpture eventually worked on the site, among them Donatello, Ghiberti, Verrocchio, and Michelozzo, crafting the niche statues and their ornate surrounds (some of the present works are copies).

Inside, the church provides a peaceful retreat from the crowds on Via dei Calzaiuoli. Patches of frescoes appear around the walls as your eyes become accustomed to the gloom—most portray the guilds' patron saints. To the rear

Florence's Mighty Medici

The Medici fortune was established by Giovanni de' Medici (1360–1429) and consolidated by Cosimo de' Medici, also known as Cosimo the Elder (1389–1464). Its fruits were enjoyed by Cosimo's heir, Lorenzo de' Medici, better known as Lorenzo the Magnificent (1449–1492). The enlightened patronage of the Medici and others, together with an upsurge in classical and humanist scholarship, provided the spur for the Renaissance, a long-flowering artistic reawakening that found a fertile breeding ground in Florence, then Europe's most dynamic, cosmopolitan, and sophisticated city.

Medici power faltered in the 1490s with Lorenzo's death, leaving the way clear for Girolamo Savonarola (1452–1498), a charismatic monk eventually removed by the papacy in 1498. By 1512, the Medici were back, albeit with reduced power, only to be ousted again in 1527 by Emperor Charles V. Just two years later, the family had returned again, this time in the person of Cosimo I, who took control of Tuscany and assumed the title of grand duke.

stands a magnificent **tabernacle** (1348–1359) by Andrea Orcagna, built partly to house a painting of the "Madonna and Child" (1347) by Bernardo Daddi, a work said to have inherited the miraculous powers of the Virgin on the pillar, which had been destroyed in a fire. The greatest work of its kind in Italy, the tabernacle was financed by a flood of votive offerings prompted by the plague of 1348.

Piazza della Signoria

Where Piazza del Duomo serves as Florence's religious heart, the city's second great square,

Piazza della Signoria

205 C3

■ **The battlements and tower of the Palazzo Vecchio dominate the Piazza della Signoria.**

Palazzo Vecchio

- 🅰 205 C3
- ✉ Piazza della Signoria
- ☎ 055 276 8325
- 🕐 Closed Thurs. p.m.
- 💲 $$

museicivicifiorentini.comune.fi.it

Piazza della Signoria, has long been its civic focus. It is home to the Palazzo Vecchio, the seat of city government for seven centuries, and plays hosts to several notable pieces of public sculpture. It is also a meeting place for visitors and Florentines alike: Rivoire, one of the city's most distinguished cafés, is here, while close by lies the entrance to the most celebrated of all Florence's museums, the Uffizi (see pp. 216–219).

Palazzo Vecchio: Dominating the Piazza della Signoria is the fortresslike Palazzo Vecchio. Building began in 1299, probably to a plan by the cathedral's architect, Arnolfo di Cambio. Initially it housed the Priori, or Signoria, the city's ruling council, but in 1540 it became home to Grand Duke Cosimo I. Cosimo remained just nine years before moving to the Palazzo Pitti, the point at which

his old *(vecchio)* palace acquired its present name. Today, the palace once again houses the city's council, although much of its interior is also open to the public.

You enter the complex via an inner **courtyard,** designed by Michelozzo and beautifully decorated by Giorgio Vasari (1565), and then climb to the **Salone dei Cinquecento,** the palace's vast centerpiece, designed to accommodate the members of the Maggior Consiglio, the republic's ruling assembly. Its ceiling painting, the "Apotheosis of Cosimo I," and bombastic wall paintings—illustrations of Florentine military triumphs—are the work of Vasari. Of greater interest are Michelangelo's statue "Victory" (1533–1534), almost opposite the room's entrance, and the small **Studiolo di Francesco I** (1569–1573), a private study adorned with the decorative efforts of more than 30 artists.

Turn left on the stairs from the Salone and a suite of rooms, the Quartiere degli Elementi, leads to the **Terrazzo di Saturno,** which offers some intriguing city views. Turn right and you enter the **Quartiere di Eleonora,** the apartments of Cosimo I's wife. The highlight here is the tiny **Cappella di Eleonora** (1540–1545), sumptuously decorated by the mannerist artist Agnolo Bronzino.

Among the following rooms, the **Sala dell'Udienza** has good views over the Piazza della Signoria and a glorious ceiling (1472–1476) by Giuliano da Maiano, who was also responsible, with his brother, for the carved doorway to the neighboring **Sala dei Gigli.** Named after its decorative lilies *(gigli),* this room features another fine Maiano ceiling, a fresco sequence (1481–1485) by Domenico Ghirlandaio, and Donatello's sublime statue of "Judith and Holofernes" (1455–1460). The adjacent **Cancelleria** was once Niccolò Machiavelli's office, while the **Sala delle Carte** next door, now filled with lovely 16th-century maps, once housed Cosimo I's costumes of state.

Loggia della Signoria: The triple-arched Loggia della Signoria on the piazza's eastern side was begun in 1376, possibly to a design by Orcagna, to protect city officials from the weather during Florence's numerous public ceremonies. In time it was also used as a site to meet visiting foreign dignitaries, and as a shelter for the Swiss *lanzi* (lancers) of Cosimo I's personal guard—hence its other name, the Loggia dei Lanzi. Today, it acts as a small outdoor museum for pieces

Statues in the Piazza

From left to right as you face the Palazzo Vecchio, a range of statues stands along the Piazza della Signoria's eastern flank: "Cosimo I" (1594), an equestrian monument to the Medici duke by Giambologna; "Fountain of Neptune" (1563–1575) by Ammannati, a work ridiculed by Michelangelo, among others; Donatello's "Il Marzocco" (1418–1420), a copy of a statue of Florence's heraldic symbol (the original is in the Museo Nazionale del Bargello); Donatello's "Judith and Holofernes," another copy of an original statue now in the Palazzo Vecchio; "David," a copy of Michelangelo's original, now in the Galleria dell'Accademia; and "Hercules and Cacus" (1534), carved by Bandinelli to act as a companion piece for the "David."

of sculpture. The most famous work is Benvenuto Cellini's prodigious "Perseus" (1545–1553), one of Europe's greatest bronze statues. To its right stands Giambologna's "Rape of the Sabine Women" (1583). Despite its title, it was originally intended simply as a study of old age, male strength, and female beauty. ∎

GALLERIA DEGLI UFFIZI

"Great" is an overused adjective in Italy, where so many monuments and works of art command the highest praise. In the case of the Galleria degli Uffizi, or Uffizi, it barely does justice to a gallery that holds the world's finest collection of Renaissance paintings. All the famous names of Italian art are here, not only the Renaissance masters but also painters from the country's medieval, baroque, and mannerist heyday. So, too, are artists from farther afield.

■ "Coronation of the Virgin" (ca 1435) by Fra Angelico

from the collection went to the Bargello, Etruscan and other antique art to the Museo Archeologico, and paintings to the Uffizi and Palazzo Pitti.

With the "Nuovi Uffizi" project, the number of permanent display halls has increased from 45 to about 100 and visitor experience has been improved with the installation of a new lighting system, a modern security system, to insure the safety of the artwork, and the creation of new spaces and connections between the galleries. The fact that work isn't finished yet hasn't discouraged visitors, who came in record-breaking numbers in 2018.

To visit the entire Uffizi would be a colossal enterprise so we suggest you select the themes that interest you the most and concentrate your effort on those display halls rather than others. Don't hesitate to use the available technology; some apps can be of great help. You should be prepared to wait in line at almost any time of the day and in any season, although note that tickets guaranteeing entry at a specific time can be arranged (see sidebar opposite).

The Collection

An assortment of sculptures and frescoes by Andrea del Castagno provide the Uffizi's prelude, and

Florence has the Medici family to thank for the Uffizi. The building that houses the collection was designed in 1560 as a suite of offices (*uffizi*) for Cosimo I, the family's first grand duke, while the collection itself, accumulated by the family over the centuries, was bequeathed to the city (on condition that it never leave Florence) by Anna Maria Luisa, sister of the last grand duke, Gian Gastone Medici. Sculpture

it is only with three great depictions of the Maestà, or Madonna Enthroned, in **Room 2** that the gallery gets into its stride. Italy's three finest 13th-century artists were responsible for the paintings—Giotto, Cimabue, and Duccio—each of whom pioneered a distinct move away from the stylized and iconic conventions of Byzantine art that had dominated Italian and other art for centuries. Thus Cimabue's depiction of the saints around the Virgin's throne improves on those of Duccio: Cimabue's saints stand in fixed positions, while those of Duccio, a painter more wedded to Byzantine tradition, seem to float haphazardly. Giotto makes the largest leap of all, adding light and shadow to denote the folds of the Madonna's cloak, one of several realistic and revolutionary departures from the Byzantine approach.

Paintings from Italy's Gothic masters fill **Rooms 3–6,** beginning with works from the city of Siena, where painters continued to borrow heavily from the fading conventions of Byzantine art. Finest of all are Simone Martini's "Annunciation" (1333) and the works by Pietro and Ambrogio Lorenzetti, two brothers who probably died during the plague epidemic that swept Italy in 1348. Then come exponents of the International Gothic, a highly detailed and courtly style exemplified by Gentile da Fabriano's exquisite "Adoration of the Magi" (1423) and Lorenzo Monaco's "Coronation of the Virgin" (1413).

The first flowering of the Renaissance is seen in **Room 7,** which presents works by early iconoclasts such as Fra Angelico, Masaccio, and Masolino. **Room 8** features a painting by one of the least known of Italian painters,

Galleria degli Uffizi

- 205 C3
- Loggiato degli Uffizi 6, off Piazza della Signoria
- 055 294 883; reservations online at uffizi.it
- Closed Mon.
- $$, $$$ in peak periods; $$$$ three-days combined ticket to Uffizi, Palazzo Pitti, and Giardino di Boboli

uffizi.it

Beat the Lines With a Prebought Ticket

At no other Italian museum or art gallery is it so necessary to secure advance tickets than at the Uffizi, where lines are extremely long year-round at any time of the day or week. Many private operators and several commercial websites offer the booking service, but it's just as easy to go through the official ticketing agency, **Firenze Musei** *(tel 055 294 883, firenze musei.it or uffizi.it).*

You must nominate a day and time, and pay a booking fee on top of the gallery standard entrance fee (extra charged for special exhibitions). Bookings must be made at least 24 hours in advance. On the day, collect your timed ticket at a separate location across the street from the gallery.

If you miss your time slot, you will forfeit the right to skip the lines.

Tickets can also be booked for the Galleria dell'Accademia, the Museo Nazionale del Bargello, the Cappelle Medicee, Giardino di Boboli, Museo di San Marco, and the Galleria Palatina in the Palazzo Pitti. These museums share a useful website *(polomuseale.firenze.it),* which offers additional practical information on tickets, plus details of how to purchase the **Firenze Card** *(firenzecard.it).* This card costs €85 ($96) and is good for entry (avoiding lines) to more than 70 museums, galleries, gardens, and villas in Florence. Valid for 72 hours, it also offers free use of public transit.

Domenico Veneziano, an artist with only 12 confidently attributed paintings to his name. Nearby hang two well-known paintings by one of Veneziano's pupils, Piero della Francesca—portraits (1460) of Federico da Montefeltro, Duke of Urbino, and his wife, Battista Sforza. Federico was always portrayed in left profile, as here, after a jousting accident disfigured the right side of his face.

Botticelli: You can almost guarantee that **Rooms 10–14** will be the Uffizi's most crowded, for this is the suite given over to the gallery's most famous paintings: Botticelli's "Primavera" (1478) and "The Birth of Venus" (1485). The latter, the famous woman in a half shell, was the first pagan nude of the Renaissance and, like the "Primavera" (Spring), drew heavily on classical myth and contemporary

humanist scholarship. Venus was impregnated following the castration of Uranus and then rose from the sea, suggesting beauty (Venus) was the result of a union of the physical and spiritual (Uranus). In the myth—and painting—the nymphs Chloris and Zephyr blow the risen Venus to the shore, where she is cloaked by Hora. The theme of the "Primavera" is more uncertain. Some critics suggest it is an allegory of spring or all four seasons, others that it represents the Triumph of Venus, the attendant Graces representing her beauty, Flora her fecundity.

On the Road to Leonardo: The octagonal Tribune, **Room 18,** was specially built by the Medici to house their most precious works of art, among which the "Medici Venus," a first-century B.C. Greek statue, figured large. Widely

■ **Sandro Botticelli used classical rather than Christian imagery in his 1485 "The Birth of Venus."**

celebrated as Europe's most erotic statue–Lord Byron stood before it "dazzled and drunk with beauty"–the figure was the only Florentine statue removed to France by Napoleon after his invasion of Italy.

Room 35 contains two of only a handful of paintings in Florence attributed to Leonardo da Vinci: an "Annunciation" (1475) and the "Adoration of the Magi" (1481), works that rather overshadow paintings by Luca Signorelli and Perugino elsewhere in the room.

Raphael & Michelangelo:

The next rooms are devoted to Florentine, Venetian, German, and Flemish canvases, but in Room 41, visitors can admire some of the most famous works by one of the most influential painters of the Renaissance: Raphael. The most notable are the "Madonna of the Goldfinch" (1506) and the portraits of Agnolo Doni and his wife, Maddalena (1504–1507), displayed in such a way as to make it possible to see the scenes from Ovid's "Metamorphosis" painted on the backs. The Doni family also commissioned the only work by Michelangelo present in the Uffizi (which, not by chance, is located in the same display hall), the "Holy Family" (1504), known as the "Doni Tondo".

The First Floor: Little of the content of Michelangelo's "Doni Tondo" is understood, but its deliberately obscure meaning, contorted composition, and often virulent coloring profoundly influenced a style of painting known

as mannerism, a genre whose leading lights are represented on the first floor. Once you walk downstairs, you will find what has become one of the greatest col-

---

INSIDER TIP:

Botticelli's "Primavera" at the Uffizi is a 10-foot-long (3 m) lush delight. Luckily there's a bench just in front for lingering.

–JOHNNA RIZZO
National Geographic author

---

lections of Italian art of the 1500s. It was further enhanced in May 2019 with a new arrangement and the addition of a number of paintings that were put on display for the first time in many years. This part of the Uffizi will undergo other transformations and the placement of the works may change, but in these halls you will find Pontormo's "Madonna with Child with the Infant St. John the Baptist" (1529–1530), Artemisia Gentileschi, Correggio, Giorgione, and Titian's much talked about "Venus of Urbino" (1538), one of the most explicit nudes in Western painting, that led Mark Twain to describe it as "the foulest, the vilest, the obscenest picture the world possesses."

Caravaggio's two masterpieces "Sacrifice of Isaac" (1603) and "Bacchus" (1598) are displayed in Room 90.

Halls dedicated to French, Dutch and Flemish artists are also located on the first floor. ∎

MUSEO NAZIONALE DEL BARGELLO

The Bargello's collection of Renaissance and Gothic sculpture is one of the most important in Italy, second only in Florence to the Uffizi. The museum takes its name from its building, the Bargello, a palace built in 1255. Once the seat of the *podestà*, the city's main magistrate, it acquired its present name in 1574 after the Medici abolished the position of podestà and made the building over to the *bargello*, the chief of police.

"Lamentation" by Giovanni della Robbia, a relief made of glazed and colored terra-cotta

Museo Nazionale del Bargello

- 205 C3
- Via del Proconsolo 4
- 055 064 9440
- Closed 1st, 3rd, 5th Mon. & 2nd & 4th Sun. of the month
- $; free 1st Sun. of the month

bargellomusei.beniculturali.it

Sculptural Masterpieces

The first room on the ground floor to the right after the ticket hall contains the best of the gallery's late Renaissance sculpture. Three works by Michelangelo take center stage: a lurching and very obviously drunk **"Bacchus"** (1497), carved when the sculptor was just 22; a delicate tondo of the **"Madonna and Child"** (1503–1505); and a proud-faced bust of **"Brutus"** (1539–1540), the only work of its kind completed by the artist.

Scattered around the room are works by Michelangelo's contemporaries. Benvenuto Cellini was responsible for a **"Bust of Cosimo I"** and several preparatory bronzes for his great statue of "Perseus" in the Loggia della Signoria (see p. 215). Giambologna is represented by his famous winged **"Mercury,"** an image that has become the standard representation of the god. In any other company, the works of Bandinelli, Ammannati, and other sculptors on display would shine. Here, they somehow appear second-rate.

Cross the Bargello's courtyard, formerly the scene of executions, to take in the less arresting Gothic works in the ground floor's remaining two rooms (the crests around the courtyard walls belong to the palace's various podestà). Then climb the courtyard's external stairs to the first floor, where you come across a wonderfully eccentric menagerie of bronze animals by Giambologna. Turn right to reach the gallery's second major salon, the **Salone del Consiglio Generale.**

Sculptures here represent the pinnacle of Renaissance achievement, with those of Donatello taking pride of place. His most famous sculpture, the androgynous bronze **"David"** (1430–1440), was described by American writer Mary McCarthy in *The Stones of Florence* (1959) as a "transvestite's and fetishist's dream of alluring ambiguity." More restrained masterpieces by the same artist include "St. George" (1416), made for the Armaiuoli, or armorers' guild; "St. George and the Dragon" (1430–1440), sculpted for Orsanmichele; a marble "David" (1408); a stone "Marzocco" (1420), Florence's heraldic symbol; and the "Atys-Amorino" (1440), a frivolous putto of unknown mythical origin.

Two other works of immense importance are a pair of **reliefs depicting the "Sacrifice of Isaac"** by Lorenzo Ghiberti and Filippo Brunelleschi. These were the joint winning entries of a 1401 competition to choose a sculptor for the Battistero di San Giovanni doors (see pp. 208–210). Also noteworthy are the distinctive 15th-century polychrome terra-cottas of Luca della Robbia, as well as works from most of the great names of Renaissance sculpture—Michelozzo, Vecchietta, Agostino di Duccio, Desiderio da Settignano, and many more.

Decorative Arts & More

Most of the rest of the first floor and the entire second floor display a ravishing collection of carpets, tapestries, silverware, enamels, ivories, glassware, and other objets d'art spanning many centuries. Highlights on the second floor include the collections of Islamic art, ivories, and the beautifully decorated **Cappella di Santa Maria Maddalena.** The chapel contains frescoes (1340) by the school of Giotto. The fine painting of "Il Paradiso" on the end wall features a depiction of Dante. The chapel's

---

INSIDER TIP:

The Museo del Bargello occasionally hosts classical concerts. Check to see if one is on while you're in town. They are usually not very expensive, and the setting is wonderful.

—JANE SUNDERLAND
National Geographic contributor

lovely pulpit, lectern, and stalls (all 1483–1488) were originally carved for the church of San Miniato al Monte (see p. 237).

On the third floor, look for the enameled terra-cottas of the della Robbia family of artists; sculptures by Antonio del Pollaiuolo and the Sienese artist Vecchietta; the **Sala dell'Armeria,** a display of arms and armor; and the **Salone del Camino,** home to Italy's finest collection of miniature bronzes. ∎

SANTA CROCE

Florence's most compelling church is not only an artistic shrine—with frescoes by Giotto, Taddeo Gaddi, and others—but also the burial place of 270 of the city's most eminent inhabitants, among them Galileo, Michelangelo, and Machiavelli. In the cloister next door stands the Cappella dei Pazzi, the church's former chapter house, widely regarded as one of the most perfect early Renaissance creations.

Santa Croce

- 🗺 205 D3
- ✉ Piazza Santa Croce
- ☎ 055 246 6105; tickets available on website
- 🕐 Closed Sun. a.m.
- 💲 $

santacroceopera.it

Santa Croce was commissioned by the Franciscans and probably designed by Arnolfo di Cambio. Begun around 1294, its purpose was partly to rival Santa Maria Novella, mother church of the city's Dominicans, then being built on the other side of the city. Vast sums were spent on the church.

■ Michelangelo was laid to rest in this Santa Croce tomb, despite spending most of the last 25 years of his life in Rome.

Rich Florentines saw it as an act of humility to be involved with, and better still buried among, the humble Franciscans, while wealthy bankers saw sponsorship of religious buildings as a way of assuaging the guilt of usury, then still considered a sin by the Church.

The patronage lavished on Santa Croce accounts for the ostentation of its many chapels, most of which were named after the families that sponsored them. It also explains the splendor of its numerous **tombs,** which begin as soon as you enter the magnificent interior with Giorgio Vasari's 1575 **monument to Michelangelo** (on the south wall). Alongside stands a cenotaph to Dante—the poet is buried in Ravenna, where he died in exile in 1321. Beyond this comes a fine pulpit (1472–1476) by Benedetto da Maiano and then the **tomb of Machiavelli** (1787). Beyond these, and past a gilded stone relief of the "Annunciation" (1435) by Donatello, are the tombs of the opera composer Gioacchino Rossini (1792–1868) and the 15th-century humanist scholar Leonardo Bruni.

Bruni's tomb (1446–1447) was the work of Bernardo Rossellino; it became one of the most influential of all early Renaissance funerary monuments, mainly

Cappella dei Pazzi

The Cappella dei Pazzi is one of Florence's architectural highlights, commissioned as a chapter house and mausoleum in 1429 from Filippo Brunelleschi by Andrea de' Pazzi, a scion of one of the city's then leading banking families. Brunelleschi worked on the project intermittently until his death in 1446, but financial shortfalls meant the chapel was only finished in the 1470s.

The chapel's austere interior is particularly notable for the manner in which its decoration complements its simple geometrical forms. Note the glazed terracotta tondi (decorated roundels) in the cupola, for example, which depict the Evangelists and were the work of Luca della Robbia (ca 1400–1482), possibly to designs by Donatello and Brunelleschi himself. Della Robbia also created the 12 tondi of the Apostles around the walls, as well as the garland of fruit clasped around the Pazzi coat of arms. The lovely frieze of medallions and angels' heads above the porch is the work of Desiderio da Settignano (ca 1430–1464).

because it was the first time a human figure was the focus of a secular tomb. Among the works it influenced was the church's other great secular tomb, Desiderio da Settignano's 1453 **monument to Carlo Marsuppini,** another humanist scholar: It lies across the nave almost opposite the Bruni tomb. Moving back down the church on the north side, look for the **tomb of Galileo** (1737), situated near the entrance opposite the monument to Michelangelo.

Frescoes & Other Art

Patches of faded fresco adorn many of Santa Croce's walls, sharpening the appetite for the church's pictorial highlights: the **Cappella Bardi** and **Cappella Peruzzi,** two chapels to the right of the high altar frescoed by Giotto between about 1317 and 1330. The murals in the latter portray scenes from the lives of St. John the Baptist and St. John the Evangelist, while those in the former depict episodes from the life of St. Francis.

Fresco cycles by artists influenced or taught by Giotto fill several nearby chapels. To the left of the Cappella Bardi, the chancel area around the high altar is frescoed with the "Legend of the True Cross" (1380–90) by Agnolo Gaddi (1333–1396). The same artist was responsible for the **Cappella Castellani** (in the south transept), whose left wall has episodes from the life of St. Antony Abbot and its right has scenes from the lives of St. John the Baptist and St. Nicholas (1385). To the chapel's left, the **Cappella Baroncelli** contains a cycle (1328–1338) by Agnolo's father, Taddeo, devoted mostly to scenes from the life of the Virgin.

Works by Giovanni da Milano and others adorn the nearby sacristy and its adjacent little Cappella Rinuccini. Other paintings, including a celebrated 13th-century "Crucifix" by Cimabue, are on display in the **Museo dell'Opera di Santa Croce** in the cloister, whose entrance lies off the right aisle of the church. ■

SAN LORENZO & AROUND

Located northwest of Santa Maria del Fiore (the Duomo), San Lorenzo served as Florence's principal church prior to the construction of the Duomo. A key feature is the stunning Cappelle Medicee, the Medici Chapels, the resting place of several Medici family members. Nearby is the Palazzo Medici-Riccardi, the Medici family's home until the mid-16th century.

■ Artists commonly show off their talent on the streets around San Lorenzo.

San Lorenzo

🗺 205 B4
✉ Piazza San Lorenzo
☎ 055 214 042
🕐 Closed Sun.
💲 $

**operamedicea
laurenziana.org**

San Lorenzo

San Lorenzo is Florence's oldest church—founded in 393—and it served for many years as the city's cathedral. It was also the Medici's parish church, and several vast grants from the family in the 15th century helped transform it into the present-day structure, a restrained Renaissance masterpiece designed by Filippo Brunelleschi.

The church's first artistic highlight is Rosso Fiorentino's painting of the "Marriage of the Virgin" (1523) in the second chapel on the south wall. In the middle of the nave stand two pulpits (1460),

their superb bronze reliefs among the last works of Donatello, who is buried in the church. To their right lies a tabernacle, the "Pala del Sacramento" (1458–1461) by Desiderio da Settignano, while beneath the dome an inscription marks the tomb of Cosimo the Elder, Donatello's chief patron and the church's main benefactor.

Additional Medici tombs lie to the left of the altar, in the **Sagrestia Vecchia,** or Old Sacristy (1422–1428), commissioned as a private chapel by Cosimo's father, Giovanni Bicci de' Medici. Giovanni and his wife are buried beneath the marble slab at the center of the chapel, while their grandsons, Giovanni and Piero de' Medici, lie in a tomb (1472) by Andrea del Verrocchio to the left of the entrance door. Donatello was responsible for the eight colored tondi, the frieze of cherubs, and the two large reliefs and bronze doors of the end wall.

Exit the church at the top of the north aisle, pausing to admire Filippino Lippi's altarpiece of the "Annunciation" (1440). Before the cloister, a door on your right leads to the **Biblioteca Medicea Laurenziana** *(tel 055 210 760, closed Sun. & p.m., $)*, a library created by Pope Clement VII, nephew of Lorenzo the Magnificent, to house the 11,000 manuscripts accumulated by Lorenzo and Cosimo de' Medici. Michelangelo designed the vestibule, or Ricetto (1559–1571), with its jet-black steps, as well as the reading room atop the stairs.

Cappelle Medicee

The Cappelle Medicee, or Medici Chapels, form the Medici mausoleum, a three-part complex annexed to San Lorenzo. Beyond the ticket hall, amid the gloom of the **crypt,** lie the bodies of 49 of the Medici's lesser lights, most of them placed here in 1791 by Grand Duke Ferdinand III. According to one contemporary account, the duke threw the corpses "together pell-mell . . . caring scarcely to distinguish one from the other." The bodies were exhumed in 1857 and arranged in their present, more dignified manner.

Steps lead from here to the **Cappella dei Principi,** or Chapel

of the Princes, the most expensive project ever undertaken by the Medici. Begun in 1604, it was still being paid for when the family line died out in 1743. The gargantuan interior features the tombs of the six Medici grand dukes— Cosimo I first adopted the ducal title in 1570. All are grotesque affairs, as are the gaudy marbles swathing the walls. The main points of interest are the stone coats of arms of the 16 major Tuscan towns under Medici control.

More beautiful examples of Medici patronage are found in the **Sagrestia Nuova,** designed by Michelangelo as a riposte to Brunelleschi's Sagrestia Vecchia in San Lorenzo (see page opposite). The sculptor was also responsible for the sacristy's **three tombs** (1520–1534): The one on the right belongs to Lorenzo, the

Cappelle Medicee

🗺 205 B4

✉ Piazza Madonna degli Aldobrandini 2

☎ 055 238 8602

🕐 Closed 2nd & 4th Sun. & 1st, 3rd, & 5th Mon. of the month

💲 $$

EXPERIENCE: Live With Florentines

Be a GeoVisions Conversation Corps volunteer—it's a great deal. Typically, you teach members of a Florentine family English for 15 hours a week, Monday to Friday, and in return you get the chance to live with the family—making friends, learning Italian, and seeing firsthand how Italians really live and work (minimum one month). Alternatively, you can join a 130-hour TEFL certificate course (that will allow you to teach English) while living in Florence (minimum one-month placement to 12). You have to be a native English-speaker and hold a bachelor's degree. Contact GeoVisions *(tel 888 586 1255 in the U.S., 203 453 5838 from outside the U.S., geovisions.org)* **for further information.**

Palazzo Medici-Riccardi

🏛 205 C4

✉ Via Cavour 3

☎ 055 276 8224

🕐 Closed Wed.; Capella dei Magi limited to groups of 15 for a 15-minute visit

💲 $$

palazzomedici riccardi.it

arrogant grandson of Lorenzo the Magnificent, depicted here as a man of thought; the tomb's two attendant figures represent Dawn and Dusk. Opposite stands the tomb of Giuliano, Lorenzo the Magnificent's feckless youngest son, portrayed as a man of action with the attendant figures of Day and Night. The third sculpture, an unfinished "Madonna and Child,"

Palazzo Medici-Riccardi has many stately, ornate rooms.

was intended to grace the tombs of Lorenzo the Magnificent and his brother, Giuliano.

Palazzo Medici-Riccardi

The Palazzo Medici-Riccardi was built for Cosimo de' Medici between 1444 and 1462, possibly to a plan by Brunelleschi. It remained the Medici's family home and business headquarters

until 1540, when Cosimo I moved to the Palazzo Vecchio. Although deliberately understated, the palace and its use of rustication—a facing of rough-cut pieces of stone—would influence other Florentine palaces for generations to come.

Today's visitors come for the **Cappella dei Magi,** a tiny chapel decorated with a three-panel fresco cycle (1460) by Benozzo Gozzoli, a pupil of Fra Angelico. The cycle is one of the most charming objects in Florence.

Ostensibly, its subject is the "Journey of the Magi." Its actual subject is probably the annual procession of the Compagnia dei Magi, the most prestigious of Florence's medieval confraternities. Several Medici were members of the order, among them Piero de' Medici, who may have commissioned the frescoes. Given the Medici's involvement, it comes as little surprise to find that many of the family feature as protagonists in the paintings.

Putting names to faces, however, has proved difficult. The figure leading the procession on a white horse is believed to be Piero; the red-hatted figure astride a mule may be Cosimo de' Medici; while the gold-cloaked king riding the gray horse is probably Lorenzo the Magnificent. Lorenzo's brother, Giuliano, may be the figure preceded by the bowman. Gozzoli also included himself in the crowd: He stands on the left a couple of rows from the rear with the words OPUS BENOTTI— the work of Benozzo—picked out in gold on his red cap. ∎

GALLERIA DELL'ACCADEMIA

Only the Uffizi is more visited than the Galleria dell'Accademia, whose crowds are lured by the most famous Renaissance image—Michelangelo's "David." The statue's home was created by grand duke Pietro Leopoldo I in 1784 to house a collection of Florentine paintings and sculpture, the purpose of which was to act as a study aid for students of the city's arts academy.

Michelangelo's **"David"** was commissioned in 1501 by the Opera del Duomo, the body responsible for the upkeep of the cathedral. Its theme—David slaying Goliath—was chosen for its parallels with Florence's recent history, evoking the city's belated liberation from Medici rule and its ability to withstand more powerful foes.

Michelangelo's achievement becomes more remarkable when you realize that not only was the statue carved from a single piece of marble but also that the marble in question—a thin and fault-riddled block—was considered too damaged to work with. Several artists, Leonardo da Vinci among them, had failed to make anything of the stone, which had been quarried from the Tuscan hills some 40 years previously. Michelangelo confounded the doubters, completing the work in three years, whereupon it was installed in the Piazza della Signoria.

The statue remained in the square until 1873; its long exposure to the elements resulted in the loss of the gilding that once adorned its hair and chest. Also gone is the skirt of copper leaves designed to placate Florence's more prudish citizens. What remain are the figure's strange proportions—notably the disproportionately long arms and overly large head and hands—created to emphasize the statue's monumentality in its original outdoor setting.

Away from the "David," the gallery contains a variety of pleasing paintings and other works by Michelangelo, notably a statue of **"St. Matthew"** (1504–1508) and four **"Slaves"** (or "Prisoners"; see sidebar this page). All five (uncompleted) sculptures were originally intended for the tomb of Pope Julius II. ∎

Galleria dell'Accademia

▣ 205 C4

✉ Via Ricasoli 58–60

☎ 055 098 7100; reservations online at firenzemusei.it

🕐 Closed Mon.

💲 $$

galleriaaccademia firenze.beniculturali .it

Michelangelo's "Slaves"

Michelangelo's unfinished sculptures of the four so-called "Slaves" (or "Prisoners"), carved between 1521 and 1523, originally formed part of a design for the tomb of Julius II, the pope who commissioned Michelangelo in 1508 to paint the ceiling of the Sistine Chapel. In the event, they were presented to Cosimo I, the Medici Grand Duke, who installed them in the Giardino di Boboli, where they languished until 1909. Two other (finished) "Slaves" found their way to the Louvre in Paris.

The statues' rough and deliberately unfinished appearance exemplified Michelangelo's notion that sculpture was the liberation of an existing form "imprisoned" within unworked stone. Others suggest the figures might have eventually been intended to represent the "Liberal Arts" left "enslaved" by Julius's death.

MUSEO DI SAN MARCO

The Museo di San Marco once formed part of the Dominican convent of San Marco, a building patronized by Cosimo de' Medici, who backed the creation of a majestic library within its walls and paid for the enlargement of its conventual buildings between 1437 and 1452. Today, the convent is a museum given over to the works of Fra Angelico, an erstwhile monk and prior of the convent, but remembered as one of the most sublime of all Renaissance painters.

■ Fra Angelico's "Annunciation" is considered one of the finest portrayals of the subject in Western art.

Museo di San Marco

◢ 205 C5

✉ Piazza San Marco 3

☎ 055 238 8608 for reservations or online at firenzemusei.it

🕒 Closed p.m. Mon.–Fri., 2nd & 4th Mon., & 1st, 3rd, 5th Sun. of the month

💲 $

polomusealetoscana .beniculturali.it

On entering the former monastic complex you find yourself in the **Chiostro di Sant'Antonino,** a cloister designed in the 1430s by Michelozzo, one of the Medici's preferred architects. It takes its name from Antonino Pierozzi (1389–1459), archbishop of Florence, the convent's first prior and Fra Angelico's religious mentor.

Look first at the faded frescoes in the cloister's four corners, all painted by Fra Angelico, before moving to the far greater works by the artist in the **Ospizio dei Pellegrini** (off the cloister on the right), a room previously used to offer hospitality

to visiting pilgrims. Paintings here have been garnered from churches and other buildings around Florence and include two of the artist's greatest works: the "Madonna dei Linaiuoli" (1433), commissioned by the linen-weavers' guild (the Linaiuoli), and the "San Marco Altarpiece" (1440), commissioned by the Medici for the church of San Marco, which you can visit next door to the convent. Note the presence in the altarpiece of the saints Cosmas and Damian, chosen by the Medici as their patron saints because of their status as *medici,* or doctors.

A door off the top right-hand corner of the cloister opens into the **Sala del Lavabo,** where the monks washed before eating (*lavare* means "to wash"). The entrance walls contain more frescoes by Fra Angelico, while the **Large Refectory** off to the right is dominated by a painting of the Last Supper, the work of 16th-century artist Giovanni Sogliani.

The *Cenacolo,* or Last Supper, was a common subject of paintings in monastic refectories (rooms where the monks gathered to eat). Several versions are found in buildings around Florence, and there is another, superior, version dating from 1480 by Domenico Ghirlandaio in San Marco's **Refettorio Piccolo** (Small Refectory). This is reached via a passage off the cloister by the old convent bell. The adjacent **Chapter House,** by the bell, retains an impressive fresco of the Crucifixion (1441) by Fra Angelico. Beyond the refectory a passage leads to the **Foresteria,** the convent's former guest rooms—today it is full of archaeological fragments and offers goods views of the Cloister of San Domenico, which is not part of the complex.

San Marco's Upper Floor

Florence has many artistic surprises, but none as wonderful as the sudden vision of Fra Angelico's **"Annunciation,"** a sublime painting at the top of the stairs leading to San Marco's upper floor. Note the work's inscription, which reminded monks to say a Hail Mary as they passed the image.

Next to catch the eye is the magnificent wooden ceiling, followed by two corridors containing 44 **dormitory cells.** Most of the latter are painted with simple, pious frescoes by Fra Angelico and his assistants, each designed as an aid to devotion for the monks. Fra Angelico's hand is most present in the frescoes of cells 1 to 11 in the corridor straight ahead of you; numbers 1, 3, 6, and 9 are worthy of special attention—these portray a "Noli me Tangere," "Annunciation," "Transfiguration," and "Coronation of the Virgin," respectively.

Turn right at the end of this corridor, and you come to a trio of rooms once occupied by Girolamo Savonarola, the monk who held Florence in thrall after the Medici's temporary fall from power in 1494. Turn right by the "Annunciation" along the nearer corridor and you pass the entrance (on the right) to the Michelozzo-designed and Medici-donated **Library** (1441–1444). Beyond this, the last two cells on the right, both larger than their neighbors, were reserved for the use of Cosimo de' Medici. ■

A WALK FROM SANTISSIMA ANNUNZIATA TO SANTA TRÌNITA

This is a good walk to follow after visiting the Galleria dell'Accademia or Museo di San Marco, as both are close to its starting point in Piazza della Santissima Annunziata.

Start your walk by first admiring Giambologna's statue of Grand Duke Ferdinand I (1608) at the center of **Piazza della Santissima Annunziata,** a stately square laid out in 1420 by Brunelleschi, before visiting the church of **Santissima Annunziata ❶** *(closed 12:30 p.m.–4 p.m.)* on its northern flank. The church's vestibule, known as the Chiostrino dei Voti, features an accomplished fresco cycle on the "Life of the Virgin" and "Life

NOT TO BE MISSED:

Chiostrino dei Voti • Ospedale degli Innocenti • Museo Bardini • Palazzo Davanzati • Santa Trìnita

of St. Filippo Benizzi" by Andrea del Sarto, Pontormo, and Rosso Fiorentino. The interior's chief attraction is Michelozzo's ornate tabernacle (1448–1461), commissioned by the Medici to enshrine a miraculous 13th-century image of the Virgin.

On the square's eastern margin stands the **Ospedale degli Innocenti** *(tel 055 20371, $).* Created as an orphanage in 1445, it is known for Brunelleschi's delightful facade (1419–1426), with a nine-bay loggia characterized by perfect proportions and decorated with terra-cotta roundels, two interior courtyards, and a modest museum of Renaissance paintings and sculptures.

Walk south on Via dei Servi to the **Piazza del Duomo** (see pp. 206–212). Skirt the east end of the Duomo and exit the piazza by walking south on Via dello Studio. The poet Dante Alighieri was born somewhere in the tangle of streets here in 1265, though not in the so-called **Casa di Dante ❷** *(Via Santa Margherita 1, tel 055 219 416, museocasadidante.it, closed Mon. Nov.–March, $),* a mock medieval pastiche given over to a modest museum devoted to the poet. Two nearby churches have associations with Dante: Santa Margherita de' Cerchi was the parish church of the Portinari, the family name of Dante's beloved Beatrice, while San Martino del Vescovo, opposite the Casa di Dante, was the Alighieri family church.

■ **Equestrian statue of Grand Duke Ferdinand I, Piazza della Santissima Annunziata**

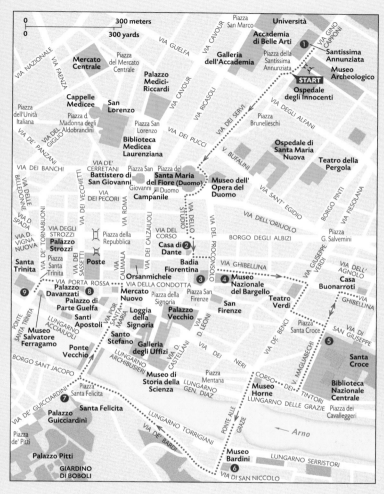

Walk east on Via Dante Alighieri and you pass the **Badia Fiorentina** ❸, a tenth-century abbey church *(open Mon. 3 p.m.–6 p.m., $)* where Dante is said to have first glimpsed Beatrice. Highlights are Filippino Lippi's painting of the "Apparition of the Virgin to St. Bernard" (1485) and the Chiostro degli Aranci, a cloister with a fresco cycle on the "Life of St. Benedict" (1436–1439) by Giovanni da Consalvo. The campanile was completed in the 14th century.

> ▲ Also see area map, p. 205 C4
> ► Piazza della Santissima Annunziata
> 🕒 Allow at least half a day
> ↔ 2 miles (3 km)
> ► Piazza Santa Trìnita

Turn onto Via Ghibellina, stopping at the **Museo Nazionale del Bargello** ❹ (see pp. 220–221) and then **Santa Croce** ❺

INSIDER TIP:

Enjoy a delicious ice cream from La Carraia (Piazza Nazario Sauro 25r) while admiring a view of the Ponte Vecchio at night from the Ponte Carraia, just a couple blocks west of Santa Trinita.

—BEATRICE LAGHI
Hotel Brunelleschi

(see pp. 222–223), in the heart of one of the city's most interesting older quarters. If time allows, make a detour to Vivoli (Via Isola delle Stinche 7r), makers of some of Florence's best ice cream. Devotees of Michelangelo may wish to deviate north to the **Casa Buonarroti** (Via Ghibellina 70, tel 055 241 752, casabuonarroti .it, closed Tues., $), a museum with a handful of minor works and much miscellaneous ephemera connected with the sculptor.

South of Santa Croce stands the **Museo Horne** (Via de' Benci 6, tel 055 244 661, museo horne.it, closed Wed. & p.m., $), a small but high-quality art collection amassed by the English art historian Herbert Percy Horne (1864–1916). The museum is housed in a charming 15th-century palazzo.

Across the Arno & Back

Now cross the Arno River via the Ponte alle Grazie to visit the similar **Museo Bardini** ⑥ (Via de' Renai 37, tel 055 234 2427, closed Tues.–Thurs., $, cultura.comune.fi.it), a wonderfully eclectic collection put together by Sergio Bardini (1836–1922), the greatest international art dealer of his day.

From the museum, walk west on Via de' Bardi to the Ponte Vecchio (see pp. 234–235), then turn left to the church of **Santa Felicita** ⑦ (closed Sun. & 12 p.m.–3:30 p.m., santafelicita firenze.it), worth a quick visit for the Cappella Capponi, known for Pontormo's strange painting of the "Deposition" (1525–1528).

Return to the Ponte Vecchio and cross the river. On reaching the Mercato Nuovo, bear west on Via Porta Rossa. Midway down the street on the left is one of Florence's most charming museums, the **Palazzo Davanzati** ⑧ (Via Porta Rossa 13, tel 055 238 8610, closed Mon.–Fri. p.m., Sat.–Sun. a.m., & some Sun. and Mon. each month, $), whose interior preserves the decor and appearance of a medieval Florentine house. The piazza at the end of the street contains the interesting church of **Santa Trinita** ⑨ (tel 055 216 912, closed 12 p.m.–4 p.m.), renowned for Domenico Ghirlandaio's fresco cycle (1483–1486) and altarpiece in the Cappella Sassetti to the right of the high altar.

High Heels, High Art

The high heel, or stiletto—from the Italian for "little dagger"—is said to have been invented in Florence by Catherine de' Medici, who compensated for her stature by wearing 2-inch (5 cm) heels at her wedding in 1533 (aged 14) to the future King Henry II of France. How appropriate, then, that Florence should also be home to a temple to the shoemaker's art, the **Museo Salvatore Ferragamo** (Piazza Santa Trinita 5r, tel 055 356 2846, $, free 1st Sun. of the month), devoted to Salvatore Ferragamo (1898–1960).

Ferragamo was born in Naples. He emigrated to the United States at age 16, later making his name—and fortune—in Hollywood by creating shoes for Greta Garbo, Vivien Leigh, Rudolph Valentino, and Gloria Swanson, among others. On his eventual return to Italy he opened a store in Florence, still home to the headquarters of the company that bears his name. The company's museum is a true shoe-lover's dream, featuring more than 16,000 pairs of shoes, exhibited in rotation.

SANTA MARIA NOVELLA

The outstanding Santa Maria Novella ranks just behind Santa Croce as Florence's most important church. The mother church of the city's Dominican order, it was begun in 1246, replacing an earlier 11th-century church on the site. It's home to a trio of captivating fresco cycles and one of the most influential paintings of the early Renaissance.

Santa Maria's interior was completed in 1360, although its Romanesque facade remained half-finished until 1456, when Giovanni Rucellai, a textile merchant, commissioned Leon Battista Alberti to complete it in a more modern, classical-influenced style.

Inside, Masaccio's fresco of the **"Trinity"** was one of the first Renaissance works in which the new ideas of mathematical proportion (in other words, perspective) were successfully employed. Florentines lined up for days in 1426 to share in the miracle of a picture that apparently created a three-dimensional space in a solid wall.

Santa Maria's first fresco cycle lies in the **Cappella di Filippo Strozzi.** The paintings by Filippino Lippi (1489–1502) deal with episodes from the life of Strozzi's namesake, St. Filippo the Apostle (Filippo is Philip).

The **chancel** holds the second, and most important, cycle, a work by Domenico Ghirlandaio. Here the themes are the "Life of John the Baptist" and the "Life of the Virgin" (1485–1490), although the cycle is crammed with numerous portraits and a wealth of insights into the daily life of 15th-century Florence.

The third cycle lies in the **Cappella Strozzi.** Its paintings (1350–1357) are the work of

The church's facade is a study in marble patterning.

Nardo di Cione (died 1366). The principal frescoes depict "Paradiso" and a pictorial version of Dante's "Inferno."

Almost immediately inside Santa Maria's museum (off the left side of the church, recently enlarged and renovated) lies the **Chiostro Verde** (1332–1350), or Green Cloister, named after the *terra verde* pigment of its frescoes. The frescoes (1425–1430) are the work of Paolo Uccello and depict "Stories from Genesis."

Leading off the cloister is the **Cappellone degli Spagnoli,** or Spanish Chapel, adorned with magnificent frescoes (1367–1369) by Andrea da Firenze: "The Triumph of Divine Wisdom" and "The Mission, Work, and Triumph of the Dominican Order." ■

Santa Maria Novella

🅐 205 B4

✉ Piazza Santa Maria Novella

☎ 055 219 257

🕐 Closed a.m. Fri. until 11 a.m. & a.m. Sun. until 12 p.m. (1 p.m. Oct.–Jun.)

💲 $

smn.it

PONTE VECCHIO & THE OLTRARNO

The Ponte Vecchio bridges the Arno River and links Florence's bustling downtown to the Oltrarno, a quieter, leafy district home to such outstanding gems as the Cappella Brancacci, the Palazzo Pitti, and San Miniato al Monte.

A cluster of houses and workshops—many more than 400 years old—overhangs the Ponte Vecchio.

Ponte Vecchio

205 B3

Ponte Vecchio

The Ponte Vecchio, with its load of overhanging shops and buildings, is one of Florence's most familiar images. Over the centuries, it has survived countless floods and the havoc of war and civil strife. In World War II, only the intervention of Hitler himself is said to have saved it, Field Marshal Kesselring having been ordered to spare the bridge during the Nazi retreat from the city.

There has probably been a bridge on the site, the Arno's narrowest point, since Etruscan times. Under the Romans it carried the Via Cassia, an important highway that linked Rome to the principal cities to the north. For centuries thereafter, the crossing remained the city's only trans-Arno link, although its wooden superstructure was replaced often in the wake of floods. The present bridge was built in 1345, whereupon it took its current name, Ponte Vecchio (Old Bridge), to distinguish it from the Ponte alla Carraia (1218), then known as the Ponte Nuovo (New Bridge).

Shops first appeared on the earlier bridge during the 13th century. Most were fishmongers and butchers attracted by the river, a convenient dump for their waste. Next came tanners, who used the river to soak their hides before tanning them in horses' urine. In time, a space was opened at the center of the bridge—still there today—to allow the tipping of rubbish straight into the water.

By 1593, Grand Duke Ferdinando I banished what he called the practitioners of these "vile arts." In their place—at double the rent—he installed some 50 jewelers and goldsmiths, many of whose descendants still trade from the bridge's pretty wooden-shuttered shops. A bust (1900) of one of Florence's most famous goldsmiths, Benvenuto Cellini, stands at the middle of the bridge.

In 1565, Cosimo I ordered the building of the Corridoio Vasariano to connect Palazzo Pitti and the Uffizi. The passageway is currently closed for renovation work that will make it more accessible for the public and will reopen in 2021.

Cappella Brancacci

In a city of magnificent paintings, few command as much attention as the frescoes of the Cappella Brancacci. The paintings are considered some of the most important in Western art, executed on the cusp of the Renaissance in a manner whose innovation and invention would influence painters for generations to come.

The paintings were commissioned by Filippo Brancacci, a silk merchant and diplomat, and begun in 1424 by Masolino (1383–1447) and his young assistant, Masaccio (1401–1428), or

---

EXPERIENCE: A Lazy Trip on the Arno

See Florence from a different perspective on an intimate and little known tour aboard a vintage *barchetto*, a small, traditional flat-bottomed boat propelled by a pole. The boats were used for centuries during floods and for light work and as ferries. Today, they offer a peaceful outlook on the city, as you are taken slowly past the Uffizi and under the Ponte Vecchio, and then past the churches of Santa Trìnita and San Jacopo. The 2.5-hour-long tour *($$$$$)* is customizable and takes you on a journey from the river to the hills. Book through **Florence and Tuscany Tours** *(Via Condotta 12, tel 055 210 301, florenceandtuscanytours.com).*

"Bad Tom." In 1426, Masolino was called to Budapest, where he was official painter to the Hungarian court. In his absence, Masaccio's genius blossomed, so much so that when Masolino returned in 1427 he became the junior partner.

The pair's frescoes surpassed anything seen in Italy, dazzling in their realism, dramatic narrative, and mastery of perspective: In the words of Giorgio Vasari, the 16th-century artist and art historian, the "most celebrated sculptors and painters . . . became excellent and illustrious in studying their art."

Masaccio, however, would die aged just 28, while, in 1428, Masolino was called to Rome, never to return. When Brancacci was exiled in 1436, all work on the chapel ceased. The frescoes were only finished some 50 years later by Filippino Lippi, whose copying skills proved so consummate that his part in the chapel was only recognized as recently as 1838.

Cappella Brancacci

🏛 205 A3

✉ Santa Maria del Carmine, Piazza del Carmine 14 (entrance to the right of the church)

☎ 055 238 2195; free recommended reservations 055 276 8224

🕐 Closed Sun. a.m. & Tues.

💲 $

cultura.comune.fi.it

NOTE: Groups of 30 are admitted to the Cappella Brancacci for a maximum of 30 minutes. Tickets are timed. You may need to return at a later time if you join the line for tickets.

Giardino di Boboli

🗺 205 A1–B2

☎ 055 294 883

🕐 Open daily

💲 $, $$ peak season, $$$$ combined ticket (see p. 217)

Palazzo Pitti

🗺 205 B2

✉ Piazza de' Pitti

☎ 055 294 883

🕐 Closed Mon.

💲 $, $$ peak season, $$$$ combined ticket (see p. 217)

uffizi.it/palazzo-pitti

Masaccio was responsible for the cycle's most famous image, the stark, emotionally charged panel portraying "The Expulsion of Adam and Eve from Paradise" (left of the entrance arch as you look at the frescoes). Compare this with Masolino's more ano-dyne rendering of "Adam and Eve" on the opposite wall. Other panels in the cycle deal with epi-sodes from the life of St. Peter, of which the three most striking, all by Masaccio, are "Christ and the

Giardino di Boboli

Behind the Palazzo Pitti lies Florence's principal park, the Giardino di Boboli, or Boboli Garden, begun by Cosimo I in 1549. Open to the public since 1766, the park's trees, formal gardens, walkways, and fountains provide a green and peaceful retreat.

Tribute Money," "St. Peter Healing the Sick," and the combined "Rais-ing of Theophilus's Son" and "St. Peter Enthroned."

Palazzo Pitti

Few palaces are as colossal as the Palazzo Pitti, begun by the Pitti family, a banking dynasty, in 1458. So financially draining was the project that the family was forced to sell its creation in 1549, when the palace was bought and further enlarged by Cosimo I. Today, it contains a cluster of museums, of which the most important is the **Galleria**

INSIDER TIP:

Consider staying in the quiet, shady Oltrarno neighborhood. It's away from the crowds but close to the sights.

—PAT DANIELS
National Geographic contributor

Palatina, home to much of the Medici art collection.

The collection's real highlights lie in the ornate state rooms, where the paintings are arranged three or four deep. This design is confusing for the modern visitor but was the preferred arrange-ment of Cosimo and the Medici. Any systematic exploration is almost impossible, so wander more or less at will until a painting catches your eye.

Your attention will be drawn quickly for the masterpieces are many. The gallery has several works by Raphael, the finest being the "Madonna del Granduca" (1507), or Madonna of the Grand Duke, and the "La Velata" (1516), or Veiled Woman (the subject was reputedly the painter's mistress, a Roman baker's daughter). Several penetrating portraits figure among the paintings by Titian: One of the most celebrated is the "Portrait of Pietro Aretino" (1545). Don't miss Cristofani Allori's erotic and curiously bloodless "Judith and Holofernes" (1610–1612), one of the pictures most admired by the palace's 17th-century visitors. It hangs in Sala dell'Educazione di Giove, one of seven smaller rooms parallel to the state rooms. Other painters represented include Caravaggio, Filippo Lippi, Andrea del Sarto, Rubens, and Tintoretto.

The ticket for the Palatina also admits you to the **Appartamenti Reali,** the palace's lavishly decorated state apartments; to the **Tesoro dei Granduchi,** a collection of silverware and other decorative arts; and to smaller exhibits at Galleria d'Arte Moderna, the Museo del Costume, and the Giardino di Boboli (see sidebar opposite).

San Miniato al Monte

San Miniato is the most beautiful church in Florence, perhaps even in Tuscany, its glorious colored marble facade visible from across the city atop its hill on the Oltrarno's leafy fringes. Begun in 1018, it sits over the site of an earlier chapel to San Miniato, a saint martyred and buried on the spot in A.D. 250.

The church was often mistaken for an antique Roman building during the Middle Ages, as was the Battistero di San Giovanni, whose patterned exterior it deliberately copies. The facade's lower section is probably 11th century, its upper reaches 12th century. The mosaic depicting "Christ between the Virgin and St. Minias" dates from 1260. Notice the eagle (1401) with its bale of cloth, a symbol of the Arte di Calimala, the cloth merchants' guild, entrusted with the church's upkeep after 1288.

The interior is beyond compare. The beautiful pavement dates from 1207, while many of

the pillars and capitals were salvaged from earlier Roman and Byzantine buildings. The center of the nave is dominated by Michelozzo's **Cappella del Crocefisso** (1448), created to house a miraculous crucifix (now removed) and graced with painted panels (1394–1396) by Agnolo Gaddi. Steps to its side lead to the **crypt.** Other steps lead up to the church's raised choir, dominated by a superlative Romanesque **pulpit, screen** (1207), and **apse mosaic** (1297). Off to the right stands the sacristy, whose walls are covered in a fresco cycle by Spinello Aretino on the "Life of St. Benedict" (1387). Back in the lower church, off the north

aisle, is the **Cappella del Cardinale del Portogallo** (1473), one of Italy's great Renaissance ensembles, a unified composite of sculpture and paintings by Antonio Rossellino, Alesso Baldovinetti, and Luca della Robbia. ∎

San Miniato al Monte

⌖ 205 D1

✉ Via del Monte alle Croci–Viale Galileo Galilei

☎ 055 234 2731

⊕ Closed 1 p.m.– 3 p.m. Nov.–Mar.

🚇 Uphill walk from the Ponte Vecchio via the Costa di San Giorgio, Forte di Belvedere, and Via di Belvedere. Alternatively, take bus 13 to Piazzale Michelangelo.

sanminiatoalmonte.it

▪ **Ancient cypresses and 17th- and 18th-century statues flank the long avenue of the Viottolone in the Giardino di Boboli.**

FLOODS

Florence is famously prone to flooding. The notorious deluge of 1966, in which many lives and myriad works of art were lost, was only the most recent of a series of inundations. The main culprits are the Arno River and the surging meltwaters of the Apennines. Also at fault is the position of Florence itself—ringed by hills, close to the river's floodplain, and situated downstream of the Sieve, the Arno's major tributary.

The Ponte Vecchio came close to collapse in 1966, when the rising river swamped the bridge.

Florence was so blighted by floods that early chroniclers concluded the city must have been founded by Noah. Accounts over the years abound with tales of watery disaster. "A great part of the city became a lake," lamented one source in 1269, when torrents swept away the Carraia and Trìnita bridges. In 1333, a four-day storm unleashed floods so violent that the city's bells were tolled to drive away the demons blamed for the inundation. And in 1557, Cosimo I introduced primitive city defenses when a flash flood crashed over the Trìnita bridge. On this last occasion, everyone standing on the bridge was killed, all except for two children, who were left stranded on a pillar for two days before being rescued.

Today, most visitors see the Arno at its kindest, in summer, when the lazy-flowing waters appear benign. Mark Twain, writing of the river in *Innocents Abroad* in 1869, could not see what all the fuss was about: "This great historical creek," he wrote, "with four feet in the channel would be a very plausible river if they would pump some water into it." Compare this with the account of another American writer, K. K. Taylor, who described a very different scene in her 1967 *Diary of Florence in Flood:* "A tumultuous mass of water stretches from bank to bank," she wrote, "a snarling brown torrent of terrific velocity, spiraling in whirlpools and countercurrents . . . this tremendous water carries mats of debris: straw, twigs, leafy branches, rags, a litter that the river sucks down and spews up again in a swelling turbulence."

The Flood of 1966

This apocalyptic scene followed 40 days of almost continuous rain. Around 19 inches (48 cm) fell on November 2 and 3 alone, the days preceding the flood. The final straw came on the night of November 4, when sluice gates above Florence were opened to prevent the collapse of a dam. Apparently, the only people warned of the river's further rise were the jewelers of the Ponte Vecchio, summoned by a night watchman to save their stock as the bridge began to shudder.

At dawn, some 500,000 tons of water crashed through the city, moving with such ferocity that commuters in the train station underpass were drowned where they stood. In all, 35 Florentines perished, and hundreds were made homeless. Women and children were winched from the rooftops. More than 16,000 cars were destroyed, and gas, water, and electricity were disrupted for days.

Longer-term damage was inflicted on buildings and works of art, many of which were submerged beneath water that in places reached 20 feet (6 m) above street level. Damage was exacerbated by vast quantities of heating oil, recently delivered for the winter and flushed out of basements by the surge of water. Slurry slopped around 8,000 paintings in the Uffizi's cellars and damaged 1.5 million books and manuscripts in the Biblioteca Nazionale.

Donations and volunteers flowed into the stricken city—the so-called Angels of Florence—to help with the cleanup. Huge progress was subsequently made in restoration techniques, albeit at vast human and artistic cost. Even today, only two-thirds of the ravaged paintings are on show, while two huge laboratories, one for sculpture, one for paintings, still operate full time to repair the damage of a single night.

One painting, Cimabue's majestic "Crucifix" from Santa Croce—caught in the 6 feet (1.8 m) of water that surged into the church—came to symbolize the effects of that terrible November morning. On the fifth anniversary of the flood, Mayor Bargellini wrote in *La Nazione,* Florence's daily newspaper: "When Cimabue's 'Crucifix' was carried past, fatally wounded, on a tank, even the most hardened men, the loudest blasphemers, stopped in their muddy labors and took off their hats in silence; every woman, however tough or dishonest, crossed herself with sincerity . . . It was as still and silent as on Good Friday."

■ **The 1966 floodwaters ripped five panels off the Battistero di San Giovanni's east doors.**

FIESOLE

The small town of Fiesole is the most popular short excursion from Florence. Cradled in the cypress-scattered hills above the city, its roots date back to Etruscan times (around 600 B.C.), predating Florence by several centuries. It fell to its more famous neighbor in 1125, and since then it has been a favored rural retreat for Florentines and visitors alike.

From its hilltop vantage point, Fiesole offers sublime vistas of the Florentine countryside.

Fiesole

🗺 243 D4

Visitor Information

✉ Via Portigiani 3–5

☎ 055 596 1323 or 055 596 1311

🕐 Closed p.m. daily Nov.– Feb., irregular opening hours March–Oct.

🚌 Bus: 7 from outside Florence's Santa Maria Novella train station runs regularly to Fiesole's Piazza Mino da Fiesole.

fiesoleforyou.it

comune.fiesole.fi.it

Fiesole's **Duomo,** founded 1028, has a plain 19th-century facade masking an interior enlivened by Bicci di Lorenzo's dazzling high altarpiece (1450); the **Cappella Salutati** has an altar frontal and tomb (1466) by Mino da Fiesole.

The steep Via San Francesco leads from the town's edge to the churches of **Sant'Alessandro** and **San Francesco,** where the views of Florence below are the real draw. Back in the square, another street leads to the pretty **archaeological zone** (Via Portigiani 1, tel 055 596 1293, museidifiesole. it, closed Tues. & p.m. Nov.–Feb., $, $$ with museum & Museo Bandini), home to Roman ruins, Etruscan walls, and a site museum. Nearby stands the **Museo Bandini** (Via Duprè 1, tel 055 59 477, closed Mon.–Thurs., $ or $$ combined ticket), devoted mainly to ivories, ceramics, and Florentine paintings.

For a 1.5-mile (2.5 km) round-trip walk, follow Via Vecchia Fiesolana from the southern side of Piazza Mino. The lane passes the **Villa Medici** (gardens irregular hours), built for Cosimo de' Medici, before arriving at the church and convent of **San Domenico.** Once the home of Fra Angelico, it contains his "Madonna with Saints and Angels" (1430). Via della Badia then leads to the **Badia Fiesolana,** the town's cathedral until 1028. The lovely Romanesque facade survives, enclosed by a later 15th-century frontage. ∎

A pastoral paradise of vineyards, poppy-strewn fields, olive groves, sun-dappled hills, and age-old towns and villages

TUSCANY

Poppies, a common springtime sight in Tuscany

TUSCANY

Tuscany is Italy at its best. In Florence, it has the greatest Renaissance city; in Siena, one of its most perfect medieval towns; and, in San Gimignano, its single most celebrated village. In addition, its landscapes fully embody the popular image of rural Italy. The region also offers beaches, outdoor activities, and some of Italy's best food and wine.

No trip to Tuscany is complete without a visit to Siena, a perfect medieval town. Less well known Lucca is almost as appealing and shares Siena's mix of churches, galleries, and stunning historical core. Nearby Pisa boasts the Leaning Tower, one of the country's most familiar sights.

If Siena is the town you should visit before any other, then San Gimignano is the village equivalent. Conveniently located just north of Siena, this quintessential medieval village is best known for its crop of ancient towers.

Foremost among the villages south of Siena, the region's heartland, is tiny Pienza, planned as a model Renaissance city in the 15th century but now little more than a sleepy backwater.

NOT TO BE MISSED:

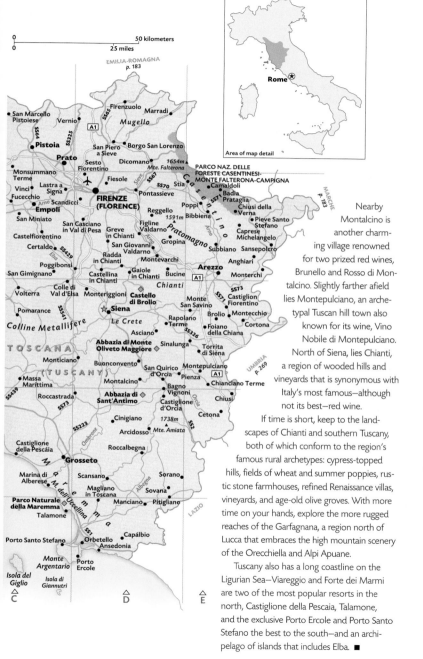

0
0
50 kilometers
25 miles

EMILIA-ROMAGNA
p. 183

Rome

Area of map detail

San Marcello
Pistoiese
Vernio
Firenzuolo Marradi
Mugello
A1
SS64 SS325
Pistoia
Prato San Piero Borgo San Lorenzo
a Sieve
Monsummano Sesto Dicomano 1654m▲
Terme Fiorentino Mte. Falterona
Vinci Lastra a Fiesole SS70 Stia
Signa Pontassieve
Fucecchio Arno Scandicci FIRENZE
Empoli (FLORENCE) Reggello Poppi
San Miniato Figline Bibbiena
San Casciano Valdarno
in Val di Pesa Greve San Giovanni Gropina
Castelfiorentino in Chianti Valdarno
Certaldo SS429 Radda Montevarchi
in Chianti Bucine Arezzo
Poggibonsi Castellina Gaiole
San Gimignano in Chianti in Chianti Monterchi
Colle di Chianti A1
Volterra Val d'Elsa Monteriggioni Castello Monte Castiglion
di Brolio San Savino Fiorentino
Pomarance Siena Brolio Montecchio
Colline Metallifere Le Crete Rapolano Cortona
Terme Foiano
TOSCANA Asciano della Chiana
Abbazia di Monte Sinalunga
Oliveto Maggiore Torrita
Monticiano di Siena
(TUSCANY) Buonconvento San Quirico Montepulciano
Massa d'Orcia Pienza A1
Marittima Montalcino Chianciano Terme
SS439 Roccastrada Bagno
Abbazia di Vignoni
Sant'Antimo Castiglione Chiusi
SS223 d'Orcia
Cinigiano 1738m Cetona
Arcidosso Mte. Amiata
Castiglione Roccalbegna
della Pescáia
Grosseto
Marina di Scansano Sorano
Alberese Magliano Sovana
Parco Naturale in Toscana Manciano Pitigliano
della Maremma LAZIO
Talamone
Porto Santo Stefano Orbetello Capálbio
Ansedonia
Monte Porto
Argentario Ercole
Isola del Isola di
Giglio Giannutri

C D E

PARCO NAZ. DELLE
FORESTE CASENTINESI-
MONTE FALTERONA-CAMPIGNA
Camaldoli
Badia
Prataglia
Chiusi della
Verna
Pieve Santo
Stefano
Caprese
Michelangelo Sansepolcro
Subbiano
Anghiari
SS73
Castiglion
Fiorentino
MARCHE
p. 183
UMBRIA
p. 269

Nearby
Montalcino is
another charm-
ing village renowned
for two prized red wines,
Brunello and Rosso di Montalcino. Slightly farther afield
lies Montepulciano, an archetypal Tuscan hill town also
known for its wine, Vino
Nobile di Montepulciano.
North of Siena, lies Chianti,
a region of wooded hills and
vineyards that is synonymous with
Italy's most famous—although
not its best—red wine.

If time is short, keep to the landscapes of Chianti and southern Tuscany,
both of which conform to the region's
famous rural archetypes: cypress-topped
hills, fields of wheat and summer poppies, rustic stone farmhouses, refined Renaissance villas,
vineyards, and age-old olive groves. With more
time on your hands, explore the more rugged
reaches of the Garfagnana, a region north of
Lucca that embraces the high mountain scenery
of the Orecchiella and Alpi Apuane.

Tuscany also has a long coastline on the
Ligurian Sea—Viareggio and Forte dei Marmi
are two of the most popular resorts in the
north, Castiglione della Pescaia, Talamone,
and the exclusive Porto Ercole and Porto Santo
Stefano the best to the south—and an archipelago of islands that includes Elba. ■

SIENA

Siena is Italy's most perfect medieval town. At its heart lies the Campo, Italy's most glorious square and the stage for the city's renowned annual horse race—the Palio—as well as the art-filled chambers of the majestic Palazzo Pubblico. Nearby are the Duomo, one of Italy's finest Gothic buildings, and the treasures of the cathedral museum, while all around a magical labyrinth of palace-lined streets and peaceful corners provides for hours of aimless exploration.

Siena's magnificent Duomo sits on a site originally occupied by a Roman temple to Minerva.

Siena

243 D3

Visitor Information

Santa Maria della Scala, Piazza del Duomo 1

0577 280 551

terresiena.it

comune.siena.it

Il Campo

Your first stop in Siena should be the Campo—literally the "field"—a scallop-shaped piazza that has long served as the city's civic and social heart. Located at the convergence of three hilly ridges, its pivotal position made it an obvious site for development. The area was also a point of intersection for the city's fiercely independent *contrade,* or parishes, and therefore the only neutral patch of ground in a combative city. The piazza acquired its present appearance around 1293, when the city's then ruling

body, the Council of Nine, began acquiring land with a view to create a new public piazza.

Palazzo Pubblico: A broad arc of palaces grew up around the square, chief among them the Palazzo Pubblico (1297–1310), now the city's town hall. Inside and upstairs is the **Museo Civico,** a rambling collection of state and other apartments adorned with frescoes and paintings. Its two most significant rooms lie side by side: the **Sala del Mappamondo** and Sala della Pace. The end walls of the former are decorated with a beautiful Maestà (1315) by Simone Martini and an equestrian portrait (1328) of Sienese general Guidoriccio da Foligno, a painting long attributed to Martini. In the **Sala della Pace** is the city's most renowned fresco cycle, Ambrogio Lorenzetti's faded "Allegories of Good and Bad Government" (1337–1339). The **Sala dei Pilastri** off the Sala della Pace contains a grand 13th-century Maestà by Guido da Siena and the violent 15th-century "Massacre of the Innocents" by Matteo di Giovanni.

The vaults of the **Sala del Concistoro** are covered in frescoes of mythical and allegorical scenes by the Sienese mannerist painter Domenico Beccafumi (1485–1551). Also noteworthy is the **Cappella del Consiglio,** graced with some beautiful inlaid choir stalls (1415–1428), an intricate screen in wrought iron (1435–1445) by Jacopo della Quercia, an altarpiece (1530) by Sodoma, and frescoes on the "Life of the Virgin" (1407–1408) by Taddeo di Bartolo.

Turn left in the palazzo's courtyard and climb the 503 steps of the 335-foot (102 m) **Torre del Mangia** (1338–1348), designed by a leading Sienese painter, Lippo Memmi. The bell tower was reputedly named after its first watchman and bell ringer, Giovanni di Balduccio, a notable profligate, or *mangiaguadagni,* literally "eater of profits." The views are magnificent, particularly those over the Campo below, where you can clearly make out the square's nine segments, designed to symbolize the nine members of the Council of Nine and the cloak of the Madonna cast protectively over the city. The tower's great bell was originally used to mark the end of the working day and the daily opening and closing of the city gates.

In front of the tower is the distinctive **Cappella di Piazza,** a stone loggia begun in 1348 to mark the passing of the Black Death. The fountain at the top of the piazza, the **Fonte Gaia,** is a 19th-century copy of a 15th-century original.

**Museo Civico &
Torre del Mangia**

✉ Palazzo Pubblico, Piazza del Campo

☎ 0577 292 232

$ $$

museisenesi.org

Palazzo Piccolomini

Most visitors just pass by the intimidating walls of the **Palazzo Piccolomini** *(Banchi di Sotto 52, tel 0577 247 145, archiviostato .si.it, closed Sun. & p.m., accompanied visits at 9:30, 10:30, & 11:30 a.m.).* But the building contains some of the city's most compelling treasures: enormous bundles of ancient papers and manuscripts—more than 60,000 documents in all—pertaining to the city and the towns and villages of the old Sienese Republic. Each is marked in ornate script and labeled with a year.

You'll see documents from as early as A.D. 736, plus papal bulls and letters of artistic commission for such famous works as the Tavolette di Biccherna and Gabelle, the city's account books and tax records, whose covers are wooden panels painted with religious and domestic scenes. Created between 1258 and 1682 by leading artists of their day, the covers offer a fascinating record of artistic and daily life in Siena over the centuries.

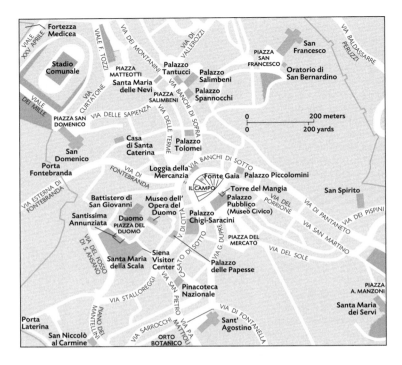

Duomo

✉ Piazza del Duomo

☎ 0577 286 300

🕐 Closed Sun. p.m., except part of Sept.–Oct.

💲 $ or Opa Sì Pass

operaduomo.siena.it

NOTE: The multisight **Opa Sì Pass** (*$–$$*) provides entry to the Duomo, Battistero di San Giovanni, Museo dell'Opera, and Oratorio di San Bernardino; buy it at Santa Maria della Scala ticket office. Single tickets are not for sale, with the exception of the Duomo.

Piazza del Duomo

Dominating the Piazza del Duomo is the **Duomo**. Its awe-inspiring facade (1284–1296), a Gothic and Romanesque mix of carvings, pillars, and intricate decorative detail, was largely the work of the Pisan architect and sculptor Giovanni Pisano (1245–1320). In the interior, your attention is drawn first to the ceiling, where sculptured heads represent busts of countless popes. The special "Porta del Cielo" tour *(for booking, visit operaduomo.siena.it)* gives you the opportunity to see both the outside and inside of the dome and to visit "high up" places that are not normally open to the

public. The marble pavement, which consists of 56 narrative panels (1349–1547) designed by a succession of Siena's leading artists, is an amazing work of art protected by a cover that is removed for only two months a year (mid-August to mid-October).

Midway down the north aisle is the **Piccolomini Altarpiece** (1503), whose lower four niche statues are the work of the young Michelangelo. Alongside lies the entrance to the **Libreria Piccolomini,** a 16th-century library with a fresco cycle (1502–1509) by the Umbrian artist Pinturicchio. The vibrant paintings portray episodes from the life of local-born nobleman Enea Silvio Piccolomini (1405–1464, Pope Pius II).

The chancel features a notable set of inlaid wooden choir stalls, while close by stands the building's foremost masterpiece: Nicola Pisano's celebrated **pulpit** and its sculpted reliefs of episodes from the "Life of Christ" (1266–1268). Just ahead of it, the wall on the left contains Tino da Camanio's tomb of Cardinal Petroni (1318), a model for many subsequent funerary monuments. In front of this lies the "Tomb of Bishop Pecci" (1426), a bronze pavement memorial by Donatello. The **Cappella di San Giovanni Battista,** in the corner of the north transept, features a statue of John the Baptist (1457) and more frescoes (1504) by Pinturicchio.

The **Battistero di San Giovanni,** the cathedral's subterranean baptistery, shelters a baptismal font (1417–1430), one of the city's best works of sculpture. Its decorative panels were executed by the most exalted Sienese and Florentine sculptors of their day—Lorenzo Ghiberti (the "Baptism of Christ" and "John in Prison"), Donatello ("Herod's Feast"), and Jacopo della Quercia ("The Angel Announcing the Baptist's Birth"). Jacopo also crafted the font's statue of the Baptist and its marble tabernacle, and Donatello produced two of the font's corner angels. The baptistery's walls are swathed in 14th-century frescoes, the work mostly of Vecchietta (1410–1480), an influential Sienese painter and sculptor.

Santa Maria della Scala:

Opposite the cathedral stands the Santa Maria della Scala. For almost 800 years it served as Siena's main hospital. Today, it is being converted to a premier art and exhibition space. After several renovation works, the museum offers a rich and complete itinerary, with brand new areas devoted to temporary exhibitions and to an art museum for children.

Works of art in situ, however, include a fresco of "St. Anne and St. Joachim" (1512) by Beccafumi in a small vestibule. The vaster halls, once shelter for pilgrims, show the most spectacular frescoes. Particularly interesting is the

Battistero di San Giovanni

✉ Piazza San Giovanni (entrance down steps behind cathedral)

Santa Maria della Scala

✉ Piazza del Duomo

☎ 0577 224 811 or 0577 224 828

🕐 Closed Tues.

💲 $$

santamariadella scala.com

The Duomo's marble-striped bell tower rises high above Siena.

Museo dell'Opera del Duomo

Piazza del Duomo 8

0577 286 300

Opa Sì Pass

operaduomo.siena.it

Pinacoteca Nazionale

Via San Pietro 29

0577 286 143

Closed p.m. both Mon. & Sun.

$

www.spsae-si.beni culturali.it

cycle on the walls of the **Pellegrinaio** (1439–1446), which tells the story and the commitment of the hospital itself.

The smaller **Sagrestia Vecchia** nearby has another fresco cycle, Vecchietta's "Articles of the Creed," and an altarpiece of the "Madonna del Manto" (1444) by Domenico di Bartolo. Vecchietta also created the statue of the "Risen Christ" (1476) on the main altar of the adjoining church, **Santissima Annunziata.**

The spectacular lower levels lead to the hayloft, to the storerooms, and to the guild headquarters, where you can admire the eerie Oratorio di Santa Caterina della Notte, a lavishly decorated underground oratory, and the hospital's huge, and often bizarre, collection of religious relics. The **Granaio,** or old hayloft, houses Jacopo della Quercia's original marble panels for the Fonte Gaia. Other rooms are dedicated to new displays that narrate the history of the city from its origins to the medieval period and to the **Museo Archeologico.**

Museo dell'Opera del Duomo:

Before you leave the Piazza del Duomo, be sure to visit the Museo dell'Opera del Duomo, with its many outstanding paintings and sculptures, most of them removed over the years from the cathedral and baptistery. The lower-floor **Galleria delle Statue** kicks off with sculptures, most notably a graceful tondo by Donatello, a bas-relief by Jacopo della Quercia, and several age-worn

Gothic statues by Giovanni Pisano. Upstairs, the darkened **Sala della Maestà** contains the greatest of all Sienese paintings, Duccio's monumental Maestà, painted for the cathedral's high altar in 1308–1311. Beyond it are a few small halls where precious illuminated manuscripts and wooden statues from the 1400s are on display.

A bit farther is the **Sala di Tesoro,** with reliquaries and liturgical objects in fine gold work. The most important masterpiece on display on the top floor is the "Madonna dagli Occhi Grossi" (1220–1230) or "Madonna of the Large Eyes," a haunting Byzantine icon that served as the cathedral's pre-Duccio altarpiece.

Pinacoteca Nazionale

Siena's superb main art gallery is housed in the imposing 15th-century **Palazzo Buonsignori.** Its many rooms offer an in-depth look at the city's Gothic school of painting, a genre heavily influenced in its early days by the stylized composition, intense coloring, and gold backgrounds of Byzantine art. All the major—and many minor—Sienese names are represented.

Rooms and paintings displayed proceed in chronological order, revealing the ever greater influence of Florentine art on the more backward-looking Sienese. Later rooms deal with offshoots such as Sienese mannerism, a genre exemplified by the 16th-century works of painters such as Sodoma.

Three Churches

Siena has three principal churches. **Santa Maria dei Servi** lies some way from the center of Siena, but it's worth the walk to get there. The oldest of its paintings (first altar of the south aisle) is the "Madonna di Bordone" (1261) by Coppo da Marcovaldo, a Florentine artist captured in battle and forced to paint this picture as part of his ransom. At the end of the same aisle is Matteo di Giovanni's harrowing "Massacre of the Innocents" (1491). A similarly violent depiction of the same event by Pietro Lorenzetti graces the right wall of the second chapel to the right of the high altar. Lorenzetti also painted in the second chapel, left of the altar, along with one of his followers, Taddeo di Bartolo, whose "Adoration of the Shepherds" (1404) also hangs here. Taddeo's pupil, Giovanni di Paolo, painted the "Madonna della Misericordia" (1431) in the north transept.

Fire and heavy-handed restoration have left **San Francesco** almost bereft of works of art. Its best remaining artifacts are the 14th-century tombs of the Tolomei at the end of the south aisle, burial places of several members of one of the city's leading medieval families. Also worth searching out are frescoes by Sassetta (right of the main door) and Pietro and Ambrogio Lorenzetti (first and third chapels left of the high altar). More remarkable still is the **Oratorio di San Bernardino** to the south of the church, whose wood-paneled salon upstairs contains frescoes on the "Life of the Virgin" (1496–1518) by Sodoma, Beccafumi, and Giralmo del Pacchia.

The Gothic outline of **San Domenico** dominates northern Siena. Begun in 1226, the austere brick church is closely associated with St. Catherine of Siena, patron saint of Siena and (with St. Francis) of Italy. It was here that she performed miracles, became a Dominican nun, and received the stigmata. Her links with the church are commemorated in the **Cappella delle Volte,** which contains her portrait, and in the **Cappella di Santa Caterina,** whose tabernacle (1466) contains part of her skull. The latter chapel also boasts two frescoes (1526) by Sodoma of episodes from her life. Chapels flanking the high altar feature several Sienese paintings, while the high altar itself is adorned with a tabernacle and angels (1465) by Benedetto da Maiano. ∎

Siena's History

Myth claims Siena was founded by Senius and Acius, sons of Remus, hence the statues around the city of the she-wolf who suckled Rome's mythical founders, Romulus and Remus. In fact, Siena began as an Etruscan settlement and evolved into a Roman colony, Saena Julia. Flourishing banking and textile concerns in the Middle Ages then made it one of Europe's most important cities. Its stature inevitably drew it into conflict with Florence, with first one, then the other city achieving dominance. In 1554, the Sienese Republic finally surrendered. Thereafter, Florence deliberately suppressed the city, its decline into a rural backwater one reason for its remarkably unsullied appearance today.

Oratorio di San Bernardino

✉ Piazza San Francesco

☎ 0577 28 055

🕐 Closed a.m. & Nov.–Feb.

💲 $

THE PALIO

Siena's Palio is Italy's most spectacular festival. Held twice yearly—July 2 and August 16—it involves a breathtaking bareback horse race around the Campo, together with many preparatory days of drama, processions, drumming, flag waving, and colorful pageantry. The spectacle and celebration are living and vivid expressions of rivalries and traditions that stretch back more than 700 years.

■ Riders in the Siena Palio make three circuits of the Campo. The race lasts just 90 seconds.

A *palio* of some description has taken place in Siena virtually every year since the 13th century. In the early days, it was run around the city streets—only since 1656 has it followed its famous three-lap circuit of the Campo. The prize has always been the same: the embroidered banner, or *pallium*, from which the race takes its name. So, too, is the dedication to the Virgin, the reason why races are run on, or close to, feast days devoted to the Madonna. The July 2 race takes place on the Feast of the Visitation, the August 16 contest on the day after the Feast of the Assumption. Very occasionally, a race is staged to mark another event, the most notable examples being the palios held to commemorate the end of World War II (1945), the sixth centennial

of St. Catherine's birth (1947), and the first lunar landing (1969).

Race contestants represent Siena's *contrade,* the districts into which the city has been divided since the 13th century. Today, there are 17 such districts. Each contrada has its own church, social club, heraldic device, museum, flag, and symbolic animal (from which a contrada usually derives its name). Allegiance to your district is absolute: Church baptisms of new contrada babies, for example, are followed by baptisms in the infants' contrada fountain. Each district also holds its own annual procession and supports a band of *tamborini* (drummers) and *alfiere* (flag throwers), many of whom can be seen practicing on the streets during the year.

Only ten contrade can take part in the Palio, drawn by lot. Riders from the unlucky seven losers are allowed to accompany the *carroccio,* or chariot, that bears the pallium in the prerace procession. Each contrada has its own rival, and as much thought goes into ensuring a rival's defeat as securing one's own victory. Alliances are forged and bribes offered. Horses may be doped, and it has been known for men and animals to be kidnapped. Riders and animals are therefore watched day and night, communication with the outside world being possible only through riders' bodyguards.

Race Day

The day of the race involves endless ceremonials, all of which make wonderful viewing whether or not you are able to squeeze into the Campo for the race itself. Horses gather for the 90-second dash at around 7 p.m. All but one of the riders are then corralled together. The race begins when the lone rider charges his rivals. From this point, almost anything goes. The only rule is that jockeys cannot interfere with another rider's reins. The race is hectic, fast, violent, and dangerous, both for riders and horses. Sand and mattresses are laid out to help prevent serious injury.

Victory is sweet. Thousands of people sit down to an outdoor banquet in the streets of the winning contrada, sonnets are written, and vast bets and other huge sums of money are called in. Defeat is invariably acrimonious, recriminations occasionally spilling over into violence, while rumors and memories of dark doings fester for years among the beaten contrade and their members.

EXPERIENCE: The Frenzy of the Palio

Siena is at fever pitch in the three days before the Palio, when the festivities and prerace rituals begin in earnest. Noise, color, and spectacle fill the streets and squares. The different *contrade* (districts) deck the streets with their respective flags and banners. Parades of drummers and others in medieval costumes march through the streets, and parties go on long into the night. Horses are chosen at random in public—evincing loud groans and cheers, depending on the horses' perceived abilities—and then blessed in contrada churches—all to the accompaniment of still more festivities.

On the day of the race, you can either sit in the expensive reserved seating around the Campo or file into the Campo. If you choose the latter, arrive early and be prepared to spend many hours on your feet, with no shade and little likelihood of being able to escape the hyperactive throng. The race does not run to a timetable—despite an official "starting time"—as part of the strategy of the race is for some riders to false-start deliberately, thus spooking and tiring rival horses that are known to be skittish. Preliminaries to the race, even with the horses and riders in the Campo, can therefore go on for hours.

After the race, the atmosphere in the Campo becomes, if possible, even more frenzied. People rush to try to touch the winning horse (doing so is said to confer good luck in matters sexual), and losing contrade vent their disappointment on their jockeys and one another. As the evening wears on, the winning contrada celebrates with an enormous outdoor street banquet.

Seats in the reserved seating (like the city's hotels) are booked months in advance and are very expensive and difficult to obtain. The visitor center (see p. 244) offers leads on how to secure these seats, but often it is easier to go through a ticket agency such as **The Palio Expert** (*jacopo dellatorre.com*) or with a hotel package.

SAN GIMIGNANO

Tuscany's most famous village is often called a "medieval Manhattan" after a skyline that bristles with ancient stone towers. Although popular—perhaps too much so in summer—it is a place that retains its charm. Visit not only for its towers but also for a fascinating art gallery, some beautiful views of the Tuscan landscape, and a pair of superb fresco-filled churches.

■ The famous towers of San Gimignano. Most Italian towns would once have had a similar skyline.

San Gimignano

▲ 243 C4

Visitor Information

✉ Piazza del Duomo 1

☎ 0577 940 008

🕐 Closed 1 p.m.– 3 p.m.

sangimignano.com

NOTE: A combined ticket (*$$*) is available to such principal sights as the Musei Civici, Palazzo Comunale, Torre Grossa, and San Lorenzo in Ponte.

San Gimignano existed in Etruscan and Roman times, and then developed during the Middle Ages thanks to its location on the Via Francigena, a trade and pilgrimage route between Rome and the north. The famous towers began to appear around 1150. Their purpose was twofold: to act as a status symbol—your tower had to be higher than your neighbor's—and to provide a defensive retreat in times of trouble.

Plague and the constant strife between aristocratic factions eventually weakened the village, which in 1348 placed itself under the protection of Florence. This immediately undermined the power of

local nobles, one reason why so many towers survived (since they posed no threat, there was no need to tear them down).

Exploring the village is easy—you can walk from one end to the other in a few minutes. Start your tour at the southern gateway, the Porta San Giovanni, and then walk north on Via San Giovanni. Stop by **San Francesco** midway up the street, a deconsecrated church now given over, like many places around town, to the sale of the local Vernaccia white wine. Its rear terrace offers memorable views.

At the top of the street, a medieval arch ushers you into the first of two linked central squares,

Piazza della Cisterna and **Piazza del Duomo.** The first is ringed with towers, medieval buildings, and tempting cafés. The second is home to the village's two principal sights: the Collegiata and Museo Civico, as well as a frescoed baptistery and the **Museo d'Arte Sacra,** a modest museum of sacred art and archaeological finds.

Collegiata

The Collegiata was once San Gimignano's cathedral, but its title was lost when the village ceased to be a bishopric. Founded in the tenth century, it was consecrated in 1148 and enlarged by the architect and sculptor Giuliano da Maiano between 1466 and 1468.

Beyond the blandest of facades (1239) lies an extraordinary interior almost completely covered in frescoes. Three principal cycles adorn the walls, beginning on the rear (entrance wall) with the **"Last Judgment"** (1410) by leading Sienese painter Taddeo di Bartolo (1363–1422); "Inferno" is portrayed on the left, "Paradiso" on the right. Between these two scenes, which are painted on protruding walls, is a fresco by Benozzo Gozzoli of "St. Sebastian" (1465), a saint invoked against infectious diseases and often painted during or after plague epidemics (one had struck San Gimignano a year before the painting was commissioned). The two wooden statues flanking the fresco, the "Archangel Gabriel" and the "Madonna Annunciate" (1421), are the work of the Sienese master Jacopo della Quercia.

The church's second cycle (1356–1367), on the left (north) wall, was executed by Bartolo di Fredi and depicts scenes from the Old Testament, with biblical scenes from the Creation in the lunettes above. The most celebrated scene (also because of a graphically depicted penis) is the "Drunkenness of Noah." (Tradition has it that Noah was the first to cultivate the vine, and the first to abuse its fruits.) Also note the lovely scene portraying the "Creation of Eve" (fourth lunette from the left), in which Eve emerges from Adam's rib. The cycle of New Testament scenes on the opposite wall is earlier (around 1333) and is attributed to one of two Sienese artists, Lippo Memmi or Barna da Siena.

Museo d'Arte Sacra
- ✉ Piazza del Duomo
- ☎ 0577 942 226
- 🕐 Closed Sun. a.m. & mid-Jan.–Feb.
- 💲 $, $$ with Collegiata

Collegiata
- ✉ Piazza del Duomo
- ☎ 0577 940 316
- 🕐 Closed Sun. a.m. & last 2 weeks of Nov. & Jan.
- 💲 Church & Cappella di Santa Fina $, $$ with Museo d'Arte Sacra

duomosangimignano.com

EXPERIENCE: Horseback Riding & Farm Stays

Tuscany is perfect for horseback riding, thanks to its ancient mule tracks, quiet country lanes, numerous woodland trails, and the preponderance of rural farm-stay accommodations, or *agriturismi*, where riding is often one of many countryside pursuits available.

Typically, farm stays offer small self-catering apartments rather than rooms, usually on properties dotted around the farm estate. Prices are often far lower than those charged by hotels.

Visitor centers in Siena, San Gimignano, and other major Tuscan towns carry lists of *agriturismo* accommodations, along with information on the riding and other activities available. Numerous online agencies also offer listings, including *agriturism italiani.it* and *agriturismo.it*. Many of the properties also offer easily arranged half- or full-day riding excursions even if you are not staying at the property.

Musei Civici

- ✉ Palazzo del Popolo, Piazza del Duomo
- ☎ 0577 940 340
- 💲 $$ combined ticket

sangimignanomusei .it

San Lorenzo in Ponte

- ✉ Via Santo Stefano 8
- ☎ 0577 286 300
- 💲 $$ combined ticket

Sant'Agostino

- ✉ Piazza Sant'Agostino
- ☎ 0577 907 012
- 🕐 Closed Mon. until 4 p.m. Jan.–March & 12 p.m.–3 p.m.

Elsewhere in the church, be sure to admire the **Cappella di San Gimignano** (left of the high altar), which contains an altar by Benedetto da Maiano (brother of Giuliano), and to visit the **Cappella di Santa Fina** off the south aisle. It is dedicated to one of San Gimignano's patron saints, the subject of lunette frescoes (1475) by the important Florentine painter Domenico Ghirlandaio (1449–1494). Benedetto was responsible for the chapel's altar, marble shrine, and bas-reliefs from 1475.

Musei Civici

San Gimignano's civic museum is divided in two. One ticket admits you to the museum proper and to the **Torre Grossa,** the only one of San Gimignano's towers currently open to the public. You enter both via a pretty courtyard dotted with archaeological fragments and three frescoes (1513) by Sodoma.

The museum opens with the **Sala del Consiglio,** or Sala Dante, dominated by Lippo Memmi's majestic Maestà (1317). Upstairs is the picture gallery proper, crammed with masterpieces by Sienese and Florentine painters, most notably Benozzo Gozzoli and Filippino Lippi. The most beguiling pictures, the work of a minor local painter, Memmo di Filipuccio, hang in a separate room (turn left at the top of the stairs): The early 14th-century panels portray three wedding scenes, including two remarkable vignettes in which the couple share a bath and then a bed.

San Lorenzo in Ponte

This church is a little gem of the Tuscan Romanesque style. It was bought by the government after having been closed for years and was restored and then reopened to the public in 2017. Although the entire cycle of frescoes wasn't preserved, Cenni di Francesco di ser Cenni's fresco, which depicts "Hell, Purgatory and Heaven" (1413) survived. It's no coincidence that it was St. Lawrence who was granted the power to liberate souls from purgatory.

Sant'Agostino

Take a circuitous route north from Piazza della Cisterna to San Gimignano's third major set piece, the church of Sant'Agostino, and enjoy some of the pretty backstreets on the way. Also spare a few moments to explore the remains of the **Rocca di Montestaffoli,** or castle (1353), and its peaceful public gardens to the west of Piazza del Duomo.

On entering the church, the west wall on your left contains the **Cappella di San Bartolo;** the tomb holds another of San Gimignano's saints. The reliefs (1495) of three episodes from his life are by Benedetto da Maiano. Frescoes also adorn the chapel, and parts of the side walls, although these and other paintings here are overshadowed by Benozzo Gozzoli's stunning **fresco cycle** around the high altar. Painted between 1464 and 1465, it depicts scenes from the "Life of St. Augustine." ■

SOUTHERN TUSCANY

For sheer variety of landscape, historical interest, and outstanding villages, the area south of Siena outshines other areas of Tuscany. It is a bounty of vineyards, cypress-ringed villas, and olive-cloaked hills. Two of Tuscany's finest abbeys are here, along with several of its loveliest little towns—all linked by a tangle of quiet roads that wend through beautiful countryside.

Countless fields of poppies turn the Tuscan countryside red in springtime.

The best way to tackle the region is by car from Siena, heading east on the SP438 road. This takes you through the **Crete,** a distinctive landscape of almost bare, sun-drilled clay hills centered on the village of **Asciano.** Pause here to admire the Collegiata di Sant'Agata, a late 13th-century Romanesque-Gothic church, and the surprisingly rich collection of medieval Sienese paintings in the **Museo Civico Archeologico e d'Arte Sacra** (Corso Matteotti 122, tel 0577 719 524, closed Mon., 1 p.m.–3 p.m., & Tues.–Thurs. Nov.–Feb., $).

From Asciano, take the minor, but very scenic, road south to **Abbazia di Monte Oliveto Maggiore,** a large and beautifully located 14th-century Benedictine abbey. It boasts a majestic artistic offering: a consummately executed fresco cycle (1495–1505) by Sodoma and Luca Signorelli on the "Life of St. Benedict" in the main cloister.

From Monte Oliveto, the SP451 takes you west to **Buonconvento,** a village whose ugly outskirts conceal a pretty medieval kernel. The main draws here are the little known **Museo d'Arte Sacra** (Via Soccini 18, tel 0577 807

Asciano
🗺 243 D3 & 257 B3

Visitor Information
✉ Via delle Fonti
☎ 0577 718 811
🕐 Closed 12 p.m.–3:15 p.m.

comune.asciano.siena.it

Abbazia di Monte Oliveto Maggiore
🗺 243 D3 & 257 B2
✉ Near Chiusure
☎ 0577 707 611
🕐 Closed 12 p.m.–3:15 p.m.

monteolivetomaggiore.it

■ The quaint streets and shops of southern Tuscany, such as in San Quirico d'Orcia, invite endless hours of exploration.

Buonconvento

🗺 243 D3 & 257 B2

Visitor Information

✉ Piazzale Garibaldi 2

☎ 0577 809 075

Montalcino

🗺 243 D3 & 257 B1

Visitor Information

✉ Costa del Municipio 8, off Piazza del Popolo

☎ 0577 849 331

Abbazia di Sant'Antimo

🗺 243 D2 & 257 B1

✉ 6 miles (10 km) S of Montalcino

☎ 0577 835 659

🕐 Closed 12:30 p.m.–3 p.m. Mon.–Sat. & 10:45 a.m.–3 p.m. Sun.

antimo.it

190, closed Mon., 1 p.m.–3 p.m., & Tues.–Fri. Nov.–March, $), with an art collection out of all proportion to the size of the village, and the **Museo della Mezzadria Senese** (Piazzale Garibaldi 10, tel 0577 809 075, closed Mon., 1 p.m.–2 p.m., & Sat.–Sun. & p.m. Nov.–Feb., $), a museum that celebrates rural life.

Montalcino

A road south of Buonconvento climbs to Montalcino, a hilltop village enclosed by walls, crowned by a picture-perfect castle, and privy to magnificent views over the hills of the Crete and the wooded slopes of the Val d'Orcia. The town probably dates from Paleolithic or Etruscan times, although its chief moment of glory came in 1555, when, as the last bastion of the Sienese Republic, it held out for four years against the besieging Florentines.

Many people are lured here by one of Italy's greatest red wines, Brunello di Montalcino, available, along with its cheaper cousin, Rosso di Montalcino, in many local shops. The **Rocca**, or castle (Piazzale della Fortezza, tel 0577 849 211, $), which has an excellent wine shop, offers bracing views from its battlements. Just up the street is the **Musei di Montalcino** (Via Ricasoli 31, tel 0577 846 014, closed Mon. & 1 p.m.–2 p.m., $), full of superbly displayed medieval paintings and sculptures. Afterward, walk down to the main square, the tiny **Piazza del Popolo,** and relax in the Fiaschetteria, a fine 19th-century café.

Isolated in verdant countryside 6 miles (10 km) south of Montalcino is the **Abbazia di Sant'Antimo,** the most glorious of central Italy's many medieval abbeys. It was founded in the eighth century, possibly by Charlemagne, and built in its present form in 1118. In its day, the abbey lay astride several ancient trade and pilgrimage routes. The most important of these was the Via Francigena, which also led directly to the growth of towns such as Siena and San Gimignano. The abbey church is beautiful in its simplicity, its interior, based on French Romanesque models, a vision of honey-colored stone and fine medieval carving.

Val d'Orcia

From Sant'Antimo, drive east on the lovely country road into the Val d'Orcia, the valley of the Orcia River, where a trio of lovely villages await. First up, 12 miles (20 km) from Sant'Antimo, is **Castiglione d'Orcia,** huddled around an imposing fortress. Close by lies the hamlet of **Bagno Vignoni,** famed for its main square, which is, in fact, a large open *piscina,* or pool, that bubbles with water from sulfurous hot springs below. You can bathe in waters from the same source in the nearby Posta Marcucci hotel for a small fee.

Some 3.5 miles (6 km) to the north lies **San Quirico d'Orcia,** a village known for the Collegiata, an outstanding Romanesque church just off Piazza Chigi. Constructed in the 12th century, the building is renowned for its earlier main portal (1080), considered the region's finest work of its kind. The interior is equally admirable—take time to see Sano di Pietro's 15th-century Sienese painting of the "Madonna and Saints" in the north transept. Also visit the Horti Leonini by the Porta Nuova, a simple Renaissance garden, and the little 11th-century church of Santa Maria Assunta in Via Dante.

Pienza

A few miles east of San Quirico is Pienza, a hamlet known to Corsignano until 1459, the year Pope Pius II (1405–1464) decided to transform his birthplace into a model Renaissance city. Pius died as the project was barely under way, but not before architects had created a cathedral, papal residence, and a palace-ringed central piazza. This hint of city survives, forming

Castiglione d'Orcia

🗺 243 D2 & 257 B1

Visitor Information

✉ Torre di Tintinnano, Rocca d'Orcia

☎ 0577 741 032

San Quirico d'Orcia

🗺 243 D3 & 257 B1

Visitor Information

✉ Piazza Chigi 2

☎ 0577 899 728

🕐 Closed Nov.– March

comunesanquirico.it

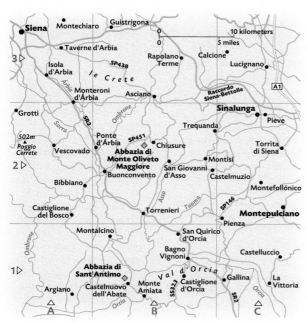

Pienza

◪ 243 D3 & 257 C2

Visitor Information

✉ Via delle Case Nuove 4

☎ 366 248 6015

prolocopienza.it

Montepulciano

◪ 243 E3 & 257 C2

Visitor Information

✉ Piazzale Don Minzoni 1

☎ 0578 757 341

🕓 Closed 12:30– 3 p.m. & Sun. p.m.

montepulcianoliving .it

the heart of one of Italy's most charming villages.

The **cathedral** has one of Tuscany's earliest Renaissance facades (1462), while inside are five specially commissioned 15th-century Sienese altarpieces. To its left are two palaces, one of which, the Palazzo Borgia, or Palazzo dei Vescovi, hosts the **Museo Diocesano** *(Corso il Rossellino 30, tel 0578 749 905, palazzoborgia.it, closed Tues., 1:30 p.m.–2:30 p.m., & Mon.–Fri. Nov.–March, $)* and its collection of medieval art and artifacts. To the cathedral's right is the **Palazzo Piccolomini** *(tel 0577 286 300, palazzopiccolominipienza .it, closed Mon., early Jan.–mid-Feb., & 2nd half Nov., $),* where guided tours showcase Pius's former state apartments.

Walk west on the main street, Corso il Rossellino, and you come to the church of San Francesco, a survivor from pre-Pius Pienza. Beyond lies Piazza Dante, from which a small lane skirts the walls for more views. Another road drops downhill to the signposted **Pieve di Corsignano,** the village's tenth-century parish church.

Montepulciano

Montepulciano is a classic hill town. Ranged over a narrow volcanic outcrop, it consists of little more than a single main street— known as the Corso—a steep road that wends past mostly 16th-century churches and palaces. Start at the bottom of the street at the Porta al Prato. As you climb, look for the **Palazzo Bucelli** at No. 70, whose base is studded with Roman and Etruscan remains; the church of **Sant'Agostino,** designed by Michelozzo in 1472; and the small **Museo Civico** *(Via Ricci 10, tel 0578 717 300, closed 1 p.m.– 3 p.m. Nov.–March & Mon. until 3 p.m., $),* with medieval paintings and sculptures.

At the top of the climb awaits the main **Piazza del Duomo,** one of several places around town with stores selling the local Vino Nobile wine. Dominating the square is the **Duomo,** known for Taddeo di Bartolo's high altarpiece (1401) and the sculpture-filled baptistery. Follow Via di San Biagio to **San Biagio** *(ten minutes' downhill walk, closed 12 p.m.–3 p.m.),* a harmonious Renaissance church designed by Antonio da Sangallo at the beginning of the 16th century. ■

EXPERIENCE: Live & Work on a Tuscan Farm

Agriculture has been the very lifeblood of Tuscany for centuries. To experience life on a farm—harvesting olives, trimming vines, picking grapes—is to experience an age-old element of traditional Tuscan life.

WWOOF, or **World Wide Opportunities on Organic Farms** *(wwoof.it),* links volunteers with organic farms in Tuscany, offering visitors the chance to learn the traditional, small-scale farming methods that have sustained generations of Tuscan peasant families. You pay a nominal fee for membership in the Italian arm of the organization, which entitles you to a contact list of affiliated farms. You then arrange a stay with one of the host farms directly. In exchange for labor, you will receive basic room and board, which varies from farm to farm.

LUCCA

Henry James once described Lucca as "overflowing with everything that makes for ease, for plenty, for beauty, for interest and good example" (*Italy Revisited,* 1877). Little has changed since. Peaceful, urbane, and embraced by tree-topped walls, the city today is still an attractive mix of atmospheric piazzas, tiny churches, museums, galleries, and cobbled lanes. Among Tuscan towns and cities, only Florence and Siena are more compelling.

■ The pillars and arcades of San Michele in Foro's facade typify Pisan Romanesque architecture.

Lucca owes the gridiron plan of its center to the Romans. It rose to medieval prominence as a result of a trade in silk—tapestries made Lucca famous in medieval time. After the 14th century, the city declined in importance, but it retained its independence until the arrival of Napoleon. The Bourbons assumed control until Italian unification.

Today, everything you want to see lies within the old walls. The best plan of attack is to start either at the Duomo and work east, or in the central square, Piazza San Michele, and work north.

San Michele in Foro

Few churches are quite as breathtaking at first glance as San Michele in Foro (*Piazza San Michele, closed 12 p.m.–3 p.m.*), built on the site of the old Roman *foro*, or forum. Its stupendous **facade** combines the marble-striped veneer that distinguishes most Pisan-Romanesque buildings with an astounding confection of miniature loggias, blind arcades, and inventively twisted columns. The plain interior is less arresting, largely because most of the church's funds were lavished on

Lucca

🗺 242 B5

Visitor Information

✉ Vecchia Porta di San Donato, Piazzale Verdi

☎ 0583 583 150

turismo.lucca.it

Casa di Puccini

- Corte San Lorenzo 9
- 0583 584 028
- Closed Tues. except Apr.–Sept.
- $$

puccinimuseum.org

Duomo di San Martino

- Piazza San Martino
- 0583 957 068
- Closed a.m. Sun.
- $–$$

museocattedrale lucca.it

Diners enjoy an alfresco meal at one of Lucca's many charming streetside restaurants.

Museo della Cattedrale

- Via Arcivescovado
- 0583 490 530
- Closed p.m. Mon.–Fri. Nov.– mid-March
- $ or $$ combined ticket

www.museo cattedralelucca.it

its exterior. It does have one major work of art, however, Filippino Lippi's "Santi Jerome, Sebastian, Roch, and Helena."

Lucca's own Giacomo Puccini (1858–1924) was born a stone's throw from the church. The composer's birthplace, **Casa di Puccini,** today is a museum.

Duomo di San Martino

Another wonderful **facade** (1060–1241) fronts the Duomo di San Martino, in Piazza San Martino. The cathedral's most important feature is a series of 13th-century carvings around the atrium and the entrance doors. The left-hand door reliefs are by the celebrated Pisan sculptor Nicola Pisano, while the panels between the doors on the "Life of St. Martin" are the work of the facade's principal architect, Guidetto da Como (active early

13th century). Midway down the nave inside, you come to the **Tempietto,** a gaudy octagonal chapel built by local sculptor Matteo Civitali (1435–1511) to house the much venerated **Volto Santo** (Holy Face), a cedarwood crucifix said to be a true likeness of Christ carved by Nicodemus, an eyewitness to the Crucifixion. In truth, it is probably a 13th-century copy of an original 8th-century work.

Of greater artistic merit is the funeral monument of Ilaria del Carretto (1410), dedicated to the wife of Paolo Guinigi, one of Lucca's leading medieval rulers, and housed in the **sacristy.** The masterpiece of Sienese sculptor Jacopo della Quercia, it is one of Italy's loveliest sculptures.

The ticket for the Duomo also gives you admission to the **Museo della Cattedrale**—an excellent collection of paintings, sculptures, and religious ephemera—in Piazza Antelminelli, and to the nearby church of **Santi Giovanni e Repa-rata** *(same hours as Museo della Cattedrale),* where excavations have revealed Roman buildings and the medieval remains of Lucca's first cathedral and baptistery.

Beyond Lucca's Principal Churches

Just south of the cathedral is a good place to climb up to Lucca's magnificent, broad walls (1544–1645). Walk east and you soon look down on the **Giardino Botanico** *(tel 0583 950 596, closed Nov.–late March except by appt., $).* To enter the garden, use the access ramp to the walls located almost at the end of Via del Fosso. Green thumbs might also want to explore the gardens of the nearby **Villa Bottini** (*Via Elisa 9, tel 0583 442 140, closed Sat.–Sun.*). A few steps west stands the 13th-century **Santa Maria Forisportam,** a charming but unfinished Pisan-Romanesque church that once marked the city's Roman and medieval limits.

Walk north from here and you come to Lucca's strangest sight, the **Palazzo & Torre Guinigi,** a medieval town house built by the Guinigi, Lucca's preeminent noble family. It is best known for its tower—which provides lovely city views—and the pair of holm oaks sprouting from the roof.

INSIDER TIP:

Allow enough time to stroll (or cycle) atop the old, tree-lined walls of Lucca. It's only about a 2.5-mile (4 km) circuit around the town, passing city gates and bastions.

—CAROLINE HICKEY
National Geographic contributor

Another former Guinigi dwelling houses the **Museo Nazionale di Villa Guinigi,** an extensive and varied collection of archaeological remains, medieval paintings, sculptures, textiles, and other arts.

From Piazza San Michele, pick up Via Fillungo, Lucca's main street, which takes you to

Barga

If you are in or around Lucca, consider driving north to this delightful village in a little-visited region known as the Garfagnana. The village sits in the lee of the Appennini, overlooking the Serchio valley and jagged peaks of the distant Apuane Alps. Its highlight is a tenth-century cathedral, a vision of honey-colored stone fronted by a panoramic terrace. The facade is adorned with shallow reliefs and other carvings, while the interior boasts a huge tenth-century statue of St. Christopher and a glorious carved pulpit by the 13th-century sculptor Bigarelli da Como.

Piazza dell'Anfiteatro, a square whose medieval houses were built into the oval of the old Roman amphitheater. A couple of blocks east lies another gem of a church, the small **San Pietro Somaldi.** A similar distance to the northwest stands the larger **San Frediano** (*1112–1147; closed 12 p.m.–3 p.m.*), distinguished by its 13th-century facade mosaic and interior treasures that include a sublimely carved 12th-century font, glazed terra-cottas by the della Robbia family, carvings and pavement tombs by Jacopo della Quercia, and Amico Aspertini's 16th-century frescoes of the "Arrival of the Volto Santo in Lucca."

Southwest of the church, explore the palace and formal 18th-century gardens of the **Palazzo Pfanner** (*Via degli Asili 33, tel 0583 491 243, closed Nov.–March, $$*) and, farther west, the **Museo Nazionale di Palazzo Mansi,** whose rococo decoration provides the backdrop for a fine collection of paintings. ∎

Palazzo & Torre Guinigi
✉ Via Sant'Andrea 41
☎ 0583 583 086
💲 $

Museo Nazionale di Villa Guinigi
✉ Via della Quarquonia
☎ 0583 496 033
🕐 Closed Sun.–Mon.
💲 $ or $$ with Palazzo Mansi

luccamuseinazionali.it

Museo Nazionale di Palazzo Mansi
✉ Via Galli Tassi 43
☎ 0583 55 570
🕐 Closed Sun.–Mon.
💲 $

Barga
🗺 242 B5
Visitor Information
✉ Via di Mezzo 45
☎ 0583 724 743

prolocobarga.it

| PISA

Most people know Pisa's famous Leaning Tower. Rather fewer know that it is one component in a lovely ensemble of medieval buildings; fewer still that the rest of the city—sadly—is a largely modern place (the result of bombing during World War II). Allow an hour to see the tower and its surroundings, and the same again to explore Pisa's medieval highlights.

Pisa

🗺 242 B4

Visitor Information

✉ Piazza Vittorio Emanuele II 16

☎ 050 42 291

🕐 Closed 1 p.m.– 2 p.m.

turismo.pisa.it

The **Leaning Tower** *(tickets sold in northeast corner of Campo dei Miracoli or online at opapisa.it, $$$)* was originally a modest component of the **Campo dei Miracoli,** or Field of Miracles, which includes the Duomo, a baptistery, and the Camposanto. Begun in 1173, the Duomo's

■ The tower once leaned 17.5 feet (5.5 m) from the vertical. Engineers in the 1990s reversed the lean by 10 percent.

now famous campanile started to lean almost immediately, the result of weak sandy subsoil underpinning its foundations.

The **Duomo** *(closed 12:45 p.m.–2 p.m. Nov.–Feb.)* was begun a century earlier and with its array of pillars, columns, and colored marbles would provide the model for similar Pisan-Romanesque churches across central Italy. It is known primarily for its bronze south doors (1180), Cimabue's apse mosaic of "Christ in Majesty" (1302), and Giovanni Pisano's pulpit (1302–1311). An equally staggering pulpit by Giovanni's father, Nicola Pisano, stands in the circular **baptistery** (begun in 1152). Treasures can be seen in the nearby **Museo dell'Opera del Duomo.** The **Camposanto** is a medieval cemetery *($),* where the "Trionfo della Morte" frescoes by Buonamico Buffalmacco (1262–1340) have been completely renewed after 70 years of difficult restoration.

Other highlights are **Piazza dei Cavallieri,** a square ringed by medieval buildings; **Santa Maria della Spina,** an exquisite church on the riverbank at Lungarno Gambacorti; and the **Museo Nazionale di San Matteo** *(Piazza San Matteo, tel 050 541 865, closed Sun. p.m. & Mon., $),* a wide-ranging collection of mostly Tuscan paintings and sculptures. ■

AREZZO

Arezzo was an important Etruscan city that maintained its elevated status during Roman and early medieval times, when its position astride important trade routes over the Apennines brought it considerable prosperity. Today, its well-being derives from a flourishing gold and jewelry industry and from the visitors lured by Piero della Francesca's "Legend of the True Cross," one of Italy's most celebrated fresco cycles.

Arezzo's modern veneer conceals a medieval core. Most visitors go straight to the church of **San Francesco** *(pierodella francesca-ticketoffice.it, closed Sun. a.m., $)* in Piazza San Francesco, where famous frescoes by Piero della Francesca (1416–1492) adorn the walls of the apse.

Most of Arezzo's other highlights lie on or close to **Piazza Grande,** the town's oddly sloping main square. At the top of the

---

INSIDER TIP:

Visit the Antiques Market held on the first weekend of the month to buy a piece of old Italy. Hundreds of booths offer everything from skeleton keys to furniture.

—ASHLEY MATHIEU
National Geographic contributor

---

slope stands the **Palazzo delle Logge** (1573), fronted by an attractive Renaissance loggia designed by the local artist and art historian Giorgio Vasari (1512–1574). In the square's top left-hand corner stands the **Fraternita dei Laici,** a Gothic palace known for

its doorway and lunette sculptures (1434), the latter the work of Bernardo Rossellino. Lower down the square is the rear apse of **Pieve di Santa Maria** *(closed 12 p.m.–3 p.m.),* a magical 12th-century Romanesque church whose entrance lies around the corner on Corso Italia. Pop inside to admire Pietro Lorenzetti's high altarpiece painting of the "Madonna and Saints" (1320).

North of the square stretches the **Passeggio del Prato,** a pleasant park flanked by the cathedral and the remnants of the Fortezza Medicea, a 16th-century castle built by Florence's Medici family (Florence captured Arezzo in 1384). The **cathedral** *(closed 12:30 p.m.–3 p.m.)* warrants a visit for its stained glass (1523), a fresco of "Mary Magdalene" by Piero della Francesca, and the bizarre tomb of Guido Tarlati, a 14th-century bishop of Arezzo (located next to Piero's fresco). ■

Piero Trail

Devotees of Piero della Francesca visit the museum in Monterchi *(Via della Reglia, tel 0575 70713, closed 1 p.m.–2 p.m., $)* **that houses his "Madonna del Parto." Sansepolcro's civic museum** *(Via Niccolò Aggiunti 65, closed 1 p.m.–2:30 p.m., $$)* **has the "Resurrection" and "Madonna della Misericordia."**

Arezzo
- 243 E4

Visitor Information
- Piazza della Repubblica 28
- 0575 26850
- Closed 1 p.m.–2 p.m.

arezzointuscany.it

Antiques Market
- Piazza Grande & surrounding streets

A DRIVE THROUGH THE CHIANTI COUNTRYSIDE

There are many possible routes through the vineyards, olive groves, small towns, and wooded hills of Chianti, Tuscany's most visited region. This loop drive allows you to see the best of the area on a day trip from Siena.

Acres upon acres of neat Chianti vineyards thrive under the hot Tuscan sun.

Leave Siena on the SR2 road (the Via Cassia) to the west, keeping your eyes peeled for signs to Castellina in Chianti and the SR222 road to the north, a specially designated scenic route known as the Chiantigiana. Ultimately, you could follow this beautiful road all the way to Florence by way of Greve in Chianti, an excellent way of linking Siena with the Tuscan capital. The route offers a good look at the Chianti region and is prettier than the *superstrada*, or two-lane highway, between the two cities.

For a circular but equally representative tour of Chianti from Siena you should remain with the SR222 as far as Castellina. All manner of diversions are possible from the basic route outlined here, but note that while roads in Chianti are well made, they are also often full of twists and turns. Distances on the ground

> ### NOT TO BE MISSED:
>
> **Radda di Chianti • Monti del Chianti • Badia a Coltibuono • Castello di Brolio**

and journey times are usually much greater than they appear on the map. The region's towns are often relatively unmemorable, making the roads themselves—and the countryside they travel—Chianti's main attractions.

With the countryside come vineyards, hundreds of them. Their grapes produce Chianti's famous wine, a vintage today that is far superior to the watery, acidic reds once found in cheap Italian restaurants almost the world over. Most of the vineyards are well signposted and open to the public for buying and tasting.

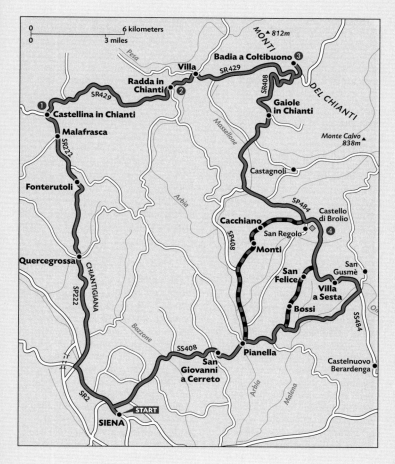

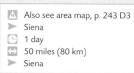

For an introduction to the region's viticulture, pause in **Castellina in Chianti 1**, 13 miles (21 km) from Siena, where local Gallo Nero wines and extra virgin olive oils are sold at the Bottega del Vino at Via della Rocca 13 (the Gallo Nero, or Black Cockerel, is a well-respected federation of Chianti producers). Be sure to walk along the town's intriguing Via delle Volte, a medieval vaulted street just inside the walls.

From Castellina head east on the SR429 to **Radda in Chianti 2**, an especially scenic

- Also see area map, p. 243 D3
- Siena
- 1 day
- 50 miles (80 km)
- Siena

stretch of road that runs for 6 miles (10 km). Radda's modern outskirts are unappetizing, although the inner core still retains its medieval aspect. Beyond Radda continue east into the heart of the heavily wooded **Monti del Chianti,** the Chianti hills, and after 2 miles (3 km) take a left turn to **Badia a Coltibuono ❸** (see sidebar this page), a beautifully located 11th-century Vallambrosan abbey, some 6 miles (10 km) from Radda. Just south of the abbey, the road joins with the SP408, where you should turn right toward **Gaiole in Chianti,** another important wine town with a quaint old center ringed by more modern development.

Three miles (5 km) south of Gaiole ignore the turns to Castagnoli and Radda off the SP408, and continue on, the same distance again, to the next main junction. Turn left on the SS484 and follow signs for the **Castello di Brolio ❹** *(near San Regolo, tel 0577 7301, ricasoli.it, closed in winter, $–$$$$ short or two-hour visit & wine tasting).* This vast crenellated castle, approached

by a cypress avenue, has been in the Ricasoli family since the 12th century. The battlements offer sweeping views of the Arbia valley and the Chianti hills, while the on-site cantina sells the noted wines produced by the estate.

Several minor roads, most of them light-color gravel-surfaced *strade bianche* (white roads), lead back to the SP408, either via San Felice or Cacchiano and Monti, the quickest route. Once back on the SP408, turn right and it is another 10 miles (16 km) to Siena.

Alternatively, return from Castello di Brolio to the SP484 and continue 5 miles (8 km) past Villa a Sesta to an intersection beneath **San Gusmè,** one of the region's most picturesque villages. From here the return to Siena is slightly longer and more circuitous.

EXPERIENCE: Wine-tasting in Chianti

Numerous small Chianti wineries between Florence and Siena offer short, informal tours and tastings. Drop by the visitor centers in the towns of Radda, Greve, and Castellina for details, or just pick one of the wineries with signs saying "Vendita Diretta" (Direct Sales) or "Degustazioni" (Tastings). For more in-depth tours of larger and more prestigious wineries, it is usually necessary to make an appointment—English will invariably be spoken.

Of Chianti's many wineries open to visitors, **Badia a Coltibuono** *(tel 0577 749 498, coltibuono.com, by appt. or set tours Mon.–Fri. May–Oct., $$–$$$$),* where you can also stay overnight (see p. 373), is a step above the rest. First, it sits high and isolated in the Chianti hills, offering glorious views across the Val di Chiana. Second, the *badia,* or abbey, and its church date from the 11th century, and for some 800 years the Benedictine monks who lived here made—and drank—wine. The abbey was dissolved at the start of the 19th century, with the arrival of Napoleon, and later passed to a Florentine banking family. Today, its owners still make wine.

Inside the abbey is an exquisite small courtyard—note the badia's ancient symbols above the main door, the grill of St. Laurence and the planting stick of the abbey's founder, San Giovanni Gualberto. You can wander the small but superb Italianate garden to the rear, then start your tour and tasting, perhaps in the abbey's frescoed former refectory.

Wine is not actually made at the abbey anymore, but the building's ancient cellars, once used to bury the monks, are a perfect temperature for storing and aging wine made at Badia a Coltibuono's wineries elsewhere in Chianti. The rows of vast French-oak barrels in the dark and chill vaults make for a memorable sight.

Other Chianti wineries that offer tours by appointment include **Castello di Volpaia** *(tel 0577 738 066, volpaia.com),* near Radda; **Castello di Verrazzano** *(tel 0577 854 243, verrazzano.com);* **Castello di Brolio** *(tel 0577 7301, ricasoli.it);* **Villa Vignamaggio** *(tel 055 854 661, vigna maggio.com),* where you can also spend the night; and **Rocca delle Macie** *(tel 0577 732 236, roccadellemacie.com).*

CORTONA

Cortona lords over the surrounding countryside, views from its hilltop ramparts extending for miles across the hazy hills and plains of Tuscany and Umbria. As old as Troy, at least according to myth, the town was already a flourishing center when the Etruscans arrived in the eighth century b.c. Today, Cortona has a prevailing medieval look and the town's two museums, several churches, steep old streets, and pleasant feel make it a fine place to visit.

Views from Cortona's commanding hilltop position stretch for miles across the plains of Tuscany.

Brave the steep grades to reach the town's upper levels and the ruined **Fortezza Medicea** (Medici fortress), where the views are especially good. Cortona's chief attraction is the **Museo Diocesano** *(Piazza del Duomo, tel 0575 62 830, closed Mon. Nov.–March, $)*, a collection of Renaissance art dominated by two riveting paintings by Fra Angelico: the "Annunciation" and "Madonna and Child with Saints" (1428–1430). Close by stands the **Museo dell'Accademia Etrusca e della Città di Cortona** *(Piazza Signorelli 9, tel 0575 630 415, closed Mon. Nov.–March, $$, cortonamaec*

.org), with displays on Cortona's rich Etruscan heritage.

San Nicolò *(closed 12 p.m.– 5 p.m.)* off Via San Nicolò has an intriguing double-sided altarpiece by Luca Signorelli (1441–1523), a noted Renaissance painter born in Cortona. Another work by him is found in **San Domenico** *(off Piazza Garibaldi)*, which also boasts a poetic "Coronation of the Virgin" (1402) by Lorenzo di Niccolò. The most celebrated local church is the austere **Santa Maria del Calcinaio,** located 2 miles (3 km) east of Cortona and often considered as Tuscany's finest Renaissance church. ∎

Cortona

▲ 243 E3

Visitor Information

✉ Piazza Signorelli 9

☎ 0575 637 223

🕐 Closed Sat. p.m., Sun., & 1 p.m.– 3:15 p.m.

comunedicortona .it/turismo

More Places to Visit in Tuscany

The Maremma

The Maremma region encompasses the medieval charms of **Massa Marittima** *(visitor information, Via Todini 3, tel 0566 902 756, turismomassamarittima.it),* a town notable for its magnificent cathedral. The area's coastline is dotted with small resorts and beaches—notably the undeveloped sands at the Marina di Alberese, the village of Castiglione della Pescaia, and the glitzy resorts of Porto Ercole and Porto Santo Stefano. The **Parco Regionale della Maremma** *(visitor information, Via del Bersaglieri 7–9, Alberese, tel 0564 407 098, parco-maremma .it)* protects the best coastal scenery; visit on foot from Talamone, a pretty little resort village, or by shuttle bus from Alberese.

Several inland villages merit a detour: Visit isolated **Capalbio,** a hilltop maze of old streets; **Pitigliano,** superbly sited on a rocky ridge; and **Sovana,** a single-street gem with a sublime parish church, Santa Maria Maggiore, and an interesting collection of Etruscan tombs.
🗺 243 C2–D1

Pistoia

Pistoia, set in unprepossessing country between Florence and Lucca, has plenty to see. Start in the central **Piazza del Duomo** and visit the 10th-century Duomo *(closed 12:30 p.m.–3 p.m.),* which contains the famous silver Dossale di San Jacopo (Altarpiece of St. James). The medieval work took some 200 years to complete. It contains 628 sculpted figures and weighs close to a ton. Elsewhere, the church of **Sant'Andrea** contains a magnificent carved pulpit (1297) by Giovanni Pisano. Also search for the **Ospedale del Ceppo** at the end of Via Pacani, a medieval hospital adorned with a colorful terra-cotta frieze (1526–1529).
territorio.pistoia.it 🗺 243 C5
Visitor Information ✉ Piazza del Duomo 4 ☎ 0573 21 622

Volterra

Volterra sits on the type of craggy, easily defended hill favored by its Etruscan founders. The **Museo Etrusco Guarnacci** *(Via Don Minzoni 15, tel 0588 86 347, closed p.m. Nov.–March, $$)* is one of Italy's most important museums outside Rome and Florence. The city's medieval streets are a pleasure to explore for their own sake. From your starting point in the central **Piazza dei Priori,** make a tour of the Rocca (castle), the Balze (part of the town's crumbling rock bastions), and the Parco Archeologico (a park with Roman and other ruins).
volterratur.it or *provolterra.it* 🗺 243 C3
Visitor Information ✉ Piazza dei Priori 19–20 ☎ 0588 87 257 🕐 Closed 1 p.m.–2 p.m.

EXPERIENCE: Join an Archaeological Dig

Paying volunteers at **Poggio del Molino,** on the Tuscan coast, help excavate the remains of a Roman villa and maritime settlement, uncovering, cleaning, and documenting finds; collecting organic samples with a paleobotanist; and surveying the area in and around the site in the search for mosaic, fresco, coins, metal, and pottery. Accommodation is near Populonia, 2.5 miles (4 km) from the site. Volunteers work with senior high-school students from the area, as well as with a technical team and trained students from U.S. and European universities. You can join the project for between 6 and 13 days from about mid-March to mid-October. Contact the locally based **Archeodig** *(archeodig.com, sessions with academic credits also available)* for more information and costs.

A peaceful region home to St. Francis, sun-hazed hills, dulcet countryside, snow-tinged mountains, and gastronomic centers

UMBRIA

■ The Valnerina, a region of valleys and mountains in southeast Umbria

UMBRIA

Once known as neighboring Tuscany's unassuming sister, Umbria has emerged as an appealing destination in its own right. Intimate and pretty, the so-called green heart of Italy is tailor-made for a self-contained vacation, thanks not only to its coronet of closely linked towns—each a cornucopia of museums, galleries, and medieval corners—but also to its wonderfully varied scenery, good wines, and honest, plain cuisine.

Castelluccio, high above the Piano Grande

Umbria's earliest known inhabitants were the Umbrii, a farming tribe who were absorbed by the Etruscans after about the seventh century B.C. Then came the Romans, whose most important town was Spoleto, a city adopted by the Lombards, the region's next rulers, as the capital of their Italian duchy.

Powerful city-states emerged around the 12th century. Only Perugia, still Umbria's capital, achieved national prominence. Its fall to the papacy in the 16th century precipitated a long period of stagnation, whose effects have only really been reversed with Umbria's emergence as a tourist destination over the last decades.

As the birthplace of Francis (1181/2–1226) and Benedict (480–550), Europe's foremost saints and founders of the Western world's most significant monastic orders, Umbria has an unrivaled claim to fame. So many other saints were also born here that Umbria is sometimes called *Umbra santa*, or *Umbra mistica*—holy or mystical Umbria.

A Wealth of Sights

There are two must-sees in Umbria: Orvieto, with its majestic Gothic cathedral, and Assisi, home to the astounding Basilica di San Francesco. The latter is the burial place of Assisi-born St. Francis and a building that helped alter the course of Italian, and thus European, art. Giotto, Cimabue, and other Italian artists of their day painted here, beginning a move away from the stilted conventions of Byzantine art to a more naturalistic style of painting that would culminate in the Renaissance.

But to leave Umbria having seen only these sights would be a mistake. One of the region's

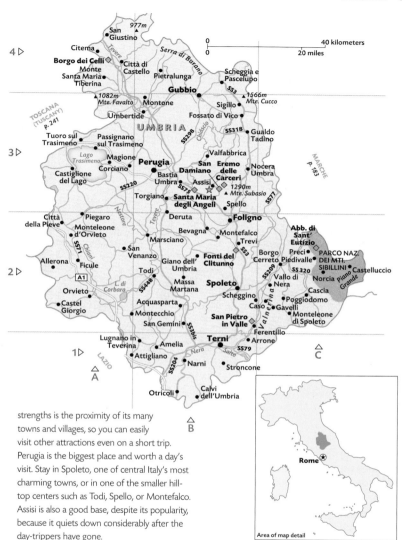

strengths is the proximity of its many towns and villages, so you can easily visit other attractions even on a short trip. Perugia is the biggest place and worth a day's visit. Stay in Spoleto, one of central Italy's most charming towns, or in one of the smaller hill-top centers such as Todi, Spello, or Montefalco. Assisi is also a good base, despite its popularity, because it quiets down considerably after the day-trippers have gone.

More remote towns, such as Gubbio, a medieval gem, are intriguing, as is Norcia in Umbria's wilder and more mountainous eastern margins. The town is a gourmet's paradise and an excellent base for exploring the Parco Nazionale dei Monti Sibillini, one of the most popular national parks. The scenery embraces the Sibillini Mountains, situated in the Marche, one of the Apennines' major massifs, and the

extraordinary Piano Grande, a beautiful flower-filled plain enclosed by a vast bowl of mountains. Hiking in the park is excellent, thanks to the scenery and the availability of good maps, a rarity in central and southern Italy.

Landscapes in western Umbria are more pastoral, their beauty subtle and insinuating, and many are similar to Tuscany at its best. ■

PERUGIA

Penetrate the jumble of highways and dispiriting suburbs encircling Umbria's capital, and you discover a wonderfully atmospheric old center still resonating with the echoes of its Etruscan, Roman, and medieval past. As well as the sights clustered around Piazza IV Novembre, the main square, there is plenty to see farther afield, so put on your walking shoes and be prepared to cover plenty of ground during the course of a day's sightseeing.

The Piazza IV Novembre contains the Fontana Maggiore, one of Italy's loveliest fountains.

Perugia

271 B3

Visitor Information

Loggia dei Linari, Piazza Matteotti 18

075 577 2686 or 075 573 6458

turismo.comune .perugia.it

perugiacittamuseo.it

www.umbriatourism .it

Corso Vannucci cuts through Perugia's medieval heart. In **Piazza IV Novembre,** at its northern end, is the **Fontana Maggiore** (1277), a fountain created by the father-and-son team of Nicola and Giovanni Pisano, sculptors best known for their pulpits in Siena and Pisa (see pp. 244–249 & p. 262). To its rear rises the **Duomo** (begun in 1345), whose interior contains the tombs of two popes who died in the city. Paintings here include the late 15th-century "Madonna delle Grazie," reputed to have miraculous powers,

hence its many votive offerings. Also see the **Cappella del Sant'Anello** (north aisle), which contains a piece of agate said to be the Virgin's wedding ring.

Palazzo dei Priori

The corner of the square and Corso Vannucci is filled by one of Italy's most formidable civic palaces, the Palazzo dei Priori (1293–1443), home to four separate sights. The first, the **Sala dei Notari** *(closed Mon.),* a meeting place for medieval lawyers, contains an impressive vaulted ceiling and the coats of arms of

Perugia's medieval *podestà,* or magistrates. Its main hall is entered via the fan-shaped steps off the piazza. Down the Corso at No. 15 lies the entrance to the **Sala del Collegio della Mercanzia,** former meeting place of the city's merchants' guild. The tiny 15th-century room is almost completely covered in intricately detailed wood paneling. A few steps away at No. 25 lies the entrance to the **Collegio del Cambio,** which once hosted the money changers' guild. The city's painter Pietro Vannucci (1446–1523), better known as Perugino, provided the decoration—the frescoes (1496) here are considered to be his masterpiece.

Save the palace's pride and joy for last, the **Galleria Nazionale dell'Umbria** *(tel 075 572 1009, closed Mon., gallerianazionaledell umbria.it, $).* Its paintings combine the best of Umbrian art over the centuries with outstanding Tuscan works, such as the two paintings of the "Madonna and Child with Saints" by Fra Angelico and Piero della Francesca (1437 and 1460).

More Sights

Head west from the Corso on picturesque Via dei Priori to reach the church of **San Francesco al Prato,** reopening after decades of redevelopment as an auditorium. Founded in the 13th century by the Franciscans, it was called the "Pantheon of Perugia" because over the centuries, members of the city's most prominent families wanted to be buried there. Next to it is the **Oratorio di San Bernardino,** celebrated for Agostino di Duccio's sculpted and multicolored facade (1457). Swing north and take in the **Arco di Augusto** (third to first century B.C.), an Etruscan-Roman gateway, before following Corso Garibaldi north to the churches of **Sant'Agostino** and **Sant'Angelo.** West of the piazza, the key sights are an Etruscan well in Piazza Danti and the church of **San Severo,** which contains a painting by Raphael. Then head south on Corso Cavour to **San Domenico** *(closed 12 p.m.–4 p.m.),* Perugia's largest church, known for the early 14th-century Gothic tomb of Benedict XI (right of the altar). Just off the same street are the **Museo Archeologico** *(Piazza Giordano Bruno 10, tel 075 572 7141, $),* whose displays explore Perugia's Roman and Etruscan heritage, and the beautiful church of **San Pietro,** which must not be missed. ■

Sala del Collegio della Mercanzia & Collegio del Cambio
- ✉ Corso Vannucci 15 & 25, respectively
- ☎ 075 573 0366
- 🕐 Sala: Hours vary. Collegio: Closed Sun. p.m., 1 p.m.–2:30 p.m.; also Mon p.m. Nov.–March
- 💲 Individual $, combined ticket $$

San Francesco al Prato
- ✉ Piazza San Francesco 5/8
- ☎ 075 573 3957

San Severo
- ✉ Piazza Raffaello
- ☎ 075 947 1766
- 🕐 Closed 1:30 p.m.–2:30 p.m., & Mon. except Apr. & Aug.
- 💲 $

Lago Trasimeno
- ▲ 271 A3
- **Visitor Information**
- ✉ Piazza Gramsci 1, Castiglione del Lago
- ☎ 075 965 8293
- 🕐 Closed 1 p.m.–3:30 p.m.

Lago Trasimeno

The lake is a pretty stretch of water amid the hills west of Perugia. It is known for the Romans' defeat in 217 B.C. at the hands of the Carthaginian general, Hannibal. You can visit the site of the battlefield near Tuoro sul Trasimeno. The new **Via del Trasimeno** is a 100-mile (160 km) circuit that takes you on a seven-leg journey, on foot or by bike, that passes through the most beautiful villages in the area. Of these, **Castiglione del Lago** is the most pleasant, with a nice old center, a handful of modest beaches, waterfront fish restaurants, and boat trips to the lake's islands. Various water sports, notably windsurfing, are available here and at other major centers.

ASSISI

Assisi is celebrated as the birthplace of St. Francis, patron saint of Italy, founder of the Franciscan order, one of the most influential religious figures of the medieval world. His twin-churched basilica, adorned with frescoes by the greatest painters of their day, is one of Europe's most important artistic and sacred shrines. At the same time Assisi is an attractive hill town, full of churches, galleries, flower-decked streets, and medieval buildings.

■ Giotto's frescoes in the Basilica di San Francesco

Assisi
🗺 271 B3
Visitor Information
✉ Piazza del Comune 22
☎ 075 813 8680

Museo e Foro Romano
✉ Via Portica 2
☎ 848 004 000
💲 $

Pinacoteca
✉ Via San Francesco 10
☎ 075 813 8680
🕐 Open daily Apr.–Oct., Nov.–March by appt.
💲 $

Assisi's principal sight, the Basilica di San Francesco (begun in 1229), lies at the town's western edge, meaning you are initially likely to find yourself in the more central **Piazza del Comune,** probably the site of the old Roman forum. Its northern flank is dominated by the first-century **Tempio di Minerva,** an almost perfectly preserved six-columned Roman temple pediment. On the western edge of the square is the **Museo e Foro Romano,** which offers the chance to explore excavations of the Roman remains below the piazza. Just west of the piazza is the **Pinacoteca,** or picture gallery, a modest but beautifully displayed collection of medieval and Renaissance Umbrian paintings.

The **Basilica di San Francesco** hit world headlines in 1997, when earthquakes brought down part of its Upper Church, killing four people and destroying several of its many frescoes. The greatest of its frescoes survived, however. In the **Upper Church,** a soaring space, you can still see Giotto's peerless fresco cycle on the "Life of St. Francis" (1290–1295), together with works by Giotto's teacher, Cimabue. In the subdued, crypt-like **Lower Church,** the walls are smothered in more frescoes by Giotto, the anonymous "Master of San Francesco," and the leading Sienese artists Simone Martini and Pietro Lorenzetti.

The Lower Church also contains the **tomb of St. Francis,** entered via a stone staircase midway down the nave. This tomb was discovered in 1818 after two months of digging, Francis having been buried in secret to prevent the theft of his body (for holy relics). Francis died in 1226 and was canonized just two years later. Donations from across Europe funded the basilica, an early example of Italian Gothic whose single-naved Upper Church influenced Franciscan and other churches for years to come.

INSIDER TIP:

Walking the hill town's honey-colored streets is the perfect palate cleanser after seeing the colorful frescoes in the Basilica di San Francesco.

—JOHNNA RIZZO
National Geographic author

Walking back from the basilica, detour south to see **San Pietro,** a pleasing 13th-century Romanesque church, and then return to Piazza del Comune either on Via Ancaiani, an atmospheric old street, or the busier Via San Francesco. On the latter, look for the 15th-century **Oratorio dei Pellegrini** at No. 11 *(closed Sun. & 12 p.m.–4 p.m.),* covered in medieval Umbrian frescoes.

From Piazza del Comune, a short walk east brings you to the **Basilica di Santa Chiara** *(closed 12 p.m.–2 p.m., assisisantachiara.it),* burial place of St. Clare (Chiara), Francis's early companion and founder of the Clarissan order of nuns. To the north is the **Duomo** *(closed 12:30 p.m.–2:30 p.m.).* Begun in 1140 over an earlier 1029 base, it has an outstanding Romanesque facade. Farther north rises the **Rocca Maggiore** *($),* the town's partly ruined castle, whose grassy ramparts offer vast views over Assisi and the countryside.

Beyond Assisi

Be sure to visit the **Eremo delle Carceri,** a Franciscan monastery 2 miles (3 km) from the town center. The interior is fascinating—you can see the primitive cell once used by St. Francis—and the lovely surrounding woods offer a pretty network of easy trails. Equally important to pilgrims is **Santa Maria degli Angeli,** a church built over the spot where St. Francis died: It is located in the village of the same name on the plain below Assisi. ■

Basilica di San Francesco

✉ Piazza San Francesco

☎ 075 819 0084

sanfrancesco assisi.org

EXPERIENCE: Monte Subasio's Wildflowers

The slopes of Monte Subasio above Assisi boast a botanical bounty, including orchids by the thousands, swaths of wild narcissi, carpets of wild tulips, and rarities such as snake's head fritillaries. The blooming starts after the snows have melted, with wild crocuses, but visit in May and early June for the real floral fireworks.

The largest numbers of flowers are found on the highest slopes, which you can access by car on the mostly gravel road that runs along much of the length of the mountain between Collepino and Assisi. The mountain is also crisscrossed with marked trails, with maps and information hikes available in stores and visitor centers in Assisi and Spello. In practice, the high slopes are bare and open, and walking directly from the mountain road is straightforward.

If you would like to visit with a botanist, contact the visitor center for lists of accredited guides, or call the local guides' association, **G.A.I.A.** *(tel 334 937 2108, guideassisi.com).* Half-day trips start from €110 ($123). For more information on the park protecting much of Monte Subasio, visit *parks.it.*

A DRIVE INTO THE HEART OF UMBRIA

The lesser known hill towns between Assisi and Spoleto are the highlights of this bucolic drive off Umbria's beaten path.

Forest-clad hills punctuated by tile-roofed towns characterize the heart of Umbria.

Leave Assisi by going east to the **Eremo delle Carceri ❶** (see p. 275), turning left beyond the monastery to follow the road as it climbs through woods to the open slopes of **Monte Subasio ❷**, the whalebacked mountain that rises above town. Much of the road is gravel but sound, but if the weather is poor, you may want to take the main SS75 road from Santa Maria degli Angeli direct to Spello. This is very much a second choice, however, as the Subasio road, which reaches 4,232 feet (1,290 m), offers incredible views and the chance to park and stroll the meadows.

The Subasio road descends to the walled town of **Spello ❸**. Park outside the medieval center and then explore on foot. Before the Roman Porta Consolare is the **Villa dei Mosaici** (*Via P. Schicchi Fagotti 7, closed Mon., hours vary in*

winter, $, villadeimosaicidispello.it), discovered by chance in 2018: 5,400 square feet (500 sq m) of mosaic flooring inside a Roman villa constructed between the first century B.C. and the second A.D. The visit is accompanied by a multimedia reconstruction. Other sights are ranged along the town's main street, beginning at the base of the hill. Farther up the street stands the church of **Santa Maria Maggiore** (*closed 12:30 p.m.–3 p.m., $*), which contains a celebrated **fresco cycle** about the "Life of the Virgin" (1501) by Pinturicchio, one of Umbria's leading Renaissance painters. More works await to the left of the church in the excellent **Pinacoteca Civica** (*Piazza G. Matteotti 10, tel 0742 301 497, closed Mon., hours vary*), while another painting by Pinturicchio stands in the south transept of the church of Sant'Andrea. Climb to the top of the town for excellent views and visit the **Villa Fidelia** (*Via Centrale Umbra, tel 0742 651 726, call for hours*) for its old furniture, sculpture, and costumes.

Take the main SS75 road from Spello toward Foligno, leaving it at the first major junction and following signs to **Bevagna ❹** on the SR316. A former staging post on the Via Flaminia—an important Roman road—Bevagna today is a classic rural backwater centered on **Piazza Filippo Silvestri**, a stunning medieval square. Two lovely 12th-century Romanesque churches face one another across the piazza, San Silvestro and San Michele. Also visit the small **Museo di Bevagna** (*Corso Matteotti 70, tel 0742 360 081, hours vary,*

$), with miscellaneous artifacts. Admission includes a visit to the **Mosaico Romano,** a well-preserved Roman mosaic at Via Porta Guelfa 4, close to the ruins of a classical temple and Roman amphitheater.

Montefalco & Beyond

A scenic road leads south from Bevagna to **Montefalco** ❺ (the name means falcon's mount), testimony to the vast views of the Vale of Spoleto available from the town's hilltop aerie. This is one of the nicest towns around and a good place to stay if you need a base in the region. It is also famous for its red wines, notably Sagrantino and Sagrantino Passito, the latter a dessert wine. Chief sight is the magnificent modern gallery housed in the former church of **San Francesco** (Via Ringhiera Umbra, tel 0742 379 598, $, museodimontefalco.it), a collection of medieval paintings based around a superb 15th-century fresco cycle by Benozzo Gozzoli. More frescoes adorn **Sant'Agostino** (Via Umberto I), **Sant'Illuminata** (Via Verdi), and **San Fortunato,** the last in a pretty setting just off the road leading south out of town.

Turn left at the intersection just beyond San Fortunato and follow signs to the village of **Trevi** ❻, which soon appears high on a spectacular pyramidal hill. The highlight here is the sleek **Raccolta d'Arte di San Francesco** (Via Lucarini, tel 0742 381 628, closed Tues.–Thurs. Nov.–March & 12:30 p.m.–2 p.m., & also Oct. closed Mon.–Wed., $), featuring magnificent Umbrian paintings from different eras and a small adjoining museum devoted to the world of olive oil. After exploring the town, return to the valley and turn south on the SS3 toward Spoleto. Stop off at the **Tempio del Clitunno,** an eighth-century church, and the **Fonti del Clitunno** ❼ ($), limpid pools and springs renowned since classical times. Both

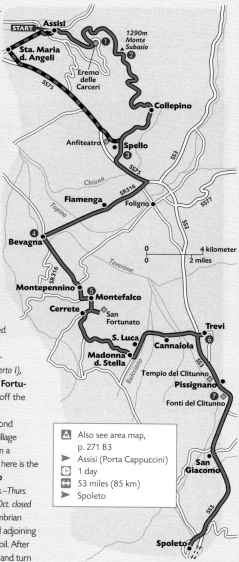

are signposted off the road south of Trevi. From the Fonti, continue south 7 miles (11 km) on the SS3 to Spoleto (see pp. 278–279).

SPOLETO

Spoleto is one of central Italy's most charming towns. Founded by the Umbrians, it subsequently became a major Roman colony and later the capital of a far-reaching Lombard duchy. Today, it is best known for its annual Festival di Spoleto, a renowned arts and music festival, and for the beauty of its cathedral, surrounding countryside, and many Romanesque churches.

■ The 755-foot-long (230 m) Ponte delle Torri carried water from the hills to the Rocca.

Spoleto

⬛ 271 B2

Visitor Information

✉ Largo Ferrer 6 (temporary)

☎ 0743 218 620

🕐 Closed Apr.– Sept. 1:30 p.m.– 3 p.m. Mon.– Sat. & 1 pm.–3 p.m. Sun.; Oct.– March closed 1:30 p.m.–2:30 p.m. Mon.–Sat. & 1 p.m.–3 p.m. Sun.

comune.spoleto.pg.it

spoletocard.it

Pick up a good map from the visitor center and start your visit in **Piazza della Libertà.** Across the square lies the first-century **Teatro Romano,** a Roman theater that is visited in conjunction with Spoleto's modest **Museo Archeologico** (Via Sant'Agata 18a, tel 0743 223 277, $). Walk up from the square through Piazza della Fontana to the church of **Sant'Ansano,** whose crypt contains fragments of a Roman temple and well-preserved Byzantine frescoes. Beyond the church lies the **Arco di Druso,** a Roman arch that opens into **Piazza del Mercato,** site of the former Roman forum.

Pause here to explore the mouthwatering food shops dotting the square. The café with lots of outdoor tables on the west side of the piazza is one of the best places in town to break. Then take the alley to the right of the fountain clock, which passes the **Casa Romana** (Via di Visiale, tel 0743 40255 , closed 1:30 p.m.–2 p.m. & Tues. in winter, $) on the left, part of a first-century Roman house.

Carry on up the cobbled alley beyond the Palazzo Comunale to emerge in Piazza Campello. From here a quiet lane encircles the majestic **Rocca,** home to a superb museum and gallery, the

Museo Nazionale del Ducato
(closed Mon., $, polomusealeumbria
.beniculturali.it), devoted to the art
and history of the town. The lane
offers superb views of the countryside and of the famous 262-
foot-high (80 m) **Ponte delle
Torri.** This medieval engineering
masterpiece was built in the 14th
century and was designed to carry
water from the slopes of Monte-
luco, the forest-covered hill above
Spoleto. You can stroll in the
woods across the bridge—climb
the steps and bear left, and a
lovely level path eventually brings
you to a peaceful olive grove, or
follow the tree-shaded lane to
San Pietro, a church known for
the 12th-century Romanesque
carvings on its facade.

Return to Piazza Campello,
where Via Saffi leads down past
the fan-shaped piazza fronting
Spoleto's idyllic **cathedral** (1198).
The cathedral's apse contains one
of Umbria's major fresco cycles,
"Scenes from the Life of the
Virgin" (1467), by Fra Lippo Lippi.
Other treasures include paintings
by Pinturicchio, one of two surviving letters written by St. Francis,
and a beautiful 12th-century patterned marble floor.

A few steps farther down Via
Saffi, a door opens on a courtyard containing the church of
Sant'Eufemia, a beautifully plain
Romanesque church remarkable
for its matroneum, an upper gallery
once used to segregate women
from the rest of the congregation. Admission to the church is
included in a ticket to the adjacent
Museo Diocesano, left of the
church. The museum's displays

include numerous interesting
medieval paintings from churches
in and around Spoleto, as well as
Tuscan and Sienese works, the
best of which is Filippino Lippi's
"Madonna and Child with Saints"
(1485). Also appealing are the glorious wooden ceilings in many of
the rooms, as well as the sculpture,
which includes a bust of Pope
Urban VIII by Gianlorenzo Bernini.

Lower Town

Three Romanesque churches
make a visit to the largely modern lower town worthwhile. The
easiest to see is **San Gregorio**
in Piazza Garibaldi, while a short
walk east brings you to **San Pon-
ziano,** which has a tremendous
facade and interesting crypt.
Nearby, in the town's main cemetery, stands **San Salvatore,** one
of Italy's oldest churches, whose
fifth-century interior is modeled
on an ancient Roman basilica. ■

Rocca

- ⊠ Piazza Campello 1
- ☎ 0743 223 055
- 🕐 Museum closed Mon.
- 💲 $

Museo Diocesano

- ⊠ Via Aurelio Saffi 13
- ☎ 0743 286 300
- 🕐 Apr.–Oct. closed 1:30 p.m.–2:30 p.m.; Nov.–March closed Mon.– Thurs.
- 💲 $–$$

duomospoleto.it

Festival di Spoleto

**One of Europe's leading arts and cultural
festivals, the Spoleto Festival is widely
known as the Festival dei Due Mondi, or
Festival of Two Worlds. Founded by composer Gian Carlo Menotti (1911–2007),
it came to Spoleto in 1958 after Menotti
chose the town over 30 others, seduced
by its scenery, numerous small venues, and
compelling artistic, historical, and cultural
heritage. The festival attracts top international names in music, opera, theater,
cinema, and other performing arts, as well
as offers many exhibitions, fringe events,
and other cultural activities over some two
weeks, beginning in late June. For more
information, visit festivaldispoleto.it; for
tickets, call 0743 776 444 or visit boxol.it.**

GUBBIO

Beautiful forested mountains frame Gubbio's skyline of towers, battlemented ramparts, and orange-tiled rooftops. Wilder than the bucolic hill towns to the west, this lovely but isolated town has long been remote from the Umbrian mainstream, having marked the limit of Etruscan expansion in the region. Today, it is known for its ceramics and extravagant May pageant.

Gubbio

🗺 271 B3

Visitor Information

✉ Via della Repubblica 15

☎ 075 922 0693

🕐 Closed 1 p.m. –2 p.m.

comune.gubbio.pg.it

Most approaches to Gubbio leave you in Piazza Quaranta Martiri, below the old town proper. Here, step into the church of **San Francesco** to see a series of frescoes (1410) by the Gubbian painter Ottaviano Nelli (left of the high apse). Opposite the church, note the 14th-century **Logge dei Tiratori,** once used for drying wool: The washed cloth dried evenly in the loggia's shade. To its right,

■ Ceramic shops line the streets of Gubbio.

Via della Repubblica climbs to the medieval quarter, culminating in a series of steps that lead to the central **Piazza Grande.**

This broad piazza provides the stage for the **Palazzo dei Consoli,** home to the **Museo Civico** (tel 075 927 4298, closed 1 p.m.–3 p.m., hours vary, $, palazzodeiconsoli.it), a

museum and picture gallery best known for the Eugubine Tablets, a unique series of first- and second-century B.C. bronzes inscribed with Latin and Etruscan characters.

INSIDER TIP:

On the plains below town are the ruins of a small Roman amphitheater rarely visited by locals, and even less so by tourists.

—MATT PROPERT

National Geographic photographer

North of the square are the **Duomo,** interesting for its gracefully arched ceiling, and the **Palazzo Ducale** (Via della Cattedrale 1, tel 075 927 5872, closed Mon. a.m., $), built by Urbino's Federico da Montefeltro, who briefly ruled Gubbio in the 15th century. West of the square, follow Via dei Consoli, watching for its many **Porte della Morte,** or Doors of Death, so-called because they were reputedly bricked up once a coffin had been taken from a house. At the town's southern end, take the funicular (tel 075 927 7507, funiviagubbio.it, $$) up Monte Ingino for wonderful views of the town and the **Basilica di Sant'Ubaldo,** burial place of Gubbio's patron saint. ■

NORCIA & THE VALNERINA

Norcia is a remote, immediately likeable mountain town that is renowned both as the birthplace of St. Benedict, founder of Western monasticism, and as the producer of some of Italy's best hams, salamis, and sausages. The Valnerina is the name given to the nearby valley of the river's main tributaries, a region dotted with tiny fortified villages and Umbria's finest abbey.

The right convergence of winds and mountains make the Monti Sibillini perfect for paragliders.

Norcia's stolid, sturdy air derives mainly from its low buttressed houses and redoubtable walls, both built to resist the earthquakes that periodically shake the region. Of prehistoric origin, the town controlled one of the lowest and thus most important passes across the Apennines, the mountains that divide the Italian peninsula. Today, it is a quietly prosperous place, and it attracts a growing number of visitors, thanks mainly to the **Parco Nazionale dei Monti Sibillini,** a national park that protects the magnificent Sibillini Mountains immediately east of the town.

The town provides an excellent base for exploring the park, the Valnerina, and the timeless pastoral countryside of the Val Castoriana to the north. As well as being a gastronomic center par excellence, with numerous mouthwatering food stores, it is also an interesting historical town. The central **Piazza San Benedetto,** in particular, is a delight, as are its principal buildings: the quaint 15th-century Palazzo Comunale; the 14th-century church of San Benedetto, reputedly built over the 5th-century birthplace of St. Benedict, today heavily damaged by a 2016 earthquake; and the Castellina (1554), a papal fortress that contains a small civic museum and art gallery, **Museo Civico Diocesano.**

Norcia
🗺 271 C2
Visitor Information
✉ Piazza San Benedetto
☎ 0743 828 173
sibillini.net

Museo Civico Diocesano
✉ Piazza San Benedetto
☎ 0743 824 911
🕐 Closed Mon. & 1 p.m.–4 p.m., curtailed winter hours
💲 $

EXPERIENCE: Fly With Eagles

The area around Castelluccio is one of Europe's finest paragliding and hang gliding destinations. This is thanks to the smooth, steep, mostly treeless slopes of the Monti Sibillini, which facilitate landing and takeoff, and to the almost constant winds and perfect thermals produced by the vast bowl of the mountains surrounding the Piano Grande.

It's possible to take a ride into the skies without equipment or previous experience. On a "tourist flight," you ride in tandem on a paraglider with an instructor, enjoying a bird's-eye view of some of central Italy's most spectacular and distinctive scenery: the vast peak of Monte Vettore; the crops, pastures, and flocks of sheep that patchwork the Piano Grande below; and the glorious sweep of the Sibillini range and the Monti della Laga mountains in the hazy distance.

If you want to learn more, contact **Prodelta** *(tel 0743 821 156 or 339 563 5456, prodelta.it),* Italy's national free-flight school, in Castelluccio. In addition to tourist flights (€120/$136), it also offers a five-day introduction to hang gliding or paragliding, with all equipment provided.

Castelluccio

🅰 271 C2

San Pietro in Valle

🅰 271 B2

✉ Signposted from Colleponte

☎ 0744 780 724 or 0744 780 990

🕐 Closed 1 p.m.–3 p.m. (Oct.–March open Sat. & Sun.)

Piano Grande

The Piano Grande—"big plain"—is an unusual and magical landscape. It lies high in the Monti Sibillini about a 40-minute drive from Norcia, its vast, almost eerie expanses ringed by smooth-sloped peaks and overlooked by the wind-battered village of Castelluccio. In spring and summer, wildflowers abound, including peonies, fritillaries, and wild tulips. Glacial in origin, the area was once a huge lake whose lack of a natural outlet meant it dried slowly over the millennia to produce today's almost level plain.

At 4,764 feet (1,452 m), **Castelluccio** is one of Italy's highest continually inhabited settlements, the preserve mainly of shepherds and hang gliders (see sidebar this page). All manner of superb hikes are possible locally, including a straightforward ascent of **Monte Vettore,** the highest point at 8,123 feet (2,476 m) in the Monti Sibillini. You can pick up good maps from stores in Norcia or in Castelluccio.

Valnerina

The best parts of the Valnerina can be seen by driving north from Norcia along the Val Castoriana to Preci, with a detour at Piedivalle to see the Benedictine abbey of **Sant'Eutizio.** From Preci, follow the SP476 road southwest along the river. Several diversions are possible, all of which will take you into glorious countryside. One excellent circuit would be to turn off the main road at Borgo Cerreto toward Monteleone di Spoleto, dropping back to the Valnerina shortly after Poggiodomo via Gavelli and Caso.

The valley boasts many fortified villages, built because this was a vital trade route from the mountains—**Scheggino** and **Vallo di Nera** are the best. The valley's most famous sight, however, is the picturesque **San Pietro in Valle,** an eighth-century abbey founded by the Lombard dukes of Spoleto. It has an important 12th-century fresco cycle, several Roman remains, and a rare Lombard altar from 739. ∎

TODI

Once a sleepy agricultural backwater, Todi has long since been discovered by expatriate incomers, although the influx of outsiders has done little to dent the charm of a hill town that has just about everything: a magnificent location, a history that goes back to Etruscan times, art and culture to spare, picturesque streets, and views that seem to stretch across half of Umbria.

Start in **Piazza del Popolo,** often described as Italy's most perfect medieval piazza. The **Duomo** (*closed 12:30 p.m.–3 p.m.*) dominates its northern end, begun in the 12th century over a temple to Apollo. Fragments from this earlier building can be seen inside in the crypt, while in the church's main body the principal attraction is an inlaid

■ The setting sun casts a warm glow over the hill town of Todi.

INSIDER TIP:

See a performance in the World's Smallest Theater (*teatropiccolo.it*) in nearby Monte Castello di Vibio.

—CAROLINE HICKEY
National Geographic contributor

wooden choir (1521–1530). Three 13th-century palaces guard the piazza, one of which, the Palazzo Comunale, houses the superb **Museo Pinacoteca,** a modern space with a wide range of exhibits and a glorious painting depicting the "Coronation of the Virgin" (1511) by Lo Spagna.

As you explore around the Duomo, note the three separate sets of walls—the town's Etruscan, Roman, and medieval limits. Head south from the piazza and you come to the grandiose

Romanesque-Gothic church of **San Fortunato** (*closed 1 p.m.–3 p.m., campanile $*). Its undoubted masterpiece is a fresco (1432) in the fourth chapel off the south aisle by Masolino da Panicale.

Enter Todi's public gardens, passing the stump of the medieval castle. Walk through the gardens and down the snaking footpath at their far end to emerge in front of **Santa Maria della Consolazione** (1508–1607; *closed Tues. & 12:30 p.m.–2:30 p.m.*), among Italy's finest Renaissance churches. A land art operation will connect it to the city's historical center: The **Beverly Pepper Park,** designed by the New York artist, populated with her sculptures, is opening in 2019. ■

Todi

◭ 271 B2

Visitor Information

✉ Via del Monte 23

☎ 075 895 6529

🕓 Closed Sun. & 1 p.m.–3:30 p.m.

visitodi.eu

Museo Pinacoteca

✉ Palazzo Comunale, Piazza del Popolo

☎ 075 894 4148 or 848 004 000

🕓 Closed Mon., Tues. & Fri. p.m. (Oct.–March Mon.–Thurs. & 1 p.m.–2 Sat.-Sun. p.m.)

💲 $

coopculture.it

ORVIETO

Orvieto enjoys the most spectacular location in Umbria, spread across a soaring cliff-edged plateau of volcanic rock. Its site attracted the Etruscans, who made this one of their most important cities, but its real fame dates from 1263, the year of a religious miracle that saw the founding of the town's famous cathedral, Orvieto's glorious and undoubted main attraction.

Try to approach Orvieto on the scenic **funicular** from the railroad station in Orvieto Scalo, the modern town on the plain. This drops you in **Piazzale Cahen,** where you should visit

■ A total of 33 architects, 152 sculptors, 68 painters, and 90 mosaicists worked on the facade of Orvieto cathedral.

the ruined medieval fortress, the public gardens—built over the site of a former Etruscan temple—and the extraordinary **Pozzo di San Patrizio** *(Viale Sangallo, tel 0763 343 768, $)*. The latter is a well, commissioned by Pope Clement VIII in 1527 to provide the town with water in the event of a siege. Two 248-step staircases allow you to drop into the structure's dank, dark bowels. Ten minutes' pleasant walk on Corso Cavour from Piazzale Cahen brings you to the heart of the old town.

Orvieto's Old Town

No visit to Umbria is complete without a visit to the **Duomo** *(opsm.it, closed Sun. a.m., $)*, described by Pope Leo XIII as the "Golden Lily of Italian cathedrals." It was inspired by the Miracle of Bolsena (1263), in which blood is said to have dripped from a consecrated host during Mass in the nearby village of Bolsena. The Romanesque-Gothic building is distinguished by the most elaborately decorated **facade** in all of Italy. All manner of detail dazzles the eye, the most accomplished being the four Sienese bas-reliefs flanking the doors at ground level, one of the masterpieces of 14th-century Italian sculpture.

Inside, the cathedral's apparent sobriety is belied by two heavily frescoed side chapels. On the left

---

INSIDER TIP:

Should you decide to descend into the depths of the well of Pozzo di San Partizio, bring a sweater.

—MARGARET ROBERTS
*National Geographic
contributor*

(north) side is the **Cappella del Corporale,** which sports a rich casket (1358) encasing the *corporale* (altar cloth) spotted with blood during the miracle of Bolsena. Its walls are blanketed in frescoes (1357–1364) by Ugolino di Prete Ilario, recalling episodes from the miracle and assorted miracles of the Sacrament. The **Cappella di San Brizio,** or Cappella Nuova, opposite, holds the even more important fresco cycle (1499–1504) of the "Last Judgment" by the Tuscan artist Luca Signorelli, one of Italy's great pictorial works. In March 2019, Francesco Mochi's two

Annunciation statues (1603–1608) were reintroduced as part of the cathedral's decorative treasures. They had been "exiled" more than two centuries ago because they were considered too sensual.

Opposite the cathedral are the **Museo Claudio Faina** and **Museo Civico,** with a variety of Etruscan and other archaeological artifacts. Etruscan fans should also make time to visit the **Necropoli Etrusca del Crocefisso del Tufo** *(tel 0763 343 611, closed Mon.–Tues., $),* an intriguing series of stone burial chambers a mile (1.6 km) outside town on the SS71 road to Orvieto Scalo. More artistic and archaeological finds are displayed in the **Museo dell'Opera del Duomo** *(Piazza del Duomo, tel 0763 342 477, closed Tues., $, museomodo .it),* alongside the cathedral.

Elsewhere in town, visit the tiny church of **San Lorenzo** on Via Ippolito Scalza, the larger **Sant'Andrea** in the main Piazza della Repubblica, and **San Gio-venale,** with medieval frescoes. ∎

Orvieto

🗺 271 A2

Visitor Information

✉ Piazza del Duomo 24

☎ 0763 341 772

🕐 Closed 1:50 p.m.–4 p.m. Mon.–Fri., 1 p.m.–3 p.m. Sat.–Sun.

inorvieto.it

Museo Claudio Faina & Museo Civico

✉ Palazzo Faina, Piazza del Duomo 29

☎ 0763 341 511

🕐 Closed Mon. Nov.–March

💲 $

museofaina.it

Orvieto Underground

Honeycombed into the soft tufa *rupe,* or rock, on which Orvieto stands is an extraordinary labyrinth of caves, cisterns, cellars, tunnels, quarries, aqueducts, storage areas, and passages that has been used and added to since Etruscan and Roman times. At least 1,200 separate caves have been identified, one-third of the entire area beneath the town having been infiltrated over the years. Much of the material removed from below ground was used to build Orvieto or mined to produce pozzolana, used to make mortar.

You can visit part of this strange world with **Orvieto Underground** *(Piazza del Duomo 23, tel 0763 344 891 or 347 383 1472, orvietounderground.it),* which offers guided one-hour tours *($)* that provide historical and archaeological background and take in Etruscan-era caves, two vast 130-foot-deep (39.5 m) Etruscan well shafts, part of an ancient pozzolana quarry, and the remains of an old olive press. Longer and more varied themed workshops are available *($$).* Tours run daily, at least four times a day, also in English.

More Places to Visit in Umbria

Amelia

Amelia lies amid gorgeous pastoral countryside in southern Umbria behind some of Italy's most redoubtable walls, parts of which date from the fifth century B.C. Four gates penetrate the defenses, including the main Porta Romana, from which medieval streets climb to Piazza Marconi, site of the much-altered, yet fascinating, Romanesque Duomo and distinctive 12-sided 11th-century tower.

The main sights are **Roman cisterns** beneath Piazza Matteotti and the Museo Archeologico (*Piazza Augusto Vera 10, tel 0744 978 120, closed Mon.–Thurs./Fri. & 1 p.m.–3:30 p.m., $*), noted for its bronze of Germanicus, father of Caligula. Amelia's other pleasures—like those of similar hill towns—are views, peace and quiet, and the charm of sleepy medieval streets.

turismoamelia.it 🗺 271 B1 **Visitor Information** ✉ Piazza Matteotti 1 ☎ 0744 981 453 🕐 Closed 12:30/1 p.m.–3:30 p.m. & Sun. p.m. July–Aug.; 1 p.m.–3:30 p.m., Sat. p.m., & Sun. Sept.–June

Città di Castello

Città di Castello, slightly isolated in the north of Umbria, is a pleasing and provincial old town, the gridiron plan of its medieval streets a monument to its Roman builders.

The main sight is the **Pinacoteca Comunale** (*Palazzo Vitelli, Via della Cannoniera 22a, tel 075 554 202, closed Mon. & 1 p.m.–2:30/3 p.m., $*), notable for Umbria's only painting wholly by Raphael. Also noteworthy are the **Duomo** and its fabulous museum (*Piazza Gabriotti 3a, tel 075 855 4705, closed Mon. except in Aug. & 12:30/1 p.m.–3 p.m., $*), filled with paintings, silverware, and several other exhibits.

cittadicastelloturismo.it 🗺 271 A4 **Visitor Information** ✉ Corso Cavour 5 ☎ 075 855 4922 🕐 Closed 1:30 p.m.–3 p.m. Mon.–Fri., 12:30 p.m.–3 p.m. Sat. & Sun. p.m.

Deruta

Deruta is a modest hill town set between Todi and Perugia with one claim to fame—its ceramics. Romans worked the local clay here, but it was the discovery of startling new yellow and blue glazes in the 15th century that put the town firmly on the map. The craft continues to this day. The roadsides are lined with workshops and stalls selling pottery in a multitude of shapes, sizes, and designs. The old town contains an interesting museum devoted to the town's specialty, the **Museo Regionale della Ceramica** (*Largo San Francesco, tel 075 971 1000, closed Mon.–Tues. Oct.–July; 1 p.m.–2:30 p.m. Oct.–March; & 1 p.m.–3 p.m. April–Sept., $*).

🗺 271 B2–B3 **Visitor Information** ✉ Piazza dei Consoli 4 (summer only) ☎ 0759 971 1559 🕐 Closed Mon. & 12:30 p.m.–3 p.m.

INSIDER TIP:

When in Umbria, be sure to try the delicious regional specialty *salame di cinghiale* (wild boar salami).

—JANE SUNDERLAND
National Geographic contributor

Narni

Most Umbrian towns and villages hold some appeal for the traveler, and hilltop Narni is no exception. There are no great set pieces, but the evocative fortress, an age-old cathedral, a good museum, a Romanesque church, and medieval nooks warrant an hour or two of aimless roaming.

turismonarni.it 🗺 271 B1 **Visitor Information** ✉ Piazza dei Priori 2 ☎ 0744 715 362 🕐 Closed Sat. p.m. & 12:30 p.m.–4:30 p.m.

A landscape peppered with active volcanoes, sublime coastal scenery, rugged mountains, and historic cities such as Naples and Lecce

THE SOUTH

■ Painted tiles depicting the Amalfi
Coast near Praiano

THE SOUTH

Southern Italy is another country, a land separated from the rest of Italy by history, geography, and economics, a world apart that is poorer, wilder, more backward, and more rooted in tradition than its northern counterpart. Yet the South can be hugely rewarding to visit.

The South, the so-called Mezzogiorno, or land of the midday sun, comes closest to resembling that fabled phenomenon, "the real Italy"—or at least the real Italy that many outsiders, ignorant of the country's modern élan, would like to imagine. Clichéd Latin vignettes still prevail—the black-clad peasant woman, the washing hung across streets—as do the classic passions of food, family, soccer, love, and religion. Poverty, crime, and other social ills may be amplified here, particularly in the cities, but so, too, by and large, are the Old World ideals of honor and hospitality.

The region's particular character has been variously molded. Geographically, it is forever isolated, far from markets and the prospect of industrial salvation. Climatically, it bakes under a hot sun, a blight to agricultural initiative.

Geologically, its soils are poor. Socially, its countryside has been desiccated by emigration. Historically, it has been endlessly conquered. And for centuries it remained in thrall to feudal tradition and the deadening hand of Spanish rule, twin afflictions that led to social, economic, and agricultural stagnation that lingers to this day.

Highlights of the South

At its most basic, the area consists of five regions—the Abruzzo, Campania, Calabria, Basilicata, and Puglia—although precisely where the South starts is a matter of debate. The Milanese will tell you Florence, the Florentines say Rome, while the Romans point to the first gas station south of Rome.

Wherever the border, by the time you reach Naples, the region's capital, there is no doubt that a threshold of some sort has been crossed. Chaotic, noisy, and ebullient, this is one of the most Italian of cities, a microcosm of all that is good and bad in the South. Many people brave its mayhem and admire its many sights as they head for two great archaeological sites to the south, Pompeii and Herculaneum, Roman settlements eerily preserved by an eruption of Mount Vesuvius, the still active volcano that broods over Naples and its surroundings. A little to the south stretches the fabled Amalfi Coast, Italy's most beautiful stretch of coastline, and the idyllic island retreats of Capri and Ischia.

NOT TO BE MISSED:

Eating a pizza margherita in Naples, where it was invented 290

The exhibits of Naples's Museo Archeologico Nazionale 291

Ascending Mount Vesuvius 295

The ruins at Herculaneum and Pompeii 295–297

The views from Ravello on the Amalfi Coast 300–301

Hiking in wolf country in the Abruzzo mountains 305

Staying in one of the unique *trulli* dwellings of Puglia 306–307

The Abruzzo is more remote and introspective, and blessed with exceptional mountain scenery, some of the best of which is protected by the Parco Nazionale d'Abruzzo, Lazio e Molise. To the south stretches Puglia, the heel of the Italian "boot," a long, narrow region whose endless plains and rolling hills are redeemed by the coast and countryside of the Gargano, the boot's spur. Lecce, a city-size shrine to the baroque, is the best of the big urban targets, while smaller centers are graced with Romanesque churches. The most unusual sights are the *trulli*, strange conical dwellings unique to the region. Few first-time visitors linger in Basilicata, the boot's instep, or in Calabria, its toe, although their empty, mountainous interiors are unspoiled, their coastlines, in places, a perfect place to rest en route to Sicily. ∎

BAY OF NAPLES

The Bay of Naples—Golfo di Napoli—has much to offer. Naples, the south's largest city, sprawls along the coast with myriad attractions. Nearby, Pompeii and Herculaneum preserve a slice of Roman life, buried under tons of ash in A.D. 79, courtesy of the still active Mount Vesuvius. In the bay, the island jewels of Capri and Ischia lure visitors with glorious sea views and pretty villages.

■ Naples's Duomo, built in the shape of a Latin cross, has a lavish baroque interior.

Naples

Set on a peerless bay and backed by Vesuvius's distinctive volcanic profile, Naples (Napoli) has been celebrated by poets and painters since classical times as one of the most beautiful and blessed places on Earth. Crime, poverty, pollution, and traffic chaos have all taken their toll on the city, but progress has now been made on several fronts, and today this most vibrant and Italian of cities is becoming more amenable.

This edge and character, of course, are also the city's most distinctive features. Naples is so Italian as to be almost clichéd—a city of pizza, opera, bustling markets, soccer, religion, Sophia Loren (born nearby), family, crime, and the sort of washing-hung streets used as visual shorthand for Italy in countless movies. Few places bring you quite so close to the teeming realities of life in the Italian south, and few people are quite as exuberant, sharp, fatalistic, and fiercely individual as the Neapolitans.

The vibrancy of Naples's streets and citizens is matched by a huge artistic and archaeological patrimony, the result of its at least 3,000-year-long history and a succession of rulers and settlers that included the Greeks, Romans, Normans, Germans, French, Aragonese, Spanish, and Bourbons.

A good plan of attack is to visit the Museo Archeologico Nazionale, one of Europe's preeminent archaeological museums and a city's must-see sight. Then walk south through the most atmospheric part of the old city, **Spaccanapoli** (meaning split Naples), the area around Via Tribunali and Via Benedetto Croce. Then continue south to arrive at the sights close to the port and waterfront. If time allows, you could also visit two outlying attractions: the Certosa di San Martino and the Palazzo Reale di Capodimonte.

Museo Archeologico Nazionale: This archaeology museum and its collection of Greek and Roman antiquities, many of them recovered from Pompeii and Herculaneum, is stunning. The basement is home to a collection of Egyptian artifacts and Roman epigraphs of extraordinary artistic and documentary value, while the ground floor is devoted primarily to sculpture, with most of the highlights in the first 15 of the floor's 49 rooms. Of particular note are statues of Athena, Harmodius and Aristogeiton, Aphrodite, and the much praised Doryphorus,

or javelin thrower. More striking still are the "Farnese Hercules," the museum's finest statue, and the "Farnese Bull," the largest surviving sculpture from the ancient world. Much of the mezzanine is devoted to fabulous mosaics from Pompeii, the right side to exhibits connected with Naples's early history.

Farther treasures grace the first floor, among them the **Sale della Villa dei Papiri,** given over to papyrus, statues, and other exhibits from the Villa dei Papiri at Herculaneum. Equally absorbing are the **Sala degli Affreschi,** with wall paintings removed from Pompeii, Herculaneum, and elsewhere, and the recent section dedicated to oriental religions in Campania. It includes the famous **Sala del Tempio di Iside,** where part of Pompeii's Temple of Isis has been re-created and filled with artifacts from the original temple and the model of the city of Pompeii from the 1800s.

The Duomo & Other Churches: Wend east to the **Duomo,** known for the relics of San Gennaro, the fourth-century martyr and city's protector. The saint's chapel contains a vial of

Naples
🅰 288 B4
Visitor Information
✉ Piazza del Gesù 7
☎ 081 551 2701
🕘 Closed Sun. p.m.

✉ Via San Carlo 9
☎ 081 402 394
🕘 Closed Sun. p.m.
inaples.it
ecampania.it

Museo Archeologico Nazionale
✉ Piazza Museo Nazionale 19
☎ 081 442 2328
🕘 Closed Tues.
💲 $$; tickets also at coopculture.it
museoarcheologico napoli.it

Duomo
✉ Via del Duomo 147
☎ 081 449 097
🕘 Closed Mon.–Sat. 12:30 p.m.–4:30 p.m. & Sun. 1:30 p.m.–5 p.m.
💲 Archaeological zone & baptistery $

What Lies Beneath

One of southern Italy's most memorable excursions involves exploring the ancient tunnels, cellars, and sewers that riddle subterranean Naples, or **Napoli Sotteranea** *(Piazza San Gaetano 68, tel 081 296 944, napolisotterranea.org).* Some tunnels date back to Greek times but have been extended throughout history for storage, drainage, and similar purposes. The **Stazioni dell'Arte** offers an alternative underground itinerary where 15 stations of the city's subway display over 200 works and installations of art and architecture by both well-known names and young emerging artists *(infoarte@anm.it, anm.it, guided $).*

NOTE: The **Campania Artecard** is valid for 3 days ($$$$, campaniarte card.it). With it, admission to many sites in the region is free or discounted.

San Giovanni a Carbonara

✉ Via Carbonara 5

blood that is paraded yearly (see sidebar opposite)—failure of the blood to liquefy during the ceremony bodes ill for the city. Also see the saint's Renaissance tomb and remnants of the palaeo-Christian basilica of Santa Restituta, rebuilt after an earthquake in the 17th century, home to the **Battistero di San Giovanni in Fonte,** considered the oldest in Western Europe.

The monumental complex of **Donnaregina** (Vico Donnaregina 26, tel 081 299 101, closed Tue., $), just to the north, has Tino da Camaino's "Tomb of Mary of Hungary" (1326) and early 14th-century frescoes by Roman painter Pietro Cavallini. A short walk north, **San Giovanni a Carbonara** is known for Andrea da Firenze's 1414 "Tomb of King Ladislas of Naples."

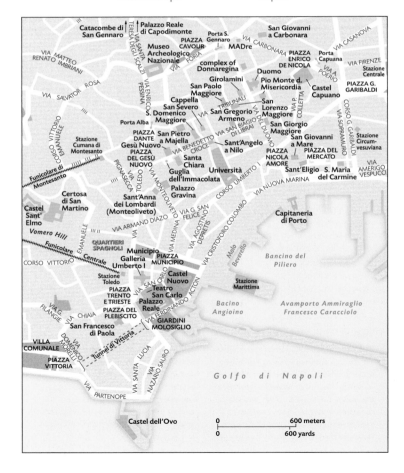

EXPERIENCE: The Festa di San Gennaro

Little is known of San Gennaro, or St. Januarius. He was probably born in Benevento, in southern Italy, and martyred during the persecutions of Diocletian at the end of the third century. His relics came to Naples's cathedral in 1497, where they became the source of numerous miracles.

You will need to book hotels early if you want to attend one of the three occasions—the first Saturday in May, September 19, and December 16—on which the saint's blood is displayed, especially on September 19. It is difficult to get into the Duomo itself for the ceremony, but events are usually broadcast on screens outside. Even if you are not inside, the whole city has a febrile atmosphere that makes these days great times to visit.

West of the Duomo stands Gothic **San Lorenzo Maggiore,** distinguished by Tino di Camaino's "Tomb of Catherine of Austria" (1323), to the right of the high altar, as well as by an underground itinerary through Greco-Romano ruins. On the same street, the **Pio Monte della Misericordia** church houses Caravaggio's majestic "Seven Acts of Mercy" (1607). To the south rises **San Gregorio Armeno** (*Via San Gregorio Armeno 1, tel 081 552 0186, closed p.m.*), one of the most opulent of Naples's myriad baroque churches.

Farther west is **San Domenico Maggiore** (*Piazza San Domenico 8a, tel 081 459 298, closed 12 p.m.– 5 p.m.*), worth visiting for its funerary sculpture. Across the square, **Sant'Angelo a Nilo** (*Piazzetta Nilo 23, tel 081 211 0860, closed 1 p.m.– 4:30 p.m. & Sun. p.m.*) contains the "Tomb of Cardinal Bracciano" by Michelozzo (1428). Just off the piazza stands the impressive **Museo Cappella San Severo,** also celebrated for its sculpture, in particular Giuseppe Sammartino's virtuoso "Veiled Christ" (1753) above the altar. The district's rich collection of churches continues on the street to the north, where

San Pietro a Majella (*Piazza Luigi Miraglia 393, tel 081 459 008, closed Sun. p.m.*) has a 17th-century painting cycle by Mattia Preti. **Santa Chiara** has three 14th-century royal tombs by Tino da Camaino and other Florentine sculptors, as well as a pretty cloister from the 1300s covered in majolica from the 1700s and with an Italian-style garden full of Mediterranean essences.

South & North of Naples's

Center: Explore south by taking Calata Trinità Maggiore from near Santa Chiara, being sure to see the church of **Monteoliveto,** begun in 1411, with more exemplary Florentine tombs and sculptures. Then visit the teeming **Quartiere Spagnoli** west of Via Toledo, full of archetypal Neopolitan street scenes, or continue to the waterfront and **Piazza del Plebiscito.** The latter is dominated by **San Francesco di Paola,** a neoclassical church modeled on Rome's Pantheon, and by the **Palazzo Reale** (*Piazza del Plebiscito 1, tel 848 800 288, closed Wed., $, polomusealecampania .beniculturali.it,)*, a 17th-century Spanish palace with lavish royal

San Lorenzo Maggiore

- ⊠ Piazzetta San Gaetano
- ☎ 081 211 0860
- 🕐 May close at lunch
- 💲 Excavations $$

laneapolissotterrata.it

Pio Monte delle Misericordia

- ⊠ Via dei Tribunali

Museo Cappella San Severo

- ⊠ Via de Sanctis 19
- ☎ 081 551 8470
- 🕐 Closed Tues.
- 💲 $

museosansevero.it

Santa Chiara

- ⊠ Via Santa Chiara 49
- ☎ 081 552 6280
- 🕐 Closed Sun. p.m.
- 💲 $

monasterodisanta chiara.it

Monteoliveto

- ⊠ Piazza Monteoliveto 44
- ☎ 081 551 3333
- 🕐 Closed 12:30 p.m.–4:30 p.m. & Sun. p.m.

Museo & Real Bosco di Capodimonte

- ✉ Via Miano 2
- ☎ 081 749 9130
- 🕐 Closed Wed.
- 💲 $$, or Campania Artecard; garden free
- 🚌 A shuttle leaves every hour from Piazza Trieste e Trento (tickets for travel only or travel with admission)

museocapodimonte .beniculturali.it

apartments. On the palace's northern flank stands the **Teatro San Carlo** (1737), one of Italy's leading opera houses. From here, Via San Carlo leads to the **Castel Nuovo,** or Maschio Angioino, *(Piazza Municipio, tel 081 795 7722, closed Sun., $),* built for Charles of Anjou in 1279. Its ramparts, offset by the delicacy of a lovely entrance arch (1454–1467), conceal several grand salons and a civic museum.

North of the center are the **Museo and Real Bosco di Capodimonte,** Naples's key attractions

Rome, Florence, and Venice. Virtually all the great names of Italian art are represented, with particularly outstanding works by Titian, Raphael, Michelangelo, Botticelli, Masolino, and Giovanni Bellini. The palace also stands at the heart of a magnificent historical park.

Outside Naples: The gargantuan Carthusian monastery (Certosa) of **San Martino** and the neighboring 14th-century **Castel Sant'Elmo** overlook Naples from a hilly spur west of the city. Both are worth a visit,

■ A sea of lights at night, Naples lives restively under the active volcano Mount Vesuvius.

Museo Nazionale di San Martino

- ✉ Largo di San Martino 5
- ☎ 081 229 4589
- 🕐 Closed Wed.
- 💲 $$

polomusealecampania .beniculturali.it

after the archaeological museum. Begun by the Bourbons as a hunting lodge in 1738, its interior is divided between a picture gallery, a series of former royal apartments, and a top floor display of contemporary art. Of these, the picture gallery is by far the most compelling, its collection on a par with those of more famous galleries in

but the Certosa also hosts the 90-room **Museo Nazionale di San Martino,** a wide-ranging collection best known for its figurines and Neapolitan *presepi,* or Christmas cribs. The Certosa's most memorable sight is the conventual church, one of Naples's most pleasing baroque creations.

Ascending Vesuvius

The easiest way to the 4,189-foot (1,277 m) summit of Vesuvius is to book a package ($$$$) at the *circumvesuviana* desk at Napoli Centrale rail station (includes train to Ercolano Pompeii Scavi and bus to volcano). Wear sturdy shoes for the 20-minute hike to the crater ($$).

Vesuvius

Italy has higher and more active volcanoes—notably Sicily's Mount Etna—but none as notorious as Vesuvius (Vesuvio), whose catastrophic eruption in A.D. 79 famously buried and preserved the Roman towns of Pompeii and Herculaneum. Today, the volcano is dormant—for the time being at least (another eruption is overdue)—and can be admired by visitors either as a backdrop to the Bay of Naples or from the closer proximity of its crater's edge.

People living on the Bay of Naples in the first century B.C. knew all was not well with Vesuvius. An earthquake in A.D. 63, 16 years before the fateful eruption, had ravaged the region and given fair warning of the forces gathering subterranean strength.

More immediate warning was issued in the days before the catastrophe, when the volcano began to smoke and rumble, a warning at first ignored by the populace—the volcano, after all, had not erupted in recorded memory. On August 24, A.D. 79, it more than lived up to its name.

On that morning, the cone's ancient basalt plug collapsed. Gas, pumice, and other debris were released with explosive force, a vast cloud blotting out the sky. Two days passed before light returned to the region. Pompeii was buried by dust and cinders within hours.

The 2,000 inhabitants who had not fled were asphyxiated by superheated gases. By evening, the volcano's inner walls had also collapsed, unleashing further destruction, including the torrent of boiling volcanic mud that engulfed Herculaneum. The most recent eruption was in 1944—another is just a matter of time.

Herculaneum

In A.D. 79, Herculaneum (Ercolano) was engulfed by the same eruption that devastated nearby Pompeii. But whereas Pompeii was a thriving commercial town, Herculaneum was an exclusive residential district, built to exploit the site's cooling breezes and far-reaching views. Like Pompeii, it remained entombed until the 18th century, and remains only half-excavated today. Where it differs from Pompeii is in its more modest and manageable size. You should allow about two hours for the site.

Beyond the entrance, an avenue passes through the ruins of the **Palestra,** or gymnasium. Nearby are the **Casa dell'Atrio a Mosaico,** which still boasts its mosaic pavements, and just

Vesuvius
🌋 289 B4
Visitor Information
☎ 081 239 5653
parconazionale delvesuvio.it

Herculaneum ruins
✉ Corso Resina 6, Herculaneum
☎ 081 777 7008
💲 $$ or Campania Artecard
ercolano. beniculturali.it

NOTE: The range of different buildings, and their generally superior state of preservation, make Herculaneum the better site to visit if time constraints force you to choose between Pompeii and Herculaneum.

Pompeii

289 B4

Visitor Information

✉ Via Sacra 1

☎ 081 850 7255

🕐 Closed Sat. p.m. & Sun.

Pompeii ruins

✉ Entrances at Piazza Porta Marina, Piazza Esedra, and Piazza Anfiteatro

☎ 081 857 5347

💲 $$ or Campania Artecard

pompeiisites.org

NOTE: Tickets are available for just Pompeii (*$$*) or for Pompeii and two other archaeological sites: Oplontis and Boscoreale (*$$$*).

beyond it on the left the **Casa a Graticcio** (House of the Wooden Trellis) and **Casa del Tramezzo di Legno** (House of the Wooden Partition). Beyond the latter, at the town's major intersection, stands a former dyer's shop (at No. 10), known for its superbly preserved wooden clothespress.

Across the street stretch the ruins of the **Terme,** or baths. The plan of the **Casa Sannitica** opposite is typical of simpler dwellings built by the Sannites, a local Italic tribe absorbed by the Romans. Next door is an old weaver's shop, and a couple of doors down the wonderful **Casa del Mosaico di Nettuno e Anfitrite,** noted both for its shop and the blue-green mosaic adorning its rear living quarters. Other outstanding structures include the **Casa del Bel Cortile** (House of the Beautiful Courtyard), the **Pistrinum,** a bakery complete with oven and flour mills, and the **Casa dei Cervi** (House of the Deer), the most sumptuous house in Herculaneum.

Pompeii

But for one of history's most famous cataclysms, Pompeii (Pompei in Italian) would have been one more minor Roman colony lost to the ravages of time. Instead, it was preserved for posterity by the eruption of Vesuvius in A.D. 79, when it and many of its inhabitants were buried beneath a mountain of volcanic debris. There they remained until the 18th century, when the study of old texts suggested Pompeii's existence.

Nowhere in Italy so vividly evokes the reality of the Roman world as Pompeii. "Nothing is wanting but the inhabitants," wrote the diarist Henry Matthews in 1820, adding that "a morning's walk through the solemn streets of Pompeii will give you a livelier idea of their modes of life than all the books in the world."

The main entrance for visitors is the old **Porta Marina,** on the site's seaward (western) flank. Exploring the huge site—Pompeii had a population of around 25,000—requires some forethought. Of the estimated 163 acres (66 ha) of surface, approximately 123 (50 ha) have been uncovered. Set off early and be prepared for the crowds, for this is one of southern Italy's most popular excursions. Note, too, that it is worth seeing the town in conjunction with Naples's Museo Archeologico Nazionale (see p. 291), which houses many of the objects removed from the site over the years. Make for the highlights first, and don't become bogged down with the lesser streets, where one small house soon looks much like another.

Just beyond the entrance, you come to the town's old **forum,** ringed by many of the site's most imposing civic structures: the Santuario di Apollo, Tempio di Giove, and the Basilica, Pompeii's largest building. To the north lie the site's most famous houses: the **Casa del Fauno** and **Casa dei Vettii.** The latter is particularly interesting. Once the property of rich merchant brothers, its painted friezes are some of the finest of

The ancient Roman city of Pompeii preserves a variety of public and private buildings.

their kind. Among the scenes is a mural of a famously rampant Priapus, one of many phallic representations around the site (most probably representing superstitious attempts to ward off the evil eye).

Another well-preserved house, the **Casa degli Amorini Dorati,** lies just to the east, while to the west you should hunt out the **Casa del Poeta Tragico,** known for its famous mosaic and graffiti—*"Cave canem"* ("Beware of the dog"). Some distance out to the west, through the Porta Ercolano, a tomb- and cypress-lined lane (Via delle Tombe) leads to a pair of villas, the **Villa di Diomede** and the **Villa dei Misteri.** Return to the forum and then head east on Via dell'Abbondanza, formerly a busy commercial street, to reach the rest of the site. Off to the right after a short distance (on Via dei Teatri) are the **Teatro Grande,** a 5,000-seat open-air theater, and the smaller 800-seat Teatro Piccolo, or **Odeon,** the name given to a smaller covered theater. Two blocks north, on the

corner with Vicolo del Lupanare, stretch the ruins of the **Terme Stabiane,** the town's main bath complex. At the end of Vicolo del Lupanare, once a thriving red-light district, is another visitors' favorite—a small brothel complete with bed stalls and frescoes illustrating the various services available.

Continuing down Via dell'Abbondanza, a right turn takes you to the **Casa del Menandro,** another outstanding patrician house adorned with mosaics and wall paintings; currently being reconstructed, it is visible only from the outside. On the opposite side of Via del Menandro is the **Casa dei Ceii,** which reopened to the public in 2018 with its splendid, Egypt-inspired murals. Two more fine houses, both with beautiful gardens, lie on the right toward the end of Via dell'Abbondanza, the **Casa di Octavius Quartius** and **Praedia di Giulia Felice.** Closing the eastern end of the site is the **Anfiteatro,** one of the oldest (80 B.C.) and best preserved Roman amphitheaters in existence.

Capri

 288 B4

Visitor Information

✉ Piazza
   Umberto I,
   Capri Town

☎ 081 837 0634

⏰ Closed 1:30
   p.m.–3:30 p.m.
   & Sun. p.m.

capritourism.com

Capri

Beauty in Italy often exists side by side with ugliness. Nowhere is the juxtaposition more marked than off the Neapolitan coast, where Naples's often hellish urban environs give way to the idyllic island havens of Capri and Ischia (see page opposite). A luxury playground of the first rank, Capri has long been a sybaritic retreat for emperors, artists, writers, and the international jet set.

The charms of Capri have been enjoyed since earliest times. The emperor Augustus called the city Apragopolis, the City of Sweet Idleness, a fitting epithet for a retreat that has become a byword for decadent self-indulgence. Today, hordes of day-trippers flood to the island—which measures a mere 2 miles (3 km) by 4 miles (6 km)—to enjoy its balmy climate, its rugged coastline, its whitewashed villages, and the almost subtropical lushness of its gardens and hilly interior.

Regular boats and hydrofoils from Naples and Sorrento dock at **Marina Grande,** the island's colorful main port and the point of departure for boat trips around the island. Such trips are an essential part of the Capri experience, offering a firsthand glimpse of the coast's jumble of cliffs, bays, caves, and rocky sea stacks. Beware the separate trips to the famous but overrated **Blue Grotto** (Grotta Azzurra), which can be extortionate.

From Marina Grande a funicular climbs to **Capri,** the island's pretty main village, centered on the fashionable Piazza Umberto I. Surrounding streets are lined with cafés, souvenir stores, and chic boutiques, but quieter corners are easily found—try following Via Madre Serafina south to the

■ The church floor of San Michele in Anacapri is made up of more than 2,500 hand-painted tiles.

EXPERIENCE: Hikes on Capri

One of the loveliest ways to experience Capri is by hiking, escaping the crowds to walk trails scented with thyme and jasmine, following ancient tracks between villages. At times you'll enjoy sweeping sea views, at others vistas of the island's bucolic interior. All the trails are easy to follow, but if you'd like to learn more about the area as you hike, contact visitor centers about hiring a licensed guide.

One walk from Capri Town leads to the Belvedere di Tragara. More demanding is the 1,149-foot (350 m) climb on the Passetiello trail from beyond the hospital near Marina Piccola to the top of Monte Solaro via the Monte Santa Maria ridge and Santa Maria a Cetrella hermitage (details at the visitor center).

From Anacapri, you can walk to Migliera (45 minutes), taking Via Caposcuro left of the Monte Solaro chairlift and following for 1.25 miles (2 km). Have lunch at Gelsomina and admire the views at the Belvedere Migliera at the path's end.

Belvedere Cannone, for example, or Via Camerelle east to the Belvedere Tragara. Both offer magnificent views. Farther east lies the **Villa Jovis** (tel 06 3996 7450, closed Tue. in Oct.–Dec. & winter, $), or Jupiter's Villa, the remains of Emperor Tiberius' Capri hideaway. To the south, the exhilarating Via Krupp drops to **Marina Piccola,** one of the island's better—but busier—places to swim and sunbathe.

To the west of Capri lies the island's second village, **Anacapri,** approached by a dramatic corniche road. Quieter than Capri, it is best known as the onetime home of Axel Munthe (1857–1949), Swedish physician and author of the best-selling Story of San Michele (1929). Be sure to visit the 19th-century **Villa San Michele** (Via Axel Munthe 34, tel 081 837 1401, closes at 3:30 p.m. Nov.–Feb., villasanmichele.eu, $) on which the book is based, and in particular the garden terrace, which offers magnificent views across the island. For more spectacular panoramas, take the chairlift from Piazza della Vittoria to the summit of nearby **Monte Solaro** (1.5 hours on foot, 12 minutes by elevator). At 1,932 feet (589 m), this is Capri's highest point.

Ischia

Ischia is a less chic island than Capri, and more favored by package tour companies, although its views, luxuriant vegetation, quaint villages, and lovely coast are almost equally appealing, so it's no less visited. Many visitors are attracted by the island's **hot springs,** a legacy of Ischia's volcanic origins—Monte Epomeo, the island's highest point at 2,585 feet (788 m), is an extinct volcano. The best of the springs bubble under the spa resorts on the northern coast—notably at Forio, Lacco Ameno, and Casamicciola. Villages on the west and south of the island are quieter. Boats dock at the town of Ischia, which divides between the modern Ischia Porto and more picturesque Ischia Ponte. Between the two lie pretty pine woods and a good beach. ∎

Anacapri

Visitor Information

✉ Via Giuseppe Orlandi 95

☎ 081 837 1524

🕐 Closed Sun. & 2:30 p.m.– 3:30 p.m.

Ischia

🗺 288 B4

Visitor Information

✉ Via Sogliuzzo 72, Ischia Town

☎ 081 507 4211

🕐 Closed 1:30 p.m. –4 p.m.

infoischiaprocida.it

AMALFI COAST

The Amalfi Coast, or Costiera Amalfitana, is Italy's most beautiful stretch of coastline, a mild-weathered enclave of towering cliffs, idyllic villages tumbling colorfully to the sea, precipitous corniche roads, luxuriant gardens, and magnificent vistas over turquoise waters and green-swathed mountains. It lies along the flanks of the Sorrento Peninsula, a cliff-edged promontory that juts from the mainland close to the southern reaches of the Bay of Naples.

■ The town of Ravello offers fine views of the Amalfi Coast.

Salerno to Ravello

The coast's most convenient access point is **Salerno,** a busy port best known as an Allied beachhead during the 1943 invasion of Italy. It has a beautiful seafront promenade and a very enjoyable historical center. From Autostrada A3, you pick up the SS163 at **Vietri sul Mare,** a village celebrated for its ceramics and one that offers sweeping views of the coastline to come. From here, the road weaves past innumerable viewpoints—**Capo d'Orso** is the best—and skirts the villages of Maiori (small sandy beach) and Minori (ruins of a first-century A.D. Roman villa) before a junction close to **Atrani** (two tempting churches) whisks you inland to Ravello.

Ravello

Ravello is one of the most romantic and beautiful small towns imaginable. Perched on steep, terraced slopes, it is a place blessed with gardens, quiet lanes, sleepy, sun-drenched corners, and a lofty position at 1,148 feet (350 m) that provides unforgettable views over the azure coast. At its heart lie an 11th-century cathedral and the **Villa Rufolo** (Piazza del Vescovado, tel 089 857 621, villarufolo.it, $). Built in the 13th century, in Arab-Norman style, the villa received guests that included popes and emperors. The Torre Maggiore, the highest point in the historical center, opened to the public in 2017. The history of the villa from its origins to the 1800s is illustrated along the climb to the top of the tower, with magnificent views, as are those from the terrace, the idyllic gardens, and the nearby **Villa Cimbrone** (*Via Santa Chiara 26, tel 089 857 459, $*).

Amalfi

Dropping back to the coast from Ravello, the corniche road brings you to Amalfi, in its day one of Italy's four powerful maritime republics (with Venice, Pisa, and Genoa). Today, the town's beauty, stunning seafront setting, and mild climate make it a hugely popular resort, so steel yourself for high prices and high-season crowds.

Pride of place goes to the **Duomo di Sant'Andrea** (*tel 089 871 059, $*), fronted by a gorgeous and intricately patterned 12th-century facade. Founded in the ninth century, the church's subsequent alterations have spared the beauty of its principal glory, the main portal's 11th-century Byzantine bronze doors. Next to the church lies the **Chiostro del Paradiso** (1268), or Cloister of Paradise (*closed 1 p.m.–2:30 p.m. Jan.–Feb., $*), whose somber Romanesque tone is enlivened by the Arab elements in its sinuous columns.

You can escape much of the hustle by hiking into the hills above town. Consult the visitor center,

or take the popular walk along the **Valle dei Mulini,** a steep-sided ravine dotted with ruined water mills—*mulini*—once used to make paper, an industry for which Amalfi was, and still is, famous. The small **Museo della Carta** offers displays related to the industry.

West of Amalfi

West from Amalfi, the increasingly spectacular corniche road passes **Grotta dello Smeraldo,** a marine cave of luminous emerald waters that you can visit by boat, elevator, or rock-cut steps. Just beyond it, the road passes the **Vallone di Furore,** one of the coast's most impressive gorges (worth exploring on foot), before arriving at the villages of Praiano and **Positano,** two more majestically situated villages, connected by the Sentiero degli Dei (7.5 miles/12 km). From here the road runs around the tip of the peninsula to **Sorrento,** a popular package tour resort. Other roads to Sorrento and the peninsula's northern coast—notably the SS366 from Conca dei Marini near Amalfi—provide firsthand views of the interior's beautiful Lattari mountains. ∎

Amalfi Coast

🅰 289 B4

Ravello

Visitor Information

✉ Via Wagner 4

☎ 089 857 096

ravellotime.it

Amalfi

Visitor Information

✉ Corso delle Repubbliche Marinare 27–29

☎ 089 871 107

🕐 Closed 1 p.m.–3 p.m., & Sun. & p.m. in winter

amalfitouristoffice.it

Museo della Carta

✉ Via delle Cartiere

☎ 081 830 4561

🕐 Closed Feb.

💲 $

museodellacarta.it

Positano

Visitor Information

✉ Via Marconi 288

☎ 089 875 067

🕐 Closed Sun. & p.m. Nov.–March

aziendaturismo positano.it

Limoncello

Limoncello **is a lemon-flavored digestif–best drunk ice cold–that has always been made on the Amalfi Coast. These days it is trendy, and ubiquitous across Italy, but is often served in badly made versions that use lemon syrup rather than real lemons. Some of the best, though, still comes from the Amalfi region. Look for the family-run La Valle dei Mulini company** (*Amalfi, Via delle Cartiere 55, tel 089 873 211, amalfilemon.it*).

PAESTUM

"Inexpressibly grand," wrote the poet Shelley of Paestum, southern Italy's most evocative and romantic archaeological ensemble. Center stage at the site goes to three almost perfectly preserved Doric temples, widely considered the greatest in the Greek world—finer even than those of Greece itself. Much of Paestum's charm, however, also derives from its flower-filled meadows and the rural beauty of its tranquil setting.

The remains of the Tempio di Cerere (Temple of Ceres), dedicated to Athena

Paestum began life as Poseidonia, the city of Neptune or Poseidon, a colony founded by Greeks in the sixth century B.C. Absorbed by Romans in 273 B.C., when it took its present name, Paestum was almost completely abandoned following the ravages of malaria and a devastating Saracen raid in A.D. 877. The city then lay hidden amid the undergrowth for hundreds of years until its discovery during road building in the 18th century, when excavations brought its magnificent temples and other ruins to light once again The site continues to be full of surprises and, in fact, in May 2019 archaeologists found parts of a small Doric temple (sixth/fifth century B.C.) with traces of red paint. It would have been located between the artisanal quarter and the city wall, which is currently under renovation.

The grandest and best preserved of the temples is the

Mozzarella

Mozzarella cheese is one of Campania's finest foodstuffs. It is made from the milk of a rare, indigenous buffalo *(bufala)*, though a poor substitute, *fior di latte,* is made from cow's milk. The smoked version is known as *provola,* the small balls *bocconcini* (small bites), and the braids *trecce.*

Mozzarella takes its name from the verb *mozzare,* to cut, after the manner in which the large mass of cheese is cut in the early stages of production. The best comes from around Caserta, Battipaglia, and the plains between Salerno and Paestum. When buying, look for the labels

"Mozzarella DOC" or "Mozzarella DOP" (visit *mozzarelladop.it* for more information). Buy directly from farms or from a delicatessen *(salumeria)* in Naples such as **Augustus** *(Via Toledo 147),* **Gran Gusto** *(Via Nuova Marina 5, gran-gusto.it),* and **Gourmeet** *(Via Alabardieri 8, gour-meet.it).*

Farm stays or visits are possible across the region, allowing you to see mozzarella production firsthand: Try **Agriturismo Seliano** *(Tenuta Seliano, tel 0828 723 634, agriturismoseliano.it, closed Nov.–March, €70–110/$80–125),* near Paestum, which has a lovely setting.

Tempio di Nettuno, or Temple of Neptune (fifth century B.C.). The temple's entablature and pediments have survived nearly intact, but the roof and part of the walls are missing. Recent discoveries have brought to light architectural elements dating to the period of its Roman renovation. Almost alongside it stands the **Tempio di Hera,** the earliest of the temples (sixth century B.C.), also known as the basilica after being wrongly identified by 18th-century archaeologists. In a more isolated position, at the site's northern extreme, stands the **Tempio di Cerere** (Temple of Ceres), actually dedicated to the goddess Athena and probably built some time between its two neighbors.

Paestum's other Greek and later Roman remains are less striking, but it is still well worth exploring the site simply to soak up the atmosphere. For a good overall picture of the area, you could walk the line of the colony's former walls, a distance of just over 3 miles (5 km).

Also be sure to visit the Museo Nazionale, a museum of finds from the site located to the east of the temples. Its most treasured exhibits are **wall paintings of the Tomb of the Diver** (ca 480 B.C.). These pictures may be the only surviving examples of Greek mural painting from this period.

The pictures—five in all—originally formed part of a coffin: Four of them show scenes of a funeral banquet and the songs, games, musicians, and former companions that accompany the deceased into the next world. The fifth panel, which probably formed the coffin's lid, is the most famous of the paintings and shows a naked diver—hence the tomb's name—diving into a blue sea. The scene may be an unusual allegory of the passage from life to death. ■

Paestum

⚠ 289 C4

Visitor Information

✉ Via Magna Graecia 887

☎ 0828 811 016

infopaestum.it

Archaeological Park & Museum

✉ Entrance from Via Magna Graecia 919 (east) and Via Nettuno (south)

☎ 0828 811 023

🕐 Museum closed Mon.

💲 $–$$

museopaestum .beniculturali.it

PARCO NAZIONALE D'ABRUZZO

The Parco Nazionale d'Abruzzo is Italy's premier national park, a mountain sanctuary that is home to some of Europe's last brown bears, many of its last remaining wolves, and more than 150 varieties of rare indigenous flora. It is also great hiking and driving country, with plenty of marked trails, good maps, and a variety of scenic touring routes. The nearby appealing town of Sulmona makes a good base for exploring this and other nearby mountain enclaves.

■ The Gran Sasso offers superb hiking and scenery.

Parco Nazionale d'Abruzzo, Lazio e Molise

🅰 288 B5

Visitor Information

✉ Via Colli dell'Oro, Pescasseroli

☎ 0863 911 3221

abruzzoturismo.it

parcoabruzzo.it

The park's 193 square miles (50,000 hectares) of wilderness centers on the Sangro valley, a broad cleft that almost bisects the park and contains its key villages—Barrea, Villetta Barrea, Alfedena, Opi, and Pescasseroli. For maps and hints for hiking, stop by the largest village, **Pescasseroli,** which hosts the park's main museum and visitor center. If you only have time for one walk, try trail I1, a 3-mile (4.7 km) trip from Civitella Alfedena to the Val di Rose, which offers a good chance of seeing some of the park's 500 or more Apennine chamois. Other walks nearer Pescasseroli include trail A1 to Bisegna (5.5 hours) and D4 to Valle Mancina (two hours). Other favored haunts are the Canala valley (north of Pescasseroli), the Camosciara (southwest of Villetta Barrea), and the Val di Fondillo (east of Opi).

The Parco Nazionale d'Abruzzo, whose complete denomination is Parco Nazionale d'Abruzzo, Lazio e Molise, balances the needs of visitors, the environment, and the local community. Originally a hunting reserve, like many Italian parks, it first achieved protected status in 1923, although the majority of the real work to establish the reserve was accomplished in the last 50 years.

Spring (late May to June) is the best time to enjoy the park's stunning flora—there are more than 2,000 species of flowers and trees, and 400 types of fungus. Three fifths of the area is forested, so fall is almost equally spectacular, thanks to the ever changing colors of the park's mixed woodlands. Bird-watchers have the chance to spot more than 230 species of birds, including at least ten pairs of golden eagles. The park's 60 or more species of mammals are likely to be more elusive—chamois aside—especially the main attractions, the bears and the wolves.

Bears were common here until the 16th century but were almost extinct by 1915, when bounties on every animal killed were still being paid. Today, between 45 and 70 are thought to exist, with number and range slowly increasing. Descended from Alpine bears (also in decline), the Abruzzo bear has developed enough features to qualify as a subspecies, *Ursus arctos marsicanus*. Wolves in the wild are few (see sidebar this page); about 30 roam the park. A few Apennine wolves are kept at the **Museo del Lupo Appenninico** *(tel 0864 890 141, closed 1:30 p.m.–3 p.m., $)* in Civitella Alfedena for study and to preserve the subspecies' thoroughbred characteristics.

Outside the Park

Timeless villages and superb mountain scenery ring the park. **Scanno** to the east of the park is a picturesque target—many of the townswomen here still wear traditional dress—as is **Sulmona,** a lovely old mountain town in the shadow of the Maiella, one of the most monumental of all the Apennine massifs. Hiking and touring here are superb—use Sulmona as your base.

The same is true of the **Gran Sasso** massif to the north, where the Corno Grande, at 9,560 feet (2,914 m), is the highest peak on the Italian peninsula. Autostrada A25/24 links Sulmona to L'Aquila, the best base for the Gran Sasso. From L'Aquila, be sure to drive up to the Campo Imperatore, a lonely upland plain, and follow the SS80 road through the scenic Valle del Vomano to the north. ∎

Pescasseroli

🗺 288 B5

Visitor Information

✉ Viale Principe di Napoli

☎ 0863 910 461

Sulmona

🗺 288 B5

Visitor Information

✉ Palazzo SS. Annunziata, Corso Ovidio

☎ 0864 567 681

🕐 Closed 12:30 p.m.–3:30 p.m.

comune.sulmona .aq.it

EXPERIENCE: Tracking the Abruzzo's Wolves

The remote mountains of central and southern Italy still support a population of wolves, a distinct Apennine subspecies protected—yet still persecuted—since 1972. The wolves are also threatened by Italy's huge numbers of feral dogs, with which they both interbreed and compete for food. An estimated 200 to 300 animals survive, principally in the Abruzzo and Majella National Parks.

In the latter it is possible to join a **Wolf Weekend,** staying in the tiny Rifugio Majo, a cozy mountain hut high in the mountains, in the centuries-old Bosco (Forest) di Sant'Antonio. Accompanied by a qualified guide from the Collegio Regionale Guide Alpine d'Abruzzo, you follow tracks left by wolves during the

night, listening for their howling, and, if lucky, catching a glimpse of the elusive creatures. You may also see wild boars and chamois, animals on which the wolves prey. At night you return to the *rifugio* for meals in front of an open fire and to learn more about wolves, local lore, and the park's other flora and fauna.

Offered most years late October through late April, the weekends cost €150–250 ($168-280), including meals and lodging. They start with an evening trek on Friday, followed by full-day outings on Saturday and Sunday. Private weekends can be arranged for a minimum of four participants, with 15 days' notice, subject to staff availability. For more information and bookings, visit *majellatrekking.eu.*

TRULLI

Puglia's *trulli* are curious dwellings of mysterious origin. Round, single-story houses, their age is unknown, as are the reasons for their curious conical appearance and oddly tapered roofs. Unknown elsewhere in Europe, they are found scattered across much of the pretty pastoral countryside south of Bari but especially in the towns and region around Alberobello and Martina Franca.

Almost everything about the trulli is mysterious. The only simple thing about them is the way they are made and their considerable practicality—they are cool in summer, warm in winter, and cheap and easy to build. But this begs the question of their absence across the Mediterranean, where conditions and locally available building materials are often identical. At their simplest, they consist of uncemented stone walls and roofs. Most are whitewashed and many are topped with strange stone markers, usually a cross or bizarre symbol, tokens of unknown magical or superstitious significance. Roofs are also often painted with arcane hieroglyphics.

INSIDER TIP:

Stay overnight in a *trullo* (homeaway.it). The unique shape of the building creates a protective, almost holy feeling.

—ILARIA CAPUTI
National Geographic contributor

Mysterious Origins

The earliest theories for their existence have their roots in peasant artfulness. During the 15th century, Ferdinand I of Aragon prohibited his Puglian subjects from building permanent houses, the idea being that he could move a servile labor force where it was most needed. In response, the Puglians—or so it is claimed—built loose-stoned houses that could be easily dismantled if their occupants needed to move, or if word came of an impending visit from one of the emperor's inspectors. Another theory has it that the houses were a sophisticated form of tax evasion—the Aragonese had imposed a levy on all houses except those that were unfinished, an exemption for which the Puglians could quickly qualify by removing (and later replacing) their loose-stoned roofs.

These theories are quaint, but in truth the origins of the trulli are probably even more exotic. The oldest trulli probably date back to the 14th century, although the majority are no more than 200 or 300 years old. Some current thinking connects the trulli with similar structures in Mycenae, in Greece, which would link them with a civilization almost 5,000 years old. Such links are not far-fetched, for Puglia's ports are the closest of any in Italy to the Greek mainland. Furthermore, much of the region fell within the realm of Magna Graecia, the area of southern Italy and Sicily colonized by the Greeks between the eighth and third centuries B.C.

Unfortunately, this theory does not explain why trulli are so limited in geographical extent. One that does suggests trulli are based on the "sugarloaf" houses of Syria and other parts of the Middle East, and that one or two were built as tombs or homes in Puglia by monks who settled there from the East. Local people then copied these and adapted them to everyday use. Another idea, along similar lines, suggests that soldiers who disembarked at Puglian ports on their way home from the Crusades introduced the building style to parts of the region.

■ *Trulli* houses mix with more recent buildings in the Puglian town of Alberobello.

Alberobello

If you want to see trulli, head for Albero-bello, where there are some 1,500 examples. Alberobello means "the war tree," perhaps from its earlier Latin name, Sylva Arboris Belli, after the oak woods that once covered the region. Be warned, however, that it is often a busy place and that while some of the trulli have been converted into evocative hotels and restaurants, others have been turned into stores selling trashy souvenirs.

You can see other trulli in more pastoral surroundings on the road to the nearby town of Martina Franca, and on the road along the Valle d'Itria from Martina Franca to Locoro-tondo. **Martina Franca,** despite its off-putting suburbs, is worth a stop in its own right for the baroque architecture of Via Cavour, the Palazzo Ducale (1668), and the church of San Martino (1747–1775). The town walls, and Viale de Gaspari in particular, offer good views over the trulli-dotted countryside.

IL GARGANO

The Gargano is the spur of the Italian "boot," an upland peninsula jutting into the Adriatic from the Puglian plains. The Foresta Umbra, a protected enclave of wild and ancient wood-lands, cloaks its interior, while a medley of cliffs, coves, beaches, fishing villages, and increasingly popular small resorts line its coastline. Off the coast to the north lie the Isole Tremiti, an archipelago of attractive islands still little-visited by outsiders.

The Gargano largely remains a closed book to foreigners. Not so to the Italians, who have discovered its charms and its beaches in particular. As a result, many of the coastal resorts are busy in summer. Several beaches are owned by hotels or camp-grounds, so access, unless you are a paying guest, is not always straightforward. If you come here in low season, however, or drive and hike in the Foresta Umbra, you will barely meet a soul.

The best approach is from the south via **Monte Sant'Angelo,** or St. Michael's Mount, a mountain town (highest point 2,634 feet/803 m) famous for three appari-tions of the Archangel Michael between A.D. 490 and 493. A fourth apparition in the eighth century led to the founding of a monastery, a foundation whose importance was sealed by the Crusades, when soldiers came to pray here before embarking for the Holy Land from Puglia's many ports. Today, the cave in which the apparitions took place is one of Italy's most important points of pilgrimage, although the original grotto has been swallowed up by the **Santuario di San Michele,** a church of 13th-century origins prized for its ornate Byzantine bronze doors (1076).

■ **The coast near Mattinata is typical of the beautiful beaches and pristine seas of the Gargano.**

From Monte Sant'Angelo, you have a choice of two itineraries. One runs north through the **Foresta Umbra** on the SP52b road. This route offers a firsthand view of the beeches, yews, limes, pines, oaks, chestnut, and other trees that comprise this wonderful tranche of relict woodland. Close to the heart of the forest, near the intersection for Vico, lies the Corpo Forestale, a visitor center *(tel 0884 88055, www.parcogargano .it)* where you can pick up details of the region's trails and outdoor activities. The second route follows the forest road and its continuation (the SP52bis) north until you come to **Peschici,** one of the smallest and nicest of the villages. To its west lies another resort village, **Rodi Garganico,** as well as several good beaches and the lagoons of Lago di Varano and Lago di Lesina (both noted bird-watching areas).

Head east and you pick up the promontory's coast road, quickly reaching **Vieste,** the area's most developed village. From here, the road climbs through wooded and rocky landscapes, offering superb coastal vistas, where the beautiful contrast of green woodland and azure seas and skies provides a constant backdrop. Continue east and you will complete a return circuit to Monte Sant'Angelo, a distance of about 95 miles (153 km). You will have seen the best the region has to offer.

Isole Tremiti

No trip would be complete, however, without an excursion to the Isole Tremiti, which can

---

EXPERIENCE:
Birding in the Gargano

The Gargano Peninsula's varied habitats make it a birding destination. Varano and Lesina on the Gargano's north coast are southern Italy's largest lakes and one of the country's most important waterfowl regions. Huge numbers of resident and migrating birds can be seen, including cormorants, shovelers, pochards, coots, and red-breasted mergansers. Breeding birds here and elsewhere on the peninsula (notably the Cesine nature reserve east of Lecce and the salt flats near Margherita di Savoia) include vultures, honey buzzards, red and black kites, short-toed eagles, eagle owls, rollers, and middle-spotted and white-backed woodpeckers. Visit *parks.it* or *lipu.it,* the website of the Italian League for the Protection of Birds, for further information.

---

be reached by regular ferries and hydrofoil *(April–Oct.)* from **Manfredonia,** Vieste, Peschici, Foggia, and Termoli (in the region of Molise). The trip from Manfredonia gives you sensational views of the promontory's coastline, an added bonus. If you want a quicker approach, the closest port, at 8 miles (13 km), is Rodi Garganico (see above).

The archipelago's principal islands are **San Nicola** and **San Domino,** both renowned for their natural beauty and translucent waters. Opportunities for swimming, diving, and other water sports are all first rate, but the less active can enjoy scenic boat trips, island strolls, and historical sights such as San Nicola's ninth-century Benedictine abbey, Santa Maria a Mare. ∎

Peschici
🏔 289 D5
Visitor Information
✉ Via Magenta 3
☎ 0884 964 966

Vieste
🏔 289 D5
Visitor Information
✉ Piazza Kennedy 13
☎ 0884 708 806

Manfredonia
🏔 289 D5
Visitor Information
✉ Piazza Libertà 1
☎ 0884 581 998
🕐 Closed p.m. & Sat.–Sun.

viaggiareinpuglia.it

visitmanfredonia.it

ROMANESQUE PUGLIA DRIVE

This drive begins in Bari, a busy modern port with an interesting historic quarter, and then takes in several towns celebrated for their Romanesque churches, Puglia's chief glory, as well as Emperor Frederick II's great fortress at Castel del Monte.

Along the Coast

Begin in the city of **Bari ❶**, whose modern port and suburbs crowd in on the **Città Vecchia** (Old City), an atmospheric labyrinth of streets and alleys that contains most of the city's principal monuments. Chief among these are the late 12th-century **Cattedrale di San Sabino** and the 1087 **Basilica di San Nicola,** both supreme examples of the Romanesque architecture for which Puglia is famed. Such architecture flourished here for several reasons. First, the strong government of Norman, Swabian, and Angevin rulers over several centuries provided the money and stability needed to create buildings that often took hundreds of years to complete. Second, the region was

NOT TO BE MISSED:

Trani cathedral • Castel del Monte • Ruvo di Puglia

a melting pot of ruling and other cultures, with the result that its buildings combined the architectural styles of Roman, Norman, Byzantine, Lombard, Arab, and imported northern Italian craftsmen. Third, Puglia was located astride several important pilgrimage routes and close to ports used by pilgrims and crusaders bound for the Holy Land.

From Bari, drive west on the SS16 coast road as far as **Trani ❷**, a bustling port of white-washed buildings that boasts an outstanding Romanesque cathedral, a building known both for its unforgettable location—hard against the sea's edge—and its remarkable 12th-century bronze portals. The cathedral is dedicated to St. Nicholas the Pilgrim, a local saint who reputedly arrived in Trani astride a dolphin.

❸ Barletta
SS16
SS170
A14
SS170
❷ Trani
Bisceglie
SS16
●ANDRIA
SP238
SP231
Molfetta
A14
Giovinazzo
Corato
Terlizzi
Sovereto
Bitonto ❻
SS170 dir.
379m
Monte
S. Marzano
❺
Ruvo di Puglia
SP231
L E
SP324
Castel del
Monte ❹
SP234
M U R G E
Matera
SP238
520m
Monte Maccarone

0   8 kilometers
0   4 miles

San Sabino, Bari's majestic cathedral, has the round arches typical of Romanesque architecture.

Next, follow the SS16 to **Barletta** ❸, a relatively drab town enlivened, again, by its Romanesque cathedral, **Chiesa del Santo Sepolcro** *(Corso Garibaldi & Corso Vittorio Emanuele),* and by the **"Colosso"** *(Corso Vittorio Emanuele),* the largest Roman bronze in existence.

Inland Sights

From Barletta drive south on SS170 through the town of **Andria** and follow signs for **Castel del Monte** ❹ *(SS170/dir., tel 0883 569 997, casteldelmonte.beniculturali.it, $),* one of the South's most memorable and mysterious sights. A huge fortress visible for miles around, it sits 1,790 feet (546 m) above Puglia's plains and low limestone hills—a region known as Le Murge—its purpose and distinctive design a puzzle to generations of historians and scholars.

Built around 1240, the castle was the brainchild of the Holy Roman Emperor Frederick II. Everything

about the building betrays an obsession with mathematical harmony and, in particular, with the number eight: The building is octagonal in plan, has an octagonal courtyard, and eight octagonal towers, each of which contains two stories of eight rooms each. Some claim that eight is a symbol of the crown or the union of God and humankind, others that the castle's proportions reflect some astrological configuration of the heavens. Alternative theories suggest it was simply a hunting lodge or a retreat for pilgrims searching for the Holy Grail. That it had some special significance is clear: It was the only octagonal fortress among some 200 quadrilateral castles commissioned by Frederick on his return from the Crusades.

After visiting the castle, turn left onto the SP234 at the junction below the fortress and follow signs to **Ruvo di Puglia** ❺, whose cathedral again encapsulates the best of the Apulian Romanesque style. In Greek and early Roman times, the town was renowned for its distinctive red-black ceramics, or Apulian ware, examples of which can be seen in the local **Museo Archeologico Nazionale Jatta** *(Piazza Giovanni Bovio 35, tel 080 361 2848, musei.puglia .beniculturali.it, closed p.m. Sun.–Wed. & Fri.).* From Ruvo, the SP231 runs east to **Bitonto** ❻, a town encircled by olive groves, and one whose Romanesque cathedral bears similarities to the cathedrals of nearby Trani and Bari. Roads from here via Modugno lead back to Bari.

LECCE

Lecce is almost universally known as the "Florence of the baroque," a sobriquet coined as a testimony to an architectural flowering unequalled in southern Italy. Greeks, Romans, Normans, Saracens, and Swabians all left their mark here, but the most lasting legacy was that of Hapsburg Spain, whose ruling denizens, fired by the fervor of the Counter-Reformation and financed by wealthy local merchants, effected a sweeping architectural transformation of the city during the 17th century.

Outstanding baroque architecture has made Lecce famous.

The city's baroque heart is **Piazza del Duomo,** dominated by the cathedral, which was rebuilt by the chief architect of the city's transformation, Giuseppe Zimbalo, between 1659 and 1670. Alongside it stands the **Palazzo Vescovile** (the Bishops' Palace, 1632) and the glorious **Seminario** (Seminary), built between 1694 and 1709 by Zimbalo's pupil, Giuseppe Cino. Walk west from the square on Via Giuseppe Libertini and you come to the **Chiesa del Rosario,** or San Giovanni Battista (1691–1728), Zimbalo's last, and to many eyes, finest work.

Then retrace your steps and head for **Piazza Sant'Oronzo,** Lecce's busy main square, named after the town's first bishop, St. Orontius, a prelate martyred by the Romans in the first century. On the piazza's southern flank lies the partially excavated remains of a Roman amphitheater, along with Lecce's former town hall, the **Sedile,** or Palazzo Seggio (1592). Nearby stands the **Colonna di Sant'Oronzo,** one of two pillars that once marked the end of the old Via Appia, an important Roman road, in the nearby town of Brindisi. Another baroque church, **Santa Maria delle Grazie,** dominates the square's southeast corner. Beyond it rises the

Lecce

🅜 289 E4

Visitor Information

✉ Castello di Carlo V

☎ 0832 246 517

comune.lecce.it

viaggiareinpuglia.it

Lecce's major buildings and decorative details—balconies, porches, pedestals, and windows—are all smothered in garlands of fruit, chubby statues, gargoyles, and intricately worked curlicues of stone. The stone is a light, golden, and close-grained local limestone, whose easily worked but durable properties proved perfectly suited to the demands of carving.

INSIDER TIP:

You can drive across the peninsula near Lecce in just over an hour. In one day you can watch the sun rise over the east coast and set over the west.

—PATRICIA DANIELS
National Geographic contributor

unmistakable **Castello,** a medieval fortress rebuilt in the 16th-century by Emperor Charles V.

From the square, walk north on Via Umberto I to **Santa Croce,** the apotheosis of Lecce's vivacious baroque style. Begun in 1549, the church was the work of several architects, including the ubiquitous Zimbalo, who was responsible for the facade's pediment and rose window. Alongside stands the **Palazzo del Governo** (1659–1695), former residence of the city's governor, also by Zimbalo. Around five minutes' walk to the north on Via Manfredi stands the church of **Sant'Angelo** (1663),

a baroque confection by another member of the Zimbalo clan, Francesco Giuseppe Zimbalo.

Return to Piazza Sant'Oronzo and explore the knot of streets to its south, heading for the church of **Santa Chiara** and its adjacent first-century A.D. **Teatro Romano,** the remains of Puglia's only Roman theater. Continue south toward the limit of old Lecce to reach the city's principal museum, the **Museo Castromediano.** Completely renovated, it is home to Greek, Roman, and Puglian vases, coins, bronzes, and terra-cottas; and reliefs removed from Piazza Sant'Oronzo's amphitheater, all in a new, modernized setting with user-friendly, immersive technology. Also visit **Museo Storico Città di Lecce,** or MUST, devoted to the history of the region.

Another major sight, **Santi Nicola e Cataldo** (1180), lies northeast of the old center on Via del Cimitero. One of the region's finest Norman monuments, the Byzantine, Arab, and Gothic elements of the original Romanesque church are complemented by a baroque facade, by Giuseppe Cino. ■

Chiesa del Rosario

✉ Via Giuseppe Libertini
☎ 0832 9547 040
🕐 Closed 12 p.m.–5 p.m. & Sun. p.m.

Santa Croce

✉ Via Umberto I 3
☎ 0832 241 957
🕐 Closed 1 p.m.–5 p.m.

Museo Castromediano

✉ Viale Gallipoli 28
☎ 0832 373 572
🕐 Closed Mon. a.m.

Museo Storico Città di Lecce (MUST)

✉ Via degli Ammirati 11
☎ 0832 183 0851
🕐 Closed Mon. & 1:30 p.m.–3:30 p.m. a.m.
💲 $

mustlecce.it

The Tarantella

Tarantism is an illness supposedly brought on by a spider bite; it resulted in a frenzied dance, the tarantella, which supposedly cured the condition. This, in turn, inspired a ritualized folk dance and musical accompaniment, first in Naples, then across southern Italy, and especially in Puglia's Salento region, where the dance and music are known as *pizzica*.

After dying out in the 1950s, the tarantella folk tradition has recently enjoyed a revival, with pizzica being danced and played at an increasing number of festivals in the region. One not to miss is the **Festa Patronale dei SS. Apostoli Pietro e Paolo,** held annually June 28–30 *(comune.galatina.le.it),* in Galatina, 15 miles (24 km) south of Lecce. Here, San Paolo (St. Paul) is invoked against bites from spiders and poisonous animals. Visit *lanottedellataranta.it* for details of similar events during August.

More Places to Visit in the South

Caserta

Caserta's industrial hinterland is dispiriting, but the town itself is redeemed by the **Palazzo Reale,** or Reggia di Caserta *(Viale Douhet, tel 0823 448 084, reggiadicaserta.beniculturali.it, closed Tues., $$),* Italy's largest royal palace. There are some 1,750 windows, 94 staircases, and more than 1,000 painted and stuccoed rooms. It was begun in 1752 for the profligate Bourbon King Charles III and finished 50 years later. The **gardens** *(close at dusk)* are equally vast: A shuttle bus drops you off at the main points of interest. *eptcaserta.it* 🔝 288 B4 **Visitor Information** ✉ Piazza Dante ☎ 0823 211 137

Matera

Matera is widely known for its unique *sassi*—cave settlements excavated from the ravines in and around the lower part of the town. You can view the labyrinth of caves, inhabited since prehistoric times, from a specially built Strada Panoramica (panoramic road), but to make the most of this fascinating town, explore on foot. Be sure to see some of the 120 or more *chiese rupestri,* or **cave churches,** carved by monks between the 8th and 13th centuries, and the **Museo Nazionale Ridola** *(Via Domenico Ridola 24, tel 0835 310 058, closed Mon. a.m., $),* a collection of locally discovered archaeological artifacts. An introduction to the exploration is a visit to **Casa Noha** *(Recinto Cavone 9, tel 0835 335 452, closed Tue., $, fondoambiente.it),* a suggestive private home that has been restored. Here, visitors can watch a movie that will take them on a trip through history. *comune.matera.it/turismo* 🔝 289 D4 **Visitor Information** ✉ Via Ridola ☎ 389 444 8799

Parco Nazionale del Pollino

Monte Pollino (7,375 feet/2,248 m) and the national park that protects it form the high instep of the Italian "boot." Utterly wild and majestic, it is a region that encapsulates the traditional ways of life of the rural south and, until recently, was all but unknown to outsiders. The village of Terranova di Pollino is the best base for exploration, while the seaside resort town of Maratea is an option if you want to mix land and sea. Walkers will find excellent hiking and car drivers will enjoy the uncompromising landscapes. Just to the east of the region you could reach **Sibari,** site of the Greek colony of Sybaris, home to the high-living Sybarites, hence the word "sybaritic." Since the 2010 flood, only few areas are open *(tel 0981 79394, hours vary). parcopollino.gov.it, parks.it* 🔝 289 D3 **Visitor Information** ✉ Complesso Monumentale S. M. della Consolazione, Rotonda ☎ 0973 669 335 🕐 Closed Sat.–Sun. & 1 p.m.–2 p.m.

Parco Nazionale della Sila

The Sila are Calabria's main mountain ranges, a jumble of massifs famous for their forests. Timber from these provided, among other things, the wood for many of Rome's church ceilings. Today this mountains enjoy national park status, although much of the scenery, while wild in the extreme, is more monotonous than that of the Abruzzo and Pollino parks. Some of the most arresting countryside lies along the scenic SP211 road and around **Camigliatello** and **San Giovanni in Fiore,** the main villages. *parcosila.it, parks.it* 🔝 289 D2 **Visitor Information** ✉ Via Nazionale, Lorica San Giovanni in Fiore ☎ 0984 53 7109

Tropea

The drive to reach Sicily from Rome or Naples is long. One place to break the journey is Tropea on the Calabrian coast, a resort that has largely withstood the modern developments that have tainted other parts of the Calabrian Riviera. Beaches, hotels, restaurants, and surrounding countryside are generally first rate. *prolocotropea.eu* 🔝 289 D2 **Visitor Information** ✉ Piazza Ercole ☎ 0963 61 475 🕐 Closed 1 p.m.–4 p.m. & Sun.

Islands of rich art, culture, language, and history at once entwined
yet fiercely separate from those of mainland Italy

SICILY & SARDINIA

Sicilian puppet, Museo Internazionale
delle Marionette, Palermo

SICILY & SARDINIA

Sicily (Sicilia) is a world apart, an island separated from the rest of Italy not only by the sea but also by centuries of history and cultural experience. Yet it is also a vital part of the country—the writer Johann Goethe observed that "to have seen Italy without seeing Sicily is not to have seen Italy at all, for Sicily is the clue to everything" (*Italian Journey*, 1789). He might have said much the same about Sardinia (Sardegna).

Castello Normanno di Venere and Torre Pepoli, viewed from Erice, Sicily

Sicily

The largest island in the Mediterranean Sea, Sicily lay between the civilizations of Africa and Europe, providing a tempting prize for

traders and invaders alike. Originally, the island was home to the Siculi and Sicani, ancient tribes from which it takes its present-day name. Between the eighth and third centuries B.C., Sicily's rulers were the Greeks; in the ninth and tenth centuries A.D., it was under Arab control; and in the 11th century, it was dominated by the Normans. Between times, the island attracted Romans, Carthaginians, Vandals, Spanish, Byzantines, French, and Bourbons—and even the British.

Sicily's invaders bequeathed the island its extraordinarily rich heritage, from art and architecture to language and cuisine. From the Greeks came the theaters at Syracuse and Taormina, and the great temples at Agrigento, Selinunte, and Segesta. From the Romans came the magnificent mosaics at Piazza Armerina, and from the Arabs a variety of Moorish-influenced architecture and much of Sicily's wonderfully eclectic cuisine. In later centuries, the Normans introduced the majesty of Romanesque architecture, a legacy seen to best effect in the sublime cathedrals of Cefalù and Monreale. From the Spanish came the decorative exuberance of the baroque, a style incorporated into many Sicilian churches and palaces.

Palermo, Sicily's capital, a teeming, decaying, fascinating, and occasionally troubled city, provides a telling introduction to Sicily's magnificent past and its occasionally sordid present. The Sicilian coastline, once one of Europe's loveliest, is now only seen to best effect at places like Cefalù, Taormina, and offshore islands such as the Aeolian (Eolie) archipelago, best known for the volcanic eruptions of Stromboli. Inland, the landscapes are less ravaged: They range from the limitless ridged plateaus and shimmering wheatfields of the interior to the Madonie and Nebrodi mountains. Finally, there is Mount Etna, Europe's greatest active volcano, a smoldering, snowcapped peak of brooding majesty.

Sardinia

Sardinia, the second largest island in the Mediterranean, draws visitors in search of beauty and traditional island life, the allure being the sun-drenched beaches of Costa Smeralda, the stark yet stunning interior mountains, and villages where the way of life has little changed over the centuries. ■

Rome

Sardinia, see map on p. 337

Area of map detail

SICILY

Sicily's coastal sights range from the charming towns of Cefalù and Taormina to the mix of history and urban seediness that is Palermo to offshore islands such as the Aeolian Islands. Inland, make time to visit the Villa Romana del Casale, near Piazza Armerina, and Segesta, a spectacularly sited Greek temple. Finally, there is Mount Etna, Europe's greatest active volcano, a smoldering peak of brooding majesty.

Corso Vittorio Emanuele II and the streets around the Quattro Canti, the hub of historic Palermo

Palermo
🅰 317 B2
Visitor Information
✉ Via Principe Belmonte 92
☎ 091 585 172
🕐 Closed Sat.–Sun. & p.m. except Thurs.

✉ Palermo airport
☎ 091 591 698
🕐 Closed Sun.

turismo.comune .palermo.it

provincia.palermo.it

visitpalermo.it

Palermo

Big, battered, and bustling, Palermo is not a city for all tastes, its traffic, poverty, and decaying sense of baroque grandeur not for the fainthearted. At the same time, it is one of Italy's most vibrant and atmospheric cities, founded by the Phoenicians in the eighth century B.C. and still bearing the stamp of its later Arab, Norman, and Spanish rulers. Monuments to past glories rise amid the modern tenements and cramped backstreets, fighting for space in a city whose Arab bazaars, flourishing port, seedy dives, and teeming thoroughfares offer a dramatic contrast between past and present.

Central Palermo's sights are dispersed, so arm yourself with a map and be prepared either for lots of walking or trips aboard the cabs or crowded buses that ply the city's three principal streets: Corso Vittorio Emanuele II, Via Maqueda, and Via Roma. The most efficient approach to the key sights is to start at the western end of the first of these, Corso Vittorio Emanuele II, working eastward to take in

INSIDER TIP:

If you're in Palermo for the Feast of Santa Rosalia *(mid-July),* don't miss the theatrical show near the Palazzo dei Normanni.

—TINO SORIANO
National Geographic photographer

the clusters of attractions near its seaward conclusion and its intersection with Via Maqueda.

Around Palazzo dei Normanni: The Palazzo dei Normanni, or Palazzo Reale, occupies the site of the city's ninth-century Saracen fortress, a building enlarged by the Normans and transformed into a palace complex that became one of Europe's leading royal courts.

Guided tours generally conduct you around the 12th-century **Sala di Re Ruggero,** or Hall of Roger II, a chamber adorned with mosaics of hunting scenes. Roger, a Norman king, was also

responsible for the magnificent **Cappella Palatina** (1129–1143), one of Palermo's highlights, a glittering private chapel that encapsulates the composite architectural style that flourished in Sicily under the Normans. Ancient Roman columns support its predominantly Romanesque interior, which is overarched by a Moorish wooden ceiling and adorned with Byzantine **mosaics:** These mosaics— along with the similar mosaics in Ravenna and Istanbul—are considered to be Europe's finest. Also be sure to stroll around the palace's palm-fringed gardens, the **Villa Bonanno,** connected with a new installation, a "cultural" garden in the middle of the square: nature that brings civilizations together and triumphs over concrete.

Palermo had more than 200 mosques during its period of Arab rule (831–1072). Many were subsequently replaced by Christian buildings, including **San Giovanni degli Eremiti,** a deconsecrated church, built between 1132 and 1148 to the south of the Palazzo dei Normanni. Its five bulging ocher domes bear

Palazzo dei Normanni & Cappella Palatina

- ✉ Piazza del Parlamento
- ☎ 091 626 2833
- 🕐 Palace apartments closed Tues.– Thurs.; chapel closed Sun. p.m.
- 💲 Palace & chapel $$; gardens $

federicosecondo.org

San Giovanni degli Eremiti

- ✉ Via dei Benedettini 16–20
- ☎ 091 651 5019
- 🕐 Closed Sun. p.m. & Mon.
- 💲 $

EXPERIENCE: Guided Literary Walks

Aristocrat Giuseppe Tomasi di Lampedusa's only novel, *The Leopard (Il Gattopardo)*—published posthumously in 1958—is not just one of the great works of Sicilian literature, it is one of the great 20th-century European novels. Join one of half a dozen literary walks around Palermo and you'll gain not only an insight into the author and his links with the city but also visit all sorts of hidden corners.

Or you can walk around the port and listen to extracts from the works of 18th- and 19th-century visitors to the city.

Two-day tours to other landmarks in Sicily associated with the author are also available and include food and accommodations. Further information on walks and tours is available from the **Parco Culturale del Gattopardo** *(tel 091 625 4011 or 327 684 4052, parcotomasi.it).*

La Martorana

- ✉ Piazza Bellini
- ☎ 091 616 1692
- 🕐 Closed 1 p.m.–3:30 p.m. Mon.–Sat., 10:30 a.m.–11:45 a.m. and p.m. Sun.

San Cataldo

- ✉ Piazza Bellini
- ☎ 091 348 728
- 🕐 Closed p.m. in winter, & 12:30 p.m.–3 p.m. & Sun. p.m. in summer
- 💲 $, guided tour

witness to the architectural legacy of its Islamic predecessor—the church's instigator, Roger II, is said to have employed Arab architects and personally insisted on the curious domed motif. As lovely as the church are its cloister and unkempt garden, the latter a scented enclave of palms, lemon trees, and subtropical plants.

A Riot of Churches: Moving east along Corso Vittorio Emanuele II, you come to Palermo's great honey-stoned **cathedral**

■ Guests dine alfresco at the Antica Foccaceria on Piazza San Francesco in the heart of old Palermo.

(begun in 1184), another monument to the city's Norman past. Its interior was much altered in the 18th century, but the exterior has retained its wonderfully exotic blend of early architectural styles. Note, in particular, the main portal, a 15th-century work executed in a flamboyant Catalan-Gothic manner. Inside,

the only surviving points of real interest are the royal tombs of Henry IV, Roger II, and the great Hohenstaufen emperor, Frederick II, and his wife, Constance of Aragon (located in two chapels in the south aisle).

Palermo's heart is marked by Corso Vittorio's intersection with Via Maqueda, known as the Quattro Canti, or Four Corners. Just south lies **Piazza Pretoria,** a ring of medieval and Renaissance buildings also known as the "Square of Shame" after the lascivious nude figures of its 16th-century fountain. To the south in Piazza Bellini stands the church of **La Martorana,** also known as Santa Maria dell'Ammiraglio, as it was founded in 1143 by Roger II's admiral *(ammiraglio),* Georgios Antiochenos, a Greek Orthodox Christian. Subsequent baroque alterations spared the church's sensational Greek-crafted 12th-century dome mosaics.

Alongside La Martorana lies the 12th-century Norman church of **San Cataldo,** whose external architecture bears marked Moorish leanings. The interior, like most of Palermo's smaller churches, is a riot of baroque overelaboration. Another example of baroque exuberance is the 1612 **San Giuseppe dei Teatini** *(closed p.m.)* on the Quattro Canti, whose plain-faced exterior conceals an interior of matchless decorative splendor.

Via Roma: Before continuing east on the Corso, head north on Via Roma, pausing to explore Palermo's vibrant market area in the streets around Piazza San

Catacombe dei Cappuccini

Long after memories of your Italian visit have faded, chances are you will recall the sights of the **Convento dei Cappuccini** (*Via G. Mosca-Via Pindemonte, tel 091 652 4156, catacombepalermo.it, closed 12 p.m.– 3 p.m., also Sun. p.m. Nov.–March, $*). Palermo's most unusual and macabre sight, it lies west of the city center—cab drivers know the way—but the journey is well worth the effort, if you can stomach the sight of corpses in various states of decay.

Preserving the dead using lime, arsenic, and the drying effects of the sun was a Capuchin tradition and one seen to eerie effect in the convent's gloomy, subterranean corridors. Rows of bodies are hung or splayed in gruesome poses. Each cluster of corpses is divided according to rank and profession: priests, monks, commoners, aristocrats—even children, the most disturbing of the catacomb's incumbents. All wear the clothes they died in, the effect morbid and comical by turns—bones and yellowing flesh poke through moldering gloves; tufts of hair sprout from crumbling top hats.

Domenico. This highly colorful district is known as the **Vucciria,** from the French *boucherie,* butchery, today an Arablike open-air market, a source of junk as well as every variety of food from swordfish to *pani ca' meuza*—rolls filled with calf's spleen, cheese, and a spicy sauce.

While in the area, stop by **San Domenico** (*Piazza San Domenico, tel 091 589 172, closed 1 p.m.–5 p.m. Sun.*), the nearby **Oratorio del Rosario** (*Via dei Bambinai 2, closed Sun. & p.m., $*), and the **Oratorio di Santa Cita** (*Via Valverde 3, tel 091 785 3181, closed Sun., $*). All three churches offer object lessons in the finer points of Sicilian baroque decoration.

Farther north, just off Via Roma, Sicily's leading archaeological museum, the extensive **Museo Archeologico Regionale Antonino Salinas,** is a repository for art and artifacts removed from the island's myriad ancient sites. It has recently reopened after careful restoration, a rearrangement of its historical display,

and the addition of a few new items, including some architectural earthenware and a group of gutters shaped like lions' heads that were originally from the Temple of Himera. Other highlights include the metopes from the Greek temple friezes at Selinunte.

East of Quattro Canti:

Return to the Quattro Canti and head east to a cluster of sights grouped between the Corso and Via Alloro to the south. Chief among these is the **Galleria Regionale della Sicilia,** an important collection of paintings and sculptures whose highlights are Antonello da Messina's painting of the "Annunciation" (1473) and an exquisite 1471 bust of Eleonora of Aragon by Francesco Laurana.

Immediately north in Piazza Marina stands the Palazzo Chiaramonte (1307), a Gothic palace best known for its garden's mighty magnolia fig trees. If gardens appeal, walk south to visit the **Villa Giulia,** laid out in 1778, and

Museo Archeologico Regionale Antonino Salinas

- ✉ Piazza Olivella 24
- ☎ 091 748 9995
- 🕒 Closed Sun. p.m.
- 💲 $

regione.sicilia.it/ bbccaa/salinas

coopculture.it

Galleria Regionale della Sicilia

- ✉ Via Alloro 4, Palermo
- ☎ 091 623 0011
- 🕒 Closed Sat.–Sun. p.m.
- 💲 $

regione.sicilia.it/ beniculturali

Orto Botanico

- ✉ Via Abramo Lincoln 2b, Palermo
- ☎ 091 623 8241
- 💲 $

ortobotanico.unipa.it

Museo Internazionale delle Marionette

- ✉ Piazza Antonio Pasqualino 5, Palermo
- ☎ 091 328 060
- 🕐 Closed Sun. & 1 p.m.–2:30 p.m.
- 💲 $

museodellemarionette .it

the 18th-century **Orto Botanico.** Otherwise, walk to Piazza Marina's southern corner to see the **Palazzo Mirto** *(tel 091 616 4751, may close Sun.),* filled with gloriously decorated period rooms.

Nearby lies the **Oratorio di San Lorenzo** *(Via Immacolatella 5),* another baroque gem. For something more unusual, head to the Corso's eastern end and the **Museo Internazionale delle Marionette.** The museum has a fine collection of puppets from across Sicily—where they were long a source of traditional satire and entertainment—and other parts of the world.

Monreale

Monreale has one of Europe's supreme cathedrals, a monument to the greatest traditions of Arab, Norman, and Byzantine art and architecture. Sadly, it has the misfortune to be stranded in a town almost subsumed by the seething suburbs of present-day Palermo. Brave the surroundings, however, for the church, and its mosaics in particular, constitutes Sicily's single greatest treasure.

The cathedral was founded in 1172 by the Norman king, William II, and drew on French, Islamic, and Byzantine models. A finely carved portal frames its main **bronze doors** (1186), which are adorned with 42 biblical scenes—notice the repeated lion and griffon emblems, symbols of the Norman royal family. Compare the Romanesque scenes here with the more Byzantine-influenced bronze door (1179) on the cathedral's left (north) side.

Inside, the building resembles a giant casket of jewels, shimmering

◾ **Monreale's cathedral represents the pinnacle of Arab-Norman art and architecture.**

with gold leaf, paintings, and richly colored marbles, its nave and wooden ceiling supported by columns salvaged from earlier classical buildings. A glorious mosaic pavement mirrors the greater **mosaics** in the main body of the church—68,000 square feet (6,340 sq m) of decoration in all—a cycle completed around 1182 by Greek, Byzantine, and Sicilian craftsmen. The royal tombs of kings William I and II lie in a chapel to the right of the apse.

On its own, Monreale's interior would be accounted a masterpiece, but the monastery's equally celebrated Norman **cloister** is an added bonus. Some 228 twin columns, most sinuously carved or inlaid with colored marbles, support the quadrangle's Arab-style arches. To the rear, a pleasing terrace and **garden** are two of several points around town offering views of the Conca d'Oro, the name given to the Golden Basin cradling the city of Palermo below.

Cefalù

Cefalù has largely escaped the modern building that has done so much to spoil Sicily's once pristine coastline. Charming and compact, this immediately likeable town, built below an immense fortresslike crag, has several pleasant beaches, one of Sicily's most perfect main squares, and a majestic Norman cathedral graced with one of the most sublime images of Christ in Western art.

Cefalù's main **Piazza del Duomo** is as satisfying a spot for a quiet drink or reflective half

hour as you could wish for. Gently curved palm trees grow in each corner, overlooked by the amber-stoned facade of the town's wondrous **cathedral** (1131–1267). Legend has it the building was raised to fulfill a vow by Roger II, Sicily's 12th-century Norman king, who survived a shipwreck nearby and pledged a church to the Madonna in gratitude for his spared life. Originally, the shrine was intended as Sicily's most important religious building and was designed as a pantheon for Roger's Norman successors. Neither ambition was realized.

The church's interior is as restrained as its exterior—much of it has remained unchanged for

more than 800 years. Note the redoubtable wooden ceiling and Arab-influenced capitals, the latter perfect examples of the composite Sicilian-Norman Romanesque style. The celebrated **apse mosaic,** which depicts Christ Pantocrator, dates from 1148, making it the earliest Sicilian example of an image much repeated across the island. A short distance from the cathedral lies the **Museo**

Monreale
🗺 317 B2

Monreale Cathedral
✉ Piazza Guglielmo II

☎ 091 640 4413 (church), 091 640 4403 (cloister)

🕐 Closed 10 a.m.– 2:30 or 3 p.m. Sun.; may close 12:45 p.m.–2:30 or 3:30 p.m. rest of week

💲 $ cathedral, $$ cathedral and cloister

monrealeduomo.it

coopculture.it

Cefalù's Best Beaches

If you want a day on the beach, Cefalù is one of the most popular resorts in Sicily. Visitors colonize the sandy town beach, the **Lungomare,** but locals make for the pebbly **Caldura** beach, east of the town, beyond the harbor. **Capo Playa** beach stretches for 9 miles (15 km) west of Cefalù to Campofelice di Roccella; it offers great surfing—the Salinelle area, 4.5 miles (7 km) west of Cefalù, is especially popular.

Cefalù
🗺 317 C2

Visitor Information

✉ Corso Ruggero 77

☎ 0921 421 050

🕐 Closed Sun. & 1 p.m.–3 p.m.

EXPERIENCE: Stromboli by Night

Volcanoes, by their nature, are rarely predictable, so it's rare to come across a volcano like Stromboli, where superheated gases throw up an almost constant barrage of magma. One of Sicily's most memorable experiences is to view these pyrotechnics by night, when the burning orange of the molten rock is dramatically visible against the night sky.

There are three ways you can do it. One way is to book a table for dinner at **L'Osservatorio** (tel 090 958 6991), a restaurant at 1,312 feet (400 m) on the volcano's slopes. The food here may be nothing special (play safe with pizzas), but the views of the eruptions are spectacular.

A second option is to take a boat trip ($$$$$). There are many operators in Porto Scari, among them **Società Navigazione Pippo** (kiosk by the Beach Bar, cell 339 222 9714 or 348 055 9296) and **Paola e**

Giovanni (stand opposite Sirenetta hotel, Ficogrande, tel 338 431 2803). The trips run about 2.5 hours.

The third way to view the volcano is to hike to the summit. Access since 2005 has been regulated: You need to hire a guide or join an organized trek to climb beyond 1,312 feet (400 m). Two good operators are **Magmatrek** (Via Vittorio Emanuele, tel 090 986 5768, magmatrek.it, group treks daily Easter–June. & Sept.–Nov., $$$$$) and **Stromboli Guide** (Agenzia Il Vulcano a Piede, Via Pizzolo, tel 090 986 144, stromboli guide.it, $$$$$).

The summit is at 3,031 feet (924 m). The groups generally walk at a fairly brisk pace over the course of five to six hours. Bring a flashlight, proper footwear, a daypack, windbreaker, and a handkerchief to protect against dust (don't wear contact lenses).

Aeolian Islands

🗺 317 C3

Visitor Information

✉ Via Vittorio Emanuele 66, Lipari, Eolie Pro Loco

☎ 090 988 0306

comunelipari.gov.it

eolieproloco.it

Mandralisca (Via Mandralisca 13, tel 0921 421 547, $, fondazione mandralisca.it), a collection of coins, pottery, vases, Greek and Roman artifacts, and an exceptional painting, the "Portrait of an Unknown Man" (1472), a work by Sicily's most eminent Renaissance artist, Antonello da Messina (1430–1479).

Aeolian Islands

None of Sicily's ravishing offshore islands are as popular or spectacular as the Aeolian Islands (Isole Eolie), legendary home of Aeolus, god of the winds. The coronet of seven islets are the remnants of volcanoes both active and extinct, and visitors come for the chance to witness raw volcanic activity

and for the ethereal light, balmy climate, stark beauty, and aquamarine seas.

Ferries run to the islands from Naples, Palermo, and Messina, but the most direct access is from Milazzo, 16 miles (26 km) away on Sicily's northern coast. Boats also ply between the islands themselves. Walking and snorkeling are major attractions, as are the volcanic black-sand beaches. Excellent wine, dessert wine in particular, is also made locally. However, you won't have the islands to yourself: The big three—Stromboli, Vulcano, and Lipari—are extremely popular, so reserve accommodations in advance. Other islands, notably Salina, are quieter.

Stromboli: This island is the one most people make for, mainly because its volcanic action is the most reliable—spectacular eruptions take place from its summit cone around four times an hour. This makes it the busiest of the Aeolians if you wish to stay overnight, but you can easily visit for the day from Lipari, Salina, or elsewhere. Boats dock near San Vincenzo, a hamlet that with its neighbors (Piscità and San Bartolo) forms a settlement known as **Stromboli Paese.** Most hotels and other facilities are here, as is the island's main black-sand beach (north of Piscità).

Only the first part of the climb up this volcano, one of the most active on Earth, can be done on your own. You must have an authorized guide to reach the peak and observe the lava eruptions (see sidebar opposite). It's not an endeavor suited to everyone but your guides will supply any equipment you may not have and they will prepare you for the climb.

Vulcano: Vulcano is the closest island to Milazzo and the Sicilian mainland. However, it has one major drawback—the last major eruption here was in 1980. The island takes its name from the myth that this was where Vulcan, god of fire, kept his forge, a notion that led to the island lending its name to all things volcanic. If the god's in-house activities are currently diminished, however, they are not entirely curtailed, for all sorts of minor volcanic activities continue unabated—smoke holes smolder, mud baths bubble, and geysers spout.

Boats dock at **Porto Levante,** nestled beneath the so-called **Great Crater** (Vulcano in effect is four separate volcanoes), whose summit offers fabulous views of the crater vicinity and the rest of the island. (Allow three hours for the round-trip on foot.) Walks elsewhere reveal landscapes of somber but striking beauty—try the hike to **Vulcanello,** another of the craters. The landscapes can also be enjoyed from one of the highly recommended summer boat trips around the island. Trips leave from **Porto Ponente** (15 minutes' walk from

INSIDER TIP:

Each of the Aeolians has its own appeal. Italian families flock to Salina and Lipari, while Filicudi and Alicudi— no cars allowed— attract adventurous travelers.

—JANE SUNDERLAND
National Geographic contributor

Porto Levante), a place also known for its (busy) black-sand beach and therapeutic sulfurous mud baths. The waters at **Porto Levante** beach are warmed by jets of volcanic steam.

Lipari: This island is the largest and most scenically varied of the Aeolians, making up what it lacks in volcanic activity with some beautiful coastal and other landscapes. Boats dock at **Lipari**

Taormina

 317 D2

Visitor Information

✉ Palazzo Corvaja, Piazza Santa Caterina

☎ 0942 23 243

🕐 Closed Sun. & 1:30 p.m.– 4 p.m. (hours may vary)

taormina.it

Town, cradled between two bays, Marina Lunga, which has a beach, and Marina Corta, from where you can pick up boats for some excellent trips around the coast. The town has a pleasant old walled quarter and the **Castello** is home to the Archaeological Museum *(Via del Castello 2, tel 090 988 0174, may have restricted winter hours, $)*, which is small but has an excellent collection of prehistoric artifacts, Greek masks, and epigraphs. In Lipari, you can rent cars, bikes, and scooters to explore the hinterland, whose highlights are the village of **Canneto,** the **Spiaggia Bianca** (the island's best beach), the headland at **Puntazze,** and the matchless viewpoint at **Quattrocchi.**

Etna's Wines

Etna's rich but well-drained volcanic soils are perfect for growing vines, and at heights up to 4,000 feet (1,200 m), its vast day-to-night temperature range—as much as 36°F (20°C)—produces a stop-start ripening process that adds complexity to the wine and can push back the harvest to the last week of October on the mountain's northern slopes.

It is only recently, however, that the wines' full potential has begun to be realized. Some critics are calling the region the "Burgundy of the Mediterranean," producing some of southern Italy's most exciting new wines. Look for Etna-specific grape varieties, notably red Nerello Mascarese and Nerello Cappuccio, or the white Carricante and Catarratto. To learn more about the wines from the people who create them, make an appointment for a tasting at **Azienda Vinicola Benanti** *(Viagrande, tel 095 789 0928, vinicolabenanti.it, $$$$$).*

Taormina

Taormina enjoys a fabled site, its beautiful location offering views across the blue expanse of the Ionian Sea to one side and the majestic profile of Mount Etna to the other. As well as enjoying some of Sicily's loveliest landscapes, the town boasts sandy beaches, chic designer stores, grand hotels, ancient monuments, and top-notch restaurants. All of these combine to make Taormina Sicily's most exclusive and visited resort.

The town is also blessed with a mild climate, which means its matchless views are fringed with borders of palms, bougainvillea, citrus trees, and swathes of luxuriant subtropical vegetation. Flowers fill the windows and balconies of its medieval houses, most of which twist around steeply rising streets and sun-dappled piazzas. Visitors intent on seeing, or being seen, make for the cafés and bars on the panoramic main square, **Piazza IX Aprile,** or the almost equally seductive establishments on **Corso Umberto I,** Taormina's main street.

More than most towns, this is a place to be enjoyed off-season, for its charms attract hordes of summer visitors, their numbers swollen by those attending the town's many arts and music festivals. Many of the festivals take place in the town's premier sight, the sublimely situated **Teatro Greco** *(tel 0942 23 220, $$).* German writer Johann Goethe considered the theater's setting the "greatest work of art and nature" *(Italian Journey, 1789).*

■ **Visible from far and wide, the still active volcano Etna looms over the Plain of Catania.**

Other sights are few and far between, but this is not a place you visit for art and architecture. Try exploring the **Giardino Publico** (Public Gardens) on Via Croce, or walk or drive the 2 miles (3 km) to the **Castello** on the 1,279-foot (390 m) Monte Tauro. Built on the site of the former Greek acropolis, the medieval fort offers tremendous views of the surrounding countryside.

Etna

Etna is Europe's highest volcano. Ancient mariners believed its snow-tinged and smoldering summit was the world's highest point. To the Arabs, it was simply the "The Mountain," while to the Greeks it was known as Aipho (meaning "I burn"). A visit close to its summit, and a car or train ride around its fertile lower slopes, are essential.

Etna is a youngster geologically. Formed about 60,000 years ago, it sprang from undersea eruptions on what is now the Plain of Catania. Unlike many volcanoes, it tends to rupture rather than explode, creating huge lateral fissures instead of a single crater—some 350 fissures have appeared to date. About 90 major and 135 minor eruptions have been documented, of which the most catastrophic occurred in 1669, when the pyrotechnics lasted for 122 days. Debris was thrown over 65 miles (104 km), and a mile-wide tongue of lava engulfed **Catania** more than 25 miles (40 km) away.

To experience Etna fully, you should visit the summit, which rises to 10,900 feet (3,322 m), and explore its lower slopes. For the latter, take the private Circumetnea railroad from Catania, which circles the volcano, or make a road trip along a similar route—the approach from the village of Linguaglossa is superb. As well as views of the mountain, you pass through groves of orange, lemon, figs, vines, olives, and the swathes

Etna

🗺 317 C2

Visitor Information

✉ Via A. Manzoni, Formazzo

☎ 095 955 159

parcoetna.it

Catania

🗺 317 C2

Visitor Information

✉ Via Etnea 63–65

☎ 095 401 4070

🕐 Closed Sat. p.m. & Sun.

turismo.citta metropolitana.ct.it

Syracuse

 317 D1

Visitor Information

✉ Info point
Via Roma 30,
Ortigia

☎ 0931 462 946

🕐 Closed Sat.–Sun.

siracusaturismo.net

Parco Archeologico della Neapolis

✉ Viale Augusto–
Via Paradiso 14,
Syracuse

☎ 0931 66 206

💲 $$

**regione.sicilia.it/
beniculturali**

of vegetation nurtured by the volcano's fertile soils.

As for the summit, volcanic activity alters the means of access and the areas you can safely approach (there was a major eruption in 2002). Guided tours are possible from Catania, Taormina, Nicolosi, and elsewhere using minibuses and off-road vehicles. Or you can drive yourself to the Rifugio Sapienza, a mountain refuge, take a cable car to the upper slopes, and then walk (allow a full day). Be sure to wear strong boots.

Syracuse

Syracuse (Siracusa) was founded by the Greeks in 733 B.C. Between the third and fifth centuries B.C., it became Europe's most powerful city. For years its only rivals were the Etruscans and Carthaginians, each of whom it defeated before succumbing to Rome in 214 B.C.

Today, its old town—Ortigia (or Ortygia)—and the extensive archaeological zone (the Parco Archeologico), are essential stops on any Sicilian itinerary. Only the modern town, raised from the ruins of World War II bombing, turns out to be a disappointment.

Parco Archeologico della Neapolis: It is a pleasant open area ranged across the site of the ancient Greek city, Neapolis, above the sea and modern suburbs. The park's entrance is marked by a small visitor center and a sprawl of souvenir stands. Beyond these on the left lies the site's first major ruin, the **Ara di Ierone II,** created as a vast sacrificial altar in the third century B.C.—as many as 450 bulls were slaughtered here in a single day. Today, its remains serve as an occasional stage. More

■ The 18th-century baroque facade of Syracuse's imposing Duomo was designed by Andrea Palma.

INSIDER TIP:

If you have time when visiting Etna, don't miss the town of Randazzo just north of the volcano, with its church built of lava and yellow pumice.

—TINO SORIANO
National Geographic photographer

survives of the fifth-century B.C. **Teatro Greco,** an amphitheater carved from the hillside's living rock—its 15,000-seat capacity made it one of the largest theaters in the Greek world.

Close to the theater lies the **Latomia del Paradiso,** site of a former quarry in which 7,000 Athenian prisoners were reputedly incarcerated in 413 B.C. and left to perish. Nearby is a grotto known as the **Orecchio di Dionisio** (Ear of Dionysius), christened by the artist Caravaggio in 1608. (Legend has it that the cave's acoustic properties allowed one of Syracuse's erstwhile rulers to overhear prisoners or conspirators talking, hence the strange name.) Another nearby cave, the **Grotta dei Cordari,** was used by Greek ropemakers, its humidity preventing hemp breaking as it was being made into ropes.

Syracuse was the birthplace in 287 B.C. of Archimedes, the eminent geometrician and scientist best known for the discovery—made in his tub—that any body in water loses weight equivalent to the weight of the water it displaces. He helped defend Syracuse from

the besieging Romans in 214 B.C. by trying to direct the sun's rays and set fire to the enemy fleet using a system of lenses and mirrors. When the Romans entered the city he was so deep in calculations that he failed to hear them and was killed by a Roman foot soldier.

Before heading for Ortigia (buses and cabs run from outside the ruins), it makes sense to visit the town's **Museo Archeologico Regionale** *(Viale Teocrito 66, tel 0931 489 511, closed Sun. p.m. & Mon., $).* A museum of finds from the archaeological zone and elsewhere, it lies on the grounds of the Villa Landolina, about ten minutes' walk east of the Parco Archeologico. Just west of the villa are the fourth-century **Catacombe di San Giovanni** *(Viale San Giovanni),* Sicily's oldest catacombs and the world's largest outside of those in Rome.

Ortigia: Ortigia, squeezed onto a tiny island linked by a causeway to the mainland and modern town, formed the heart of ancient Syracuse for some 2,700 years, its easily defended island location and freshwater springs making it a natural fortress. It was here that the besieging Romans were held at bay for 13 years in the third century B.C. The ancient Greek chronicler Thucydides described the former encounter as the "greatest battle in Hellenic history." Today, much of the island has a pretty baroque and medieval appearance, largely the result of rebuilding that followed

EXPERIENCE: Olives & Olive Oil

Olive groves are found across much of Italy, but in the South, where you will find some of the country's oldest and largest trees, they are everywhere. The olive is part of the Oleaceae family (along with ash, lilac, and jasmine); it is drought-resistant but susceptible to cold—temperatures below minus 10°F (−12°C) can often kill trees.

Southern Italy produces a variety of exceptional olives.

The International Olive Oil Council has declared Ravidà olive oil from Menfi, Sicily, one of Europe's finest. The oil can be bought outside Italy, or visit the **Ravidà Estate** by appointment between March and November (head office, Via Roma 173, Menfi, tel 39 0925 71 109, ravidaoil.com). Cooking classes can also be arranged by appointment and according to availability.

The harvest takes place from late October to January. The timing is crucial: Pick too early and the oil's acidity will be low—a good thing— but so will the yields, and the taste will be bitter. Too late, and yields will be high, along with the acidity, rendering the oil rancid. Picking by hand is best, because farmers can select the best olives and return to individual trees, as olives on the same tree ripen at different times.

The traditional method of harvesting is to surround the trees with nets and beat the branches with poles or, recently, to use mechanical claws that grasp the tree and vibrate in order to dislodge the fruit.

The olives are then washed and stored, ideally for no more than a day (or they may ferment). The olives, including the pits, are then crushed or chopped, traditionally between water- or mule-driven millstones, but now more often using metal grinders.

The resulting paste is pressed to extract the oil. Traditionally, this was achieved by spreading the paste on hemp mats and stacking them in a column, which was then compressed using weights or a wooden lever or screw press to squeeze out the oil. Today, fiber mats and a hydraulic press are used, usually in combination with a centrifuge, which removes excess water.

More oil can be extracted from the paste if it is heated, if the paste is re-pressed, or if chemicals are used, but this affects flavor. As a result, the best oils come from the first "natural" pressing and are "cold pressed." European Union (EU) rules state that only oils extracted at temperatures below 80°F (27°C) can be called "cold pressed."

Low acidity is important in olive oil. Extra-virgin oils should have acidity levels below 0.8 percent and virgin olive oil below 2 percent. However, acidity is not all, and low levels don't guarantee quality—tiny differences, in any case, will be imperceptible to most palates. Buy cold-pressed oils from small producers, and don't be taken in by deep green oils, which are not necessarily better than amber or light gold oils.

a calamitous earthquake in 1693. The Ponte Nuovo from the mainland leads into Piazza Pancali, home of the fragmentary **Tempio di Apollo** (565 B.C.), Sicily's oldest Doric temple.

The town's most famous sight is the **Duomo,** whose baroque facade conceals the Tempio di Atena, a fifth-century B.C. temple incorporated into the fabric of the later Christian building. Also worth seeing are the **Fonte Aretusa,** Ortigia's precious original spring; the **Passeggio Adorno,** a scenic promenade; and the **Galleria Regionale** *(Palazzo Bellomo, Via Capodieci 14, tel 0931 69 511, closed Sun. a.m. & Mon., $),* a museum of paintings (including works by Caravaggio and Antonello da Messina) and artifacts.

Piazza Armerina

Piazza Armerina is a village lost in Sicily's central heartlands; a place of little note save for the **Villa Romana del Casale,** an isolated Roman villa 3 miles (5 km) to the southwest. Here are preserved some of Europe's most extensive and unspoiled

Roman mosaics, a priceless treasure buried by a landslip in the 12th century and thus protected from the elements until full-scale excavations between 1929 and 1950 brought their glories to light.

No one is sure to whom the Villa Casale belonged, but to judge from its opulence and huge extent—it contains more than 50 rooms—its owner must have been a figure of considerable renown. The most persuasive theories suggest it was a hunting lodge and country retreat built for the emperor Maximianus Herculius, who reigned as co-emperor with the better-known emperor Diocletian between A.D. 286 and 305. Its role as a hunting lodge would seem to be borne out by the hunting scenes of many of its floor mosaics and by its rustic position.

While the villa's superstructure may have gone—skillfully fashioned modern walls and roofs suggest how it might once have appeared—the original mosaics survive in an almost pristine state. Their style resembles similar mosaics discovered in Roman villas

Piazza Armerina

🗺 317 C2

Visitor Information

✉ Via Generale Muscarà 47a

☎ 0935 680 201

🕐 Closed Sat.–Sun. & p.m. daily except Wed.

comune.piazza armerina.en.it

Villa Romana del Casale

🗺 317 C1

✉ Casale

☎ 0935 680 036

💲 $$

villaromanadelcasale .it

The Ceramics of Caltagirone

The town of Caltagirone, 20 miles (32 km) southeast of Piazza Armerina, is famous across Italy for its ceramics, the legacy of high-quality local clays that have sustained the craft for more than a thousand years. Although it is not possible to tour local factories, you can watch craftspeople at work—often painting the yellow and blue motifs that characterize the local majolica—in some of the 120 stores around town. This is especially true of those on

Via Roma and those on the famous **Scalinata di Santa Maria del Monte** *(Piazza Municipio),* 142 steps adorned with hand-painted tiles. The staircase is at its most beautiful during the town's Festa di San Giacomo (July 24–25), when it is lit by more than 4,000 oil lamps. Information is available online at *ceramichecaltagirone .com* or from the visitor center *(Via Duomo 15, tel 0933 490 836),* which can help make appointments to visit specific ceramicists.

Agrigento

⚑ 317 B1

Visitor Information

✉ Via Empedocle 73

☎ 0922 20 391

parcovalledeitempli.it

Valle dei Templi

✉ Piazzale dei Templi

☎ 0922 183 9996

💲 $$ or combined ticket with Museo Archeologico Regionale

parcovalledeitempli.it

Selinunte

⚑ 317 B2

✉ Via Selinunte, off Via Caboto, Castelvetrano

☎ 0924 46 251 or 0924 46 277 (ticket office)

💲 $$

selinunte.gov.it

across North Africa, suggesting their creators may have been Carthaginian. This notion is borne out by the villa's centerpiece, an African hunting scene some 200 feet (61 m) long. Woven into this scene's rippling narrative are vivid depictions of exotic animals such as tigers, ostriches, and elephants, many of them being captured and caged for transportation to Rome for use in circuses and gladiatorial games.

INSIDER TIP:

Arrive at the Villa Romana del Casale as early as possible in the morning to avoid lines of people pouring from tour buses.

—SHEILA F. BUCKMASTER
National Geographic Traveler
magazine editor at large

Virtually every room features similarly fascinating mosaics, although the scene that attracts most visitors is the one depicting ten female athletes in bikinis.

Agrigento

Modern Agrigento provides an ugly backdrop to Sicily's principal archaeological sight—the **Valle dei Templi,** or Valley of the Temples, site of the ancient Greek city of Acragas. Once this "loveliest of mortal cities," as the classical Greek writer Pindar described it, was among the most important of Sicily's Greek colonies. Today,

much of its former grandeur is still apparent in the valley's extensive ruins and its nine temples, the finest classical Greek remains outside Greece.

The city was founded in 582 B.C. by settlers from nearby Gela, a town that had originally been established by pioneers from the Greek island of Rhodes. Although earthquakes over the years laid much of the city low, the worst damage was inflicted by early Christian settlers, who deliberately vandalized the temples, sparing only the **Tempio di Concordia** (430 B.C.), and only because it was converted into a church in the sixth century.

This magnificent Doric temple is the finest in Sicily and the finest anywhere in the Greek world after the Temple of Hephaestus in Athens. Other only marginally less impressive temples lie close by along the so-called Via Sacra. Among them are the 470 B.C. **Tempio di Giunone** (Juno) and the fifth-century B.C. **Tempio di Ercole** (Herakles). The site's western margins, reached by crossing the street known as the Via dei Templi, include the ruins of the half-finished **Tempio di Giove** (Jupiter). Had this been completed—work was interrupted by a Carthaginian raid in 406 B.C.—it would have been the largest temple in the Greek and Roman world.

To the north, at the end of the Via dei Templi, lies the **Quartiere Ellenistico-Romano,** the ruins of part of a later Greco-Roman town. Also here is the **Museo Archeologico Regionale** (Viale dei Templi, tel 0922 401 565, closed Sun. p.m. & Mon., $), an extensive collection devoted to art and artifacts discovered in the valley.

Selinunte

Selinunte was among Sicily's most powerful Greek colonies, but it fell into ruin following Carthaginian raids in 409 B.C. and 250 B.C. What survives places it second to Agrigento in archaeological terms, although only portions of its eight massive temples remain standing (much of the site is still being excavated). The best of its treasures have been removed to Palermo's Museo Archeologico Regionale (see p. 321), but a small on-site museum displays some of the lesser artifacts. Like Segesta, the site has a pretty location.

Segesta

No Greek temple in Sicily occupies such dramatic surroundings as the tawny-stoned Segesta. The Doric temple (430 B.C.), almost encircled by a shallow ravine, stands in majestic isolation at the heart of glorious countryside. Myth claims the original colony, still largely unexcavated, was founded by Trojan companions of Aeneas. In truth, the site probably dates back to the pre-Hellenic cultures of the 12th century B.C. Work on the temple was probably abandoned after a Syracusan raid in 307 B.C. A short road from the site leads about a mile (2 km) toward the summit of **Monte Barbaro,**

whose hilly slopes offer glorious views and a dainty Greek theater (third century B.C.) still used for performances on summer evenings.

Erice

Some of Sicily's medium-size towns, notably Enna and Erice, are worth a visit if you are in the vicinity. Others, such as Catania and Messina—both mainly modern and earthquake-damaged horrors—you should avoid. Erice appeals by virtue of its panoramic setting, hunched 2,461 feet (750 m) above the port of Trapani, and the charm and medievalism of its alleys,

◾ **Dawn breaks on the ruins of one of Selinunte's temples.**

streets, and squares (unusual in Sicily). The main sights are the 16th-century cathedral and **Castello di Venere** (Largo Castello 9, $), a 12th-century Norman castle that occupies the site of the Eryx, a fortress and ancient shrine dating back to Greek and Phoenician times. ◾

Segesta
🅰 317 B2
Visitor Information
✉ Located 25 miles (40 km) east of Trapani, signed just south of Calatafimi exit of A29 Autostrada
☎ 0924 952 356
💲 $

regione.sicilia.it/ beniculturali

Erice
🅰 317 A2
Visitor Information
✉ Pro Loco, Via Castello di Venere
☎ 329 065 8244
🕐 Closed p.m. & Sat.–Sun.

prolocoerice.it

THE MAFIA

Everyone has heard of the Mafia. The word first appeared in Italian around 1860. By 1866, it was quoted by Sicily's British consul, who reported to his superiors that "*maffie*-elected juntas share the earnings of the workmen, keep up intercourse with outcasts and take malefactors under their wing and protection." Both the word and the organizations of which the consul spoke have ancient origins: The linguistic roots are uncertain and may probably lie in an Arab word.

■ In this historic photograph, children mimic the style of Sicilian-born gangster Charles "Lucky" Luciano (center), walking down a street in Sicily.

The organizational roots of the Mafia are more elusive. Many scholars believe the seeds were sown as early as the 12th century, when secret societies were created to resist the imposition of rule by the Holy Roman Empire. Others point to the Bourbons, who used ex-brigands to police the remote Sicilian interior, a system that quickly led to the brigands taking bribes in exchange for ignoring the activities of their former criminal colleagues. Many experts also cite the rise of the so-called *gabellotti*, middlemen who acted as rent collectors or mediators between peasants or landowners and quickly grew rich by intimidating the former and acting as agents for the latter. The gabellotti quickly became a separate class, bound by distinct codes of honor, behavior, and semiformal organization.

All theories are linked by a common thread: the centuries-old gulf between Sicilians and agents of authority, a gulf fostered by Sicily's long succession of foreign rulers. Nowhere was the breach more keenly felt than by landless peasants forced to work on the island's *latifondi*, vast feudal estates owned by absentee landlords in Naples or Palermo. The system went back to Roman times and survived until well after World War II. Where conventional justice and authority were either lacking or despised, the gap soon was filled by all manner of local arbitrators—the so-called *amici* (friends) or *uomini d'onore* (men of honor).

Traveler Patrick Brydone, writing in *A Tour through Sicily and Malta*, summarized the situation in 1773: "These banditi," he wrote, "are the most respectable of the island, and have the highest and most romantic notions of what they call their point of honour . . . with respect to one another, and to every person to whom they have once professed it, they have ever maintained the most unshaken fidelity. The magistrates have often been obliged to protect them, and even pay them court, as they are known to be extremely determined and desperate; and so extremely vindictive, that they will certainly put any person to death who has ever given them just cause of provocation." He might easily have been describing events two centuries later.

A Growing Power

Under Mussolini, the legendary police chief Cesare Mori used brutal and entirely illegal measures to combat the Mafia and, but for World War II, might have crushed it entirely. Ironically, the Americans foiled the venture. In preparing for the invasion of Sicily in 1943, the Allies had only one source of intelligence and logistical support—the Mafia—with whom it forged links by exploiting the contacts of Italian-American gangsters such as Lucky Luciano (Luciano's sentence was reassessed in light of his assistance).

Once the Allies had taken the island, they further reinforced Mafia power by drafting its often highly placed members onto the new Allied Military Government—of 66 Sicilian towns, 62 were entrusted to men with criminal connections. Mafia power was further consolidated in Italy's postwar boom, when huge fortunes were made in construction. Money was then laundered into legitimate businesses or funneled into narcotics, a trade that altered forever the nature of Mafia business. Despite occasional judicial successes, the Mafia's dismemberment remains highly unlikely, largely because its tentacles are now so tightly entwined in Italy's legitimate economy: Not for nothing do the Italians refer to the Mafia as *la piovra*—the octopus.

Mafia Locations

Towns such as **Prizzi** and **Corleone** in the Sicilian interior receive a stream of curious visitors drawn by their appearance in Mario Puzo's Mafia novels. Fewer people visit **Savoca**, a village in the Monti Peloritani northwest of Taormina, featured in Francis Ford Coppola's classic movie *The Godfather*. Much of the sequence where Michael Corleone (Al Pacino) is sent to Sicily and marries the ill-fated Apollonia Vitelli was shot in and around Savoca, not least in the village bar, the Vitelli, where you can still stop for coffee or an iced lemon *granita*. A visit to Savoca, and to nearby villages such as **Forza d'Agrò** and **Casalvecchio Siculo**, reveals landscapes and ways of life little changed in centuries.

SARDINIA

Sardinia is blessed with a peerless coastline—especially along the Costa Smeralda—of golden sands and emerald seas; the opportunities here for diving, sailing, and other water sports are unparalleled. Invaders did leave their mark on the island, but its starkly beautiful interior was far more inhospitable. Venture inland today, preferably to the Gennargentu mountains, and you will discover traditions and ways of life that have remained unchanged for centuries.

■ Sun-seeking Italians flock to the beaches of Sardinia's Costa Smeralda, or Emerald Coast.

Costa Smeralda

🅰 337 D5

Costa Smeralda

Ask almost any Italian where they would like to spend an Italian beach vacation and chances are they will say Costa Smeralda, or Emerald Coast. The rags-to-riches story of this stretch of the inortheast coastline began when the Aga Khan built a single luxury resort village—Porto Cervo—in the 1960s. Similar resorts soon followed, turning the area into one of Europe's most exclusive summer retreats.

Porto Rotondo, Portisco, Baja Sardinia, and of course, the granddaddy of them all, **Porto Cervo,** are all similarly chic and exclusive and based mostly around upscale hotel resorts or self-contained resort villages. Choose well and you will have a relaxing time—but don't expect much by way of local color or character.

Relatively undeveloped adjacent resorts include Santa Teresa Gallura, Palau, Cannigione, and the beaches at Punta Falcone, Capo Testa, and La Marmorata.

Some of the island's northern highlights are within a morning's drive. For example, from the SS199 east of Olbia, or from Castelsardo, you can visit a succession of Pisan-Romanesque churches. Take roads south and west toward Ozieri and Sassari, and you pass half a dozen of these churches, including **Santissima Trinità di Saccargia,** Sardinia's loveliest religious building. This itinerary also gives you the chance to drive along the **Valle dei Nuraghi** (on the SS131), scattered with the mysterious *nuraghi*—ancient prehistoric dwellings (see sidebar p. 340)—for which the island is celebrated and leaves you well placed for Alghero, one of northern Sardinia's most attractive towns.

Alghero

Alghero is a prettily situated port gathered around a walled and atmospheric old quarter. The town is popular with visitors, but its role as a fishing port means that it retains a role of its own.

Alghero owes much of its culture and appearance to the Spanish, and to the Catalans in particular, who ruled the town for some four centuries after landing here in 1354. The Catalan presence was so pervasive that the region

Alghero

🗺 337 B4

Visitor Information

✉ Largo Lo Quarter

☎ 079 979 054

🕐 Closed Sun. Nov.–March & Sun. p.m. April–Oct.

sardegnaturismo.it

algheroturismo.eu

Grotta di Nettuno

✉ 15 miles (24 km) W of Alghero

☎ 368 353 6824 or 333 619 6855

🕐 Boat tours daily April–Oct.; caves close 3 p.m. Nov.– March

💲 $$$$$, caves $$$$

grottedinettuno.it

acquired the nickname "Barcelo-netta" or Little Barcelona. Catalan influence survives to this day, both in language—*plaça* and *iglesia* are used for piazza and church, for example—and in the decidedly Spanish look of the town's religious and domestic architecture.

Key sights in the old town's web of twisting cobbled lanes are the **Cattedrale** in Piazza del Duomo (*off Via Roma*) and the

■ Prehistoric *nuraghi* (conical dwellings) near Cala Gonone

Cala Gonone

🅰 337 C3–D3

Visitor Information

✉ Comune, Viale Umberto 37, Dorgali

☎ 0784 927 235

🕐 Restricted hours Nov.–Easter

enjoydorgali.it

church of **San Francesco** on Via Carlo Alberto. The former is a Catalan-Gothic building enlivened by an Aragonese portal, the latter a 14th-century Catalan-Gothic affair overlaid with Renaissance detailing and annexed to an exquisite cloister.

The town's best beaches lie to the north, as does the **Grotta di Nettuno,** a cave system best reached by boat, although road access offers far-reaching views of the region's cliff-edged coastline. Arriving by car, however, means climbing down the 654-step

Escala del Cabriol (Catalan for "goat's steps"). Allow ten minutes. The point of **Capo Caccia** has a new museum dedicated to prison memory and a theme park for children inspired by Antoine de Saint-Exupéry's *The Little Prince.*

Cala Gonone

Cala Gonone is a small but increasingly popular resort on Sardinia's east coast. It lies at the heart of the island's most spectacular coastal scenery, much of which is accessible by boat from the resort or visible from above on the gloriously scenic road (SS125) that runs between the neighboring towns of Arbatax and Dorgali.

Ideally, aim to stay in Cala Gonone itself, a former fishing village gradually surrendering its former identity—but not its charm—to the march of modern hotels, restaurants, and other visitor facilities. If accommodations are full, then **Dorgali,** just 6 miles (10 km) inland, makes a good alternative base.

Approaching Cala Gonone from Arbatax and the south offers views of the **Gola su Gorroppu,** one of the island's most breathtaking canyons. Views around Cala Gonone itself are best enjoyed from a boat, the most popular trips being to coves south of the village at **Cala di Luna** and **Cala Sisine.** Cliffs in the vicinity tumble from the 3,000-foot (900 m) mountains that rear up along much of this stretch of coast. Boats will also drop you for the day at secluded coves along the coast or provide

INSIDER TIP:

Near the Gennargentu, stop by Orgosolo, where incredible graffitists have decorated the walls, some calling for revolution.

—TINO SORIANO
National Geographic photographer

access to the **Grotta del Bue Marino** *(tel 347 720 9696, excursionscalagonone.com, $$$$$)*, a spellbinding cave studded with stalactites and stalagmites.

Barbagia

The Barbagia is one of the wildest regions in Sardinia, which is to say one of the wildest regions in Western Europe. It lies near the island's center, between Nuoro and the almost equally remote Monti del Gennargentu to the south. It is full of tiny villages such as **Mamoida** and **Arizo** that, in the words of the Sardinian poet Sebastiano Satta (1867–1914), are "as remote from one another as are the stars." Older people still wear traditional dress, one of the few places in Sardinia where this is the case. Sheep farming provides virtually the only income. Hiking is possible on the remote hills, but a car is necessary to get the best from the area.

Monti del Gennargentu

Sardinia's interior is one of western Europe's most traditional rural enclaves, an upland fastness where sheep are often more in evidence than people, and where ancient customs, dress, and ceremonies are still preserved in time-forgotten villages. No area is more starkly beautiful than the mountains of the Gennargentu.

Situated midway down the east of the island, the Gennargentu rise to a height of 6,017 feet (1,834 m) of mostly barren, rounded summits. The name means "silver gate," a reference to the snow that covers them in winter. Their heart is protected by the **Parco Nazionale del Gennargentu** *(parco gennargentu.it)*. This wilderness is so remote that even the Romans did not fully penetrate its depths. The only practical way of seeing the region is by car, following roads such as the SS125 from Arbatax to Dorgali (see p. 338), or the scenic drives from Aritzo, the main resort center, to **Arcu Guddetorgiu, Seui,** or **Fonni,** the highest of the island's villages at 3,281 feet (1,000 m).

Giara di Gesturi

A *giara* is a basalt outcrop, a geological feature found across Sardinia. The best is the Giara di Gesturi, a lofty plateau about 2,000 feet high (600 m) and 8 miles (13 km) across. Its summit is cloaked in lush vegetation and forests of cork oak, the last a refuge for the once-common and reclusive Sardinian pony. The plateau is good for walking and is also known for its birds and flora—the best access point is the village of Gesturi. While in the region you should also visit **Las Plassas,** a distinctive conical

Barbagia

🔼 337 C3

Visitor Information

✉ Piazza del Popolo 12, Orosei

☎ 0784 998 184

🕐 Closed 1 p.m.–4 p.m. & Nov.–April

Monti del Gennargentu

🔼 337 C3

Giara di Gesturi

🔼 337 B2–C2

Visitor Information

✉ Info point Palazzo Comunale, Via Roma 145, Cagliari

☎ 070 677 7397

parcodellagiara.it

cagliariturismo.it

Cagliari

🅰 337 C1

Visitor Information

✉ Info point
Palazzo
Comunale,
Via Roma 145,
Cagliari

☎ 070 677 7397

**www.cagliariturismo
.it**

Museo
Archeologico
Nazionale

✉ Piazza Arsenale 1,

☎ 070 6051 8245

🕓 Closed Mon.

💲 $

**museoarcheocagliari
.beniculturali.it**

Pinacoteca
Nazionale

✉ Piazza Arsenale 1

☎ 070 662 496 or
340 982 4303

🕓 Closed Mon.

💲 $

**pinacoteca.cagliari
.beniculturali.it**

hill visible for miles around and topped by a ruined 12th-century castle. Be sure to visit 15th-century B.C. **Su Nuraxi,** the most important of the island's *nuraghi,* or prehistoric dwellings (see sidebar this page). It lies about half a mile (1 km) west of Barumini, a village some 30 miles (50 km) north of Cagliari.

Cagliari

Sardinia's capital has a large port, substantial population, lots of industry, and a surfeit of modern building, yet it is a surprisingly appealing place, blessed with a pleasant old center, a couple of major monuments, and easy access to nearby beaches and flamingo-filled lagoons.

Head first for Sardinia's major museum, the **Museo Archeo-logico Nazionale,** perched on the northern flanks of the historic quarter, an area enclosed by 13th-century Pisan-built fortifications. The highlights of the museum's wide-ranging collection are a series of bronze statuettes, the artistic high point of the island's prehistoric Nuraghic culture. In the same complex is the **Pinacoteca Nazionale,** devoted to Sardinian paintings from different eras.

Elsewhere in the old quarter, make for the **Bastione Saint Remy,** one of several terraces offering views over the city, and the cathedral of **Santa Maria,** whose main portal is guarded by 12th-century carvings originally destined for Pisa cathedral on the mainland. Be certain to descend into the lavishly decorated crypt, hewn from solid rock. Farther afield, try to see the remains of the **Roman amphitheater** *(Viale Fra Ignazio)* and the churches of **Sant'Agostino** *(near Largo Carlo Felice),* **San Saturno** *(Piazza San Cosimo),* and **Nostra Signora di Bonara** *(Viale Armando Diaz).* San Saturno dates from the fifth century and is one of the most important early Christian churches on the island. To the northwest, just outside the center, is **Tuvixeddu,** one of the largest Punic burial grounds in the Mediterranean. ∎

Nuraghi

Myth suggests the Sards are descended from Sardus, legendary son of Hercules. In truth, they could have come from almost anywhere in the Mediterranean. All that is known for certain is that an indigenous population existed before the arrival of the Phoenicians and Carthaginians in the first millennium B.C. Evidence of its presence lies scattered across the island, from the rock tombs—*Domus de Janas* (elves' dwellings)—of about 2000 B.C. to 1800 B.C., to the 7,000 or more mysterious *nuraghi* established by

the tribes who inhabited Sardinia from around 1500 B.C. to 500 B.C.

Nuraghi were probably houses or fortified citadels. No two are the same, but most are conical, with circular vaulted interiors linked by passages to terraces and upper stories. They occur across Sardinia, but the three most famous are found at Su Nuraxi, outside Barumini; Losa, near Abbasanta; and Sant'Antine, between Macomer and Sassari. Anghelu Ruiu, 6 miles (10 km) north of Alghero, has the best concentration of ancient tombs.

TRAVELWISE

Bike, moped, bus—just some of the transportation opportunities in Italy

TRAVELWISE

PLANNING YOUR TRIP

When to Go

Deciding when to visit Italy depends on the activities you plan during your vacation. Spring and fall (April–June & late Sept.–Oct.) are best for sightseeing, summer (July–Aug.) is extremely busy but best for the beach, and winter (Jan.–March) is the time for skiing. Most big cities—save Venice—are quieter in winter, with fewer lines and lower prices. Easter, however, is always busy.

See pp. 389–390 for more details if you wish to plan your trip around one of the many artistic, religious, cultural, and other festivals and events that take place across Italy throughout the year.

Further help in planning your trip is available from various Italian State Tourist Offices outside Italy (see p. 348 for details). Some cities and organizations also have useful websites:
italia.it
visiteurope.com
initaly.com
wel.it
traveleurope.it
turismoroma.it
veneziaunica.it
firenzeturismo.it

Climate

As a general rule, Italy has mild winters and hot summers, but its varied topography produces a wide range of climatic conditions. Climate is generally warmer and drier the farther south you go. Winters in the Alps, Apennines, and high ground of the south can be severe, with snow and temperatures below freezing. Winter across the rest of northern and central Italy is shorter but otherwise broadly comparable to the colder climate of northern Europe. Spring tends to be short and fall more drawn out, but summers are hot across the country—and more so in the south.

Winter daytime temperatures in Italy range from around 5° to 59°F (-15° to 14°C), and summer temperatures from 65° to 90°F (18° to 38°C), although temperatures may often exceed these extremes. Italy uses degrees Celsius (°C) as its unit of temperature. To convert degrees Celsius to degrees Fahrenheit, multiply °C by 9, divide by 5, and add 32.

What to Take

You should be able to buy everything you need in Italy. Pharmacies offer a wide range of drugs, medical supplies, and toiletries, along with expert advice, but you should bring any prescription drugs you might need. Many brand-name drugs are different in Italy. A pharmacy (farmacia) is indicated by a green cross outside the store. It is also useful to bring a second pair of glasses or contact lenses if you wear them. Sunscreen and bug spray products are advisable in summer.

Clothing will depend on your destination, when you travel, and the activities you plan: You will only really need to dress up for the grandest city restaurants and casinos. Don't be too casual, however, because Italians generally dress more smartly than most U.S., Canadian, and northern European visitors. Make some effort for any meal out, and always dress appropriately in churches—ideally no bare shoulders or shorts for women. Note, too, that dress codes are more conservative in the south and most rural areas. Bring a sweater, even in summer, for evenings can be chilly. Come prepared for some rain and cool temperatures outside midsummer. Hiking, skiing, camping, and other sports equipment can easily be bought or rented, but you may prefer to bring equipment such as hiking boots.

Electricity in Italy is 220V, 50 Hz, and plugs have two (sometimes three) round pins. If you bring electrical equipment, you will need a plug adapter plus a transformer for U.S. appliances.

Lastly, don't forget the essentials: passport, driver's license, tickets, traveler's checks, and insurance documents.

Insurance

Make sure you have adequate travel and medical coverage for treatment and expenses, including repatriation and baggage and money loss. Keep all receipts for expenses. Report losses or thefts to the police, and obtain a signed statement (una denuncia) from police stations to help with insurance claims.

FURTHER READING

Italy has spawned a huge amount of poetry, fiction, and nonfiction from native and foreign writers. The following is a highly selective list of books you might want to read before your vacation. The Italians by Luigi Barzini was first published in 1964, but no writer, before or since, has produced a more penetrating or better-written analysis of Italy and the Italians. This is an essential read.

The best relatively modern Italian or Italian-set novels include The Leopard, Giuseppe di Lampedusa; A Room with a View, E. M. Forster; Christ Stopped at Eboli, Carlo Levi; The Name of the Rose, Umberto Eco; The Aspern Papers, Henry James; and the works of Primo Levi and

Italo Calvino. Evocative travelogues and nonfictional accounts include *Italian Journey*, Johann Goethe; *Italian Hours*, Henry James; *Innocents Abroad*, Mark Twain; *Naples '44*, Norman Lewis; *Venice*, Jan Morris; *The Stones of Florence/Venice Observed*, Mary McCarthy; *Love and War in the Apennines*, Eric Newby; and *Romans*, Michael Sheridan.

HOW TO GET TO ITALY
Passports
U.S., Canadian, and U.K. citizens need a passport to enter Italy for stays of up to 90 days. No visa is required.

Airlines
All the major airlines have flights to Italy, and many arrange package tours and budget-price flights. Alitalia, the main Italian carrier, has booking offices in most major cities around the world. Direct flights from North America land in Milan, Venice, or Rome, with occasional (summer only) flights to Pisa and Palermo. Rome is the more convenient hub and has a wider and more easily accessible network of internal flights. Flying time to Italy is about 8–9 hours from New York, 10–11 hours from Chicago, and 12–13 hours from Los Angeles.

Useful Numbers in the United States & Canada
Alitalia (U.S.), tel 800/223-5730, alitalia.com
Alitalia (Canada), 800/361-8336, alitalia.com
American Airlines, tel 800/433-7300, aa.com
Delta, tel 800/221-1212 or 404/765-4000, delta.com
Air Italy, tel 800/746-1888 (Canada), 866/387-6359 (U.S.), airitaly.com
United, tel 800/864-8331, united.com

Airports
Direct flights to Italy from the United States or Canada land at Milan's Malpensa airport, Rome's Leonardo da Vinci (better known by its colloquial name of Fiumicino), or, more infrequently, at Venice's Marco Polo airport (veniceairport.it).

Fiumicino–Leonardo da Vinci *(tel 06 65 951, adr.it)* is about 19 miles (30 km) west of Rome's city center. The best way into the city is on the express rail service (every 15 minutes in peak hours, between about 6:08 a.m. and 11:23 p.m.), taking 35 minutes to reach Stazione Termini, Rome's central station. Onward rail connections leave from Termini. Tickets are available from automated machines in the airport arrivals *(arrivi)* terminal or from a ticket office *(biglietteria)* on the right as you face the rail platforms. The same office sells tickets for the state network: Buy tickets here to avoid the long lines at Termini.

Cabs outside arrivals are plentiful, but be sure to take a licensed cab (yellow or white), and *never* accept offers from taxi (or hotel) touts inside the terminal buildings. Follow the signs for "Roma" and "Centro" if you're driving to the center, but be aware that city traffic can be intimidating. Parking is also very difficult. If you're renting a car to travel onward, tour Rome without a vehicle and then rent a car in the city, or return to the airport to rent a vehicle there.

Milan's major intercontinental airport, Milan-Malpensa *(flight information, tel 02 232 323, milanairports.com or milanomalpensa-airport.com)*, is an impractical 31 miles (50 km) northwest of the city center. A dedicated rail link, the Malpensa Express *(tel 02 7249 4949, malpensaexpress.it)*, connects to Garibaldi, Cadorna, and Centrale stations in Milan. Alternatively, you can board a special bus for the

hour's journey to the Stazione Centrale, Milan's main railroad station. Buses are timed to meet incoming and departing international and intercontinental flights. Buses also run from Malpensa to other cities and regions. Milan's Stazione Centrale offers onward rail connections to major cities in northern Italy.

If you begin your vacation in the United Kingdom, you can fly direct to a variety of Italian destinations. Scheduled flights with British Airways, Alitalia, and a host of smaller cut-rate carriers leave from Heathrow, Gatwick, Stansted, Luton, and Manchester for airports in Rome, Milan, Venice, Genoa, Bologna (for Florence), Florence, Pisa (for Florence), and Naples. Charter flights and smaller no-frills operators also often fly to lesser airports such as Verona and Catania (for Sicily). Note that charter flights and low-cost airlines often use second-string airports near the major cities, namely Ciampino in Rome and Treviso for Venice (both have bus connections to their respective city centers).

GETTING AROUND
Traveling in Italy
By Airplane
Some 40 Italian cities are connected by internal flights: Rome and Milan are the main hubs. Flights within Italy are operated mainly by Alitalia's domestic service, plus smaller companies such as Air Italy.
Alitalia, tel 06 65649, alitalia.it
Air Italy, tel 892 928 (call center) in Italy or 0039 0789 58682 from abroad, airitaly.com

By Bus
Trains are usually quicker and cheaper than inter-town buses *(pullman* or *corriere)*, but in more remote areas such buses (usually blue) may be the only viable means of public transportation.

Services are operated by many different companies and usually depart from a town's major square, outside the railroad station, or from a bus depot. Tickets must generally be bought before boarding the bus, usually from the depot or the nearest bar or station kiosk. Inquire at local visitor centers for details.

By Car

Italian city centers may be congested, but the rest of the country has an excellent network of clearly signposted and numbered roads, from the ordinary highway—known as a *nazionale* or *strada statale* (S or SS) to the fast three- or four-lane expressways known as *autostrade*, where tolls are payable. Sometimes you pay a fixed rate, but usually you take a card from automated machines on joining the road and then pay at a manned booth (*alt stazione*) when exiting. Prepaid *viacards*, available from *autostrada* service stations (24-hour gas and food stops), make toll payment quicker, especially at busy times. Gravel-surfaced roads known as *strade bianche* (white roads) are common in rural areas, but they are intended for cars and are often marked on maps. They are slow but passable.

Maps are widely available from bookstores and other outlets: The best are the *Touring Club of Italy* (TCI) 1:200,000 ratio sheet maps.

Renting a Car

It is easy to rent a car in Italy—international companies have offices in some railroad stations, most airports, and all major cities. Costs are high by U.S. standards, and it may be worth arranging car rental through your travel agent before leaving home. Cheaper deals in Italy can often be obtained through smaller

local companies—look under "*Autonoleggio*" in the Yellow Pages (*paginegialle.it*). Drivers must be over 21 and hold a full license to rent a car.

Driving Information

Busy periods Italian roads are especially busy on Friday and Sunday evenings and immediately before and after major public holidays such as August 15. The first and last weekends of August, when many Italians begin and end their vacations, are also very busy. City traffic builds up in the early morning, evening, and pre-lunch periods.

Breakdowns Put on hazard lights if you break down, and place a warning triangle behind the car. Call the Automobile Club d'Italia (*aci.it*) emergency number (*tel 803 116*), giving your location, car make, and registration. The car will be towed to the nearest ACI-approved garage. Car rental firms often have their own arrangements for breakdowns and accidents. Inquire when renting.

Distances All distances on signposts in Italy are shown in kilometers (1 km = 0.62 mile).

Gas In Italy, gas (*benzina*) is more expensive than in the U.S. and priced by the liter (0.26 U.S. gallon). Gas stations on *autostrade* are open 24 hours and generally accept credit cards. Other gas stations usually close between 1 p.m. and 3 p.m., after 7 p.m., and all day Sunday, and some only accept cash. Be sure all pump meters are set to zero before the attendant starts filling your tank. Some stations have automatic dispensers that take a range of large denomination notes to use in closed periods.

Headlights It is obligatory to drive with headlights on main roads even during daylight. You will be fined if you don't.

Licenses U.S. and Canadian drivers in Italy require a full home

driver's license (*patente*) or international driver's license. They are also legally bound to carry a translation of the license to help police, but this obligation is rarely enforced. For details of current regulations and how to obtain translations and an international driver's license, contact any branch of the American Automobile Association or Canadian Automobile Association.

Parking Parking is often difficult in major towns and cities. Most street slots and parking lots (*parcheggi*) are filled with local cars. Almost all the historic centers have restricted traffic zones (*ZTL*) or pedestrian areas that are closed to traffic. Others may have restrictions at busy times of the day. Metered parking (*parcometro*) is introduced almost everywhere, but in some cases you will need to buy a ticket at a tobacconist. Try to park your car in supervised lots, and never leave valuables or luggage in parked vehicles. Illegally parked cars, especially those in a "removal zone" (*zona rimozione*), may be towed or receive a ticket.

Rules of the road Most regulations in Italy are similar to those in the U.S., notably the fact that you drive on the right. Passing is on the left only. Seat belts are compulsory in front seats, and licenses, insurance, and other documentation must be carried at all times. Drunk-driving penalties are severe, with heavy fines and the possibility of six months' imprisonment. A red warning triangle for use during breakdowns or accidents must be carried by law.

Speed limits The limit in built-up areas is 50 kph (31 mph) and 110 kph (68 mph) outside them, unless marked at 90 kph (56 mph). *Autostrade* limits are 130 kph (80 mph) or 150 kph (93 mph) on designated stretches and 110 kph (68 mph) for vehicles with engine capacity under 1100 cc.

By Ferry

Car and passenger ferries (traghetti) and/or hydrofoils operate between Reggio di Calabria and Messina on Sicily; Naples to Capri and Ischia; Naples to Palermo (Sicily); from Genoa, Livorno, and Civitavecchia to several ports on Sardinia; between Piombino and ports on the island of Elba; from Tuscan ports to islands in the Tuscan archipelago such as Capraia; and from Sicilian ports to a large number of islands off the Sicilian coast. For more details, contact visitor centers in the relevant ports.

By Train

The train provides an excellent way of traveling around Italy. Fares on the state-run railroad network—Trenitalia (tel 892 021, trenitalia.com), often referred to by its old name, Ferrovie dello Stato, or FS—are inexpensive, and standards of service and comfort are improving, especially on the country's new superfast trains (Frecciarossa, Frecciargento, and Frecciabianca, or Red, Silver, and White Arrow).

Train tickets (biglietti) can be bought at railway stations and through some travel agents and are issued in first (prima) or second (seconda) class. Fast trains may have also business and executive class. These trains are more expensive and you have to buy the ticket before getting on board (at the ticket office of the station, at self service machines, or online) and make seat reservations in advance: Seats are often reservable until a few minutes before a train departs.

A second railway company, Italo (italotreno.it), also offers good service and good deals.

Reservations can be made for most other services, including long-distance overnight sleeper (cuccetta) services, available in first class (single or double berths) or second class (six-berth compartments). Note that larger stations may have separate ticket windows for such services, so check if you are in the right line: Look for the word prenotazioni (reservations).

A Eurail Italy Pass is available for 3, 4, 5, or 8 days within a month. First- and second-class options are available, plus "saver" passes for groups of 2–5 people. Supplements are payable on Frecciarossa and Pendolino services. (Visit eurail.com or raileurope.com for more information and to purchase passes.)

Before boarding the train, you must validate all tickets in the special machines (small gold or yellow boxes) on platforms and station ticket halls: A heavy fine is payable if you travel with a non-validated ticket.

Transportation in Towns & Cities

Most historic town and city centers are small enough to explore on foot. In many towns you can rent bicycles. Elsewhere, motor scooters are available, but inexperienced riders should treat these with caution in busy cities such as Rome or Naples.

By Bus

In cities and towns, trams and buses (autobus) are usually orange, and the procedure for using them is virtually identical across Italy. You buy your ticket beforehand, usually from designated bars—look for bus company logos or bar-tobacconists signs with a white "T" on a blue background. Some cities such as Rome also have ticket machines in the streets. You then validate your ticket by stamping it in a small machine on the bus. Generally you board a bus by the rear or the front doors and leave by its central doors. A bus stop is una fermata. Often, as in Rome or Florence, a ticket allows a limited number of journeys within a set period (usually 1 hour, 30 minutes). Otherwise it is valid for a single journey. Day passes giving unlimited travel are available in Rome, Florence, and elsewhere. Inspectors board buses at random, and passengers without valid tickets are subject to fines.

By Cab

Cabs are difficult to hail on the streets. Most gather at taxi stands on the main piazzas or outside rail stations. Supplements can legally be charged for luggage placed in the trunk, rides early or late in the day, on Sundays and public holidays, or trips to airports or outside city limits. It's best to agree on nonmetered prices for longer trips in advance. You can usually reserve a cab by phone: The operator will give you the number and call sign of the cab that has been dispatched. A supplement is charged for a reserved cab. Round up fares to the nearest euro, or tip about 10 percent.

By Subway

Rome and Milan have the most extensive networks (la Metropolitana or Metro for short). Stations and trains are drab, but both systems are generally safe. Although limited in extent, the networks are useful for crossing these cities in a hurry. Buy tickets from the same sources as bus tickets (see above) or from station machines and ticket offices. In Rome, a bus ticket allows one Metro trip within its 100-minute time limit. In Milan, tickets are valid for a single metro journey within 90 minutes of purchase. Integrated day passes in both cities give unlimited journeys on bus, tram, and metro services.

PRACTICAL ADVICE

Communications

Post Offices

Buy stamps *(francobolli)* from a post office *(ufficio postale; poste .it)* or most tobacconists *(tabacchi)*, the latter indicated by a blue sign with a white "T." Offices are open from about 8, 8:30, or 9 a.m. to 2 p.m. Monday to Friday and 8 or 8:30 a.m. to noon Saturday. Main post offices in large towns and cities usually open from 8, 8:30, or 9 a.m. to 7 or 8 p.m. Monday to Saturday. The Italian mail system can be slow. Allow 15 days for letters between Italy and North America, longer for postcards. Priority post is now available. Post is guaranteed to arrive at its destination within three days for the United States and next day in Europe. It costs an average of $2 more than standard postage. Its advisable to use email for hotel reservations.

Mail boxes Small red mail boxes (blue in the Vatican) are found outside post offices or on walls in towns and cities. They are marked "Poste" and usually have two slots: one marked "Per La Città" (city mail), the other "Per Tutte Le Altre Destinazioni" (other destinations). Priority post boxes are usually separate.

Receiving mail You can arrange to have mail waiting for you at general delivery (or *fermo posta* in Italian, €3/$3,40). Mail must carry your name and be addressed to the "Ufficio Postale Centrale, Fermo Posta" plus the name of the town or city. It must be collected from the town's main post office, and you need to present a passport or photo ID and pay a small fee. American Express also has a general delivery service.

Telephones & SIM Cards

Italy's telephone network is operated mainly by TIM. Public phone booths are still found on streets, in bars, and in restaurants. Look for red or yellow signs showing a telephone receiver. Most take coins and cards *(schede telefoniche)*, on sale at *tabacchi* and newspaper stands in a range of euro denominations. Cards have a perforated corner that must be removed before use. To make a call, pick up the phone, insert money or card, and then dial the number. Most booths have instructions in English. Telephone numbers may have anything between four and eleven digits. Call 1254 or visit *1254.it* for all telephone inquiries. Calling rates are lowest on Sundays and national holidays. Hotels always add a significant surcharge to calls made from rooms.

If your mobile phone is set for European roaming, then it could be a good idea to buy an Italian prepaid sim card. The main operators, TIM *(tim.it)*, Vodafone *(vodafone. it)*, and Wind *(wind.it)*, offer cheap solutions that include access to voice, text, and data packages.

To call an Italian number within Italy, dial the full number, including the town or city code (for example, 06 in Rome and 055 in Florence). The code must also be used when calling *within* a city. To call Italy from abroad, dial the international code (011 from the U.S. and Canada, 00 from the U.K.), then the code for Italy (39), followed by the area code (including the initial 0) and number.

Conversions

1 kilo = 2.2 pounds
1 liter = 0.2642 U.S. gallon
1 kilometer = 0.62 mile
1 meter = 1.093 yards

Women's Clothing

U.S.	8	10	12	14	16	18
Italian	40	42	44	46	48	50

Men's Clothing

U.S.	36	38	40	42	44	46
Italian	46	48	50	52	54	56

Women's shoes

U.S.	6–6½	7–7½	8–8½	9–9½
Italian	38	39	40–41	42

Men's shoes

U.S.	8	8½	9½	10½	11½	12
Italian	41	42	43	44	45	46

Etiquette & Local Customs

Italians may have a reputation for being passionate and excitable, but they are also generally polite and considerate in social and public situations. On meeting people or entering or leaving stores, bars, hotels, and restaurants, use a simple *buon giorno* (good day) or *buona sera* (good afternoon/ evening). Do not use the informal *ciao* (hi or goodbye) with strangers. "Please" is *per favore*, "thank you" *grazie*, and *prego* means "you're welcome." Before a meal you might say *buon appetito* (enjoy your meal), to which the reply is *grazie, altrettanto* (thank you, and the same to you). Before a drink, the toast is *salute* (good health) or *cin cin*. Say *permesso* when you wish to pass people and *mi scusi* if you wish to apologize, excuse yourself, or stop someone to ask for help. A woman is addressed as *signora*, a young woman *signorina*, and a man as *signore.* More vocabulary can be found at the end of Travelwise, see p. 391.

Kissing on both cheeks is a common form of greeting among men and women who know each other well. Dress appropriately in churches, respect those at worship, and do not sightsee in churches when services are in progress. Italians dress conservatively for most occasions, and unusual dress will be noticed. For advice on tipping, see p. 348.

Italians are generally more assertive in lines, when they form them at all, and in stores, banks, and other offices you should not expect "fairness" or for people to "wait their turn." You can be equally assertive in such situations—such pushiness is not generally considered rude in Italy.

Smoking in bars, cafés, restaurants, and other public places is prohibited.

Holidays

Stores, banks, offices, and schools close on the following national holidays:
January 1 (New Year's Day)
January 6 (Epiphany)
Easter Sunday
Easter Monday
April 25 (Liberation Day)
May 1 (Labor Day or May Day)
June 2 (Republic Day)
August 15 (Ferragosto or Assumption)
November 1 (All Saints' Day)
December 8 (Immaculate Conception)
December 25 (Christmas)
December 26 (Santo Stefano)

Some cities have special holidays when businesses close: Rome (June 29, St. Peter's Day); Florence and Genoa (June 24, St. John's Day); and Venice (November 21, Festa della Salute).

Media

Publications

Most Italian newspapers are sold from a street newsstand *(edicola)*, many of which, in larger cities and tourist centers, also stock American, British, and other foreign language newspapers and periodicals. The *International New York Times*, *USA Today*, and most U.K. papers are available on the day of issue from about 2 p.m. Airports and railroad stations often have the largest selection of foreign publications.

Italy has a buoyant newspaper market. Among national papers, *Corriere della Sera* is one of the most authoritative, followed by *La Repubblica* and *Il Sole 24 Ore* (economy). Other best-selling daily newspapers are sports publications such as the pink *Gazzetta dello Sport*. Many papers have strong city or regional links, notably *La Stampa* in Turin, *Il Messagero* in Rome, and *La Nazione* in Florence. Regional and city papers are often read in preference to national newspapers. Newspapers are a good source of information on local events, museum opening times, and so forth.

Television

Italian television has three main state channels (RAI 1, 2, and 3), many prominent privately owned channels (notably Rete Quattro, Canale 5, and Italia Uno), and a plethora of cable, local, and other private channels. In most parts of the country you can expect to have 15 or more channels. Foreign movies and shows are almost always dubbed into Italian, never with English subtitles, but up-to-date hotels provide access to CNN, Sky, BBC World, and other foreign stations via cable and satellite. The main RAI 1 news bulletin is at 8 p.m.

Radio

Italian radio is generally of a poor standard, although the number of stations, particularly FM music stations, is enormous. The only English-language broadcasts are those of the BBC World Service and similar organizations.

Money Matters

The euro is Italy's official currency. Euro notes come in denominations of 5, 10, 20, 50, 100, and 200 euros. There are 100 cents to the euro. Coins come in denominations of 1 and 2 euros and 1, 2, 5, 10, 20, and 50 cents *(centesimi)*.

Most major banks, airports, and railroad stations have automatic teller machines *(Bancomat* in Italian) for money (ATM) cards and international credit cards *(carta di credito)*. Before leaving home, ask your credit card company for a four-digit PIN number to enable you to withdraw money. Currency and traveler's checks—best bought in euros before you leave—can be exchanged in most banks and Bureaux de Change *(cambio)*, but lines are often long and the procedures slow. In rural areas, small towns, and much of the south, ATMs and *cambio* facilities are rarer—sometimes nonexistent.

Credit cards are accepted in hotels and restaurants in most major towns and cities. Look for Visa, Mastercard, or American Express stickers (Diners Card is less well known), or the Italian Carta Sì (literally, "yes to cards") sign. Many businesses still prefer cash, and smaller stores and hotels, especially in rural areas, may not take credit cards. Always check before ordering a meal or reserving a room.

Opening Times

Opening hours present a problem in Italy. There are few hard and fast rules, and opening times of museums and churches, in particular, can change with little or even no notice. Stores, banks, and other institutions in big cities are also increasingly moving to northern European hours (with no lunch and afternoon closing). Look for the words *orario continuato* displayed. Mind to treat the following times as a general guide only:

Banks 8:30 a.m.–1:30 p.m. Monday to Friday. Major banks may also open for an hour in the afternoon and Saturday morning. Hours are becoming longer and more flexible.

Churches 8 or 9 a.m.–12 p.m. and 3 or 4 p.m.–6 or 8 p.m. daily excluding services; many churches close Sunday afternoon.

Gas stations 24 hours only on *autostrade.*

Museums State-run national museums usually close Sunday afternoon and all day Monday. Most close for lunch (1 p.m.–3 or 4 p.m.), although major museums are increasingly open 9 a.m. to 7 p.m. and all day Sunday. Winter hours are usually shorter, especially in churches and open-air sites.

Post offices 8 or 9 a.m.–2 p.m. Monday to Saturday, but larger offices 8 or 9 a.m.–6 or 8 p.m. Monday to Saturday.

Restaurants Many restaurants close on Sunday evening and all day Monday or one other day a week *(la chiusura settimanale).* Many close for some of January and for periods in July or August.

Stores Generally 8:30 or 9 a.m.–1 p.m. and 3:30 or 4 p.m.–8 p.m. Monday to Saturday. Many stores close Monday morning and another half-day a week. Department stores and major city stores may stay open seven days a week from 9 a.m. to 8 p.m. or later (10 p.m.), but Sunday and late hours are still unusual.

Restrooms

There are few restrooms in the city centers outside public buildings (such as museums). Generally you need to use facilities in bars, railroad stations, and gas stations where standards are generally low. Ask for *il bagno* (eel BAN-yo), take a few tissues, and don't confuse *Signori* (Men) with *Signore* (Women). Tip attendants 25 to 50 cents or, in a bar, order a coffee, just like the Italians do.

Time Differences

Italy runs on CET (Central European time), one hour ahead of Greenwich mean time and six hours ahead of eastern standard

time. Noon in Italy is 6 a.m. in New York. Clocks change for daylight saving in late April/May (one hour forward) and late September/October (one hour back). Italy uses the 24-hour clock.

Tipping

In restaurants where a service charge *(servizio)* is not levied, leave 10–15 percent; even where it is, you may wish to leave 5–10 percent for the waiter. In bars, tip a few cents for drinks consumed standing at bars, and 25–50c for waiter service. In hotel bars be slightly more generous.

Service is included in hotel rates, but tip chambermaids and doormen about 50c (1 euro for calling a cab), the bellhop 1–3 euros for carrying your bags, and the concierge or porter *(portiere)* 3–7 euros if he has been helpful. Double these figures in the most expensive hotels.

Tip restroom and checkroom attendants up to 25c. Porters at airports and railroad stations generally work to fixed tariffs, but tip up to 2 euros extra at your discretion. Cab drivers expect around 10 percent. Barbers merit around 2 euros, a hairdresser's assistant 2–4 euros depending on the level of establishment. Tip church or other custodians 1–2 euros.

Italian State Tourist Offices

italiantourism.com, enit.it, or *italia.it.* The last has a useful list of countrywide links to attractions for which tickets can be bought online. Search under "info" on the homepage.

United States
Los Angeles 10850 Wilshire Blvd., Suite 575, Los Angeles, CA 90024, tel 310/820-1898,

fax 310/470-7788
email losangeles@enit.it

New York 686 Park Ave., 3rd Floor, New York, NY 10111, tel 212/245-5618, fax 212/586-9249 email newyork@enit.it

Canada
Toronto 365 Bay Street, Suite 503, tel 416/925-4882, fax 416/925-4799 email toronto@enit.it

United Kingdom
London 1 Princes St., London W1B 2AY email info.london@enit.it london@enit.it

Traveling With Disabilities

Museums, galleries, and public buildings across Italy are making great progress in providing wheelchair access, but much remains to be done. Few buses or trains have dedicated facilities, and virtually no cabs. Many historic cities present special problems, notably Venice, which has a large number of stepped bridges. Only hotels in higher star categories provide dedicated rooms, but hotels and restaurants will almost always do their best to provide appropriate help if you call in advance. Consult your nearest Italian embassy or consulate for details of the procedures required to bring a guide dog into Italy.

Useful contact bodies in Italy include Rome-based Rome & Italy *(romeanditaly.com),* a tour operator which provides a wide range of touristic services across the country. Other information agencies dealing with travel for visitors with disabilities include SATH *(tel 212/447-7284, sath.org)* and Mobility International *(tel 541/343-1284, miusa.org).*

EMERGENCIES
Embassies in Italy
U.S. Embassy Via Vittorio Veneto 121, Rome, tel 06 46 741, *it.usembassy.gov*

U.S. Consulate Lungarno Vespucci 38, Florence, tel 055 266 951, *it.usembassy.gov/ embassy-consulates/florence*

U.S. Consulate Via Principe Amedeo 2/10, Milan, tel 02 290 351, *it.usembassy.gov/ embassy-consulates/milan*

Canadian Embassy Via Salaria 243 (visa and consular section at Via Zara 30), Rome, tel 06 854 441, *canadainternational.gc.ca*

U.K. Embassy Via XX Settembre 80, Rome, tel 06 4220 0001, *gov.uk*

Emergency Phone Numbers
Police, tel 112
Emergency services, tel 112
Fire services, tel 112
Car breakdown, tel 803 116
Ambulance, tel 112 or 118

For legal assistance in an emergency, contact your embassy or consulate (see above) for a list of English-speaking lawyers.

For general help, contact Yellow Pages or White Pages (*paginegialle .it, paginebianche.it*).

Lost Property
If you lose property, go first to the local visitor center and ask for assistance. Bus, tram, train, and subway systems in cities usually have special offices to deal with lost property, but they can be hard to find and are usually only open a few hours a day. Ask for directions at visitor centers, and also try bus depots and rail stations. Hotels should also be able to provide assistance.

To report a more serious loss or theft, go to the local police station or Questura. In Rome, the main Questura office is off Via Nazionale at Via di San Vitale 15 (*tel 06 46861*). Many have special English-speaking staff to deal with visitors' problems. You will be asked to help fill in and sign a form (*denuncia* in Italian) reporting any crime. Keep your copy for relevant insurance claims.

Report the loss or theft of a passport to the police and then notify your embassy (see above).

What to Do in a Traffic Accident
Put on hazard lights and place a warning triangle 165 feet (50 m) behind the car. Call the police (*tel 112*) from a public phone (see p. 346): *Autostrade* have emergency telephones at regular intervals. At the scene, do not admit liablity or make potentially incriminating statements to police or onlookers. Ask any witnesses to remain, make a police statement, and exchange insurance and other relevant details with the other driver(s). Call the car rental agency, if necessary, to inform it of the incident.

HEALTH
Check that your health insurance covers visits to Italy and that any travel insurance also includes sufficient medical coverage. For minor complaints, first visit a drugstore or pharmacy (*una farmacia*), indicated by a green-lit cross outside the store. Staff is well trained and will be able to offer advice as well as help find a doctor (*un medico*) if necessary. Also consult your hotel, the Yellow Pages (*paginegialle.it*), or visitor centers for help in choosing a doctor or dentist (*un dentista*). Bring an ample supply of any prescription drugs (*medicina*). Should you need to refill a prescription, pharmacies will direct you to a doctor. Visit a hospital (*un ospedale*) for serious complaints. Emergency treatment is provided at the *pronto soccorso;* if you need an ambulance, call the emergency number 118. Some Italian hospitals can look run-down, but the treatment standards are generally good.

Before leaving home, consider contacting the International Association for Medical Assistance to Travelers (*iamat.org*), a nonprofit organization anyone can join free of charge. Members receive a directory of English-speaking IAMAT doctors on call 24 hours a day and are entitled to services at set rates. Tel 716/754-4883 in the U.S. and 416/652-0137 in Canada.

Common minor complaints include overexposure to the sun and insect bites. Poison ivy is not a major problem, but Italy does have poisonous snakes (*vipere*), though bites are usually only fatal if you have an allergic reaction.

Tap water is generally safe. However, do not drink water if marked *acqua non potabile,* and never drink from streams in the mountains or elsewhere. Milk is pasteurized and safe.

Hospitals
Rome Rome American Hospital, Via Emilio Longoni 83, tel 06 22 551, *hcir.it/rome-american-hospital*
Genoa Istituto Giannina Gaslini, Via Gerolamo Gaslini 5, tel 010 56361, *gaslini.org*
Milan Ospedale Maggiore Policlinico, Via Francesco Sforza 35, tel 02 55031, *policlinico.mi.it*
Venice Ospedale Civile, Campo S.S. Giovanni e Paolo, tel 041 529 4111, *aulss3.veneto.it*
Florence Ospedale di Santa Maria Nuova, Piazza Santa Maria Nuova 1, tel 055 69 381 *uslcentro.toscana.it*
Palermo Ospedali Riuniti Vila Sofia-Cervello, Via Trabucco 180, tel 091 680 2111 *ospedaliriunitipalermo.it*

HOTELS & RESTAURANTS

Italy has a variety of accommodations and restaurants to suit all tastes and budgets. Choose from fine hotels in old palaces and castles, intimate family-run establishments, or the increasingly popular *agriturismo*, or farm holidays. And enjoy one of the world's great cuisines in restaurants that range from humble pizzerias to centuries-old classics, found in every town and village. A selection of interesting places to stay and eat follows.

HOTELS
Grading System

Hotels are officially graded from one star (the simplest accommodations) to five star (luxury). In a three-star establishment and above, all rooms should have private bath/shower rooms, a telephone, and a television. Most two-star hotels also have private bathrooms.

Even in the smartest hotels, bathrooms may only have a shower and no tub. Always ask to see a selection of rooms—you may be shown the worst first. Rooms are often small by U.S. standards, even in upscale hotels. All-day room service and air-conditioning are also comparatively rare.

Recommended hotels have a restaurant unless stated otherwise. A restaurant symbol is given where the restaurant is outstanding.

Reservations

It is advisable to reserve all hotels in advance, especially in the major cities, and particularly in high season (June–Aug.). Note that in Rome, Florence, and Venice, high season often means Christmas, New Year, and Easter to October.

Make your reservation by telephone and confirm by fax; it's also a good idea to reconfirm a couple days ahead of your arrival. Hoteliers must register every guest, so you will be asked for your passport at check-in. It will be returned within a few hours or when you check out.

Checkout times range from around 10 a.m. to 12 p.m., but you should be able to leave luggage at reception for collection later on.

Prices

All prices are officially set, and room rates must be displayed by law at reception and in each room. Prices for different rooms can vary within a hotel, but all taxes and services should be included in the rate.

Hotels often levy additional charges for air-conditioning and garage facilities, while laundry, drinks from minibars, and phone calls made from rooms invariably carry large surcharges.

Price categories given in the entries are for double (*una matrimoniale*) or twin (*una camera doppia*) rooms and are for guidance only. Seasonal variations often apply, especially in coastal resorts, where high-season (summer) rates are usually higher.

At busy times, there may also be a two- or three-day minimum stay policy, and you may be obliged to take full- or half-board packages, always priced on a per person basis. Half-board (*mezza pensione*) includes breakfast and lunch, while full-board (*pensione completa*) includes all meals.

Prices usually include breakfast (*colazione*), but where breakfast is optional (see rate cards in rooms), it always costs less to eat at the nearest bar. Breakfasts in upscale hotels are improving—U.S.-style buffets are now more common—but colazione usually means coffee, a roll, and jelly.

Hotel Groups

Best Western, tel 800/780-7234, 800/820 080 (Italy), bestwestern.com

Hilton, tel 800/445-8667, hilton.com

Leading Hotels of the World, tel 800/745-8883 (U.S. & Canada), 800 2888 8882 (U.K.), lhw.com

Marriott Bonvoy, tel 800/627-7468 (U.S. & Canada), 800/6277-4680 (international), marriott.com

NH-Hotels, tel 212/219-7607 (U.S.), 020 3499 8271 (U.K.), nh-hotels.com

Relais & Châteaux, tel 800/735-2478 (U.S. & Canada), 020 3519 1967 (U.K.), relais chateaux.com

Contact information in Italy:

Dimore Storiche Italiane (historic hotels), dimorestoricheitaliane.it

Starhotels, tel 800/816-6001 (U.S.), 00 800 0022 0011 (U.K.), 055 36925 (Italy), starhotels.com

Unahotels, tel 02 6982 6982, gruppouna.it

RESTAURANTS
Types of Restaurant

Italy's restaurant categories are increasingly blurred. Once an *osteria* was a simple inn, a trattoria was a basic neighborhood eatery, and a *ristorante* was an upscale establishment. Now some of the best places to eat can be *osterie*, revamped as informal restaurants with innovative cooking.

Old-fashioned trattorias with bright lights and checkered tablecloths are also largely consigned to the past, while ristorante is a term now applied to just about any eating place. A pizzeria remains the one constant—a simple, usually modern place that often serves basic pasta, main courses, and desserts as well as pizzas.

Neither a restaurant's appearance nor price necessarily reflect the quality of the dining experience. A pizza in a boisterous Neapolitan pizzeria may be every bit as good—and memorable—as a five-course feast in a sleek Milanese restaurant.

When a range of seats is given, the first is the number inside, the second the number outside.

Dining Hours

Breakfast (colazione) usually consists of a cappuccino and bread roll or sweet pastry (una brioche) taken standing in a bar between about 7 and 9 a.m. Lunch (pranzo) starts around 12:30 p.m. and finishes at about 2 p.m.—the long lunch and siesta are increasingly a thing of the past. Dinner (cena) begins about 8 p.m., with last orders at around 10 p.m., although hours may be later in southern Italy and earlier in rural areas or smaller towns.

Pizzerias often only open in the evenings, especially those with wood-burning ovens (forno a legna) that take time to fire. Most restaurants in every category close once a week (la chiusura settimanale), and many take long vacation breaks (ferie) in July or August.

Meals

Meals traditionally begin with appetizers or antipasto—literally "before the meal"—a first course (il primo) of soup, pasta, or rice; and a main course (il secondo) of meat or fish. Vegetables (contorni) or salads (insalata) often are served with or after il secondo. Desserts (dolci) may include or be followed by fruit (frutta) and cheese (formaggio). Italians often finish a meal with an espresso (never cappuccino) and brandy, grappa (a clear, brandylike spirit), or an amaro (a bitter digestif).

Ordering only a primo and salad is acceptable in all but the grandest restaurants. Many Italians opt to visit an ice-cream parlor (gelateria) afterward instead of having dessert.

Meals are usually accompanied by bread and mineral water, for which you pay extra.

Set Menus

Fixed-price menus are available in many restaurants in tourist areas. The menù turistico usually includes two courses, a simple dessert, and half a bottle of wine and water per person. Quantity and quality of food are invariably poor. Of better value in more upscale restaurants is the menù degustazione, where you pay a fixed price to sample a selection of the restaurant's special dishes.

Bars, Cafés, & Snacks

Bars and cafés are perfect for breakfast and often provide snacks such as sandwiches (panini, tramezzini) throughout the day. A few may offer a light meal at lunch. Stands or small stores selling slices of pizza (pizza al taglio) with different toppings are common.

It costs less to stand at the bar. Specify what you want and pay at the separate cash desk (la cassa), then take your receipt (lo scontrino) to the bar and repeat your order. A small coin slapped on the bar often helps secure prompt service. Where a bar has tables, especially outside tables, you pay more to sit and place your order with a waiter. Only in small rural bars can you pay at the bar and then sit down.

Wine bars (enoteche) are becoming common. All serve wine by the glass or bottle, often in informal surroundings, and most provide bread, cheeses, other snacks, and good-quality light meals. A birreria, or beer cellar, is similar, but usually appeals to a younger crowd.

Retain your receipt when you leave the bar. If you are stopped outside the bar by plainclothes finance police and you do not have it, you will be liable to pay for what you ordered again plus a fine.

Paying

The check (il conto) must be presented by law as a formal receipt. You are within your rights to demand an itemized ricevuta. Bills once included a cover charge (pane e coperto), a practice the authorities are trying to outlaw. Many restaurants attempt to get around the law by charging for bread brought to your table whether you want it or not.

Smaller, simpler restaurants, and those in rural areas, are less likely to accept credit cards. Check if your card is acceptable even in places displaying card signs outside.

Tipping & Dress

Tip between 10 and 15 percent where service has been good and where a service charge (servizio) is not included. As a rule, Italians dress well but informally to eat out, especially in better restaurants. A relaxed casual style is a good rule of thumb. Jacket and tie for men are rarely necessary, but often the better dressed you are, the better service you receive.

LISTINGS

The hotels and restaurants are grouped first according to their region, then listed alphabetically by price category. For disabled access, you should check with the establishment to verify the extent of their facilities.

Credit Cards

Abbreviations used are AE (American Express), DC (Diners Club), MC (MasterCard), and V (Visa). As a general rule, AE and DC are less widely accepted than V and MC.

L = lunch   D = dinner

▶ ROME

HOTELS

🏨 GRAND HOTEL DE LA MINERVE
$$$$$ ✪✪✪✪✪
PIAZZA DELLA MINERVA 69
TEL 06 695 201
grandhoteldelaminerve.com
It is hard to imagine a better
centrally placed hotel than
the Minerve, which occu-
pies a beautifully restored
17th-century palazzo almost
directly behind the Pantheon.
Its position, comfort, service,
facilities, rooms, and the stylish
reception are beyond reproach.
Nonsmoking rooms available.
ⓘ 131 + 4 suites 🅿 🚇 Bus:
119 to Piazza della Rotonda
or 70, 81, 87 to Corso del
Rinascimento 🔄 💺 🎦
🎙 Free 🃏 All major cards

🏨 HASSLER
🍽 $$$$$ ✪✪✪✪✪
PIAZZA TRINITÀ DEI MONTI 6
TEL 06 699 340
hotelhasslerroma.com
Rooms in this hotel above the
Spanish Steps are in the grand
style and have views of Rome
or the gardens of the Villa
Medici. The rooftop restau-
rant, **Imàgo**, has a Michelin
star and superb views.
ⓘ 82 + 13 suites 🅿
🚇 Metro: Spagna
🕐 Restaurant closed L
& 2 weeks in Jan. 🔄 💺 🎙
🃏 All major cards

🏨 D'INGHILTERRA
$$$$–$$$$$ ✪✪✪✪
VIA BOCCA DI LEONE 14
TEL 06 699 811
starhotelscollezione.com
A hotel that retains the
old-fashioned charm and
traditions of the 19th century.
Past guests have included
the composer Franz Liszt and
Ernest Hemingway. Its central

position is convenient to the
Spanish Steps and the major
shopping streets.
ⓘ 88 + 9 suites 🅿 🚇 Metro:
Spagna 🔄 💺 🎙 Free
🃏 All major cards

🏨 SCALINATA DI SPAGNA
$$$$ ✪✪✪
PIAZZA TRINITÀ DEI MONTI 17
TEL 06 4568 6150
hotelscalinata.com
This romantic, quiet, and
welcoming hotel is situated at
the top of the Spanish Steps.
Rooms are Old World in style
and furnished with antiques.
There is a lovely roof terrace
but no restaurant.
ⓘ 16 🚇 Metro: Spagna 💺
🎙 Free 🃏 All major cards

🏨 ALBERGO CESÀRI
$$$ ✪✪✪
VIA DI PIETRA 89/A
TEL 06 674 9701
albergocesari.it
A reliable family-run concern
tucked away in a central back
street between the Corso and
the Pantheon.
ⓘ 47 🚇 Bus: 56, 60, 62,
& others to Via del Corso
🔄 🎙 Free 🃏 All major cards

🏨 ALBERGO SANTA CHIARA
$$$
VIA SANTA CHIARA 21
TEL 06 687 2979
albergosantachiara.com
In the same family since 1830;
rooms are spacious and comfortable, if occasionally low on
light, but the hotel's biggest
draw is its location, one block
south of the Pantheon.
ⓘ 93 🅿 🚇 Bus: 119 to 64 &
all services to Largo di Torre
Argentina 🔄 💺 🎙 Free
🃏 All major cards

🏨 CAMPO DE' FIORI
$$$ ✪✪✪✪
VIA DEL BISCIONE 6
TEL 06 687 4886

PRICES

HOTELS
An indication of the cost of
a double room in the high
season is given by **$** signs.

$$$$$	Over $300
$$$$	$200–$300
$$$	$130–$200
$$	$100–$130
$	Under $100

RESTAURANTS
An indication of the cost of
a three-course meal without
drinks is given by **$** signs.

$$$$$	Over $80
$$$$	$50–$80
$$$	$35–$50
$$	$20–$35
$	Under $20

---

hotelcampodefiori.com
The location is excellent—close
to Campo de' Fiori and Piazza
Navona, two of Rome's loveliest squares. Traces of fresco
and open brickwork in the
public spaces create a homey
and romantic atmosphere.
ⓘ 23 🅿 🚇 Bus: 64 & all
other buses along Corso
Vittorio Emanuele II 🔄 💺
🎙 Free 🃏 All major cards

🏨 LOCARNO
$$$ ✪✪✪
VIA DELLA PENNA 22
TEL 06 361 0841
hotellocarno.com
On a relatively quiet side
street, it is located a stone's
throw from Piazza del Popolo.
Attractive art nouveau decor
distinguishes many of the
rooms. You will love the out-
door garden, excellent for a
drink after a sightseeing day.
ⓘ 83 🅿 🚇 Bus: 119 to
Via di Ripetta 🔄 💺 🎙 Free
🃏 All major cards

PORTOGHESI
$$$ ✪✪✪

VIA DEI PORTOGHESI 1
TEL 06 686 4231
hotelportoghesiroma.it
A peaceful hotel housed in
a 17th-century palazzo just
north of Piazza Navona close
to the Palazzo Altemps gallery.
Rooms are simple but pleasant,
and there is the bonus of a
summer terrace for breakfast.
🛏 27 🚌 Bus: 70, 81, 87 ⬗
💲 📶 Free 🅿 All major cards

HOTEL SANTA MARIA
$$–$$$ ✪✪✪

VICOLO DEL PIEDE 2
TEL 06 589 4626
hotelsantamariatrastevere.it
A charming addition in the
Trastevere quarter, this is a
beautifully converted 16th-
century former convent built
around a courtyard dotted
with orange trees.
🛏 18 + 2 suites 🚌 Bus: 8,
44, 75 to Viale di Trastevere
💲 📶 Free 🅿 All major cards

TEATRO DI POMPEO
$$–$$$ ✪✪✪

LARGO DEL PALLARO 8
TEL 06 8778 4391
hotelteatrodipompeo.it
A central and intimate hotel
near Campo de' Fiori, with
enchanting wood-beamed
rooms and vestiges of the
site's Roman past—parts of
Pompey's ancient theater are
incorporated into the building.
🛏 13 🚌 Bus: 64 & others
along Corso Vittorio
Emanuele II ⬗ 💲 📶 Free
🅿 All major cards

NAVONA
$$ ✪✪✪

VIA DEI SEDIARI 8, OFF CORSO
DEL RINASCIMENTO
TEL 06 6830 1252
hotelnavona.com
A star among Rome's inexpensive hotels, thanks to its tremendous location—just off the

southeastern corner of Piazza
Navona—and the welcome
of its English-speaking Italo-
Australian family owners. The
quality of the rooms is good
for this class of hotel. If there
are no rooms, inquire about
availability at the co-owned and
nearby Zanardelli.
🛏 21 🚌 Bus: 70, 81, 87, 116
to Corso del Rinascimento
💲 A few rooms 📶 Free
🅿 Cash only

RESTAURANTS

IL CONVIVIO
$$$$–$$$$$

VICOLO DEI SOLDATI 31
TEL 06 686 9432
ilconviviotroiani.it
The sublime and often inven-
tive Roman-based cuisine at
this tiny restaurant north of
Piazza Navona has earned a
Michelin star. The wine list is
one of the best in the capital.
Reservations essential.
🍴 30 🚌 Bus: 70, 81, 87
to Corso del Rinascimento
📅 Closed L, Sun., & a week in
Aug. 💲 🅿 All major cards

LA ROSETTA
$$$$–$$$$$

VIA DELLA ROSETTA 8–9
TEL 328 613 0384
larosetta.com
A small restaurant of long-
standing repute in a small
street immediately north of
the Pantheon. Patrons usually
include politicians from the
nearby parliament building.
Fish and seafood only.
🍴 50 🚌 Bus: 119 to Piazza
della Rotonda 📅 Closed
parts of Jan. & Aug. 💲
🅿 All major cards

ANTONELLO COLONNA
OPEN
$$$$

VIA MILANO 9A
TEL 06 4782 2641
antonellocolonna.it

Antonello Colonna won
Michelin stars over several
years for his cooking in this
striking contemporary restaurant in the Palazzo delle Espo-
sizioni. When available, the
lunch menu and the weekend
brunch are good value.
🍴 35 🚌 Bus: 40, 60, 64, 70,
71, & other services to Via
Nazionale 📅 Closed Sun. D,
Mon., & Aug. 💲
🅿 All major cards

GLASS HOSTARIA
$$$$

VICOLO DEL CINQUE 58
TEL 06 5833 5903
glass-restaurant.it
The bold, contemporary styl-
ing of this Trastevere restau-
rant breaks the mold of the
normal and more traditional
Roman trattoria. The creative
Italian cooking earned a
Michelin star in 2015.
🍴 50 🚌 Bus: H, 23, 280 to
Ponte Sisto-Piazza Trilussa
📅 Closed Mon., L, & parts of
Jan. & late July–Aug. 💲
🅿 All major cards

IL PAGLIACCIO
$$$$

VIA DEI BANCHI VECCHI 129
TEL 06 6880 9595
ristoranteilpagliaccio.com
A pleasing and restrained
restaurant in one of the most
characteristic corners of
the old center. The creative
cooking (two Michelin stars)
is occasionally unusual (a
starter of small fried fish with
tomato and basil ice cream, for
example) but never less than
perfectly executed.
🍴 45 📅 Closed Sun., Mon.,
Tues. L in winter, L July–mid-
Sept., & periods in Jan. & Aug.
💲 🅿 All major cards

CHECCHINO DAL 1887
$$$–$$$$

VIA MONTE TESTACCIO 30
TEL 06 574 3816
checchino-dal-1887.com

⬗ Elevator 💲 Air-conditioning 🏊 Indoor Pool 🏖 Outdoor Pool 🏋 Health Club 📶 Wi-Fi 🅿 Credit Cards

The cooking at this historic restaurant in the old cattle yards area south of the historic center is of a very particular kind. Dishes revolve largely around offal and such quintessential Roman ingredients as *cervello* (brain), *trippa* (tripe), and *pajata* (intestine).

🔢 105–125 🅿 🚇 Bus: 23, 75, 280, 716. Metro: Piramide 🕐 Closed Sun. D, Mon., Aug., & 1 week in Dec. ♿
💳 All major cards

🍴 ENOTECA FERRARA
$$$–$$$$

PIAZZA TRILUSSA 41
TEL 06 5833 3920
enotecaferrara.com

A modern establishment, but with solid traditional foundation. It offers three alternatives: wine bar for an aperitif, gourmet restaurant, or pub for something less formal.

🔢 120 🚇 Bus: 25 to Lungotevere Farnesina. Tram: 8 🕐 Closed Sun. only in Aug. ♿ 💳 All major cards

🍴 PIPERNO
$$$–$$$$

VIA MONTE DEI CENCI 9
TEL 06 6880 6629
ristorantepiperno.it

Rome has a strong tradition of Jewish culture and cooking, and this old-fashioned and rustic restaurant in the former Ghetto is the best place to sample specialties such as *carciofi alla giudia* (deep-fried artichoke) and *fiori di zucca ripieni* (deep-fried zucchini flowers filled with mozzarella).

🔢 100–30 🚇 Bus: 23, 63 🕐 Closed Sun. D, Mon., & Aug. ♿ 💳 All major cards

🍴 VECCHIA ROMA
$$$–$$$$

VIA TRIBUNA DI CAMPITELLI 18
TEL 06 686 4604
ristorantevecchiaroma.com

One of the city's prettiest restaurants, situated on a

charming piazza at the heart of the old Ghetto—reserve a table outside. The food is merely notable, though salads are excellent, and pastas are innovative, while the main courses tend toward fish and seafood.

🔢 100–120 🚇 Bus: 64 & other buses to Piazza Venezia 🕐 Closed Wed. ♿ 💳 AE, DC

🍴 GRANO
$$$

PIAZZA RONDANINI 53
TEL 06 6819 2096
ristorantegrano.it

The virtually all-white decor of this rustic-styled bar and restaurant east of San Luigi dei Francesi will not be to all tastes, but the excellent pastas and creative, mostly southern Italian cooking are first-rate.

🔢 60–30 🚇 70, 80, 87, 116, & other services to Corso del Risorgimento 💳 All major cards

🍴 SORA LELLA
$$$

VIA DI PONTE QUATTRO CAPI 16,
ISOLA TIBERINA
TEL 06 686 1601
trattoriasoralella.it

The two cozy dining rooms and their wood-paneled walls and rows of bottles still bear witness to the simple trattoria origins of this restaurant on Tiber Island, but the food has increased in sophistication.

🔢 45 🚇 Bus: 23, 44, 63, 95, 280, & others to Piazza Bocca della Verità 🕐 Closed Sun. & 3 weeks in Aug. ♿
💳 All major cards

🍴 TRATTORIA DA TEO
$$$

PIAZZA DEI PONZIANI 7
TEL 06 581 8355

In a quiet corner, its ambience is intimate and friendly with a few tables outdoors when the weather is good (advance reservations are essential). Great classics of Roman cuisine.

🔢 60 🚇 Bus: 23, 44, 280 to Lungotevere Ripa. Tram: 8 🕐 Closed Sun. & Jan. ♿
💳 All major cards

🍴 HOSTARIA L'ORSO 80
$$–$$$

VIA DELL'ORSO 33
TEL 06 686 4904
orso80.it

Invariably filled with vacationers, but none the worse for that, this big restaurant close to Piazza Navona is a reliable standby for pizza and basic meat and fish dishes at a moderate price.

🔢 170 🚇 Bus: 70, 81, 87 to Corso del Rinascimento 🕐 Closed Mon. & Aug.
♿ 💳 All major cards

🍴 MACCHERONI
$$–$$$

PIAZZA DELLE COPPELLE 44
TEL 06 6830 7895
ristorantemaccheroni.com

Popular and informal, with attractive, rustic dining rooms (and outdoor tables on a pretty piazza). It serves good-value and quality traditional Italian dishes; convenient for the Pantheon.

🔢 120–60 🚇 🚌 Bus: 8, 64, 87, & other services to Largo di Torre Argentina 💳 All major cards

🍴 MATRICIANELLA
$$–$$$

VIA DEL LEONE 4
TEL 06 683 2100
matricianella.it

In business since 1957, close to Via del Corso and the parliament building, offering classic Roman cooking in understated, traditional-looking dining rooms.

🔢 45–25 🕐 Closed Sun. & 3 weeks in Aug. 🚇 Bus: 116 to Via della Scrofa and all services to Via del Corso
💳 All major cards

CANTINA E CUCINA
$$
VIA DEL GOVERNO VECCHIO 87
TEL 06 689 2574
cantinaecucina.it
It has a pleasant, rustic atmosphere with brick walls and bottles of wine on display. The menu includes pizza, meat-based dishes, and good cheeses. Also coffee bar and aperitifs.
60 Bus: 40, 46, 62, 64, 190 to Corso Vittorio Emanuele II All major cards

HOSTARIA DA NERONE
$$
VIA DELLE TERME DI TITO 96
TEL 06 481 7952
This friendly, old-fashioned trattoria very convenient to the Colosseum is noted for its buffet of cold antipasti (appetizers) and robust Abruzzese and Roman cooking. In summer, there are tables outdoors.
30–50 Metro: Colosseo Closed Sun. & Aug. All major cards

OPPIO CAFFÈ
$$
VIA DELLE TERME DI TITO 72
TEL 06 474 5262
oppiocaffe.it
Great views of the Colosseum are the main attraction here, plus light meals and café snacks; open until 2 a.m., with live music some nights.
120–75 Metro: Colosseo All major cards

CAFFÈ GRECO
$
VIA DEI CONDOTTI 86
TEL 06 679 1700
anticocaffegreco.eu
Rome's oldest and most atmospheric coffeehouse was founded in 1760 and has hosted the likes of Goethe, Casanova, and Lord Byron.
Metro: Spagna. Bus: 119 to Piazza di Spagna

CAVOUR 313
$
VIA CAVOUR 313
TEL 06 678 5496
cavour313.it
Perfect for a snack or glass of wine after visiting the Forum.
Bus: 11, 27, 81, 85, 87 Closed Sun. in July & Aug.

ENOTECA CORSI
$
VIA DEL GESÙ 87–88
TEL 06 679 0821
enotecacorsi.com
Little has changed at this simple wine bar-trattoria in more than 30 years. The food is simple Roman cooking at its best—you can eat a full meal or simply have a glass of wine and a snack.
Bus: 64 Closed Sun., Mon. & Tues. L, & Aug.

GELATERIA DELLA PALMA
$
VIA DELLA MADDALENA 19–23
TEL 06 6880 6752
dellapalma.it
A big, bright, and modern emporium just north of the Pantheon selling more than a hundred flavors of ice cream, cakes, chocolates, and other calorie-filled treats.
Bus: 119 to Piazza della Rotonda

GIOLITTI
$
VIA UFFICI DEL VICARIO 40
TEL 06 699 1243
giolitti.it
Once the most celebrated of Rome's cafés–ice cream parlors—and noted for its sulky service.
Bus: 119 to Piazza della Rotonda

IL PICCOLO
$
VIA DEL GOVERNO VECCHIO 74–75
TEL 06 6880 1746

This intimate small wine bar just a few steps west of Piazza Navona is perfect for a quiet glass of wine by candlelight.
20 Bus: 46, 62, 64 to Corso Vittorio Emanuele II All major cards

IVO A TRASTEVERE
$
VIA DI SAN FRANCESCO A RIPA 158
TEL 06 581 7082
ivoatrastevere.it
A great success since the 1960s, everybody should sample the Ivo experience. This is one of the most popular of Trastevere's pizzerias. You may have to wait, but turnover is quick and the atmosphere lively.
200 Bus: 44, 75 to Viale di Trastevere. Tram: 8 Closed L (except Sun.), Tues., & 3 weeks in Aug. All major cards

ROSATI
$
PIAZZA DEL POPOLO 4/5A
TEL 06 322 5859
barrosati.it
Rosati is a 1922 art nouveau delight that is serves tempting cakes, pastries, and cocktails.
60 Bus: 119 to Piazza del Popolo All major cards

▶ NORTHWEST ITALY

CINQUE TERRE

PALAZZO VANNONI
$$$ ✪✪✪
VIA MARCONI 4, LEVANTO
TEL 0187 808146 OR 334 119 6687
hotelpalazzovannoni.it
Levanto makes a good base for exploring the Cinque Terre villages. The hotel is in the historical center in an elegant 16th-century building that has been restored to enhance its original frescoes.
7 + 4 suites Free All major cards

Elevator Air-conditioning Indoor Pool Outdoor Pool Health Club Wi-Fi Credit Cards

🏨 PORTO ROCA
🍴 $$$ ○○○○
VIA CORONE 1, MONTEROSSO
TEL 0187 817 502
portoroca.it
Set on steep slopes affording
fine views of the sea and village, this hotel has a romantic,
flower-filled terrace and pleasant bar and restaurant. Rooms
are filled with pictures, rugs,
antiques, and old furniture.
🛏 32 🕒 Closed Nov.–mid-
March 🍽 🛗 📶 Free in public
areas 💳 All major cards

🏨 CA' D'ANDREAN
$$ ○○○
VIA DISCOVOLO 101,
MANAROLA
TEL 0187 920 040
cadandrean.com
A former mill, wine cellar, and
private home. Rooms are plain,
simple, and clean.
🛏 10 🕒 Closed mid-Nov.–
Dec. 📶 Free 💳 All major cards

🍴 MIKY
$$$
VIA FEGINA 104,
MONTEROSSO
TEL 0187 817608
ristorantemiky.it
Eat fish and seafood on the
seafront terrace or in the pretty
little garden to the rear.
🪑 60–60 🕒 Closed Dec.–
mid-March & Tues. except Aug.
🛗 💳 All major cards

🍴 A CANTINA DE
MANANAN
$$
VIA FIESCHI 117, CORNIGLIA
TEL 0187 821 166
An appealing, old-fashioned
trattoria in the former wine
vaults of the 14th-century
Palazzo Fieschi. Fish and seafood dominate the menu, but
pasta dishes are also available.
Small, and booking is essential.
🪑 30 🕒 Closed Mon. (except
summer) & L June–Sept.
💳 Cash only

🍴 GAMBERO ROSSO
$$
PIAZZA MARCONI 7, VERNAZZA
TEL 0187 812265
ristorantegamberorosso.net
One of several small and
welcoming restaurants around
the square on Vernazza's tiny
beach and harbor. Delightful
outdoor dining (mainly fish
and seafood, but be sure to try
the pesto) and a cozy interior
for colder days.
🪑 40–40 🕒 Closed Thurs. &
Jan.–March 💳 All major cards

GENOA

🏨 BRISTOL PALACE
$$$–$$$$ ○○○○
VIA XX SETTEMBRE 35
TEL 010 592 541
hotelbristolpalace.it
The best known of Genoa's
grand old hotels, although the
grandeur and elegance are a
little faded in places.
🛏 128 + 5 suites 🅿 🍽 🛗
📶 Free 💳 All major cards

🏨 CITY
🍴 $$$ ○○○○
VIA SAN SEBASTIANO 6
TEL 010 584 707
bwcityhotel-ge.it
A comfortable, central hotel
affiliated with the reliable Best
Western chain. **Pesciolino** res-
taurant is good.
🛏 63 + 3 suites 🅿
🕒 Restaurant closed Sun. L
🍽 🛗 📶 Free
💳 All major cards

🏨 METROPOLI
$$$ ○○○
PIAZZA FONTANA MOROSE
TEL 010 246 8888
hotelmetropoli.it
An upscale hotel in a romantic
square at the heart of Genoa's
historic center. First-floor
rooms are especially pleasant.
🛏 48 🅿 🍽 🛗 📶 Free
💳 All major cards

🍴 SAN GIORGIO
$$$
VIALE BRIGATA BISAGNO 69r
TEL 010 595 5205
ristorantesangiorgiogenova.it
In its bright dining rooms,
guests are treated to delectable
dishes from both land and
sea. The cuisine is traditional
and uses high quality, seasonal
ingredients. Professional service and elegant atmosphere.
🪑 60 🕒 Closed Sun. 🛗 💳 All
major cards

🍴 ANTICA OSTERIA DI
VICO PALLA
$$
VICOLO PALLA 15/R
TEL 010 246 6575
osteriadivicopalla.com
This venerable inn in the old
port area (convenient for the
Acquario) has been in business
since the 17th century, serving
the freshest fish and seafood.
🪑 95 🕒 Closed Mon. & 10
days in Aug. 💳 All major cards

🏨 Hotel 🍴 Restaurant 🛏 No. of Guest Rooms 🪑 No. of Seats 🅿 Parking 🚇 Metro 🚢 Boat/ferry 🕒 Hours

TRATTORIA DA FRANCA

$$

VICO LEPRE 4

TEL 010 247 4473

facebook.com/
trattoriadafranca

This fish restaurant in the historical center has only a few tables in a well-decorated dining room. Savory tartes, bread, and sweets are all homemade.

35 Closed Tue. & Wed. MC, V

PARCO NAZIONALE DEL GRAN PARADISO

BELLEVUE

$$$$ ✪✪✪✪

VIA GRAN PARADISO 22, COGNE

TEL 0165 74 825

hotelbellevue.it

The hotel's communal areas are decorated with rustic antiques, and rooms, although varying in age and style, are all attractively decorated. The hotel's **Le Petit Restaurant** is the town's finest.

38 + 8 suites
Closed early Oct.–early Dec., restaurant closed Wed. & L Mon.–Fri. Free
All major cards

PETIT DAHU

$$ ✪✪

FRAZIONE VALNONTEY 27, VALNONTEY

TEL 393 8285300

hotelpetitdahu.com

A tiny hotel with small, simple rooms fashioned from two traditional wooden houses built in 1729. Situated in the pretty village of Valnontey, 1 mile (1.5 km) from Cogne–perfectly positioned for hiking.

8 Closed May & Oct.–Nov. Free AE, V

LOU RESSIGNON

$$

VIA MINES DE COGNE 23, COGNE

TEL 0165 74 034

louressignon.it

Warm welcome, homey atmosphere, rustic appearance—wooden ceiling and old fireplace—and authentic Valle d'Aosta cooking, such as *seupetta cogneintze* (a soup of rice, local fontina cheese, herbs, and croutons). Also offers five rooms for B&B ($).

75 Closed Mon. D, Tues. except summer & Christmas, & 2-week periods Sept., Oct., & Nov. All major cards

PORTOFINO

SOMETHING SPECIAL

SPLENDIDO

$$$$$ ✪✪✪✪✪

SALITA BARATTA 16

TEL 0185 267 801

belmond.com

One of Italy's finest, most notable, and most expensive hotels. Originally a medieval monastery, it opened as a hotel in 1901. Stunning location set on four acres (1.5 ha) of semitropical gardens. All rooms are individually styled. Spa, tennis courts, and countless other facilities.

56 + 8 suites Closed mid-Nov.–late March (may vary) Free
All major cards

EDEN

$$$ ✪✪✪

VICO DRITTO 18

TEL 0185 269 091

hoteledenportofino.com

A traditional Ligurian house dating from 1929 near the village square. Set in a small palm-dotted garden. Hotels in this lower price range are rare.

12 Free
All major cards

PICCOLO

$$$ ✪✪✪✪

VIA DUCA DEGLI ABRUZZI 31

TEL 0185 269 015

hotelpiccoloportofino.it

A comfortable and intimate hotel set among parkland and gardens, a five-minute walk from the Piazzetta. Most rooms have balconies with sea views.

23 Closed Nov.–mid-March (may vary) Free
All major cards

DA PUNY

$$$

PIAZZA MARTIRI DELL' OLIVETTA 5

TEL 0185 269 037

A Portofino institution, this long-established restaurant is set on the chic square overlooking the harbor, with two comfortable salons and tables set under trees on a terrace. A predominantly fish and seafood menu.

40–70 Closed Thurs. & mid-Dec.–mid-Feb.
All major cards

LA GRITTA

$$$

CALATA MARCONI 20

TEL 0185 269 126

lagrittaportofino.com

One of Portofino's oldest bars. Rex Harrison once shared cocktails here with the Duke of Windsor, just two among many illustrious past habitués.

MC, V

TURIN

GOLDEN PALACE

$$$$ ✪✪✪✪✪

VIA DELL'ARCIVESOVADO 18

TEL 011 551 2727

allegroitalia.it

This luxury hotel opened in 2006 on the occasion of the Winter Olympics. Part of the architecturally distinguished Palazzo Toso, it has a perfect central location a block off Piazza Solferino and a minimalist, art deco–inspired design, with a host of facilities.

183 + 12 suites Free All major cards

🏨 VICTORIA
$$$ ✪✪✪✪
VIA NINO COSTA 4
TEL 011 561 1909
hotelvictoria-torino.com
An elegant hotel distinguished
by its courteous service and
fine attention to detail. Modern
and older wings, with uniformly
good rooms in various styles.
🛏 106 ➡ 🅢 🅢 🅦 📶 Free
🅢 All major cards

🍴 DEL CAMBIO
$$$$
PIAZZA CARIGNANO 2
TEL 011 546 690
delcambio.it
A historic restaurant founded
in 1757 that boasts a Michelin
star from 2016 and a reno-
vated beautiful interior, com-
plete with chandeliers, ornate
lamps, and huge mirrors.
Cooking is Piedmontese, the
wine list superb.
🍽 60–150 🕐 Closed Sun. D,
Mon., Tues. L, periods in Jan. &
Aug. 🅢 🅢 All major cards

🍴 VINTAGE 1997
$$$$
PIAZZA SOLFERINO 16/H
TEL 011 535 948
vintage1997.com
An elegant restaurant just
west of the old center with a
Michelin star, and a good choice
if you want to dress up and
enjoy a fusion of Piedmontese
and Mediterranean cuisine.
Tasting menus are available.
🍽 60 🕐 Closed Sun., L Sat.,
& periods in Jan. & Aug. 🅢
🅢 All major cards

🍴 AL GARAMOND
$$$–$$$$
VIA GIUSEPPE POMBA 14
TEL 011 812 2781
algaramond.it
Traditional Italian meat and
seafood dishes with a modern
twist are offered in this small,
elegant, brick-vaulted restaurant
a few minutes' walk southeast
of the main Piazza San Carlo.

🍽 40 🕐 Closed L Sat., Sun., 1
week in Jan., & 3 weeks in Aug.
🅢 🅢 All major cards

🍴 TRE GALLINE
$$
VIA BELLEZIA 37
TEL 011 436 6553
3galline.it
There has been an inn of
this name here for three centuries or more. The present
patrons continue a strong
tradition of classic Piedmontese cooking in a tranquil city-
center setting just northwest
of Piazza Reale.
🍽 70 🅿 🕐 Closed Sun.,
L Mon.–Fri., 1 week in Jan.,
Easter, & 3 weeks in Aug.
🅢 🅢 All major cards

VALLE D'AOSTA

🏨 G.H. ROYAL E GOLF
🍴 **$$$$$ ✪✪✪✪✪**
VIA ROMA 87, COURMAYEUR
TEL 0165 831 611
hotelroyalegolf.com
One of Courmayeur's best
hotels, with a renowned
restaurant boasting elaborate
cooking with regional and
French influences. Reservations
are essential.
🛏 80 + 6 suites 🅿
🕐 Restaurant closed L &
Mon. except Aug. & Christmas;
hotel may close May–June
🅢 🅱 🅦 📶 Free
🅢 All major cards

🏨 AUBERGE DE LA MAISON
$$$$ ✪✪✪✪
VIA PASSERON D'ENTRÈVES,
ENTRÈVES 2.5 MILES (4 KM)
FROM COURMAYEUR
TEL 0165 869 811
aubergemaison.it
A new-build mountain chalet
in peaceful out-of-town setting, with lots of cozy touches
such as wood-burning stoves
and individually decorated
rooms, most with a view of
Mont Blanc.

🛏 33 🅿 ➡ 🅢 🅦 📶 Free
🅢 All major cards

🏨 DUCA D'AOSTA
$$$ ✪✪✪✪
PIAZZA NARBONE 8, AOSTA
TEL 0165 236363
alpissima.it
A traditional, comfortable inn
in Aosta's main square that
was renovated in 2015.
🛏 60 ➡ 🅢 📶 Free
🅢 All major cards

▶ LOMBARDY & THE LAKES

BERGAMO

🏨 EXCELSIOR SAN
🍴 MARCO
$$$ ✪✪✪✪
PIAZZA DELLA REPUBBLICA 6
TEL 035 366 111
hotelsanmarco.com
A modern but comfortable
hotel in Bergamo Bassa. Plus
points are the roof terrace, the
Michelin-starred **Roof Garden**
restaurant, and easy walking
distance from the historic hilltop part of the city.
🛏 147 + 8 suites 🕐 Restaurant
closed Sat. L, Sun. & parts of Jan.
& Aug. 🅿 🅢 🅢 🅱 🅦 📶 Free
🅢 All major cards

🏨 PIAZZA VECCHIA
$$–$$$ ✪✪✪✪
VIA COLLEONI 3/5
TEL 035 253 179
hotelpiazzavecchia.it
The best of only a hand-
ful of hotels at the heart of
Bergamo's historic upper city.
It lies on one of the old city's
principal streets.
🛏 13 🅿 ➡ 🅢 📶 Free
🅢 All major cards

🍴 SANT'AMBROEUS
$$$
PIAZZA VECCHIA 2
TEL 035 237 494
trattoriasantambroeus.it
In the heart of the upper town,

dinner is served by candlelight, either inside the antique walls or in the spectacular square. The cuisine is regional, reinterpreted but traditional, but there are also specialties from the rest of the country such as *burrata* or *vitel tonné*.

🍴 40 🕐 Period in Jan. 🅰
🅰 All major cards

🍴 TRATTORIA LA COLOMBINA
$$
VIA BORGO CANALE 12
TEL 035 261 402 OR 346 303 2342
trattorialacolombina.it
Just a few steps from the house where Gaetano Donizetti was born, the restaurant offers good local cuisine: polenta, a variety of salamis and cheeses from the Alps, and stuffed pasta. In good weather, the terrace is open for dining.

🍴 70 🅰 🅰 All major cards

LAGO DI COMO

SOMETHING SPECIAL

🏨 GRAND HOTEL 🍴 VILLA SERBELLONI
$$$$$ ⭕⭕⭕⭕⭕
VIA ROMA 1, BELLAGIO
TEL 031 950 216
villaserbelloni.com
The first choice for a treat in Lake Como's prettiest village. Rooms are all superlative but vary in size and splendor—the best look out over the lake. The **Mistral** restaurant has a Michelin star.

ℹ️ 91 + 4 suites 🅿
🕐 Closed Nov.–March
🅰 🅰 🅰 🅰 Free
🅰 All major cards

SOMETHING SPECIAL

🏨 VILLA D'ESTE 🍴
$$$$$ ⭕⭕⭕⭕⭕
VIA REGINA 40, CERNOBBIO
TEL 031 3481
villadeste.com

The lakeside Villa d'Este was built in 1568 and became a hotel in 1873. Today, it is not only one of Italy's grandest and most luxurious hotels, but it also has one of the country's finest gardens. Public areas are magnificent—full of frescoes, statues, vast chandeliers, and precious antiques—while rooms are decorated in a similarly grand 19th-century style.

ℹ️ 145 + 7 suites
🅿 🕐 Closed Dec.–Feb.
🅰 🅰 🅰 🅰 🅰 Free
🅰 All major cards

🏨 TERMINUS 🍴 $$$–$$$$ ⭕⭕⭕⭕
LUNGO LARIO TRIESTE 14, COMO
TEL 031 329 111
albergoterminus.it
This is a 19th-century, family-run villa hotel in the center of town near the lakefront. It has a pleasant terrace for sunny days with lakeside views for dining, and good rooms with elegant furniture.

ℹ️ 50 + 3 suites 🅿
🅰 🅰 🅰 Free
🅰 All major cards

🏨 DU LAC $$–$$$ ⭕⭕⭕
PIAZZA MAZZINI 32, BELLAGIO
TEL 031 950 320
bellagiohoteldulac.com
Charming Anglo-Italian-run hotel at the center of the village, close to the ferry landing stage. Roof terrace and plenty of rooms offering views of the lake.

ℹ️ 42 🅿 🅰 🅰 Free
🅰 All major cards

🍴 BARCHETTA 🏨 $$$ ⭕⭕⭕⭕
SALITA MELLA 13, BELLAGIO
TEL 031 951 389
ristorantebarchetta.com
Dine on the charming terrace in summer or indoors in front of the fire, amid a clutter of objets d'art and antiques. Fish

and meat dishes, including excellent *maialino arrosto del Monte Primo* (local roast suckling pig). Four rooms available *(tel 031 951 030)*.

ℹ️ 4 🍴 80 🕐 Closed mid. Oct.–March 🅰 Free
🅰 AE, MC, V

🍴 IL SOLITO POSTO
$$$
VIA LAMBERTENGHI 9, COMO
TEL 031 271 352
ilsolitoposto.net
Stone-walled dining rooms give a traditional look to this historic restaurant on the west side of the town center, but the cooking is modern, with dishes such as *gamberi con salsa ai frutti di bosco* (shrimp with a wild berry sauce).

🍴 80–20 🕐 Closed Mon. & 1 week in Feb. & Nov. 🅰
🅰 All major cards

LAGO MAGGIORE

🏨 GRAND HOTEL DES ÎLES BORROMÉES & SPA
$$$$$ ⭕⭕⭕⭕⭕
CORSO UMBERTO I 67, STRESA
TEL 0323 938 938
borromees.it
A classic villa hotel set on the lakeside amid gardens and parkland. It has been a byword for luxury and elegance since its opening in 1863. The 27 rooms in the hotel's *residenza* (annex) are less costly and decorated in a more contemporary style.

ℹ️ 164 + 15 suites
🅿 🅰 🅰 🅰 🅰 Free
🅰 All major cards

🏨 VERBANO 🍴 $$$ ⭕⭕⭕
VIA UGO ARA 12,
ISOLA DEI PESCATORI
TEL 0323 30 408
hotelverbano.it
This is one of the few places to stay on the Borromean Islands. The restaurant is good but obviously busy, with a pleasant

outdoor terrace dining in summer.

(i) 12 **P** **(!)** Hotel closed Dec.–Feb., restaurant closed Wed. Oct.–mid-April **Free** **All major cards**

LA PIEMONTESE
$$$

VIA MAZZINI 25, STRESA
TEL 0323 30 235
ristorantepiemontese.com
A pleasant family-run restaurant in the town center where you can dine outside under a vine-covered pergola in summer. Robust local dishes, with an emphasis on fish.

(=) 50–50 **P** **(!)** Closed Mon., D Sun. Oct.–March, Dec., & Jan. **All major cards**

LAGO D'ORTA

VILLA CRESPI
$$$$–$$$$$ ✪✪✪✪

VIA G. FAVA 8–10 (1 MILE/2 KM E OF ORTA SAN GIULIO)
TEL 0322 911 902
villacrespi.it
The restaurant has two Michelin stars, and the handful of rooms in the park-enclosed 19th-century villa boast ornate Moorish decoration, canopied beds, marble bathrooms, and valuable furniture and antiques.

(i) 8 + 6 suites **P** **(!)** Hotel closed Jan., restaurant closed Mon. & L Tues. **Free** **All major cards**

SAN ROCCO
$$$ ✪✪✪✪

VIA GIPPINI 11,
ORTA SAN GIULIO
TEL 0322 911 977
hotelsanrocco.it
A converted 17th-century monastery with a panoramic view of the lake. Rooms are comfortable and modern, if a little dated; half have lake views.

(i) 78 + 2 suite **P** **Free** **All major cards**

MANTUA

CASA POLI
$$$ ✪✪✪✪

CORSO GARIBALDI 32
TEL 0376 288 170
hotelcasapoli.it
A hotel half a mile (1 km) from the town center, with modern facilities and a minimalist approach to decor.

(i) 34 **P** **Free** **All major cards**

BROLETTO
$$ ✪✪✪

VIA ACCADEMIA 1
TEL 0376 326 784
hotelbroletto.com
Central Mantua has few good hotels. This adequate but unexceptional establishment lies just a stone's throw from the Palazzo Ducale. Some rooms suffer traffic noise.

(i) 16 **(!)** Closed parts of Jan. & July **Free** **All major cards**

AQUILA NIGRA
$$$$

VICOLO BONACOLSI 4
TEL 0376 327 180
aquilanigra.it
Mantua's best restaurant has a Michelin star, a central location, frescoed walls, medieval vaulted ceilings, and a refined range of Mantuan specialties that might include *tortelli di zucca* (pasta parcels with sweet squash filling) and *filetto di manzo* (beef fillet).

(=) 75 **P** **(!)** Closed Sun. L except April–May & Sept.–Oct., **All major cards**

MILAN

FOUR SEASONS
$$$$$ ✪✪✪✪✪

VIA GESÙ 8
TEL 02 77 088
fourseasons.com
One of historical Milan's luxury-class hotel is a

converted 14th-century monastery, located on one of the city's premier shopping streets, northeast of the Duomo. Its **La Veranda** and **Il Foyer** restaurants are highly rated but expensive.

(i) 67 + 51 suites **P** **Metro: Montenapoleone** **Free** **All major cards**

UNA HOTEL CUSANI
$$$$–$$$$$ ✪✪✪✪

VIA CUSANI 13
TEL 02 85 601
gruppouna.it
A good central location in front of the Castello Sforzesco. Attentive service and spacious rooms furnished with style.

(i) 87 + 5 suites **P** **Metro: Cairoli** **Free** **All major cards**

SPADARI AL DUOMO
$$$–$$$$$ ✪✪✪✪

VIA SPADARI 11

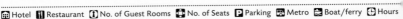

Hotel **Restaurant** **(i)** No. of Guest Rooms **No. of Seats** **P** Parking **Metro** **Boat/ferry** **(!)** Hours

TEL 02 7200 2371
spadarihotel.com
A tremendous location on a side street just off the central Piazza del Duomo. Decor is elegant and sophisticated, and the hotel is particularly known for its precious collection of contemporary art.

🏙 40 🅿 🚇 Metro: Duomo
📅 Closed Christmas ⬅ 📶
📶 Free 📇 All major cards

🏨 GRAN DUCA DI YORK
$$$ ○○○
VIA MONETA 1/A
TEL 02 874 863
ducadiyork.com
Price and a central location, moments from the Pinacoteca Ambrosiana, are the main attractions of this small, reliable hotel, with simple rooms, housed in a former 19th-century seminary.

🏙 33 🅿 📶 📶 Free
📇 All major cards

🍴 SADLER
$$$$$
VIA ASCANIO SFORZA 77
AT VIA CONCHETTA
TEL 02 5810 4451
sadler.it
Superb meat and fish cooking has earned Sadler one Michelin stars. However, you'll need to take a cab here because the restaurant lies south of the city center. Eat more informally at the adjoining, co-run **Chic'n Quick** (tel 02 8950 3222).

🏙 40 📅 Closed L & Sun., Jan. 1–15, & some of Aug.
📶 📇 All major cards

🍴 EMILIA E CARLO
$$$$
VIA GIUSEPPE SACCHI 8
TEL 02 875 948
Three period dining rooms with wooden beams and stone vaults in a palazzo in the Brera neighborhood, a short walk east of the Castello Sforzesco. Cooking is bright and modern

without straying too far from the Italian classics, with fish, meat, and vegetarian options.

🏙 60 📅 Closed period in Jan. & Aug. 📶

SOMETHING SPECIAL

🍴 CRACCO
$$$–$$$$$
GALLERIA VITTORIO EMANUELE II
TEL 02 876 774
ristorantecracco.it
Carlo Cracco has moved to the iconic Galleria. The new restaurant has a number of lavish, elegant dining rooms and private rooms. The cuisine hasn't changed—the level is still among the highest in Italy. The wine list is worthy of the menu.

🏙 50 🚇 Metro: Duomo
📅 Closed Sat. L, Sun.
📶 📇 All major cards

🍴 IL LUOGO DI AIMO E NADIA
$$$–$$$$$
VIA MONTECUCCOLI 6
TEL 02 416 886
aimoenadia.com
Known for its fanatical use of the best ingredients available and inventive interpretations of Milanese and other northern Italian dishes. Menus change regularly and can range from simple dishes such as *crostini* (toasts) with the finest olive oil and sweetest tomatoes to *melanzane farcite d'aragosta* (eggplant stuffed with lobster). Less expensive for lunch.

🏙 40 🚇 Metro: Primaticco
📅 Closed Sat. L, Sun., & periods in Jan. & Aug. 📶
📇 All major cards

🍴 TRATTORIA MILANESE
$$$
VIA SANTA MARTA 11
TEL 02 8645 1991
santamartamilano.com
A busy, central, traditional, two-room trattoria. Popular with a range of Milanese, from

businesspeople to young lovers. Located just west of the Biblioteca Ambrosiana.

🏙 80 📅 Closed Sun. & Aug.
📇 All major cards

🍴 CHARLESTON
$–$$
PIAZZA DEL LIBERTY 8
TEL 02 798 631
ristorantecharleston.it
Big, busy, and often noisy, just as pizzerias should be, and convenient to the center, just west of the Duomo. Antipasti (appetizers) and nonpizza dishes, such as simple pastas, are also available.

🏙 180 🅿 🚇 Metro: Duomo
📶 📇 All major cards

▶ VENICE

HOTELS

🏨 CIPRIANI
$$$$$ ○○○○
FONDAMENTA SAN GIOVANNI, ISOLA DELLA GIUDECCA 10
TEL 041 240 801
belmond.com
The Cipriani lies on the island of the Giudecca rather than the Grand Canal. This makes it quieter and calmer—guests also have use of a pool, garden, and tennis courts—but you may feel cut off from the life of the city.

🏙 80 + 24 suites ⬅ Zitelle 2, 4.1, 4.2, or private hotel launch from San Marco
⬅ 📶 📶 📶 Free
📇 All major cards

🏨 DANIELI
$$$$$ ○○○○○
RIVA DEGLI SCHIAVONI-CALLE DELLE RASSE, CASTELLO 4196
TEL 041 522 6480
danielihotelvenice.com
To indulge fully in the opulent Old World splendor, make sure to reserve a room in

the original hotel, housed in a 13th-century palazzo, not the 1948 annex.

ℹ️ 215 + 10 suites 🚤 S. Zaccaria 1, 2, 4.1, 4.2, 5.1, 5.2, 14, 15 🅿️ 📶 Free 🗝 All major cards

🏨 GRITTI PALACE
$$$$$ 😊😊😊😊😊
CAMPO SANTA MARIA DEL GIGLIO, SAN MARCO 2467
TEL 041 794 611
thegrittipalace.com
A peaceful hotel housed in a historic building—the 15th-century palace home of a former doge. It exudes comfort and elegance.

ℹ️ 85 + 6 suites 🚤 Giglio 1 🅿️ 🗝 📶 Free 🗝 All major cards

🏨 BAGLIONI HOTEL LUNA
🍴 $$$$–$$$$$ 😊😊😊😊😊
CALLE LARGA DELL'ASCENSIONE, SAN MARCO 1243
TEL 041 852 0730
baglionihotels.com
Venice's oldest hotel, once the Venetian headquarters of the Knights Templar. Public spaces have beautiful old touches, such as the frescoes of the Marco Polo lounge, while rooms—some overlooking the Grand Canal—are elegant and well designed. Its **Canova** restaurant is one of the city's best.

ℹ️ 89 + 15 suites 🚤 Vallaresso 1, 2 🅿️ 🗝 📶 Free 🗝 All major cards

🏨 ACCADEMIA VILLA MARAVEGE
$$$ 😊😊😊
FONDAMENTA BOLLANI, DORSODURO 1058–1060
TEL 041 521 0188
pensioneaccademia.it
A well-known and popular hotel, thanks to its location, garden, setting—a 17th-century palazzo that once housed the Russian Embassy—and the grand style and antique decoration of its rooms and public

spaces. Some rooms are very small. No restaurant. Reservations essential.

ℹ️ 27 🚤 Accademia 1, 2 🅿️ 📶 Free 🗝 All major cards

🏨 ALA
$$$ 😊😊😊
CAMPO SANTA MARIA DEL GIGLIO, SAN MARCO 2494
TEL 041 520 8333
hotelala.it
The Ala is a short walk from St. Mark's. Rooms are generally either small and decorated in a contemporary manner or large and furnished in an older style.

ℹ️ 84 🚤 Giglio 1 🅿️ 🗝 📶 Free 🗝 All major cards

🏨 AMERICAN
$$$ 😊😊😊
FONDAMENTA BRAGADIN-SAN VIO, DORSODURO 628
TEL 041 520 4733
hotelamerican.com
A perfect mid-priced hotel in a quiet and pretty canalside location within a few minutes' walk of the Accademia and Guggenheim galleries.

ℹ️ 30 🚤 Accademia 1, 2 📶 Free 🗝 All major cards

🏨 FLORA
$$$ 😊😊😊
CALLE DEI BERGAMESCHI, SAN MARCO 2283A
TEL 041 520 5844
hotelflora.it
A small inner garden lends this hotel much of its charm. Period-style rooms are a bit small, but the location, just off Calle Larga XXII Marzo to the west of St. Mark's, is perfect.

ℹ️ 43 🚤 Giglio 1 🅿️ 🗝 📶 Free 🗝 All major cards

🏨 GIORGIONE
$$$ 😊😊😊😊
CAMPO SS. APOSTOLI, CANNAREGIO 4587
TEL 041 522 5810
hotelgiorgione.com
The hotel has a small courtyard

garden and tranquil location, plus a range of facilities and well-presented rooms that raise it above the standard of most other four-star hotels.

ℹ️ 76 🚤 Ca' d'Oro 1 🅿️ 🗝 📶 Free 🗝 All major cards

🏨 NOVECENTO BOUTIQUE HOTEL
$$$
SAN MARCO 2683–84
TEL 041 241 3765
novecento.biz
A rich mix of Venetian, Mediterranean, and Oriental fabrics and decorative motifs lend this small, family-run hotel, in a quiet street close to the appealing Campo Santo Stefano, an exotic yet elegant air. Breakfast is served in a small courtyard in fine weather.

ℹ️ 9 🚤 Giglio 1 🗝 📶 Free 🗝 All major cards

🏨 OLTRE IL GIARDINO
$$$
FONDAMENTA CONTARINI, SAN POLO 2542
TEL 041 275 0015
oltreilgiardino-venezia.com
A large garden, plus calm, understated rooms in a gently contemporary style make this distinctive and graciously run B&B hotel a genuine place of quiet and retreat close to the Frari church.

ℹ️ 2 + 4 suites 🚤 San Tomà 1, 2 🗝 📶 Free 🗝 All major cards

🏨 PALAZZO ABADESSA
$$$ 😊😊😊😊
CALLE PRIULI, OFF STRADA NOVA, CANNAREGIO 4011
TEL 041 241 3784
abadessa.com
Antiques, rich fabrics, and frescoed ceilings evoke the Venice of the 16th century in this historic lodging, with spacious, elegant rooms, a small beautiful garden, and gracious service.

🏨 Hotel 🍴 Restaurant ℹ️ No. of Guest Rooms 🔧 No. of Seats 🅿️ Parking 🚇 Metro 🚤 Boat/ferry 🕐 Hours

🛏 8 + 5 suites 🚊 Ca' d'Oro 1
🅿 🛜 Free 🅰 All major cards

RESTAURANTS

🍴 ANTICO MARTINI
$$$$$
CAMPO TEATRO FENICE 2007
TEL 041 522 4121
anticomartini.com
The refined Venetian cuisine
is almost overshadowed by
the decor, a grand ensemble
of chandeliers, paneled walls,
and precious paintings. The
restaurant, in the shadow of
Teatro La Fenice opera house,
is almost three centuries old.
The restaurant's 350-label
wine list is outstanding. Special
for a drink, overlooking the
square from the terrace.
🍽 50 🚊 Giglio 1 🕐 Closed
Tues., open D only Nov.–March
🅿 🅰 All major cards

🍴 BANCOGIRO
$$$$
CAMPO SAN GIACOMETTO,
SAN POLO 122
TEL 041 523 2061
osteriabancogiro.it
This refined, successful *osteria*
near the waterfront close to
the Rialto markets offers the
option of a glass of wine in the
bar downstairs, with a view of
the Grand Canal, or a meal of
creative Venetian dishes in the
dining room upstairs. It stays
open late.
🍽 35 🚊 Rialto 1, 2 🕐 Closed
Mon. 🅰 All major cards

🍴 AL COVO
$$$–$$$$
CAMPIELLO DELLA PESCARIA,
CASTELLO 3968
TEL 041 522 3812
ristorantealcovo.com
A wonderful little two-room
restaurant that produces
exquisite and often innovative
takes on Venetian classics such
as *fritto misto* (mixed fish and
seafood grill).

🍽 60–100 🚊 Arsenale 1, 4.1,
4.2 or San Zaccaria also 5.1, 5.2,
14, 15 🕐 Closed Wed., Thurs.,
& 2 weeks in Jan. & Aug. 🅿
🅰 All major cards

🍴 ANTICO MONTIN
$$$–$$$$
FONDAMENTA DI BORGO,
DORSODURO 1147
TEL 041 522 7151
locandamontin.com
Artists, writers, and the rich
and famous have patronized
the Montin for decades. The
rear garden is one of the
loveliest places in Venice to
eat alfresco, but the main
dining rooms are equally cozy
and appealing. They have an
old-fashioned atmosphere and
painting-covered walls.
🍽 125 🚊 Zattare or Ca'
Rezzonico 1, 2, 5.1, 5.2, 6, 8, 10
🕐 Closed Wed.
🅰 All major cards

🍴 CORTE SCONTA
$$$–$$$$
CALLE DEL PRESTIN,
CASTELLO 3886
TEL 041 522 7024
cortescontavenezia.it
It is difficult to secure a table in
this simple, trattoria-style res-
taurant, a favorite of locals and
foreigners in the know. The
atmosphere is lively, at times
almost chaotic, and there is no
real menu: The waitstaff brings
a selection of appetizers and
a limited choice of main and
pasta dishes. Quality is good,
but perhaps not reflective of
the price and reputation.
🍽 50–70 🚊 Arsenale 1, 4.1,
4.2 🕐 Closed Sun.–Mon.
🅿 🅰 All major cards

🍴 NARANZARIA
$$$
SOTTOPORTEGO DEL BANCO
GIRO, SAN POLO 130
TEL 041 724 1035
naranzaria.it
One of the more recent breed
of bars and restaurants near

the Rialto markets (see also
Bancogiro, this page), this
small establishment on two
levels (there is a bar on the
lower level) offers an unusual
but popular hybrid of Venetian and Japanese food in an
attractive brick-vaulted
dining room, plus a few
tables outside overlooking
the Canal Grande.
🍽 30 🚊 Rialto 1, 2 🕐 Closed
Mon. from Nov.–March
🅰 MC, V

🍴 OSTERIA ANICE STELLATO
$$$
FONDAMENTA DE LA SENSA,
CANNAREGIO 3272
TEL 041 720 744
osterianicestellato.com
The menu includes fish,
meat, and a good number
of vegetarian options. All
the dishes are inspired by
traditional Veneto cuisine, but
propose some intriguing and
interesting combinations. A
good selection of wines and a
congenial atmosphere.
🍽 35 🚊 S. Alvise 4.1, 4.2, 5.1,
5.2 🕐 Closed Mon. L & Sun.,
& period in Aug., Nov., & Dec.
🅿 🅰 All major cards

🍴 TRATTORIA ALLA MADONNA
$$$
CALLE DELLA MADONNA,
SAN POLO 594
TEL 041 522 3824
ristoranteallamadonna
.com
A trattoria of the old school:
big, busy, and low on frills.
The mainly fish-oriented
cooking is unexceptional,
but as a dining experience
it is far more genuine and
earthy than the tourist-filled
haunts on the nearby Rialto
waterfront.
🍽 220 🚊 Rialto 1, 2 🕐 Closed
Wed. & some of Jan. & Aug.
🅿 🅰 All major cards

🍴 VINI DA GIGIO

$$$

FONDAMENTA SAN FELICE,
CANNAREGIO 3628/A
TEL 041 528 5140
vinidagigio.com

A perfect little canalside
restaurant for a quiet lunch
or romantic dinner. Simple
but elegantly cooked and
presented Venetian cooking,
and two plain dining rooms
with bar, beamed ceilings, and
wooden cabinets around the
walls. Try the *carpaccio di spada*
(thin slices of raw swordfish).

🪑 40 🚢 Ca' d'Oro 1
🕐 Closed Mon.–Tues., 2 weeks
in Jan., & 3 weeks in Aug.
🅿️ 🅰️ All major cards

🍴 LA BITTA

$$

CALLE LUNGA SAN BARNABA,
DORSODURO 2753
TEL 041 523 0531

La Bitta is on Calle Lunga
San Barnaba, the focus of an
emerging dining and drinking
quarter, and is a tiny *osteria* and
bar that's ideal for an *ombra*
(aperitif), wine by the glass, or
cicheti (snacks), as well as light
meals of often creative, mostly
meat-based regional dishes
(with vegetarian options).

🪑 28–12 🚢 Ca' Rezzonico 1
🕐 Closed L, Sun., & part of
July 🅰️ Cash only

🍴 DONA ONESTA

$$

PONTE DE LA DONA ONESTA,
DORSODURO 3922
TEL 041 710 586

The "Honest Woman" is true
to her name, and this simple
trattoria charges fair prices
for good, basic Venetian fish
and meat dishes in a plain,
one-room restaurant near San
Rocco and the Frari. There
are some tables for two on
a lovely balcony looking the
canal.

🪑 45 🚢 San Tomà 1, 2
🅿️ 🅰️ All major cards

🍴 ACIUGHETA

$–$$

CAMPO SS. FILIPPO E GIACOMO,
CASTELLO 4357
TEL 041 522 4292
aciugheta.com

Revamped in a sleek
contemporary style, this
bacaro-pizzeria-trattoria just
west of St. Mark's is one of
the most reasonably priced
places in this busy quarter
for a simple meal.

🪑 70–70 🚢 San Zaccaria 1, 2,
4.1, 4.2 🅰️ MC, V

🍴 ANTICO DOLO

$

RUGA VECCHIA SAN GIOVANNI,
SAN POLO 778
TEL 041 522 6546
anticodolo.it

A café not quite as old as
nearby Do Mori (see this
page), but an almost equally
authentic and atmospheric
source of wines and snacks
(*cicheti* in Venetian dialect).
Limited seating.

🚢 Rialto 1, 82 🅰️ AE, DC, V

🍴 CAFFÈ ROSSO

$

CAMPO SANTA MARGHERITA,
DORSODURO 2963
TEL 041 528 7998
cafferosso.it

A tiny red-fronted café with a
spread of busy outdoor tables
on a lovely and lively square
a few minutes' walk from the
Frari church.

🚢 Ca' Rezzonico 1
🕐 Closed Sun.

🍴 DO MORI

$

CALLE DO MORI, OFF RUGA
VECCHIA SAN GIOVANNI,
SAN POLO 429
TEL 041 522 5401

Venetians and market traders
have been crowding this dark,
cramped *bacaro*, since 1462. No chairs or tables,
but tasty snacks and more

---

than 350 different wines. An
essential Venetian experience.

🚢 Rialto 1, 2 🕐 Closed Sun.
& Wed. D

▶ NORTHEAST ITALY

DOLOMITI

🏨 PARK HOTEL LAURIN

$$$$ ⬤⬤⬤⬤

VIA LAURIN 4, BOLZANO
TEL 0471 311 000
laurin.it

This hotel is an art nouveau
gem on the eastern edge of
the old town. Over the years it
has played host to royalty and
other visiting VIPs.

🛈 100 🕐 Restaurant closed
Sun. L 🅿️ 🔁 🅿️ 🚢 📶
🅰️ All major cards

🏨 ROSA ALPINA

🍴 $$$–$$$$ ⬤⬤⬤⬤⬤

VIA MICURÀ DE RÜ,
SAN CASSIANO

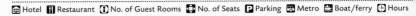

TEL 0471 849 500
rosalpina.it
This superb winter or summer base is a few miles northwest of Cortina d'Ampezzo in the eastern Dolomites. The lovely rooms spread over five floors are individually furnished and adorned with original local rural antiques. Even if you are not staying, it is worth making a detour for the two-Michelin-star restaurant, **St. Hubertus,** one of Italy's best.

① 51 **🍴** 35 **P** **🕐** Hotel & restaurant closed April–early June & Oct.–Nov., restaurant closed Tues. & L **🔼** **❄️** **🏊** **💪** **📶** Free

🏨 BIOHOTEL HERMITAGE
🍴 $$$ ✪✪✪✪
VIA CASTELLETTO INFERIORE 69, MADONNA DI CAMPIGLIO
TEL 0465 441 558
biohotelhermitage.it
Set among gardens and woodland, with wonderful mountain views, about 1 mile (1.5 km) from the center of Madonna. It has a refined hotel restaurant.

① 25 **🕐** Closed Oct.–mid-Dec. & Easter–late June, restaurant closed Mon. & L **📶** Free **🔲** All major cards

🏨 LUNA-MONDSCHIEN
$$$ ✪✪✪✪
VIA PIAVE 15, BOLZANO
TEL 0471 975 642
hotel-luna.it
This central but peaceful garden-fringed hotel dates from 1798; the superior wood-paneled rooms have balconies overlooking the garden.

① 73 + 4 suites **P** **🔼** **📶** Free **🔲** All major cards

🏨 GOLF HOTEL CAMPIGLIO
$$–$$$$ ✪✪✪✪
VIA CIMA TOSA 3, CAMPO CARLO MAGNO (2 MILES/ 3 KM FROM MADONNA DI CAMPIGLIO)
TEL 0465 441 003
thcampiglio.it

There are numerous hotels in the winter and summer resorts of the Dolomites. This hotel stands out by virtue of its nine-hole golf course.

① 109 **🕐** Closed April–June & mid-Sept.–Nov. **P** **🔼** **❄️** **🏊** **💪** **📶** Free **🔲** All major cards

🍴 EL FILÒ
$–$$
PIAZZA SCUOLE 5, MOLVENO
TEL 0461 586 151
A medieval house at the center of town where you can go for a snack and a glass of wine or a full meal. Choose from game specialties such as *cervo* (venison), *cinghiale* (wild boar), and Trentino dishes like *gnocchi alle ortiche* (small potato dumplings with a nettle sauce).

🍴 55 **🕐** Closed Mon.–Fri. mid-Oct.–mid-Dec. **❄️** **🔲** All major cards

LAGO DI GARDA

SOMETHING SPECIAL

🏨 GRAND HOTEL A VILLA FELTRINELLI
$$$$$ ✪✪✪✪✪
VIA RIMEMBRANZA 38–40, GARGNANO
TEL 0365 798 000
villafeltrinelli.com
Many rank this one of Italy's best hotels, an intimate yet exquisitely restored villa from 1892 in immaculate gardens with a lakefront setting. Rooms and public spaces (including a superb library) are decorated with paintings, frescoes, and antiques. The room in the tower is lovely.

① 17 + 4 suites **🍴** 40 **P** **🕐** Closed mid-Oct.–mid-April **🔼** **❄️** **🏊** **📶** Free **🔲** All major cards

🏨 PALACE HOTEL VILLA CORTINE
$$$$$ ✪✪✪✪✪
VIALE C. GENNARI 2 , SIRMIONE

TEL 030 990 5890
palacehotelvillacortine.it
Sublime, almost overly luxurious 1905 villa hotel set on parkland away from the town center overlooking the lake.

① 52 + 2 suites **P** **🕐** Closed mid-Oct.–Easter **🔼** **❄️** **🏊** **📶** Free **🔲** All major cards

🏨 VILLA DEL SOGNO
$$$$$ ✪✪✪✪✪
VIA ZANARDELLI 107, GARDONE RIVIERA
TEL 0365 290 181
villadelsogno.it
This grand 1920s mock-Renaissance "Villa of the Dream" overlooks the lake and the countryside. The hotel, one of the area's best, and its grounds are oases of tranquility.

① 32 **P** **🕐** Closed Nov.–March **🔼** **❄️** **🏊** **📶** Free **🔲** All major cards

🏨 LAURIN
$$$$ ✪✪✪✪
VIALE LANDI 9, SALÒ
TEL 0365 22 022
hotellaurinsalo.it
One of Italy's finest art nouveau villas, this romantic hotel is set on the lake and surrounded by parks and gardens.

① 33 **P** **🔼** **❄️** **🏊** **💪** **📶** Free **🔲** All major cards

🏨 VILLA FIORDALISO
🍴 $$$$ ✪✪✪✪
CORSO ZANARDELLI 150, GARDONE RIVIERA
TEL 0365 20 158
villafiordaliso.it
A temple to refined regional Lombard and Veneto cooking. This 19th-century villa—once home to Mussolini's mistress—is surrounded by parkland. There are five four-star standard rooms, some with lake views.

① 5 **🍴** 60 **🕐** Closed mid-Nov.–mid-March, restaurant closed Mon., L Tues. **❄️** **🔲** All major cards

---

🔼 Elevator **❄️** Air-conditioning **🏊** Indoor Pool **🌊** Outdoor Pool **💪** Health Club **📶** Wi-Fi **🔲** Credit Cards

🏨 HOTEL DU LAC ET DU PARC
$$$–$$$$$
VIALE ROVERETO 44,
RIVA DEL GARDA
TEL 0464 566 600
dulacetduparc.com
The town of Riva has numerous mid-range hotels, but for style and recreational activities (sauna, tennis courts), this smart, Spanish-style villa hotel has no equal.
🛈 159 + 5 suites 🅿 🔁
🅢 🈺 🛏 🛜 Free
🅢 All major cards

🏨 LA MAISON DU RELAX
$$$–$$$$ ◯◯◯◯
VIA ZANARDELLI 126,
GARDONE RIVIERA
TEL 0365 290 484
villaparadiso.com
In its day, the 180-room Grand Hotel nearby was more famous, but today this much more intimate villa on the lake is Gardone's most elegant place to stay, though it offers only week-long "well-being" stays most of the year.
🛈 13 🔁 🅢 🛜 Free
🅢 All major cards

🍴 LA RUCOLA 2.0
$$$$
VIA STRENTELLE 3, SIRMIONE
TEL 030 916 326
ristorantelarucola.it
Exemplary modern Italian cooking with seasonal specialties that embrace meat, fish, and seafood dishes.
🍽 45 🕐 Closed Thurs. & mid-Dec.–Jan. 🅢 🅢 All major cards

🍴 OSTERIA DELL'OROLOGIO
$–$$$
VIA MATTIA BUTTURINI 26, SALÒ
TEL 0365 290 158
facebook.com/osteriadellorologiosal
A find among the generally expensive restaurants in Lake Garda's resorts. The setting is simple and informal, and there are good cheeses, wines, snacks, and a handful of hot dishes.
🍽 70 🕐 Closed Wed. & 2 weeks each in Jan. & June or July 🅢 All major cards

PADUA

🏨 MAJESTIC TOSCANELLI
$$$ ◯◯◯◯
VIA DELL'ARCO 2
TEL 049 663 244
toscanelli.com
Housed in a 16th-century palazzo on a tranquil square south of the central Piazza delle Erbe. The rooms are decorated in a 19th-century style.
🛈 34 + 3 suites 🔁 🅢 🛜 Free
🅢 All major cards

🏨 AL FAGIANO
$–$$ ◯◯
VIA LOCATELLI 45
TEL 049 875 0073
alfagiano.com
An inexpensive hotel with a courteous welcome and perfect central location close to the Basilica di Sant'Antonio. Many rooms are adorned with striking works of modern art.
🛈 40 🅿 🔁 🅢 🛜 Free
🅢 All major cards

🍴 ANTICO BROLO
$$$–$$$$
CORSO MILANO 22
TEL 049 664 555
anticobrolo.it
An elegant, formal restaurant with first-rate service and good food. Signature dishes include *ravioli ai fiori di zucca* (filled pasta with zucchini flowers).
🍽 55–50 🕐 Closed L Mon. 🅢 🅢 All major cards

🍴 L'ANFORA
$–$$
VIA DEI SONCIN 13
TEL 049 656 629
Meat and fish dishes are available at this traditional trattoria near Piazza delle Erbe. Try the grilled fish of the day, *zuppa di vongole e cozze* (a soup of clams and mussels).
🍽 40 🕐 Closed Sun. & part of Aug. 🅢 🅢 All major cards

VERONA

🏨 GABBIA D'ORO
$$$$$ ◯◯◯◯
CORSO PORTA BORSARI 4/A
TEL 045 800 3060
hotelgabbiadoro.it
This superb, discreet hotel lies close to Piazza delle Erbe at the center of the city. All its rooms are different and beautifully appointed with beamed ceilings, frescoes, canopy beds, and other period touches.
🛈 27 🔁 🅢 🛜 Free
🅢 All major cards

🏨 COLOMBA D'ORO
$$$–$$$$ ◯◯◯◯
VIA C. CATTANEO 10
TEL 045 595 300
colombahotel.com
A bright and enticing family-run hotel housed in a thoughtfully restored 14th-century palazzo close to Piazza Brà.
🛈 51 🔁 🅢 🛜 Free
🅢 All major cards

🏨 AURORA
$$–$$$ ◯◯◯
PIAZZETTA XIV NOVEMBRE 2
TEL 045 594 717
hotelaurora.biz
The hotel is centrally located, overlooking the Piazza delle Erbe. It offers a variety of room types, all of which are comfortable. Breakfast buffet and 24-hour reception desk.
🛈 18 🔁 🅢 🛜 Free
🅢 All major cards

🏨 TORCOLO
$$ ◯◯
VICOLO LISTONE 3
TEL 045 800 7512
hoteltorcolo.it
A welcoming, good-value hotel

that looks onto a quiet square close to the main Piazza Brà.

(i) 19 **⊟** 🟦 🛜 Free
🔲 AE, MC, V

🍴 IL DESCO
$$$$$
VIA DIETRO SAN SEBASTIANO 7
TEL 045 595 358
ristoranteildesco.it
Ranked among northern Italy's best restaurants by many critics, including Michelin, which has regularly awarded it. Appetizers might include small medallions of quail or exquisite flans, and main courses like duck with honey.

🍽 50 🕐 Closed Sun.–Mon. (open Mon. D July, Aug., & Dec.), 1st week in Jan., Easter, 2 weeks in June, & some of Aug. 🟦 🔲 All major cards

🍴 LA GREPPIA
$$–$$$
VICOLO SAMARITANA 3
TEL 045 800 4577
ristorantegreppia.it
A bright, spacious restaurant with vaulted ceilings in the city's historic center. Local and regional cooking.

🍽 80–150 🕐 Closed Mon. & some of Jan. & July 🟦 🔲 All major cards

🍴 AL DUOMO
$$
VIA DUOMO 7/A
TEL 045 800 4505
Two small dining rooms between the Duomo and Sant'Anastasia, with wood paneling and walls adorned with musical instruments. A touchstone for traditional Veronese cooking, it also has fair prices, good local wine by the glass, and friendly service. Reservations essential (bookings not taken on weekends).

🍽 35 🕐 Closed Sun. 🟦
🔲 AE, MC, V

🍴 OSTERIA A LE PETARINE
$$
VICOLO SAN MAMASO 6/A
TEL 045 597 388
This tiny, traditional, two-roomed *osteria* is tucked away in a small alley not far from Piazza delle Erbe and is a popular spot for a glass of wine and a quick snack from the buffet or a meal based on one of the dishes of the day.

🍽 30 🕐 Closed Sun. D, Mon., & 2 weeks in Aug. 🟦
🔲 Cash only

VICENZA

🏨 DUE MORI
$$ 🔵🔵
CONTRÀ DO RODE 24
TEL 0444 321 886
albergoduemori.it
Vicenza has several bland modern hotels on its outskirts, but remarkably few places to stay in the city's historic heart. This simple hotel lies close to Piazza dei Signori, the central piazza.

(i) 30 🕐 Closed 2 weeks in Aug. **⊟** 🔲 AE, MC, V

🍴 ANTICA CASA DELLA MALVASIA
$$
CONTRÀ DELLE MORETTE 5
TEL 0444 543 704
anticacasadellamalvasia.it
A restaurant at the heart of the city whose atmosphere lends it the feel of a large medieval diner. Food can be innovative and is strictly regional, and includes *cavallo* (horse meat), a local specialty. Good salads are among the wide choice of alternatives. Excellent drinks, including more than 150 different teas, 75 herbal infusions, 70 malt whiskies, and 150 grappas.

🍽 140–180 🕐 Closed Sun. D & Mon. 🟦 🔲 All major cards

▶ EMILIA-ROMAGNA & THE MARCHE

ASCOLI PICENO

🏨 🍴 PALAZZO GUIDEROCCHI
$$$ 🔵🔵🔵🔵
VIA CESARE BATTISTI 3
TEL 0736 254 753
hotelguiderocchi.it
A central and recently converted 16th-century palazzo, with charming rooms in period style (there is a more modern annex 200 yards/ 200 m away).

(i) 37 **P** 🕐 Restaurant closed Tues. 🟦 🛜 Free
🔲 All major cards

🍴 IL DESCO
$$$
VIA VIDACILIO 10
TEL 0736 250 757
Fine regional food is served in romantic medieval-era dining rooms that have been given an elegant, contemporary look. The service is welcoming and the restaurant is conveniently located on the northern edge of Ascoli's old center.

🍽 60 🕐 Closed Mon. 🟦 🔲 All major cards

🍴 OSTERIA NONNA NINA
$$
PIAZZA DELLA VIOLA 11
TEL 0736 251 523
osterianonnanina.com
A classic trattoria on a peaceful town square with a small terrace for the summer; simple dining rooms and a mixture of straightforward local food and more sophisticated truffle and other seasonal dishes.

🍽 30–40 🕐 Closed Mon.
🔲 MC, V

BOLOGNA

⊞ G. H. MAJESTIC
$$$$–$$$$$ ✪✪✪✪✪
VIA DELL'INDIPENDENZA 8
TEL 051 225 445
grandhotelmajestic
.duetorrihotels.com
English royalty has stayed at
the Grand during visits to
Bologna. It is the city's finest
hotel, and rooms are opulent.
ⓘ 103 + 6 suites 🅿 🔁 📶
📶 Free 📇 All major cards

⊞ CORONA D'ORO 1890
$$$–$$$$$ ✪✪✪✪
VIA OBERDAN 12
TEL 051 745 7611
hco.it
Art nouveau decoration in
the public areas and medi-
eval touches such as painted
wooden ceilings in the rooms
make this a memorable place
to stay.
ⓘ 40 + 3 suites 🅿 🔁 📇
📶 Free 📇 All major cards

⊞ OROLOGIO
$$–$$$ ✪✪✪
VIA IV NOVEMBRE 10
TEL 051 745 7411
bolognarthotels.it
Perfect for sightseeing, the
hotel lies just off Piazza Grande
in a quiet pedestrians-only
zone of the historic city center.
ⓘ 33 + 6 suites 🅿 🔁 📇
📶 Free 📇 All major cards

⊞ ROMA
$$–$$$ ✪✪✪
VIA MASSIMO D'AZEGLIO 9
TEL 051 226 322
hotelroma.biz
A calm atmosphere, profes-
sional service, and central
location are the hallmarks of
the Roma.
ⓘ 85 🔁 📇 📶 Free
📇 All major cards

🍴 BATTIBECCO
$$$–$$$$$

VIA BATTIBECCO 4
TEL 051 223 298
battibecco.com
A stylish, centrally located restaurant with a bias toward fish
and seafood, but plenty of pastas, risottos (including porcini
mushrooms and saffron), and
meat dishes such as *maialino*
(roast suckling pig).
🪑 60 🅿 🕐 Closed Sun. & Sat.
L & periods in Feb. & late June
📇 📇 All major cards

🍴 DA CESARI
$$–$$$
VIA DEI CARBONESI 8
TEL 051 237 710
da-cesari.it
A classic old trattoria—in the
same family for more than 30
years—with traditional Bolognese dishes, home-produced
wine, and occasionally adventurous offerings such as *capret-
to* (goat) and *ravioli di coniglio*
(pasta and rabbit).
🪑 65 🕐 Closed Sun., 1 week
in Jan., & 3 weeks in Aug.
📇 📇 All major cards

🍴 DA GIANNI
$$
VIA CLAVATURE 18
TEL 051 229 434
trattoria-gianni.it
Da Gianni's two dining rooms
at the heart of the old city have
no decorative frills, but locals
flock here for classic Bolognese
dishes such *bollito misto* (mixed
meats), *tortellini in brodo* (filled
homemade pasta in broth),
and *tagliatelle al ragù* (pasta rib-
bons with a meat sauce).
🪑 45 🕐 Closed Sun. D, Mon.,
& Aug. 📇 📇 All major cards

FERRARA

⊞ DUCHESSA ISABELLA
$$$$$ ✪✪✪✪✪
VIA PALESTRO 70
TEL 0532 185 8096
duchessaisabella.com
A sumptuous hotel housed
in an opulent 16th-century

palazzo, adorned with rich
fabrics and antiques, and other
period details; located just
northeast of the historic center.
ⓘ 26 🅿 🕐 Closed Aug.
🔁 📇 📶 Free 📇 All major
cards

⊞ ANNUNZIATA
$$$ ✪✪✪✪
PIAZZA REPUBBLICA 5
TEL 0532 201 111
annunziata.it
It is impossible to be more
central than this reliable
family-run hotel directly in
front of the Castello Estense.
ⓘ 21 🅿 🔁 📇 📶 Free
📇 All major cards

🍴 L'OCA GIULIVA
$$–$$$
VIA BOCCACANALE DI SANTO
STEFANO 38–40
TEL 0532 207 628
ristorantelocagiuliva.it
A tiny establishment where the
menus make innovative use

of fish and meat. Dishes may include simply grilled fish or a more decadent pâté of pheasant with *uva passita* (rich, sugary grapes).

🛏 30–15 🕐 Closed Tues. & 2 weeks in June–July
❄ 🅒 All major cards

🍴 QUEL FANTASTICO GIOVEDÌ
$$–$$$
VIA CASTELNUOVO 9
TEL 0532 760 570
quelfantasticogiovedi.it
"That Fantastic Thursday" is named after a John Steinbeck story. Its food can be as unusual as its sobriquet, with dishes such as salmon and bream sushi with an herb mayonnaise and tagliatelle with saffron and squid.

🛏 38–10 🕐 Closed Wed. & 4 weeks in July–Aug. ❄
🅒 All major cards

PARMA

🏨 BUTTON
$$ ☺☺☺
VIA DELLA SALINA 7
TEL 0521 208 039
hotelbutton.it
This hotel is the best choice for sightseeing at the heart of the historic quarter.

ⓘ 40 🅿 ⬆ 🛜 Free
🅒 All major cards

🍴 PARIZZI
🏨 $$$$
STRADA REPUBBLICA 71
TEL 0521 285 952
ristoranteparizzi.it
Parma-based cuisine in this comfortable and relaxed Michelin one-star restaurant that has been a byword for fine food and courteous service for years. Try the *manzo stracotto* (beef steak in a rich sauce). It also now operates as an inn, with 13 rooms ($$$).

🛏 60 🅿 🕐 Closed Mon., Aug., & part of Jan. ❄
🅒 All major cards

🍴 LA FILOMA
$$$
BORGO XX MARZO 15
TEL 0521 206 181
ristorantelafiloma.it
Romantic if faintly kitsch dining rooms just south of the Duomo set in a 17th-century palazzo, plus classic Parmesan dishes such as *petto di faraona farcito* (stuffed breast of guinea fowl).

🛏 40 🕐 Closed Sat. L & Sun. from June–Aug., Tues. L & Wed. Sept.–May ❄
🅒 All major cards

🍴 TRATTORIA DEL TRIBUNALE
$$–$$$
VICOLO POLITI 5,
OFF STRADA FARINI
TEL 0521 285 527
trattoriadeltribunale.it
Excellent traditional food at good prices in a trattoria behind the Palazzo di Giustizia, just a few moments' walk south of the city's main historic core.

🛏 80–40 🕐 Closed a period in Aug. 🅒 All major cards

🍴 GALLO D'ORO
$$
BORGO DELLA SALINA 3
TEL 0521 208 846
gallodororistorante.it
The Gallo d'Oro is a traditional inn, with *salumi* hanging from beamed ceilings, that offers classic Parmesan trattoria dishes a block off the main Strada Repubblica. Don't miss *tortelli* and horse meat.

🛏 45 🅒 All major cards

RAVENNA

🏨 BISANZIO
$$$ ☺☺☺☺
VIA SALARA 30
TEL 0544 217 111
bisanziohotel.com
A stylish traditional hotel at the center of town with bright public spaces, a pretty internal garden, and attractive, restful modern-style rooms, different in type and size.

🛏 38 ⬆ ❄ 🛜 Free
🅒 All major cards

🍴 LA GARDELA
$$
VIA PONTE MARINO 3
TEL 0544 217 147
ristorantelagardela.com
An unpretentious dining room with straightforward local cooking in a convenient spot between the Basilica di San Vitale and Piazza del Popolo.

🛏 80–95 🕐 Closed Thurs. & some of Feb. & Aug. ❄
🅒 All major cards

URBINO

🏨 BONCONTE
$$–$$$ ☺☺☺☺
VIA DELLE MURA 28
TEL 0722 2463
viphotels.it
Some rooms can be small, especially on upper floors, but the Bonconte's comforts and location—by the town walls—make it a perfect sightseeing base.

ⓘ 23 🅿 ⬆ ❄ 🛜 Free
🅒 All major cards

🍴 VECCHIA URBINO
$$–$$$
VIA DEI VASARI 3-5
TEL 0722 4447
vecchiaurbino.it
This pretty, central restaurant comes into its own in the fall and winter, when the menu is enlivened with seasonal truffle and mushroom dishes.

🛏 50–120 🕐 Closed Tues. in winter & periods in Jan., July, & Dec. ❄ 🅒 All major cards

🍴 ANTICA OSTERIA DA LA STELLA
$–$$
VIA SANTA MARGERITA 1,
CORNER OF VIA RAFFAELLO
TEL 0722 320 228

anticaosteriadalastella.com
Pretty and homey, Urbino's
first-choice osteria has rustic
touches and seasonal, regional
dishes, including mushrooms
and truffles.

🔲 40 🕐 Closed Mon.
& periods in Jan. & Aug.
🅵 🅰 MC, V

▶ **FLORENCE**

HOTELS

🏨 **EXCELSIOR**
$$$$$ ✪✪✪✪✪
PIAZZA OGNISSANTI 3
TEL 055 27151
westinflorence.com
Florence's second grandest
hotel is undermined only by
its location on one of the city's
less attractive piazzas. Otherwise, the antiques-filled rooms
are visions of Old World
elegance, while the public
areas are sumptuous.

🛏 166 + 5 suites 🅿 🔁 🅵
🛜 Free 🅰 All major cards

🏨 **FOUR SEASONS
HOTEL FLORENCE
$$$$$**
BORGO PINTI 99
TEL 055 26 261
fourseasons.com/florence
Four Seasons' Florence hotel
is the most luxurious in the
city, a sumptuously restored
palace and former convent set
in glorious gardens and rooms
and public spaces that feature
a wealth of frescoes, fine art,
antiques, and other period
details. Removed from the
bustle of the historic center, it
is calmer but also less convenient for sightseeing.

🛏 94 + 24 suites 🅿 🔁 🅵
🚇 🔇 🛜 Free
🅰 All major cards

🏨 **HELVETIA & BRISTOL
$$$$$ ✪✪✪✪✪**
VIA DEI PESCIONI 2

TEL 055 26651
starhotelscollezione.com
Luxurious and exclusive, this
superb hotel has been in business since the 18th century.
Facilities and bathrooms are
state of the art, but rooms
(some of which are relatively
small) are in a more sober,
traditional style, with antiques
and old paintings.

🛏 52 + 15 suites 🅿 🔁 🅵
🛜 Free 🅰 All major cards

<hr>

SOMETHING SPECIAL

🏨 **VILLA SAN MICHELE**
🍽 **$$$$$ ✪✪✪✪✪**
VIA DOCCIA 4, FIESOLE
TEL 055 567 8200
belmond.com
Everything about this converted monastery is special,
from the spot-on service and
Michelangelo-designed facade
to the period decor and sublime swimming pool at the top
of the gardens. The hotel is
set in the hills, 7 miles (11 km)
from Florence, an excellent
base away from the bustle and
crowds of the city (regular free
shuttle service to and from the
city center). The terrace views
from the **Loggia Restaurant**
are some of the best of any
restaurant in Tuscany.

🛏 422 + 24 suites 🅿
🕐 Closed mid-Nov.–
mid-March 🅵 🚇 🔇 🛜 Free
🅰 All major cards

<hr>

🏨 **BRUNELLESCHI
$$$$–$$$$$ ✪✪✪✪**
PIAZZA SANTA ELISABETTA 3
TEL 055 27 370
hotelbrunelleschi.it
This central hotel, ideally
placed for sightseeing, has
been stylishly converted
from a Byzantine chapel and
fifth-century tower. Ancient
brick and stone have been preserved in the public areas and
complemented by the use of
wood. The rooms are bright,
airy, and comfortable. Professional and helpful staff.

🛏 96 + 9 suites 🅿 🔁 🅵
🛜 Free 🅰 All major cards

🏨 **MONNA LISA
$$$$ ✪✪✪✪**
BORGO PINTI 27
TEL 055 247 9751
monnalisa.it
A somber facade conceals a
marvelous and charming
14th-century palazzo, complete with sweeping staircase,
frescoed ceilings, and terra-
cotta floors. Rooms vary in
size but preserve an aristocratic, Old World feel, with
oil paintings and expensive
antiques. Some rooms over-
look a peaceful rear garden,
others an inner courtyard.

🛏 45 🅿 🔁 🅵 🛜 Free
🅰 All major cards

🏨 **TORRE DI
BELLOSGUARDO
$$$–$$$$$ ✪✪✪✪**
VIA ROTI MICHELOZZI 2
TEL 055 229 8145
torrebellosguardo.com
This glorious Renaissance villa
lies amid fascinating hilltop
gardens with lovely views,
just a five-minute drive south
of the Oltrarno. The frescoes
and vast stone fireplaces of
the vaulted public areas cre-
ate a wonderful atmosphere,
while the spacious rooms are
individually decorated in an
old-fashioned style. Breakfast
and light meals served, but no
restaurant.

🛏 10 + 6 suites 🅿 🔁
🔇 3 rooms 🚇 🛜 Free
🅰 All major cards

🏨 **MORANDI ALLA
CROCETTA
$$$ ✪✪✪**
VIA LAURA 50
TEL 055 234 4748
hotelmorandi.it
This quiet, intimate hotel—part
of a former monastery—near
Piazza S.S. Annunziata is a gem,
thanks both to the charm and

<hr>

friendly welcome of the owner and the considerable style with which the rooms and public spaces have been decorated. Colorful rugs cover polished wooden floors, and old prints and antiques decorate the walls. Reserve well in advance.

🛏 10 ❄ 🛜 Free
🌐 All major cards

🏨 CASCI
$$ 😊😊
VIA CAVOUR 13
TEL 055 211 686
hotelcasci.com
One of the best in its class, this two-star family-run hotel enjoys a perfect location just two minutes' walk north of the cathedral. The modestly sized rooms are immaculate and modern, and the courtesy and welcome of the multilingual staff and family owners is faultless. Buffet breakfast included.

🛏 25 ⬆ ❄ 🛜 Free
🌐 All major cards

🏨 RELAIS CAVALCANTI
$$
VIA PELLICERIA 2
TEL 055 210 962
relaiscavalcanti.com
Two sisters run this refined little B&B on the fourth floor of a 13th-century palazzo in a perfect (if busy) location close to the Ponte Vecchio and Porcellino market. The rooms are bright and spacious by the standards of central Florence, with pretty fittings and views over the rooftops.

🛏 8 ⬆ ❄ 🛜 Free
🌐 All major cards

RESTAURANTS

SOMETHING SPECIAL

🍴 ENOTECA PINCHIORRI
$$$$$
VIA GHIBELLINA 87
TEL 055 26311
enotecapinchiorri.it

Florence's best and most expensive restaurant has three Michelin stars and—at more than 80,000 bottles—one of Europe's finest wine cellars. The setting—a Renaissance palazzo with frescoed ceilings—and Tuscan-international cuisine are predictably chic, although the formality and ceremony may not be to all tastes. Jacket requested for men.

🍴 60 🕐 Closed L, Sun. & Mon. ❄ 🌐 AE, MC, V

🍴 CIBRÈO
$$$$
VIA DEL VERROCCHIO 8r
TEL 055 234 1100
cibreo.com
The first choice of most Florentine gastronomes and the city's best place to enjoy creative interpretations of traditional Tuscan dishes such as the delicious *trippa in insalata* (cold tripe salad) and the celebrated *fegato brasato* (braised liver). The dining room is plain—simple wooden tables and painted walls—and the service and atmosphere relaxed. Prices are set for each course—leave room for the desserts. A reservation several days in advance is essential. Note the nearby **Caffè Cibrèo** (see p. 372) and the less expensive **Cibrèo Trattoria**.

🍴 70 🅿 🕐 Closed Aug. & 1 week early in Jan. ❄ 🌐 All major cards

🍴 ORA D'ARIA
$$$$
VIA DE' GEORGOFILI 11–13r
TEL 055 200 1699
oradariaristorante.com
Success encouraged rising young chef Marco Stabile to move his original restaurant to this location just south of Piazza della Signoria. The modern Tuscan and Italian cooking is light, imaginative, beautifully presented, and has earned a Michelin star.

🍴 40 🕐 Closed Sun., Mon. L, & Aug. ❄ 🌐 AE, MC, V

🍴 BACCAROSSA
$$$
VIA GHIBELLINA 46r
TEL 055 240 620
baccarossa.it
Tasty pan-Mediterranean fish and meat dishes and homemade pastas are served in this informal bistro-style restaurant two blocks north of Santa Croce. The restaurant's eclectic and attractive decor includes old wooden tables and vivid furnishings.

🍴 35 🕐 Closed L, Sun., & part of late Aug.–Sept. ❄ 🌐 AE, MC, V

🍴 OLIVIERO
$$$
VIA DELLE TERME 51r
TEL 055 389 6135
facebook.com/
olivieroristorante1962
Oliviero enjoys a reputation for excellent regional cooking with a twist. Typical dishes include *tagliatelle all'ortica* (pasta with a green nettle sauce) or pigeon with a purée of peas and potato. The ambience is warm and welcoming.

🍴 80 🕐 Closed 3 weeks in Aug. ❄ 🌐 All major cards

🍴 CAFFÈ ITALIANO
$$–$$$
VIA ISOLE DELLE STINCHE 11–13r
TEL 055 289 080
osteriacaffeitaliano.com
This restaurant is split into four areas: a formal restaurant, a wine bar for snacks and lighter meals, a simple trattoria for lunches and less formal dining, and a brand new friendly pizzeria. All serve good-value Tuscan food and have a fine medieval setting, with vast beams, brick vaults, and terra-cotta floors.

🍴 50–120 ❄ 🌐 MC, V

⬆ Elevator ❄ Air-conditioning 🏊 Indoor Pool 🏊 Outdoor Pool 🏋 Health Club 🛜 Wi-Fi 🌐 Credit Cards

🍴 OSTERIA DE' BENCI
$$
VIA DE' BENCI 13r
TEL 055 234 4923
facebook.com/osteriadebenci
A busy dining room painted in tasteful pastel colors that lend it a fresh modern air. Staff is young, energetic, and informal, and the food offers light, well-cooked takes on Tuscan staples such as *zuppa di verdura* (vegetable soup) and *agnello alla scottaditto* (grilled lamb).
🔢 50–80 🕐 Closed L Tue.–Thurs. 💳 All major cards

🍴 PAOLI
$$
VIA DEI TAVOLINI 12r
TEL 055 216 215
casatrattoria.com
A tempting place to eat at the very heart of the city (just off Via dei Calzaiuoli), although the temptation lies not so much in the perfectly good food—Tuscan-style grilled meats, pastas, and soups—as in the beautiful frescoed dining room.
🔢 80 🕐 Closed part of Aug. 💳 💳 All major cards

🍴 IL SANTO BEVITORE
$$
VIA SANTO SPIRITO 64–66r
TEL 055 211 264
ilsantobevitore.com
The Saintly Drinker is just across the Carraia bridge, in the Oltrarno district. The atmosphere is young and welcoming, and the Tuscan food has a creative edge.
🔢 60 🕐 Closed Sun. L 💳 💳 MC, V

🍴 ZÀ-ZÀ
$$
PIAZZA DEL MERCATO CENTRALE 26r
TEL 055 215 411
trattoriazaza.it
This former market-traders' retreat has increased in size and popularity without sacrificing its reasonable prices and reliable Florentine food. Forgo the outside tables on a forgettable square for the cheerful and informal old-style trattoria atmosphere inside.
🔢 90–30 💳 💳 All major cards

🍴 YELLOW BAR
$–$$
VIA DEL PROCONSOLO 39r
TEL 055 211 766
Yellow Bar is conveniently located in eastern Florence, close to the Bargello, and is big, busy, and bustling, with welcoming and friendly staff but brisk service. This is not a place for a lingering meal, but the Tuscan food (plus fine pizzas, *foccace*, and salads) is excellent, if straightforward; it is also good value, which makes it popular with young Florentines. Expect fast-moving lines. Lunch is quieter.
🔢 150+ 🕐 Closed Mon. 💳 💳 All major cards

🍴 CAFFÈ CIBRÈO
$
VIA ANDREA DEL VERROCCHIO 5r
TEL 055 234 5853
cibreo.com
This entrancing café lies some way off the beaten path, to the north of Santa Croce, but is well worth the detour. The interior is beautifully old-fashioned, and cakes, snacks, and light meals come from the **Cibrèo** restaurant, just across the street (see p. 371). Open all day, it is excellent for a break.
💳 💳 Cash only

🍴 CAFFÈ GILLI
$
VIA ROMA 1r
TEL 055 213 896
caffegilli.com
This vast square is distinguished by its four historic cafés, of which Gilli is the best, known for its pastry shop. Founded in 1733, it moved to its present corner site in 1910, the date of its magnificent belle epoque interior. Its large terrace is a fine place for an aperitif.
💳 All major cards

🍴 CANTINETTA DEI VERRAZZANO
$
VIA DEI TAVOLINI 18r
TEL 055 268 590
verrazzano.com
A tempting retreat for take-out snacks, cakes, or slices of pizza, or a more leisurely lunch and glass of wine at the tables to the rear. Choose from the mouthwatering array of food under the huge glass-fronted display. Owned by a notable Chianti vineyard, so the wines are as good as the food.
🕐 Closed D & part of Aug. 💳 All major cards

PRICES

HOTELS
An indication of the cost of a double room in the high season is given by **$** signs.

$$$$$	Over $300
$$$$	$200–$300
$$$	$130–$200
$$	$100–$130
$	Under $100

RESTAURANTS
An indication of the cost of a three-course meal without drinks is given by **$** signs.

$$$$$	Over $80
$$$$	$50–$80
$$$	$35–$50
$$	$20–$35
$	Under $20

🏨 Hotel 🍴 Restaurant 🛏 No. of Guest Rooms 🔢 No. of Seats 🅿 Parking 🚇 Metro ⛴ Boat/ferry 🕐 Hours

¶¶ DEL FAGIOLI

$

CORSO TINTORI 47r
TEL 055 244 285

The same family has run this trattoria close to Santa Croce for more than 40 years, perfecting both traditional Florentine standards such as *ribollita* (vegetable soup) and house specialties like *involtini alla Gigi* (rolled and filled meat).

➕ 50 ⏲ Closed Sat.–Sun. & Aug. 🔅 Cash only

¶¶ LE VOLPI E L'UVA

$

PIAZZA DE' ROSSI 1r
TEL 055 239 8132
levolpieluva.com

A discreet wine bar tucked away off Piazza di Santa Felicita south of Ponte Vecchio. It offers a well-chosen selection of wines and a first-rate selection of cheese and snacks.

🔅 AE, MC, V

▶ **TUSCANY**

AREZZO

¶¶ CASTELLO DI GARGONZA

$$–$$$ ✪✪✪

CASTELLO DI GARGONZA,
MONTE SAN SAVINO
TEL 0575 847 021
gargonza.it

A converted medieval hamlet just west of Monte San Savino. Rooms must be taken for at least three nights; apartments and cottages in the village are available for weekly rental.

ⓘ 45 🅿 ⏲ Closed for a period in Jan.–Feb. 🌊 🛜 Free in some rooms & public areas 🔅 All major cards

¶¶ BUCA DI SAN FRANCESCO

$$–$$$

VIA SAN FRANCESCO 1
TEL 0575 23 271
bucadisanfrancesco.it

Has served simple Tuscan staples such as thick *ribollita* (vegetable soup) and *agnello* (roast lamb) since 1929. The dining room, with its ancient floor and medieval paintings, is well placed for the church of San Francesco.

➕ 60 ⏲ Closed Mon. D, Tues., & July 🔅 All major cards

CHIANTI

¶¶ CASTELLO DI SPALTENNA

$$$–$$$$ ✪✪✪✪

PIEVE DI SPALTENNA,
GAIOLE IN CHIANTI
TEL 0577 749 483
spaltenna.it

The buildings and rooms at this former castle-monastery retain many medieval features. The first-rate restaurant occupies the old refectory.

ⓘ 29 + 8 suites 🅿 ⏲ Closed Jan.–mid-March 🔅 🌊 🛀 🛜 Free 🔅 All major cards

¶¶ RELAIS FATTORIA VIGNALE

$$$–$$$$ ✪✪✪✪

VIA PIANIGIANI 9,
RADDA IN CHIANTI
TEL 0577 738 300
vignale.it

A roadside setting makes this hotel less enticing than some Chianti hotels, but the gardens and rooms in the farmhouse, with simple country furniture and wooden beams, compensate. The **Palazzo San Niccolò** (*hotelsanniccolo.com*) offers a fine and similarly priced four-star in-village alternative.

ⓘ 32 + 5 suites 🅿 ⏲ Closed mid-Nov.–March 🔅 🌊 🛜 Free 🔅 All major cards

¶¶ TENUTA DI RICAVO

$$$–$$$$ ✪✪✪✪

LOCALITÀ RICAVO 4,
CASTELLINA IN CHIANTI
TEL 0577 740 221
ricavo.com

Amid countryside 2 miles (3 km) from Castellina, this medieval hamlet serves as both a base and a place to relax. The **Pecora Nera** restaurant serves refined Tuscan cuisine.

ⓘ 23 🅿 ⏲ Closed Oct.–April, restaurant closed Sun. 🌊 🛜 Free 🔅 All major cards

¶¶ BADIA A COLTIBUONO

$$$

BADIA A COLTIBUONO (3 MILES/
5 KM NE OF GAIOLE)
TEL 0577 74481
coltibuono.com

Situated in a restored monastery founded in 770, this exclusive family-owned Chianti vineyard and estate offers a handful of B&B rooms in a delightful rural location, with a separate restaurant housed in the monastery's former stables.

ⓘ 8 ➕ 65–110 🅿 ⏲ Closed early Jan.–early March, plus restaurant closed Mon. Nov.–April 🔅 🔅 All major cards

CORTONA

¶¶ IL FALCONIERE

$$$–$$$$ ✪✪✪✪

LOCALITÀ SAN MARTINO A
BOCENA 370
TEL 0575 612 679
ilfalconiere.it

A beautifully restored, 17th-century villa outside the town walls, off the SS71 road to Arezzo. Rooms are furnished in period style. The restaurant (with summer terrace) offers fine meat and fish dishes and boasts an excellent wine list.

ⓘ 19 🅿 ⏲ Hotel closed part of Jan.–Feb., restaurant closed Tues. L Nov.–Feb. 🔅 🔅 🌊 🛜 Free 🔅 All major cards

📷 SAN MICHELE
$$–$$$ ♦♦♦♦
VIA GUELFA 15
TEL 0575 604 348
hotelsanmichele.net
Comfortable converted
Renaissance palace at the
town's historic heart. The
room in the old tower is a
gem. The staff can arrange
tours and cooking classes.
🛏 43 🅿 🕐 Closed Nov.–
mid-March 🛗 📺 📶 Free
🚫 All major cards

🍴 AD BRACERIA
$$$
VIA NAZIONALE 10
TEL 0575 638 185
A locals' favorite, in a central
but tucked-away little alley off
one of the town's main streets,
with wonderful stone- and
brick-vaulted dining rooms
that include fragments of a
Roman-era road. Meat dishes
are especially good (many are
grilled on an open fire), but
there are plenty of seafood,
vegetarian, fresh pasta, and
other options.
🪑 50 🕐 Closed Mon.–Thurs. L
📺 🚫 All major cards

🍴 LA LOGGETTA
$$
PIAZZA PESCHERIA 3
TEL 0575 630 575
laloggetta.com
A tasteful restaurant with a
brick-vaulted medieval interior, white walls, and honest
Tuscan cooking. The central
location just off the main
square is also a plus, as is dining alfresco on the terrace in
fine weather.
🪑 70 🕐 Closed Wed. & Nov.
🚫 All major cards

LUCCA

📷 LA BOHÈME
$$
VIA DEL MORO 2
TEL 0583 462 404

boheme.it
The rooms in this B&B are
named after Puccini's operas.
The structure is in a 16th-cen-
tury building in the center. The
La Bohème room can accom-
modate a family of four.
🛏 7 📺 📶 Free
🚫 All major cards

📷 LA LUNA
$$ ♦♦♦
VIA FILLUNGO,
CORTE COMPAGNI 12
TEL 0583 493 634
hotellaluna.it
A family-run hotel in a sleepy
courtyard just off old Lucca's
main street.
🛏 27 🅿 🕐 Closed some of
Jan. 📶 Free 🚫 All major cards

📷 PICCOLO HOTEL PUCCINI
$$ ♦♦♦
VIA DI POGGIO 9
TEL 0583 55 421
hotelpuccini.com
Bright, tasteful rooms in a
Renaissance palace at the heart
of the old city. It is essential
to request private parking in
advance of your stay.
🛏 14 🅿 📶 Free
🚫 All major cards

🍴 BUCA DI SANT'ANTONIO
$$
VIA DELLA CERVIA 3
TEL 0583 55881
bucadisantantonio.com
Established in 1782, its cooking
is based on old Lucchese traditions but does not shy from
innovation. Try the celebrated
Buccellato semifreddo, the house
dessert, a mix of chilled cream
and wild berries.
🪑 90 🕐 Closed Sun. D,
Mon., & some of Jan. & July
📺 🚫 All major cards

MONTALCINO

📷 DEI CAPITANI

$$ ♦♦♦
VIA LAPINI 6
TEL 0577 847 227
deicapitani.it
A comfortable, lovely, modern
hotel in an old town house
with panoramic terrace and
garden, bar area, and swim-
ming pool.
🛏 29 🅿 🏊 📶 Free in
public areas 🚫 All major cards

🍴 TAVERNA DEI BARBI
$$–$$$
FATTORIA DEI BARBI, LA CROCE,
LOCALITÀ PODERNOVI
TEL 0577 847 143
Annexed to a well-known
Brunello vineyard 3 miles
(5 km) southeast of Mon-
talcino, this restaurant serves
superb local dishes. A huge
stone fireplace dominates the
tasteful, rustic dining room.
🪑 70–40 🅿 🕐 Closed Wed.
🚫 All major cards

🍴 GRAPPOLO BLU
$$
VIA SCALE DI MOGLIO 1
TEL 0577 847 150
grappoloblu.it
In a stepped alley off the main
Via Mazzini, the cool stone
walls of the medieval interior
house two small dining rooms.
The high-quality pasta dishes
are all good.
🪑 50 🚫 All major cards

MONTEPULCIANO

📷 DUOMO
$$ ♦♦♦
VIA DI SAN DONATO 14
TEL 0578 757 473
albergoduomo
montepulciano.it
Just a few steps from the
town's cathedral and main
piazza, this is a friendly, family-
run hotel with bright, straight-
forward rooms.
🛏 13 🛗 📶 Free
🚫 All major cards

LA CHIUSA

$$$$$

VIA DELLA MADONNINA 88,
MONTEFOLLONICO
TEL 0577 669 668
ristorantelachiusa.it
For the best food close to
Montepulciano, drive 5 miles
(8 km) northwest to Mon-
tefollonico village. Here, this
former mill has become a
hotel-restaurant. Meals are
expensive but outstanding. A
light creative touch enhances
the mostly Tuscan cuisine. The
restaurant has also added 15
rooms ($$$$) around the mill
and former farm buildings.
⊞ 45 🅿 🕒 Closed Tues.
& mid-Jan.–mid-March
🚫 All major cards

LA GROTTA
$$

LOCALITÀ SAN BIAGIO 16
TEL 0578 757 479
lagrottamontepulciano.it
La Grotta is a good place for
lunch, thanks largely to its
location opposite the noted
church of San Biagio. Without
a car or cab, however, it is a
steep climb back up to town.
⊞ 50–30 🅿 🕒 Closed
Wed. & Jan.–Feb. 🅰
🚫 All major cards

PIENZA

IL CHIOSTRO DI PIENZA
$$$ ❍❍❍

CORSO ROSSELLINO 26
TEL 0578 748 129
anghelhotels.it
This central hotel takes its
name from the *chiostro* (courtyard) of the 15th-century
convent from which it was converted. Simple, elegant rooms.
🛏 37 🅿 🖒 🚱 🛜 Free
🚫 All major cards

DAL FALCO
$–$$

PIAZZA DANTE ALIGHIERI 3
TEL 0578 748 551
ristorantedalfalco.it

Locals and visitors alike frequent this outlying trattoria
with a medieval decor. Try the
local pecorino cheese melted
and wrapped in prosciutto.
⊞ 80 🅿 🕒 Closed Thurs.
🚫 All major cards

PISA

RELAIS DELL'OROLOGIO
$$$$ ❍❍❍❍❍

VIA DELLA FAGGIOLA 12–14
TEL 050 805 6138
hotelrelaisorologio.com
The Relais dell'Orologio, part
of a converted 14th-century
town house and tower, provides an intimate, stylish, and
comfortable place to stay
at the heart of the old city
(within easy walking distance
of the Leaning Tower and
Piazza del Duomo).
🛏 19 + 2 suites 🅿 🖒
🚱 🛜 Free 🚫 All major cards

ROYAL VICTORIA
$$–$$$ ❍❍❍

LUNGARNO PACINOTTI 12
TEL 050 940 111
royalvictoria.it
On the banks of the Arno, ten
minutes' walk from the Leaning
Tower, this hotel's been in the
same family since 1839. Attentive service makes up for the
occasionally rather tired rooms.
🛏 48 🅿 🖒 🛜 Free in public
areas 🚫 All major cards

OSTERIA DEI CAVALIERI
$$

VIA SAN FREDIANO 16
TEL 050 580 858
osteriacavalieri.pisa.it
A welcoming trattoria at the
heart of the old city. The well-
priced Tuscan dishes include
cinghiale (wild boar) and a
sprinkling of more adventurous
meat and fish dishes.
⊞ 60 🕒 Closed Sat. L, Sun., &
a period in Aug. 🅰
🚫 All major cards

SAN GIMIGNANO

LA COLLEGIATA
$$$$$ ❍❍❍❍

LOCALITÀ STRADA 27
TEL 0577 943 201
lacollegiata.it
A dazzlingly stylish hotel with
a good restaurant housed in
a converted 16th-century con-
vent 1 mile (1.5 km) from the
town wall. Fine views of San
Gimignano and its towers.
🛏 20 🅿 🕒 Closed Jan.–
mid-March 🖒 🚱 🛜 Free
🚫 All major cards

LA CISTERNA
$$ ❍❍❍

PIAZZA DELLA CISTERNA 24
TEL 0577 940 328
hotelcisterna.it
The village's oldest established
hotel is perched on the main
piazza. Rooms with a view
command higher prices.
🛏 49 🅿 🕒 Closed Jan.–
mid-March, restaurant closed
Wed. L & Tues. 🖒 🛜 Free
🚫 All major cards

LEON BIANCO
$$ ❍❍❍

PIAZZA DELLA CISTERNA 13
TEL 0577 941 294
leonbianco.com
This hotel shares La Cisterna's
perfect position, but is smaller
and more intimate.
🛏 26 🕒 Closed parts of mid-
Nov.–early Feb. 🅿 🖒 🅰
🛜 Free 🚫 All major cards

DORANDÒ
$$$–$$$$

VICOLO DELL'ORO 2
TEL 0577 941 862
ristorantedorando.it
A small, welcoming, intimate
restaurant in a medieval
setting but with a modern
ambience. It re-creates ancient
recipes from Etruscan, Medici,
and early medieval periods.
⊞ 50 🕒 Closed mid-Jan.–
mid-March & Mon.

🛗 Elevator 🅰 Air-conditioning 🚱 Indoor Pool 🏊 Outdoor Pool 🏋 Health Club 🛜 Wi-Fi 🚫 Credit Cards

except Easter–Oct. 🔆
🃏 All major cards

SIENA

🏨 GRAND HOTEL CONTINENTAL
$$$$ ⓞⓞⓞⓞⓞ
VIA BANCHI DI SOPRA 85
TEL 0577 56 011
starhotelscollezione.com
Rooms in this historic palace are stylish, and public spaces are a mix of frescoed and beautifully appointed salons.
ⓘ 46 + 5 suites 🅿️ 🔄 🔆
📶 Free 🃏 All major cards

🏨 PALAZZETTO ROSSO
$$$–$$$$ ⓞⓞⓞ
VIA DEI ROSSI 38–42
TEL 0577 236 197
OR 347 956 8096
palazzettorosso.com
This building's red bricks gave the hotel its name. Located in the historical center, it was probably an inn in the medieval period, too. Today, its ancient walls are home to charming rooms with modern lines. Breakfast features local products, both sweet and savory. Wine bar for a good glass at the end of the day.
ⓘ 9 🔄 📶 Free in public areas
🃏 All major cards

🏨 ANTICA TORRE
$$–$$$ ⓞⓞⓞ
VIA FIERAVECCHIA 7
TEL 0577 222 255
anticatorresiena.it
Siena's most appealing small hotel has just eight modest rooms with small bathrooms squeezed into an old medieval tower (torre) a few minutes' walk from the historic center.
ⓘ 8 📶 Free 🃏 All major cards

🏨 PALAZZO RAVIZZA
$$–$$$ ⓞⓞⓞ
VIA PIAN DEI MANTELLINI 34
TEL 0577 280 462
palazzoravizza.it

A charming mid-range hotel that occupies an 18th-century palace on the fringes of the old center.
ⓘ 30 + 4 suites 🅿️ 🔄 🔆
📶 Free 🃏 All major cards

🍴 ANTICA OSTERIA DA DIVO
$$$
VIA FRANCIOSA 25–29
TEL 0577 286 054
osteriadadivo.it
The remarkable subterranean dining rooms at Da Divo include ancient Etruscan-era caves carved from the volcanic tuff that underpins the nearby Duomo. The first-rate Tuscan food—beef, wild boar, soups, game, chestnuts, mushrooms—lives up to its surroundings, with an often creative menu..
🪑 65 🕐 Closed Tues. & Feb.
🔆 🃏 All major cards

🍴 LE LOGGE
$$–$$$
VIA DEL PORRIONE 33
TEL 0577 48 013
osterialelogge.it
No Sienese restaurant is prettier than this former medieval pharmacy just off the Campo. Innovative but occasionally hit-and-miss Sienese cuisine. Avoid the bland upstairs dining room.
🪑 40–80 🕐 Closed Sun. & periods in Jan. & June 🔆
🃏 AE, DC

🍴 IL CARROCCIO
$$
VIA DEL CASATO DI SOTTO 32
TEL 0577 41165
A tiny and discreet one-room trattoria barely two minutes from the Campo. Simple Sienese dishes (excellent antipasti), plus pleasant, easy-going service.
🪑 35–20 🕐 Closed Wed. & periods in Nov. & Feb.
🃏 Cash only

PRICES

HOTELS
An indication of the cost of a double room in the high season is given by $ signs.

$$$$$	Over $300
$$$$	$200–$300
$$$	$130–$200
$$	$100–$130
$	Under $100

RESTAURANTS
An indication of the cost of a three-course meal without drinks is given by $ signs.

$$$$$	Over $80
$$$$	$50–$80
$$$	$35–$50
$$	$20–$35
$	Under $20

VOLTERRA

🏨 SAN LINO
$$ ⓞⓞⓞⓞ
VIA SAN LINO 26
TEL 0588 85 250
hotelsanlino.net
This converted convent is probably Volterra's best central option.
ⓘ 44 🅿️ 🕐 Closed periods Nov.–Jan. 🔄 🔆 🏊 📶 Free
🃏 All major cards

🍴 SACCO FIORENTINO
$–$$
VIA GIUSTO TURAZZA 13
TEL 0588 88 537
This central eatery offers such genuine traditional dishes as homemade fettuccine, as well as salsicce e fagioli (Tuscan sausages and beans) and tagliata di Chianina (sliced beef fillet).
🪑 40 🕐 Closed Wed., 10 days in June, & periods in Dec.–Feb.
🔆 🃏 All major cards

🏨 Hotel 🍴 Restaurant ⓘ No. of Guest Rooms 🪑 No. of Seats 🅿️ Parking 🚇 Metro ⛴ Boat/ferry 🕐 Hours

▶ UMBRIA

ASSISI

🏨 FONTEBELLA
🍽 $$$ ○○○○
VIA FONTEBELLA 25
TEL 075 812 883
fontebella.com
An intimate hotel with attractive, antiques-furnished rooms (all different) and good views from upper floors. Its **Frantoio** restaurant is also excellent.
ⓘ 43 🅿 ⊟ ⧉ 🔊 Free
⧉ All major cards

🍽 MEDIOEVO
$$$
VIA ARCO DEI PRIORI 4B
TEL 075 813 068
A beautiful medieval vaulted dining hall is the setting for refined and exquisite food that mixes Italian and pan-European culinary styles.
⊞ 80–120 🕒 Closed Mon., some of Jan., & a week in July
⧉ ⧉ All major cards

GUBBIO

🏨 BOSONE PALACE
$$–$$$ ○○○○
VIA XX SETTEMBRE 22
TEL 075 922 0688
hotelbosone.com
A converted medieval palace in a central location combining modern facilities with period touches such as decorative antiques and frescoed ceilings.
ⓘ 30 ⊟ 🔊 Free
⧉ All major cards

🍽 TAVERNA DEL LUPO
$$–$$$
VIA DELLA REPUBBLICA 47
TEL 075 927 3291
tavernadellupo.it
Pretty medieval dining rooms and well-presented Umbrian specialties, including truffle, game, and mushroom dishes.
⊞ 150 🕒 Closed Mon. except Aug.–Sept. ⧉ ⧉ All major cards

MONTEFALCO

🏨 VILLA PAMBUFFETTI
🍽 $$$ ○○○○
VIA DELLA VITTORIA 20
TEL 0742 379 417
villapambuffetti.it
A tastefully converted villa in gardens on the edge of the village. Excellent restaurant. Try the **Palazzo Bontadosi Hotel & Spa** *(hotelbontadosi .it)* if you prefer to be right in the village.
ⓘ 15 🅿 ⊕ Hotel closed Jan., restaurant closed L & Jan.– March ⊟ ⧉ ⧉ 🔊 Free
⧉ All major cards

🍽 COCCORONE
$$–$$$
LARGO TEMPESTIVI,
OFF VIA TEMPESTIVI
TEL 0742 379 535
coccorone.com
An attractive medieval dining room whose open fire is used to cook meats and other Umbrian specialties. The *crespelle* (stuffed pancakes) and tiramisu are notable.
⊞ 40 🕒 Closed Wed. Nov.– March ⧉ All major cards

NORCIA

🏨 PALAZZO SENECA
🍽 $$$$ ○○○○
VIA CESARE BATTISTI 10–12
TEL 0743 817 434
palazzoseneca.com
The Palazzo Seneca at the heart of Norcia is one of the finest new hotels in central Italy. State-of-the-art facilities combine with contemporary decorative touches without compromising the palazzo's historical character. The **Vespasia** restaurant is excellent.
ⓘ 23 + 1 suite ⊞ 25 🅿 ⊟ ⧉ 🔊 Free ⧉ All major cards

🍽 GRANARO DEL MONTE
$$–$$$

VIA ALFIERI 7–12
TEL 0743 816 513
bianconi.com
A large, bustling restaurant in a fine medieval setting attached to the central and good-value **Hotel Grotta Azzurra.** Umbrian country cooking, with regional and truffle-based specialties.
⊞ 50–150 🕒 Closed Tues.
⧉ ⧉ All major cards

ORVIETO

🏨 LA BADIA
$$$ ○○○○
LOCALITÀ LA BADIA 8
TEL 0763 301 959
labadiahotel.it
In a beautiful pastoral setting, 2 miles (3 km) from Orvieto, this glorious hotel was converted from a 12th-century Romanesque *badia* (abbey).
ⓘ 22 + 5 suites 🅿
🕒 Closed Jan.–Feb. ⧉ ⧉
🔊 Free ⧉ All major cards

🏨 VALENTINO
$$ ○○○
VIA ANGELO DA ORVIETO 30–32
TEL 0763 342 464
valentinohotel.com
Some of the rooms of the hotel have a view of the Duomo, located just a few minutes away on foot. The structure, which dates to the 16th century, has been well renovated and furnished. Convenient services such as free Wi-Fi, paid parking on request, and a bar are available.
ⓘ 19 ⊟ 🔊 Free
⧉ All major cards

🍽 AL POZZO ETRUSCO DA GIOVANNI
$$
PIAZZA DE' RANIERI 1
TEL 0763 341 050
alpozzoetruscodagiovanni.it
A typical restaurant with a

special attraction: a well from the sixth century B.C. that clients can admire. The cuisine is Umbria inspired with home-made pasta and wild game.

🔲 50 🕒 Closed Tues. & 2 weeks in July 🖪 MC, V

🍴 ETRUSCA
$$
VIA MAITANI 10
TEL 0763 344 016
A trattoria set in a 16th-century building, with courteous service, pleasantly relaxed atmosphere, and traditional Umbrian dishes.

🔲 90 🕒 May close periods in Nov. or Jan.–Feb. 🖪
🖪 All major cards

PERUGIA

🏨 LOCANDA DELLA POSTA
$$$ ✪✪✪✪
CORSO VANNUCCI 97
TEL 075 572 8925
locandadellapostahotel.it
There has been a hotel on this central street since the 18th century. Good, modern rooms.

🛈 40 🅿 🖪 🖪 🛜 Free
🖪 All major cards

🍴 ANTICA TRATTORIA SAN LORENZO
$$$
PIAZZA DANTI 19/A
TEL 075 572 1956
anticatrattoriasanlorenzo.com
A perfect central position, just behind the Duomo, good service, and a pretty setting under old vaulted ceilings make this a convenient place to sample refined Umbrian cooking.

🔲 30 🖪 🖪 All major cards

🍴 OSTERIA A PRIORI
$$$
VIA DEI PRIORI 39
TEL 075 572 7098

osteriaapriori.it
This charming spot a few minutes' walk west of the main Corso is serious about its food and wine. It has a small restaurant space upstairs and a *bottega* (store) and wine bar downstairs where you can eat light meals or buy wines, oils, and other regional produce. For fuller meals in a more traditional setting make for **La Taverna** (*Via delle Streghe 8, tel 075 572 4128, $$$*), five minutes' walk south.

🔲 28 🕒 Closed Sun.
🖪 🖪 All major cards

SPELLO

🏨 PALAZZO BOCCI
🍴 $$$ ✪✪✪✪
VIA CAVOUR 17
TEL 0742 301 021
palazzobocci.com
A converted 17th-century palazzo on the main street, with frescoed public areas and large modern rooms full of charm. Breakfast can be served in the garden. The co-owned **Il Molino** restaurant opposite is one of the best in town.

🛈 21 + 2 suites 🖪 🖪 🛜 Free
🖪 All major cards

🍴 CACCIATORE
🏨 $$ ✪✪
VIA GIULIA 24
TEL 0742 301 140
hoteldelteatro.it
Food here is not the best you can find in town, but the outdoor terrace, especially on summer evenings, is one of the most poetic places to dine in Umbria. There are 17 rooms available in the three-star hotel, and 12 more in the newer and co-owned three-star **Teatro** a few doors away.

🔲 100–150 🅿 🕒 Closed Mon. & 3 weeks in July
🛜 Free 🖪 All major cards

SPOLETO

🏨 GATTAPONE
$$–$$$ ✪✪✪✪
VIA DEL PONTE 6
TEL 0743 223 447
hotelgattapone.it
A marvelous hotel overlooking a wooded gorge and the medieval aqueduct. Intimate and discreet with individually decorated rooms, a garden, and a bar. More central is the **Palazzo Leti** with lovely period rooms (*$$$$*).

🛈 15 🅿 🖪 🖪 🛜 Free
🖪 All major cards

🍴 APOLLINARE
$$
VIA SANT'AGATA 14
TEL 0743 223 256
ristoranteapollinare.it
Innovative and carefully pre-pared food—the truffle-filled *caramella soffiata* appetizer is sensational—served in cozy medieval dining rooms.

🔲 55–45 🅿 🕒 Closed Tues.
🖪 All major cards

TODI

🏨 FONTE CESIA
$$$ ✪✪✪✪
VIA LORENZO LEONI 3
TEL 075 894 3737
fontecesia.it
A consummately restored 17th-century palace at the heart of town, with rooms in different period styles.

🛈 35 🅿 🖪 🖪 🛜 Free
🖪 All major cards

🍴 CAVOUR
$
CORSO CAVOUR 21–23
TEL 075 894 3730
ristorantecavour-todi.com
A simple trattoria-pizzeria, in a 15th-century building, patronized by locals and visitors alike.

🔲 180 🕒 Closed Thurs
🖪 All major cards

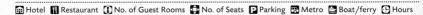

▶ THE SOUTH

AMALFI COAST

🏨 CARUSO
$$$$$ ○○○○○
PIAZZA GIOVANNI DEL TORO 2,
RAVELLO
TEL 089 858 801
belmond.com
The Caruso is a historic lodging with one of the village's best positions that has been given a new lease on life by a far-reaching restoration.
ℹ️ 42 + 6 suites 🅿️ 🕐 Closed early Nov.–late March or early April 🔌 🅰️ 🏊 🎾 📶 Free
🅰️ All major cards

🏨 IL SAN PIETRO
$$$$$ ○○○○○
VIA LAURITO 2, POSITANO
TEL 089 812 080
ilsanpietro.it
Positano has a surfeit of five-star hotels, with little to choose between them. San Pietro, about 1 mile (1.5 km) from the village, is probably the best, thanks to its pool, views, beach, tennis courts, and tastefully understated rooms.
ℹ️ 55 + 7 suites 🕐 Closed Nov.–March 🅿️ 🔌 🅰️ 🎾 📶 Free 🅰️ All major cards

🏨 SANTA CATERINA
$$$$$ ○○○○○
VIA NAZIONALE 9, LOCALITÀ
PASTENA, AMALFI
TEL 089 871 012
hotelsantacaterina.it
This luxurious hillside mansion on the coast road just outside the town of Amalfi provides a good base for exploring but is dated in places.
ℹ️ 62 + 9 suites 🅿️ 🔌 🅰️ 🏊 📶 Free 🅰️ All major cards

🏨 POSEIDON
🍽️ **$$$$ ○○○○**
VIA PASITEA 148, POSITANO
TEL 089 811 111
hotelposeidonpositano.it
A romantic hotel with a superb panoramic location overlooking the sea and village. Elegant rooms and a pretty terrace garden with bar and restaurant.
ℹ️ 48 + 4 suites 🅿️ 🔌 🅰️ 🏊 🎾 📶 Free
🅰️ All major cards

🏨 VILLA CIMBRONE
$$$$ ○○○○○
VIA SANTA CHIARA 26, RAVELLO
TEL 089 857 459
villacimbrone.com
Greta Garbo vacationed at this lovely villa set among gardens before it was converted into a hotel. Although a beautiful place to stay, it is a steep walk from the rest of the village.
ℹ️ 19 + 2 suites 🕐 Closed mid-Nov.–March 📶 Free
🅰️ All major cards

🏨 AMALFI
$$$–$$$$ ○○○
VIA DEI PASTAI 3
TEL 089 872 440
hamalfi.it
A perfect location near the Duomo if you want a simple, comfortable, and inexpensive base in town. Friendly service, panoramic terrace, and a pretty garden with orange trees.
ℹ️ 40 🅿️ 🔌 📶 Free
🅰️ All major cards

🍽️ LA CARAVELLA
$$$–$$$$
VIA MATTEO CAMERA 12,
AMALFI
TEL 089 871 029
ristorantelacaravella.it
Much thought here goes into re-creating traditional, and sometimes unusual, fish and seafood dishes such as *fettucine nere con sugo nero* (black pasta noodles with squid's ink black sauce).
🍴 40–50 🅿️ 🕐 Closed parts of Nov.–mid-Feb., & Tues. except Aug. 🔌
🅰️ All major cards

🍽️ DA COSTANTINO
$$$
VIA CORVO 95, POSITANO
TEL 089 875 738
dacostantino.net
Costantino opened this traditional restaurant and pizzeria in 1978 but has passed the reins to his family. The dining rooms are high above Positano, which means glorious views over the village to the sea and beyond. The food is varied, reliable, and fairly priced.
🍴 70 🕐 Closed mid-Nov.–Easter 🅰️ All major cards

🍽️ DA GEMMA
$$$
VIA FRÀ GERARDO SASSO 9,
AMALFI
TEL 089 871 345
trattoriadagemma.com
Reserve a table on the terrace of this family-run restaurant that is considered the Amalfi Coast's best trattoria. Try the *ziti alla genovese*, with a sauce of meat and onions.
🍴 45 🕐 Closed early Jan.–early March 🅰️ All major cards

🍽️ CUMPÀ COSIMO
$$
VIA ROMA 48, RAVELLO
TEL 089 857 156
A simple pizzeria-restaurant in the middle of the village that has been run by the Bottone family for more than 70 years.
🍴 100 🅰️ All major cards

CAPRI

🏨 GRAND HOTEL
🍽️ QUISISANA
$$$$–$$$$$ ○○○○○
VIA CAMERELLE 2
TEL 081 090 1333
quisisana.com
The grandest hotel on Capri, and much patronized by U.S. visitors. The two main restaurants are among the island's best, but, like the hotel, are very expensive.

🔌 Elevator 🅰️ Air-conditioning 🏊 Indoor Pool 🏊 Outdoor Pool 🎾 Health Club 📶 Wi-Fi 🅰️ Credit Cards

🛈 148 + 13 suites 🅿
🕐 Closed Nov., restaurant closed D Sun. (except mid-June–mid-Sept.) & L 🚢
🔳 🔳 🔳 🔳 🔳 🔳 Free
🔳 All major cards

🏨 VILLA SARAH
$$–$$$ ✪✪✪
VIA TIBERIO 3/A
TEL 081 837 7817
villasarahcapri.com
A welcoming family-run hotel with garden, about ten minutes' walk from the center of Capri Town. Reserve well in advance.
🛈 19 🕐 Closed Nov.–Easter
🔳 Free 🔳 All major cards

🍴 LA CAPANNINA
$$$$–$$$$$
VIA LE BOTTEGHE 12-14
TEL 081 837 0732
capanninacapri.it
A glamorous but unstuffy restaurant just off the main piazzetta that was founded in 1931. Predominantly modern fish-based creations, with some meat dishes. La Capannina Più, a few steps away, sells a superb selection of wines, many available in the wine bar adjoining the restaurant.
🔳 100–120 🕐 Closed Nov.–mid-March 🔳
🔳 All major cards

IL GARGANO

🏨 PIZZOMUNNO VIESTE PALACE
$$$$$ ✪✪✪✪✪
LUNGOMARE ENRICO MATTEI KM 1, VIESTE
TEL 0884 708 741
hotelpizzomunno.it
More a luxurious hotel-village than a hotel, this is the Gargano's premier establishment. It boasts many sports facilities and a private beach.
🛈 183 🕐 Closed Nov.–March
🅿 🔳 🔳 🔳 Free
🔳 All major cards

🏨 SEGGIO
$$ ✪✪✪
VIA VESTA 7, VIESTE
TEL 0884 708 123
hotelseggio.it
A small hotel with a private beach housed in a 17th-century palazzo.
🛈 30 🅿 🕐 Closed Nov.– March 🔳 🔳 🔳
🔳 All major cards

ISCHIA

🏨 REGINA ISABELLA
$$$$–$$$$$ ✪✪✪✪✪
PIAZZA SANTA RESTITUTA 1, LACCO AMENO
TEL 081 994 322
reginaisabella.com
Ischia's top luxury hotel is situated in the northwest of the island and has every comfort.
🛈 125 + 3 suites 🅿
🕐 Closed Nov.–Easter
🔳 🔳 🔳 🔳 🔳 🔳 Free
🔳 All major cards

🍴 GARDENIA MARE
$$$–$$$$
VIA NUOVACARTAROMANA 66, SCOGLI SANT'ANNA
TEL 081 991 107
gardeniamare.it
Take a water taxi from Ischia town to Gardenia Mare's seafront setting just south of the castle headland; the restaurant is part of a larger complex that can be busy by day, so this is not necessarily an intimate experience, but the refined fish, seafood, and other dishes are good. For dining in town, visit Da Ciccio (Via Luigi Mazzella 32, tel 081 991 686, $$$).
🕐 May close for dinner
🔳 All major cards

LECCE

🏨 PATRIA PALACE
$$$$$ ✪✪✪✪✪
PIAZZETTA GABRIELE RICCARDI 13
TEL 0832 245 111
patriapalace.com
A beautifully restored 18th-century palazzo at the heart of the historic city center, facing the church of Santa Croce.
🛈 67 🅿 🔳 🔳 🔳 Free
🔳 All major cards

🍴 OSTERIA DEGLI SPIRITI
$$$
VIA CESARE BATTISTI 4
TEL 0832 246 274
osteriadeglispiriti.it
An attractive vaulted dining room in the former stables of a centrally located noble palazzo near the Villa Comunale. Excellent local food and good wines from the Salento peninsula to the south.
🔳 55 🕐 Closed Sun., L except Mon., & 2 weeks in Sept.
🔳 🔳 All major cards

MATERA

🏨 SANT'ANGELO
$$ ✪✪✪✪
VIA MADONNA DEL VIRTÙ 63
TEL 0835 314 010
hotelsantangelosassi.it
The Sant'Angelo offers a unique hotel experience, for the rooms are caves—restored sassi excavated from the soft tufa stone of the town's ravine.
🛈 16 🅿 🔳 🔳 🔳 Free
🔳 All major cards

NAPLES

🏨 GRAND HOTEL
🍴 VESUVIO
$$$$ ✪✪✪✪
VIA PARTENOPE 45
TEL 081 764 0044
vesuvio.it
Built in 1882, this fine hotel has welcomed the likes of Humphrey Bogart and Errol Flynn over the years. The rooftop Caruso restaurant is named after the opera star, another famous guest.
🛈 161 🅿 🔳 🔳 🔳 🔳
🔳 Free 🔳 All major cards

GRAND HOTEL PARKER'S

$$$–$$$$ ✪✪✪✪

CORSO VITTORIO EMANUELE 135

TEL 081 761 2474

grandhotelparkers.it

Its location west of the center affords wonderful views of the Bay of Naples. Established in 1870, the hotel's atmosphere and style are elegant, and the panoramic **George** restaurant, with views of the Bay of Naples, rates highly.

🛏 82 🅿 ⬆ ❄ 📶 📶 Free ⬛ All major cards

IL CONVENTO

$$$ ✪✪✪

VIA SPERANZELLA 137/A

TEL 081 403 977

hotelilconvento.it

This family-run hotel is (just) in the Quartieri Spagnoli, one of Naples's most distinctive neighborhoods. Wooden beams, creamy pastel-colored walls, and stone floors recall the 17th-century convent from which the hotel was converted. Rooms and bathrooms are contemporary, and the junior suites on the top floor (with private roof gardens) and two family rooms are appealing.

🛏 14 🅿 ⬆ ❄ 📶 Free ⬛ All major cards

LA BERSAGLIERA

$$$–$$$$

VIA SANTA LUCIA 10–11, BORGO MARINARI

TEL 081 764 6016

labersagliera.it

Most visitors of note who have visited Naples since 1919 have eaten at this waterfront restaurant. Prices are perhaps higher than the food merits, and it can be busy with vacationers, but the busy atmosphere and sense of history make this a fun place to visit at least once.

🍴 200 🅿 ⏲ Closed Tues. (except May) & some of Jan. & Aug. ❄ ⬛ All major cards

BIANCOMANGIARE

$$–$$$

VICO SAN NICOLA ALLA CARITÀ 13–14

TEL 081 552 0226

Proximity to Pignasecca market ensures the freshest produce at this two-room traditional restaurant on the northern fringes of the Quartieri Spagnoli, serving classic Neapolitan food.

🍴 50 ⏲ Closed 1 week in Aug. ❄ ⬛ All major cards

HOSTERIA TOLEDO

$$–$$$

VICO GIARDINETTO 78

TEL 081 421 257

hosteriatoledo.it

This restaurant in a Quartieri Spagnoli tenement from the 17th century has served simple but perfect Neapolitan fare such as *pasta alle cozze e vongole* (pasta with clams and mussels) since 1951. Ask for a table on the more amenable upper floor.

🍴 70 ⏲ Closed Tues. ❄ ⬛ All major cards

BRANDI

$–$$

SALITA SANT'ANNA DI PALAZZO 1–2, OFF VIA CHIAIA

TEL 081 416 928

brandi.it

Naples's most famous pizzeria and birthplace of the Margherita (tomato, basil, and mozzarella cheese). It is often full of vacationers, but the atmosphere, pizzas, and pasta dishes are good.

🍴 100 ❄ ⬛ All major cards

GRAN CAFFÈ GAMBRINUS

$

VIA CHIAIA 1–PIAZZA TRENTO E TRIESTE

TEL 081 417 582

grancaffegambrinus.com

Dating from 1860, this is the city's most famous, expensive, and opulent café. Wonderful coffees and widely celebrated cakes and pastries.

🍴 170 ❄ ⬛ All major cards

PAESTUM

ESPLANADE

$$ ✪✪✪

VIA POSEIDONIA 291

TEL 0828 851 005

hotelesplanadepaestum.com

This hotel on the edge of pine woods close to the sea with its own pool and private beach makes a comfortable overnight stop.

🛏 28 🅿 ⬆ ❄ 🏊 📶 Free ⬛ All major cards

PARCO NAZIONALE D'ABRUZZO

VILLA MON REPOS

$$$$ ✪✪✪✪✪

VIA SANTA LUCIA 2, PESCASSEROLI

TEL 0863 912 858

villamonrepos.it

A century-old villa in a peaceful park setting.

🛏 11 + 2 suites 🅿 📶 Free ⬛ All major cards

PAGNANI

$$ ✪✪✪

VIA COLLACCHI 4, PESCASSEROLI

TEL 0863 912 866

hotelpagnani.it

This modern mountain hotel just outside the village offers bright, spacious rooms, many with flower-filled balconies.

🛏 36 🅿 ⬆ 🏊 📶 Free in public areas ⬛ V

POMPEII

FORUM

$$ ✪✪✪

VIA ROMA 99–101

TEL 081 850 1170

hotelforum.it

Most people visit Pompeii on a day trip, but if you do stay, this is the best of the hotels.

🛏 35 ⬆ 📶 Free ⬛ All major cards

⬆ Elevator ❄ Air-conditioning 🏊 Indoor Pool 🏖 Outdoor Pool 💪 Health Club 📶 Wi-Fi ⬛ Credit Cards

PUGLIA

🏨 PALACE HOTEL BARI
🍴 $$$ ✪✪✪✪
VIA LOMBARDI 13, BARI
TEL 080 521 6551
palacehotelbari.com
Bari's best Old World hotel is within walking distance of the old quarter. The Murat hotel restaurant is also first-class.
ℹ️ 190 + 6 suites 🅿️
🕐 Restaurant closed Sun. & Aug. 🔁 🅂 🛜 Free
🕷️ All major cards

🍴 LA BUL
$$$–$$$$
VIA VILLARI 52, BARI
TEL 080 523 0576
ristorantelabul.it
A suggestive atmosphere with candid stone walls and vintage furnishings. With important professional experiences to his credit, the chef proposes an innovative menu that uses local products. The wine list has been well researched.
🔢 40 + 30 🕐 Closed L & Mon., open Sun. L. 🅂 🕷️ D, MC, V

TRULLI COUNTRY

SOMETHING SPECIAL

🏨 MASSERIA SAN DOMENICO
$$$$$ ✪✪✪✪✪
STRADA PROVINCIALE 90
SAVELLETRI DI FASANO
TEL 080 482 7769
masseriasandomenico.com
The 15th-century Masseria San Domenico is one of the best of Puglia's *masserie*, or traditional fortified farm and manor houses converted to luxury hotels—a glorious collection of historic white-washed buildings half a mile or so from the sea set amid olive groves. The large spa is exceptional. So, too, is the large pool, the focal point of the expansive and well-kept gardens. There is also access to an 18-hole golf course.

ℹ️ 44 + 6 suites 🅿️ 🔁 🅂 🈂️ 🏊 (sea water) 🚭 🛜 Free
🕷️ All major cards

🍴 IL POETA CONTADINO
$$$–$$$$
VIA INDIPENDENZA 21, ALBEROBELLO
TEL 080 432 1917
ilpoetacontadino.it
An elegant central restaurant with one of Italy's best wine cellars and delightful local cooking, including a seasonal appetizer of warm salad with scallops and wild porcini.
🔢 70 🅿️ 🕐 Closed Thurs. & part of Jan. 🅂
🕷️ All major cards

🍴 TRULLO D'ORO
$$–$$$
VIA FELICE CAVALLOTTI 27, ALBEROBELLO
TEL 080 432 1820
trullodoro.it
The setting, in five *trulli* with wooden beams and white-washed walls, makes for a memorable meal of local fare.
🔢 100–150 🕐 Closed Sun. D, Mon. (except Aug.), & part of Jan. 🅂 🕷️ All major cards

▶ SICILY & SARDINIA

SICILY

AEOLIAN ISLANDS

🏨 GATTOPARDO PARK HOTEL
$$$–$$$$ ✪✪✪
VIALE DIANA 1, LIPARI
TEL 090 981 1035
gattopardoparkhotel.com
Choose from comfortable, rustic rooms in a 19th-century villa or quiet bungalows in the surrounding gardens. Breakfast and lunch must be reserved with accommodations.
ℹ️ 47 🅿️ 🅂 🛜 Free
🕷️ All major cards

🏨 HOTEL RESIDENCE ACQUACALDA
$$$ ✪✪✪
VIA LUNGOMARE DI ACQUACALDA
TEL 090 988 0201
residenceacquacalda.it
This charming seafront hotel is in a quiet village around 15 minutes' drive from Lipari Town and the ferry terminal (free transfers can be arranged through the hotel). Most of the bright, clean rooms have terraces and fine sea views (ground-floor rooms look on to a garden, with the sea beyond), and the apartment suites have kitchens or kitchenettes. Scooter and car rental is available, and the hotel is linked to the well-priced Al Tramonto *(Via Mazzini, tel 090 982 1094)* restaurant nearby, which has a fine panoramic terrace; half-board is possible by dining here; otherwise the hotel offers breakfast only.
ℹ️ 20 🅿️ 🅂 🛜 Free in common areas 🕷️ All major cards

🍴 FILIPPINO
$$$–$$$$
PIAZZA MUNICIPIO 8–16, LIPARI
TEL 090 981 1002
filippino.it
A welcoming restaurant founded in 1910 with lovely views from its terrace and first-rate fish and seafood.
🔢 200 🅿️ 🕐 Closed mid-Nov.–Dec. 🅂 🕷️ All major cards

🍴 BARBABLÙ
🏨 $$$
VIA VITTORIO EMANUELE 17–19, STROMBOLI
TEL 090 986 118
barbablu.it
This celebrated and romantic fish restaurant, in a former fisherman's house, has added five small but charming rooms, with colorful, elegant decor and period furnishings.
🔢 25 ℹ️ 5 🅂
🕷️ All major cards

🏨 Hotel 🍴 Restaurant ℹ️ No. of Guest Rooms 🔢 No. of Seats 🅿️ Parking 🚇 Metro 🚢 Boat/ferry 🕐 Hours

🍴 E' PULERA
$$$
VIA ISABELLA CONTI ELLER VAINICHER, LIPARI
TEL 090 981 1158
Less renowned than the Filippino (see above), but the predominantly fish-based cooking is almost as good and less expensive. A pretty garden setting among citrus trees.
🛏 100 🕐 Closed L mid-Oct.–mid-April 🔲 All major cards

AGRIGENTO

🏨 VILLA ATHENA
$$$$ ✪✪✪✪✪
VIA PASSEGGIATA ARCHEOLOGICA 33
TEL 0922 596 288
hotelvillaathena.it
Reserve early for this peaceful 18th-century villa at the heart of the archaeological zone. A pool and pretty rooms complement the superb location.
ⓘ 40 🅿 🔲 ⊠ 🔵 Free 🔲 All major cards

🏨 COLLEVERDE PARK HOTEL
$$$–$$$$ ✪✪✪✪
VALLE DEI TEMPLI
TEL 0922 29 555
colleverdehotel.it
A modern hotel ringed by gardens, north of the temples and archaeological zone.
ⓘ 52 🅿 🔵 🔲 🔵 Free 🔲 All major cards

CEFALÙ

🏨 KALURA
$$$ ✪✪✪
VIA VINCENZO CAVALLARO 13
TEL 0921 421 354
hotel-kalura.com
About 1 mile (1.5 km) east of town, so you may need a car or cab, but worth the inconvenience for its lovely seaside setting, beach, simple rooms, and sports facilities.
ⓘ 65 🅿 🔵 🔲 ⊠

🔵 In business center
🔲 All major cards

🍴 LA BRACE
$$
VIA XXV NOVEMBRE 10
TEL 0921 423 570
ristorantelabrace.com
Run by a Dutch-Indonesian couple, this restaurant offers regional food to rival that of native chefs. Try the *spaghetti all'aglio e peperoncino* (pasta with garlic and chili) and the cannoli for dessert. Both are classic Sicilian dishes.
🛏 50 🕐 Closed L, Mon., & period mid-Dec.–mid-Jan.
🔵 🔲 All major cards

PALERMO

🏨 CENTRALE PALACE HOTEL
$$$$$ ✪✪✪✪
CORSO VITTORIO EMANUELE II 327
TEL 091 8539
eurostarshotels.it
Palermo's best city center hotel occupies a 19th-century building two blocks west of the Quattro Canti. The rooms are well furnished, the service is excellent, and there is a roof garden with restaurant.
ⓘ 102 + 2 suites 🅿 🔵 🔵
🔵 Free 🔲 All major cards

🍴 GAGINI
$$$–$$$$
VIA CASSARI 35
TEL 091 589 918
gaginirestaurant.com
Modern tables and chairs contrast with aged stone walls in this central restaurant close to the Vucciria market district. This is a quite young venture, and the food here is creative, ambitious (small servings, refined presentation), and more expensive than most in Palermo, but it makes a good place for a treat and a change

from the more robust cooking in much of the city.
🛏 50 🔵 🔲 MC, V

🍴 DAL MAESTRO DEL BRODO
$$$
VIA PANNIERI 7
TEL 091 329 523
Market-fresh ingredients from the Vucciria go into traditional dishes such as *pasta con le sarde* (pasta with sardines) and *pesce spada e menta* (swordfish with mint) at this welcoming, family-run trattoria.
🛏 60 🕐 Closed Mon. year-round, D Sun.–Thurs. Sept.–mid-June, 2 weeks in Aug., Sun. in summer, & Tues. in winter
🔵 🔲 AE, MC, V

SYRACUSE

🏨 GRAND HOTEL ORTIGIA
$$$–$$$$ ✪✪✪✪✪
VIALE MAZZINI 12
TEL 0931 464 600
grandhotelortigia.it
This comfortable Old World hotel was founded in 1898 on the western edge of Ortigia, the town's ancient heart. Its roof terrace restaurant has fine sea and harbor views.
ⓘ 41 + 17 suites
🅿 🔵 🔵 🔵 Free
🔲 All major cards

🏨 DOMUS MARIAE
$$ ✪✪✪✪
VIA VITTORIO VENETO 76
TEL 0931 60087
domusmariaebenessere.com
The attractive Domus in Ortigia is warmly and professionally run.
ⓘ 33 🅿 🔵 🔵 Free in public areas 🔲 All major cards

🍴 ARCHIMEDE
$$$
VIA GEMMELLARO 8
TEL 0931 69 701
trattoriaarchimede.it

🔵 Elevator 🔵 Air-conditioning 🔵 Indoor Pool ⊠ Outdoor Pool 🔵 Health Club 🔵 Wi-Fi 🔲 Credit Cards

Contented diners have come to this restaurant in Ortigia since 1930 to enjoy mainly fish and seafood dishes. Service may suffer at busy times.
🍴 150 🕐 Closed Sun. except July–Aug. 🅂 🚫 All major cards

TAORMINA

SOMETHING SPECIAL

🏨 **SAN DOMENICO PALACE**
$$$$$ ○○○○○
PIAZZA SAN DOMENICO 5
TEL 0942 613 111
san-domenico-palace.com
A central and consummately converted 15th-century convent with gorgeous garden, antique-decorated rooms, and views of Etna and the sea.
🛏 97 + 8 suites 🅿 🔁 🅂
🏊 🛜 Free 🚫 All major cards

🏨 **VILLA DUCALE**
$$$–$$$$ ○○○○
VIA LEONARDO DA VINCI 60
TEL 0942 28 153
villaducale.com
This romantic little hotel, with lovely terrace views, is part of a late 19th-century villa.
🛏 11 + 6 suite 🅿 🕐 Closed mid-Jan.–mid-Feb. 🅂 🛜 Free 🚫 All major cards

🏨 **VILLA BELVEDERE**
$$–$$$ ○○○
VIA BAGNOLI CROCE 79
TEL 0942 23 791
villabelvedere.it
Panoramic views distinguish this comfortable hotel, situated amid palm and olive trees a little east of the town center by the public gardens.
🛏 49 🅿 🕐 Closed Dec. & mid-Jan.–mid-March 🔁 🅂
🏊 🛜 Free 🚫 All major cards

🍴 **AL DUOMO**
$$$$
VICO EBREI 11, PIAZZA DUOMO
TEL 0942 625 656

Tucked away in a small alley off the cathedral square, this lively restaurant has marble tables, homey atmosphere, good service, and well-prepared dishes.
🍴 40–35 🕐 Closed Wed., Dec.–Jan., & Mon. Nov.–March
🅂 🚫 All major cards

🍴 **TISCHI TOSCHI**
$$$
VICO FRANCESCO PALADINI 3
TEL 339 364 2088
tischitoschitaormina.com
Chef Luca is exuberant and full of ideas. He has created a "gourmet trattoria" where the central theme is respect for the area and its resources. Every ingredient is selected with passion and the dishes on the menu take diners on a trip through the real Sicily. The wines are also from the area, from local grapes grown in small vineyards.
🍴 32 🕐 Periods may vary 🚫 All major cards

SARDINIA

ALGHERO

🏨 **VILLA LAS TRONAS**
$$$ ○○○○
LUNGOMARE VALENCIA 1
TEL 079 981 818
hotelvillalastronas.com
An art nouveau villa on a promontory overlooking the sea. The hotel's gardens and beach provide a wonderful sense of peace and privacy.
🛏 22 + 3 suites 🅿 🔁
🅂 🏊 🛜 Free
🚫 All major cards

🍴 **AL TUGURI**
$$–$$$
VIA MAIORCA 113
TEL 079 976 772
altuguri.it
The cuisine combines Sardinian and Catalan traditions, with an emphasis on fish and seafood. Try the homemade pasta with cozze, piselli, and

gamberi (mussels, peas, and lobster).
🍴 35 🕐 Closed mid-Dec.–Jan. & Sun. except in summer
🅂 🚫 All major cards

CAGLIARI

🏨 **REGINA MARGHERITA**
$$$ ○○○○
VIALE REGINA MARGHERITA 44
TEL 070 670 342
hotelreginamargherita.com
The best of the hotels close to Cagliari's old quarter.
🛏 98 + 2 suites 🅿 🔁 🅂
📺 🛜 🚫 All major cards

🍴 **DAL CORSARO**
$$$
VIALE REGINA MARGHERITA 28
TEL 070 664 318
stefanodeidda.it
A local institution with creative Sardinian cooking. Reservations essential.
🍴 80 🅿 🕐 Closed Sun. & part of Jan. 🅂
🚫 All major cards

CALA GONONE

🏨 **COSTA DORADA**
$$–$$$ ○○○○
LUNGOMARE PALMASERA 45
TEL 0784 93332
hotelcostadorada.it
A straightforward, comfortable hotel with some suites, in a pleasant coastal setting.
🛏 28 🕐 Closed Nov.–Easter
🅂 🛜 Free 🚫 All major cards

COSTA SMERALDA

🏨 **CALA DI VOLPE**
$$$$$ ○○○○○
CALA DI VOLPE, PORTO CERVO
TEL 0789 976 111
caladivolpe.com
An elegant re-creation of a traditional Sardinian village. Tennis courts, access to a nine-hole golf course, and more.
🛏 112 + 11 suites 🅿 🔁 🅂
🛜 🚫 All major cards

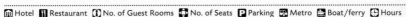
🏨 Hotel 🍴 Restaurant 🛏 No. of Guest Rooms 🍴 No. of Seats 🅿 Parking 🚇 Metro ⛴ Boat/ferry 🕐 Hours

SHOPPING

Shopping is one of the great pleasures of visiting Italy. From the smallest mountain town to the grandest city street, Italian stores offer superb arrays of food and wine, wonderful clothes, inspired design, beautiful fabrics, precious jewelry, exquisite shoes, leatherware and accessories, precious art, antiques, objets d'art, and a host of craft and artisan articles such as ceramics, metalware, and marbled paper. But be prepared for high prices: Italy is not a country of bargains.

Stores

Most Italian stores are small, family-run affairs, even in big cities. Many neighborhoods still have their own baker *(panificio)*, fruit seller *(fruttivendolo)*, pastry store *(pasticceria)*, butcher *(macellaio)*, and food shop *(alimentari)*. Department stores and supermarkets are gradually gaining ground, especially in larger towns and cities, but the shopping mall is still an almost alien concept.

Markets

All towns and cities have at least one street market *(un mercato)*. In cities, these usually run daily except Sunday, starting at dawn and closing early afternoon. Opening times are the same in towns, but generally such provincial markets are held just once weekly. Many larger towns also hold antique fairs, usually once monthly or over a weekend, or coinciding with special events devoted to local food or artisanal produce. These are the only places you may be able to bargain—haggling over prices in food markets or other stores is not appropriate.

Specialties

Many Italian products are unique to one area and to one season of the year. Fruit and vegetables only appear in stores when they are in season, so don't expect to find grapes in spring or cherries in fall. All regions, and many towns, have their own food and wine specialties. Some are found across Italy—such as Parma ham

and Parmesan cheese—but often, as in the truffles of Umbria and Piedmont, or the spicy *panforte* cake of Siena, the products are confined to a small area. The same applies to handicrafts, with glassware and lace both specialties of Venice, for example, or the marbled paper and fine leatherware typical of Florence.

What to Buy

Italy is a cornucopia of exquisite gifts and treats. Food delicacies are obvious purchases, but check import restrictions on meat and produce into North America. Lingerie, silks, lace, linens, soaps, shoes, bags, wallets, marbled paper products, and jewelry are all easily transportable items. Also leave space for wine, clothes, and design objects, particularly kitchenware, an area in which Italian designers excel. Most reputable stores should be able to arrange shipping for larger items such as ceramics, furniture, and antiques.

Payment

Supermarkets and department stores usually accept credit cards, as do larger clothes and shoe stores, but cash is required for virtually all transactions in small food and other stores.

Exports

Most Italian luxury items and many clothing purchases include a value-added goods and services tax of 22 percent (known as IVA in Italy). Non–European Union residents can claim an IVA refund for purchases

over about 154.94 euros (before tax) made in one store. Shop with your passport and ask for invoices to be made out clearly, showing individual articles and tax components of prices. Many department stores have special counters for this purpose.

Keep all receipts and invoices and have them stamped at the customs office at your point of departure, or the last exit from EU territory if you are traveling beyond Italy. Then mail the invoice to the store, within 90 days of arriving home, for your rebate.

Many stores are members of the Tax-Free Shopping System and issue a timesaving "tax-free check" for the amount of the rebate, which can be cashed directly at special tax-free counters at airports or credited to your bank or credit card account.

■ ROME

Rome's key shopping streets cluster around Via dei Condotti, home to most of the big names in designer clothes and shoes. Less expensive stores line Via del Corso, Via Nazionale, and Via del Tritone. Antique and art stores are found on Via del Babuino, Via Margutta, Via Giulia, Via Monserrato, and Via dei Coronari. The best food stores are on Via Santa Croce and Via Cola di Rienzo.

Department Store

La Rinascente Via del Tritone 61, tel 06 879 161, rinascente.it; also located at Piazza Fiume. The largest and most stylish of Rome's big stores.

Food & Wine

Ai Monasteri Piazza Cinque Lune 2, tel 06 6880 2783, aimona steri.it. Jams, preserves, honey, liqueurs, chocolates, soaps, and perfumes, all made in monasteries and convents across Italy.
Buccone Via di Ripetta 19–20, tel 06 361 2154, www.enoteca buccone.com. One of Rome's best stocked wine stores.
Castroni Via Cola di Rienzo 196, tel 06 687 4383, castroni.it. The ultimate Roman food store. Eight other locations, including Via Frattina 79 and Via Nazionale 71.
Trimani Via Goito 20, tel 06 446 9661, trimani.com. A wine store that opened in 1821 and will ship bottles home.

Jewelry

Bulgari Via dei Condotti 10, tel 06 696 261, bulgari.com. Italy's foremost jewelers, but prices start high and climb to stratospheric.

Linen & Fabrics

Bassetti Corso Vittorio Emanuele II 73, tel 06 689 2326, fratelli bassetti.com. A large selection of Italian silks and other fabrics.
Frette Via del Corso 381, tel 06 678 6862; Piazza di Spagna 11, tel 06 679 0673, frette.com. A national chain selling superb sheets, towels, and other linens.

Markets

Campo de' Fiori Colorful and central food, fruit, and flower market held in Campo de' Fiori (Mon.–Sat. a.m.). Also see p. 61.
Porta Portese Massive flea market held in streets off Viale Trastevere near Porta Portese. Very crowded. Beware of pickpockets (Sun. a.m.).

Men's Clothing

Davide Cenci Via Campo Marzio 1–7, tel 06 699 0681, davidecenci.com. A huge store,

founded in 1926, selling clothes in classic Italian-English country gentleman styles.

Paper & Pens

Pineider Via dei Due Macelli 68, tel 06 678 9013; Via della Fontanella Borghese 22, tel 06 687 8369, pineider.com. Everyone from Napoleon to Elizabeth Taylor has shopped for pens and paper at Pineider. Also located in Florence at Piazza de' Rucellai, 4r–7r, tel 055 284 656.

Pictures & Prints

Alberto di Castro Piazza di Spagna 5, tel 06 679 2269, dicastro.com. Hundreds of old prints and engravings.

Religious Objects

Via dei Cestari A treasure trove of religious objects and souvenirs. Stores on this street sell everything from rosaries to cardinals' hats.

▪ NORTHWEST ITALY

TURIN

Turin's streets are filled with good stores, especially Via Roma and Via Garibaldi. Antique shops abound on Piazza San Carlo, Via Maria Vittoria, and the streets around Via Pietro Micca. The city is especially known for its vermouths and chocolates.

Food & Wine

Paissa Piazza San Carlo 196, tel 011 562 8462, paissa.it. Selection of food and drinks, including Turin's locally produced vermouths Cinzano and Martini.

Markets

Balôn Piazza della Repubblica. Flea market on Saturday morning plus huge "Gran Balôn" antiques and flea market every second Sunday of the month.

GENOA

Genoa's Via Soziglia is a good place to pick up Ligurian handicrafts such as lace, ceramics, marble, gold, and silverware. Jewelers line Via dei Orefici and luxury shops cluster on Via XX Settembre and Via Luccoli.

Department Stores

COIN Via XX Settembre 16a, tel 010 570 5821, coin.it.

Food & Wine

Drogheria Viganego Via Colombo, 22r, tel 331 595 6753, drogheriaviganego.com. The best spices you can find in the city.
Pietro Romanengo Via Soziglia 74r, tel 010 247 4574; Via Roma 51–53r, tel 010 580 257, romanengo.it. Fantastic chocolates and candies.
Vinoteca Sola Piazza Colombo 13r, tel 010 561 329, vinoteca sola.it. Hundreds of wines from Italy and around the world.

▪ LOMBARDY & THE LAKES

MILAN

Milan is probably Italy's premier shopping city. Armani, Prada, Versace, Ferré, Krizia, Moschino, and Dolce & Gabbana all originated here. Most of these, and other designer names, abound on the Golden Quadrangle, a quartet of streets on and around Via Montenapoleone. Antiques, accessories, and other luxury stores are also found here. Less expensive high-quality clothing can be found on Corso Buenos Aires and Corso Vittorio Emanuele II, and the more attractive Brera district has an oasis of interesting and unique stores: Via Solferino, Via Madonnina, and Via Fiori Chiari are the key streets.

Books

Vecchi Libri in Piazza Piazza Diaz, piazzadiaz.com. An historical appointment for bibliophiles and the inquisitive. It offers rare, antique, artistic and out-of-print books, held on the second Sunday of the month.

Clothes

Giorgio Armani Via Manzoni 31, tel 02 7231 8600, armani.com. The most famous name in Milan's fashion firmament.

Prada Via della Spiga 18, tel 02 780 465; Via Montenapoleone 8; Corso Venezia 3, prada.com. Fashionable bags, accessories, and clothes.

Department Store

La Rinascente Piazza del Duomo, tel 02 88 521, rinascente.it. Has Italy's largest fashion floors in a single store.

Jewelry

Mario Buccellati Via Montenapoleone 23, tel 02 7600 2154, buccellati.com. Only Rome's Bulgari rivals Buccellati for the title of Italy's finest jeweler.

Leather

Valextra Via A. Manzoni 3, tel 02 9978 6060, valextra.it. Has sold superior bags, wallets, and other leather goods since 1937.

Linens

Frette Via della Spiga 31, tel 02 783 950; Via Manzoni 11, 02 864 433, frette.com. Sublime bed linens, plus luxurious homewear.

Markets

Mercantone dell'Antiquariato Via Brera-Via Fiori Chiari. Massive antiques market (3rd Sat. of each month).

Mercato Papiniano Viale Papiniano. New and secondhand goods (Sat.).

Paper & Stationery

Papier Via San Maurilio 4, tel 02 865 221, papier-milano.it. A large selection of beautiful, and often unusual, papers.

Prints & Engravings

Raimondi di Pettinaroli Corso Venezia 43, tel 02 7600 2412; Corso Venezia 3; pettinaroli .it. Hundreds of old prints and engravings.

■ VENICE

Venice's most famous products are glass, lace, fabrics, and marbled paper. Beware, however, for much cheap glass and lace is foreign and machine-made. Many glass shops are on the Fondamenta dei Vetrai on the island of Murano, as well as around San Marco. Lace can be found on the island of Burano, and paper and fabric stores are dotted across the city.

The key shopping streets are around Calle dei Fabbri, the Frezzeria, and Le Mercerie between San Marco and the Rialto Bridge and on and around Calle Largo XXII Marzo west of Piazza San Marco. Antiques stores cluster around the churches of San Maurizio and Santa Maria Zobenigo, west of Piazza San Marco. Antiques fairs are held periodically in Campo San Maurizio: Details of forthcoming fairs are available from the visitor center.

Beads

Anticlea Campo San Provolo, Castello 4719/a, tel 041 528 6946. A tiny gem of a store, crammed with thousands of new and antique Venetian beads.

Department Store

DFS-Fondaco dei Tedeschi Calle del Fontego dei Tedeschi, Ponte di Rialto, tel 041 3142 000, dfs.com. Luxury brands and artisanship in a renovated historical building.

Food

Casa del Parmigiano Campo della Corderia, Ruga Vecchia San Giovanni, San Polo 214, tel 041 520 6525, casadelparmigiano .ve.it. Venice's best food emporium has cheeses, fresh pasta, and ready-made delicacies.

Glass

Venini Fondamenta Vetrai 47-50, Murano, tel 041 273 7211, venini .com. Innovative designs.

Gondoliers' Goods

Ceccato Sottoportico di Rialto, San Polo 1617, tel 041 522 2700. If you must buy a gondolier's straw hat as a souvenir, then at least buy the real thing from this store, which sells hats, tunics, and pants to real gondoliers.

Jewelry

Missiaglia Dorsoduro 586, tel 041 522 4464, missiaglia1846. com. Classic and contemporary gold and silver jewelry at top prices from Venice's best jeweler.

Nardi Piazza San Marco 69, tel 041 522 5733, nardi-venezia.com. The only place that produces work close to nearby Missiaglia.

Lace

Jesurum Calle Larga XXII Marzo 2401, San Marco, tel 041 523 8969, jesurum.it. Venice's finest lace retailer since 1868. Products and quality are guaranteed.

Leather

Bottega Veneta Campo San Moisé, San Marco 1461, tel 041 520 5197. Flagship store of this chic label; bags, belts, wallets, and other high-quality leather goods.

Markets

Rialto Don't miss the goods and food markets (the Erberia) in the streets north of the Rialto Bridge (Mon.–Sat. 8 a.m.–1 p.m.).

Pescheria The fish market operates alongside the Erberia north of the Rialto Bridge (Tues.–Sat. 8 a.m.–1 p.m.).

Masks

Mask stores are everywhere in Venice. **Mondonovo** (*mondonovo maschere.it*) was perhaps the best, but sales are now only available online at maskedart.com. Currently worth visiting is **Ca'Macana** (*Calle delle Botteghe, Dorsoduro 3172, tel 041 277 6142*).

Paper

Alberto Valese Campo Santo Stefano, San Marco 3471, tel 041 523 8830. Some of Venice's most beautiful marbled paper. The designs are also applied to silk and various ornaments.

Polliero Campo dei Frari, San Polo 2995, tel 041 528 5130. Tiny shop by the Frari church selling beautiful leather- and paper-bound books and diaries and other marbled paper products.

■ FLORENCE

Florence is a great shopping city for luxury goods. Leather, clothes, jewelry, and antiques are top buys, thanks to a long tradition of fine artisanal work. Less expensive gift possibilities include marbled paper and goods from the city's thriving markets. Most clothes and other luxury goods stores are found on and around Via de' Tornabuoni. Antique stores group together south of the Arno River on and around Via Maggio. Jewelers congregate on the Ponte Vecchio.

Clothes & Accessories

Gianfranco Lotti Via de' Tornabuoni 59r, tel 055 238 2945, gianfrancolotti.com. If the chic handbags do not tempt you, the exquisite scarves, stoles, gloves, hats, and jewelry, almost certainly will.

Gucci Via de' Tornabuoni 73r, tel 055 264 011, gucci.com. The famous double "G" label originated in Florence. Clothes are sold at this store, accessories at Via Roma 32r *(tel 055 759 221)*.

Madova Via Guicciardini 1r, tel 055 239 6526, madova.com. Has sold a glorious selection of summer and winter gloves since 1919.

Pucci Via de' Tornabuoni 20–22r, tel 055 265 8082, emiliopucci .com. One of the city's best known designers, Emilio Pucci made his name with signature silks and prints in the 1960s.

Department Stores

COIN Via de' Calzaiuoli 56r, tel 055 280 531, coin.it. Florentines crowd this central mid-range store.

La Rinascente Piazza della Repubblica 1, tel 055 219 113. Of generally higher quality than COIN.

Food

Pegna Via dello Studio 26r, tel 055 282 701, pegnafirenze.com. Founded in 1860, this superb deli sells more than 7,000 items.

Household Goods

Bartolini Via dei Servi 72r, tel 055 289 223, bartolinifirenze.it. Founded in 1921, and purveyors of kitchenware, china, porcelain, glassware, and other home items.

Casa dei Tessuti Via de' Pecori 20r–24r, tel 055 215 961, casa deitessuti.com. A staggering collection of silk, linen, wool, and other fabrics.

Jewelry

Torrini Piazza del Duomo 12r, tel 055 230 2401, torrini.it. Torrini registered its half cloverleaf trademark in 1369. Classic and modern designs, with an emphasis on gold.

Leather

Cellerini Via del Sole 9, tel 055 282 533, www.cellerini.it. More than 600 types of wallets, shoes, suitcases, belts, and bags.

Desmo Via de' Tornabuoni 7r, tel 055 267 0509, desmo.it. A long-established name with a huge selection of leather goods.

Linens

Loretta Caponi Piazza Antinori 4r, tel 055 213 668, lorettacaponi.com. Beautiful lace, embroidery, linens, and lingerie.

Markets

Cascine Parco del Cascine. A vast weekly flea market held in a large park west of the city center (Tues. 8 a.m.–2 p.m., Bus: 1, 9, 17, Tram: T2).

Mercato Centrale Piazza del Mercato Centrale. Europe's largest indoor food market is a bustling must-see. A good place both for buying and dining (Mon.–Sat. 9 a.m.–5 p.m.).

San Lorenzo Piazza San Lorenzo. The streets off the square are crammed with stalls selling clothes and other goods (Mon.–Sun. 9 a.m.–7 p.m.).

Shoes

Salvatore Ferragamo Via de' Tornabuoni 4r–14r, tel 055 292 123, ferragamo.com. Ferragamo made his name in the United States, but his Italian base was Florence. Also sells clothing and accessories.

Soaps & Perfumes

Farmaceutica di Santa Maria Novella Via della Scala 16r, tel 055 216 276, www.smnovella.it. Sells soaps, perfumes, and cosmetics, many made from ancient recipes created in monasteries and convents.

Farmacia del Cinghiale Piazza del Mercato Nuovo 4r, tel 055 212 128, farmaciadelcinghiale.it. Has sold cosmetics and toiletries since the 18th century.

FESTIVALS

Italy has countless fascinating and colorful festivals, religious ceremonies, historic pageants, fairs, markets, and local events. A few are vast, showy affairs such as the Venice Carnevale or Siena's Palio. Many are cultural extravaganzas of Europe-wide significance, notably Verona's summer opera festival or Venice's Biennale. The majority, however, are tiny affairs, restricted to a town or village.

If you plan to attend one of the larger events, make reservations well in advance, as tickets and hotel rooms go quickly.

The selection below lists by town the main arts and musical festivals, plus several of the largest and most colorful other annual events. An excellent source on festivals is italiafestival.it.

Arts & Music Events

Città di Castello Major international festival of chamber music. *(Aug.–Sept., tel 075 852 2823, festivalnazioni.com)*

Fiesole Estate Fiesolana, a festival of music and other performing arts held in a hill town above Florence. *(Mid-June–Aug., tel 055 596 1293, estatefiesolana.it)*

Florence Maggio Musicale, widely considered Italy's most prestigious classical music festival. *(Late April–early July, tel 055 277 9309, maggiofiorentino.com)*

Lucca Lucca Summer Festival, one of Tuscany's leading summer musical festivals. *(July–Aug., tel 0584 46477, summer-festival.com)*

Macerata Small but highly regarded opera festival. *(Mid-July–mid-Aug., tel 0733 261 335, sferisterio.it)*

Milan Opera season and other classical music staged at La Scala, Italy's premier opera house. *(Opera: Dec.–July; classical: Sept.–Nov., tel 02 7200 3744, teatroallascala.org)*

Naples Opera season at San Carlo, Italy's second-ranked opera house. *(Opera season: Dec.–May; tel 081 797 2331, teatrosancarlo.it)*

Perugia Umbria Jazz, a festival attracting the world's leading jazz musicians to Perugia in July. *(Tel 075 573 2432, umbriajazz.com)*

Pesaro Opera festival devoted to the composer Giacchino Rossini. *(Aug., tel 0721 380 0294, rossinioperafestival.it)*

Ravenna Wide-ranging festival with opera, jazz, and contemporary music. *(Mid-June–mid-July, tel 0544 249 244, ravennafestival.org)*

Siena Classical concerts season organized by the prestigious Accademia Chigiana. *(Nov.–April, tel 0577 22091, chigiana.it)*

Spoleto Festival dei Due Mondi, performance arts festival especially popular with U.S. visitors, thanks to its former links with a sister festival in Charleston, South Carolina. *(Late June–July, tel 0743 221 689, festival dispoleto.com)*

Stresa Stresa Settimane Musicali, a short season of classical concerts. *(July–early Sept., tel 0323 31095 or 0323 30459, stresafestival.eu)*

Syracuse Festival of Greek drama with performances in the outdoor Greek theater. *(May–July, tel 0931 487 248, indafondazione.org)*

Taormina International film festival, plays, and concerts held in the Sicilian town's outdoor Greek theater. *(late June–early July, tel box office 0942 21142, taorminafilmfest.it)*

Torre del Lago Puccini Outdoor opera festival near Viareggio devoted to composer Giacomo Puccini. *(Mid-July–mid-Aug., tel 0584 359 322, puccinifestival.it)*

Urbino Festival Internazionale di Musica Antica, one of Europe's leading festivals of early and baroque music. *(10 days late July, tel 06 321 0806, fima-online.org/umafest)*

Venice (art) Biennale, one of Europe's best contemporary art shows. Held in pavilions in the Giardini Pubblici (public gardens).

(June–Sept. in odd-numbered years, tel 041 521 8711, labiennale.org)

Venice (film) Venice International Film Festival, second only to Cannes among European movie festivals. *(10 days late Aug.–early Sept., tel 041 521 8711, labiennale.org)*

Venice (opera) Concerts, mostly held in the Fenice opera house. *(Nov.–June, tel 041 786 511 or 041 2424, teatrolafenice.it)*

Verona Opera festival, staged in the Arena, the city's vast Roman amphitheater. *(July–Aug., tel 045 800 5151, arena.it)*

Calendar of Events

January–February

Epiphany Celebrations across Italy to celebrate the feast of the Epiphany, especially in Rome where a 3-week Christmas fair concludes in Piazza Navona. *(Jan. 5–6)*

Festa di Sant'Orso Aosta, Valle d'Aosta. An ancient local festival celebrating Aosta's patron saint. *(Late Jan., fieradisantorso.it)*

Festival della Canzone Italiana Sanremo, Liguria. This 3-day "Festival of Italian Song" is hugely popular in Italy, where it is televised nationwide, but little known outside the country. *(Early Feb.)*

Carnevale Italy's most celebrated carnival festivities take place in Venice (street parties, costumes, and masked balls) and Viareggio on the Tuscan coast, where a huge procession of floats takes place. *(10 days before Ash Wednesday, carnevale.venezia.it)*

Sagra del Tartufo Norcia, Umbria. "Nero Norcia" is the biggest of several food and truffle *(tartufo)* fairs in truffle-producing areas of Italy, notably Tuscany, Umbria, and the Marche. *(Late Feb.)*

Sagra del Mandorlo in Fiore Agrigento, Sicily. International festival of folk music and world music, dancing, and folklore held to coincide with the "Festival of the Almond Blossom." (*Early March, mandorloinfiore.online*)

March–April

Easter Torchlit and other processions, plus religious services take place across Italy on Good Friday and Easter Sunday. The pope traditionally leads Rome's Good Friday procession past the Colosseum and conducts a service at St. Peter's on Easter Sunday.

Festa di San Marco Venice. The city's patron saint, St. Mark, is commemorated with a gondola race and other festivities. (*April 25*)

Scoppio del Carro Florence. Florence's Easter Sunday ceremonies conclude with the igniting of a cart of flowers and fireworks at noon by a mechanical dove that "flies" along a wire from the altar of the cathedral to the piazza outside.

May–June

Calcio Storico Florence. Three soccer games played in medieval dress in Piazza Santa Croce or Piazza della Signoria to commemorate a game first played in 1530. (*mid-June*)

Cavacata Sassari, Sardinia. Thousands of people in traditional island dress parade on foot and horseback, followed by horse races and traditional songs and dances. (*Late May*)

Corsa dei Ceri Gubbio, Umbria. Processions and medieval pageantry precede a race of teams carrying huge wooden candles, or *ceri*, to the hill above town. (*Early or mid-May*)

Festa di San Domenico Cocullo, Abruzzo. Live snakes are handled by local people and draped over a statue of the village's patron saint. (*1st week May*)

Festa di San Gennaro Naples. Celebrations to honor the city's

patron saint, including the miraculous liquefaction of a vial of the saint's blood. (*Three times yearly: 1st Sun. May, Sept. 19, & Dec. 16*)

Festa di Sant'Efisio Cagliari, Sardinia. Mass processions on foot or horseback, with participants in medieval dress, to commemorate the city's patron saint. (*May 1*)

Sagra di San Nicola Bari. Festivities centered on a boat carrying the image of Bari's patron saint for a ceremony at sea. (*Early May*)

Festa di San Pietro St. Peter's, Vatican City. Important religious festival to celebrate the feast day of St. Peter. (*June 29*)

Festa di San Ranieri Pisa, Tuscany. Candlelit processions followed by a rowing regatta in medieval dress to celebrate Pisa's patron saint. (*June 16*)

Festa di Sant'Andrea Amalfi, Campania. Festivities to celebrate Amalfi's patron saint. (*June 27*)

Gioco del Ponte Pisa, Tuscany. A tug-of-war in medieval costume held on Pisa's Ponte di Mezzo. (*Last Sun. June*)

Vogalonga Venice. A popular 20-mile (32 km) rowing race to the island of Burano, returning along the Grand Canal in the early afternoon. (*One Sun. in May, vogalonga.com*)

July–August

Bravio delle Botti Montepulciano, Tuscany. A barrel-rolling contest up the town's steep main street, plus processions and displays of medieval drumming and flag throwing. (*Last Sun. Aug., braviodellebotti.com*)

Festa del Redentore Venice. Pontoon bridges are laid across the Giudecca canal to link Venice with the church of the Redentore (Redeemer), a celebration of Venice's deliverance from the plague in 1576. People picnic in boats, fireworks. (*3rd Sat. & Sun. July*)

Festa de' Noantri Rome. Eight days of festivals, pageants, outdoor feasts, and folk music in Rome's colorful Trastevere quarter. (*Mid-July*)

Il Palio Siena. Processions and displays of flag throwing by participants in medieval costume before a bareback horse race around the Campo, the city's main square. (*July 2 & Aug. 16*)

Torneo della Quintana Ascoli Piceno, Marche. Jousting involving knights in armor plus medieval pageant. (*1st weekend Aug.*)

September–October

Giostra del Saracino Arezzo, Tuscany. Jousting knights and processions and events in medieval costume. (*1st Sun. Sept.*)

Luminara di Santa Croce Lucca, Tuscany. Torchlit procession bearing the Volto Santo, the city's most sacred relic, around the streets. (*Sept. 13*)

Regata Storica Venice. A medieval pageant with a procession of boats on the Grand Canal, followed by a boat race. (*1st Sun. Sept.*)

Sagra del Tartufo Alba, Piedmont. A fair held in the country's white truffle (*tartufo*) capital to celebrate the expensive fungus. (*Early Oct. to Late Nov., fieradel tartufo.org*)

November–December

Christmas Eve Special religious services across Italy. (*Dec. 24*)

Christmas Day Rome. Papal blessing in St. Peter's Square. (*Dec. 25*)

Festa della Salute Venice. The "Festival of Health" sees a pontoon bridge built across the Grand Canal to the church of the Salute to commemorate the passing of a plague epidemic in 1630. (*Nov. 21*)

Festa di Sant'Ambrogio Milan. Large market and other celebrations to commemorate the city's patron saint. (*Dec. 7*)

Presepi Ornate and precious old Christmas crèches (*presepi*) are features of churches across Italy in the lead up to Christmas, especially in Naples, where the tableau figures are a popular craft tradition.

LANGUAGE GUIDE

Useful Words & Phrases
Yes/No *Sì/No*
Okay/that's fine/sure *Va bene*
I don't understand *Non capisco*
Do you speak English? *Parla inglese?*
What? *Quale?*
Why? *Perchè?*
When? *Quando?*
Where? *Dove?*
How much is it? *Quant'è?*
Good morning *Buon giorno*
Good afternoon/good evening
    Buona sera
Good night *Buona notte*
Hello/goodbye (informal) *Ciao*
Goodbye *Arrivederci*
Please *Per favore*
Thank you *Grazie*
You're welcome *Prego*
How are you? (polite/informal)
    Come sta/stai?
I'm sorry *Mi dispiace*
Excuse me/I beg your pardon
    Mi scusi
Excuse me (in a crowd) *Permesso*

MENU READER

General
breakfast *la colazione*
lunch *il pranzo*
dinner *la cena*
I'm a vegetarian *Sono vegetariano/a*
The check, please *Il conto, per favore*
cover charge *il coperto*

The Menu
l'antipasto appetizer
il primo first course
la zuppa soup
il secondo main course
il contorno vegetable, side dish
l'insalata salad
la frutta fruit
il formaggio cheese
i dolci sweets/desserts
la lista dei vini wine list

Pasta Sauces
al pomodoro tomato
amatriciana tomato and bacon
arrabbiata spicy chilli tomato
bolognese veal or beef
carbonara bacon, cheese and egg

parmigiano Parmesan cheese
peperoncino oil, garlic, and chilli
pesto pine nuts, basil, and cheese
puttanesca tomato, anchovy, olive,
    caper, and oregano
ragù any meat sauce
vongole wine, clams, and parsley

Meats
agnello lamb
anatra duck
bistecca beef steak
cinghiale wild boar
coniglio rabbit
fritto misto mixed fried
maiale pork
manzo beef
ossobuco cut of veal
pancetta pork belly/bacon
pollo chicken
prosciutto cotto cooked ham
prosciutto crudo (Parma) ham
salsiccia sausage
saltimbocca veal with ham and sage
trippa tripe
vitello veal

Fish & Seafood
acciughe anchovies
aragosta lobster
baccalà dried salt cod
calamari squid
cappesante scallops
coda di rospo monkfish
cozze mussels
dentice sea bream
gamberi prawns
granchio crab
merluzzo cod
ostriche oysters
pesce spada swordfish
polpo octopus
salmone salmon
sarde sardines
seppie cuttlefish
sgombro mackerel
sogliola sole
tonno tuna
triglie red mullet
trota trout
vongole clams

Vegetables
aglio garlic

asparagi asparagus
basilico basil
capperi capers
carciofi artichokes
carote carrots
cavolo cabbage
cipolle onions
fagioli beans
funghi mushrooms
funghi porcini porcini mushrooms
insalata mista mixed salad
insalata verde green salad
melanzane eggplant
patate potatoes
patate fritte French fries
peperoni peppers
piselli peas
pomodoro tomato
radicchio red salad leaf
rucola/rughetta arugula
spinaci spinach
tartufo truffle
zucchine zucchini

Fruit
albicocca apricot
ananas pineapple
arance oranges
banane bananas
ciliegie cherries
fichi figs
fragole strawberries
limone lemon
mele apples
melone melon
pere pears
pesca peach
pompelmo grapefruit
prugna plum

Drinking
acqua water
una birra beer
una bottiglia bottle
una mezza bottiglia half-bottle
caffè coffee
caffè Hag/caffè decaffeinato
    decaffeinated coffee
latte milk
tè tea
vino wine
vino della casa house wine
zucchero sugar

INDEX

ILLUSTRATIONS CREDITS

National Geographic

TRAVELER

Italy

SIXTH EDITION

Since 1888, the National Geographic Society has funded more than 13,000 research, exploration, and preservation projects around the world. National Geographic Partners distributes a portion of the funds it receives from your purchase to National Geographic Society to support programs including the conservation of animals and their habitats.

National Geographic Partners
1145 17th Street NW
Washington, DC 20036-4688 USA

Get closer to National Geographic explorers and photographers, and connect with our global community. Join us today at nationalgeographic.com/join

For information about special discounts for bulk purchases, please contact National Geographic Books Special Sales: specialsales@natgeo.com

For rights or permissions inquiries, please contact National Geographic Books
Subsidiary Rights: bookrights@natgeo.com

Cutaway illustrations drawn by Maltings Partnership, Derby, England

Sixth edition edited by White Star s.r.l.
Licensee of National Geographic Partners, LLC.
Update by Iceigeo (Alice Avanzi, Cynthia Anne Koeppe, Maria-Angela Silleni, Francesca Mottadelli)

The information in this book has been carefully checked and to the best of our knowledge is accurate. However, details are subject to change, and the publisher cannot be responsible for such changes, or for errors or omissions. Assessments of sites, hotels, and restaurants are based on the author's subjective opinions, which do not necessarily reflect the publisher's opinion.

ISBN: 978-88-544-1583-6

Printed by
Rotolito S.p.A. - Seggiano di Pioltello (MI) - Italy

 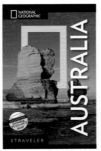 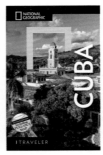